GW01418145

THE COMPLETE BOOK OF
BASEBALL

1991

THE COMPLETE HANDBOOK OF

BASEBALL

EDITED BY

ZANDER HOLLANDER

AN ASSOCIATED FEATURES BOOK

A SIGNET BOOK

ACKNOWLEDGMENTS

We thank all who helped make possible this 21st edition of *The Complete Handbook of Baseball*: contributing editor Howard Blatt, the writers listed on the contents page and Lee Stowbridge, Eric Compton, Fred Cantey, Kevin Mulroy, Linda Spain, Phyllis Merhige, Brian Small, Katy Feeney, Susan Aglietti, the team publicity directors, Elias Sports Bureau, MLB-IBM Baseball Information System, Dot Gordineer of Libra Graphics, and Westchester/Rainsford Book Composition.

Zander Hollander

PHOTO CREDITS: Cover—Focus on Sports. Inside photos—Ira Golden, Vic Milton, Mitch Reibel, Joe Sebo, Wide World and the major-league team photographers.

CONTENTS

Editor's Note: The material herein includes trades and rosters up to final printing deadline.

THE VINDICATION OF NAILS DYKSTRA

By GEORGE KING

Go ahead and admit it. You checked the daily leaders in the National League in May and were surprised to see Lenny Dykstra's name atop the charts.

May turned to June, the Phillies' leadoff man and center fielder was still the best hitter in the NL—with an average over .400—and you figured this couldn't last.

However, June melted into July, which gave way to the dog days of August, and there was Dykstra still leading the league in hitting. And when the final numbers came in, showing Dykstra had finished fourth in the batting derby with a .325 average, you didn't have the nerve to claim you knew it all along. After all, here was a guy who entered the 1990 season as a career .268 hitter. And a platoon player to boot.

Join the crowd. You were surprised. So was the league. Players, teammates and opposition alike, knew Dykstra had talent. Still, they were taken aback by his emergence.

"Nails can play," said Dwight Gooden, his ex-teammate with the Mets, during the lockout last spring. But not even Gooden would have predicted that Dykstra would lead the NL with 192 hits and a .418 on-base percentage, bat .325, be the NL's starting center fielder in the All-Star Game, put together the longest hitting streak in the NL (23 games) and finish in the top 10 in seven offensive categories.

Even Lee Thomas, the Phillies' general manager who engi-

As a beat writer on the Mets and later the Phillies, George King of the Trenton Times *has covered Lenny Dykstra all the way in the bigs.*

Down-and-dirty Lenny Dykstra thrives as a Phillie.

neered the deal that brought the scrappy Dykstra to Philadelphia along with reliever Roger McDowell from the Mets for Juan Samuel in June 1989, was surprised.

In fact, the only guy who wasn't surprised by Dykstra's sterling season was the architect.

After missing the first five games of the season with a pulled muscle in the rib cage, Dykstra hit the ground running and never stopped. That's the speed at which he plays the game. With a jaw full of tobacco, Dykstra has been running—and sliding head-first—since before the Mets drafted him in the 12th round in 1981. He always knew that, given a chance to play every day, he was capable of joining the elite.

"Ever since I have known him, he knew he could play and play well in the big leagues," said Alan Meersand, Dykstra's agent since 1983. "He just knew he was going to play there. He is the most focused person I know. There is an air about him. If he went to the Gulf, he would be the leading Marine there."

When he was hitting over .400 in mid-June, Dykstra eschewed all talk of being the first player to hit .400 since Ted Williams in 1941.

"Can't do it," he said. "They pay guys $3 million a year to come out of the bullpen today. Nobody will ever hit .400 again."

That didn't mean Dykstra had no idea where the strong start would lead. In fact, he knew he was in for a solid year before the labor disagreement between the players and management was resolved.

"I am not saying what my goals are, but I have them in mind," Dykstra said in spring training. "Just say some people are going to be surprised come September."

On the last weekend of the season, Dykstra revealed what he wrote down in March.

"I wanted three things," he said in Montreal. "I wanted to hit .300, score 100 runs and sign a big contract."

He did all three and much more. Even winding up fourth in the batting race that he had led from May 12 to Aug. 15 couldn't take the luster off Dykstra's season. Especially since NL batting champion Willie McGee's title was tainted by the deal that sent him out of the league, from St. Louis to Oakland, in late August and froze his NL average at .335.

"It's like he hit .335 for the month of September and that's hard to do," Dykstra said of McGee. "So, I am not real disappointed."

With every passing month, it was apparent that the Phillies were becoming Dykstra's club. Once the Phillies' clubhouse belonged to Mike Schmidt and Pete Rose, but now it was Dykstra's room. Dykstra developed into the clubhouse presence with the Phillies, assuming the role filled by Keith Hernandez and Gary Carter during Lenny's early years with the Mets.

When rookie second baseman Mickey Morandini struggled in September, it was a chat with Dykstra that got him straightened out. When a pitcher failed to help himself at the plate, Dykstra often reminded the pitcher his job was to pitch, not hit. The biggest impression Dykstra had on rookie third baseman Dave Hollins dealt with monetary rewards.

"We were in the trainer's room and he said, 'Head [Hollins' nickname], you can make a lot of money in this game if you work at it,'" Hollins recalled.

"Since I did what I did, I have become more accepted," Dykstra said. "In New York, I wasn't one of the main guys they counted on. Here I am. I like that, but you have to do something for the players to respect you. You just can't say you are a team

He made a run at hitting crown in his first .300 season.

leader. Now that I have hit .325, people will know where I am coming from.''

It was Dykstra's locker at which the media gathered, whether he had gone 4-for-4 or 0-for-5. He has become the voice of the Phillies. In a quiet moment, he will grudgingly tell you he likes that. And Dykstra learned how to play the media game perfectly. He used the papers to get the pace of his contract negotiations stepped up.

Throughout the season—especially after he was voted to the starting lineup on the All-Star team—the question everybody asked was this: ''Do you feel the Mets made a mistake in trading you?''

No matter how many times or how many ways he was asked it, Dykstra refused to put the knock on his former club, which was desperately seeking a center fielder and leadoff hitter. And when the Mets axed manager Davey Johnson—the man responsible for getting him traded—Dykstra again chose not to bury his former club.

''Do I feel vindicated?'' Dykstra repeated after having six weeks to reflect on his coming-out season. ''I don't think about things like vindication. For me, I always knew that I could play like this.''

Since he first began playing organized sports, the 5-foot-8 Dykstra has been told he was too small. That was one reason he lasted until the 12th round of the 1981 draft. The other was that many teams thought he was going to Arizona State on a football scholarship to play cornerback.

While scouts usually shy away from 5-8, 160-pounders, Thomas, a former farm director with St. Louis, knows why Mets' scout Myron Pines took a chance on Dykstra.

''The scout probably saw him dive and hustle all over the place and said, 'Boy, I would love to have him.' The way he hustles and runs had to catch the scout's eye. He also had talent, don't forget,'' said Thomas.

And the confidence that some day he was going to put together the type of year he did in 1990. Nothing intimidates him. Not 95-mph fastballs aimed at his head by pitchers who genuinely hate him. Not the brick walls of Chicago's Wrigley Field. Not the catcher in full gear blocking home plate. Nothing.

But that's the way it has been for as long as he can remember. Not even the presence of Rod Carew and Bobby Grich at a 1981 California Angels batting practice session could unnerve Dykstra, then a senior at Garden Grove High School in Southern California.

''I drove up to Anaheim Stadium in my Volkswagen Bug,

Lenny celebrates game-winning homer in 1986 NLCS.

because they wanted to take a look at me. They wanted to draft me,'' Dykstra said. ''I get to the gate and tell the guard what I am there for and he looks at me like I am crazy. Finally, I get in and take batting practice. It was awesome. Carew, Grich and the rest of those guys were there watching.''

So how did he do?

''I hit ropes, of course,'' Dykstra said in a tone of voice that said you were a fool to ask.

Seemingly, ropes were all Dykstra hit during 1990. But, to say that all Lenny Dykstra was about in 1990 was a lofty batting average would be wrong. As a leadoff man, it was Dykstra's job to get on base and his .418 on-base percentage was the best in the NL. According to Phillies' first-base coach John Vukovich, that took precedent over any personal goals Dykstra set.

''He was really concerned about his on-base average, which was his biggest job,'' Vukovich said. ''There were a number of times during his hitting streak when he was down to his last at-bat and hadn't had a hit yet. Still, even though he was ahead 2-0 in the count, he was still trying to work the pitcher for a walk.

''He was sending his teammates a message. He was saying, 'Hey, I got something personal going, but us winning is more important.' ''

Ah, winning. Dykstra thrives on it, no matter what the arena. ''That's what it's all about, winning,'' Dykstra said. ''Golf, cards, baseball. That's what it's all about. Winning. Nothing else matters.''

And when he isn't part of a winner, he loses interest. Just look at the final eight weeks of the 1989 season, when he took an admitted nap. He hit .170 in August and .189 in September, finishing with a career-low .237 average for a last-place team.

''I thrive on the pressure winning produces,'' Dykstra said. ''There was no pressure to win because we were so bad.''

Not only did he hit .237 overall, he hit only .222 against left-handers. Those were the pitchers the Mets said he couldn't hit. Bull, Dykstra said. Immediately after the 1989 season, he went to work on sculpting his body with weights back home in Jackson, Miss. Four hours a day, Dykstra was in the weight room, figuring the added pounds would help his stamina for the long season.

''I had never played every day and really didn't know what it took, both mentally and physically,'' Dykstra said upon showing up at spring training with 30 pounds of muscle that weren't there at the end of the 1989 season.

Suddenly, he had shoulders. And forearms. And a butt. ''Nails'' had been transformed into a 195-pound railroad spike.

"I am going to have a huge year," Dykstra said more than once during the spring.

Of course, he was right. He scored 106 runs and, late in the season, signed a three-year contract that, with incentives, could be worth $11.2 million. And he hit .290 against lefties. But the most impressive stat he produced last year was his .427 average with runners in scoring position. In those 110 at-bats, he struck out only eight times. And he turned in solid defense night after night.

Vindication? No, he insisted.

But what else can you call it? Here was a guy whom the Mets judged expendable because privately they questioned his commitment to being a team player. Well, he was a one-man team against his former team last year, hitting .366 (26-for-71) with one homer and nine RBI and, after a year and a half, Dykstra's career average against the Mets is .317.

"Just another team, Dude," Dykstra said about the Mets, though he played an integral part in their 1986 World Series victory with a strong postseason. "Just another team."

Now his team is the Phillies. From his infectious "Dude" salute to just about everyone . . . to the respect he has commanded from his teammates, he is a Phillie. And he's a down-and-dirty player, perfect for a blue-collar city like Philadelphia, which has embraced him with open arms.

When Frank Coppenbarger, the Phillies' clubhouse manager, was asked why Veterans Stadium was getting new dirt, Coppenbarger's response was: "All of the old dirt is on Lenny's uniform." He was only half-kidding.

On the field, Dykstra is same grimy pest at the top of the Phillies' lineup that he was back in 1984 for Jackson (AA).

"He is still the same guy," said McDowell, who has been with Dykstra on and off since 1982. "You know what I mean, nobody on the other team liked him because of his antics on base, the way he steps out of the box and those faces he makes."

Off the field, Dykstra removes that large wad of tobacco from his mouth and is pretty much a loner. Occasionally, he can be seen moving through a hotel lobby with a teammate, but he dances to his own beat in his own world, a world he doesn't let many people visit.

Dykstra is as hard to keep still for a conversation as he is to throw out stealing—and he has been successful 80 percent of the time (166-for-207) in his six-year, big-league career. His thoughts drift in and out. Ask him a question and his reply could be about anything. However, there is one thing he thinks about most often—

Bunting is one of Lenny's many skills.

improving the Phillies.

Above all else, that is why Thomas dealt for him.

"I knew we needed a leadoff hitter and a center fielder, but I also knew we needed a crap-kicker in the clubhouse and dugout," Thomas said. "I knew I hated his little butt when he played against us. You hated to see him come to town. He still ticks me off at times, but he can play.

"And I will tell you another thing. Lenny Dykstra is no dummy. He's a pretty smart guy. He's street smart and baseball smart."

Look at that Eddie Haskell face and you might wonder about Thomas' assessment of Dykstra's knowledge of the game. But, listen to Dykstra talk about hitting, fielding and the game in general and you know differently.

Thomas gets to listen to Dykstra probably more than he cares to since Dykstra is always talking about what the Phillies need to do to improve.

His trips to the front office didn't start in Philadelphia, however. "With the Mets, I always went to the office and told them I was capable of doing things they didn't think I could do," Dykstra said. "After that, I told them I wanted to be traded."

His two-month coma in 1989 aside, he has been everything the Phillies could have expected. And yet that two-month period will serve as fodder for his critics, who are expecting the 28-year-old Dykstra to roll over now that he has secured a big contract.

"The only reason I hesitate to put him in a class with Pete Rose is because I saw the flip side," Vukovich said of Dykstra's disappointing finish in 1989. "But if all you saw was last year, when he was mentally prepared, he paralleled Pete."

Lofty praise, indeed. Especially coming from Vukovich, who played with Rose and makes no bones about his respect for baseball's all-time hit leader and the player who taught the Phils how to win in 1980.

"He's baseball smart. He's got some street in him just like Pete," Vukovich continued. "When he would get to first base and there would be a break in the action, he would say some things that had great logic to them."

Without the huge 1990 season, Dykstra wouldn't have inked that large contract. And his strong season has paid off in other ways, too. He was selected to tour Japan with a team of U.S. All-Stars after the World Series. Meersand says the requests for endorsements have been "absolutely unreal." And the Phillies, striking while the iron is hot, are marketing him like no other player in the club's history.

The season-ticket brochure features pictures of "Dr. Dirt" (Dykstra) and "Mr. Clean" (Dale Murphy) on its cover. In addition, the same picture in poster form will be given out on Opening Day 1991 at Veterans Stadium.

"He fits," says marketing director Dennis Mannion. "For once we have a player who is concurrent with the marketing department's ideas."

Considering Hall of Fame locks Steve Carlton, Schmidt and Rose all played for the Phillies' that is some compliment.

All-Star starter. Fourth-leading hitter in the league. Big contract. Endorsements. Cover-boy status. All for a player whom the Mets never thought would be a regular.

If that's not vindication, what is?

JOSE RIJO AND THE NASTY BOYS

By HAL McCOY

They refer to themselves singularly as "The Officer," "The Genius" and "Mr. Mellow." Collectively, they are "The Nasty Boys"—the heart, the soul and the substance of the Cincinnati Reds' bullpen.

Rob Dibble is "The Officer." Norm Charlton is "The Genius." Randy Myers is "Mr. Mellow."

Jose Rijo's dressing cubicle in the Cincinnati clubhouse is close enough for him to overhear anything any of the Nasties utter, but he wants no part of them.

That's because Rijo is a starting pitcher who strives to finish what he starts. Rijo, a 25-year-old Dominican right-hander, won two games during the Reds' four-game destruction of Oakland in the 1990 World Series and earned MVP honors, but Myers finished both of Jose's victories.

Late in Game 4, manager Lou Piniella strode to the mound to ask Rijo how he felt as Myers pumped his left arm to life in the bullpen.

"Do what you want to do," Rijo told Piniella, knowing exactly what Piniella wanted to do. When a game is on the line, Piniella always dials 1-800-NASTY. Myers finished the A's and, in three World Series appearances, gave up no runs, two hits, no walks and struck out three in three innings. Dibble dazzled, too, in his three appearances—one victory, no runs, three hits, one walk and four strikeouts in 4⅔ innings. Charlton pitched one scoreless inning and gave up a hit.

From the big-league beginnings of Pete Rose through The Nasty Boys, Hal McCoy of the Dayton News *has covered the Cincinnati Reds.*

Jose Rijo checks "The Officer's" jewelry at Series workout.

But cold, hard statistics don't begin to describe "The Nasty Boys."

The saga began last spring in Plant City, Fla., when Myers, newly acquired from the New York Mets in a stunning trade for John Franco, watched Dibble throw fast, faster and fastest. He mixed in some 88-mph sliders with 100-mph fastballs—speeds that could get you arrested in the Mojave Desert.

"Man, that's some nasty stuff," Myers said. And a nickname was born for the three fire-shooting bullpenners.

The Nasty Boys.

The name already was in use for a Friday night television series and copyrighted by NBC television. David Fishof, Myers' agent, approached NBC and was given permission for the Reds' relievers to use the name. NBC was so enthralled over Myers, Dibble and Charlton promoting the name that they dispatched black baseball caps with "Nasty Boys" scrawled in pink on the front.

The TV version didn't survive the season. The baseball version was a bombastic hit, heavily marketed all season with Nasty Boys T-shirts and posters.

In addition, on each Nasty Boy's locker is a black sticker with the Legend, "Bad to the Bone." And after each Cincinnati victory last season, home or away, Myers inserted a tape into the clubhouse stereo system and, with the volume at ear-busting levels, the rap group M.C. Hammer sang "U Can't Touch This."

Dibble, 27, nicknamed "The Officer" after Saturday morning cartoon character Officer Dibble, has a collection of police officers' caps across the top shelf of his dressing cubicle. It was a strange twist for a man who served three different league and team suspensions and was fined more than $3,000 for varying indiscretions during the 1989 season.

Charlton, 28, nicknamed "The Genius" because he graduated from prestigious Rice University with a triple major—political science, religion and physical education—began 1990 in the bullpen. But when injuries sidelined starters Danny Jackson and Rijo early in the season, Piniella moved Charlton into the rotation.

"He is on temporary loan," Myers said. "He is still a Nasty Boy." Myers was correct. When the playoffs and World Series commenced, Charlton was back in the bullpen.

During last year's playoffs, Pirates' manager Jim Leyland uttered an unforgettable assessment of Dibble: "Right-handed, left-handed, cross-handed. If Dibble is throwing 100 miles an hour, it doesn't make a damned bit of difference from which side of the plate you bat."

Dibble and Charlton, road roommates, are inseparable, eating

RIJO AND THE NASTY BOYS   19

cheeseburgers for lunch every day, a ritual, and dressing alike. They had no nicknames before Myers arrived, just reputations.

Dibble's fastball was clocked at 100 mph in three parks in 1989 and it has gotten faster. In one game against the Pirates in the NLCS last year, the right-hander was caught at 100 mph six times and at 101 twice. Lefties Charlton and Myers are consistently between 92 and 96 mph on the speed guns.

The Nasty Boys took shape with Myers' arrival in the deal that sent Franco, owner of a club-record 148 saves in six Cincinnati seasons, home to New York. As a Met, Myers was known as "Psycho"—he once shot up the Mets' clubhouse with a BB gun— but he took one look around the Cincinnati clubhouse and said, "Dibble and Charlton are the crazy ones. I'm mellow compared to them."

Evidence refutes the claim. The 28-year-old Myers' tailor is Uncle Sam. He leans toward camouflage shirts, hats and pants. His locker is an ammunition depot—disarmed hand grenades (well, he says they're disarmed), metal drab olive ammunition boxes he uses to store valuables and a hunting knife with an eight-inch blade jammed into the wood of his dressing stall.

"Myers is crazy all the time," Dibble says. "I don't do anything off the field. I'm a nice, quiet, family man with a religious background. People have the conception that if I weren't pitching, I'd be a mass murderer. I'm not, but if that's the reputation I have with hitters, that's fine with me."

Of course, Dibble did nothing to damage his reputation as an intimidator when he gave his honest, unfavorable opinions of people such as National League president Bill White and deceased baseball commissioner A. Bartlett Giamatti during the '89 season. Dibble was one of banished manager Pete Rose's staunchest supporters during the investigation of Rose's gambling habits, calling Giamatti "a Yale, Yuppie egghead who knows nothing about baseball."

But when Rose heard that Piniella planned to use Dibble as a stopper, Rose said Dibble couldn't do it, that his mechanics were bad and he'd come down with a sore arm. Dibble retaliated. "To my face, Pete said I was the best he'd ever seen in my job," Dibble said. "He used me like a side of beef and I never complained. What's he know? I take care of my arm and I've never had a sore arm in my life."

How crazy is Myers? You decide.

During spring training, he fished a half-dead water moccasin out of a pond next to the Reds' clubhouse and carried it into the building, scattering teammates to far locations. He also comman-

Norm ("The Genius") Charlton went 12-9 with 2.74 ERA.

deered equipment manager Bernie Stowe's mini-bike and whizzed around the clubhouse at breathtaking speeds. He borrowed a small pay-loader from a construction crew and tried to guide it into the clubhouse, but the doors weren't wide enough.

Dibble attracts the most attention on the field, because he wears his emotions publicly, from the scowl on his face to the angry eruptions when things don't go his way. Once last season, after giving up a couple of hits, Dibble barged into the dugout and tried to rip out a bolted temporary wall that sometimes separates the photographers' booth from the dugout. "I never do well when that thing is up," Dibble explained. "Why do people always focus on me? Other guys throw things and show emotion and nobody makes a big deal of it."

Maybe folks watch Dibble closely because of a series of incidents in 1989:

In the spring, after giving up a home run to Mike Laga, Dibble

Randy ("Mr. Mellow") Myers was second in NL saves (31).

assaulted some picnic tables outside the clubhouse with a bat and tossed several metal folding chairs into the pond. For that, he was fined.

Also during spring training, Dibble was ticketed by a Plant City police officer for speeding. Dibble claimed the officer was harassing him because he was a ballplayer and he represented himself in court. Case dismissed.

In April, he fired a fastball behind Dodger Willie Randolph's head and, after the game, was quoted as saying, "If he wants to do something about it, he knows where I am. He can come and get me." Dibble was fined for throwing at Randolph and for the inflammatory remarks, but beat the inflammatory remarks portion of his fine by pleading his case with White.

In May, after giving up a run-scoring hit to Terry Pendleton, Dibble picked up Pendleton's bat and hurled it against the backstop. It came within six inches of whizzing over it and into the stands. For that, he was fined by both the club and the league and suspended by the NL.

In July, he was suspended again after he hit the Mets' Tim Teufel between the 1's on the No. 11 that Teufel wears on his back. Teufel knew where Dibble was and went after him, torching a brawl.

Enter Charlton.

Charlton bolted from the bullpen to help his buddy. During the skirmish, Charlton ended up on the ground and said Juan Samuel kicked him in the back. After the fight was sorted out, Dibble and Charlton were ejected. Charlton telephoned the Mets' clubhouse and Darryl Strawberry answered the phone.

"Put Samuel on the phone," Charlton demanded. When Strawberry answered with some obscenities, according to Charlton, Charlton said, "Well, then, you come out and I'll whip you." Contingents from both clubs were on their way to a tunnel rumble under Shea Stadium when security police intervened.

Late in the 1989 season, after Rose was banned, interim manager Tommy Helms ordered Dibble to bunt, but he swung away. An incensed Helms fined and suspended Dibble and wanted to ship him to Class-AAA Nashville, but Dibble pleaded his case to owner Marge Schott and remained with the Reds. Helms was fired after the season.

Mix in Myers and his GI Joe Soldier of Fortune reputation and what do you get?

"I hated him when he was in New York," Charlton admits. "Why not? He was on the other team and he was good. And we didn't accept him right away when he joined us."

It didn't take long for Myers to win over his new teammates. How can you dislike a guy who invites you to play croquet?

During an exhibition game last spring in Plant City, Myers grabbed a coat hanger and twisted it into a croquet wicket, planting it atop the bullpen pitcher's mound. He, Charlton and Dibble used baseballs and bats to play croquet.

"We concentrated more on hitting each other's balls into the weeds than putting our balls through the wicket," Myers said. Once the croquet game ended, Myers placed a resin bag atop a paper cup and honed his golf swing. Tiring of that, he boarded the mini-bike and played polo, making laps around the fenced-in confines of the bullpen, whacking paper cups with a bat.

Explaining their modus operandi, Charlton says, "We want to be just like television's Nasty Boys. They're bad . . . and I mean in the good sense."

Charlton didn't forget the incident with Samuel. Twice during the 1990 season, Charlton's message pitches came close to Samuel. Early in the season, he hit Philadelphia's Von Hayes. The Phillies remembered. Later in the season, they buzzed Charlton, touching off another fight.

In a game against the Dodgers in midseason, Charlton tried to score from second base on a shallow single to left, running through a stop sign from third-base coach Sam Perlozzo. Catcher Mike Scioscia, known for putting bold baserunners on the disabled list, blocked home, but Charlton lowered his valuable left shoulder and sent Scioscia sprawling.

"That's my job," said Charlton, who went 12-9 with a 2.74 ERA. "I don't just pitch, I play the game, too."

His shoulder was sore for a week, but his teammates were amazed.

"I loved it," outfielder Glenn Braggs said. "To see a pitcher do something like that, man it just fired everybody up."

As the season progressed, Myers (4-6, 2.08, 31 saves) raked in the saves and Dibble (8-3, 1.74, 11 saves, 136 strikeouts in 98 innings) served mostly as his set-up man, the same as he had done for Franco. And his salary status rankled him.

Dibble used the National League playoffs as a personal forum, holding daily mass press conferences to state his case and demand a trade.

"If I'm going to keep going out there and blowing away my arm every year, I want to be paid like a stopper," he said. "Pay me or trade me. This is my third year. I'm unhappy and I just want to go somewhere else where there is a stopper's role for Rob Dibble."

And of "The Nasty Boys" theme, Dibble said, "You just psyche the other team up with crap like that. It's good for posters and T-shirt sales, but the problem with labels is they end up in lockerroom walls. I was intimidating before the Nasty Boys got here."

Even manager Piniella agreed.

"They put pressure on themselves by coming up with a nickname like that," he said. "It stirs up the opposition and you have to live up to it. Those guys did."

And how did the other Nasties feel about Dibble's remarks?

Charlton, standing next to Dibble during one of his tirades, said, "Dibs, you have more problems than a run-over dog."

Meanwhile, in actuality, it was the 25-year-old Rijo who felt like the run-over dog the first half the season. He started fine, going 4-1 in his first 10 starts, but he couldn't finish what he started and needed The Nasties to bail him out.

Series MVP Rijo was pretty nasty himself.

A sore shoulder put him on the disabled list June 28 and, during the All-Star break, he had a chat with his father-in-law, Hall of Fame pitcher Juan Marichal.

Marichal put it on the line for Rijo.

"All you ever talk about is that your shoulder hurts," Marichal said. "Cut it out. If you hurt, don't pitch. If you pitch, don't complain."

Rijo told Marichal that his shoulder ached after every start and Marichal said, "Your shoulder is supposed to hurt after each start. That's natural."

Rijo took his father-in-law's advice at face value. Maybe he was right.

"He is my hero," Rijo said. "I talk to him on the telephone before I pitch. Every time. He gives me advice and confidence."

Heeding Marichal's advice to ignore the between-starts pain was the best thing Rijo ever did.

He came off the disabled list July 21 and pitched seven complete games while going 9-5 in his last 15 starts. He finished 13-6, lowering his ERA from 3.52 to 2.70.

"By the end of the season, Jose was the best pitcher in the National League, maybe in baseball," Piniella said.

Rijo proved it in the NLCS and the World Series and displayed a trait that qualified him as an honorary Nasty Boy—some intimidating talk.

After the Reds swept four games from the Padres in San Diego, including a complete-game, five-hitter by Rijo Sept. 21, Rijo said concerning the NL West race, "I don't care what Yogi Berra said about it not being over until it's over, it is over."

At the time, the Reds led the division by five games with nine to play. Some of his teammates admonished him for his honesty, but he didn't back down.

In fact, after Rijo beat Bob Walk, 5-3, in Game 4 of the NLCS to give the Reds a 3-1 lead in games, Rijo once again said, "It's over. Pittsburgh can pack for home. The pennant is ours."

Pittsburgh won Game 5, but the Reds wrapped it up in Game 6, sending them to the World Series.

The media tried to bait Rijo after the Reds beat Oakland in Games 1 and 2, trying to get him to repeat his "It's over" message. This time, Rijo wouldn't crow.

But, before Game 1, Rijo called a Cincinnati writer aside and lifted his uniform jersey to display a T-shirt. Inscribed on the T-shirt was, "It's over."

The Nasty Boys couldn't have said it better.

FAR EAST TO FAR OUT: FIELDER'S FIFTY

By GENE GUIDRY

It was a typically raw late January day in Detroit more than a year ago when Cecil Fielder arrived at Tiger Stadium. Just a week before, he had joined the Tigers as a free agent after tours of duty with the Toronto Blue Jays and Hanshin Tigers of the Japanese League.

General manager Bill Lajoie, the man who signed Fielder to a two-year, $3-million contract, spotted the club's newest employee, greeted him with a handshake and said, "Hi Cecil, I'm Bill Lajoie."

Bo Schembechler, the ex-University of Michigan coaching legend who has started a second career as Tigers' president, watched the exchange between Lajoie and Fielder with widening eyes.

"You mean to tell me you gave this guy $3 million without even laying eyes on him?" Schembechler said, only half-jokingly.

But as winter turned to spring and then the long summer and baseball took its hold on the country, Fielder became the biggest story of the 1990 season—and perhaps the biggest bargain in the sport.

On the last day of the Tigers' season in New York, Fielder hit his 50th and 51st homers to become only the 11th player in big-league history—and only the second in the last 25 years—to reach the magical 50 mark. The last major-league player to hit 50 had been George Foster, who slugged 52 in 1977.

How tough is it to hit 50 homers? Consider that, among the

Gene Guidry, a sportswriter for the Detroit Free Press *since 1978, started covering baseball in 1984, the year the Tigers won their fourth world championship.*

Cecil Fielder: Tiger clout unmatched since Hank Greenberg.

14 players who hit 500 career homers, 10 never hit 50 in a season: Hank Aaron, Frank Robinson, Harmon Killebrew, Reggie Jackson, Mike Schmidt, Ted Williams, Willie McCovey, Eddie Mathews, Ernie Banks and Mel Ott. No Tiger had turned the trick since Hank Greenberg slugged 58 in 1938.

If someone like Killebrew or Schmidt had put together a 50-homer season, no one would have been the least bit surprised. But Fielder, whose previous major-league homer high was 14 with Toronto in 1987? He was a guy who came into last season with the modest goal of just wanting to be wanted.

"After what happened in Toronto, I didn't want the Tigers to think they had a big mistake by taking a chance on me," Fielder said. "I didn't want them to have any second thoughts."

Second thoughts? The only second thoughts have to be coming from north of the border, where the Blue Jays considered Fielder expendable. There are certainly no misgivings in Detroit, a city that normally takes a dim view of Japanese imports. When Fielder switched his Tiger stripes from Hanshin to Detroit, he quickly became the exception to that rule.

After the Tigers finished 59-103 in 1989, Detroit fans needed something positive to hang their baseball hopes upon. Fielder gave them that. As the homers piled up, each Fielder at-bat at Tiger Stadium became a happening. Local newspapers prominently displayed a daily "Cecil Watch." The most-asked question around the breakfast table changed from "Did the Tigers win last night?" to "Did Cecil hit one?"

Fielder, 27, is built for power at 6-foot-3, 250 pounds. But his sudden emergence as major-league baseball's premier home-run hitter was unexpected if only because he never played regularly in the majors before last season. In Toronto, he was behind Willie Upshaw and then Fred McGriff on the Blue Jays' depth chart at first base.

"Hitting is tough enough as it is without having to worry about going back to the bench after a couple of hitless games," Fielder said. "They would say I was 0-for-12 or 1-for-15, but that was going in and out of the lineup. It's tough to get started like that."

The Blue Jays had a chance to sell Fielder to Japan prior to the 1989 season and he okayed the deal.

Each Japanese baseball team is allowed two Americans, called gaijin, on the active roster. Japanese scouts come to America in search of talent—usually big, strong power hitters who can easily reach the shorter fences in Japanese stadiums.

One of the reasons Fielder decided to give Japan a try was money, lots of it. With the Blue Jays, he was making $125,000.

Japan gave "Wild Bear" a hero's welcome last fall.

The Hanshin Tigers paid him $1,050,000. "I had a chauffeur and a full-time interpreter, too," Fielder said.

But the big reason Fielder went to Japan at age 25 was the opportunity to play every day. Fielder said the competition was better than most American baseball fans think.

"The position players aren't as good, but they've got some tough pitchers," Fielder said. Maybe more than anything, the Japanese pitching style—heavy on breaking balls—helped Fielder become a dangerous hitter upon his return to the U.S.

Throughout the 1990 season, even when he was down to his last strike and knew he would see a steady diet of curves, Fielder was a threat to hit the ball with authority. Unlike many power hitters, he was particularly adept at going down to get a low curve and putting it into orbit.

More than once, an opposing pitcher shook his head after a Fielder home run and commented, "I thought I made a good pitch."

During his one season in Japan, Fielder hit 38 homers in 384 at-bats. He led the Japanese League in slugging percentage (.628), was third in RBI (81) and became a hero to the local baseball fans. They nicknamed him "Wild Bear"—wild is the image of power in Japan—even though he was more of a mild bear. Fielder, whose hulking presence was easy to spot in a crowd of smallish Japanese, caused a stir wherever he went.

People would point at him and talk in wonderment about the game in which he hit two home runs that went entirely out of the stadium in Yokohama, a heretofore unheard of feat.

Fielder was a returning hero when he played for the major leagues in a postseason tournament last fall in Japan. Young children were particularly impressed, bowing deeply when Fielder honored a autograph request, which he always did.

It brought back pleasant memories for him.

"I miss it [playing in Japan] sometimes," Fielder said. "They treated us [the players] beautifully. The Japanese love the game. And they never boo."

While playing for Hanshin, Fielder and his family lived in a large three-bedroom home with a view of the ocean. The club provided him with a satellite dish that picked up American baseball games. In fact, the Hanshin team picked up the tab for everything, right down to the silverware and plates.

On road trips, Fielder and Matt Keough, a former Oakland pitcher who was the other American on the Hanshin team, stayed at Western-style hotels while their Japanese teammates stayed at more traditional lodgings.

"The beds were too small for us in those places," Fielder said. "They sleep on mats on the floor. We were too big for that."

Baseball is baseball, no matter where it is played, but some things about the Japanese version took a little getting used to.

Like spring training. In America, spring training is six laid-back weeks in the warmth of Florida or Arizona. In Japan, it's two months of tough eight-hour days filled with strenuous work—often in cold weather. It's nothing for a player in Japan to take 1,000 batting practice swings a day during spring drills. And don't try to get by with only 975 swings, because someone is standing behind the batting cage and counting.

Fielder actually signed a two-year contract with the Hanshin club, but his agent had built an escape clause into the agreement that would let Fielder return to the U.S. after one year. At first, Fielder balked when his agent suggested that he go back to the major leagues.

"I was comfortable in Japan. My wife [Stacey] and son [Prince] liked it there," Fielder said.

What his family thinks is important to Fielder. He credits Stacey with keeping him from giving up on baseball when it looked like the sport was giving up on him.

But the Tigers, rejected by free-agent first basemen Kent Hrbek and Pete O'Brien, showed a strong interest. The Tigers dispatched a scout to get an up-close and personal view of Fielder. After 10 minutes, the scout was convinced that Fielder was worth the multi-million-dollar gamble.

What might have finally convinced Fielder to come back home was what happened to his friend, Larry Parrish. The season after Parrish, also an ex-major leaguer, led the Japanese League in homers, he was released by a fickle Japanese team intent on switching to a speed-oriented offense.

So, when the Tigers offered Fielder a $1.5-million signing bonus, $500,000 for the 1990 season and $1 million in 1991, he decided to say sayonara to Japan.

An even-tempered, quick-to-smile Fielder was immediately accepted by his new teammates, one of whom was his old high-school buddy, catcher Mark Salas. While his incredible season was unfolding, Fielder would always rather talk with Salas about the good old days at Nogales High School in Los Angeles. Fielder was a three-sport star there, excelling in football as well as baseball and basketball.

His mother, Tina, will tell you that her son made an impact in the sports arena right from the start. She said that when he was an eight-year-old Little League pitcher, a group of parents signed a petition to remove Cecil after he struck out 17 of their kids in one game. He was so big and so good that the parents figured he belonged at a higher level.

After high school, Fielder was chosen by the Kansas City Royals in the fourth round of the June 1982 draft and then traded to Toronto for outfielder Leon Roberts in 1983.

Fielder split the 1985 and 1986 seasons between the minors and majors. He stuck with the Blue Jays throughout 1987 and 1988, but got less than 200 at-bats each year.

Even after his big year in Japan, no one quite knew what to expect from Fielder. Tigers manager Sparky Anderson, who often elevates unknown talents to the doorstep of immortality, was uncharacteristically reserved when discussing Fielder.

"Truthfully, I didn't know what to expect," Anderson said. "I didn't know if he would hit, and I didn't know if he could field well enough to play regularly."

Fielder turned out to be a surprisingly good defensive first baseman. "He catches what he gets to," Anderson said.

Fielder flashed power in spring training, including a three-homer exhibition game against the Cardinals. But the feat didn't cause high excitement, mainly because it was accomplished in a tiny Florida ballpark against pitchers who were behind in their development because of the lockout.

More media attention was paid to the Tigers' other new free agents, Tony Phillips and Lloyd Moseby. Fielder remained more of a curiosity than anything else as a player trying to make it back to the majors after a year in Japan. Teammate Paul Gibson teased Fielder, saying, "Canada. Japan. America. You played in three countries and nobody wants you."

But when the season started, Fielder showed that he was for real. He hit 15 homers in 31 days, starting with a three-homer game in Toronto on May 6 and ending with a three-homer game in Cleveland on June 6.

Most power hitters are streaky, but after that early homer cluster, Fielder became a model of consistency. On his climb to 50, Fielder produced a homer every three or four games over the last half of the season. The only time he went more than a week without a homer was a span of 11 homerless games from June 18 through June 29.

Entering the game of June 30, he was halfway there with 25 homers. He homered June 30 in Kansas City. In July and August, he hit one homer in 12 of the Tigers' 16 series. He had two multi-homer series and two homerless series. Fielder entered September with 42 homers and the pressure started to build.

With each succeeding homer, another out-of-town writer or two would show up in the Tigers' clubhouse looking for Fielder. He tried to accommodate everyone, answering questions thoughtfully, even though he had answered the same ones yesterday and the day before that.

Finally, in the last week of the season, the Tigers moved to give Fielder a little breathing room by calling a halt to pre-game interviews. "I really believe that sort of thing wears on you," said Anderson. "It takes away your concentration."

Fielder later admitted that he almost didn't get to 50, "because I was trying to please everybody by trying to hit every ball out of the park. That's not my style. It's not my game. I don't go up there swinging for home runs—at least I didn't before those last few games, when I became a different hitter. It wasn't me anymore."

Fielder hit his 49th homer with six games left. After going homerless in 21 plate appearances over the next five games, he had one last chance in the season finale against the Yankees at Yankee Stadium. In his third at-bat in the fourth inning, Fielder

When he wasn't slugging, Cecil played a tidy first base.

crunched a 2-1 fastball from from rookie left-hander Steve Adkins, who was making his fifth big-league start. The drive, never more than 15 feet fair, banged off the facing on the left-field upper deck.

Throughout the season, when he homered, Fielder, his head down, had trotted around the bases almost apologetically.

''I don't think it's right to show up the pitcher,'' Fielder said. ''He feels bad enough as it is. They respect you more if you just run around the bases and get out of there.''

But when Fielder made contact on No. 50, he just couldn't help himself. He threw his bat in the air and clapped his hands. Home-plate umpire Rocky Roe said Fielder exclaimed loudly "Yes! Yes!" as soon as he hit the ball.

With the pressure from chasing 50 homers finally gone, Fielder added to his super season with No. 51. He finished with 51 homers and 132 RBI, both major-league highs.

No one was more proud of Fielder's accomplishment than his mother.

"I always thought of Cecil as my little boy," she said. "But then I watched the way he handled himself with the press and everybody. He was so polite and a gentleman. Then, it really hit me that my son was a man."

Happily for his mom, all the attention Fielder received helped set the world straight that his first name is pronounced 'Ceh-cil,' not 'Cee-cil.'

"We named him after his Uncle Cecil," she said. "We changed the pronunciation, so they wouldn't get mixed up."

Not much ruffles Fielder and he would patiently correct anyone who called him 'Cee-cil.' But he would also warn them—"Don't let my mother hear you call me that."

As satisfying as the season was for Fielder, he often talked about looking forward to retreating to his offseason home in Arlington, Tex., when it was over. The fan adulation was nice, Fielder said, but he's smart enough to understand the flip side.

"People can be such front-runners," Fielder said. "No one even thought about me a few years ago."

Maybe that's why Fielder says he won't go home and brood about being underpaid. In these days of huge contracts signed by power hitters like Jose Canseco and Darryl Strawberry, what is a 51-homer season worth?

Fielder just shrugs off that kind of speculation. His agent has talked to the Tigers about a contract extension, but Fielder says he will not demand a renegotiation. Of course, "If everyone was happy" with a contract extension, he'd accept one. "I'm human—I like security," Fielder said.

The big question going into Fielder's second season with the Tigers is: what will he do for an encore?

The pressure to produce will be there from Opening Day this time.

"Don't expect another 50," Anderson said. "That just doesn't happen back-to-back. But they won't stop him from hitting in the 30s—they can't stop him from getting that many. And that ain't bad."

INSIDE ROTISSERIE LEAGUE BASEBALL®

By GLEN WAGGONER

The best team in baseball in 1990? Not the Cincinnati Reds, despite their World Series sweep. Not the Oakland Athletics, despite their 103 regular-season victories. No, the best team in baseball last year was the Stein Brenners, winner of the Rotisserie League pennant and early favorite to repeat as champion in 1991.

The Stein Who? The Stein Brenners? I thought he was out of baseball. And what's that about a Rotisserie League? Does that have something to do with backyard barbecues? I don't understand . . .

You and me, both. As a founding father of Rotisserie League Baseball, I simply do not understand why the Stein Brenners keep on winning. What's that? You mean you don't understand Rotisserie League Baseball? No problem. You've come to the right place.

Hatched by a cadre of crazed geniuses at a now-defunct Manhattan bistro that lent part of its moniker to the fledgling enterprise, Rotisserie League Baseball exploded onto the national scene in 1980. For those who fault the lack of imagination in the distinctly low-concept name, consider this: it could have been "La Rotisserie Francaise Baseball." Or worse still, we could have been having lunch at our second-favorite place, and today the summer game's

---

Glen Waggoner, a contributing editor for Esquire *and co-editor of* Rotisserie League Baseball, *is a founding father of what he describes as baseball's third major league.*

most astonishing craze would be called ''Blimpy League Baseball.'' And, for mean-spirited carpers who think ''exploded'' is too strong a word, maybe ''plunked'' is more like it for that first year, when we stumbled blindly into a magnificent obsession that would transform millions . . . well, dozens of lives.

But five books—all of them called, cleverly enough, *Rotisserie League Baseball*—and about a zillion wacky trades later, there is definitely something going on in America. It's Rotisserie Fever and if you haven't caught it yet, you soon will.

Although we have done everything in our power to make it as complicated as possible, Rotisserie League Baseball is simplicity itself: It's a way for you to own your own major-league baseball team, and make all the decisions on how it's run, without having to put up $75 million or so to buy one of the 26 teams already around. Here's how it works:

At the beginning of the baseball season, you and a bunch of other certified baseball crazies get together to form a league. If you prefer the National League, your league will have 10 teams. If you favor the American League, you will need 12 teams. (That's the ideal number; you can play with fewer.)

Each of the teams in your league then acquires, at open auction, a team of nine pitchers and 14 batters. The batters have to be distributed as follows: two catchers, three first basemen-third basemen, three middle infielders, five outfielders and one utility man-DH. Each owner-general manager may spend a maximum of 260 Rotissedollars (R$) and players go to the highest bidder, one by one, until each team is fully stocked.

We use real money, by the way, but that's not necessary. Many teams across the country use pocorobas or bocabellas or some other imaginary unit of measure. This is a game about baseball savvy, not cash. What is important is that you have a 260-unit limit on the amount you spend to acquire your 23 players.

Team performance is tracked in eight statistical categories, the raw data for which is found in the morning boxscores: home runs, RBI, stolen bases and batting average for position players; wins, saves, ERA and ratio (walks plus hits divided by innings pitched) for pitchers. Teams are ranked according to totals in each category (10 points for first, nine for second, etc.) and points are added to determine weekly standings.

If you draft brilliantly, all you do is sit back, put your feet up, and spend the summer watching your team accumulate stats that, measured against the performances of other teams, will confirm that you astutely selected the best starters, the speediest basestealers, the most powerful sluggers, the craftiest relievers—in

**ERIC DAVIS
R$38**

*When will the performance
catch up to the potential?*

**DELINO DeSHIELDS
R$30**

*Look for more SB, more HR,
more everything. A rising star.*

other words, the best team in your league.

The catch is, you probably didn't draft all that brilliantly—you
overpaid here, let a bargain slip by there, loaded up on power but
ignored pitching, made all the mistakes that owners-GMs make
in real baseball. And a couple of superstars get off to super-flop
starts. And then you have a couple of injuries. And all of a sudden,
a certain pennant winner is sinking towards the cellar. Remember,
if it can happen in major-league baseball, it can happen in Rotisserie Baseball.

So what do you do? Sit there helplessly and watch your season,
your team, your life turn to shambles? No way. That's second-
division thinking. You do what any rational person would do. You
give up sleep. You start going to strange religious services, the
kind that begin at the stroke of midnight outside cemeteries. You
kick the dog. And you wheel and deal.

Unlike our major-league counterparts, who cite the complex-
ities and restrictions of modern contracts to rationalize their lack
of guts and imagination, we Rotisserie League owners-GMs show

about as much restraint as Jose Canseco demonstrates when he sees a belt-high fastball.

Wheeling and dealing is the whole point of Rotisserie League Baseball. It's what gives you the strength each morning to look at the baseball news when your team is struggling. You're looking for that key rookie call-up, that change in a pitching rotation, that important inter-league trade that will give you new leverage in the deal you've been cooking for a couple of weeks. If Strat-O-Matic and APBA are "manager's games"—Rotisserie League Baseball is a "general manager's game"—if you can imagine a general manager who is one part rug merchant, one part carnival huckster and two parts Sandy Alderson.

Let's say you bought Cecil Fielder for 11 Rotissedollars at last year's preseason auction draft. That's the price of an "average" Rotisserie regular (260 units divided by 23, remember?). At the time, it seemed like a pretty big risk. Fielder hadn't shown much in his four seasons with Toronto and who knew whether all those homers in Japan would translate into big power numbers in Detroit? But you had this feeling, so you went to R$11 and he was yours. So, this year, you're sitting pretty, right? All you have to is sit back while Cecil bangs those dingers.

Wrong. Now may be the best time in the world for a Rotisserie owner to trade Cecil Fielder. As much as you like Fielder, maybe you don't believe he's going to hit 50 homers and drive in 100-plus runs again. But if someone else in your league does believe he is capable of back-to-back bonanza years, you might be able to get a bundle for him. How about Jeff Montgomery (R$12, a great price for a closer), Randy Milligan (R$8, good value), Alex Cole (R$10, a midseason callup in 1990), and Mike MacFarlane (R$2, more RBI than most AL catchers) for Fielder?

Done. Why? Because you pick up a lot of saves from Montgomery, you get back most of the RBI with Milligan and MacFarlane and you get a stolen-base bonus from Cole.

A deal like that would never be made in major-league baseball, but it actually happened during the offseason in a league I play in. And that sort of deal is commonplace in Rotisserie League Baseball.

Beyond wheeling and dealing, a Rotisserie League owner-GM keeps his team in contention by watching the waiver wire, selecting wisely from the free-agent pool when one of his players goes on a major-league disabled list, fine-tuning his farm system so it can help the big club in midseason, and picking up a role player who can drive in a few crucial runs or notch a key victory when rosters are expanded from 23 in September.

BO JACKSON
R$35
Bo, how about this football thing? Give it up.

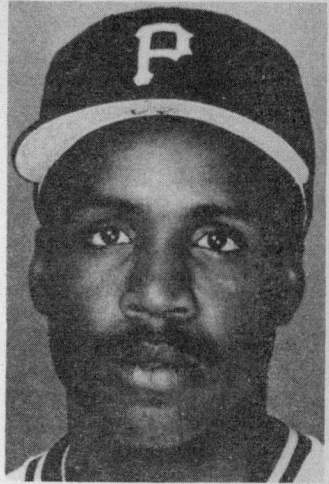

BARRY BONDS
R$40
He is what Bo would be if Bo would give up this football thing.

During the season, running a Rotisserie League team is pretty much a 24-hour preoccupation. Oh, we all hold jobs and pay the rent and stay in touch with our families (sort of), but Rotisserie League Baseball seeps into your life until it takes over. It fills gaps that you never even knew existed. It becomes the mortar between your bricks. Go to a dull business meeting and keep your face looking interested by letting your mind tinker with your starting lineup. Get caught in traffic and keep your blood pressure down by plotting a blockbuster deal. Pretty soon you find yourself wondering whatever in the world you did with your time before Rotisserie baseball.

The first Sunday after Opening Day, if you follow a Rotisserie pattern set in 1980, determines whether the rest of the year is worth staying awake for. In our case, for example, at precisely 10:00 A.M., 10 ostensibly reasonable, mature adults assemble in the dining room of our Beloved Commissioner for Life, Cork Smith, who is former owner of the ill-fated Smith Coronas and an original member of the famed La Rotisserie Francaise Roundtable.

DENNIS ECKERSLEY
R$43
The best in the business. And priced accordingly.

RON GANT
R$36
Last year he went for R$1 in most drafts. Guess he deserves a raise.

Sitting at the table masking their nervousness in mindless banter are mercurial Steve Wulf, a *Sports Illustrated* editor who heads the Wulfgang (winners of the 1981 Rotisserie League pennant); Michael Pollet, a lawyer whose Pollet Burros never win anything; studious Bob Sklar, New York University cinema studies professor and chief astronomer of the Sklar Gazers (1984 champs); crafty insurance exec Cary Schneider, chairperson of the Cary Nations (1985 and 1989 victors); philosopher Harry Stein, managing partner of the despised Brenners, the only four-time pennant winners (1983, 1986, 1988, 1990) in league history; magazine editor Lee Eisenberg of the Furriers, who have one title (1982) under their pelts; New York bon vivant Peter Gethers, Sturgeon-General of Peter's Famous Smoked Fish, named after a St. Petersburg seafood joint; and yours truly, whose Glenwag Goners won the first-ever Rotisserie League pennant back in 1980; Rob Fleder, head mouse-keteer of the Fleder Mice (1987 winners); and last (usually), writer, editor and jazz musicologist Daniel Okrent, our Beloved Founder and Former Commissioner for Life, and also the environmental protector of the Okrent Fenokees (who have never won anything but the hoots and jeers of their fan).

The auction draft commences when the preceding season's cellar-dweller announces the name of a player and a minimum bid of R$1. As soon as that player is sold to the highest bidder, the next owner introduces a player, and so it goes until every team has been fully stocked.

The process takes the better part of a day, not to mention the better part of your heart and soul. You love Von Hayes, but is he ever going to have a R$32 season? Will Eric Davis stay healthy? Can Don Mattingly come back? Is Mo Vaughn going to make it in Boston? Does Carney Lansford have another good year left in him? Is Roger Clemens going to break down again and waste your R$28 investment? Is Ray Lankford for real? What about Geronimo Pena? Will Eric Anthony hit enough dingers to make up for his putrid batting average? Do you have enough speed? Can you get by with just four starters and a strong pen? Who will be the Ron Gant of 1991?

It's precious little consolation if you find yourself caught up in this madness, but upwards of one million dazed, bleary-eyed Rotisserie owners-GMs are, that same weekend in April, going to be in the throes of that same sweet agony. That's the estimated number of people who are playing Rotisserie League Baseball or some reasonable facsimile thereof.

Some people are nuts enough to play in two leagues, if you can believe it. Like me, for instance. I play in an outfit called Tony's Italian Kitchen League, whose flag was won last year by a brand-new franchise last year, the John Paul Popes (owned by a couple of guys named John and Paul who resisted league pressure to call their team the Ringos). I play in the Kitchen League because they use American League players. How else would I ever learn the Texas Rangers' starting rotation? How would I learn the name of the California Angels' fourth outfielder or the guy who might step in for the White Sox if Bobby Thigpen were hurt? I would only be half a man.

What do Rotisserie League players get out of the game, besides spousal estrangement, overheated brains, funny looks from baseball-hating friends, flinty stares from bosses, bags under their eyes from studying boxscores, social leper status at parties and insomnia when your best starter gives up five earned runs, four hits and three walks in two-thirds of an inning?

If you have a good draft, and make a few smart deals, and catch a break on injuries, and are very, very lucky, you get a

ELLIS BURKS
R$24
Why did he stop running in 1990?

IVAN CALDERON
R$26
Why did he start running in 1990?

bottle of Yoo-Hoo poured over your head.

Yes, Yoo-Hoo, the delicious chocolate beverage that Yogi Berra used to endorse. At least, we assume it's delicious. Actually, we never touch the stuff. But we do pour a bottle over our pennant winner's head every year, just after we hand him a cheesy trophy signifying his victory and a winner's check (we play for dollars, but you can play for acorns and still have fun).

The dough is gone within days, the trophy gathers dust on a bookshelf, but the memory of Yoo-Hoo trickling over your nose and down your neck will live forever—because no winner to date has been able to wash it off.

Rotisserie League Baseball is all about buying your own team of major leaguers at auction. It's about shoring up weaknesses during the season with trades, free-agent signings and waiver moves. It's about twisting in agony when watching a game and all of a sudden, one of your hitters steps up against one of your pitchers with the bases loaded. It's about buying every baseball magazine and newspaper at the newsstand for shreds of information that might help your pennant drive. It's about calling 900-226-STAT (at 95 cents a minute) before going to bed to see who got the save in a night game on the West Coast and whether Jose Canseco hit another homer in Oakland.

And it's about forgetting, after years of being a diehard fan, to root, root, root for the home team, because now you have another team to root for. Your own.

HOW TO GET STARTED

1. Round up enough other baseball fanatics like yourself to form a league. Ideally, you should have 10 teams if you use National League players and 12 teams if you use American League players, but it's okay to have fewer.

2. Get a copy of the new, 1991 edition of *Rotisserie League Baseball*. It's the official rulebook, and it contains complete player ratings and a lot of crucial stats.

3. Set a date just after Opening Day for your auction draft. It will take five or six hours. If possible, get somebody who doesn't own a team to serve as auctioneer. You're going to have your hands full trying to build a pennant-winner without the added burden of keeping a dozen or so crazy people in hand.

4. Join the Rotisserie League Baseball Association. The RLBA provides member leagues with all sorts of useful information, including position eligibility lists, four newsletters, and a championship certificate for your league's pennant winner. Write RLBA, 41 Union Square West, Suite 1226, New York, N.Y. 10003 for information. Or call 212-691-7846.

5. Play Ball!

HOW TO KEEP SCORE

The only thing not fun about Rotisserie League Baseball is keeping score. You have to tally the numbers each week and you have to keep track of players traded, put on reserve, and released. It takes five-to-seven hours to do it by hand with a calculator or two or three hours if you have a computer and a spread-sheet program (you still have to enter the data and record the transactions). Fortunately, there is a better way. Rotisserie League Stats, the official stats service of the Rotisserie League Baseball Association, will compile team stats, record transactions and mail you weekly standing reports, all for only a few bucks a week per team.

For complete information, including instructions on how to do keep you own standings by hand, write Rotisserie League Stats, 41 Union Square West, Suite 1226, New York, N.Y. 10003; or call 212-691-7846.

HOW TO BUILD A WINNER

1. **Go after players you like.** Yeah, you're supposed to be a hard-headed, unsentimental GM, but unless you have a couple of players on your teams that you really like, you're going to lose interest and fall into the second division.

2. **Maintain your balance.** While it's possible to win with a handful of high-priced superstars (e.g., Rickey Henderson, Jose Canseco, Roger Clemens) and a supporting cast of mediocrities, the teams that usually fare best in Rotisserie League Baseball are balanced clubs, solid in all categories with lots of steady, capable regulars.

3. **You've got to have a strong bench.** That's the way it is in the American and National Leagues, so why should it be any different in the Rotisserie League? This means figuring out which fourth infielders and fifth starters are going to help you the most. It means finding a set-up man (Barry Jones of Chicago, for example) capable of getting you from eight to ten wins.

4. **Hang back for bargains at the draft.** The owner who

comes out of the auction draft with the strongest team is the owner who manages his budget the best. At the start, there is a feeding frenzy, as everyone overspends on the first superstars to come up for auction. Hold steady. Be patient. Let the other owners deplete their resources, then you waltz in and scoop up bargains.

5. **Don't forget the end game.** As in chess, the end game in Rotisserie League Baseball is a game unto itself. When everybody has only a few positions left to fill and not many Rotissedollars to spend, the concept of value no longer pertains. It may make sense at this stage to spend R$8 on an outfielder who's worth only R$2 simply because he's the best one available.

6. **Don't feel bad if you hate your team after the auction draft.** *Every* owner hates his team after the auction draft. It'll take a couple of days before you get a handle on what kind of team you really have, to know your own strengths and weaknesses and to begin to think about what kind of moves you need to make.

7. **Don't be afraid to trade.** Just because you buy a dog doesn't mean you have to live with fleas. As an owner, you simply have to take chances, unless your team is obviously so strong that it's going to win the pennant in a landslide. If Kent Hrbek is your best power hitter and your best base-stealing threat, you know you're in trouble in stolen bases. Do something about it.

8. **You've got to have an ace closer.** If there's one huge way that the game has changed over the last 40 years, it's in the importance of a strong bullpen—and the emergence of superstar relief specialists. An ace closer will cost a lot of R$, but you have to have one to be a contender.

9. **Cream rises.** Don't panic if Jack Clark is under .200 on Memorial Day; he never starts hitting until June. If Glenn Davis has only three dingers in April and May, don't worry about it— he's been the most consistent slugger in baseball the last five years. You can take this to the bank: Established veterans who start slow will play up to their career standard—George Brett was the rule last year and Robin Yount was the exception—and younger players who start off hot will cool down.

INSIDE THE
NATIONAL LEAGUE

By KEVIN KERNAN and JOHN BELIS
San Diego Union   *Bridgewater*
                          Courier-Post

	West	East
PREDICTED ORDER OF FINISH	Los Angeles Dodgers San Francisco Giants Cincinnati Reds Atlanta Braves San Diego Padres Houston Astros	Chicago Cubs Pittsburgh Pirates New York Mets Philadelphia Phillies Montreal Expos St. Louis Cardinals

Playoff Winner: Los Angeles

WEST DIVISION		Owner		Morning Line Manager
1	**DODGERS** New blood makes difference	Peter O'Malley Royal blue & white	**1990** W 86 L 76	2-1 Tommy Lasorda
2	**GIANTS** White, orange & black Will make it a tight race	Bob Lurie	**1990** W 85 L 77	5-2 Roger Craig
3	**REDS** Red & white Need blinders to win	Marge Schott	**1990** W 91 L 71	5-1 Lou Piniella
4	**BRAVES** Improving, but not ready to run distance	W. Bartholomay/S. Kasten Royal blue & white	**1990** W 65 L 97	40-1 Bobby Cox
5	**PADRES** Brown, gold & white Not armed for victory	Tom Werner	**1990** W 75 L 87	50-1 Greg Riddoch
6	**ASTROS** Orange & white Time for pasture	John McMullen	**1990** W 75 L 87	100-1 Art Howe

Bolstered **DODGERS** get off to fast start and hold on when **GIANTS** make bid down the stretch. **REDS** can't keep up the pace and fall back at clubhouse turn. **BRAVES** make early strides, **PADRES** stumble out of the gate and **ASTROS** never leave the barn.

Strawberry Stakes

115th Running. National League Race. Distance: 162 games plus playoff. Payoff (based on '90): $112,533 per winning player, World Series; $69,995 per losing player, World Series. A field of 12 entered in two divisions.

Track Record: 116 wins—Chicago, 1906

EAST DIVISION		Owner		Morning Line Manager
1	**CUBS** Royal blue & white Return to '89 form	Tribune Co.	1990 W 77 L 85	3-1 Don Zimmer
2	**PIRATES** Old gold, white & black Unlikely to repeat	Douglas Danforth	1990 W 95 L 67	4-1 Jim Leyland
3	**METS** Orange, white & blue Not enough heart	N. Doubleday/F. Wilpon	1990 W 91 L 71	5-1 Buddy Harrel-son
4	**PHILLIES** Crimson & White Must prove they can go distance	Bill Giles	1990 W 77 L 85	10-1 Nick Levya
5	**EXPOS** Scarlet, white & royal blue Always fade down the stretch	Claude Brochu	1990 W 85 L 77	15-1 Buck Rodgers
6	**CARDINALS** Red & white Out of their class	August A. Busch III	1990 W 70 L 92	100-1 Joe Torre

CUBS have the horses and lead wire-to-wire as **PIRATES** have trouble duplicating last race. **METS** make strong bid but don't sustain it. **PHILLIES** lead back of the pack, edging **EXPOS** and tail-end **CARDINALS**.

ATLANTA BRAVES

TEAM DIRECTORY: Chairman: Bill Bartholomay; Pres.: Stan Kasten; Sr.VP/Asst. to Pres.: Hank Aaron; GM: John Schuerholz: Dir. Scouting and Player Development: Chuck LaMar; Dir. Pub. Rel.: Jim Schultz; Trav. Sec.: Bill Acree; Mgr.: Bobby Cox. Home: Atlanta-Fulton County Stadium (52,007). Field distances: 330, l.f. line; 402, c.f.; 330, r.f. line. Spring training: West Palm Beach, Fla.

SCOUTING REPORT

HITTING: Following last summer's departure of icon Dale Murphy, there is Justice for Braves' fans. NL Rookie of the year Dave Justice (.282, 28, 78) has the sweetest left-handed swing this side of Will Clark. Add Ron Gant (.303, 32, 84, 33 steals) and the Braves have two serious weapons. When Lonnie Smith (.305, 9, 42) is motivated, he can be dangerous, too. Only the Mets hit more homers than the Braves' 162, but no team had a lower on-base percentage than Atlanta's .311, which explains why the Braves ranked seventh in runs with 682.

New GM John Schuerholz opened the safe to Ted Turner's millions and signed free agents Terry Pendleton and Sid Bream. Though Pendleton (.230, 6, 58 with Cards) is coming off a bad year, he'll replace free agent Jim Presley at third. Bream (.270, 15, 67 with Pirates), a leader, will play first and hit behind Justice, giving the Braves their first left-handed four-five hitters since moving to Atlanta. If Nick Esasky beats vertigo, the disorder that ruined his 1990 season, the Braves will have another thumper.

PITCHING: For years, we've heard about the potential of these guys, but this southern-fried staff finished dead last in ERA with a bloated 4.58 mark last year.

Only John Smoltz (14-11, 3.85, 170 Ks) has proven to be the real thing among the starters. Tom Glavine (10-12, 4.28) was a huge disappointment and rookie Steve Avery (3-11, 5.64) paid the price for being rushed. Newly re-signed Charlie Leibrandt (9-11, 3.16) pitched better than his record indicates while Pete Smith (5-6, 4.79) is a question mark because of rotator cuff woes.

The Braves' bullpen managed just 30 saves all year—27 less than the White Sox' Bobby Thigpen. Left-handed Kent Mercker (4-7, 3.17, 7 Sv) did a decent job at the end of last season and is being counted upon heavily.

David Justice was served in Rookie-of-Year balloting.

FIELDING: The infield at Atlanta-Fulton County is the worst cow pasture in the majors, but that still doesn't excuse Presley's 26 errors at third. That's why Braves went after two-time Gold Glove winner Pendleton. Pendleton and Bream join second baseman Jeff Treadway and shortstop Jeff Blauser in a vastly improved infield, but there are still gaping holes elsewhere—left fielder Smith, to name one. Smith's .956 fielding percentage was the poorest among NL starting outfielders.

OUTLOOK: Last year, the Braves finished dead last for the fourth time in five seasons at 65-97 and Bobby Cox had to step down as GM and take over as manager. If his club doesn't get off to a good start, Cox' next move will be out of the tepee. The Braves have added enough position help to move all the way up to third if the arms come around.

ATLANTA BRAVES 1991 ROSTER

MANAGER Bobby Cox
Coaches—Jim Beauchamp, Pat Corrales, Clarence Jones, Leo Mazzone, Jimy Williams

PITCHERS

No. Name	1990 Club	W-L	IP	SO	ERA	B-T	Ht.	Wt.	Born
42 Avery, Steve	Richmond	5-5	82	69	3.50	L-L	6-4	180	4/14/70 Trenton, MI
	Atlanta	3-11	99	75	5.64				
36 Castillo, Tony	Richmond	3-1	25	27	2.52	L-L	5-10	188	3/1/63 Venezuela
	Atlanta	5-1	77	64	4.23				
40 Freeman, Marvin	SWB-Rich.	4-7	74	56	4.84	R-R	6-7	222	4/10/63 Chicago, IL
	Phil.-Atl.	1-2	48	38	4.31				
47 Glavine, Tom	Atlanta	10-12	214	129	4.28	L-L	6-0	175	3/25/66 Concord, MA
56 Gomez, Pat	Richmond	1-1	15	8	8.80	L-L	5-11	185	3/17/68 Roseville, CA
	Greenville	6-8	124	94	4.49				
55 Grant, Mark	SD-Atl.	2-3	91	69	4.73	R-R	6-2	215	8/24/63 Aurora, IL
32 Leibrandt, Charlie	Greenville	1-0	13	12	0.00	R-L	6-3	200	10/4/56 Chicago, IL
	Atlanta	9-11	162	76	3.16				
34 Marak, Paul	Richmond	9-8	148	75	2.49	R-R	6-2	175	8/2/65 England
	Atlanta	1-2	39	15	3.69				
50 Mercker, Kent	Richmond	5-4	58	69	3.55	L-L	6-2	195	2/1/68 Dublin, OH
	Atlanta	4-7	48	39	3.17				
49 Parrett, Jeff	Phil.-Atl.	5-10	109	86	4.64	R-R	6-3	193	8/26/61 Indianapolis, IN
51 Rivera, Ben	Greenville	1-4	52	32	6.58	R-R	6-3	160	8/21/66 Dominican Republic
	Durham	5-3	75	64	3.60				
25 Smith, Pete	Greenville	0-0	3	2	0.00	R-R	6-2	200	2/27/66 Weymouth, MA
	Atlanta	5-6	77	56	4.79				
29 Smoltz, John	Atlanta	14-11	231	170	3.85	R-R	6-3	185	5/15/67 Detroit, MI
30 Stanton, Mike	Atlanta	0-3	7	7	18.00	L-L	6-1	190	6/2/67 Houston, TX
	Greenville	0-1	6	4	1.59				
	Richmond	2-0	20	20	0.00				
57 Turner, Matt	Greenville	6-4	68	60	2.66	R-R	6-5	215	2/18/67 Lexington, KY
	Richmond	2-3	42	36	3.86				
58 Wendell, Turk	Durham	1-3	39	26	1.86	L-R	6-3	175	5/19/67 Greenville, TN
	Greenville	4-9	91	85	5.74				

CATCHERS

No. Name	1990 Club	H	HR	RBI	Pct.	B-T	Ht.	Wt.	Born
19 Cabrera, Francisco	Richmond	30	7	20	.227	R-R	6-4	193	10/10/66 Dominican Republic
	Atlanta	38	7	25	.277				
17 Kremers, Jim	Richmond	44	6	24	.232	L-R	6-3	205	10/8/65 Little Rock, AR
	Atlanta	8	1	2	.110				
38 Mann, Kelly	Greenville	49	7	27	.316	R-R	6-3	215	8/17/67 Santa Monica, CA
	Richmond	41	3	20	.202				
	Atlanta	4	1	2	.143				
10 Olson, Greg	Atlanta	78	7	36	.262	R-R	6-0	200	9/16/60 Marshall, MN
	Richmond	0	0	0	.000				

INFIELDERS

No. Name	1990 Club	H	HR	RBI	Pct.	B-T	Ht.	Wt.	Born
11 Bell, Mike	Greenville	118	6	42	.291	L-L	6-1	175	4/22/68 Lewiston, NJ
	Atlanta	11	1	5	.244				
6 Belliard, Rafael	Pittsburgh	11	0	6	.204	R-R	5-6	150	10/24/61 Dominican Republic
4 Blauser, Jeff	Atlanta	104	8	39	.269	R-R	6-0	170	11/8/65 Los Gatos, CA
— Bream, Sid	Pittsburgh	105	15	67	.270	L-L	6-4	220	8/3/60 Carlisle, PA
62 Castilla, Vinny	Sumter	91	9	53	.268	R-R	6-1	175	7/4/67 Pittsfield, MA
	Greenville	40	4	16	.235				
17 Esasky, Nick	Atlanta	6	0	0	.171	R-R	6-3	215	2/24/60 Hialeah, FL
20 Lemke, Mark	Bradenton	4	1	5	.364	S-R	5-9	167	8/13/65 Utica, NY
	Atlanta	54	0	21	.226				
9 Pendleton, Terry	St. Louis	103	6	58	.230	S-R	5-9	180	7/16/60 Los Angeles, CA
18 *Presley, Jim	Atlanta	131	19	72	.242	R-R	6-1	190	10/23/61 Pensacola, FL
8 Rosario, Victor	Scranton	120	5	42	.251	R-R	5-11	145	8/26/66 Dominican Republic
	Atlanta	1	0	0	.143				
14 Thomas, Andres	Atlanta	61	5	30	.219	R-R	6-1	185	11/10/63 Dominican Republic
15 Treadway, Jeff	Atlanta	134	11	59	.283	L-R	5-11	170	1/22/63 Columbus, GA

OUTFIELDERS

No. Name	1990 Club	H	HR	RBI	Pct.	B-T	Ht.	Wt.	Born
37 Berroa, Geronimo	Richmond	134	12	80	.269	R-R	6-0	195	3/18/65 Dominican Republic
	Atlanta	0	0	0	.000				
5 Gant, Ron	Atlanta	174	32	84	.303	R-R	6-0	172	3/2/65 Victoria, TX
16 Gregg, Tommy	Atlanta	63	5	32	.264	L-L	6-1	190	7/29/63 Boone, NC
61 Hunter, Brian	Greenville	77	14	55	.241	R-L	6-0	195	3/4/68 Torrance, CA
	Richmond	27	5	16	.197				
23 Justice, David	Richmond	16	2	7	.356	L-L	6-3	195	4/14/66 Cincinnati, OH
	Atlanta	124	28	78	.282				
1 McDowell, Oddibe	Atlanta	74	7	25	.243	L-L	5-9	160	8/25/62 Hollywood, FL
63 Mitchell, Keith	Durham	134	6	48	.294	R-R	5-10	180	8/6/69 San Diego, CA
27 Smith, Lonnie	Atlanta	142	9	42	.305	R-R	5-9	170	12/22/55 Chicago, IL
59 Tomberlin, Andy	Greenville	61	4	25	.311	L-L	5-11	160	11/7/66 Monroe, NC
	Richmond	86	4	31	.304				
24 Vatcher, Jim	Scranton	46	5	22	.254	R-R	5-9	165	5/27/66 Santa Monica, CA
	Phil.-Atl.	19	1	7	.260				

*Free agent at press time

BRAVE PROFILES

RON GANT 26 6-0 172   Bats R Throws R

No longer a man without a position . . . Has found a home in center . . . Started 1989 as Braves' third baseman after playing second in 1988 . . . Was eventually sent to Sumter (A) in '89 to learn to become a center fielder . . . Lashed 32 homers, stole 33 bases and batted .303 to rank as Comeback Player of the Year candidate . . . Along the way, he joined some pretty good company . . . Only two other Braves have produced 30-30 seasons—Hank Aaron in 1963 and Dale Murphy in 1983 . . . Is playing center on raw instinct and figures to improve . . . Arm is less than average, but that seems to be the norm these days at that spot . . . Set career highs in every offensive category . . . Born March 2, 1965, in Victoria, Tex. . . . Braves' fourth-round selection in 1983 draft . . . Due for a big raise, he made just $125,000 in '90.

Year Club	Pos.	G	AB	R	H	2B	3B	HR	RBI	SB	Avg.
1987 Atlanta.	2B	21	83	9	22	4	0	2	9	4	.265
1988 Atlanta.	2B-3B	146	563	85	146	28	8	19	60	19	.259
1989 Atlanta.	3B-OF	75	260	26	46	8	3	9	25	9	.177
1990 Atlanta.	OF	152	575	107	174	34	3	32	84	33	.303
Totals		394	1481	227	.388	74	14	62	178	65	.262

DAVE JUSTICE 24 6-3 195   Bats L Throws L

There was Justice for the Braves once they traded Dale Murphy . . . First baseman moved to right field and became one of the biggest home-run threats in baseball and NL Rookie of the Year . . . Though he wasn't called up from Richmond (AAA) until May 28, he still finished with 28 home runs . . . Imagine how many homers he would have hit if he had started season with Braves . . . Really started rolling when he took over for Murphy in right Aug. 4 . . . Hit 10 homers in 12-game stretch that month . . . Bashed 67 homers in five years in the minors . . . Born April 14, 1966, in Cincinnati . . . Earned $100,000 last year . . . Selected by Braves in fourth round of 1985 draft.

Year Club	Pos.	G	AB	R	H	2B	3B	HR	RBI	SB	Avg.
1989 Atlanta.	OF	16	51	7	12	3	0	1	3	2	.235
1990 Atlanta.	1B-OF	127	439	76	124	23	2	28	78	11	.282
Totals		143	490	83	136	26	2	29	81	13	.278

LONNIE SMITH 35 5-9 170   Bats R Throws R

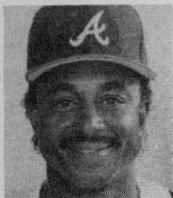

Perhaps he spoke at too many hot-stove functions after being named NL Comeback Player of the Year in 1989, because he came to spring training at 223 pounds and did not begin to get into shape until season was in progress . . . Decent leadoff hitter, he batted over .300 for second straight year . . . Had only 42 RBI and hit .233 with runners in scoring position . . . Past drug woes caused him to go begging for work . . . Was finally given tryout by Braves and signed as a minor-league free agent in March 1988, after winning MVP honors in Puerto Rico Winter League . . . His two-year, $1.75-million contract runs out at end of this season . . . Weak defensively, he made 12 errors in left . . . Played on three world championship teams with Phils and Cards . . . Born Dec. 22, 1955, in Chicago . . . Phils' first-round pick in 1974 draft.

Year Club	Pos.	G	AB	R	H	2B	3B	HR	RBI	SB	Avg.
1978 Philadelphia . . .	OF	17	4	6	0	0	0	0	0	4	.000
1979 Philadelphia . . .	OF	17	30	4	5	2	0	0	3	2	.167
1980 Philadelphia . . .	OF	100	298	69	101	14	4	3	20	33	.339
1981 Philadelphia . . .	OF	62	176	40	57	14	3	2	11	21	.324
1982 St. Louis	OF	156	592	120	182	35	8	8	69	68	.307
1983 St. Louis	OF	130	492	83	158	31	5	8	45	43	.321
1984 St. Louis	OF	145	504	77	126	20	4	6	49	50	.250
1985 St. Louis	OF	28	96	15	25	2	2	0	7	12	.260
1985 Kansas City . . .	OF	120	448	77	115	23	4	6	41	40	.257
1986 Kansas City . . .	OF	134	508	80	146	25	7	8	44	26	.287
1987 Kansas City . . .	OF	48	167	26	42	7	1	3	8	9	.251
1988 Atlanta.	OF	43	114	14	27	3	0	3	9	4	.237
1989 Atlanta.	OF	134	482	89	152	34	4	21	79	25	.315
1990 Atlanta.	OF	135	466	72	142	27	9	9	42	10	.305
Totals		1269	4377	772	1278	237	51	77	427	347	.292

SID BREAM 30 6-4 220   Bats L Throws L

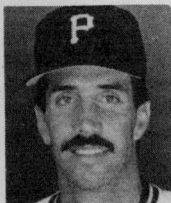

Left Pirates as free agent, signing three-year, $5.5-million contract with Braves . . . First baseman homered off Jose Rijo in NLCS Game 1 to spark 4-3 Pirate victory . . . Altered stance and swing last season to improve power . . . His 15 homers were one short of his career high and his ratio of one homer for each 26 at-bats was his best since 1985 . . . Born Aug. 3, 1960, in Carlisle, Pa. . . . Selected by Dodgers in second round of 1981 draft . . . Traded to Pirates with Cecil Espy and R.J. Reynolds for Bill Madlock, Sept. 9, 1985 . . . Earned $510,000 in 1990.

Year	Club	Pos.	G	AB	R	H	2B	3B	HR	RBI	SB	Avg.
1983	Los Angeles . . .	1B	15	11	0	2	0	0	0	2	0	.182
1984	Los Angeles . . .	1B	27	49	2	9	3	0	0	6	1	.184
1985	L.A.-Pitt.	1B	50	148	18	34	7	0	6	21	0	.230
1986	Pittsburgh	1B-OF	154	522	73	140	37	5	16	77	13	.268
1987	Pittsburgh	1B	149	516	64	142	25	3	13	65	9	.275
1988	Pittsburgh	1B	148	462	50	122	37	0	10	65	9	.264
1989	Pittsburgh	1B	19	36	3	8	3	0	0	4	0	.222
1990	Pittsburgh	1B	147	389	39	105	23	2	15	67	8	.270
	Totals		709	2133	249	562	135	10	60	307	40	.263

NICK ESASKY 31 6-3 215   Bats R Throws R

Weirdest story of one weird year . . . After setting career highs with 30 homers and 108 RBI with Red Sox in 1989, this first baseman signed a three-year pact with Braves for $5.6 million as free agent . . . Proceeded to play in just nine games and batted .171 with no homers and no RBI because he suffered from vertigo . . . "We don't know if he'll ever play again," said Braves manager Bobby Cox . . . Born Feb. 24, 1960, in Hialeah, Fla. . . . Selected to Cincinnati in first round of 1978 draft . . . Red Sox acquired him and Rob Murphy for Todd Benzinger, Jeff Sellers and Luis Vasquez before 1989 season.

Year	Club	Pos.	G	AB	R	H	2B	3B	HR	RBI	SB	Avg.
1983	Cincinnati	3B	85	302	41	80	10	5	12	46	6	.265
1984	Cincinnati	3B-1B	113	322	30	62	10	5	10	45	1	.193
1985	Cincinnati	3B-OF-1B	125	413	61	108	21	0	21	66	3	.262
1986	Cincinnati	1B-OF-3B	102	330	35	76	17	2	12	41	0	.230
1987	Cincinnati	1B-3B-OF	100	346	48	94	19	2	22	59	0	.272
1988	Cincinnati	1B	122	391	40	95	17	2	15	62	7	.243
1989	Boston	1B-OF	154	564	79	156	26	5	30	108	1	.277
1990	Atlanta	1B	9	35	2	6	0	0	0	0	0	.171
	Totals		810	2703	336	677	120	21	122	427	18	.250

JEFF BLAUSER 25 6-0 170   Bats R Throws R

Pure hustle enabled him to take the job at short from brooding Andres Thomas, who demanded to be traded several times during the season . . . Ended up playing 93 games at short in his second season . . . Also played 14 at second . . . His future could be as utility man, the Braves' answer to Jose Oquendo . . . If there is a trade rumor, he's usually in the middle of it . . . Earned $180,000 last year . . . Born Nov. 8, 1965, in Los Gatos,

Cal. . . . Braves' No. 1 selection in secondary phase of 1984 draft . . . Hit .241 with runners in scoring position.

Year Club	Pos.	G	AB	R	H	2B	3B	HR	RBI	SB	Avg.
1987 Atlanta.......	SS	51	165	11	40	6	3	2	15	7	.242
1988 Atlanta.......	2B-SS	18	67	7	16	3	1	2	7	0	.239
1989 Atlanta.......	3B-2B-SS-OF	142	456	63	123	24	2	12	46	5	.270
1990 Atlanta.......	SS-2B-3B-OF	115	386	46	104	24	3	8	39	3	.269
Totals		326	1074	127	283	57	9	24	107	15	.264

JEFF TREADWAY 28 5-11 170   Bats L Throws R

Second baseman is never given a shot, but somehow he survives . . . Put together excellent offensive year, batting .283, the third-best mark on the team . . . Hit .341 with runners in scoring position . . . Produced the offensive highlight film of his life when he smashed three homers in 6-1 win at Philadelphia May 27 . . . Hit 11 homers, none after July 17 . . . Reds sold him to Braves, March 25, 1989 . . . Earned $250,000 last year . . . Resident of Griffin, Ga. . . . Born Jan. 22, 1963, in Columbus, Ga. . . . Attended University of Georgia.

Year Club	Pos.	G	AB	R	H	2B	3B	HR	RBI	SB	Avg.
1987 Cincinnati.....	2B	23	84	9	28	4	0	2	4	1	.333
1988 Cincinnati.....	2B-3B	103	301	30	76	19	4	2	23	2	.252
1989 Atlanta.......	2B-3B	134	473	58	131	18	3	8	40	3	.277
1990 Atlanta.......	2B	128	474	56	134	20	2	11	59	3	.283
Totals		388	1332	153	369	61	9	23	126	9	.277

TERRY PENDLETON 30 5-9 195   Bats S Throws R

After seven seasons as a Cardinal, he signed four-year, $10.2-million contract with Braves as free agent . . . Coming off most disappointing year . . . Was pushed into background during final month of 1990 season as Cardinals played Todd Zeile at third base . . . Drove in 55 runs by Aug. 27, but picked up just three more RBI during last five weeks . . . Committed 19 errors while playing only 117 games . . . Won Gold Glove at third in 1987 and '89 . . . Batted .429 in 1987 World Series against Twins . . . Most celebrated homer was a two-out, ninth-inning September shot against Mets' Roger McDowell which propelled Cardinals to 1987 pennant . . . Born July 16, 1960, in Los Angeles . . . Selected by St. Louis in first round of 1982 draft . . . Earned $1,850,000 in 1990.

Year	Club	Pos.	G	AB	R	H	2B	3B	HR	RBI	SB	Avg.
1984	St. Louis	3B	67	262	37	85	16	3	1	33	20	.324
1985	St. Louis	3B	149	559	56	134	16	3	5	69	17	.240
1986	St. Louis	3B-OF	159	578	56	138	26	5	1	59	24	.239
1987	St. Louis	3B	159	583	82	167	29	4	12	96	19	.286
1988	St. Louis	3B	110	391	44	99	20	2	6	53	3	.253
1989	St. Louis	3B	162	613	83	162	28	5	13	74	9	.264
1990	St. Louis	3B	121	447	46	103	20	2	6	58	7	.230
	Totals		927	3433	404	888	155	24	44	442	99	.259

JOHN SMOLTZ 23 6-3 185   Bats R Throws R

Will be the ace of this staff for years to come . . . Topped the Braves in wins (14), innings pitched (231⅓) and strikeouts (170) . . . Groin injury caused him to get off to a slow start . . . Throws serious cheese . . . In 1989, he opened the season as the youngest pitcher in the NL . . . That year, he also became the youngest All-Star pitcher in franchise history . . . Earned $210,000 last season . . . Born May 15, 1967, in Detroit . . . Signed by Tigers as free agent in September 1985 . . . Traded to Braves for Doyle Alexander, Aug. 12, 1987.

Year	Club	G	IP	W	L	Pct.	SO	BB	H	ERA
1988	Atlanta	12	64	2	7	.222	37	33	74	5.48
1989	Atlanta	29	208	12	11	.522	168	72	160	2.94
1990	Atlanta	34	231⅓	14	11	.560	170	90	206	3.85
	Totals	75	503⅓	28	29	.491	375	195	440	3.68

TOM GLAVINE 25 6-0 175   Bats L Throws L

Took a step backward last season to 10-12, after posting 14-8 mark in 1989 . . . Has a tendency to overthrow and that's when he gets in trouble . . . Control faltered as a result . . . Dominated the NL West two years ago, running up 9-1 record, but was 0-4 in own division in 1990 . . . Born March 25, 1966, in Concord, Mass. . . . Braves' second-round pick in 1984 draft, he also was fourth-round pick of Los Angeles Kings' hockey team . . . Made $285,000 last year.

Year	Club	G	IP	W	L	Pct.	SO	BB	H	ERA
1987	Atlanta	9	50⅓	2	4	.333	20	33	55	5.54
1988	Atlanta	34	195⅓	7	17	.292	84	63	201	4.56
1989	Atlanta	29	186	14	8	.636	90	40	172	3.68
1990	Atlanta	33	214⅓	10	12	.455	129	78	232	4.28
	Totals	105	646	33	41	.446	323	214	660	4.29

KENT MERCKER 23 6-2 195   Bats L Throws L

Became savior in battered bullpen, which blew 20 save opportunities in 50 tries . . . Started the year at Richmond (AAA), but was called up when projected closer Mike Stanton went down with bad shoulder . . . For Richmond, where he was 5-4, 10 of his 12 appearances were starts . . . A power pitcher whose control is sometimes a problem . . . Recalled June 28 . . . His seven saves tied him with Stanton (1989) and Paul Assenmacher (1986) for most saves by a lefty Atlanta reliever . . . Born Feb. 1, 1968, in Dublin, Ohio . . . First-round selection in 1986 draft and the fifth player chosen overall . . . Earned $102,000 last year.

Year	Club	G	IP	W	L	Pct.	SO	BB	H	ERA
1989	Atlanta	2	4⅓	0	0	.000	4	6	8	12.46
1990	Atlanta	36	48⅓	4	7	.364	39	24	43	3.17
	Totals.	38	52⅔	4	7	.364	43	30	51	3.93

TOP PROSPECTS

RYAN KLESKO 19 6-3 220   Bats L Throws L

Big first baseman is considered the best power-hitting prospect in the organization . . . Started the season at Sumter (A), where he hit 10 homers, drove in 38 runs and batted .368 in 63 games . . . Was promoted to Durham (AA) for next 77 games and he hit seven homers and drove in 47 runs while batting .274 . . . Born June 12, 1971, in Westminster, Cal. . . . Braves' sixth-round selection in 1989 draft.

PAUL MARAK 25 6-2 175   Bats R Throws R

Sinkerballer was 9-8 with a 2.49 ERA for Richmond (AAA) . . . ERA was best mark in the International League . . . Earned late-season call-up to Braves . . . Posted a 1-2 mark with a 3.69 ERA in seven starts for Atlanta . . . Born Aug. 2, 1965, in Lakenheath, England . . . Taken in the 11th round of January 1985 draft.

GERONIMO BERROA 26 6-0 195   Bats R Throws R

Outfielder may be best suited for American League style of play . . . Was third in International League in RBI with 80 for Richmond (AAA) . . . Batted .269 and hit 12 homers . . . Born March 18,

1965, in Santo Domingo, Dominican Republic . . . Drafted from the Toronto organization after 1988 season . . . Signed by the Blue Jays as a free agent in 1983.

MANAGER BOBBY COX: Came down from the front office on June 22, when Russ Nixon was fired . . . The Braves, 20-35 at the time, went 45-62 under him . . . Excellent field manager who knows how to get the most out of his players . . . Spent five years as Braves' GM . . . Joined the Braves in October 1985, ending 25-year on-the-field career as player, coach and manager . . . Managed Blue Jays from 1982-85 . . . Took team that finished seventh in 1984 to within one game of the World Series in 1985, but Toronto lost Game 7 of ALCS to eventual world champion Kansas City . . . For his work, he was named Manager of the Year in 1985 . . . Third baseman spent 12 years in baseball as a player, 10 years in the minors . . . Started managing in Yankee farm system in 1971 and his clubs never finished lower than fourth . . . Won Eastern League pennant with West Haven (AA) in 1972 . . . Placed second twice and third twice with Syracuse, winning the International Governor's Cup in 1976 . . . Yankee first-base coach in 1977 . . . In his first time around as Atlanta manager, from 1978-81, he posted a 266-323 record . . . Built foundation for Braves' Western Division championship in 1982 . . . Overall major-league managerial record is 666-677.

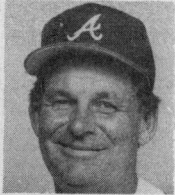

ALL-TIME BRAVE SEASON RECORDS

BATTING: Rogers Hornsby, .387, 1928
HRs: Eddie Mathews, 47, 1953
      Hank Aaron, 47, 1971
RBI: Eddie Mathews, 135, 1953
STEALS: Ralph Myers, 57, 1913
WINS: Vic Willis, 27, 1902
      Charles Pittinger, 27, 1902
      Dick Rudolph, 27, 1914
STRIKEOUTS: Phil Niekro, 262, 1977

CINCINNATI REDS

TEAM DIRECTORY: Principal Owner-Pres.: Marge Schott; Exec. VP: Stephen Schott; GM: Bob Quinn; Dir. Scouting: Julian Mock; Dir. Player Development: Howie Bedell; Dir. Inf. and Publications: Jon Braude; Trav. Sec.: Joel Pieper; Mgr.: Lou Piniella. Home: Riverfront Stadium (52,392). Field distances: 330, l.f. line; 404, c.f.; 330, r.f. line. Spring training: Plant City, Fla.

SCOUTING REPORT

HITTING: It's almost like the days of Big Red Machine again. There's not an easy out in the lineup. The Reds, who led the league in hitting (.265) and ranked fourth in runs (693), will give the power-laden Giants a run for the money for the title of best-hitting club in the NL this year.

For Eric Davis (.260, 24, 86), it was an off year, leaving room for rejuvenated Chris Sabo (.270, 25, 71) to carry the load. Paul O'Neill (.270, 16, 78) and Glenn Braggs (.299, 6, 28) provide pop in right. World Series dynamo Billy Hatcher (.276, 5, 25) is set in center and Barry Larkin (.301, 7, 67) may be the top-hitting shortstop in the majors. Mariano Duncan (.306, 10, 55) should become a super utility man with the addition of free-agent re-signee Bill Doran (.300, 7, 37). Hal Morris (.340, 7, 36) more than filled the need for a left-handed-hitting first baseman.

PITCHING: Nasty, nasty, nasty. Even with the loss of free-agent defector Danny Jackson to the Cubs, this is the best staff in the division. Only the Expos' 3.37 ERA was better than the Reds' 3.39 mark last season.

The starting staff is anchored by boisterous Jose Rijo (14-8, 2.70) and durable Tom Browning (15-9, 3.80). Opponents hit just .212 against Rijo. Enough said.

Expect former Nasty Boy Norm Charlton (12-9, 2.74) to dominate as a fulltime starter. The rotation is rounded out by first-half whiz Jack Armstrong (12-9, 3.42) and either Scott Scudder, prospect Chris Hammond or free-agent addition Ted Power.

In the bullpen, Randy Myers had 31 saves, second in the NL, but Rob Dibble is the reason this pen is the most feared in baseball. One look at Dibble's lifetime stats (19-9, 1.90 ERA, 336 strikeouts, 94 walks and 167 hits in 256.2 innings) shows he's the most overpowering reliever in the NL.

Billy Hatcher hit cool .750 to help sink Athletics.

FIELDING: Pitching and defense wins and the Reds had both in '90. They committed the least amount of errors in the NL (102) and tied the Giants for the best fielding percentage (.983).

Only Ozzie Smith and Spike Owen had better fielding percentages than the rangy Larkin (.977) among NL shortstops and Larkin led in double plays with 86. Hatcher topped the league's outfielders with a .997 percentage and Joe Oliver was the most successful catcher in the league at throwing would-be base-stealers (40.2 percent). And, Davis, Hatcher and O'Neill had a combined total of 33 assists.

OUTLOOK: Once rid of the Pete Rose circus, the Reds dominated under the leadership of the underrated Lou Piniella as they rolled to a 50-28 start and a 91-71 record last year. Everybody tried to catch them in the offseason, but the world champions can't be stopped in '91 unless they lose their focus, suffer key injuries like in '89 or owner Marge Schott destroys the team from within. All three are possibilities.

CINCINNATI REDS 1991 ROSTER

MANAGER Lou Piniella
Coaches—Jackie Moore, Tony Perez, Sam Perlozzo, Larry Rothschild, Stan Williams

PITCHERS

No.	Name	1990 Club	W-L	IP	SO	ERA	B-T	Ht.	Wt.	Born
40	Armstrong, Jack	Cincinnati	12-9	166	110	3.42	R-R	6-5	220	3/7/65 Englewood, NJ
38	Brown, Keith	Nashville	7-8	94	50	2.39	S-R	6-4	210	2/14/64 Flagstaff, AZ
		Cincinnati	0-0	11	8	4.76				
32	Browning, Tom	Cincinnati	15-9	228	99	3.80	L-L	6-1	190	4/28/60 Casper, WY
37	Charlton, Norm	Cincinnati	12-9	154	117	2.74	S-L	6-3	205	1/6/63 Ft. Polk, LA
49	Dibble, Rob	Cincinnati	8-3	98	136	1.74	L-R	6-4	235	1/24/64 Bridgeport, CT
59	Gross, Kip	Nashville	12-7	127	62	3.33	R-R	6-2	190	8/24/64 Scottsbluff, NE
		Cincinnati	0-0	6	3	4.26				
45	Hammond, Chris	Nashville	15-1	149	149	2.17	L-L	6-0	190	1/21/66 Atlanta, GA
		Cincinnati	0-2	11	4	6.35				
—	Hill, Milt	Nashville	4-4	71	58	2.27	R-R	6-0	180	8/22/65 Atlanta, GA
54	Imes, Rodney	Nashville	10-8	170	97	3.71	R-R	6-5	210	11/19/66 Cumberland, MD
43	Layana, Tim	Nashville	5-3	80	53	3.49	R-R	6-2	195	3/2/64 Inglewood, CA
33	Minutelli, Gino	Chattanooga	9-5	108	75	3.99	L-L	6-0	185	5/23/64 Wilmington, DE
		Nashville	5-2	78	61	3.22				
		Cincinnati	0-0	1	0	9.00				
28	Myers, Randy	Cincinnati	4-6	87	98	2.08	L-L	6-1	210	9/19/62 Vancouver, WA
48	Power, Ted	Pittsburgh	1-3	52	42	3.66	R-R	6-4	220	1/31/55 Guthrie, OK
27	Rijo, Jose	Nashville	0-0	4	2	8.31	R-R	6-2	200	5/13/65 Dominican Republic
		Cincinnati	14-8	197	152	2.70				
—	Risley, Bill	Cedar Rapids	8-9	138	123	2.81	R-R	6-2	210	5/29/67 Chicago, IL
—	Sanford, Mo	Cedar Rapids	13-4	158	180	2.74	R-R	6-6	220	12/24/66 Americus, GA
47	Scudder, Scott	Nashville	7-1	81	60	2.34	R-R	6-2	185	2/14/68 Paris, TX
		Cincinnati	5-5	72	42	4.90				
46	Vasquez, Luis	Nashville	4-6	99	54	3.64	R-R	6-1	180	3/23/67 Venezuela

CATCHERS

No.	Name	1990 Club	H	HR	RBI	Pct.	B-T	Ht.	Wt.	Born
9	Oliver, Joe	Cincinnati	84	8	52	.231	R-R	6-3	210	7/24/65 Memphis, TN
34	Reed, Jeff	Cincinnati	44	3	16	.251	L-R	6-2	190	11/12/62 Joliet, IL
55	Sutko, Glenn	Cedar Rapids	3	0	0	.300	R-R	6-3	225	5/9/68 Atlanta, GA
		Chattanooga	29	2	11	.167				
		Cincinnati	0	0	0	.000				

INFIELDERS

No.	Name	1990 Club	H	HR	RBI	Pct.	B-T	Ht.	Wt.	Born
12	Bates, Billy	Milwaukee	3	0	2	.103	L-R	5-7	165	12/7/63 Houston, TX
		Den.-Nash.	106	0	34	.293				
		Cincinnati	0	0	0	.000				
57	Benavides, Freddie	Chattanooga	51	1	28	.259	R-R	6-2	180	4/7/66 Laredo, TX
		Nashville	56	2	20	.211				
25	Benzinger, Todd	Cincinnati	95	5	46	.253	S-R	6-1	190	2/11/63 Dayton, KY
19	Doran, Bill	Hou.-Cin.	121	7	37	.300	S-R	6-0	175	5/28/58 Cincinnati, OH
7	Duncan, Mariano	Cincinnati	133	10	55	.306	R-R	6-0	185	3/13/63 Dominican Republic
58	Jefferson, Reggie	Nashville	34	5	23	.270	S-L	6-4	210	9/25/68 Tallahassee, FL
51	Lane, Brian	Chattanooga	70	6	51	.239	R-R	6-3	215	6/15/69 Waco, TX
		Nashville	31	6	20	.193				
11	Larkin, Barry	Cincinnati	185	7	67	.301	R-R	6-0	185	4/28/64 Cincinnati, OH
26	Lee, Terry	Chattanooga	51	8	20	.327	R-R	6-5	220	3/13/62 San Francisco, CA
		Nashville	79	15	67	.304				
		Cincinnati	4	0	3	.211				
23	Morris, Hal	Nashville	22	1	10	.344	L-L	6-4	215	4/9/65 Fort Rucker, AL
		Cincinnati	105	7	36	.340				
10	Quinones, Luis	Cincinnati	35	2	17	.241	S-R	5-11	180	4/28/62 Puerto Rico
17	Sabo, Chris	Cincinnati	153	25	71	.270	R-R	6-0	185	1/19/62 Detroit, MI

OUTFIELDERS

No.	Name	1990 Club	H	HR	RBI	Pct.	B-T	Ht.	Wt.	Born
15	Braggs, Glenn	Milwaukee	28	3	13	.248	R-R	6-3	220	10/17/62 San Bernardino, CA
		Cincinnati	60	6	28	.299				
44	Davis, Eric	Cincinnati	118	24	86	.260	R-R	6-3	185	5/29/62 Los Angeles, CA
22	Hatcher, Billy	Cincinnati	139	5	25	.276	R-R	5-9	185	10/4/60 Williams, AZ
—	Jones, Chris	Nashville	114	10	52	.261	R-R	6-2	205	12/16/65 Utica, NY
21	O'Neill, Paul	Cincinnati	136	16	78	.270	L-L	6-4	210	2/25/63 Columbus, OH
—	Sanders, Reggie	Cedar Rapids	133	17	63	.285	R-R	6-1	180	12/1/67 Florence, SC
29	Winningham, Herm	Cincinnati	41	3	17	.256	L-R	5-11	185	12/1/61 Orangeburg, SC

RED PROFILES

ERIC DAVIS 28 6-3 185   Bats R Throws R

"Eric the Red" rose to the challenge late last season and quieted his critics... Was in the midst of the worst season of his life before turning it on down the stretch... On Aug. 22, he was hitting .224... From then until Sept. 27, when he injured his left shoulder crashing into the wall at Riverfront Stadium, he hit .357 with nine homers and 29 RBI, carrying the Reds to the division title... Led the team in RBI with 86... Had all kinds of injury woes, including sprained right knee that prompted his move from center to left, bruised shoulder and lacerated kidney ... Last injury occurred in World Series Game 4 victory over A's, when he tried to make a diving catch of Willie McGee's drive in the first inning... Although he hit just .174 in NLCS, he made huge play in late innings of Game 4, hustling from left to center to throw out Pittsburgh's Bobby Bonilla at third base... Started the Reds on their World Series sweep over A's with a two-run homer off Dave Stewart in first inning of Game 1... Hit .276 with five RBI in World Series... Reds' eighth-round selection in 1980 draft... Born May 29, 1962, in Los Angeles... Earned $2.1 million last year.

Year	Club	Pos.	G	AB	R	H	2B	3B	HR	RBI	SB	Avg.
1984	Cincinnati.....	OF	57	174	33	39	10	1	10	30	10	.224
1985	Cincinnati.....	OF	56	122	26	30	3	3	8	18	16	.246
1986	Cincinnati.....	OF	132	415	97	115	15	3	27	71	80	.277
1987	Cincinnati.....	OF	129	474	120	139	23	4	37	100	50	.293
1988	Cincinnati.....	OF	135	472	81	129	18	3	26	93	35	.273
1989	Cincinnati.....	OF	131	462	74	130	14	2	34	101	21	.281
1990	Cincinnati.....	OF	127	453	84	118	26	2	24	86	21	.260
	Totals.......		767	2572	515	700	109	18	166	499	233	.272

BARRY LARKIN 26 6-0 185   Bats R Throws R

"If I were picking a team," Padres manager Greg Riddoch says, "I'd take Barry Larkin first."... Solidified his reputation as the best all-around shortstop in the game... Hit .301 and had career highs in hits (185), RBI (67), triples (six) and at-bats (614)... Played in 158 games, equaling high mark by a Reds shortstop in last 10 years... Finished fourth in NL in hits and sixth in multi-hit games (54) . . . Reds won division in April and he was a big reason, hitting .564 with 10 runs and eight RBI during season-opening, nine-game winning streak . . . It all starts with defense and he was glue that held Reds together in regular season, playoffs and World Series . . . Hit .353 in World Series . . . Member of 1984 Olympic team . . . Was named Big 10 MVP twice at Michigan . . . Reds' first-round selection and the fourth player chosen overall in 1985 . . . Born April 28, 1964, in Cincinnati . . . Made $750,000 last year.

Year	Club	Pos.	G	AB	R	H	2B	3B	HR	RBI	SB	Avg.
1986	Cincinnati	SS-2B	41	159	27	45	4	3	3	19	8	.283
1987	Cincinnati	SS	125	439	64	107	16	2	12	43	21	.244
1988	Cincinnati	SS	151	588	91	174	32	5	12	56	40	.296
1989	Cincinnati	SS	97	325	47	111	14	4	4	36	10	.342
1990	Cincinnati	SS	158	614	85	185	25	6	7	67	30	.301
	Totals		572	2125	314	622	91	20	38	221	109	.293

CHRIS SABO 29 6-0 185   Bats R Throws R

"Chris is such a quiet guy, then he takes the field and he's one of the meanest guys you've ever met. He's an incredibly tough competitor. He's like a Ty Cobb, a guy from another era," says teammate Rob Dibble . . . That's for sure . . . Was on a mission to prove the first half of his rookie season was no fluke . . . Third baseman led Reds in homers (25), doubles (38), extra-base hits (65) and runs (95) . . . Finished third in NL in doubles, fifth in extra-base hits and 10th in runs . . . Benefitted greatly from manager Lou Piniella's hitting instruction . . . Never more clutch than in World Series, when he batted .563 and ended up with eight hits in last 11 at-bats (.727), including two homers . . . Extremely underpaid at $200,000 last season . . . Born Jan. 19, 1962, in Detroit . . . Reds' second-round selection in 1983 draft, out of Michigan . . . As a youth, he played on two national championship hockey teams as a goalie . . . Probably played without a mask.

Year	Club	Pos.	G	AB	R	H	2B	3B	HR	RBI	SB	Avg.
1988	Cincinnati	3B-SS	137	538	74	146	40	2	11	44	46	.271
1989	Cincinnati	3B	82	304	40	79	21	1	6	29	14	.260
1990	Cincinnati	3B	148	567	95	153	38	2	25	71	25	.270
	Totals		367	1409	209	378	99	5	42	144	85	.268

PAUL O'NEILL 28 6-4 210   **Bats L Throws L**

Right fielder gets the job done quietly . . . Set personal highs in hits (136), RBI (78) and doubles (28) . . . Hit .387 in August when Reds needed him most . . . May really explode this season . . . Platooned the last few weeks with Glenn Braggs . . . Came on strong and was Reds' leading hitter in NLCS, batting .471 in five games . . . Picked up just one hit in World Series, but, with Billy Hatcher and Chris Sabo going crazy, that was enough . . . Born Feb. 25, 1963, in Columbus, Ohio . . . A pitcher in high school, he was Reds' fourth selection in 1981 draft . . . Made $625,000 last year . . . Giants' pitcher Don Robinson must have O'Neill nightmares considering he belted five homers off the right-hander.

Year Club	Pos.	G	AB	R	H	2B	3B	HR	RBI	SB	Avg.
1985 Cincinnati	OF	5	12	1	4	1	0	0	1	0	.333
1986 Cincinnati	PH	3	2	0	0	0	0	0	0	0	.000
1987 Cincinnati	OF-1B-P	84	160	24	41	14	1	7	28	2	.256
1988 Cincinnati	OF-1B	145	485	58	122	25	3	16	73	8	.252
1989 Cincinnati	OF	117	428	49	118	24	2	15	74	20	.276
1990 Cincinnati	OF	145	503	59	136	28	0	16	78	13	.270
Totals		499	1590	191	421	92	6	54	254	43	.265

BILLY HATCHER 30 5-9 185   **Bats R Throws R**

No one ever had a World Series like his . . . Set a World Series record for the highest batting average of any player with at least 10 at-bats, going 9-for-12, a crisp .750 . . . That bettered Babe Ruth's .625 mark (10-for-16) in 1928 World Series . . . Started the Series by going 7-for-7, a record for consecutive hits in a World Series . . . Only way the A's could stop him was by hitting him. Dave Stewart nailed him on the hand in first inning of Game 4, sending him to the hospital . . . Also hit .333 in NLCS against Pirates . . . One of those guys who come alive in postseason ·. . . Batted .280 for Astros in 1986 NLCS against the Mets, leading club in hits, runs and stolen bases . . . His Game 6 homer off Jesse Orosco in the bottom of the 14th tied game and held off elimination . . . Born Oct. 4, 1960, in Williams, Ariz. . . . Made $690,000 . . . That was more money than cheapskate Pirates wanted to pay for a fourth outfielder, so they traded him to Reds for Mike Roesler and Jeff Richardson, April 3 of last season . . . Eventually, he made the Pirates pay . . . Hit .333 in April, winning a steady job in center . . . Originally taken by Cubs in sixth round of 1981 draft.

Year Club	Pos.	G	AB	R	H	2B	3B	HR	RBI	SB	Avg.
1984 Chicago (NL) ..	OF	8	9	1	1	0	0	0	0	2	.111
1985 Chicago (NL) ..	OF	53	163	24	40	12	1	2	10	2	.245
1986 Houston.	OF	127	419	55	108	15	4	6	36	38	.258
1987 Houston.	OF	141	564	96	167	28	3	11	63	53	.296
1988 Houston.	OF	145	530	79	142	25	4	7	52	32	.268
1989 Hou.-Pitt.	OF	135	481	59	111	19	3	4	51	24	.231
1990 Cincinnati	OF	139	504	68	139	28	5	5	25	30	.276
Totals		748	2670	382	708	127	20	35	237	181	.265

BILL DORAN 32 6-0 175   Bats S Throws R

Helped put Reds over the top down the stretch after being acquired from Houston on August 31 for Butch Henry, Keith Kaiser and Terry McGriff . . . Second baseman did not play in postseason because of recurring back injuries that eventually required surgery . . . Hit .370 in 17 games for the Reds with one HR, five RBI . . . That was good enough to convince Reds to sign him to a three-year, $7.3-million contract in December . . . Born May 28, 1958, in Cincinnati . . . Houston's sixth-round pick in 1979 draft out of University of Miami (Ohio) . . . Earned $934,000 last year.

Year Club	Pos.	G	AB	R	H	2B	3B	HR	RBI	SB	Avg.
1982 Houston.	2B	26	97	11	27	3	0	0	6	5	.278
1983 Houston.	2B	154	535	70	145	12	7	8	39	12	.271
1984 Houston.	2B-SS	147	548	92	143	18	11	4	41	21	.261
1985 Houston.	2B	148	578	84	166	31	6	14	59	23	.287
1986 Houston.	2B	145	550	92	152	29	3	6	37	42	.276
1987 Houston.	2B-SS	162	625	82	177	23	3	16	79	31	.283
1988 Houston.	2B	132	480	66	119	18	1	7	53	17	.248
1989 Houston.	2B	142	507	65	111	25	2	8	58	22	.219
1990 Hou.-Cin.	2B	126	403	59	121	29	2	7	37	23	.300
Totals		1182	4323	621	1161	188	35	70	409	196	.269

HAL MORRIS 25 6-4 215   Bats L Throws L

One of GM Bob Quinn's sharpest deals . . . Stole him from Yankees along with Rodney Imes in deal for Tim Leary and Van Snider before last season . . . Yankees didn't know what to do with the rookie because they had Don Mattingly at first base . . . Mattingly wishes he hit .340 like this guy did . . . Became the regular first baseman the second half of the season, supplanting Todd Benzinger . . . Spent two months with

Nashville (AAA) and hit .350 after returning to majors on June 16 . . . Although he hit .417 in NLCS, he posted .071 mark in World Series . . . Born April 9, 1965, in Fort Rucker, Ala. . . . Eighth-round selection of Yankees in 1986 . . . Teammate of Barry Larkin at Michigan . . . Made $114,500 last year.

Year Club	Pos.	G	AB	R	H	2B	3B	HR	RBI	SB	Avg.
1988 New York (AL)	OF	15	20	1	2	0	0	0	0	0	.100
1989 New York (AL)	OF-1B	15	18	2	5	0	0	0	4	0	.278
1990 Cincinnati	1B-OF	107	309	50	105	22	3	7	36	9	.340
Totals.		137	347	53	112	22	3	7	40	9	.323

RANDY MYERS 28 6-1 208   Bats L Throws L

Brash lefty came up with "Nasty Boys" nickname . . . Saved Game 4 of World Series and three of the Reds' four victories in NLCS vs. Pirates . . . Pitched 8⅔ scoreless innings in postseason . . . Mr. October is 2-0 with four saves lifetime in postseason . . . Was the winning pitcher on Opening Night in Houston and never stopped, rolling up 31 saves, a 4-6 record and 2.08 ERA . . . Born Sept. 19, 1962, in Vancouver, Wash., he was the Mets' No. 1 pick in secondary phase of 1982 draft . . . Made $875,000 last year . . . Came over from Mets for John Franco prior to last season . . . Saved 50 games for Mets in 1988 and 1989.

Year Club	G	IP	W	L	Pct.	SO	BB	H	ERA
1985 New York (NL)	1	2	0	0	.000	2	1	0	0.00
1986 New York (NL)	10	10⅔	0	0	.000	13	9	11	4.22
1987 New York (NL)	54	75	3	6	.333	92	30	61	3.96
1988 New York (NL)	55	68	7	3	.700	69	17	45	1.72
1989 New York (NL)	65	84⅓	7	4	.636	88	40	62	2.35
1990 Cincinnati	66	86⅔	4	6	.400	98	38	59	2.08
Totals.	251	326⅔	21	19	.525	362	135	238	2.56

JOSE RIJO 25 6-2 200   Bats R Throws R

Irritated opponents and teammates with proclamation that NLCS was "over" after Game 4 . . . In World Series, he made sure it was over by winning Games 1 and 4, beating Dave Stewart both times . . . His ERA was astounding 0.59 against mighty A's, earning him World Series MVP award . . . Was 16th pitcher to receive the award and fifth in last six years . . . His World Series ERA was lowest by a starting pitcher with 10 or more innings since Bret Saberhagen posted 0.50 mark for Royals in 1985 . . . His nasty slider and power pitching carried Reds through closing weeks of season . . . In nine starts between Aug. 22 and Sept. 30, he went 6-2 with a 1.27 ERA . . . Fanned a season-high 12 batters Sept. 17 in 4-0 win over the Giants . . . Was 1-0 vs. Pirates in NLCS . . . Earned $630,000 last year . . . Born May 13, 1965, in San Cristobal, D.R. . . . Father-in-law is Hall of Fame pitcher Juan Marichal . . . Originally signed as free agent by the Yankees in 1981, he was traded to Oakland in Rickey Henderson deal in 1984 . . . A's didn't know what they had and dealt him to Reds with Tim Birtsas for Dave Parker following 1987 season . . . Earned $630,000 in 1990.

Year	Club	G	IP	W	L	Pct.	SO	BB	H	ERA
1984	New York (AL)	24	62⅓	2	8	.200	47	33	74	4.76
1985	Oakland	12	63⅔	6	4	.600	65	28	57	3.53
1986	Oakland	39	193⅔	9	11	.450	176	108	172	4.65
1987	Oakland	21	82⅓	2	7	.222	67	41	106	5.90
1988	Cincinnati	49	162	13	8	.619	160	63	120	2.39
1989	Cincinnati	19	111	7	6	.538	86	48	101	2.84
1990	Cincinnati	29	197	14	8	.636	152	78	151	2.70
	Totals.	193	872	53	52	.505	753	399	781	3.60

ROB DIBBLE 27 6-4 235   Bats R Throws R

You can't hit him and you can't shut him up . . . Throughout the postseason, he told the world he wanted to be traded to a team that would use him as a closer . . . Did not allow a hit in five innings in NLCS and gave up just three hits in World Series en route to postseason ERA of 0.00 . . . Struck out 10 of the 16 Pirates he faced in NLCS . . . Best set-up man in baseball, he might be the best closer, too, if given the opportunity . . . No one throws the ball harder . . . Often goes over 100 mph on the radar gun . . . All-Star posted 11 saves, 8-3 record and 1.74 ERA in regular season . . . Hates the "Nasty Boys" nickname . . . Born Jan. 24, 1964, in Bridgeport, Conn. . . . First selection in January 1983 draft . . . Pitched four no-hitters during high school and one season for Florida Southern College . . . Loves hockey and still plays in offseason . . . Chicago Blackhawks offered him a tryout at All-Star Game in Chicago, but he said no thanks. "I'm too old to take that kind of punishment," he explained . . . Earned $200,000 last season.

Year	Club	G	IP	W	L	Pct.	SO	BB	H	ERA
1988	Cincinnati	37	59⅓	1	1	.500	59	21	43	1.82
1989	Cincinnati	74	99	10	5	.667	141	39	62	2.09
1990	Cincinnati	68	98	8	3	.727	136	34	62	1.74
	Totals.	179	256⅓	19	9	.679	336	94	167	1.90

TOP PROSPECTS

CHRIS HAMMOND 25 6-1 190　　　　**Bats L Throws L**
Owned some of the best minor-league numbers around . . . Was 15-1 with a 2.17 ERA for Nashville (AAA) . . . Struck out 149 batters in 149 innings . . . Led all Triple-A pitchers in ERA . . . Reds' sixth-round draft choice in January 1986 . . . Born Jan. 21, 1966, in Atlanta.

TERRY LEE 29 6-5 215　　　　**Bats R Throws R**
Should be recognized as Comeback Player of the Year in all of baseball because he came back from four years of relative inactivity . . . First baseman sat out most of that time because of severe right ankle problems . . . Fractured ankle in May 1986 and then had to have three operations . . . Batted .327 for Chattanooga (AA) and .304 with 15 homers and 67 RBI in 72 games for Nashville (AAA) . . . Born March 13, 1962, in San Francisco . . . Signed by Reds as undrafted free agent in July 1982.

GINO MINUTELLI 26 6-0 180　　　　**Bats L Throws L**
Appeared in only seven games during two seasons previous to 1990 because of injuries . . . Was 9-5 with a 3.99 ERA for Chattanooga (AA) and 5-2 with a 3.22 ERA for Nashville (AAA) last year . . . Born May 23, 1964, in Wilmington, Del. . . . Purchased from Tri-Cities, Sept. 20, 1985.

TIM LAYANA 27 6-2 195　　　　**Bats R Throws R**
Spent all season on Reds' roster only because he was drafted out of Yankees' organization after 1989 season . . . Has been a reliever for just two years . . . For Albany (AA), he was 7-4 with 1.73 ERA in 1989 . . . Was winning pitcher on Opening Night for Reds and finished 5-3 with 3.49 ERA and two saves in 55 games . . . Born March 2, 1964, in Inglewood, Cal. . . . Third-round choice by Yankees in June 1986 draft.

MANAGER LOU PINIELLA: "Sweet Lou" earned sweet revenge, going 91-71 and winning world championship in his first year with Reds and showing up one-time Yankee boss George Steinbrenner . . . "George, I can manage," he said after World Series sweep of A's . . . In second year of three-year, $1-million contract . . . Batted .295 in 11 years with Yankees from 1974-84 and .291 lifetime . . . Was AL Rookie of the

Year with Kansas City in 1969 . . . Became a Yankee coach in 1985 and Yankee manager in 1986, replacing Billy Martin, and had a 179-145 record in two years . . . That wasn't good enough for Steinbrenner, so he was kicked upstairs as a VP-GM in 1988 . . . In 1989, he became a commentator, doing color for Yankee games on MSG television network . . . When the Blue Jays fired Jimy Williams in the summer of '89, they wanted to sign him but Steinbrenner refused to release him without excessive compensation . . . Lifetime managerial record is 270-216 . . . Born Aug. 28, 1943, in Tampa, he was teammate of current A's manager Tony La Russa on local American Legion team.

ALL-TIME RED SEASON RECORDS

BATTING: Cy Seymour, .377, 1905
HRs: George Foster, 52, 1977
RBI: George Foster, 149, 1977
STEALS: Bob Bescher, 81, 1911
WINS: Adolfo Luque, 27, 1923
         Bucky Walters, 27, 1939
STRIKEOUTS: Mario Soto, 274, 1972

HOUSTON ASTROS

TEAM DIRECTORY: Chairman: Dr. John J. McMullen; GM: Bill Wood; Asst. GM: Bob Watson; Coordinator Minor League Instruction: Jimmy Johnson; Dir. Pub. Rel.: Rob Matwick; Trav. Sec.: Barry Waters; Mgr.: Art Howe. Home: Astrodome (54,816). Field distances: 330, l.f. line; 380, l.c.; 400, c.f.; 380, r.c.; 330, r.f. line. Spring training; Kissimmee, Fla.

SCOUTING REPORT

HITTING: No wonder first baseman Glenn Davis (.251, 22, 64) had rib cage problems last year: he had been carrying this offense on his back for too long. And now Davis has been traded to the Orioles.The Astros scored the fewest runs (573) in the NL, had the second-lowest team BA (.242) in the majors and struck out a club-record 997 times last year.

The hitting was so bad that Craig Biggio became the first catcher in club history to lead the team in average, at .276. Eric Anthony

Eric Yelding made Astros go with 64 stolen bases.

(.192, 10, 29) was supposed to supply power, but too much may have been expected of him and he couldn't hit his weight. Ken Caminiti (.242, 4, 51) could lose his job to prospect Jeff Bagwell. Eric Yelding can steal bases (64), but who's going to drive him in?

Last winter, Houston let free agent Franklin Stubbs (.261, 23, 71) leave for Milwaukee. That's a strange way to rebuild.

PITCHING: Astros may not be able to find 10 warm bodies to form a staff. NL ERA champ Danny Darwin (11-4, 2.21) was the best pitcher in baseball the second half of the season, but he signed with Boston as a free agent. Dave Smith (6-6, 2.39, 23 Sv), who has saved 20 or more games for six straight seasons, signed with the Cubs. Juan Agosto (9-8, 4.29) set a club record with 82 appearances to lead the majors, but he signed with the Cardinals. And Bill Gullickson (10-14, 3.82), went to Detroit.

The starters are shaky. Aging Mike Scott (9-13, 3.81) is looking to rebound from a horrible year that saw him give up a career-high 27 home runs. Durable lefty Jim Deshaies (7-12, 3.78) could have used more help: he allowed two or less earned runs a game while earning only a no-decision or a loss in 14 starts last year. Pete Harnisch (11-11, 4.34), acquired in the Davis deal, and Mark Portugal (11-10, 3.62) will be the other starters. The Astros have high hopes for young reliever Al Osuna and starter Randy Hennis, and Curt Schilling, young ex-Oriole, may help in relief, but that won't be nearly enough to make up for all the exiting talent.

FIELDING: The good news is that Biggio improved on throwing out would-be base-stealers. The bad news is that he nailed just 33 percent. Third baseman Caminiti has too much talent to make 21 errors again. Shortstop Rafael Ramirez has made 55 errors in the last two years. It's time for new blood.

In the outfield, center fielder Gerald Young can run 'em down with the best, when he's not in the minors because of his weak bat. Glenn Wilson, unsigned at press time, led all NL outfielders with six double plays and compiled 12 assists.

OUTLOOK: This is a bad team in baseball's best division. The Astros had the worst road record (26-55) in the game and finished tied for fourth last year at 75-87. And that was before they were ravaged by free-agent desertions. Credit owner John McMullen with knowing when to get out of the game. Pity good-guy manager Art Howe because Houston may wind up with the worst record in the majors this season.

HOUSTON ASTROS 1991 ROSTER

MANAGER Art Howe
Coaches—Bob Cluck, Matt Galante, Phil Garner, Rudy Jaramillo, Ed Ott

PITCHERS

No.	Name	1990 Club	W-L	IP	SO	ERA	B-T	Ht.	Wt.	Born
56	Allen, Harold	Columbus	7-9	114	78	3.71	L-L	6-0	210	10/16/65 Terre Haute, IN
41	Bowen, Ryan	Columbus	8-4	113	109	3.74	R-R	6-0	185	2/10/68 Hanford, CA
		Tucson	1-3	35	29	9.35				
38	Clancy, Jim	Houston	2-8	76	44	6.51	R-R	6-4	220	12/18/55 Chicago, IL
		Tucson	3-2	42	34	2.98				
43	Deshaies, Jim	Houston	7-12	209	118	3.78	L-L	6-4	220	6/23/60 Massena, NY
—	Harnisch, Pete	Baltimore	11-11	189	122	4.34	R-R	6-0	195	9/23/66 Commack, NY
54	Hennis, Randy	Tucson	10-8	159	101	4.41	R-R	6-6	220	12/16/65 Clearlake, CA
			0-0	10	4	0.00				
—	Henry, Butch	Chattanooga	8-8	143	95	4.22	L-L	6-1	195	10/7/68 El Paso, TX
31	Hernandez, Xavier	Houston	2-1	62	24	4.62	L-R	6-2	185	8/16/65 Port Arthur, TX
—	Kaiser, Keith	Chattanooga	9-11	171	123	5.74	S-R	6-4	205	5/24/67 San Antonio, TX
57	Kile, Darryl	Tucson	5-10	123	77	6.64	R-R	6-5	185	12/2/68 Garden Grove, CA
56	Mallicoat, Rob	Gulf Coast	0-1	16	21	4.96	L-L	6-3	180	11/16/65 St. Helen's, OR
		Osceola	0-0	12	10	0.00				
35	Meyer, Brian	Tucson	5-7	100	54	2.97	R-R	6-1	190	1/29/63 Camden, NJ
		Houston	0-4	20	6	2.21				
52	Osuna, Al	Columbus	7-5	69	82	3.38	L-L	6-3	200	8/10/65 Inglewood, CA
		Houston	2-0	11	6	4.76				
51	Portugal, Mark	Houston	11-10	197	136	3.62	R-R	6-0	190	10/30/62 Los Angeles, CA
—	Schilling, Curt	Rochester	4-4	87	83	3.92	R-R	6-4	214	11/14/66 Anchorage, AK
		Baltimore	1-2	46	32	2.54				
33	Scott, Mike	Houston	9-13	206	121	3.81	R-R	6-3	215	4/26/55 Santa Monica, CA

CATCHERS

No.	Name	1990 Club	H	HR	RBI	Pct.	B-T	Ht.	Wt.	Born
7	Biggio, Craig	Houston	153	4	42	.276	R-R	5-11	180	12/14/65 Smithtown, NY
64	Eusebio, Tony	Columbus	90	4	37	.283	R-R	6-2	180	4/27/67 Dominican Republic
2	*Gedman, Rich	Boston	3	0	0	.200	L-R	6-0	222	9/26/59 Worcester, MA
		Houston	21	1	10	.202				
9	McGriff, Terry	Nashville	91	9	54	.280	R-R	6-2	195	9/23/63 Ft. Pierce, FL
		Cin.-Hou.	0	0	0	.000				
28	Nichols, Carl	Tucson	43	4	33	.253	R-R	6-0	192	10/14/62 Los Angeles, CA
		Houston	10	0	11	.204				

INFIELDERS

No.	Name	1990 Club	H	HR	RBI	Pct.	B-T	Ht.	Wt.	Born
11	Caminiti, Ken	Houston	131	4	51	.242	S-R	6-0	200	4/21/63 Hanford, CA
1	Candaele, Casey	Tucson	6	0	2	.214	S-R	5-9	165	1/21/61 Lompoc, CA
		Houston	75	3	22	.286				
17	Cedeno, Andujar	Columbus	119	19	64	.240	R-R	6-1	168	8/21/69 Dominican Republic
		Houston	0	0	0	.000				
26	Gonzalez, Luis	Columbus	131	24	89	.265	L-R	6-2	180	9/3/67 Tampa, FL
		Houston	4	0	0	.190				
—	Mota, Andy	Columbus	118	11	62	.286	R-R	5-10	180	3/4/66 Dominican Repubhlic
10	Oberkfell, Ken	Houston	31	1	12	.207	L-R	6-1	210	5/4/56 Maryville, IL
16	Ramirez, Rafael	Houston	116	2	37	.261	R-R	5-11	190	2/18/59 Dominican Republic
6	Rhode, David	Tucson	60	0	20	.353	S-R	6-2	182	5/8/64 Los Altos, CA
		Houston	18	0	5	.184				
30	Simms, Mike	Tucson	115	13	72	.273	R-R	6-4	185	1/12/67 Orange, CA
5	Yelding, Eric	Houston	130	1	28	.254	R-R	5-11	165	2/22/65 Montrose, AL

OUTFIELDERS

No.	Name	1990 Club	H	HR	RBI	Pct.	B-T	Ht.	Wt.	Born
23	Anthony, Eric	Houston	46	10	29	.192	L-L	6-2	205	11/8/67 San Diego, CA
		Columbus	2	1	3	.167				
		Tucson	46	6	26	.286				
22	Davidson, Mark	Houston	38	1	11	.292	R-R	6-2	190	2/15/61 Knoxville, TN
		Tucson	61	4	46	.335				
—	Finley, Steve	Baltimore	119	3	37	.256	L-L	6-2	178	3/12/65 Union City, TN
65	Hunter, Bert	Columbus	103	9	39	.233	S-R	6-4	200	8/23/67 Pacoima, CA
—	Lofton, Kenny	Osceola	159	2	35	.331	L-L	6-0	180	5/31/67 Chicago, IN
29	Ortiz, Javier	Tucson	63	5	39	.352	R-R	6-4	220	1/22/63 Boston, MA
4	Rhodes, Karl	Houston	106	3	59	.275	L-L	5-11	170	8/21/66 Cincinnati, OH
12	*Wilson, Glenn	Houston	90	10	55	.245	R-R	6-1	190	12/22/58 Baytown, TX
13	Young, Gerald	Houston	27	1	4	.175	S-R	6-2	185	10/22/64 Honduras
		Tucson	61	0	24	.333				

*Free agent at press time

ASTRO PROFILES

ERIC YELDING 26 5-11 165   **Bats R Throws R**

Shortstop of the future . . . Ranked second in NL and third in majors in stolen bases with 64, one shy of Gerald Young's club record set in 1988 . . . Led majors in caught stealings with 25 . . . Had double figures in steals every month after April . . . Started at five different positions: left, center, right, shortstop and second . . . Loves to hit against Frank Viola. At one point, he was 7-for-7 against Viola . . . Mets' pitchers now say when a hitter has an exceptional game against one of them, the pitcher "took a Yelding." . . . Hit his first major-league home run Sept. 13 against Reds' Rick Mahler . . . Went 534 at-bats before going deep . . . Claimed on waivers from Cubs, April 3, 1989 . . . Born Feb. 22, 1965, in Montrose, Ala. . . . Selected by Toronto in first round of 1984 draft as the 19th pick overall . . . Stole a total of 132 bases in last two years in minors . . . Made major-league minimum of $100,000 last year.

Year	Club	Pos.	G	AB	R	H	2B	3B	HR	RBI	SB	Avg.
1989	Houston	SS–2B–OF	70	90	19	21	2	0	0	9	11	.233
1990	Houston	OF–SS–2B–3B	142	511	69	130	9	5	1	28	64	.254
	Totals		212	601	88	151	11	5	1	37	75	.251

KEN CAMINITI 27 6-0 200   **Bats S Throws R**

Led team in games played for second straight year with 153 . . . Loves Dome cooking . . . Hit .288 at Astrodome and .191 on the road . . . Has Pat Tabler Syndrome . . . Hit .533 with bases loaded (8-for-14) and drove in 14 runs . . . However, he slipped badly overall this season after getting career highs in RBI, runs and homers in 1989 . . . Had 21 fewer RBI, six fewer homers and 19 fewer runs scored while average dipped 13 points . . . May be his own worst enemy . . . Tends to get down on himself too easily . . . Third baseman has one of the best infield arms in majors, but made 21 errors . . . Born April 21, 1963, in Hanford, Cal. . . . Astros' third-round selection in 1984 draft, out of San Jose State . . . A durable player, he has missed just 10 games the last two seasons . . . Hit homers May 27-28 and then went 90 games before hitting another one . . . Earned $240,000 last season.

Year Club	Pos.	G	AB	R	H	2B	3B	HR	RBI	SB	Avg.
1987 Houston......	3B	63	203	10	50	7	1	3	23	0	.246
1988 Houston......	3B	30	83	5	15	2	0	1	7	0	.181
1989 Houston......	3B	161	585	71	149	31	3	10	72	4	.255
1990 Houston......	3B	153	541	52	131	20	2	4	51	9	.242
Totals		407	1412	138	345	60	6	18	153	13	.244

ERIC ANTHONY 23 6-2 205   Bats L Throws L

When he makes contact, he can hit 'em a long way . . . Became third Houston player to reach Astrodome upper deck and the first player to do so since '83, when he crushed Mike Bielecki pitch on May 17 . . . After being minor-league home run leader the previous three seasons, outfielder couldn't make the grade in the majors, hitting just .192 and striking out 78 times in 239 at-bats . . . That's one whiff every three at-bats . . . Too much of a wild swinger . . . Has to learn to be patient at the plate . . . Don't blame him for his problems . . . Astros may have rushed him because they desperately needed power . . . On Opening Night, he strained his hamstring, costing him a month . . . Finished with 10 homers . . . Born Nov. 8, 1967, in San Diego . . . Selected in 34th round of 1986 draft . . . Earned $125,000 last season.

Year Club	Pos.	G	AB	R	H	2B	3B	HR	RBI	SB	Avg.
1989 Houston......	OF	25	61	7	11	2	0	4	7	0	.180
1990 Houston......	OF	84	239	26	46	8	0	10	29	5	.192
Totals		109	300	33	57	10	0	14	36	5	.190

CRAIG BIGGIO 25 5-11 180   Bats R Throws R

Is he a catcher, second baseman or outfielder? . . . Astros aren't sure, but they've got to make up their minds sometime . . . Caught 113 games and played 50 in the outfield . . . Prefers catching . . . Club says his best position may be second . . . Made 13 errors . . . Has a lot of trouble throwing out would-be base-stealers . . . Nailed 17 percent two years ago and 23 percent last season . . . Became first catcher to lead Astros in batting with .276 average . . . Stole 25 bases, 17 as a catcher . . . His 38 multiple-hit games led club . . . Selected by Astros in first round of 1987 draft . . . A bargain for Astros at a $240,000 price tag last season . . . Born Dec. 14, 1965, in Smithtown, N.Y. . . . Attended Seton Hall . . . Became too defensive at the plate last year and his RBI total dropped from 60 to 42.

Year	Club	Pos.	G	AB	R	H	2B	3B	HR	RBI	SB	Avg.
1988	Houston	C	50	123	14	26	6	1	3	5	6	.211
1989	Houston	C-OF	134	443	64	114	21	2	13	60	21	.257
1990	Houston	C-OF	150	555	53	153	24	2	4	42	25	.276
	Totals		334	1121	131	293	51	5	20	107	52	.261

GERALD YOUNG 26 6-2 185   Bats S Throws R

Flop of the year for Astros . . . Sent down May 22, when he was batting .179 . . . Home run off Mets' Bob Ojeda April 28 ended a streak of 1,195 at-bats without a homer . . . Has the tools, but hasn't produced . . . Center fielder has gone from phenom to enigma in three years . . . Hit .398 for Tucson (AAA) in first 21 games, then dislocated middle finger of his right hand . . . Surgery kept him out until early August . . . Played in just 57 games and batted .175 . . . "I know I'm better than this, but if the Astros are looking for somebody like Casey Candaele, jumping up and down and always full of vigor, they're looking in the wrong place. That's just not me," he says . . . Made $280,000 last year . . . Acquired from Mets with Manny Lee and Mitch Cook for Ray Knight, Sept. 1, 1984 . . . Born Oct. 22, 1964, in Tele, Honduras.

Year	Club	Pos.	G	AB	R	H	2B	3B	HR	RBI	SB	Avg.
1987	Houston	OF	71	274	44	88	9	2	1	15	26	.321
1988	Houston	OF	149	576	79	148	21	9	0	37	65	.257
1989	Houston	OF	146	533	71	124	17	3	0	38	34	.233
1990	Houston	OF	57	154	15	27	4	1	1	4	6	.175
	Totals		423	1537	209	387	51	15	2	94	131	.252

PETE HARNISCH 24 6-0 195   Bats R Throws R

Acquired from Orioles in January with Curt Schilling and Steve Finley for Glenn Davis . . . Needs to develop consistency after roller-coaster season . . . Jumped off to 5-1 start, then went 4-4, then dropped six of last eight decisions . . . Topped Orioles with 31 starts, 188⅔ innings, 122 strikeouts and three complete games . . . Only Oriole to stay in rotation all year . . . Known for tenacious disposition on mound . . . Born Sept. 23, 1966, in Commack, N.Y. . . . Selected by Orioles in 1987 draft . . . Was bonus choice between second and third rounds for Cleveland's signing of free agent Rick Dempsey . . . Earned $120,000 in 1990.

Year	Club	G	IP	W	L	Pct.	SO	BB	H	ERA
1988	Baltimore	2	13	0	2	.000	10	9	13	5.54
1989	Baltimore	18	103⅓	5	9	.357	70	64	97	4.62
1990	Baltimore	31	188⅔	11	11	.500	122	86	189	4.34
	Totals.	51	305	16	22	.421	202	159	299	4.49

JIM DESHAIES 30 6-4 220   Bats L Throws L

Tied for fourth in NL with 35 games started in 1990 but completed just two . . . Held opposition to .245 BA . . . Surrendered 21 homers . . . Fourth in league with 84 walks allowed . . . Experienced control problems for first time in career and was victimized by big innings, usually set up by walks . . . Had 52 walks and 56 strikeouts through first 21 starts . . . Until 1990, he averaged 1.9 strikeouts for every walk . . . Was among top NL left-handers in 1989, holding opponents to .217 average and pitching three shutouts . . . Born June 23, 1960, in Massena, N.Y. . . . Selected by Yankees in 21st round of 1982 draft . . . Traded to Astros for Joe Niekro on Sept. 15, 1985 . . . Led New York-Penn League (A) with 137 strikeouts in 1982 . . . Pitched no-hitter for Nashville (AA) in 1984 . . . Went 33-9 with 2.59 ERA in four years at LeMoyne College, where he was teammate of Tom Browning . . . Yankees' Minor League Player of Year in 1984 . . . Earned $1,050,000 in 1990.

Year	Club	G	IP	W	L	Pct.	SO	BB	H	ERA
1984	New York (AL)	2	7	0	1	.000	5	7	14	11.57
1985	Houston	2	3	0	0	.000	2	0	1	0.00
1986	Houston	26	144	12	5	.706	128	59	124	3.25
1987	Houston	26	152	11	6	.647	104	57	149	4.62
1988	Houston	31	207	11	14	.440	127	72	164	3.00
1989	Houston	34	225⅔	15	10	.600	153	79	180	2.91
1990	Houston	34	209⅓	7	12	.368	119	84	186	3.78
	Totals.	155	948	56	48	.538	638	358	818	3.50

MIKE SCOTT 35 6-3 215   Bats R Throws R

After finishing second to Mark Davis in the NL Cy Young voting two years ago, he slipped badly in 1990 . . . His 9-13 mark represented first time he has been under .500 since 1984, when he was 5-11 . . . That's not a lot of production for a $2,187,500 salary . . . In previous five years, however, Astros more than got their money's worth as he compiled 86-49 record . . . String of five straight 14-plus victory seasons is over . . . Equaled career high for losses with 13 . . . Winless in first five starts for first time in his career . . . Gave up 27 home runs, 17 by right-handed hitters, and only Padres' Dennis Rasmussen surrendered more . . . His 205⅔ innings pitched was sixth straight year over 200, but lowest total since 1984 . . . Ranks third on the club's all-time victory list with 110 and is tied for second with 21 career shutouts . . . Born April 26, 1955, in Santa Monica, Cal. . . . Mets' second-round pick in 1976 draft . . . Had a dream season in 1986, going 18-10, winning the ERA title (2.22) and leading the NL in strikeouts (306) . . . Finished it off by no-hitting the Giants Sept. 25 to clinch division crown.

Year	Club	G	IP	W	L	Pct.	SO	BB	H	ERA
1979	New York (NL)	18	52	1	3	.250	21	20	59	5.37
1980	New York (NL)	6	29	1	1	.500	13	8	40	4.34
1981	New York (NL)	23	136	5	10	.333	54	34	130	3.90
1982	New York (NL)	37	147	7	13	.350	63	60	185	5.14
1983	Houston	24	145	10	6	.625	73	46	143	3.72
1984	Houston	31	154	5	11	.313	83	43	179	4.68
1985	Houston	36	221⅔	18	8	.692	137	80	194	3.29
1986	Houston	37	275½	18	10	.643	306	72	182	2.22
1987	Houston	36	247⅔	16	13	.552	233	79	199	3.23
1988	Houston	32	218⅔	14	8	.636	190	53	162	2.92
1989	Houston	33	229	20	10	.667	172	62	180	3.10
1990	Houston	32	205⅔	9	13	.409	121	66	194	3.81
	Totals	345	2061	124	106	.539	1466	623	1847	3.51

MARK PORTUGAL 28 6-0 190   Bats R Throws R

Started career-high 32 games in 1990, but completed just one . . . Opponents batted .250 against him and hit 21 homers . . . Combined with Larry Andersen (now a Padre) to blank Cubs, 1-0, Aug. 29, despite allowing 11 hits and four walks . . . Put together strong second half after being 1-7 on June 17 . . . In both seasons with Astros, his record improved dramatically following All-Star break . . . Won five straight decisions against Giants over two-year period, compiling 1.78 ERA, before 5-1 loss at San Francisco, Sept. 9 . . . During second half of '89 went 7-0 with 2.39 ERA in 17 games . . . Born Oct. 30, 1962, in Los Angeles . . . Signed with Twins as amateur free agent in 1980 . . . Traded to Astros before 1989 season for Todd McClure . . . At Orlando (AA) in 1984, went 14-7 with 2.98 ERA, 10 complete games, 3 shutouts . . . Was International League's toughest pitcher to steal against in 1985 . . . Earned $202,000 in 1990.

Year	Club	G	IP	W	L	Pct.	SO	BB	H	ERA
1985	Minnesota	6	24⅓	1	3	.250	12	14	24	5.55
1986	Minnesota	27	112⅔	6	10	.375	67	50	112	4.31
1987	Minnesota	13	44	1	3	.250	28	24	58	7.77
1988	Minnesota	26	57⅔	3	3	.500	31	17	60	4.53
1989	Houston	20	108	7	1	.875	86	37	91	2.75
1990	Houston	32	196⅔	11	10	.524	136	67	187	3.62
	Totals	124	543⅓	29	30	.491	360	209	532	4.11

TOP PROSPECTS

JEFF BAGWELL 22 6-0 195   **Bats R Throws R**
Third baseman came over from Red Sox organization in September deal for reliever Larry Andersen . . . Could be a big mistake for Boston . . . Hit .333 for New Britain (AA) . . . Deal was a surprise because Red Sox were predicting big things for him . . . Born May 27, 1968, in Boston . . . Chosen by Red Sox in 19th round of 1989 draft.

AL OSUNA 25 6-3 200   **Bats R Throws L**
Astros are counting on this left-hander to become their closer . . . Has outstanding fastball and good breaking ball . . . Appears the only thing missing is experience . . . Was 7-5 with 3.38 ERA for Columbus (AA) . . . Led club with 60 appearances, 82 strikeouts in 69⅓ innings and six saves . . . Born Aug. 10, 1965, in Inglewood, Cal. . . . Selected by Astros in 16th round of 1987 draft.

RANDY HENNIS 25 6-6 220   **Bats R Throws R**
UCLA product was 10-8 with 4.41 ERA for Tucson
(AAA)... Struck out 101 and walked 92 in 159⅓ innings...
Born Dec. 16, 1965, in Clearlake, Cal.... Selected by Astros in
second round of 1987 draft... Look for him to move into the
rotation... Did not allow a run in 9⅔ innings of September work
with Houston.

KARL RHODES 22 5-11 170   **Bats L Throws L**
Outfielder hit .275 and had 11 triples in 107 games for Tucson
(AAA)... Had 98 at-bats for Astros, hitting just .184... Born
Aug. 21, 1968, in Cincinnati... Selected by Astros in third round
of 1986 draft... Drafted out of Western Hills High, the same
school that produced Pete Rose, Don Zimmer, Jim Frey and Eddie
Brinkman.

MANAGER ART HOWE: Team's lack of offense resulted in
75-87 finish, after 86-76 debut season at helm
in 1989... A go-go guy... Younger guys re-
spond better to him... Was an 11-year big-
leaguer, six of them with Houston, mainly as
infielder... Born Dec. 15, 1946, in Pittsburgh
... Played on Astros' 1980 division champions
... Came up with Pittsburgh, but was traded
for Tommy Helms in 1976... Tenth manager
in Houston history... This is his 21st season in pro ball... Played
baseball and football at University of Wyoming, but his football
career ended with back injury... Graduated with degree in business administration... Was a computer programmer when he attended Pirates' tryout camp... Served as coach for Rangers from
1985-88 and gained managerial experience in Puerto Rican League
during winters.

ALL-TIME ASTRO SEASON RECORDS

BATTING: Rusty Staub, .333, 1967
HRs: Jimmy Wynn, 37, 1967
RBI: Bob Watson, 110, 1977
STEALS: Gerald Young, 65, 1988
WINS: Joe Niekro, 21, 1979
STRIKEOUTS: J. R. Richard, 313, 1979

Astros must decide where Craig Biggio can help the most.

LOS ANGELES DODGERS

TEAM DIRECTORY: Pres.: Peter O'Malley; Exec. VP-Player Pers.: Fred Claire; VP-Marketing: Barry Stockhammer; VP-Communications: Tommy Hawkins; Dir. Minor League Oper.: Charlie Blaney; Dir. Scouting: Terry Reynolds; Publicity Dir.: Jay Lucas; Trav. Sec.: Billy DeLury; Mgr.: Tom Lasorda. Home: Dodger Stadium (56,000). Field distances: 330, l.f. line; 370, l.c.; 395, c.f.; 370, r.c.; 330, r.f. line. Spring training: Vero Beach, Fla.

SCOUTING REPORT

HITTING: Straw will stir the drink. Now that he's back home, after signing that five-year, $20.25-million contract with the Dodg-

Dodger GM Fred Claire expects Darryl to be Strawsome.

ers, Darryl Strawberry (.277, 37, 108) should put up MVP-type numbers. Strawberry averaged 31 homers and 92 RBI in eight years with the Mets and he could go off the charts this year—if he doesn't get distracted.

Strawberry, first baseman Eddie Murray (.330, 26, 95) and brittle but gifted Kal Daniels form the nucleus of a volcanic lineup. That's 90 homers and 297 RBI between the three sluggers. Free-agent Brett Butler (.309, 108 runs, 51 steals with the Giants) and Lenny Harris (.304, 2, 29) are solid table-setters.

PITCHING: This always has been the Dodgers' strong suit and, if Orel Hershiser comes back from major shoulder surgery, the Dodgers could be invincible. Ramon Martinez (20-6, 2.92) might be the most dominating pitcher in the game this year and Tim Belcher (9-9, 4.00) is expected to recuperate fully following arm woes in 1990.

Some may have laughed when Dodgers signed Kevin Gross (9-12, 4.57 with Expos) to a three-year, $6.4-million contract last winter, but Gross is Hershiser insurance and more. Insiders believe improved mechanics will turn the right-hander around. The fifth starter could be Jim Neidlinger (5-3, 3.28), Mike Morgan (11-15, 3.75), Fernando Valenzuela (13-13, 4.59) or ex-Met lefty Bob Ojeda (7-6, 3.66), who was obtained for Hubie Brooks.

Once again, the bullpen appears too dependent on Jay Howell (5-5, 2.18, 16 Sv) and only the Cubs' Paul Assenmacher blew more saves than Howell (eight) last year. Jim Gott (3-5, 2.90) should help and so should Tim Crews (4-5, 2.77) and Mike Hartley (6-3, 2.95). But the Dodgers still haven't found a lefty to replace Steve Howe.

FIELDING: Center fielder Butler has the speed to cover for some of the mistakes that will be committed by his outfield mates, Daniels in left and Strawberry in right. Shortstop Jose Offerman has a ways to go, but is a big improvement over Alfredo Griffin (26 errors). Mike Scioscia is the best defensive catcher in the NL.

The overall defense is less than average and lacks range, but Dodger management is gambling that a super-charged offense will make up for any defensive liabilities.

OUTLOOK: The addition of Strawberry puts the pressure on Tommy Lasorda this season, after the manager did one of the best jobs of his career in guiding the Dodgers to a second-place, 86-76 finish in '90. If Hershiser and Belcher are healthy, La-La land could go ga-ga over this team.

LOS ANGELES DODGERS 1991 ROSTER

MANAGER Tom Lasorda
Coaches—Joe Amalfitano, Mark Cresse, Ben Hines, Ron Perranoski, Bill Russell

PITCHERS

No.	Name	1990 Club	W-L	IP	SO	ERA	B-T	Ht.	Wt.	Born
49	Belcher, Tim	Los Angeles	9-9	153	102	4.00	R-R	6-3	210	10/19/61 Sparta, OH
25	Cook, Dennis	Phil.-LA	9-4	156	64	3.92	L-L	6-3	185	10/4/62 Lamarque, TX
52	Crews, Tim	Los Angeles	4-5	107	76	2.77	R-R	6-0	195	4/3/61 Tampa, FL
35	Gott, Jim	Bakersfield	0-0	13	16	2.77	R-R	6-4	220	8/3/59 Hollywood, CA
		Los Angeles	3-5	62	44	2.90				
—	Gross, Kevin	Montreal	9-12	163	111	4.57	R-R	6-5	215	6/8/61 Downey, CA
46	Hartley, Mike	Albuquerque	0-0	3	3	0.00	R-R	6-1	197	8/31/61 Hawthorne, CA
		Los Angeles	6-3	79	76	2.95				
55	Hershiser, Orel	Los Angeles	1-1	25	16	4.26	R-R	6-3	192	9/16/58 Buffalo, NY
50	Howell, Jay	Los Angeles	5-5	66	59	2.18	R-R	6-3	220	11/26/55 Miami, FL
—	James, Mike	San Antonio	11-4	157	97	3.32	R-R	6-3	180	8/15/67 Fort Walton, FL
48	Martinez, Ramon	Los Angeles	20-6	234	223	2.92	R-R	6-4	170	3/22/68 Dominican Republic
36	Morgan, Mike	Los Angeles	11-15	211	106	3.75	R-R	6-2	222	10/8/59 Tulare, CA
31	Neidlinger, Jim	Albuquerque	8-5	120	81	4.29	S-R	6-4	180	9/24/64 Vallejo, CA
		Los Angeles	5-3	74	46	3.28				
19	Ojeda, Bob	New York (NL)	7-6	118	62	3.66	L-L	6-1	195	12/17/57 Los Angeles, CA
63	Opperman, Dan	San Antonio	12-8	156	96	3.41	R-R	6-2	175	11/13/68 Las Vegas, NV
54	Poole, Jim	San Antonio	6-7	64	77	2.40	L-L	6-2	190	4/28/66 Rochester, NY
		Los Angeles	0-0	11	6	4.22				
59	Searage, Ray	Bakersfield	1-2	14	17	3.21	L-L	6-1	201	5/1/55 Freeport, NY
		Los Angeles	1-0	32	19	2.78				
64	Shinall, Zakary	San Antonio	6-3	91	43	3.55	R-R	6-4	220	10/14/68 St. Louis, MO
34	Valenzuela, Fernando	Los Angeles	13-13	204	115	4.59	L-L	5-11	202	11/1/60 Mexico
51	Walsh, Dave	Albuquerque	6-0	62	66	2.61	L-L	6-1	185	9/25/60 Arlington, MA
		Los Angeles	1-0	16	15	3.86				
57	Wetteland, John	Albuquerque	2-2	29	26	5.50	R-R	6-2	195	8/21/66 San Mateo, CA
		Los Angeles	2-4	43	36	4.81				

CATCHERS

No.	Name	1990 Club	H	HR	RBI	Pct.	B-T	Ht.	Wt.	Born
41	Hernandez, Carlos *	Albuquerque	45	0	16	.315	R-R	5-11	185	5/24/67 Venezuela
		Los Angeles	4	0	1	.200				
40	Lyons, Barry	Tidewater	28	0	17	.171	R-R	6-1	200	6/3/60 Biloxi, MS
		NY (NL)-LA	20	3	9	.235				
14	Scioscia, Mike	Los Angeles	115	12	66	.264	L-R	6-2	229	11/27/58 Upper Darby, PA

INFIELDERS

No.	Name	1990 Club	H	HR	RBI	Pct.	B-T	Ht.	Wt.	Born
7	Griffin, Alfredo	Los Angeles	97	1	35	.210	S-R	5-11	166	3/6/57 Dominican Republic
3	Hamilton, Jeff	Los Angeles	3	0	1	.125	R-R	6-3	207	3/19/64 Flint, MI
43	Hansen, Dave	Albuquerque	154	11	92	.316	L-R	6-0	180	11/24/68 Long Beach, CA
		Los Angeles	1	0	1	.143				
29	Harris, Lenny	Los Angeles	131	2	29	.304	L-R	5-10	205	10/28/64 Miami, FL
1	Hatcher, Mickey	Los Angeles	28	0	13	.212	R-R	6-2	205	3/15/55 Cleveland, OH
—	Karros, Eric	San Antonio	179	18	78	.352	R-R	6-4	205	11/4/67 Hackensack, NJ
51	Lopez, Luis	Albuquerque	158	11	81	.353	R-R	5-11	190	9/1/64 Brooklyn, NY
		Los Angeles	0	0	0	.000				
33	Murray, Eddie	Los Angeles	184	26	95	.330	S-R	6-2	224	2/24/56 Los Angeles, CA
30	Offerman, Jose	Albuquerque	148	0	56	.326	S-R	6-0	160	11/8/68 Dominican Republic
		Los Angeles	9	1	7	.155				
10	Samuel, Juan	Los Angeles	119	13	52	.242	R-R	5-11	170	12/9/60 Dominican Republic
27	Sharperson, Mike	Los Angeles	106	3	36	.297	R-R	6-3	190	10/4/61 Orangeburg, SC
18	Smith, Greg	Iowa	116	5	44	.291	S-R	5-11	170	4/5/67 Baltimore, MD
		Chicago (NL)	9	0	5	.205				

OUTFIELDERS

No.	Name	1990 Club	H	HR	RBI	Pct.	B-T	Ht.	Wt.	Born
2	Butler, Brett	San Francisco	192	3	44	.309	L-L	5-10	160	6/15/57 Los Angeles, CA
—	Castillo, Braulio	San Antonio	55	3	24	.228	R-R	6-0	160	5/13/68 Dominican Republic
28	Daniels, Kal	Los Angeles	133	27	94	.296	L-R	5-11	205	8/20/63 Vienna, GA
38	Gonzalez, Jose	Los Angeles	23	2	8	.232	R-R	6-2	200	11/23/64 Dominican Republic
15	Gwynn, Chris	Los Angeles	40	5	22	.284	L-L	6-0	210	10/13/64 Los Angeles, CA
6	Javier, Stan	Oakland	8	0	3	.242	S-R	6-0	185	1/9/65 Dominican Republic
		Los Angeles	84	3	24	.304				
—	Rodriguez, Henry	San Antonio	144	28	109	.291	L-L	6-1	180	11/8/67 Dominican Republic
44	Strawberry, Darryl	New York (NL)	150	37	108	.277	L-L	6-6	200	3/12/62 Los Angeles, CA

DODGER PROFILES

BRETT BUTLER 33 5-10 160   Bats L Throws L

Center fielder and leadoff hitter signed three-year, $10-million contract as new-look free agent after most productive season with Giants ... Tied Len Dykstra for the NL lead in hits with career-high 192 ... Became the first Giant to top NL in that category since Willie Mays in 1960 ... Was third-toughest batter to double up (once per 207.3 at-bats) ... Walked five times at Atlanta April 12, tying the modern NL record, and had a single, four runs scored, two stolen bases and an RBI ... One of the best bunters in baseball ... Has over 150 stolen bases in each league, only fourth player in history to accomplish the feat (Jose Cardenal, Bill North and Dave Collins) ... Earned $1,100,000 in 1990 ... Born June 15, 1957, in Los Angeles ... Atlanta's 23rd-round pick in 1979 draft ... Traded to Cleveland with Brook Jacoby and Rick Behenna for Len Barker after 1983 season ... Signed by Giants as free agent after 1987 season ... Attended Southern Oklahoma State.

Year	Club	Pos.	G	AB	R	H	2B	3B	HR	RBI	SB	Avg.
1981	Atlanta	OF	40	126	17	32	2	3	0	4	9	.254
1982	Atlanta	OF	89	240	35	52	2	0	0	7	21	.217
1983	Atlanta	OF	151	549	84	154	21	13	5	37	39	.281
1984	Cleveland	OF	159	602	108	162	25	9	3	49	52	.269
1985	Cleveland	OF	152	591	106	184	28	14	5	50	47	.311
1986	Cleveland	OF	161	587	92	163	17	14	4	51	32	.278
1987	Cleveland	OF	137	522	91	154	25	8	9	41	33	.295
1988	San Francisco	OF	157	568	109	163	27	9	6	43	43	.287
1989	San Francisco	OF	154	594	100	168	22	4	4	36	31	.283
1990	San Francisco	OF	160	622	108	192	20	9	3	44	51	.309
	Totals		1360	5001	850	1424	189	83	39	362	358	.285

EDDIE MURRAY 35 6-2 224   Bats S Throws R

After 12 years in AL, first baseman needed a full 1989 season to adjust to NL before becoming a batting terror again last year ... Had second-best average in NL (.330) to batting champion Willie McGee (.335 with Cardinals) ... Tied Expos' Tim Wallach for NL lead in multi-hit games (58) and was third in slugging percentage (.414), behind Mets' Dave Magadan and Phils' Len Dykstra ... Also finished among NL leaders in RBI (95), hits (184), runs (96), total bases (290) and walks (82)... Exploded after the All-Star break, hitting .361 with 15 homers and 54 RBI... Twice hit homers from both sides of the plate in one game, tying Mickey Mantle's all-time career record of 10 such games... Made $2.7 million in 1990 and will receive $2.8 million this year on contract he signed as free agent prior to 1989 season... Born Feb. 24, 1956, in Los Angeles... Selected by Orioles in third round of 1973 draft.

Year	Club	Pos.	G	AB	R	H	2B	3B	HR	RBI	SB	Avg.
1977	Baltimore.....	OF-1B	160	611	81	173	29	2	27	88	0	.283
1978	Baltimore.....	1B-3B	161	610	85	174	32	3	27	95	6	.285
1979	Baltimore.....	1B	159	606	90	179	30	2	25	99	10	.295
1980	Baltimore.....	1B	158	621	100	186	36	2	32	116	7	.300
1981	Baltimore.....	1B	99	378	57	111	21	2	22	78	2	.294
1982	Baltimore.....	1B	151	550	87	174	30	1	32	110	7	.316
1983	Baltimore.....	1B	156	582	115	178	30	3	33	111	5	.306
1984	Baltimore.....	1B	162	588	97	180	26	3	29	110	10	.306
1985	Baltimore.....	1B	156	583	111	173	37	1	31	124	5	.297
1986	Baltimore.....	1B	137	495	61	151	25	1	17	84	3	.305
1987	Baltimore.....	1B	160	618	89	171	28	3	30	91	1	.277
1988	Baltimore.....	1B	161	603	75	171	27	2	28	84	5	.284
1989	Los Angeles ...	1B-3B	160	594	66	147	29	1	20	88	7	.247
1990	Los Angeles ...	1B	155	558	96	184	22	3	26	95	8	.330
	Totals.......		2135	7997	1210	2352	402	29	379	1373	76	.294

DARRYL STRAWBERRY 29 6-6 200   Bats L Throws L

Made good on vow to leave Mets, signing five-year, $20.25-million contract with Dodgers as free agent last winter... Felt unappreciated in New York and was happy to return to hometown... Despite distraction of stalled contract negotiations and pending free agency, right fielder broke Mets' single-season RBI record (105)... Hit 250th career homer, becoming 95th to reach that milestone... Tied for 90th place on all-time homer list... Ranks 13th in homers among active players... Only Met ever to record 100 RBI in three seasons... Recorded 1,000th hit on Sept. 1... Hit fourth career grand slam Aug. 30, his first since 1986... Has 22 multiple-homer games... Had career-high 18-game hitting streak in June, when Mets went 21-7... Was having outstanding September until lower back spasms forced him to miss final six games, costing him a shot at his first 40-homer season... Following offseason alcohol rehab, he finished second in NL in homers and fifth in RBI... Born March 12, 1962, in

Los Angeles . . . First player chosen in 1980 draft . . . Was underpaid at 1990 prices, earning $1,800,000, but not now.

Year	Club	Pos.	G	AB	R	H	2B	3B	HR	RBI	SB	Avg.
1983	New York (NL)	OF	122	420	63	108	15	7	26	74	19	.257
1984	New York (NL)	OF	147	522	75	131	27	4	26	97	27	.251
1985	New York (NL)	OF	111	393	78	109	15	4	29	79	26	.277
1986	New York (NL)	OF	136	475	76	123	27	5	27	93	28	.259
1987	New York (NL)	OF	154	532	108	151	32	5	39	104	36	.284
1988	New York (NL)	OF	153	543	101	146	27	3	39	101	29	.269
1989	New York (NL)	OF	134	476	69	107	26	1	29	77	11	.225
1990	New York (NL)	OF	152	542	92	150	18	1	37	108	15	.277
	Totals		1109	3903	662	1025	187	30	252	733	191	.263

KAL DANIELS 27 5-11 205   Bats L Throws R

Left fielder lashed career-high 27 homers and drove in 94 runs in his first full season with Dodgers . . . The 27 homers tied a Los Angeles Dodger record by a left-handed batter . . . Became the first Dodger to hit three grand slams in one season . . . Named NL Player of the Month for September, when he hit .354 with eight home runs and 31 RBI . . . Suffered a partially collapsed lung Sept. 28 . . . Established career highs in home runs, RBI and strikeouts (104) . . . His three grand slams led NL . . . Finished ninth in the league in homers, seventh in slugging percentage (.531) and sixth in on-base percentage (.389) . . . Born Aug. 20, 1963, in Vienna, Ga. . . . Earned $600,000 last season . . . Acquired from Reds with Lenny Harris for Tim Leary and Mariano Duncan, July 18, 1989 . . . Selected by Reds in secondary phase of 1982 draft . . . His 1989 season ended Aug. 9, after arthroscopic knee surgery . . . Has had chronic knee problems, prompting promise he would perform better on grass than turf . . . Kept his word.

Year	Club	Pos.	G	AB	R	H	2B	3B	HR	RBI	SB	Avg.
1986	Cincinnati	OF	74	181	34	58	10	4	6	23	15	.320
1987	Cincinnati	OF	108	368	73	123	24	1	26	64	26	.334
1988	Cincinnati	OF	140	495	95	144	29	1	18	64	27	.291
1989	Cin.-LA	OF	55	171	33	42	13	0	4	17	9	.246
1990	Los Angeles . . .	OF	130	450	81	133	23	1	27	94	4	.296
	Totals		507	1665	316	500	99	7	81	262	81	.300

LENNY HARRIS 26 5-10 205   Bats L Throws R

Made good in leadoff spot, where he hit .321 over 79 games, scored 43 runs and drove in 23 . . . Overall, he hit a career-high .304 . . . Also set career bests in at-bats (431), hits (131), runs (61), doubles (16), triples (4) and walks (29) . . . Played 94 games at third and 44 at second . . . Platooned at third with Mike Sharperson . . . Needs to work on his base-running . . . Born Oct. 28, 1964, in Miami . . . Came over with Kal Daniels from Reds for Tim Leary and Mariano Duncan, July 18, 1989 . . . Made $145,000 last season . . . Selected by the Reds in fifth round of 1983 draft.

Year	Club	Pos.	G	AB	R	H	2B	3B	HR	RBI	SB	Avg.
1988	Cincinnati	3B–2B	16	43	7	16	1	0	0	8	4	.372
1989	Cin.-L.A.	2B–3B-OF-SS	115	335	36	79	10	1	3	26	14	.236
1990	Los Angeles . . .	3B–2B-OF-SS	137	431	61	131	16	4	2	29	15	.304
	Totals		268	809	104	226	27	5	5	63	33	.279

RAMON MARTINEZ 23 6-4 170   Bats R Throws R

What a year . . . His 20 wins were second to Pirate ace Doug Drabek's 22 in NL . . . Led NL in complete games with 12, was second in strikeouts (223) and second in winning percentage (.796), tied for second in shutouts (3) and ranked third in innings pitched (234⅓) . . . When he struck out 18 Braves June 4, he tied Sandy Koufax' all-time Dodger single-game record . . . Youngest Dodger to win 20 games since Ralph Branca won 21 at 21 in 1947 . . . Only fifth Dodger to win 20 or more in first or second season . . . He won the West, even though Dodgers didn't . . . Was 13-0 against Western Division teams . . . Born March 22, 1968, in Santo Domingo, Dominican Republic . . . Signed as free agent at age 16 . . . Could be the most dominating pitcher in the NL for years to come . . . Made $150,000 last season.

Year	Club	G	IP	W	L	Pct.	SO	BB	H	ERA
1988	Los Angeles.	9	35⅔	1	3	.250	23	22	27	3.79
1989	Los Angeles.	15	98⅔	6	4	.600	89	41	79	3.19
1990	Los Angeles.	33	234⅓	20	6	.769	223	67	191	2.92
	Totals.	57	368⅔	27	13	.675	335	130	297	3.08

Fireballing Ramon Martinez is the new Fernando.

OREL HERSHISER 32 6-3 192   Bats R Throws R

Three years after winning the Cy Young award, he finds his career in jeopardy . . . Made only four starts before shoulder blew out, requiring reconstructive surgery April 27 . . . Was 1-1 with a 4.26 ERA . . . Only someone with his bulldog tenacity would attempt to come back from such a serious injury . . . By the end of the year, he was throwing off the mound . . . Would have had a great year in '89 with some support . . . Dodgers scored only 17 runs in his 15 losses . . . Has impeccable timing . . . Signed a three-year, $7.9-million contract after winning World Series and NLCS MVP awards in 1988 . . . Born Sept. 16, 1958, in Buffalo, N.Y. . . . Dodgers' 17th selection in 1979 draft.

Year	Club	G	IP	W	L	Pct.	SO	BB	H	ERA
1983	Los Angeles.	8	8	0	0	.000	5	6	7	3.38
1984	Los Angeles.	45	189⅔	11	8	.579	150	50	160	2.66
1985	Los Angeles.	36	239⅔	19	3	.864	157	68	179	2.03
1986	Los Angeles.	35	231⅓	14	14	.500	153	86	213	3.85
1987	Los Angeles.	37	264⅔	16	16	.500	190	74	247	3.06
1988	Los Angeles.	35	267	23	8	.742	178	73	208	2.26
1989	Los Angeles.	35	256⅔	15	15	.500	178	77	226	2.31
1990	Los Angeles.	4	25⅓	1	1	.500	16	4	26	4.26
	Totals.	235	1482⅓	99	65	.604	1027	438	1266	2.71

TIM BELCHER 29 6-3 210   Bats R Throws R

Another Dodger pitcher with arm woes . . . Underwent arthroscopic shoulder surgery Aug. 18 to remove torn cartilage . . . Expects to make a full recovery . . . Pitched a shutout his first start of the year and one-hit the Pirates July 21 . . . Produced five complete games in 24 starts and had 10 in 30 starts in '89 . . . His 9-9 record marked the first time in his major-league career he did not finish over .500 . . . Born Oct. 19, 1961, in Sparta, Ohio . . . Yankees' first-round pick in January 1984, but he was lost one week later when he was drafted as free-agent compensation by Oakland . . . Made $450,000 last season . . . Came to Dodgers from A's in September 1987 deal for Rick Honeycutt . . . Was first selection in the nation by the Twins in 1983 draft, but did not sign.

Year	Club	G	IP	W	L	Pct.	SO	BB	H	ERA
1987	Los Angeles	6	34	4	2	.667	23	7	30	2.38
1988	Los Angeles	36	179⅔	12	6	.667	152	51	143	2.91
1989	Los Angeles	39	230	15	12	.556	200	80	182	2.82
1990	Los Angeles	24	153	9	9	.500	102	48	136	4.00
	Totals	105	596⅔	40	29	.580	477	186	491	3.12

KEVIN GROSS 29 6-5 215   Bats R Throws R

Expo free agent hit jackpot at winter meetings when he signed three-year, $6.5-million contract... Not bad for someone who hasn't posted a winning record since 1985... Dodgers have slotted him for starting rotation and hope he can master another pitch to go with his outstanding curve... Had a rough 1990 season, landing on disabled list for 22 days in midsummer when he broke middle finger of his pitching hand while trying to bunt... Lost eight decisions in a row over 10 starts, his longest losing streak... Had some success in the bullpen with 1-0 record and 0.69 ERA in five appearances... Born June 8, 1961, in Downey, Cal.... Phillies' first-round pick in secondary phase of January 1981 draft... Out of Cal-Lutheran... Dealt to Expos prior to 1989 season for Jeff Parrett and Floyd Youmans.

Year	Club	G	IP	W	L	Pct.	SO	BB	H	ERA
1983	Philadelphia	17	96	4	6	.400	66	35	100	3.56
1984	Philadelphia	44	129	8	5	.615	84	44	140	4.12
1985	Philadelphia	38	205⅔	15	13	.536	151	81	194	3.41
1986	Philadelphia	37	241⅔	12	12	.500	154	94	240	4.02
1987	Philadelphia	34	200⅔	9	16	.360	110	87	205	4.35
1988	Philadelphia	33	231⅔	12	14	.462	162	89	209	3.69
1989	Montreal	31	201⅓	11	12	.478	158	88	188	4.38
1990	Montreal	31	163⅓	9	12	.429	111	65	171	4.57
	Totals	265	1469⅓	80	90	.471	996	583	1447	4.02

FERNANDO VALENZUELA 30 5-11 202 Bats L Throws L

Hard to believe he threw a no-hitter against the Cardinals June 29 with the kind of stuff he had for most of the season... Finished 13-13 but collapsed down the stretch... Over his last six starts, this left-hander allowed 28 runs in 30 innings, an 8.40 ERA... Made $2 million last year... Born Nov. 1, 1960, in Navajoa, Mexico... Dodgers purchased his contract from Puebla of the Mexican League in July 1979... Created a sensation on both sides of the border by winning NL Cy Young Award as a rookie and leading the Dodgers to World Series in 1981 ... Is pitching on pure baseball smarts and not much arm anymore ... Tested free-agent waters last winter, but remained in LA.

Year	Club	G	IP	W	L	Pct.	SO	BB	H	ERA
1980	Los Angeles........	10	18	2	0	1.000	16	5	8	0.00
1981	Los Angeles........	25	192	13	7	.650	180	61	140	2.48
1982	Los Angeles........	37	285	19	13	.594	199	83	247	2.87
1983	Los Angeles........	35	257	15	10	.600	189	99	245	3.75
1984	Los Angeles........	34	261	12	17	.414	240	106	218	3.03
1985	Los Angeles........	35	272⅓	17	10	.630	208	101	211	2.45
1986	Los Angeles........	34	269⅓	21	11	.656	242	85	226	3.14
1987	Los Angeles........	34	251	14	14	.500	190	124	254	3.98
1988	Los Angeles........	23	142⅓	5	8	.385	64	76	142	4.24
1989	Los Angeles........	31	196⅔	10	13	.435	116	98	185	3.43
1990	Los Angeles........	33	204	13	13	.500	115	77	223	4.59
	Totals............	331	2348⅔	141	116	.549	1759	915	2099	3.31

TOP PROSPECTS

JOSE OFFERMAN 22 6-0 160   Bats R Throws R
Manager Tommy Lasorda has tabbed him as his everyday shortstop after 29-game sneak preview ... Batted just .155 for the Dodgers and committed four errors ... For Albuquerque (AAA), he hit .326 in 117 games with 104 runs, 56 RBI, 16 doubles, 11 triples and 60 stolen bases ... Was named Pacific Coast League MVP and *The Sporting News* tabbed him as its Minor League Player of the Year ... Selected by *Baseball America* as the top prospect after the 1989 season ... Born Nov. 8, 1969, in San Pedro de Macoris, Dominican Republic ... Signed by Dodgers as a free agent in July 1986.

JAMIE McANDREW 23 6-2 190   Bats R Throws R
Named the organization's Minor League Pitcher of the Year ... Son of former Met right-hander Jim, he was 10-3 with a 2.27 ERA for Bakersfield (A) ... Moved up to San Antonio (AA), where he continued to shine, going 7-3 with a 2.04 ERA ... Was 11-0 with a 1.65 ERA for Great Falls (Rookie League) in 1989 ... Born Sept. 2, 1967, in Williamsport, Pa. ... Dodgers' third-round selection in 1989 draft.

DAN OPPERMAN 22 6-2 175   Bats R Throws R
Another comeback kid ... After missing the 1987 and 1988 seasons due to two elbow surgeries, the hard-throwing right-hander was 0-7 with a 3.54 ERA for Vero Beach (A) in 1989 ... Last

season, he was 12-8 with a 3.41 ERA for San Antonio (AA)... Born Nov. 13, 1968, in Las Vegas... Dodgers' No. 1 selection in 1987 draft.

GREG SMITH 23 5-11 170   **Bats S Throws R**
Acquired from Cubs for Jose Vizcaino last winter... Batted .291 with five homers, 44 RBI and 26 steals for Iowa (AAA)... In last 45 games, he batted .355, including 14-game hitting streak ... Started 96 games at shortstop and seven at third base, committing 18 errors... After being recalled to Cubs in September, he went 5-for-12 with four RBI during three-game series against Cardinals... Born April 5, 1967, in Baltimore... Selected by Cubs in second round of 1985 draft.

MANAGER TOM LASORDA: He is to the Dodgers what friend Frank Sinatra is to music... Has won six division titles, three pennants and two world championships since replacing Walt Alston 14 years ago, but may have done his best job last season, keeping tattered Dodgers on the fringe of the race until the last week en route to 86-76 finish... The world's most-recognized manager following his work for a diet company ... Covers both ends of the scale, so to speak, because he also markets his own pasta sauce... His managerial record is 1,183-1,031... Not only bleeds Dodger blue, he bleeds Dodger green, too... This will be his 42nd year on Dodger payroll... Had short-lived major-league career as southpaw pitcher (1954 and 1955 with the Dodgers, 1956 with Kansas City)... Appeared in 26 games and had an 0-4 record... Born Sept. 22, 1927, in Norristown, Pa.

ALL-TIME DODGER SEASON RECORDS

BATTING: Babe Herman, .393, 1930
HRs: Duke Snider, 43, 1956
RBI: Tommy Davis, 153, 1962
STEALS: Maury Wills, 104, 1962
WINS: Joe McGinnity, 29, 1900
STRIKEOUTS: Sandy Koufax, 382, 1965

SAN DIEGO PADRES

TEAM DIRECTORY: Chairman: Tom Werner; Vice Chairmen: Russell Goldsmith, Art Engel, Art Rivkin; Pres.: Dick Freeman; Exec. VP/GM: Joe McIlvaine; Dir. Minor Leagues: Ed Lynch; Dir. Scouting: Randy Smith; Dir. Media Rel.: Jim Ferguson; Trav. Sec.: John Mattei; Mgr.: Greg Riddoch. Home: San Diego Jack Murphy Stadium (59,022). Field distances: 327, l.f. line; 405, c.f.; 327, r.f. line. Spring training: Yuma, Ariz.

SCOUTING REPORT

HITTING: After the Padres finished eighth in runs (673) with an offense that had been expected to be explosive in 1990, new GM Joe McIlvaine put his stamp on the team last winter. He traded All-Star second baseman Roberto Alomar and slugger Joe Carter to Toronto for All-Star shortstop Tony Fernandez (.276, 4, 66) and home-run-hitting first baseman Fred McGriff (.300, 35, 88).

Left-handed power is a valuable commodity and that's why Carter and his 115 RBI were dealt away. McGriff was the AL home run champ in '89 and his arrival made disgruntled clubhouse problem and second-look free agent Jack Clark expendable. You can expect four-time batting champ Tony Gwynn (.309, 4, 72) to rebound from a disappointing year. Bip Roberts (.309, 9, 44 steals, 104 runs) has developed into one of the best leadoff hitters in the majors, but the other table-setter, Alomar, will be missed.

Benito Santiago (.270, 11, 53) was off to the best year of his career when he broke his arm in June. In center, disappointing Shawn Abner (.245, 1, 15) should get a second life under McIlvaine, who made him the top pick in the nation in 1984 with the Mets.

PITCHING: The Padres' 3.68 team ERA ranked sixth in the NL last year and they gave up the most homers (147).

Other than Andy Benes (10-11, 3.60), the Padres do not have a legitimate power pitcher—although ageless Ed Whitson (14-9, 2.60) could have won 20 with more support. Bruce Hurst (11-9, 3.14) had his problems with former pitching coach Pat Dobson and should welcome Mike Roarke. Greg Harris (8-8, 2.30, 9 Sv, 7 blown Sv) never seemed at home in the pen and will return to a starting role. Either Dennis Rasmussen (11-15, 4.51) unsigned at press time, or Derek Lilliquist (3-3, 4.33 as a Padre) could

Crafty Ed Whitson lived on corners en route to 2.60 ERA.

wind up in the rotation.

The bullpen still hasn't recovered from the devastating loss of Mark Davis to the Royals. Craig Lefferts (7-5, 2.53, 23 Sv) did more than expected, but blew seven saves, so right-hander Wes Gardner (3-7, 4.89) was acquired from the Red Sox to help Lefferts.

FIELDING: Only the Braves were a worst fielding team than the Padres (.977, 144 errors). McIlvaine knew he had to get a replacement for no-range Garry Templeton (26 errors) at short and Fernandez is a four-time Gold Glove winner who committed just nine errors in 161 games. McGriff will have much more range than Clark at first. Right fielder Gwynn and catcher Santiago were the only two NL West players to win Gold Gloves last year. Santiago threw out 34.1 percent of would-be base-stealers in 1990, the fifth-best percentage in the league. There's a hole at third base.

OUTLOOK: Nearly everyone picked the Padres to finish first last year. When it was over, Jack McKeon, who started the season as GM and manager, was out of both jobs and the Padres had limped home fourth at 75-87. McIlvaine's work has just begun. The Padres will have a new look this year, but the record figures to be about the same.

SAN DIEGO PADRES 1991 ROSTER

MANAGER Greg Riddoch
Coaches—Bruce Kimm, Rob Picciolo, Merv Rettenmund, Mike Roarke, Jim Snyder

PITCHERS

No.	Name	1990 Club	W-L	IP	SO	ERA	B-T	Ht.	Wt.	Born
—	Andersen, Larry	Houston	5-2	74	68	1.95	R-R	6-3	205	6/6/53 Portland, OR
		Boston	0-0	22	25	1.23				
40	Benes, Andy	San Diego	10-11	192	140	3.60	R-R	6-6	235	8/20/67 Evansville, IN
56	Bones, Ricky	Wichita	6-4	137	96	3.48	R-R	5-10	175	4/7/69 Puerto Rico
		Las Vegas	2-1	36	25	3.47				
45	Costello, John	St. L-Mont.	0-0	11	2	5.91	R-R	6-1	180	12/24/60 New York, NY
		Indianapolis	0-3	31	32	7.04				
41	Dunne, Mike	Las Vegas	1-2	28	12	3.21	L-R	6-4	221	10/27/62 South Bend, IN
		San Diego	0-3	29	15	5.65				
44	Gardner, Wes	Boston	3-7	77	58	4.89	R-R	6-4	205	4/29/61 Benton, AR
14	Hammaker, Atlee	SF-SD	4-9	87	44	4.36	S-L	6-2	204	1/24/58 Carmel, CA
46	Harris, Greg	San Diego	8-8	117	97	2.30	R-R	6-2	187	12/1/63 Greensboro, NC
50	Hernandez, Jeremy	Wichita	7-6	155	101	4.53	R-R	6-5	195	7/6/66 Burbank, CA
47	Hurst, Bruce	San Diego	11-9	224	162	3.14	L-L	6-3	214	3/24/58 St. George, UT
1	Lefferts, Craig	San Diego	7-5	79	60	2.52	L-L	6-1	210	9/29/57 West Germany
26	Lilliquist, Derek	Atl.-SD	5-11	122	63	5.31	L-L	6-0	214	2/20/66 Winter Park, FL
		Richmond	4-0	33	24	2.57				
49	Maysey, Matt	Las Vegas	6-10	139	72	5.58	R-R	6-4	210	1/8/67 Canada
37	Nolte, Eric	Las Vegas	2-11	123	79	8.58	L-L	6-3	200	4/28/64 Canoga Park, CA
43	*Rasmussen, Dennis	San Diego	11-15	188	86	4.51	L-L	6-7	233	4/18/59 Los Angeles, CA
42	Rodriguez, Rich	Las Vegas	3-4	59	46	3.51	R-L	5-11	200	3/1/63 Downey, CA
		San Diego	1-1	48	22	2.83				
32	Schiraldi, Calvin	San Diego	3-8	104	74	4.41	R-R	6-5	216	6/16/62 Houston, TX
48	Sierra, Candy	Riverside	3-4	67	71	2.14	R-R	6-2	190	3/27/67 Puerto Rico
		Las Vegas	2-1	18	16	5.89				
35	Valdez, Rafael	Las Vegas	4-7	86	79	4.92	R-R	5-11	185	12/17/68 Dominican Republic
		San Diego	0-1	6	3	11.12				
31	Whitson, Ed	San Diego	14-9	229	127	2.60	R-R	6-3	197	5/19/55 Johnson City, TN

CATCHERS

No.	Name	1990 Club	H	HR	RBI	Pct.	B-T	Ht.	Wt.	Born
25	Lampkin, Tom	Col. Sp.-Las Vegas	45	1	18	.224	L-R	5-11	183	3/4/64 Cincinnati, OH
		San Diego	14	1	4	.222				
9	Santiago, Benito	San Diego	93	11	53	.270	R-R	6-1	185	3/9/65 Puerto Rico

INFIELDERS

No.	Name	1990 Club	H	HR	RBI	Pct.	B-T	Ht.	Wt.	Born
—	Coolbaugh, Scott	Oklahoma City	66	6	30	.225	R-R	5-11	195	6/13/66 Binghamton, NY
		Texas	36	2	13	.200				
5	Cora, Joey	Las Vegas	74	0	24	.351	S-R	5-8	152	5/14/65 Puerto Rico
		San Diego	27	0	2	.270				
53	Faries, Paul	Las Vegas	172	5	64	.311	R-R	5-10	165	2/20/65 Berkeley, CA
		San Diego	7	0	2	.189				
—	Fernandez, Tony	Toronto	175	4	66	.276	S-R	6-2	175	6/30/62 Dominican Republic
15	Garner, Kevin		Injured					L-R	6-2	205	10/21/65 Freeport, TX
—	McGriff, Fred	Toronto	167	35	88	.300	L-L	6-3	208	10/31/63 Tampa, FL
20	Redington, Tom	Greenville	103	12	52	.252	R-R	6-1	190	2/13/69 Fullerton, CA
5	Roberts, Bip	San Diego	172	9	44	.309	S-R	5-7	165	10/27/63 Berkeley, CA
21	Stephenson, Phil	San Diego	38	4	19	.209	L-L	6-1	201	9/19/60 Guthrie, OK
1	Templeton, Garry	San Diego	125	9	59	.248	S-R	6-0	209	3/24/56 Lockey, TX
22	Williams, Eddie	Las Vegas	110	17	75	.316	R-R	6-0	192	11/1/64 Shreveport, LA
		San Diego	12	3	4	.286				

OUTFIELDERS

No.	Name	1990 Club	H	HR	RBI	Pct.	B-T	Ht.	Wt.	Born
28	Abner, Shawn	San Diego	45	1	15	.245	R-R	6-1	194	6/17/66 Hamilton, OH
—	Azocar, Oscar	Columbus	109	5	52	.291	L-L	6-1	195	2/21/65 Venezuela
		New York (AL)	53	5	19	.248				
24	Clark, Jerald	Las Vegas	49	12	32	.304	R-R	6-4	202	8/10/63 Crockett, TX
		San Diego	27	5	11	.267				
19	Gwynn, Tony	San Diego	177	4	72	.309	L-L	5-11	210	5/9/60 Los Angeles, CA
33	Howard, Thomas	Las Vegas	112	5	51	.328	S-R	6-2	198	12/11/64 Middletown, OH
		San Diego	12	0	0	.273				
18	Humphreys, Mike	Wichita	116	17	79	.276	R-R	6-0	185	4/10/67 Dallas, TX
		Las Vegas	10	2	6	.238				
4	Jackson, Darrin	Las Vegas	27	5	15	.276	R-R	6-0	186	8/22/63 Los Angeles, CA
		San Diego	29	3	9	.257				
8	*Lynn, Fred	San Diego	47	6	23	.240	L-L	6-1	190	2/3/52 Chicago, IL

*Free agent at press time

PADRE PROFILES

TONY GWYNN 30 5-11 210   Bats L Throws L

Suffered the most disappointing year of his career, even though his .309 average marked his eighth straight season over .300 . . . Batted .305 with runners in scoring position . . . Reign of three straight NL batting titles came to an end . . . Was the focus of May 24 meeting that split the Padres apart . . . Several teammates said he was selfish . . . Weight was also a problem as right fielder put on 10 unwanted pounds and his stolen bases dropped from 40 to 17 . . . Was second in the league in triples with 10 . . . Then there was the mutilated ''voodoo doll'' in his likeness that was placed in Padres' dugout Sept. 8 . . . A week after doll was discovered, he was out for the year when he fractured tip of right index finger . . . Season ended with him refusing to go into clubhouse with teammates around because he did not want to have confrontation with Jack Clark and Garry Templeton . . . Born May 9, 1960, in Los Angeles . . . Brother Chris is outfielder with Dodgers . . . Third-round pick in 1981 draft . . . Will receive $2 million in 1991 . . . Won fourth Gold Glove in five seasons in 1990.

Year	Club	Pos.	G	AB	R	H	2B	3B	HR	RBI	SB	Avg.
1982	San Diego	OF	54	190	33	55	12	2	1	17	8	.289
1983	San Diego	OF	86	304	34	94	12	2	1	37	7	.309
1984	San Diego	OF	158	606	88	213	21	10	5	71	33	.351
1985	San Diego	OF	154	622	90	197	29	5	6	46	14	.317
1986	San Diego	OF	160	642	107	211	33	7	14	59	37	.329
1987	San Diego	OF	157	589	119	218	36	13	7	54	56	.370
1988	San Diego	OF	133	521	64	163	22	5	7	70	26	.313
1989	San Diego	OF	158	604	82	203	27	7	4	62	40	.336
1990	San Diego	OF	141	573	79	177	29	10	4	72	17	.309
	Totals		1201	4651	696	1531	221	61	49	488	238	.329

FRED McGRIFF 27 6-3 208   Bats L Throws L

Padres' new first baseman, replacing Jack Clark, came from Toronto with Tony Fernandez in blockbuster trade in December for Roberto Alomar and Joe Carter . . . Ranked second in AL in on-base percentage (.400), third in total bases (295), fourth in homers (35) and slugging (.530) . . . Has slammed 30-plus homers each of last three seasons . . . Twenty of his 35 homers were solo shots . . . Finished third among first basemen in fielding percentage (.996), committing six errors . . . Born Oct. 31, 1963, in Tampa . . . Acquired from Yankees with Dave Collins, Mike Morgan and cash for Dale Murray and Tom Dodd, Dec. 9, 1982 . . . His 1990 salary: $1.45 million.

Year	Club	Pos.	G	AB	R	H	2B	3B	HR	RBI	SB	Avg.
1986	Toronto	1B	3	5	1	1	0	0	0	0	0	.200
1987	Toronto	1B	107	295	58	73	16	0	20	43	3	.247
1988	Toronto	1B	154	536	100	151	35	4	34	82	6	.282
1989	Toronto	1B	161	551	98	148	27	3	36	92	7	.269
1990	Toronto	1B	153	557	91	167	21	1	35	88	5	.300
	Totals		578	1944	348	540	99	8	125	305	21	.278

New Padre Fred McGriff seeks fourth 30-HR year in row.

TONY FERNANDEZ 28 6-2 175　　　**Bats S Throws R**

One of game's best shortstops landed in San Diego in deal that also brought Fred McGriff from Toronto for Roberto Alomar and Joe Carter... Placed second to Baltimore's Cal Ripken Jr. among AL shortstops with .989 fielding percentage... Tied for fifth in AL with 52 multiple-hit games and was eighth in AL with 175 hits... Smashed major-league-leading 17 triples... Topped club with 26 stolen bases... Born June 30, 1962, in San Pedro de Macoris, Dominican Republic... Originally signed as free agent by Blue Jays, April 24, 1979... Made $1.5 million in 1990.

Year Club	Pos.	G	AB	R	H	2B	3B	HR	RBI	SB	Avg.
1983 Toronto	SS	15	34	5	9	1	1	0	2	0	.265
1984 Toronto	SS-3B	88	233	29	63	5	3	3	19	5	.270
1985 Toronto	SS	161	564	71	163	31	10	2	51	13	.289
1986 Toronto	SS	163	687	91	213	33	9	10	65	25	.310
1987 Toronto	SS	146	578	90	186	29	8	5	67	32	.322
1988 Toronto	SS	154	648	76	186	41	4	5	70	15	.287
1989 Toronto	SS	140	573	64	147	25	9	11	64	22	.257
1990 Toronto	SS	161	635	84	175	27	17	4	66	26	.276
Totals		1028	3952	510	1142	192	61	40	404	138	.289

BIP ROBERTS 27 5-7 165　　　**Bats S Throws R**

Mr. Roberts was Mr. Everything, starting eight games at second, 13 at short, 46 at third and 68 in left... Also was one of the best bargains in baseball at a price tag of $195,000 in 1990 ... Established career bests in almost every category... His .309 average tied Tony Gwynn for team lead and was sixth-best mark in NL ... Ranked sixth in runs (104), seventh in stolen bases (46) and sixth in doubles (36)... Only Padre to hit more doubles in a season was Terry Kennedy (42 in 1982)... Figures to be the third baseman in 1991, replacing Mike Pagliarulo... Born Oct. 27, 1963, in Berkeley, Cal.... Another talented player stolen away from the Pittsburgh organization... Signed by Pirates in first round of secondary phase of 1982 draft, but was left unprotected in 1985 and was taken by the Padres.

Year Club	Pos.	G	AB	R	H	2B	3B	HR	RBI	SB	Avg.
1986 San Diego	2B	101	241	34	61	5	2	1	12	14	.253
1988 San Diego	2B-3B	5	9	1	3	0	0	0	0	0	.333
1989 San Diego	OF-3B-SS-2B	117	329	81	99	15	8	3	25	21	.301
1990 San Diego	OF-3B-SS-2B	149	556	104	172	36	3	9	44	46	.309
Totals		372	1135	220	335	56	13	13	81	81	.295

BENITO SANTIAGO 26 6-1 185   Bats R Throws R

If you're looking for a day when Padres went down the drain in 1990, look no further than June 14, the day his left arm was fractured by a fastball from San Francisco's Jeff Brantley . . . Before the injury, he was off to best start of his career and was hitting .317 with nine homers and 33 RBI . . . He hit just .215 with two homers and 20 RBI after returning . . . Owns most feared arm in baseball . . . Catcher has perfected throwing from his knees . . . Big reason for his early success last season was fact he matured . . . Sought help from a psychologist prior to season to adjust to American lifestyle . . . Made $1.25 million . . . Born March 9, 1965, in Ponce, Puerto Rico . . . Signed as a free agent in September 1982 . . . Won another Gold Glove in '90.

Year	Club	Pos.	G	AB	R	H	2B	3B	HR	RBI	SB	Avg.
1986	San Diego	C	17	62	10	18	2	0	3	6	0	.290
1987	San Diego	C	146	546	64	164	33	2	18	79	21	.300
1988	San Diego	C	139	492	49	122	22	2	10	46	15	.248
1989	San Diego	C	129	462	50	109	16	3	16	62	11	.236
1990	San Diego	C	100	344	42	93	8	5	11	53	5	.270
	Totals		531	1906	215	506	81	12	58	246	52	.265

ED WHITSON 35 6-3 197   Bats R Throws R

After 15 years in the majors, he feels "I've learned how to pitch, not just throw" and that is reason ERA has dropped each of last three years . . . Established a career-best 2.60 ERA, which ranked third in NL . . . That was best mark by a Padre pitcher in 15 years, dating back to Randy Jones' league-leading 2.24 mark in 1975 . . . Finished strong by winning seven of last nine decisions . . . Had outstanding August when he went 3-0 in five starts, allowing four earned runs in 42 innings (0.86 ERA) . . . Also set a career high with three shutouts . . . Control is secret to success . . . Was second in majors at keeping the ball in the strike zone, allowing just 1.8 walks per nine innings . . . In seven of his starts, he did not give up a single walk . . . Earned $1,125,000 in 1990 . . . Winningest Padre pitcher over last four years . . . One of Jack McKeon's best acquisitions, he came to San Diego from Yankees for Tim Stoddard, July 9, 1986 . . . Born

May 19, 1955, in Johnson City, Tenn. . . . Originally a sixth-round pick by Pittsburgh in 1974 draft.

Year	Club	G	IP	W	L	Pct.	SO	BB	H	ERA
1977	Pittsburgh	5	16	1	0	1.000	10	9	11	3.38
1978	Pittsburgh	43	74	5	6	.455	64	37	66	3.28
1979	Pitt.-S.F.	37	158	7	11	.389	93	75	151	4.10
1980	San Francisco	34	212	11	13	.458	90	56	222	3.10
1981	San Francisco	22	123	6	9	.400	65	47	130	4.02
1982	Cleveland	40	107⅔	4	2	.667	61	58	91	3.26
1983	San Diego	31	144⅓	5	7	.417	81	50	143	4.30
1984	San Diego	31	189	14	8	.636	103	42	181	3.24
1985	New York (AL)	30	158⅔	10	8	.556	89	43	201	4.88
1986	New York (AL)	14	37	5	2	.714	27	23	54	7.54
1986	San Diego	17	75⅔	1	7	.125	46	37	85	5.59
1987	San Diego	36	205⅔	10	13	.435	135	64	197	4.73
1988	San Diego	34	205⅓	13	11	.542	118	45	202	3.77
1989	San Diego	33	227	16	11	.593	117	48	198	2.66
1990	San Diego	32	228⅔	14	9	.609	127	47	215	2.60
	Totals.	439	2162	122	117	.510	1226	681	2147	3.75

BRUCE HURST 33 6-3 214   Bats L Throws L

Finished strong, winning six of his last seven decisions . . . Over his last 13 games, his ERA was 1.51 . . . His 11 wins marked eighth straight season he has hit double figures . . . Pitched two two-hitters, the fourth and fifth of his career . . . Recorded two of Red Sox' three wins in 1986 World Series . . . Born March 24, 1958, in St. George, Utah . . . Boston's first pick in 1976 draft . . . Close friend with Portland Trail Blazers' Danny Ainge . . . His 3.14 ERA was 10th-best in NL . . . Ranked second in league in complete games with nine and tied for NL lead with four shutouts . . . Opponents hit just .228 against him . . . Earned $1,633,333 last season.

Year	Club	G	IP	W	L	Pct.	SO	BB	H	ERA
1980	Boston	12	31	2	2	.500	16	16	39	9.00
1981	Boston	5	23	2	0	1.000	11	12	23	4.30
1982	Boston	28	117	3	7	.300	53	40	161	5.77
1983	Boston	33	211⅓	12	12	.500	115	62	241	4.09
1984	Boston	33	218	12	12	.500	136	88	232	3.92
1985	Boston	35	229⅓	11	13	.458	189	70	243	4.51
1986	Boston	25	174⅓	13	8	.619	167	50	169	2.99
1987	Boston	33	238⅔	15	13	.536	190	76	239	4.41
1988	Boston	33	216⅔	18	6	.750	166	65	222	3.66
1989	San Diego	33	244⅓	15	11	.577	179	66	214	2.69
1990	San Diego	33	223⅔	11	9	.550	162	63	188	3.14
	Totals.	303	1927⅔	114	93	.551	1384	608	1971	3.91

CRAIG LEFFERTS 33 6-1 210   Bats L Throws L

After being signed as free agent, he said he could do closer's job if given the chance and he came up with a career-high 23 saves . . . Successful in 23 of 31 save situations . . . Converted 11 of his first 12 save opportunities and then suffered tired arm because of overuse . . . Only four of his first 30 inherited runners scored, but six of last 15 came home . . . Six of his saves came against Mets . . . Born Sept. 29, 1957, in Munich, West Germany . . . Selected by Cubs in ninth round of 1980 draft, after leading Arizona to College World Series crown . . . His 2.52 ERA was best since 1984, when he a posted 2.13 during his first stint with Padres . . . Earned $1,266,667 in 1990 as heir to Mark Davis' job.

Year	Club	G	IP	W	L	Pct.	SO	BB	H	ERA
1983	Chicago (NL)	56	89	3	4	.429	60	29	80	3.13
1984	San Diego	62	105⅔	3	4	.429	56	24	88	2.13
1985	San Diego	60	83⅓	7	6	.538	48	30	75	3.35
1986	San Diego	83	107⅔	9	8	.529	72	44	98	3.09
1987	SD-SF	77	98⅔	5	5	.500	57	33	92	3.83
1988	San Francisco	64	92⅓	3	8	.273	58	23	74	2.92
1989	San Francisco	70	107	2	4	.333	71	22	93	2.69
1990	San Diego	56	78⅔	7	5	.583	60	22	68	2.52
	Totals.	528	762⅓	39	44	.470	482	227	668	2.95

ANDY BENES 23 6-6 235   Bats R Throws R

Bullpen may be in his future . . . Padres are thinking about converting him to a closer because of blazing fastball . . . His 10-11 record is deceiving because he was involved in 11 no-decisions . . . In six of those NDs, game went into extra innings and Padres won five . . . Born Aug. 20, 1967, in Evansville, Ind. . . . First player selected in 1988 draft . . . Ranked seventh in league by fanning 6.6 men per nine innings . . . On the verge of becoming one of the best pitchers in baseball . . . Strange stat of the year: He was starter seven times this season when there were rain delays or postponements, including a rare delay in San Diego on April 23 . . . Earned $130,000 last year.

Year	Club	G	IP	W	L	Pct.	SO	BB	H	ERA
1989	San Diego	10	66⅔	6	3	.667	66	31	51	3.51
1990	San Diego	32	192⅓	10	11	.476	140	69	177	3.60
	Totals.	42	259	16	14	.533	206	100	228	3.58

TOP PROSPECTS

DAVE STATON 22 6-5 215   **Bats R Throws R**
Named the Padres' Minor League Player of the Year . . . Plays
first and third . . . Tabbed the top prospect in the California League
by *Baseball America* after hitting 20 home runs for Riverside
(A) . . . Promoted to Wichita (AA), where after a slow start, he
wound up hitting .305 with six homers and 31 RBI in 45 games
. . . Born April 12, 1968, in Seattle . . . Selected in fifth round of
1989 draft.

JERALD CLARK 27 6-4 189   **Bats R Throws R**
After two years of riding the Las Vegas shuttle, he appears ready
for the majors . . . Had two short stints with Padres last season . . .
Only Padre to hit two homers in a game, accomplishing the feat
Oct. 2 against the Dodgers . . . In his last three games, he went
5-for-12 with three homers and seven RBI . . . Hit 12 homers in
40 games for Las Vegas (AAA) . . . Born Aug. 10, 1963, in Crock-
ett, Tex. . . . Selected in the 12th round of 1985 draft.

RICKY BONES 21 5-10 175   **Bats R Throws R**
Started the year at Wichita (AA), where he posted 6-4 mark with
3.48 ERA, and advanced to Las Vegas (AAA), where he went
2-1, 3.47 . . . Has 45-25 mark over the last four years in the minors
. . . Born April 7, 1969, in Salinas, Puerto Rico . . . Signed as a
free agent in May 1986.

PAUL FARIES 26 5-10 165   **Bats R Throws R**
One of those players who is expected to fail at each new level,
but never does . . . Infielder led Pacific Coast League in hits (172)
and runs (109) . . . Also stole 47 bases for Las Vegas (AAA)
. . . Born Feb. 20, 1965, in Berkeley, Cal. . . . Selected in 23rd
round of 1987 draft.

RAFAEL VALDEZ 22 5-11 165   **Bats R Throws R**
After a spectacular season in 1989, this right-hander suffered elbow problems last year at Las Vegas (AAA) . . . Though his record
was 4-7 with a 4.92 ERA, he still is considered the top pitching
prospect in the organization . . . Born April 17, 1968, in Niza Bani,
Puerto Rico . . . Selected in second round of the Dominican draft
in March 1985.

MANAGER GREG RIDDOCH: Took over for Jack McKeon on July 11 . . . Padres lost 10 of first 11 under him, but went 37-34 the rest of the way . . . Former first-base coach had managed in Rookie ball from 1973-81 in Reds' chain . . . Has a strong background in player development and could eventually wind up in that role . . . Former high school psychology teacher . . . That may be the best background to have if you've got to handle today's ballplayer . . . Still serves as a substitute teacher during the offseason . . . Born July 17, 1945, in Greeley, Col. . . . Was high school classmate of comedian Steve Martin at Garden Grove High in California . . . Anything but a wild and crazy guy, this mild-mannered man approaches game on intellectual level . . . Big believer in charts, proper mental attitude, computers and the like . . . One of baseball's new breed.

ALL-TIME PADRE SEASON RECORDS

BATTING: Tony Gwynn, .370, 1987
HRs: Nate Colbert, 38, 1970, 1972
RBI: Dave Winfield, 118, 1979
STEALS: Alan Wiggins, 70, 1984
WINS: Randy Jones, 22, 1976
STRIKEOUTS: Clay Kirby, 231, 1971

SAN FRANCISCO GIANTS

TEAM DIRECTORY: Owner: Bob Lurie; Pres.-GM: Al Rosen; Exec. VP-Adm.: Corey Busch; VP-Baseball Oper.: Bob Kennedy; Sr. VP-Business Oper.: Pat Gallagher; Asst. GM: Ralph Nelson; VP-Scouting: Bob Fontaine; Dir. Media Rel.: Matt Fischer; Trav. Sec.: Dirk Smith; Mgr.: Roger Craig. Home: Candlestick Park (58,000). Field distances: 335, l.f. line; 365, l.c.; 400, c.f.; 365, l.c.; 335, r.f. line. Spring training: Scottsdale, Ariz.

SCOUTING REPORT

HITTING: Money doesn't buy happiness, but it can buy hitters. The free-spending Giants bought NL batting champ Willie McGee

Kevin Mitchell has averaged 41 HRs the last two years.

(.324, 3, 77, 31 steals with Cards and A's) for $13 million over four years in the free-agent market last winter.

The only crack in McGee's armor is that he is a much more dangerous player on turf than on grass, so maybe likely second-look free-agent defector Brett Butler will be missed. Strikeout-prone Robby Thompson (.245, 15, 56) may not be an ideal leadoff man, but opposing pitchers have anxiety attacks when Will Clark (.295, 19, 95), Kevin Mitchell (.290, 35, 93) and NL RBI king Matt Williams (.277, 33, 122) come to the plate. And if Kevin Bass (.252 in just 61 games) stays healthy this year, the Giants may put bigger numbers on the scoreboard than the 49ers.

PITCHING: The Giants suffered from a staff infection all of 1990 as manager Roger Craig was forced to use 26 pitchers, one shy of the major-league record. And you wonder why the Giants shelled out a four-year, $10-million contract to free agent lefty Bud Black (13-11, 3.57 with Indians and Blue Jays)?

Scott Garrelts (12-11, 4.15) and John Burkett (14-7, 3.79) are durable, but the other starters will come from a suspect group that includes Rick Reuschel (3-6, 3.93), Don Robinson (10-7, 4.57) and Kelly Downs (3-2, 3.43).

The Giants made another major free-agent acquisition in ex-Yank reliever Dave Righetti, another four-year, $10-million purchase. The lefty Righetti (1-1, 3.57, 36 Sv) steps in for Steve Bedrosian, who was dealt to Minnesota. Righetti should get plenty of help from righty Jeff Brantley (5-3, 1.56, 19 Sv).

FIELDING: Solid all around, the Giants committed just 107 errors in 1990, breaking the franchise record for the fewest errors in a season (115 in 1989), and they tied the Reds for the NL's top fielding percentage at .983.

Butler will be missed in this department, even though he has a weak arm. Center fielder McGee made 16 errors in his 125 games with the Cards, but also rang up 13 assists. Craig thinks two rookies could be big plusses—shortstop Mike Benjamin (.251 for Phoenix) and catcher Steve Decker (.293, 15, 80 for Shreveport), who could make the jump all the way from Class AA.

OUTLOOK: Give GM Al Rosen credit. He could have sat back and attributed last year's third-place finish and 85-77 record to injuries, but instead he went out and spent $33 million on three free agents. If the pitching staff doesn't crumble, that money will be well-spent, because the Giants will win the West on brute strength.

SAN FRANCISCO GIANTS 1991 ROSTER

MANAGER Roger Craig
Coaches—Dusty Baker, Bill Fahey, Wendell Kim, Bob Lillis, Norm Sherry

PITCHERS

No.	Name	1990 Club	W-L	IP	SO	ERA	B-T	Ht.	Wt.	Born
—	Ard, Johnny	Orlando	12-9	180	101	3.79	R-R	6-5	220	6/1/67 Las Vegas, NV
21	Black, Bud	Clev.-Tor.	13-11	207	106	3.57	L-L	6-2	185	6/30/57 San Mateo, CA
49	Brantley, Jeff	San Francisco	5-3	87	61	1.56	R-R	5-11	180	9/5/63 Florence, AL
33	Burkett, John	Phoenix	2-1	23	9	2.74	R-R	6-3	205	11/28/64 New Brighton, PA
		San Francisco	14-7	204	118	3.79				
14	Dewey, Mark	Shreveport	1-5	38	23	1.88	R-R	6-0	185	1/3/65 Grand Rapids, MI
		Phoenix	2-3	30	27	2.67				
		San Francisco	1-1	23	11	2.78				
37	Downs, Kelly	San Jose	0-1	5	3	1.80	R-R	6-4	205	10/25/60 Ogden, UT
		Phoenix	0-0	5	4	1.80				
		San Francisco	3-2	63	31	3.43				
50	Garrelts, Scott	San Francisco	12-11	182	80	4.15	R-R	6-4	205	10/30/61 Urbana, IL
53	Gunderson, Eric	San Francisco	1-2	20	14	5.49	R-L	6-0	175	3/29/66 Portland, OR
		Phoenix	5-7	82	41	8.23				
		Shreveport	2-2	53	44	3.25				
29	**LaCoss, Mike	San Francisco	6-4	78	39	3.94	R-R	6-6	200	5/30/56 Glendale, CA
		San Jose	1-0	6	6	1.50				
54	Myers, Jim	San Jose	5-8	84	61	3.21	R-R	6-1	185	4/28/69 Oklahoma City, OK
36	Novoa, Rafael	Clinton	9-2	98	113	2.40	L-L	6-0	185	10/26/67 New York, NY
		Shreveport	5-4	72	66	2.64				
		San Francisco	0-1	19	14	6.75				
45	Oliveras, Francisco	Portland	3-4	62	56	2.90	R-R	5-10	180	1/31/63 Puerto Rico
		San Francisco	2-2	55	41	2.77				
		San Jose	0-0	4	3	2.45				
51	Remlinger, Mike	Shreveport	9-11	148	75	3.90	L-L	6-0	195	3/23/66 Middletown, NY
48	Reuschel, Rick	San Francisco	3-6	87	49	3.93	R-R	6-3	250	5/16/49 Quincy, IL
—	Righetti, Dave	New York (AL)	1-1	53	43	3.57	L-L	6-4	212	11/28/58 San Jose, CA
31	Robinson, Don	San Jose	1-0	7	8	3.86	R-R	6-4	240	6/8/57 Ashland, KY
		San Francisco	10-7	158	78	4.57				
52	Rogers, Kevin	San Jose	14-5	172	186	3.61	S-L	6-1	190	8/20/68 Cleveland, MS
—	Williams, Jimmy	Portland	4-6	64	62	5.04	L-L	6-7	232	5/18/65 Butler, AL
41	Wilson, Trevor	Phoenix	5-5	66	45	3.82	L-L	6-0	195	6/7/66 Torrance, CA
		San Francisco	8-7	110	66	4.00				

CATCHERS

No.	Name	1990 Club	H	HR	RBI	Pct.	B-T	Ht.	Wt.	Born
47	Decker, Steve	Shreveport	118	15	80	.293	R-R	6-3	205	10/25/65 Rock Island, IL
		San Francisco	3	0	8	.296				
16	Kennedy, Terry	San Francisco	84	2	26	.277	L-R	6-4	220	6/4/56 Euclid, OH
19	Manwaring, Kirt	Phoenix	58	3	14	.235	R-R	5-11	190	7/15/65 Elmira, NY
		San Francisco	2	0	1	.154				
28	Tucker, Scooter	San Jose	123	5	71	.280	R-R	6-2	205	11/18/66 Greenville, MS

INFIELDERS

No.	Name	1990 Club	H	HR	RBI	Pct.	B-T	Ht.	Wt.	Born
10	Anderson, Dave	San Francisco	35	1	6	.350	R-R	6-2	184	8/1/61 Louisville, KY
51	Benjamin, Mike	Phoenix	104	5	38	.251	R-R	6-3	195	11/22/65 Euclid, OH
		San Francisco	12	2	3	.214				
22	Clark, Will	San Francisco	177	19	95	.295	L-L	6-1	190	3/13/64 New Orleans, LA
46	Colbert, Craig	Phoenix	112	8	47	.280	R-R	6-1	205	2/13/65 Iowa City, IA
15	Litton, Greg	Phoenix	6	0	4	.273	R-R	6-0	190	7/13/64 New Orleans, LA
		San Francisco	50	1	24	.245				
39	Perezchica, Tony	San Francisco	1	0	0	.333	R-R	5-11	175	4/20/66 Mexico
		Phoenix	105	9	49	.268				
35	Santana, Andres	Shreveport	98	0	24	.292	S-R	5-11	150	3/19/68 Dominican Republic
		Phoenix	0	0	1	.000				
6	Thompson, Robby	San Francisco	122	15	56	.245	R-R	5-11	170	5/10/62 West Palm Beach, FL
23	Uribe, Jose	San Francisco	103	1	24	.248	S-R	5-10	170	1/21/60 Dominican Republic
9	Williams, Matt	San Francisco	171	33	122	.277	R-R	6-2	205	11/28/65 Bishop, CA

OUTFIELDERS

No.	Name	1990 Club	H	HR	RBI	Pct.	B-T	Ht.	Wt.	Born
17	Bass, Kevin	San Francisco	54	7	32	.252	S-R	6-0	190	5/12/59 Redwood City, CA
		San Jose	8	0	4	.364				
		Phoenix	8	0	4	.242				
26	Kingery, Mike	Phoenix	24	1	16	.240	L-L	6-0	185	3/29/61 St. James, MN
		San Francisco	61	0	24	.295				
25	Leach, Rick	San Francisco	51	2	16	.293	L-L	6-0	195	5/4/57 Ann Arbor, MI
8	Leonard, Mark	Phoenix	130	19	84	.333	L-R	6-1	195	8/14/64 Mountain View, CA
		San Francisco	3	1	2	.176				
—	Lewis, Darren	Huntsville	64	3	23	.296	R-R	6-0	175	8/28/67 Berkeley, CA
		Tacoma	72	2	26	.291				
		Oakland	6	0	1	.229				
51	McGee, Willie	St. Louis	168	3	62	.335	S-R	6-1	195	11/2/58 San Francisco, CA
		Oakland	31	0	15	.274				
7	Mitchell, Kevin	San Francisco	152	35	93	.290	R-R	5-11	210	1/13/62 San Diego, CA
32	Parker, Rick	Phoenix	58	1	18	.335	R-R	6-0	185	3/20/63 Kansas City, MO
		San Francisco	26	2	14	.243				

**New look free agent

GIANT PROFILES

KEVIN MITCHELL 29 5-11 210   **Bats R Throws R**

Although 1989 NL MVP ranked among league leaders in home runs (third with 35), slugging percentage (third at .544), total bases (eighth with 285) and extra-base hits (ninth with 61) in 1990, he thought it was a bad year . . . "I never felt comfortable," he said . . . Plans to cut back on lifting weights because he feels too bulky . . . Signed a four-year, $15-million extension in August . . . Left fielder hit a home run completely out of Shea Stadium May 8 off Sid Fernandez . . . Born Jan. 13, 1962, in San Diego . . . Five RBI vs. Pirates on May 25 was a career high . . . Two teams are now kicking themselves for trading him away . . . Came to Giants from Padres with Craig Lefferts and Dave Dravecky for Mark Davis, Chris Brown, Keith Comstock and Mark Grant, July 7, 1987 . . . Mets dealt him to Padres after world championship season in 1986 as part of package for Kevin McReynolds and haven't been the same since . . . Originally signed by the Mets as a free agent in November 1980.

Year	Club	Pos.	G	AB	R	H	2B	3B	HR	RBI	SB	Avg.
1984	New York (NL)	3B	7	14	0	3	0	0	0	1	0	.214
1986	New York (NL)	OF-SS-3B-1B	108	328	51	91	22	2	12	43	3	.277
1987	S.D.-S.F.	3B-SS-OF	131	464	68	130	20	2	22	70	9	.280
1988	San Francisco	3B-OF	148	505	60	127	25	7	19	80	5	.251
1989	San Francisco	3B-OF	154	543	100	158	34	6	47	125	3	.291
1990	San Francisco	OF	140	524	90	152	24	2	35	93	4	.290
	Totals		688	2378	369	661	125	19	135	412	24	.278

WILL CLARK 27 6-1 190   **Bats L Throws L**

The man with the sweetest swing in baseball . . . Hit .310 in April, his seventh straight month with an average over .300 . . . Dipped to .209 in May . . . First baseman was second in NL in All-Star voting, behind Cubs' Ryne Sandberg . . . Forever clutch, he hit .362 with men in scoring position and two outs and .379 with a runner on third . . . Now ranks among the all-time SF leaders in RBI (third with 447), home runs (eighth with 117), runs (eighth with 452) and doubles (10th with 150) . . . Key to Giants' defense . . . Led NL first basemen in putouts (1,455), total chances (1,587) and double plays (118), ranked second in assists (120) and games (153)... Hit .489 in 1989 NLCS with five doubles, three homers and 11 RBI... Earned $2,250,000 last season... Born March 13, 1964, in New Orleans... Giants' first selection in the 1985 draft, out of Mississippi State, and the second player picked overall... Hit .429 with eight RBI in five games for U.S. Olympians... Middle name is Neuschler.

Year	Club	Pos.	G	AB	R	H	2B	3B	HR	RBI	SB	Avg.
1986	San Francisco	1B	111	408	66	117	27	2	11	41	4	.287
1987	San Francisco	1B	150	529	89	163	29	5	35	91	5	.308
1988	San Francisco	1B	162	575	102	162	31	6	29	109	9	.282
1989	San Francisco	1B	159	588	104	196	38	9	23	111	8	.333
1990	San Francisco	1B	154	600	91	177	25	5	19	95	8	.295
	Totals		736	2700	452	815	150	27	117	447	34	.302

WILLIE McGEE 32 6-1 195   Bats S Throws R

Crossed bay from Oakland and returned to NL in December with four-year, $13-million contract... First player in history to win a batting title while finishing season in the other league ... Trailed Phils' Lenny Dykstra most of year, but Dykstra dropped off in September while he was stuck at .335... Hit .274 in 29 games for the A's, so his combined average was .324— not good enough to win title in either league... Acquired from Cards Aug. 29 for outfielder Felix José, infielder Stan Royer and pitcher Daryl Green... Made $1.5 million in final year of contract with Cards last season... Played center field and hit second down the stretch for Oakland... Started slowly with the A's (3-for-24), but caught on and hit in 10 straight games... In his first game with A's, he scored from first on a wild pickoff attempt... Could probably beat Rickey Henderson in a sprint... Stunk up the joint on defense in NL, committing 16 errors, but made only one miscue with A's... Born Nov. 2, 1958, in San Francisco... Played at Diablo Valley College.

Year	Club	Pos.	G	AB	R	H	2B	3B	HR	RBI	SB	Avg.
1982	St. Louis	OF	123	422	43	125	12	8	4	56	24	.296
1983	St. Louis . . / . . .	OF	147	601	75	172	22	8	5	75	39	.286
1984	St. Louis . . . . , .	OF	145	571	82	166	19	11	6	50	43	.291
1985	St. Louis	OF	152	612	114	216	26	18	10	82	56	.353
1986	St. Louis	OF	124	497	65	127	22	7	7	48	19	.256
1987	St. Louis	OF-SS	153	620	76	177	37	11	11	105	16	.285
1988	St. Louis	OF	137	562	73	164	24	6	3	50	41	.292
1989	St. Louis	OF	58	199	23	47	10	2	3	17	8	.236
1990	St. Louis	OF	125	501	76	168	32	5	3	62	28	.335
1990	Oakland	OF	29	113	23	31	3	2	0	15	3	.274
	Totals		1193	4698	650	1393	207	78	52	560	277	.297

MATT WILLIAMS 25 6-2 205   Bats R Throws R

His presence gives Giants most feared 3-4-5 hitters in NL... Led NL in RBI with 122 and was fourth in homers with 33... Made the most of his opportunities by hitting .331 with men in scoring position, .308 with the bases loaded and .359 with a man on third... Hard to believe he was sent to Phoenix on May 1, 1989 after dreadful .130 start... Besides all that power, he can field, too... Ranked second among NL third basemen in fielding at .959 (19 errors in 465 total chances) and led third basemen in putouts (140) and double plays (33)... Earned $190,000 in 1990, about $700,000 less than Jose Uribe... Born Nov. 28, 1965, in Bishop, Cal.... Attended Nevada-Las Vegas and Giants made him third player taken overall in 1986 draft... Has four grand slams in short career while Kevin Mitchell has yet to hit one.

Year	Club	Pos.	G	AB	R	H	2B	3B	HR	RBI	SB	Avg.
1987	San Francisco	SS-3B	84	245	28	46	9	2	8	21	4	.188
1988	San Francisco	3B-SS	52	156	17	32	6	1	8	19	0	.205
1989	San Francisco	3B-SS	84	292	31	59	18	1	18	50	1	.202
1990	San Francisco	3B	159	617	87	171	27	2	33	122	7	.277
	Totals		379	1310	163	308	60	6	67	212	12	.235

ROBBY THOMPSON 28 5-11 170   Bats R Throws R

Compiled the most productive power numbers of his career—15 homers, 56 RBI and 22 doubles... Fifteen homers tied Bill Madlock's San Francisco mark for most homers by a second baseman... Tied for NL lead among second basemen with 94 double plays... Ranked third in assists (441) and putouts (286)... Earned $900,000 in 1990... Born May 10, 1962, in West Palm Beach, Fla.... Giants' first-round selection in secondary phase of 1983 draft, out of University of Florida.

Year	Club	Pos.	G	AB	R	H	2B	3B	HR	RBI	SB	Avg.
1986	San Francisco	2B-SS	149	549	73	149	27	3	7	47	12	.271
1987	San Francisco	2B	132	420	62	110	26	5	10	44	16	.262
1988	San Francisco	2B	138	477	66	126	24	6	7	48	14	.264
1989	San Francisco	2B	148	547	91	132	26	11	13	50	12	.241
1990	San Francisco	2B	144	498	67	122	22	3	15	56	14	.245
	Totals		711	2491	359	639	125	28	52	245	68	.257

DAVE RIGHETTI 32 6-4 212   Bats L Throws L

A four-year, $10-million contract made him a Giant after 11 years as a Yankee . . . Recorded 36 saves last season, the second-highest total of career . . . Had set major-league record with 46 saves in 1986, a mark that stood until Bobby Thigpen broke it last season . . . Ranks seventh on all-time saves list with 224 . . . Total is most by any left-hander since stat became official in 1969 . . . Registered 200th career save June 12 against Boston . . . Surpassed Whitey Ford for all-time lead in games by a Yankee pitcher with 522 . . . Fired 4-0 no-hitter against Boston, July 4, 1983 . . . Converted to relief after that season, replacing departed closer Rich Gossage . . . AL Rookie of the Year in 1981 . . . Born Nov. 28, 1958, in San Jose, Cal. . . . Acquired by Yankees as part of 10-player blockbuster with Texas after 1978 season . . . Yankees' best-paid pitcher in 1990 at a salary of $1.55 million.

Year	Club	G	IP	W	L	Pct.	SO	BB	H	ERA
1979	New York (AL)	3	17	0	1	.000	13	10	10	3.71
1981	New York (AL)	15	105	8	4	.667	89	38	75	2.06
1982	New York (AL)	33	183	11	10	.524	163	108	155	3.79
1983	New York (AL)	31	217	14	8	.636	169	67	194	3.44
1984	New York (AL)	64	96⅓	5	6	.455	90	37	79	2.34
1985	New York (AL)	74	107	12	7	.632	92	45	96	2.78
1986	New York (AL)	74	106⅔	8	8	.500	83	35	88	2.45
1987	New York (AL)	60	95	8	6	.571	77	44	95	3.51
1988	New York (AL)	60	87	5	4	.556	70	37	86	3.52
1989	New York (AL)	55	69	2	6	.250	51	26	73	3.00
1990	New York (AL)	53	53	1	1	.500	43	26	48	3.57
	Totals	522	1136	74	61	.548	940	473	999	3.11

SCOTT GARRELTS 29 6-4 205   Bats R Throws R

This was his first full year as a starter . . . Led NL in ERA in 1989 after shifting from bullpen . . . Got off to a brutal 1-6 start with a 6.88 ERA last year . . . Rebounded by winning eight of next nine decisions . . . Came within one out of no-hitter July 29 against the Reds, but Paul O'Neill's single broke it up . . . Missed the final two weeks of the season with tendinitis in his right elbow . . . Set career high with 31 starts . . . Earned

$1,400,000 in 1990 . . . Born Oct. 30, 1961, in Urbana, Ill. . . . Giants' first selection in 1979 draft.

Year	Club	G	IP	W	L	Pct.	SO	BB	H	ERA
1982	San Francisco	1	2	0	0	.000	4	2	3	13.50
1983	San Francisco	5	35⅔	2	2	.500	16	19	33	2.52
1984	San Francisco	21	43	2	3	.400	32	34	45	5.65
1985	San Francisco	74	105⅔	9	6	.600	106	58	76	2.30
1986	San Francisco	53	173⅔	13	9	.591	125	74	144	3.11
1987	San Francisco	64	106⅓	11	7	.611	127	55	70	3.22
1988	San Francisco	65	98	5	9	.357	86	46	80	3.58
1989	San Francisco	30	193⅓	14	5	.737	119	46	149	2.28
1990	San Francisco	31	182	12	11	.522	80	70	190	4.15
	Totals.	344	939⅔	68	52	.567	695	404	790	3.23

JOHN BURKETT 26 6-3 205   Bats R Throws R

After seven years in the minors, he became overnight sensation, topping the Giants in wins (14), innings pitched (204), strikeouts (118), ERA (3.79) and starts (32) . . . Only one other San Francisco rookie has ever won more his first year (John Montefusco had 15 wins in 1975) . . . Right-hander's real goal is to become pro bowler after baseball career ends . . . Bowling pins are 60 feet away, too . . . "I'm a cocky guy when I'm bowling," he says. "I can beat anybody." . . . Keeps two bowling balls in custom bag. He says one is for strikes, the other for picking up spares . . . Has bowled three perfect games, but has yet to pitch one . . . Earned major-league minimum of $100,000 last year, but figures to get a healthy raise . . . Born Nov. 28, 1964, in New Brighton, Pa. . . . Selected in sixth round of the 1983 draft.

Year	Club	G	IP	W	L	Pct.	SO	BB	H	ERA
1987	San Francisco	3	6	0	0	.000	5	3	7	4.50
1990	San Francisco	33	204	14	7	.667	118	61	201	3.79
	Totals.	36	210	14	7	.667	123	64	208	3.81

BUD BLACK 33 6-2 185   Bats L Throws L

Left Blue Jays when he signed four-year, $10-million free-agent contract with Giants . . . Made 31 starts and also finished one game as a reliever in 1990 while pitching five complete games and two shutouts . . . Finished 15th among AL qualifiers for ERA title . . . Traded from Indians to Blue Jays as September pennant insurance for pitcher Mauro Gozzo . . . Born June 30, 1957, in San Mateo, Cal. . . . Selected by Mariners in

17th round of 1979 draft . . . Traded to Royals for Manny Castillo before 1982 season . . . Traded to Indians for Pat Tabler June 3, 1988 . . . Pitched two seasons at San Diego State, where he was teammate of Tony Gwynn.

Year	Club	G	IP	W	L	Pct.	SO	BB	H	ERA
1981	Seattle	2	1	0	0	.000	0	3	2	0.00
1982	Kansas City	22	88⅓	4	6	.400	40	34	92	4.58
1983	Kansas City	24	161⅓	10	7	.588	58	43	159	3.79
1984	Kansas City	35	257	17	12	.586	140	64	226	3.12
1985	Kansas City	33	205⅔	10	15	.400	122	59	216	4.33
1986	Kansas City	56	121	5	10	.333	68	43	100	3.20
1987	Kansas City	29	122⅓	8	6	.571	61	35	126	3.60
1988	K.C.-Clev.	33	81	4	4	.500	63	34	82	5.00
1989	Cleveland	33	222⅓	12	11	.522	88	52	213	3.36
1990	Clev.-Tor.	32	206⅔	13	11	.542	106	61	181	3.57
	Totals.	299	1466⅔	83	82	.503	746	428	1397	3.70

JEFF BRANTLEY 27 5-11 180   Bats R Throws R

Filled void created when closer Steve Bedrosian was struggling . . . Ended the year on the sidelines because of back and shoulder injuries . . . Successful on 19 of 24 save opportunities . . . Ranked eighth in NL in saves . . . Named to his first All-Star team and was the losing pitcher July 10 at Wrigley Field . . . Born Sept. 5, 1963, in Florence, Ala. . . . Giants' sixth-round selection in 1985 draft . . . Earned $170,000 in 1990 . . . Was Will Clark's teammate at Mississippi State.

Year	Club	G	IP	W	L	Pct.	SO	BB	H	ERA
1988	San Francisco	9	20⅔	0	1	.000	11	6	22	5.66
1989	San Francisco	59	97⅓	7	1	.875	69	37	101	4.07
1990	San Francisco	55	86⅔	5	3	.625	61	33	77	1.56
	Totals.	123	204⅔	12	5	.706	141	76	200	3.17

TOP PROSPECTS

ERIC GUNDERSON 25 6-0 175   Bats R Throws L

Bounced around last year . . . Started season with the Giants, then was optioned to Phoenix (AAA) April 27 . . . Was 5-7 with 8.23 ERA in 16 starts for Phoenix before being sent down to Shreveport (AA) . . . Went 2-2 with 3.25 ERA there as Shreveport won its first Texas League crown in 35 years . . . Recalled by Giants Sept. 16 . . . Was 1-2 with 5.49 ERA for Giants . . . Born March 29, 1966, in Torrance, Cal. . . . Giants' second-round selection in 1987 draft.

DARREN LEWIS 23 6-0 175   **Bats R Throws R**
Giants obtained this promising outfielder from Oakland in December deal for Ernest Riles . . . Hit .296 in 71 games for Huntsville (AA) and .291 in 60 games for Tacoma (AAA) . . . Played 35 games for A's and hit .291 . . . Born Aug. 28, 1967, in Berkeley, Cal. . . . Played college ball at Cal. . . . Was 18th-round pick in 1988 draft.

TED WOOD 24 6-2 178   **Bats L Throws L**
Outfielder boasts unique combination of size and speed . . . Hit .265 with 17 homers and 11 triples and stole 17 bases for Shreveport (AA) . . . Born Jan. 4, 1967, in Chagrin Falls, Ohio . . . Giants' second selection in 1988 draft . . . Attended University of New Orleans and was member of the 1988 Olympic team.

KEVIN ROGERS 22 6-1 190   **Bats S Throws L**
Impressed Giants' brass with 14-5 record and 3.61 ERA for San Jose (A) . . . Struck out 186 in 172 innings . . . He has gone 27-12 over last two years . . . Born Aug. 20, 1968, in Cleveland, Miss. . . . Selected in ninth round of 1988 draft.

ROD BECK 22 6-1 215   **Bats R Throws R**
Posted impressive 10-3 record and 2.23 ERA for Shreveport (AA) . . . Was 18-5 in '89 for San Jose (A) and Shreveport . . . Born Aug. 3, 1968, in Burbank, Cal. . . . Acquired from A's for Charlie Corbell, March 23, 1988 . . . Selected by A's in 13th round of 1986 draft.

MIKE REMLINGER 25 6-0 195   **Bats L Throws L**
His most impressive stat was his 147 ⅔ innings pitched for Shreveport (AA) after suffering arm problems in 1989 . . . Finished 9-11 with a 3.90 ERA . . . Cut down on walks . . . In '89, he allowed more walks (52) than hits (51) . . . Gave up 72 walks and 149 hits last year . . . Giants' No. 1 selection and the 16th taken overall in 1987 draft . . . Born March 23, 1966, in Middletown, N.Y.

MANAGER ROGER CRAIG: Has a knack for keeping tattered pitching staffs together . . . He's a regular mound doctor . . . Managed to keep the Giants on the outer fringes of NL West race, despite using 26 different pitchers . . . Used 21 different pitchers, including 15 starters to win NL pennant in 1989 . . . Surpassed Charlie Fox for most games managed in San Francisco history . . . The first manager since 1971 to lead San Francisco to five consecutive winning seasons . . . His record with Giants is 439-389 since taking over, Sept. 18, 1985 . . . "Humm Baby" . . . Led Giants to 1987 NL West title, club's first since 1971 . . . Former pitcher has managed, coached or scouted for 22 years and has become known as guru of split-finger fastballs . . . Stepped down as Detroit pitching coach and became scout after club won World Series in 1984 . . . Managed Padres in 1978 and 1979 . . . Lifetime managerial record is 591-560 . . . Over 12 major-league seasons as pitcher, he was 74-98 with 3.82 ERA . . . Lost 24 games for expansion Mets in 1962 and 22 in 1963 . . . Born Feb. 17, 1930, in Durham, N.C.

ALL-TIME GIANT SEASON RECORDS

BATTING: Bill Terry, .401, 1930
HRs: Willie Mays, 52, 1965
RBI: Mel Ott, 151, 1929
STEALS: George Burns, 62, 1914
WINS: Christy Mathewson, 37, 1908
STRIKEOUTS: Christy Mathewson, 267, 1903

CHICAGO CUBS

TEAM DIRECTORY: Pres.-CEO: Donald Grenesko; Exec. VP-Dir. Baseball Operations: Jim Frey; Dir. Scouting: Dick Balderson; Dir. Media Rel./Publications: Ned Colletti; Trav. Sec.: Peter Durso; Mgr.: Don Zimmer. Home: Wrigley Field (39,012). Field distances: 355, l.f. line; 400, c.f.; 353, r.f. line. Spring training: Mesa, Ariz.

SCOUTING REPORT

HITTING: The Cubs, sixth in the NL in runs (690) last season, have finished either first or second in batting during each of manager Don Zimmer's three years in Chicago and they added even more pop to their lineup last winter. Free-agent signee George Bell (.265, 21, 86 with the Blue Jays) figures to make the Friendly Confines even more unfriendly for opposing pitchers.

Three Cubs were among the NL's top 10 hitters last year. Andre Dawson (.310, 27, 100) still loves to hit at Wrigley, NL home-run champ Ryne Sandberg (.306, 40, 100) is coming off the most spectacular season of an outstanding career and Mark Grace (.309, 9, 82) wants to extend his strong play of late 1990.

Catcher Joe Girardi (.270, 1, 38) and shortstop Shawon Dunston (.262, 17, 66) give the Cubs significant offensive punch while playing positions that are associated with defense. Jerome Walton (.263, 2, 21) should bounce back from a disappointing sophomore year ruined by injuries.

PITCHING: Obviously, the pitching must improve if the Cubs expect to contend. Their 4.34 team ERA was 11th in the league last year, when they had only 13 complete games and seven shutouts and they used 15 different starters.

Free-agent addition Danny Jackson (6-6, 3.61 with the Reds) could make a big difference if he remains healthy and regains his 20-win form. Rick Sutcliffe missed most of last season after undergoing shoulder surgery. Can he bounce back at 34? Ace Greg Maddux (15-15, 3.46) suffered through an inexplicable eight-game losing streak and relief ace Mitch Williams, following a spectacular 1989 season, slumped to a 1-8 record and saved just 16 games after requiring midseason knee surgery. So, the Cubs signed free agent Dave Smith (6-6, 2.39, 23 Sv with the Astros) to share closing duties with Paul Assenmacher (7-2, 2.80, 10 Sv).

This year's rotation should revolve around Jackson and three

NL home-run champ Ryne Sandberg is still second to none.

youngsters: Maddux, Mike Harkey (12-6, 3.26) and Shawn Boskie (5-6, 3.69). Harkey was having an outstanding rookie season until he was sidelined with shoulder stiffness. Boskie showed promise before undergoing minor elbow surgery. Lance Dickson, last year's No. 1 draft choice, also will be given a chance to make the rotation.

FIELDING: Three-quarters of the Cubs' infield is as good as any in baseball. Grace is smooth at first base, Sandberg (eight errors) is nearly flawless at second and Dunston has the best arm of any shortstop in the business. Girardi is a fine defensive catcher and two-thirds of the outfield is more than adequate, Walton in center and Dawson in right. Bell will be a liability in left, but that's the price the Cubs are willing to pay for the 30-plus home runs he figures to hit.

OUTLOOK: The Cubs have been on a rollercoaster—down in '88, up in '89, down (77-85) in '90. It's not unreasonable to expect them to rise again in 1991. They'll only go as far as their pitching allows, but there's every reason to believe it will improve dramatically.

CHICAGO CUBS 1991 ROSTER

MANAGER Don Zimmer
Coaches—Joe Altobelli, Chuck Cottier, Jose Martinez, Dick Pole, Phil Roof

PITCHERS

No.	Name	1990 Club	W-L	IP	SO	ERA	B-T	Ht.	Wt.	Born
45	Assenmacher, Paul	Chicago (NL)	7-2	103	95	2.80	L-L	6-3	200	12/10/60 Detroit, MI
36	Bielecki, Mike	Chicago (NL)	8-11	168	103	4.93	R-R	6-3	195	7/31/59 Baltimore, MD
47	Boskie, Shawn	Iowa	4-2	51	51	3.18	R-R	6-3	205	3/28/67 Hawthorne, NV
		Chicago (NL)	5-6	98	49	3.69				
52	Bullinger, Jim	Winston-Salem	7-6	90	85	3.70	R-R	6-2	180	8/21/65 New Orleans, LA
		Charlotte	3-4	44	33	5.11				
49	Castillo, Frank	Charlotte	6-6	111	112	3.88	R-R	6-1	180	4/1/69 El Paso, TX
33	Dickson, Lance	Geneva	2-1	17	29	0.53	R-L	6-1	185	10/19/69 Fullerton, CA
		Peoria	3-1	36	54	1.51				
		Charlotte	2-1	24	28	.038				
		Chicago (NL)	0-3	14	4	7.24				
22	Harkey, Mike	Chicago (NL)	12-6	174	94	3.26	R-R	6-5	220	10/25/66 San Diego, CA
35	Jackson, Danny	Charleston	0-0	3	2	6.00	R-L	6-0	205	1/5/62 San Antonio, TX
		Nashville	1-0	11	3	0.00				
		Cincinnati	6-6	117	76	3.61				
43	Kraemer, Joe	Chicago (NL	0-0	25	16	7.20	L-L	6-2	185	9/10/64 Olympia, WA
		Iowa	7-6	122	84	3.76				
50	Lancaster, Les	Chicago (NL)	9-5	109	65	4.62	R-R	6-2	200	4/21/62 Dallas, TX
		Iowa	0-1	18	15	4.08				
31	Maddux, Greg	Chicago (NL)	15-15	237	144	3.46	R-R	6-0	170	4/14/66 San Angelo, TX
39	Nunez, Jose	Iowa	7-6	107	109	3.94	R-R	6-3	190	1/13/64 Dominican Republic
		Chicago (NL)	4-7	61	40	6.53				
46	Pavlas, Dave	Iowa	8-3	99	96	3.26	R-R	6-7	195	8/12/62 West Germany
		Chicago (NL)	2-0	21	12	2.11				
41	Pico, Jeff	Iowa	0-0	5	1	5.79	R-R	6-2	170	2/12/66 Antioch, CA
		Chicagto (NL)	4-4	92	37	4.79				
51	Slocumb, Heath	Charlotte	3-1	50	37	2.15	R-R	6-3	180	7/7/66 Jamaica, NY
		Iowa	3-2	27	21	2.00				
—	Smith, Dave	Houston	6-6	60	50	2.39	R-R	6-1	195	1/21/55 San Francisco, CA
40	Sutcliffe, Rick	Iowa	0-2	13	12	7.82	L-R	6-7	215	6/21/56 Independence, MO
		Chicago (NL)	0-2	21	7	5.91				
28	Williams, Mitch	Chicago (NL)	1-8	66	55	3.93	L-L	6-4	205	11/17/64 Santa Ana, CA
44	Wilson, Steve	Chicago (NL)	4-9	139	95	4.79	L-L	6-4	195	12/13/64 Canada

CATCHERS

No.	Name	1990 Club	H	HR	RBI	Pct.	B-T	Ht.	Wt.	Born
9	Berryhill, Damon	Peoria	10	3	8	.385	S-R	6-0	205	12/3/63 South Laguna, CA
		Iowa	17	3	6	.215				
		Chicago (NL)	10	1	9	.189				
7	Girardi, Joe	Chicago (NL)	113	1	38	.270	R-R	5-11	195	10/14/64 Peoria, IL
1	Pappas, Erik	Iowa	101	16	55	.249	R-R	6-0	190	4/25/66 Chicago, IL
32	Villanueva, Hector	Iowa	47	8	34	.266	R-R	6-1	220	10/2/64 Puerto Rico
		Chicago (NL)	31	7	18	.272				
2	Wilkins, Rick	Charlotte	102	17	71	.227	L-R	6-2	210	7/4/67 Jacksonville, FL

INFIELDERS

No.	Name	1990 Club	H	HR	RBI	Pct.	B-T	Ht.	Wt.	Born
21	Arias, Alex	Charlotte	103	4	38	.246	R-R	6-3	185	11/20/67 New York, NY
12	Dunston, Shawon	Chicago (NL)	143	17	66	.262	R-R	6-1	175	3/21/63 Brooklyn, NY
3	Grace, Mark	Chicago (NL)	182	9	82	.309	L-L	6-2	190	6/28/64 Winston-Salem, NC
15	Ramos, Domingo	Chicago (NL)	60	2	17	.265	R-R	5-10	170	3/29/58 Dominican Republic
1	Salazar, Luis	Chicago (NL)	104	12	47	.254	R-R	5-9	180	5/19/56 Venezuela
23	Sandberg, Ryne	Chicago (NL)	188	40	100	.306	R-R	6-2	180	9/18/59 Spokane, WA
—	Vizcaino, Jose	Albuquerque	77	2	36	.279	S-R	6-1	150	3/26/68 Dominican Republic
		Los Angeles	14	0	2	.275				

OUTFIELDERS

No.	Name	1990 Club	H	HR	RBI	Pct.	B-T	Ht.	Wt.	Born
—	Bell, George	Toronto	149	21	86	.265	R-R	6-1	194	10/21/59 Dominican Republic
30	Clark, Dave	Chicago (NL)	47	5	20	.275	L-R	6-2	210	9/3/62 Tupelo, MS
29	Dascenzo, Doug	Chicago (NL)	61	1	26	.253	S-L	5-8	160	6/30/64 Cleveland, OH
8	Dawson, Andre	Chicago (NL)	164	27	100	.310	R-R	6-3	195	7/10/54 Miami, FL
27	May, Derrick	Iowa	136	8	69	.296	L-R	6-4	205	7/14/68 Rochester, NY
		Chicago (NL)	15	1	11	.246				
18	Smith, Dwight	Chicago (NL)	76	6	27	.262	L-R	5-11	175	11/8/63 Tallahassee, FL
24	Varsho, Gary	Iowa	69	7	33	.301	L-R	5-11	190	6/20/61 Marshfield, WI
		Chicago (NL)	12	0	1	.250				
20	Walton, Jerome	Chicago (NL)	103	2	21	.263	R-R	6-1	175	7/8/65 Newnan, GA
		Iowa	3	1	1	.188				

CUB PROFILES

RYNE SANDBERG 31 6-2 180   Bats R Throws R

One of baseball's top all-around performers . . . Led NL in homers (40), runs (116) and total bases (344) while finishing 10th in batting race (.306) . . . Joined Hank Aaron (1963) and Jose Canseco (1988) as only players in major-league history to hit 40 homers and steal 25 bases in same season . . . Achieved third-highest single-season homer total for a second baseman, trailing only Davey Johnson and Rogers Hornsby (42) . . . Only sixth Cub to have consecutive 30-homer seasons . . . Has 17 two-homer games . . . Did not commit an error from June 20, 1989 until May 18, 1990, a span of 123 games and 584 chances, and won eighth consecutive Gold Glove . . . Made seventh straight All-Star appearance and was top vote-getter . . . Born Sept. 18, 1959, in Spokane, Wash. . . . Drafted by Phillies in 20th round in 1978, then dealt to Cubs with Larry Bowa for Ivan DeJesus prior to 1982 season . . . Still a bargain, earning $1,550,000 in 1990.

Year	Club	Pos.	G	AB	R	H	2B	3B	HR	RBI	SB	Avg.
1981	Philadelphia . . .	SS-2B	13	6	2	1	0	0	0	0	0	.167
1982	Chicago (NL) . .	3B-2B	156	635	103	172	33	5	7	54	32	.271
1983	Chicago (NL) . .	2B-SS	158	633	94	165	25	4	8	48	37	.261
1984	Chicago (NL) . .	2B	156	636	114	200	36	19	19	84	32	.314
1985	Chicago (NL) . .	2B-SS	153	609	113	186	31	6	26	83	54	.305
1986	Chicago (NL) . .	2B	154	627	68	178	28	5	14	76	34	.284
1987	Chicago (NL) . .	2B	132	523	81	154	25	2	16	59	21	.294
1988	Chicago (NL) . .	2B	155	618	77	163	23	8	19	69	25	.264
1989	Chicago (NL) . .	2B	157	606	104	176	25	5	30	76	15	.290
1990	Chicago (NL) . .	2B	155	615	116	188	30	3	40	100	25	.306
	Totals		1389	5508	872	1583	256	57	179	649	275	.287

ANDRE DAWSON 36 6-3 195   Bats R Throws R

Right fielder bounced back impressively from sub-par 1989 season, when he was troubled by right knee problems . . . Stole 300th base, joining Willie Mays as only two players in history to record at least 2,000 hits, 300 homers and 300 stolen bases . . . Drove in 100 runs for third time . . . "Hawk" had 24 RBI during 28 games in September after surviving 8-for-56 August slump . . . Was 16-for-18 in stolen-base attempts . . . Finished fifth in NL batting race (.310) . . . Reached 20-homer mark for sixth straight season and 11th time overall . . . Was intentionally walked a major-league record five times by Reds May 22 . . . Selected as All-Star for seventh time . . . Had pair of two-homer games, giving him 33 for career . . . Born July 10, 1954, in Miami . . . Attended Florida A&M for three years . . . Picked by Expos in 11th round of 1975 draft and signed with Cubs as free agent prior to 1987 season . . . Highest-paid Cub in 1990, earning $2,100,000.

Year	Club	Pos.	G	AB	R	H	2B	3B	HR	RBI	SB	Avg.
1976	Montreal	OF	24	85	9	20	4	1	0	7	1	.235
1977	Montreal	OF	139	525	64	148	26	9	19	65	21	.282
1978	Montreal	OF	157	609	84	154	24	8	25	72	28	.253
1979	Montreal	OF	155	639	90	176	24	12	25	92	35	.275
1980	Montreal	OF	151	577	96	178	41	7	17	87	34	.308
1981	Montreal	OF	103	394	71	119	21	3	24	64	26	.302
1982	Montreal	OF	148	608	107	183	37	7	23	83	39	.301
1983	Montreal	OF	159	633	104	189	36	10	32	113	25	.299
1984	Montreal	OF	138	533	73	132	23	6	17	86	13	.248
1985	Montreal	OF	139	529	65	135	27	2	23	91	13	.255
1986	Montreal	OF	130	496	65	141	32	2	20	78	18	.284
1987	Chicago (NL) . .	OF	153	621	90	178	24	2	49	137	11	.287
1988	Chicago (NL) . .	OF	157	591	78	179	31	8	24	79	12	.303
1989	Chicago (NL) . .	OF	118	416	62	105	18	6	21	77	8	.252
1990	Chicago (NL) . .	OF	147	529	72	164	28	5	27	100	16	.310
	Totals		2018	7785	1130	2201	396	88	346	1231	300	.283

MARK GRACE 26 6-2 190   Bats L Throws L

After hitting just two homers and driving in 32 runs before All-Star break, he put together an outstanding second half, batting .359 during a 70-game stretch . . . Wound up tied for sixth in NL batting race (.309) . . . Had career-high 18-game hitting streak stopped Aug. 10 . . . Ended first half of season going 0-for-10 in double-header against Giants and claimed the three-day break helped turn around his year as he decided to stop swinging for fences . . . ''It took about 3½ months to realize I'm not that kind of player,'' he said. ''I went back to what got me here.'' . . . Smooth first baseman finished second, behind Reds' Chris Sabo, in 1988 Rookie-of-the-Year voting . . . Born June 28, 1964, in Winston-Salem, N.C. . . . Attended San Diego State University . . . Eastern League MVP in 1987 . . . Selected by Cubs in 24th round of 1985 draft . . . Earned $325,000 in 1990.

Year	Club	Pos.	G	AB	R	H	2B	3B	HR	RBI	SB	Avg.
1988	Chicago (NL) . .	1B	134	486	65	144	23	4	7	57	3	.296
1989	Chicago (NL) . .	1B	142	510	74	160	28	3	13	79	14	.314
1990	Chicago (NL) . .	1B	157	589	72	182	32	1	9	82	15	.309
	Totals		433	1585	211	486	83	8	29	218	32	.307

SHAWON DUNSTON 28 6-1 175 Bats R Throws R

Has best arm of any shortstop in baseball and has finally gained recognition as one of best at his position despite committing 20 errors in 1990 . . . Played in his first All-Star Game . . . Equaled career high with 17 homers . . . Tied modern major-league record with three triples in game against Expos, becoming first Cub to accomplish that feat since Ernie Banks in 1966 . . . In 1988, he became first Cub shortstop to earn trip to All-Star Game since Don Kessinger in 1974, but he did not play . . . Career-high 30 stolen bases in 1988 was most by a Cub shortstop since Ivan DeJesus had 44 in 1980 . . . Born March 21, 1963, in Brooklyn, N.Y. . . . First player chosen in 1982 draft . . . During senior year at Thomas Jefferson High School, he was 37-for-37 in stolen-base attempts and batted .790 . . . Earned $1,250,000 in 1990.

Year	Club	Pos.	G	AB	R	H	2B	3B	HR	RBI	SB	Avg.
1985	Chicago (NL) . .	SS	74	250	40	65	12	4	4	18	11	.260
1986	Chicago (NL) . .	SS	150	581	66	145	36	3	17	68	13	.250
1987	Chicago (NL) . .	SS	95	346	40	85	18	3	5	22	12	.246
1988	Chicago (NL) . .	SS	155	575	40	143	23	6	9	56	30	.249
1989	Chicago (NL) . .	SS	138	471	52	131	20	6	9	60	19	.278
1990	Chicago (NL) . .	SS	146	545	73	143	22	8	17	66	25	.262
	Totals		758	2768	340	712	131	30	61	290	110	.257

JEROME WALTON 25 6-1 175 Bats R Throws R

Rookie of the Year in 1989 suffered through injury-plagued sophomore year . . . Broke left hand when hit by pitch from Phillies' Ken Howell June 17 . . . After returning from disabled list, he was hit on same hand by Mets' Alejandro Pena Aug. 12 . . . As a result of injuries, all of his numbers were down . . . Three of his seven major-league homers have come leading off a game . . . Scored 27 runs in his last 36 games, but missed final week after suffering seven-inch cut on left index finger . . . Center fielder was near-unanimous choice as top 1989 NL rookie, receiving 22 of 24 first-place votes as the only player named on all 24 ballots . . . Rookie season was highlighted by 30-game hitting streak . . . Won Eastern League (AA) batting title in 1989 . . . Born July 8, 1965, in Newnan, Ga. . . . Selected by Cubs in second round of January 1986 draft . . . Earned $185,000 in 1990.

Year	Club	Pos.	G	AB	R	H	2B	3B	HR	RBI	SB	Avg.
1989	Chicago (NL) . .	OF	116	475	64	139	23	3	5	46	24	.293
1990	Chicago (NL) . .	OF	101	392	63	103	16	2	2	21	14	.263
	Totals		217	867	127	242	39	5	7	67	38	.279

JOE GIRARDI 26 5-11 195   Bats R Throws R

Became Cubs' No. 1 catcher because Damon Berryhill was rehabilitating for most of 1990 season following surgery to repair torn rotator cuff . . . Took advantage of opportunity, establishing himself as solid hitter and excellent catcher with outstanding arm . . . Was batting .292 through Aug. 1, but failed in bid to become first Cub catcher to hit .300 since Gabby Hartnett in 1937 . . . "If we were winning, this guy would be headlines all over the place," said manager Don Zimmer. "When it comes to throwing, I rate Girardi No. 1 or No. 2 with (San Diego's) Benito Santiago." . . . His eight stolen bases (in 11 attempts) were most by a Cub catcher since 1942 . . . Born Oct. 14, 1964, in Peoria, Ill. . . . Selected by Cubs in fifth round of 1986 draft . . . Earned $115,000 in 1990.

Year	Club	Pos.	G	AB	R	H	2B	3B	HR	RBI	SB	Avg.
1989	Chicago (NL) . .	C	59	157	15	39	10	0	1	14	2	.248
1990	Chicago (NL) . .	C	133	419	36	113	24	2	1	38	8	.270
	Totals		192	576	51	152	34	2	2	52	10	.264

GEORGE BELL 31 6-1 194   Bats R Throws R

Wrigley Field bleachers will be inviting home-run target for the nine-year Blue Jay slugger who tested free-agent waters and wound up with a three-year, $9.8-million contract in December . . . Was generally unhappy with Jays, who wanted to move him out of left field and make him a permanent designated hitter . . . Is Toronto's all-time leader in total bases (2,201), RBI (740) and home runs (202) . . . Reached 20 home runs for sixth time in seven years. . . . Has totaled at least 80 RBI each of last seven seasons . . . Left fielder experienced vision problems in late August due to collection of fluid around retina of right eye and had late-season shoulder problems . . . Honored as league MVP in 1987, when he amassed a league-leading 134 RBI . . . Born Oct. 21, 1959, in San Pedro de Macoris, Dominican Republic . . . Acquired from Philadelphia in major-league draft, Dec. 8, 1980 . . . Toronto's best-paid player in 1990 at $2 million.

Year	Club	Pos.	G	AB	R	H	2B	3B	HR	RBI	SB	Avg.
1981	Toronto	OF	60	163	19	38	2	1	5	12	3	.233
1983	Toronto	OF	39	112	5	30	5	4	2	17	1	.268
1984	Toronto	OF-3B	159	606	85	177	39	4	26	87	11	.292
1985	Toronto	OF-1B	157	607	87	167	28	6	28	95	21	.275
1986	Toronto	OF-3B	159	641	101	198	38	6	31	108	7	.309
1987	Toronto	OF-2B-3B	156	610	111	188	32	4	47	134	5	.308
1988	Toronto	OF	156	614	78	165	27	5	24	97	4	.269
1989	Toronto	OF	153	613	88	182	41	2	18	104	4	.297
1990	Toronto	OF	142	562	67	149	25	0	21	86	3	.265
	Totals		1181	4528	641	1294	237	32	202	740	59	.286

GREG MADDUX 24 6-0 170   Bats R Throws R

Survived early-season dry spell in which he suffered eight straight losses and 13 winless starts in succession . . . Ended skid by beating Padres, 4-2, July 18 . . . One of best-hitting pitchers in 1988 and 1989, he went 0-for-25 before collecting first hit of 1990 . . . During first five starts of losing streak, he gave up 33 hits and 19 earned runs in 22 innings . . . Pitched six-hit shutout against Dodgers April 29, his first complete game since April 27, 1989 . . . Also set major-league record for putouts by a pitcher (seven) in that game . . . During stretch of 14 starts in August and September, he went 10-4 with 1.98 ERA . . . Born April 14, 1966, in San Angelo, Tex. . . . Selected by Cubs in second round of 1984 draft . . . Earned $437,500 in 1990 and won Gold Glove.

Year	Club	G	IP	W	L	Pct.	SO	BB	H	ERA
1986	Chicago (NL)	6	31	2	4	.333	20	11	44	5.52
1987	Chicago (NL)	30	155⅔	6	14	.300	101	74	181	5.61
1988	Chicago (NL)	34	249	18	8	.692	140	81	230	3.18
1989	Chicago (NL)	35	238⅓	19	12	.613	135	82	222	2.95
1990	Chicago (NL)	35	237	15	15	.500	144	71	242	3.46
	Totals	140	911	60	53	.531	540	319	919	3.68

PAUL ASSENMACHER 30 6-3 200   Bats L Throws L

Supplanted Mitch Williams as Cubs' primary closer late in season and finished with 10 saves and club-best 2.80 ERA . . . Was particularly effective against Mets, going 3-0 with four saves . . . Made career-high 74 appearances . . . Made his only major-league start June 5, a 6-5 loss to Pirates, giving up four hits, two walks and four earned runs while lasting only one inning . . . Pitched 3⅔ innings to save 9-6 victory over Giants

May 2, his first save since Sept. 17, 1988, a span of 78 appearances . . . In final appearance with Braves in 1989, he tied major-league record with four strikeouts in an inning . . . As a rookie in 1986, his 2.50 ERA was third-lowest among NL relievers with 50 or more appearances . . . Born Dec. 10, 1960, in Detroit . . . Signed as non-drafted free agent with Braves in 1983 . . . Traded to Cubs for two minor leaguers, Aug. 24, 1989 . . . Earned $450,000 in 1990.

Year	Club	G	IP	W	L	Pct.	SO	BB	H	ERA
1986	Atlanta	61	68⅓	7	3	.700	56	26	61	2.50
1987	Atlanta	52	54⅔	1	1	.500	39	24	58	5.10
1988	Atlanta	64	79⅓	8	7	.533	71	32	72	3.06
1989	Atl.-Chi. (NL)	63	76⅔	3	4	.429	79	28	74	3.99
1990	Chicago (NL)	74	103	7	2	.778	95	36	90	2.80
	Totals	314	382	26	17	.605	340	146	355	3.37

DAVE SMITH 36 6-1 195   Bats R Throws R

After 11-season career with Astros, new-look free agent joins Cubs with two-year, $4.9-million contract . . . Cubs obviously don't think he's lost it . . . Gave up four homers in 60⅓ innings last year after allowing two homers in his previous 190⅔ innings . . . Sprained right knee helped limit him to 23 saves, his lowest total since 1984 . . . Had 199 career saves with Astros. Only two players, Dan Quisenberry (238 with Kansas City) and Dave Righetti (224 with Yankees), have 200 saves with one club . . . Since 1985, he has converted 159 of 187 save opportunities . . . Born Jan. 21, 1955, in San Francisco . . . Astros' eighth-round selection in 1976 draft . . . Made $1.1 million last season.

Year	Club	G	IP	W	L	Pct.	SO	BB	H	ERA
1980	Houston	57	103	7	5	.583	85	32	90	1.92
1981	Houston	42	75	5	3	.625	52	23	54	2.76
1982	Houston	49	63⅓	5	4	.556	28	31	69	3.84
1983	Houston	42	72⅔	3	1	.750	41	36	72	3.10
1984	Houston	53	77⅓	5	4	.556	45	20	60	2.21
1985	Houston	64	79⅓	9	5	.643	40	17	69	2.27
1986	Houston	54	56	4	7	.364	46	22	39	2.73
1987	Houston	50	60	2	3	.400	73	21	39	1.65
1988	Houston	51	57⅓	4	5	.444	38	19	60	2.67
1989	Houston	52	58	3	4	.429	31	19	49	2.64
1990	Houston	49	60⅓	6	6	.500	50	20	45	2.39
	Totals	563	762⅓	53	47	.530	529	260	646	2.53

DANNY JACKSON 29 6-0 205   **Bats R Throws L**

Left Reds after signing four-year, $10-million, free-agent contract with Cubs . . . Started three postseason games in 1990, earning victory in third game of NL playoffs . . . Placed on disabled list three times last season and was sidelined much of 1989 with shoulder injury . . . Finished second in 1988 Cy Young voting while making spectacular NL debut, sharing league lead in wins (23) and complete games (15) and finishing among top four in innings, shutouts, starts and winning percentage . . . Born Jan. 5, 1962, in San Antonio . . . First player chosen in January 1982 draft . . . Traded from Royals to Reds for Ted Power and Kurt Stillwell before 1988 season.

Year	Club	G	IP	W	L	Pct.	SO	BB	H	ERA
1983	Kansas City	4	19	1	1	.500	9	6	26	5.21
1984	Kansas City	15	76	2	6	.250	40	35	84	4.26
1985	Kansas City	32	208	14	12	.538	114	76	209	3.42
1986	Kansas City	32	185⅔	11	12	.478	115	79	177	3.20
1987	Kansas City	36	224	9	18	.333	152	109	219	4.02
1988	Cincinnati	35	260⅔	23	8	.742	161	71	206	2.73
1989	Cincinnati	20	115⅔	6	11	.353	70	57	122	5.60
1990	Cincinnati	22	117⅓	6	6	.500	76	40	119	3.61
	Totals	196	1206⅓	72	74	.493	734	473	1162	3.66

TOP PROSPECTS

DERRICK MAY 22 6-4 210   **Bats L Throws R**

Despite getting off to slow start for Iowa (AAA), this outfielder finished with .296 average, 27 doubles, eight homers and 69 RBI . . . Hit safely in 23 consecutive games and also had 20-game hitting streak . . . Has five-year minor-league average of .301 . . . Batted .246 in 17-game September trial with Cubs . . . First major-league hit was two-run double off Expos' Mel Rojas . . . Born July 14, 1968, in Rochester, N.Y. . . . Ninth player chosen in 1986 draft.

KEVIN COFFMAN 26 6-3 206   **Bats R Throws R**

Pitched five complete games for Charlotte (AA), going 7-3 with 2.03 ERA in 14 starts . . . Promoted to Iowa (AAA) and held opponents to .204 average in nine starts . . . Overall, he struck out 133 batters in 153 innings . . . In September trial with Cubs, he walked 19 batters in 18⅓ innings, resulting in 0-2 record and 11.29 ERA . . . Born Jan. 19, 1965, in Austin, Tex. . . . Selected by Brewers in 11th round of 1983 draft . . . Traded by Braves to Cubs with Kevin Blankenship for Jody Davis, Sept. 29, 1988.

DAVE PAVLAS 28 6-7 190   Bats R Throws R

Pitched 99 innings for Iowa (AAA), went 8-3 with eight saves and started three games . . . Struck out 96 batters, walked 48 and compiled 3.26 ERA . . . Earned first major-league victory Sept. 8, working two innings against Cardinals in 5-4 win . . . Finished with 2.11 ERA in 13 appearances with Cubs . . . Born Aug. 12, 1962, in Frankfurt, Germany . . . Signed with Cubs as non-drafted free agent in 1984 . . . Traded to Rangers in 1987, but his contract was sold back to Cubs in January 1990.

MANAGER DON ZIMMER: Perhaps the most unorthodox manager in majors, he's never afraid to take a chance . . . His unique style paid dividends in 1989, when he took Cubs to surprising NL East championship and was a near-unanimous selection as NL Manager of the Year, receiving 23 of 24 first-place votes . . . Injuries to pitching staff derailed Cubs' bid to repeat in 1990, when team had to settle for a 77-85 mark and a fourth-place tie . . . Holds rare distinction of managing in all four of baseball's divisions: Padres (1972-73), Red Sox (1976-80), Rangers (1981-82) and Cubs (1988-90) . . . Zim's Red Sox teams won 91 or more games in three consecutive seasons and were 411-304 during his tenure, but never finished first . . . Was third-base coach in 1984 when Cubs won NL East title, was Giants' third-base coach in 1987 when they won NL West title and was Red Sox' third-base coach when they won AL pennant in 1975 . . . Overall managerial record for 12 seasons is 867-849 . . . Born Jan. 17, 1931, in Cincinnati, where he grew up with Cubs' GM Jim Frey . . . Batted .235 in a 12-year major-league playing career, despite a career-threatening beaning.

ALL-TIME CUB SEASON RECORDS

BATTING: Rogers Hornsby, .380, 1929
HRs: Hack Wilson, 56, 1930
RBI: Hack Wilson, 190, 1930
STEALS: Frank Chance, 67, 1903
WINS: Mordecai Brown, 29, 1908
STRIKEOUTS: Ferguson Jenkins, 274, 1970

MONTREAL EXPOS

TEAM DIRECTORY: Pres.-Chief Oper. Off.: Claude Brochu; VP-Baseball Oper.: Bill Stoneman; VP-GM: Dave Dombrowski; Media Relations: Monique Giroux, Richard Griffin; Trav. Sec.: Erik Ostling; Mgr.: Buck Rodgers. Home: Olympic Stadium (43,739). Field distances: 325, l.f. line; 375, l.c.; 404, c.f.; 375, r.c.; 325, r.f. line. Spring training: West Palm Beach, Fla.

SCOUTING REPORT

HITTING: Lack of punch proved to be the Expos' undoing in 1990 as their offense totally shut down during a late September swoon which derailed their pennant hopes. Houston was the only NL team with a lower batting average than the Expos (.250), who were 11th in runs (662) and ninth in home runs (114). No Expo

Dennis Martinez owns one of NL's nastiest curves.

batted .300.

Tim Wallach (.296, 21, 98) is a big run producer, but he needs more help and it may come in the form of Ivan Calderon (.273, 14, 74), who joined the Expos in the trade that sent Tim Raines (.287, 9, 62), no longer the offensive threat he was, to the White Sox. Andres Galarraga (.256, 20, 87) struck out a team-record 169 times.

Delino DeShields (.289, 4, 45), Marquis Grissom (.257, 3, 29) and Larry Walker (.241, 19, 51) all made big contributions during their rookie years and the Expos will need even more from them in 1991. Walker can be a real force if he cuts down on his strikeouts (112 in just 419 at-bats).

PITCHING: The Expos surprised everybody by leading the NL with a 3.37 ERA and their bullpen tied the world champion Reds for the league lead in saves (50), buoyed by the resurgence of Tim Burke (3-3, 2.52, 20 Sv). However, last year's contributions came from some unexpected sources and there's some question about whether the Expos can duplicate those numbers in 1991.

Oil Can Boyd (10-6, 2.93) had good stats, but his health is always questionable and he rarely pitched beyond the sixth inning. Moody Dennis Martinez (10-11, 2.95), who spurned new-look free agency to stay in Montreal, figures to be the ace again. Rookie reliever Bill Sampen (12-7, 2.99) was the team's leading winner. Rookie Mark Gardner (7-9, 3.42) must recover from a "tired arm."

Late-season callups Chris Nabholz (6-2, 2.83) and Brian Barnes (1-1, 2.89) each looked brilliant at times during brief trials and the Expos have bullpen help with the arrival of Barry Jones (11-4, 2.31) in the Raines-Calderon deal.

FIELDING: Defense was no problem in 1990 and it figures to be a strong point again. Galarraga, at first base, and Wallach, at third base, are two of the best. DeShields should be even better at second base. Spike Owen made just six errors in 148 games at shortstop. Nelson Santovenia and Mike Fitzgerald are solid behind the plate while Calderon, Walker, Grissom and Dave Martinez are all fine outfielders.

OUTLOOK: Rookies delivered beyond anyone's expectations in 1990 as Buck Rodgers' Expos were surprising pennant contenders until mid-September before running out of gas and finishing 85-77. If those rookies continue to develop, this team can contend again.

MONTREAL EXPOS 1991 ROSTER

MANAGER Buck Rodgers
Coaches—Larry Bearnarth, Tommy Harper, Rafael Landestoy, Ken Macha, Hal McRae, Tom Runnells

PITCHERS

No.	Name	1990 Club	W-L	IP	SO	ERA	B-T	Ht.	Wt.	Born
47	Barnes, Brian	Jacksonville	13-7	201	213	2.77	L-L	5-9	170	3/25/67 Roanoke Rapids, NC
		Montreal	1-1	28	23	2.89				
—	Bottenfield, Kent	Jacksonville	12-10	169	121	3.41	S-R	6-3	215	11/14/68 Portland, OR
23	Boyd, Oil Can	Montreal	10-6	191	113	2.93	R-R	6-1	160	10/6/59 Meridian, MS
56	Brito, Mario	Jacksonville	9-7	116	49	3.19	R-R	6-3	185	4/9/66 Dominican Republic
44	Burke, Tim	Montreal	3-3	75	47	2.52	R-R	6-3	205	2/19/59 Omaha, NE
49	Farmer, Howard	Indianapolis	7-9	148	99	3.89	R-R	6-3	190	1/18/66 Gary, IN
		Montreal	0-3	23	14	7.04				
41	Frey, Steve	Montreal	8-2	56	29	2.10	L-L	5-9	170	7/29/63 Meadowbrook, PA
		Indianapolis	0-0	3	3	0.00				
28	Gardner, Mark	Montreal	7-9	153	135	3.42	R-R	6-1	190	3/1/62 Los Angeles, CA
45	Hall, Drew	Montreal	4-7	58	40	5.09	L-L	6-5	220	3/27/63 Louisville, KY
—	Jones, Barry	Chicago (AL)	11-4	74	45	2.31	R-R	6-4	225	2/15/63 Centerville, IN
32	Martinez, Dennis	Montreal	10-11	226	156	2.95	R-R	6-1	180	5/14/55 Nicaragua
—	Masters, David	Iowa	1-4	26	22	12.30	R-R	6-9	225	8/13/64 San Diego, CA
		Jacksonville	2-0	42	49	3.46				
43	Nabholz, Chris	Jacksonville	7-2	74	77	3.03	L-L	6-5	210	1/5/67 Harrisburg, PA
		Indianapolis	0-6	63	44	4.83				
		Montreal	6-2	70	53	2.83				
—	Piatt, Doug	Jacksonville	5-1	49	51	2.20	L-R	6-1	185	9/26/65 Beaver, PA
59	Rivera, Hector	Jacksonville	6-6	105	60	3.60	R-R	6-4	210	2/8/70 Mexico
51	Rojas, Mel	Indianapolis	2-4	98	64	3.13	R-R	5-11	175	12/10/66 Dominican Republic
		Montreal	3-1	40	26	3.60				
34	Ruskin, Scott	Pitt.-Mont.	3-2	75	57	2.75	R-L	6-2	185	6/6/63 Jacksonville, FL
55	Sampen, Bill	Montreal	12-7	90	69	2.99	R-R	6-1	185	1/18/63 Lincoln, IL
24	*Schmidt, Dave	Montreal	3-3	48	22	4.31	R-R	6-1	188	4/22/57 Niles, MI

CATCHERS

No.	Name	1990 Club	H	HR	RBI	Pct.	B-T	Ht.	Wt.	Born
20	Fitzgerald, Mike	Montreal	76	9	41	.243	R-R	5-11	190	7/13/60 Long Beach, CA
19	Goff, Jerry	Indianapolis	41	5	26	.287	L-R	6-3	205	4/12/64 San Rafael, CA
		Montreal	27	3	7	.227				
2	Reyes, Gilberto	Indianapolis	72	9	45	.233	R-R	6-2	200	12/10/63 Dominican Republic
22	Santovenia, Nelson	Montreal	31	6	28	.190	R-R	6-3	205	7/27/61 Cuba
		Indianapolis	14	1	10	.318				

INFIELDERS

No.	Name	1990 Club	H	HR	RBI	Pct.	B-T	Ht.	Wt.	Born
4	DeShields, Delino	Montreal	144	4	45	.289	l-R	6-1	170	1/15/69 Seaford, DE
16	Foley, Tom	Montreal	35	0	12	.213	L-R	6-1	180	9/9/59 Columbus, GA
14	Galarraga, Andres	Montreal	148	20	87	.256	R-R	6-3	235	6/18/61 Venezuela
3	Noboa, Junior	Montreal	42	0	14	.266	R-R	5-10	165	11/10/64 Dominican Republic
11	Owen, Spike	Montreal	106	5	35	.234	S-R	5-10	170	4/19/61 Cleburne, TX
29	Wallach, Tim	Montreal	185	21	98	.296	R-R	6-3	200	9/14/57 Huntington Park, CA

OUTFIELDERS

No.	Name	1990 Club	H	HR	RBI	Pct.	B-T	Ht.	Wt.	Born
25	Aldrete, Mike	Montreal	39	1	18	.242	L-L	5-11	185	1/29/61 Carmel, CA
18	Alou, Moises	Buff.-Ind.	86	5	37	.264	R-R	6-3	175	7/3/66 Atlanta, GA
		Harrisburg	39	3	22	.295				
		Pitt.-Mont.	4	0	0	.200				
—	Calderon, Ivan	Chicago (AL)	166	14	74	.273	R-R	6-1	221	3/19/62 Puerto Rico
—	Faulk, James	Jacksonville	49	2	12	.258	L-L	6-2	185	6/1/68 Whitville, NC
9	Grissom, Marquis	Montreal	74	3	29	.257	R-R	5-11	190	4/17/67 Atlanta, GA
		Indianapolis	4	2	3	.182				
—	Hansen, Terrell	Jacksonville	109	24	83	.260	R-R	6-3	210	9/25/66 Bremerton, WA
—	Hernandez, Cesar	Jacksonville	95	10	50	.242	R-R	6-0	160	9/28/66 Dominican Republic
1	Martinez, Dave	Montreal	109	11	39	.279	L-L	5-10	170	9/26/64 New York, NY
35	Nixon, Otis	Montreal	58	1	20	.251	S-R	6-2	180	1/9/59 Evergreen, NC
33	Walker, Larry	Montreal	101	19	51	.241	L-R	6-2	205	12/1/66 Canada

*Free agent at press time

EXPO PROFILES

TIM WALLACH 33 6-3 200   Bats R Throws R

Re-established himself as one of top all-around third basemen by putting together his most productive season since 1987 . . . Ranked in tie for fourth spot in NL in doubles (37) and finished fifth in hits (185) and total bases (295) and eighth in RBI (98) . . . Had career-high eight-RBI game at San Diego . . . Had five four-RBI games . . . Batted .345 with four homers from May 7-13 . . . Had fifth career grand slam . . . Had three four-hit games . . . Went without a homer in August, but hit .355 . . . Batted .314 with nine homers and 25 RBI during May . . . Played in fourth All-Star Game . . . Has averaged 154 games a season since 1982 and was never on disabled list in 1980s . . . Won second Gold Glove in 1990 . . . Born Sept. 14, 1957, in Huntington Park, Cal. . . . Was 10th player selected in 1979 draft . . . Earned $1,250,000 in 1990.

Year	Club	Pos.	G	AB	R	H	2B	3B	HR	RBI	SB	Avg.
1980	Montreal	OF-1B	5	11	1	2	0	0	1	2	0	.182
1981	Montreal	OF-1B-3B	71	212	19	50	9	1	4	13	0	.236
1982	Montreal	3B-OF-1B	158	596	89	160	31	3	28	97	6	.268
1983	Montreal	3B	156	581	54	156	33	3	19	70	0	.269
1984	Montreal	3B-SS	160	582	55	143	25	4	18	72	3	.246
1985	Montreal	3B	155	569	70	148	36	3	22	81	9	.260
1986	Montreal	3B	134	480	50	112	22	1	18	71	8	.233
1987	Montreal	3B-P	153	593	89	177	42	4	26	123	9	.298
1988	Montreal	3B-2B	159	592	52	152	32	5	12	69	2	.257
1989	Montreal	3B-P	154	573	76	159	42	0	13	77	3	.277
1990	Montreal	3B	161	626	69	185	37	5	21	98	6	.296
	Totals		1466	5415	624	1444	309	29	182	773	46	.267

IVAN CALDERON 29 6-1 221   Bats R Throws R

White Sox left fielder landed in Montreal in December with Barry Jones in trade for Tim Raines, Jeff Carter and a minor leaguer to be named . . . Was Chicago leader in RBI (74), runs (85), hits (166) and doubles (44) . . . His 44 doubles were one shy of club record, set by Floyd Robinson in 1962 . . . Was inserted into leadoff spot for 18 of the season's final 20 games . . . Swiped three bases vs. Orioles May 16 . . . Set career high with 32 steals . . . Obtained from Seattle as player to be named in Scott Bradley trade in 1986 . . . Was Rookie-of-the-Year candidate in '85 before season ended Aug. 9 because of a hand injury . . . Earned $925,000 in 1990 . . . Born March 19, 1962, in Fajardo, Puerto Rico . . . Played volleyball as a kid.

Year	Club	Pos.	G	AB	R	H	2B	3B	HR	RBI	SB	Avg.
1984	Seattle.......	OF	11	24	2	5	1	0	1	1	1	.208
1985	Seattle.......	OF-1B	67	210	37	60	16	4	8	28	4	.286
1986	Sea.-Chi. (AL)	OF	50	164	16	41	7	1	2	15	3	.250
1987	Chicago (AL) ..	OF	144	542	93	159	38	2	28	83	10	.293
1988	Chicago (AL) ..	OF	73	264	40	56	14	0	14	35	4	.212
1989	Chicago (AL) ..	OF-1B	157	622	83	178	34	9	14	87	7	.286
1990	Chicago (AL) ..	OF-1B	158	607	85	166	44	2	14	74	32	.273
	Totals		660	2433	356	665	154	18	81	323	61	.273

ANDRES GALARRAGA 29 6-3 235   Bats R Throws R

A dangerous hitter when he makes contact, but his strikeout totals have climbed every season . . . Has fanned more than 150 times each of the last three years as he keeps breaking his own club single-season record (now 169) . . . During a September stretch, he had 18 strikeouts in 39 at-bats . . . Had career-high six-RBI game July 18 at Cincinnati . . . Had two four-RBI games . . . Homered in three straight games from July 17-19 . . . Hit first career inside-the-park homer against Mets' Julio Machado . . . Hit second career grand slam against Reds' Randy Myers . . . Went without a homer from June 2 until July 15 . . . Ended 3-for-12 slump with three hits against Giants May 7 . . . Won second Gold Glove at first base in 1990 . . . Born June 18, 1961, in Caracas, Venezuela . . . Signed with Expos as amateur free agent in 1979 after being recommended by Felipe Alou . . . Earned $1,866,667 in 1990, making him the second-highest-paid Expo.

Year	Club	Pos.	G	AB	R	H	2B	3B	HR	RBI	SB	Avg.
1985	Montreal	1B	24	75	9	14	1	0	2	4	1	.187
1986	Montreal	1B	105	321	39	87	13	0	10	42	6	.271
1987	Montreal	1B	147	551	72	168	40	3	13	90	7	.305
1988	Montreal	1B	157	609	99	184	42	8	29	92	13	.302
1989	Montreal	1B	152	572	76	147	30	1	23	85	12	.257
1990	Montreal	1B	155	579	65	148	29	0	20	87	10	.256
	Totals		740	2707	360	748	155	12	97	400	49	.276

DELINO DeSHIELDS 22 6-1 170   Bats L Throws R

Brightest star in an outstanding Expos rookie class . . . Made transition from shortstop to second base more easily than anyone anticipated . . . Manager Buck Rodgers compared him to "a young Rod Carew" . . . Ranked third on team in doubles (28) and was so productive Rodgers switched him from leadoff to No. 3 hole in September . . . Made spectacular major-league debut with four hits at St. Louis April 9 . . . Missed from June 16 to July 12 with fractured left index finger . . . Had 15-game hitting streak in September . . . Reached base in 26 consecutive games . . . Caught stealing 22 times in 64 tries . . . Stole a combined 53 bases in 1989, which he split between Jacksonville (AA) and Indianapolis (AAA) . . . Born Jan. 15, 1969, in Seaford, Del. . . . Selected by Expos in seventh round of 1987 draft . . . A huge bargain, he earned major-league minimum $100,000 in 1990.

Year Club	Pos.	G	AB	R	H	2B	3B	HR	RBI	SB	Avg.
1990 Montreal	2B	129	499	69	144	28	6	4	45	42	.289

LARRY WALKER 24 6-2 205   Bats L Throws R

Won roster spot during spring training and surprised everybody by finishing third on team in homers, tying Andre Dawson's club record for rookies . . . Right fielder led Expos in outfield assists (12) . . . Became only second Expo rookie to steal over 15 bases and hit over 15 homers . . . Spent all of 1988 on major-league roster, but was on disabled list with injury to right knee suffered while playing winter ball . . . Underwent surgery to repair tear of two ligaments, necessitating seven-month rehabilitation . . . As 19-year-old playing for Burlington (A) in 1986, he hit 29 homers in 95 games and led Midwest League in slugging percentage . . . Made major-league debut Aug. 16, 1989, reaching base four times and scoring twice in a 4-2 win over Giants . . . Born Dec. 1, 1966, in Maple Ridge, B.C. . . . Became fifth Canadian to play with Expos . . . Signed as undrafted free agent in 1984 . . . Another Expo bargain, earning just $103,500 in 1990.

Year Club	Pos.	G	AB	R	H	2B	3B	HR	RBI	SB	Avg.
1989 Montreal	OF	20	47	4	8	0	0	0	4	1	.170
1990 Montreal	OF	133	419	59	101	18	3	19	51	21	.241
Totals		153	466	63	109	18	3	19	55	22	.234

OIL CAN BOYD 31 6-1 160   Bats R Throws R

After spending 120 days on Red Sox' disabled list in 1989 due to blood clots in right shoulder, the flamboyant Can rewarded Expos' confidence by turning in a fine season . . . His 2.93 ERA was eighth-best in NL . . . Pitched three shutouts, including two against Padres, after going five years without a shutout . . . Had spectacular July, compiling 2.08 ERA and 3-0 record in six starts . . . Overcame numerous injuries: numbness in middle finger, strained left hip flexor and sprained left knee . . . In 1985, his first full season in majors, he led Bosox in wins, ERA, complete games, shutouts and innings . . . Spent 332 days between 1987-89 inactive with various shoulder problems . . . Born Oct. 6, 1959, in Meridian, Miss. . . . Selected by Red Sox in 16th round of 1980 draft . . . Signed with Expos as free agent prior to last season . . . Earned $400,000 in 1990 . . . First name is Dennis.

Year	Club	G	IP	W	L	Pct.	SO	BB	H	ERA
1982	Boston	3	8	0	1	.000	2	2	11	5.40
1983	Boston	15	99	4	8	.333	43	23	103	3.28
1984	Boston	29	197⅔	12	12	.500	134	53	207	4.37
1985	Boston	35	272⅓	15	13	.536	154	67	273	3.70
1986	Boston	30	214⅓	16	11	.615	129	45	222	3.78
1987	Boston	7	36⅔	1	3	.250	12	9	47	5.89
1988	Boston	23	129⅔	9	7	.563	71	41	147	5.34
1989	Boston	10	59	3	2	.600	26	19	57	4.42
1990	Montreal	31	190⅔	10	6	.625	113	52	164	2.93
	Totals	183	1207⅓	70	62	.530	684	311	1231	3.96

DENNIS MARTINEZ 35 6-1 180   Bats R Throws R

Re-signed three-year, $9.5-million contract before he would have become new-look free agent . . . Victory total was down, but he turned in fourth straight solid season in Montreal and his record should have been better . . . Led eight games in sixth inning or later in which he did not earn a victory . . . Has made at least 30 starts in three consecutive seasons . . . Among league leaders in ERA (2.95), innings pitched (226), games started (32), complete games (7), strikeouts (156) and opponents' batting average (.228) . . . Set career high while leading Expos in strikeouts . . . Had 10-strikeout game against Reds . . . Missed start in September after being struck on right clavicle by Wally Backman line drive . . . Pitched perfect inning in All-Star Game . . . Pitched two-hit shutout against Phillies . . . Born May 14, 1955, in Granada, Nicaragua . . . Signed by Orioles as amateur free agent in 1973 . . . Became first Nicaraguan in majors in 1976 . . . Traded to Expos for Rene Gonzalez in June 1986 . . . Beat drinking problem and was re-signed by Expos as free agent before 1988 season . . . Earned $1,400,000 in 1990.

Year	Club	G	IP	W	L	Pct.	SO	BB	H	ERA
1976	Baltimore	4	28	1	2	.333	18	8	23	2.57
1977	Baltimore	42	167	14	7	.667	107	64	157	4.10
1978	Baltimore	40	276	16	11	.593	142	93	257	3.25
1979	Baltimore	40	292	15	16	.484	132	78	279	3.67
1980	Baltimore	25	100	6	4	.600	42	44	103	3.96
1981	Baltimore	25	179	14	5	.737	88	62	173	3.32
1982	Baltimore	40	252	16	12	.571	111	87	262	4.21
1983	Baltimore	32	153	7	16	.304	71	45	209	5.53
1984	Baltimore	34	141⅓	6	9	.400	77	37	145	5.02
1985	Baltimore	33	180	13	11	.542	68	63	203	5.15
1986	Baltimore	4	6⅔	0	0	.000	2	2	11	6.75
1986	Montreal	19	98	3	6	.333	63	28	103	4.59
1987	Montreal	22	144⅔	11	4	.733	84	40	133	3.30
1988	Montreal	34	235⅓	15	13	.536	120	55	215	2.72
1989	Montreal	34	232	16	7	.696	142	49	227	3.18
1990	Montreal	32	226	10	11	.476	156	49	191	2.95
	Totals	460	2711⅓	163	134	.549	1423	804	2691	3.82

MARK GARDNER 29 6-1 190 Bats R Throws R

Door was opened for him to move into Expos' starting rotation in 1990 when Bryn Smith, Mark Langston and Pascual Perez all opted for free agency . . . Went to Instructional League before last season and perfected changeup and cut down his delivery time to plate . . . His 135 strikeouts were second-most on staff . . . Struck out career-high 11 Giants Aug. 28 . . . Had 1.96 ERA in first four games, but remained winless until beating Giants May 6 for first major-league victory . . . Led all Triple-A pitchers with 175 strikeouts in 163 innings for Indianapolis in 1989, when he went 12-4 with 2.37 ERA . . . Had most strikeouts in American Association since Jim Kern's 220 in 1974 . . . Born March 1, 1962, in Los Angeles . . . Selected by Expos in eighth round of 1985 draft . . . Earned $103,500 in 1990.

Year	Club	G	IP	W	L	Pct.	SO	BB	H	ERA
1989	Montreal	7	26⅓	0	3	.000	21	11	26	5.13
1990	Montreal	27	152⅔	7	9	.438	135	61	129	3.42
	Totals	34	179	7	12	.368	156	72	155	3.67

TIM BURKE 32 6-3 205   Bats R Throws R

One of top relievers in baseball . . . Led Expos in saves with 20 in 25 chances, but most of his numbers were down due to injury . . . Suffered hairline fracture of right leg when he was kicked on a play at first base May 30 in Atlanta and was eventually placed on 21-day disabled list . . . Picked up seven saves in his first 14 appearances, but allowed 20 hits in 13⅔ innings and had 5.93 ERA at a time when his fastball lacked movement . . . Salvaged season with a solid September . . . Did not allow a run in 13 September appearances in which he pitched 19 innings, retired 58 of 63 hitters and picked up a victory and four saves . . . Established himself as Expos' stopper in 1989 with career-high 28 saves . . . Born Feb. 19, 1959, in Omaha, Neb. . . . Selected by Pirates in second round of 1980 draft . . . Traded to Yankees in 1983 and to Expos for Pat Rooney before 1984 season . . . Earned $1,766.667 in 1990.

Year	Club	G	IP	W	L	Pct.	SO	BB	H	ERA
1985	Montreal	78	120⅓	9	4	.692	87	44	86	2.39
1986	Montreal	68	101⅓	9	7	.563	82	46	103	2.93
1987	Montreal	55	91	7	0	1.000	58	17	64	1.19
1988	Montreal	61	82	3	5	.375	42	25	84	3.40
1989	Montreal	68	84⅔	9	3	.750	54	22	68	2.55
1990	Montreal	58	75	3	3	.500	47	21	71	2.52
	Totals	388	554⅓	40	22	.645	370	175	476	2.48

BILL SAMPEN 28 6-1 185   Bats R Throws R

Made jump from Double-A to majors in spring training and led entire staff in victories with 12 while being used primarily as a set-up man out of bullpen . . . ''I didn't even expect to make the team, so don't ask me if my record surprises me,'' he said . . . Won first six major-league decisions . . . Made spot start in place of Oil Can Boyd May 8 and pitched five strong innings for 9-1 victory over Dodgers . . . Started four games overall, earned two saves and finished 26 games as reliever . . . In 1989, pitching for Harrisburg (AA), he tied for Eastern League lead in starts (26) and tied for second in strikeouts (134) . . . Born Jan. 18, 1963, in Lincoln, Ill. . . . Selected by Pirates in 12th round of 1985 draft . . . Claimed by Expos from Harrisburg roster in December 1989 . . . Earned major-league-minimum $100,000 in 1990.

Year	Club	G	IP	W	L	Pct.	SO	BB	H	ERA
1990	Montreal	59	90⅓	12	7	.632	69	33	94	2.99

TOP PROSPECTS

CHRIS NABHOLZ 24 6-5 210   **Bats L Throws L**
Won first six major-league decisions after being called up to Expos
Aug. 12 . . . Pitched one-hit shutout against Mets, his first complete game on any level since August 1989, when he was pitching
for Rockford (A) . . . Began 1990 at Jacksonville (AA), going
7-2 with 3.03 ERA . . . For Indianapolis (AAA), he was 0-6 in 10
starts with 4.83 ERA . . . In 11 games with Expos, he went 6-2
with 2.83 ERA . . . Born Jan. 5, 1967, in Harrisburg, Pa. . . .
Selected by Expos in second round of 1988 draft . . . Attended
Towson State University.

BRIAN BARNES 24 5-9 170   **Bats L Throws L**
Struck out nine Pirates in major-league debut Sept. 14, a club
record for a first game . . . For Jacksonville (AA), he went 13-7
with 2.77 ERA, striking out 213 batters in 201 innings . . . Made
four starts for Expos, going 1-1 with 2.89 ERA and 23 strikeouts
in 28 innings . . . Born March 25, 1967, in Roanoke Rapids,
N.C. . . . Selected by Expos in fourth round of 1989 draft . . . At
Clemson University, he was ACC Player of the Year . . . Ranks
third in NCAA history with 513 strikeouts.

HOWARD FARMER 25 6-3 190   **Bats R Throws R**
Compiled 7-9 record with 3.89 ERA for Indianapolis (AAA) before being called up to Expos Sept. 1 . . . Limited Cubs to four
hits and two runs in seven innings two days later . . . In 1989, he
was 12-9 for Jacksonville (AA) and was third in Southern League
in ERA (2.20), innings pitched (184) and strikeouts (151) while
limiting opponents to .185 batting average . . . Born Jan. 18, 1966,
in Gary, Ind. . . . Selected by Expos in seventh round of 1987
draft.

GREG COLBRUNN 21 6-0 190   **Bats R Throws R**
Following in steps of Gary Carter, this former infielder was converted into a catcher and could be a star . . . For Jacksonville (AA),
he established career highs in on-base average and slugging percentage while batting .301 with 76 RBI . . . Hard-nosed performer
with leadership qualities . . . Born July 26, 1969, in Fontana,
Cal. . . . Selected by Expos in sixth round of 1987 draft . . . Turned
down scholarship offer to Stanford.

MANAGER BUCK RODGERS: His job appeared in jeopardy at tail end of 1989 season, when Expos faded from contention, but his contract was extended by one year in December 1989 and he turned in his best managing job in 1990 . . . Fielding a team filled with rookies and rebuilding a pitching staff devastated by free-agent defections, he surprised everybody by keeping Expos in contention until final 10 days . . . Broke Gene Mauch's club record for victories when he won his 500th game on final day of 85-77 season . . . Has 500-464 record after six years as Expos' manager . . . Overall major-league managerial record is 624-565 . . . Has second-longest tenure in NL, trailing only Dodgers' Tommy Lasorda . . . Named NL Manager of the Year in 1987 after leading overachieving Expos team to 91-71 record and third-place finish . . . Managed Brewers from 1980-82, winning second-half title during 1981 strike year but losing divisional playoff to Yankees . . . Veteran of 34 years in baseball, he was switch-hitting catcher with Angels from 1961-69, batting .232 . . . Hit just 32 homers, but was only Angel to homer in all three home parks . . . Born Aug. 16, 1938, in Delaware, Ohio.

ALL-TIME EXPO SEASON RECORDS

BATTING: Tim Raines, .334, 1986
HRs: Andre Dawson, 32, 1983
RBI: Tim Wallach, 123, 1987
STEALS: Ron LeFlore, 97, 1980
WINS: Ross Grimsley, 20, 1978
STRIKEOUTS: Bill Stoneman, 251, 1971

NEW YORK METS

TEAM DIRECTORY: Chairman: Nelson Doubleday; Pres'.: Fred Wilpon; VP-GM: Frank Cashen; Sr. VP-Adm.: Al Harazin; Dir. Baseball Oper.: Gerry Hunsicker; Dir. Scouting: Roland Johnson; Minor League Coordinator: Bobby Floyd; Dir. Pub. Rel.: Jay Horwitz; Trav. Sec.: Bob O'Hara; Mgr.: Buddy Harrelson. Home: Shea Stadium (55,300). Field distances: 338, l.f. line; 371, l.c.; 410, c.f.; 371, r.c.; 338, r.f. line. Spring training: Port St. Lucie, Fla.

SCOUTING REPORT

HITTING: The 1990 Mets led the NL in home runs (172) and runs (775), but those were deceptive stats because this team struggled through a feast-or-famine season. They couldn't produce against left-handed pitching and had a 23-28 record in one-run games.

When Darryl Strawberry (.279, 37, 108) wasn't hitting, the Mets stumbled and now they have to play without the free-agent defector. Free-agent addition Vince Coleman (.292, 6, 39 with the Cards) adds a dimension as the NL stolen-base king (77 last year), but it's Hubie Brooks (.266, 20, 91 with the Dodgers) who must go a long ways toward replacing Strawberry's run production. Kevin McReynolds (.269, 24, 82) runs hot-and-cold and drove in just 15 runs against lefties in 1990. He must improve his production dramatically now that he takes over the cleanup role.

Dave Magadan (.328, 6, 72) should drive in more runs if he spends a full season in the No. 3 hole. Gregg Jefferies (.283, 15, 68) led the NL with 40 doubles and should get even better. Howard Johnson (.244, 23, 90, 34 steals) had a productive season, but those numbers could go up if his sore shoulder heals. Mackey Sasser (.307, 6, 41), who looked great until spraining his ankle at midseason, must show he can do it for a full season.

PITCHING: This is still the best rotation in baseball, featuring four starters among the NL's top five strikeouts in 1990. Frank Viola (20-12, 2.67) had three shutouts and 182 strikeouts as he contended for the Cy Young. Dwight Gooden (19-7, 3.83) fanned 223 batters and was almost unbeatable during the last four months. David Cone (14-10, 3.23) led the NL with 233 strikeouts. Sid Fernandez (9-14, 3.46) held opponents to a .200 batting average. John Franco (5-3, 2.53) led the NL with 33 saves despite a shaky September. Alejandro Pena (3-3, 3.20) was a disappointment, but could play a bigger role this year.

Change paved way to Frank Viola's second 20-win year.

FIELDING: Mediocre at best. Johnson committed 28 errors while splitting time between third and shortstop and his range at short is questionable. Jefferies is a liability, although he does less damage at third base than at second. Magadan is adequate at first. Kevin Elster is a fine shortstop, but he's coming off shoulder surgery and has apparently lost his job to Johnson. Second baseman Tommy Herr has lost a step at 35, but makes up for it with experience.

Sasser is still suspect behind the plate. Charlie O'Brien is a solid defensive catcher, but hasn't hit and may not play regularly. Coleman, barely adequate in left, will be asked to play center, between the dependable McReynolds in left and the plodding Brooks in right.

OUTLOOK: These Mets, 91-71 last year and 71-49 under manager Bud Harrelson, and there's no way they can be a better team without Strawberry's bat. The pitching is good enough to keep the Mets respectable and there's still some offensive talent, but probably not enough to win the East.

NEW YORK METS 1991 ROSTER

MANAGER Bud Harrelson
Coaches—Mike Cubbage, Doc Edwards, Greg Pavlick, Tom Spencer, Mel Stottlemyre

PITCHERS

No.	Name	1990 Club	W-L	IP	SO	ERA	B-T	Ht.	Wt.	Born
38	Beatty, Blaine	New York (NL)	Injured				L-L	6-2	190	4/25/64 Victoria, TX
46	Bross, Terry	Jackson	3-4	72	51	2.64	R-R	6-9	230	3/30/66 El Paso, TX
44	Cone, David	New York (NL)	14-10	212	233	3.23	L-R	6-1	190	1/2/63 Kansas City, MO
15	Darling, Ron	New York (NL)	7-9	126	99	4.50	R-R	6-3	195	8/19/60 Honolulu, HI
50	Fernandez, Sid	New York (NL)	9-14	179	181	3.46	L-L	6-1	230	10/12/62 Honolulu, HI
31	Franco, John	New York (NL)	5-3	68	56	2.53	L-L	5-10	185	9/17/60 Brooklyn, NY
16	Gooden, Dwight	New York (NL)	19-7	233	223	3.83	R-R	6-3	210	11/16/64 Tampa, FL
63	Hillman, Eric	St. Lucie	2-0	27	23	0.67	L-L	6-10	225	4/27/66 Gary, IN
		Jackson	6-5	89	61	3.93				
40	Innis, Jeff	Tidewater	5-2	53	42	1.71	R-R	6-0	170	7/5/62 Decatur, GA
		New York (NL)	1-3	26	12	2.39				
62	Johnstone, John	St. Lucie	15-6	173	120	2.24	R-R	6-1	175	11/25/68 Liverpool, NY
26	Pena, Alejandro	New York (NL)	3-3	76	76	3.20	R-R	6-1	203	6/25/59 Dominican Republic
48	Schourek, Pete	St. Lucie	4-1	37	28	0.97	L-L	6-5	195	5/10/69 Austin, TX
		Tidewater	1-0	14	14	2.57				
		Jackson	11-4	124	94	3.04				
34	Valera, Julio	Tidewater	10-10	158	133	3.02	R-R	6-2	185	10/13/68 Puerto Rico
		New York (NL)	1-1	13	4	6.92				
29	Viola, Frank	New York (NL)	20-12	250	182	2.67	L-L	6-4	210	4/19/60 Hempstead, NY
47	Whitehurst, Wally	Tidewater	1-0	9	10	2.00	R-R	6-3	185	5/11/64 Shreveport, LA
		New York (NL)	1-0	66	46	3.29				
61	Young, Anthony	Jackson	15-3	158	95	1.65	R-R	6-2	200	1/19/66 Houston, TX

CATCHERS

No.	Name	1990 Club	H	HR	RBI	Pct.	B-T	Ht.	Wt.	Born
49	Hundley, Todd	Jackson	74	1	35	.265	S-R	5-11	170	5/27/69 Martinsville, VA
		New York (NL)	14	0	2	.209				
5	O'Brien, Charlie	Milwaukee	27	0	11	.186	R-R	6-2	190	5/1/61 Tulsa, OK
		New York (NL)	11	0	9	.162				
2	Sasser, Mackey	New York (NL)	83	6	41	.307	L-R	6-1	210	8/3/62 Fort Gaines, GA

INFIELDERS

No.	Name	1990 Club	H	HR	RBI	Pct.	B-T	Ht.	Wt.	Born
36	Baez, Kevin	Jackson	76	2	29	.232	R-R	6-0	160	1/10/67 Brooklyn, NY
		New York (NL)	2	0	0	.167				
23	Donnels, Chris	Jackson	114	12	63	.272	L-R	6-0	185	4/21/66 Los Angeles, CA
21	Elster, Kevin	New York (NL)	65	9	45	.207	R-R	6-2	200	8/3/64 San Pedro, CA
28	Herr, Tom	Phil.-NY(NL)	143	5	60	.261	S-R	6-0	196	4/4/56 Lancaster, PA
9	Jefferies, Gregg	New York (NL)	171	15	68	.283	S-R	5-10	180	8/1/67 Burlingame, CA
20	Johnson, Howard	New York (NL)	144	23	90	.244	S-R	5-10	195	11/29/60 Clearwater, FL
10	Magadan, Dave	New York (NL)	148	6	72	.328	L-R	6-3	200	9/30/62 Tampa, FL
11	Teufel, Tim	New York (NL)	43	10	24	.246	R-R	6-0	175	7/7/58 Greenwich, CT

OUTFIELDERS

No.	Name	1990 Club	H	HR	RBI	Pct.	B-T	Ht.	Wt.	Born
7	Boston, Daryl	Chicago (AL)	0	0	0	.000	L-L	6-3	195	1/4/63 Cincinnati, OH
		New York (NL)	100	12	45	.273				
—	Brooks, Hubie	Los Angeles	151	20	91	.266	R-R	6-0	190	9/24/58 Los Angeles, CA
1	Coleman, Vince	St. Louis	145	6	39	.292	S-R	6-0	170	9/22/61 Jacksonville, FL
27	Carr, Chuck	Jackson	93	3	24	.258	S-R	5-10	155	8/10/68 San Bernardino, CA
		New York (NL)	0	0	0	.000				
45	Carreon, Mark	New York (NL)	47	10	26	.250	R-L	6-0	195	7/9/63 Chicago, IL
0	McDaniel, Terry	Jackson	61	5	37	.286	R-R	5-9	195	12/6/66 Kansas City, MO
22	McReynolds, Kevin	New York (NL)	140	24	82	.269	R-R	6-1	215	10/16/59 Little Rock, AR
25	Miller, Keith	New York (NL)	60	1	12	.258	R-R	5-11	180	6/12/63 Midland, MI
—	Puhl, Terry	Houston	12	0	8	.293	L-R	6-2	197	7/8/56 Canada
6	Reed, Darren	Tidewater	95	17	74	.265	R-R	6-1	190	10/16/65 Ventura, CA
		New York (NL)	8	1	2	.205				

MET PROFILES

DAVE MAGADAN 28 6-3 200   Bats L Throws R

During his fourth big-league season, he finally became an everyday player and silenced his critics, including former manager Davey Johnson . . . Became Mets' starting first baseman in June, when Mike Marshall was injured, and immediately went on a tear, batting .402 and raising his average from .300 to .361 . . . Finished third in NL batting race (.328) and second in on-base percentage (.417) . . . Led Mets with six triples . . . Hit three doubles against Expos July 31 . . . Had 11-game hitting streak in June . . . Had seven hits in seven consecutive official at-bats June 12-13 and drove in six runs in game against Cubs . . . Born Sept. 30, 1962, in Tampa . . . Selected by Mets in second round of 1983 draft . . . Attended University of Alabama, where he batted .525 in 1983, leading Crimson Tide to final game of College World Series . . . A cousin and godson of Reds' manager Lou Piniella . . . A huge bargain in 1990, earning just $395,000.

Year	Club	Pos.	G	AB	R	H	2B	3B	HR	RBI	SB	Avg.
1986	New York (NL)	1B	10	18	3	8	0	0	0	3	0	.444
1987	New York (NL)	3B-1B	85	192	21	61	13	1	3	24	0	.318
1988	New York (NL)	1B-3B	112	314	39	87	15	0	1	35	0	.277
1989	New York (NL)	1B-3B	127	374	47	107	22	3	4	41	1	.286
1990	New York (NL)	1B-3B	144	451	74	148	28	6	6	72	2	.328
	Totals		478	1349	184	411	78	10	14	175	3	.305

VINCE COLEMAN 29 6-0 170   Bats R Throws R

Left fielder equaled Maury Wills' NL record by winning sixth straight stolen-base title (77) . . . Enjoyed best all-around season of career with the Cardinals and capped it as a free agent when he signed a four-year, $11.95-million contract with the Mets in December . . . Batted .343 during career-high 15-game hitting streak in August . . . Sat out week with hamstring injury before returning to lineup with four-hit game against Pirates . . . Stole four bases, including home, against Cubs July 24 . . . Suspended for seven games after accidentally butting umpire Ed Montague with helmet . . . Reached 500th stolen base faster than any player in history (804 games) . . . Established major-league rookie steal record in 1985, topping Juan Samuel's mark of 72 set in 1989 . . . Born Sept. 22, 1961, in Jacksonville, Fla. . . . Selected by Cardinals in 10th round of 1982 draft . . . Attended Florida A&M . . . Earned $1,012,500 in 1990.

Year	Club	Pos.	G	AB	R	H	2B	3B	HR	RBI	SB	Avg.
1985	St. Louis	OF	151	636	107	170	20	10	1	40	110	.267
1986	St. Louis	OF	154	600	94	139	13	8	0	29	107	.232
1987	St. Louis	OF	151	623	121	180	14	10	3	43	109	.289
1988	St. Louis	OF	153	616	77	160	20	10	3	38	81	.260
1989	St. Louis	OF	145	563	94	143	21	9	2	28	65	.254
1990	St. Louis	OF	124	497	73	145	18	9	6	39	77	.292
	Totals		878	3535	566	937	106	56	15	217	549	.265

TOMMY HERR 34 6-0 196   Bats S Throws R

Batted .250 for Mets after being traded by Phillies for two minor leaguers at start of final month of 1990 pennant race . . . May have lost a step, but can still field his position and figures to be starting second baseman in 1991 . . . Homered in first game as a Met in 6-5 win over the Giants . . . From All-Star break through Aug. 8, he led Phillies with .310 BA . . . Had steady season despite toe injury . . . Played 54 straight errorless games from Sept. 30, 1989 until May 19, 1990 . . . Had five-hit game at L.A. on May 19 . . . Drove in 100 runs for Cards in 1985, becoming only seventh second baseman ever to reach 100 RBI and first player in 35 years to drive in 100 runs without hitting at least 10 HRs . . . Born April 4, 1956, in Lancaster, Pa. . . . Re-signed by Mets for guaranteed $1.4-million contract following 1990 season . . . Earned $825,000 in 1990.

Year	Club	Pos.	G	AB	R	H	2B	3B	HR	RBI	SB	Avg.
1979	St. Louis	2B	14	10	4	2	0	0	0	1	1	.200
1980	St. Louis	2B-SS	76	222	29	55	12	5	0	15	9	.248
1981	St. Louis	2B	103	411	50	110	14	9	0	46	23	.268
1982	St. Louis	2B	135	493	83	131	19	4	0	36	25	.266
1983	St. Louis	2B	89	313	43	101	14	4	2	31	6	.323
1984	St. Louis	2B	145	558	67	154	23	2	4	49	13	.276
1985	St. Louis	2B	159	596	97	180	38	3	8	110	31	.302
1986	St. Louis	2B	152	559	48	141	30	4	2	61	22	.252
1987	St. Louis	2B	141	510	73	134	29	0	2	83	19	.263
1988	St. Louis	2B	15	50	4	13	0	0	1	3	3	.260
1988	Minnesota	2B	86	304	42	80	16	0	1	21	10	.263
1989	Philadelphia . . .	2B	151	561	65	161	25	6	2	37	10	.287
1990	Phil.-NY (NL) . .	2B	146	547	48	143	26	3	5	60	7	.261
	Totals		1412	5134	653	1405	246	40	27	553	179	.274

HOWARD JOHNSON 30 5-10 195   Bats S Throws R

A sore left shoulder hampered his right-handed swing, yet he remained in lineup all season . . . His batting average was down, but he had a productive year . . . Led Mets in stolen bases (34), was second in RBI (90) and third in homers (23) . . . Tied for fourth in NL in doubles (37) . . . Had difficult year defensively at third base, but did a fine job filling in at shortstop over final two months after Kevin Elster was disabled . . . Committed just one error in 41-game stretch at shortstop, but had 28 errors for season . . . May be headed to outfield in 1991 . . . Batted in seven different positions in lineup and homered in each spot . . . Had 10-game hitting streak snapped July 3 . . . Hit fifth career grand slam . . . Two-time member of 30-homer, 30-steal club . . . Born Nov. 29, 1960, in Clearwater, Fla. . . . Tigers' first choice in secondary phase of January 1979 draft . . . Traded to Mets for Walt Terrell before 1985 season . . . Earned $1,666,667 in 1990.

Year	Club	Pos.	G	AB	R	H	2B	3B	HR	RBI	SB	Avg.
1982	Detroit	3B-OF	54	155	23	49	5	0	4	14	7	.316
1983	Detroit	3B	27	66	11	14	0	0	3	5	0	.212
1984	Detroit	3B-SS-1B-OF	116	355	43	88	14	1	12	50	10	.248
1985	New York (NL)	3B-SS	126	389	38	94	18	4	11	46	6	.242
1986	New York (NL)	3B-SS-OF	88	220	30	54	14	0	10	39	8	.245
1987	New York (NL)	3B-SS-OF	157	554	93	147	22	1	36	99	32	.265
1988	New York (NL)	3B-SS	148	495	85	114	21	1	24	68	23	.230
1989	New York (NL)	3B-SS	153	571	104	164	41	3	36	101	41	.287
1990	New York (NL)	3B-SS	154	590	89	144	37	3	23	90	34	.244
	Totals		1023	3395	516	868	172	13	159	512	161	.256

KEVIN McREYNOLDS 31 6-1 215   Bats R Throws R

His final numbers weren't bad, but he had a streaky season with most homers and RBI coming in bunches . . . Too often, he failed to deliver in clutch situations . . . Was riding seven-game hitting streak when his season ended abruptly in late September because of ingrown toenail . . . Led NL outfielders with 14 assists and committed just three errors in left . . . Had four multi-homer games . . . Equaled career high with six-RBI game at San Francisco Aug. 19 . . . Had three four-hit games . . . Hit fifth career grand slam and has accounted for three of Mets' last seven slams . . . Second on team in homers (24) and walks (71), third in RBI (82) in 1990 . . . Born Oct. 16, 1959, in Little Rock, Ark. . . . Selected by Padres in first round of 1981 draft . . . Traded to Mets in deal that sent Kevin Mitchell to San Diego before 1987 season . . . Attended University of Arkansas, where he hit .386 as sophomore and was picked as Southwest Conference Player of the Year . . . Earned $1,266,667 in 1990 and signed three-year, $10-million contract extension last winter.

Year	Club	Pos.	G	AB	R	H	2B	3B	HR	RBI	SB	Avg.
1983	San Diego	OF	39	140	15	31	3	1	4	14	2	.221
1984	San Diego	OF	147	525	68	146	26	6	20	75	3	.278
1985	San Diego	OF	152	564	61	132	24	4	15	75	4	.234
1986	San Diego	OF	158	560	89	161	31	6	26	96	8	.288
1987	New York (NL)	OF	151	590	86	163	32	5	29	95	14	.276
1988	New York (NL)	OF	147	552	82	159	30	2	27	99	21	.288
1989	New York (NL)	OF	148	545	74	148	25	3	22	85	15	.272
1990	New York (NL)	OF	147	521	75	140	23	1	24	82	9	.269
	Totals		1089	3997	550	1080	194	28	167	621	76	.270

HUBIE BROOKS 34 6-0 190   Bats R Throws R

Returned to Mets in winter deal that sent Bob Ojeda and Greg Hansell to the Dodgers . . . His presence in Dodger batting order last season gave Eddie Murray the protection he had lacked in 1989 . . . Right fielder was third on the team in home runs (20) and RBI (91) . . . Homers equaled a career high and RBI were the most since he knocked in 100 for Expos in 1985 . . . Always has been a clutch player . . . Hit .349 with men on third base and .471 (8-for-17) with the bases loaded . . . Born Sept. 24, 1956, in Los Angeles . . . Drafted third overall by Mets in 1978, he came to majors as third baseman . . . Expos acquired him and four others from Mets in Gary Carter deal after '84 season . . . Starred at Arizona State . . . Earned $1,333,333 last season.

Year	Club	Pos.	G	AB	R	H	2B	3B	HR	RBI	SB	Avg.
1980	New York (NL)	3B	24	81	8	25	2	1	1	10	1	.309
1981	New York (NL)	3B-OF-SS	98	358	34	110	21	2	4	38	9	.307
1982	New York (NL)	3B	126	457	40	114	21	2	2	40	6	.249
1983	New York (NL)	3B-2B	150	586	53	147	18	4	5	58	6	.251
1984	New York (NL)	3B-SS	153	561	61	159	23	2	16	73	6	.283
1985	Montreal	SS	156	605	67	163	34	7	13	100	6	.269
1986	Montreal	SS	80	306	50	104	18	5	14	58	4	.340
1987	Montreal	SS	112	430	57	113	22	3	14	72	4	.263
1988	Montreal	OF	151	588	61	164	35	2	20	90	7	.279
1989	Montreal	OF	148	542	56	145	30	1	14	70	6	.268
1990	Los Angeles . . .	OF	153	568	74	151	28	1	20	91	2	.266
	Totals		1351	5082	561	1395	252	30	123	700	57	.274

GREGG JEFFERIES 23 5-10 180   Bats S Throws R

An outstanding pure hitter, he finally lived up to expectations following a disappointing 1989 rookie year . . . A September slump dropped his final batting average below .300, but he led NL in doubles (40) . . . Equaled career high with 11-game hitting streak in June . . . Batted lead-off early in season before being switched to No. 3 hole when Bud Harrelson took over as manager . . . Excelled as No. 3 hitter until late-season drop . . . Played second base until Tommy Herr joined team Sept. 1, then was switched to third base . . . Lacked range at second and still has trouble turning pivot after two seasons at position . . . Committed 16 errors . . . Had 24-game hitting streak for Tidewater (AAA) in 1988 . . . Born Aug. 1, 1967, in Burlingame, Cal. . . . Selected by Mets in first round of 1985 draft . . . Named *Baseball America's* Minor League Player of the Decade . . . Earned $300,000 in 1990.

Year	Club	Pos.	G	AB	R	H	2B	3B	HR	RBI	SB	Avg.
1987	New York (NL)	PH	6	6	0	3	1	0	0	2	0	.500
1988	New York (NL)	3B-2B	29	109	19	35	8	2	6	17	5	.321
1989	New York (NL)	2B-3B	141	508	72	131	28	2	12	56	21	.258
1990	New York (NL)	2B-3B	153	604	96	171	40	3	15	68	11	.283
	Totals		329	1227	187	340	77	7	33	143	37	.277

FRANK VIOLA 30 6-4 210   Bats L Throws L

Became 18th pitcher to post 20-win seasons in both leagues . . . During his first full season back home in New York, he was Mets' best pitcher . . . Led NL in innings pitched (249⅔), tied for second in victories (20) and was fourth in strikeouts (182) and ERA (2.67) . . . His nasty changeup was devastating as he won first seven starts, giving up just five runs . . . Tied career high with 11 strikeouts against Reds May 2 . . . Pitched scoreless inning in All-Star Game . . . Won 1988 AL Cy Young . . . Named MVP in 1987 World Series . . . Born April 19, 1960, in Hempstead, N.Y. . . . Selected by Twins in second round of 1981 draft . . . Traded to Mets for five pitchers, July 31, 1989 . . . Attended St. John's University, where he was teammate of John Franco . . . Beat Ron Darling and Yale, 1-0, in 12-inning NCAA

Regional game in 1981... Was 26-2 with 1.67 ERA in three collegiate seasons... Highest-paid Met at $1,966,667 in 1990.

Year	Club	G	IP	W	L	Pct.	SO	BB	H	ERA
1982	Minnesota	22	126	4	10	.286	84	38	152	5.21
1983	Minnesota	35	210	7	15	.318	127	92	242	5.49
1984	Minnesota	35	257⅔	18	12	.600	149	73	225	3.21
1985	Minnesota	36	250⅔	18	14	.563	135	68	262	4.09
1986	Minnesota	37	245⅔	16	13	.552	191	83	257	4.51
1987	Minnesota	36	251⅔	17	10	.630	197	66	230	2.90
1988	Minnesota	35	255⅓	24	7	.774	193	54	236	2.64
1989	Minnesota	24	175⅓	8	12	.400	138	47	171	3.79
1989	New York (NL)	12	85⅓	5	5	.500	73	27	75	3.38
1990	New York (NL)	35	249⅔	20	12	.625	182	60	227	2.67
	Totals	307	2107⅔	137	110	.555	1469	608	2077	3.70

DWIGHT GOODEN 26 6-3 210   Bats R Throws R

No longer dominates games, but "Doc" still has uncanny knack for winning... Had highest ERA of career (3.83), yet won 16 of last 18 decisions... Tied for second in NL in strike-outs (223) and was fourth in victories (19) and innings pitched (232⅔)... Was 5-0 with 1.98 ERA in six September starts... Bounced back convincingly from shoulder problem which wiped out second half of 1989 season... Fanned 15 Dodgers May 11... Won eight straight decisions before losing to Cardinals Aug. 4, then won seven more before losing to Pirates Oct. 2, when he failed to pick up 20th victory while pitching on short rest... Pitched 20th career shutout, a two-hitter against Phillies, his first shutout since 1988... Hit third career homer... Became youngest to win Cy Young in 1985... Named Rookie of the Year in 1984... Born Nov. 16, 1964, in Tampa... Fifth player chosen in 1982 draft... Earned $1,866,667 in 1990, making him the second-highest-paid Met.

Year	Club	G	IP	W	L	Pct.	SO	BB	H	ERA
1984	New York (NL)	31	218	17	9	.654	276	73	161	2.60
1985	New York (NL)	35	276⅔	24	4	.857	268	69	198	1.53
1986	New York (NL)	33	250	17	6	.739	200	80	197	2.84
1987	New York (NL)	25	179⅔	15	7	.682	148	53	162	3.21
1988	New York (NL)	34	248⅓	18	9	.667	175	57	242	3.19
1989	New York (NL)	19	118⅓	9	4	.692	101	47	93	2.89
1990	New York (NL)	34	232⅔	19	7	.731	223	70	229	3.83
	Totals	211	1523⅔	119	46	.721	1391	449	1282	2.82

JOHN FRANCO 30 5-10 185   Bats L Throws L

Brooklyn-born and a Met fan in his youth, he was a hero in front of home fans during his first season at Shea . . . For most of the year, he was Mets' only reliable reliever and he kept them in pennant race while leading NL with 33 saves in 39 chances . . . Named to All-Star team for fourth time and pitched a perfect inning . . . Faded in September, failing in his last three appearances at home . . . Didn't save a game after Sept. 15 . . . Posted saves in nine straight outings in July . . . Started season with saves in seven straight opportunities over nine outings . . . Has 165 saves over past five seasons . . . Born Sept. 17, 1960 . . . Selected by Dodgers in fifth round of 1981 draft . . . Traded by Reds for Randy Myers before 1990 season . . . Was Frank Viola's teammate at St. John's University . . . Earned $1,633,333 after signing three-year contract in February 1990.

Year	Club	G	IP	W	L	Pct.	SO	BB	H	ERA
1984	Cincinnati	54	79⅓	6	2	.750	55	36	74	2.61
1985	Cincinnati	67	99	12	3	.800	61	40	83	2.18
1986	Cincinnati	74	101	6	6	.500	84	44	90	2.94
1987	Cincinnati	68	82	8	5	.615	61	27	76	2.52
1988	Cincinnati	70	86	6	6	.500	46	27	60	1.57
1989	Cincinnati	60	80⅔	4	8	.333	60	36	77	3.12
1990	New York (NL)	55	67⅔	5	3	.625	56	21	66	2.53
	Totals	448	595⅔	47	33	.588	423	231	526	2.49

DAVID CONE 28 6-1 190   Bats L Throws R

By August, he was Mets' most effective pitcher . . . Despite slow start, he won NL strikeout title with 233 . . . Didn't get first victory until May 19 and didn't win second until June 9, then won six straight . . . Tossed three consecutive complete games in August . . . Hurled seventh and eighth career shutouts . . . Set career high with 13 strikeouts against Giants . . . Fanned 10 or more batters in four straight starts . . . Often pitched in hard luck, losing 1-0 to Cardinals and 2-1 to Dodgers . . . Pitched three-hit, 2-1 win over Pirates during heat of pennant race and finished season with pair of gems, blanking Expos for eight innings on two hits before throwing three-hit, 12-strikeout game in Pittsburgh . . . His .870 winning percentage in 1988 set Met record and he finished third in Cy Young voting . . . Born Jan. 2, 1963, in Kansas

City . . . Selected by Royals in third round of 1981 draft . . . Traded to Mets before 1987 season . . . Earned $1,300,000 in 1990.

Year	Club	G	IP	W	L	Pct.	SO	BB	H	ERA
1986	Kansas City	11	22⅔	0	0	.000	21	13	29	5.56
1987	New York (NL)	21	99⅓	5	6	.455	68	44	87	3.71
1988	New York (NL)	35	231⅓	20	3	.870	213	80	178	2.22
1989	New York (NL)	34	219⅔	14	8	.636	190	74	183	3.52
1990	New York (NL)	31	211⅔	14	10	.583	233	65	177	3.23
	Totals	132	784⅔	53	27	.663	725	276	654	3.14

TOP PROSPECTS

JULIO VALERA 22 6-2 185　　　　**Bats R Throws R**
Stepped into middle of pennant race Sept. 1, made major-league debut against Giants and gave up three runs on five hits through six innings in 6-5 Met victory . . . Made two more starts and finished 1-1 with 6.92 ERA . . . For Tidewater (AAA), he went 10-10 with 3.02 ERA and 133 strikeouts in 158 innings . . . Born Oct. 13, 1968, in San Sebastian, P.R. . . . Signed with Mets as amateur free agent in 1986 . . . Played at three levels of farm system in 1989, compiling 15-9 record and 2.11 ERA while striking out 162 in 195 innings.

TERRY BROSS 25 6-9 230　　　　**Bats R Throws R**
Using 90-plus-mph fastball, he led Texas League with 28 saves in 33 opportunities . . . Tied Jackson (AA) club record for appearances (58) . . . Converted 19 straight save opportunities and had 18 consecutive appearances without giving up a run . . . Finished with 3-4 record, 2.64 ERA and 51 strikeouts in 71⅔ innings, yielding just 46 hits . . . Born March 30, 1966, in El Paso, Tex. . . . Selected by Mets in 14th round of 1987 draft . . . Played basketball for four years at St. John's University.

TODD HUNDLEY 21 5-11 170　　　　**Bats S Throws R**
Probably the Mets' catcher of the future . . . Has good bloodlines, being the son of former major-league catcher Randy Hundley . . . Batted .265 with 12 doubles in 81 games for Jackson (AA) . . . Threw out 49 percent of would-be base-stealers down there . . . Called up to big leagues three different times and had three two-hit games, batting .209 in 67 at-bats overall . . . Named to 1989 South Atlantic League All-Star team . . . Born May 27, 1969, in Martinsville, Va. . . . Selected by Mets in second round of 1987 draft.

KEVIN BAEZ 24 6-0 160   **Bats R Throws R**
A smooth-fielding shortstop, he was promoted from Jackson (AA)
to the majors Aug. 28, providing Mets with infield insurance for
pennant run . . . Batted just .232 with 11 doubles for Jackson, but
his glove could get him to big leagues . . . In 1989, he led South
Atlantic League shortstops in fielding percentage and had two
eight-game hitting streaks . . . Born Jan. 10, 1967, in Brooklyn,
N.Y. . . . Selected by Mets in eighth round of 1988 draft.

MANAGER BUD HARRELSON: Took over underachieving
Mets team with 20-22 record when Davey Johnson was fired May 29 . . . Stressed fundamentals, made a few lineup changes and immediately got his team back into pennant race with
sizzling 21-7 June . . . Mets returned to their inconsistent ways following All-Star break and a
mediocre   September   doomed   them   to
a second-place finish in his first season as a
major-league manager . . . His 71-49 record added up to .592 percentage, which would have been best in NL if extended over a
full season . . . His most important decision was installing Dave
Magadan as regular first baseman . . . His most controversial decision was using rookie pitcher Julio Valera for three starts during
September pennant race . . . A member of Mets' Hall of Fame, he
played shortstop in New York from 1965-77 and is among club's
all-time leaders in numerous categories . . . Named to NL All-Star
team in 1970 and '71 . . . Also played with Phillies and Rangers
. . . Managed Little Falls (A) to New York-Penn League championship and was named Manager of the Year in 1984 . . . Began
1985 season managing Columbia (A) before replacing Bobby Valentine as Mets' third-base coach . . . Born on D-Day, June 6, 1944,
in Niles, Cal.

ALL-TIME MET SEASON RECORDS

BATTING: Cleon Jones, .340, 1969
HRs: Darryl Strawberry, 39, 1987, 1988, 1990
RBI: Darryl Strawberry, 108, 1990
STEALS: Mookie Wilson, 58, 1982
WINS: Tom Seaver, 25, 1969
STRIKEOUTS: Tom Seaver, 289, 1971

PHILADELPHIA PHILLIES

TEAM DIRECTORY: Pres.: William Y. Giles; Exec. VP: David Montgomery; VP/GM: Lee Thomas; Player Pers. Adm.: Ed Wade; VP-Pub. Rel.: Larry Shenk; Trav. Sec.: Eddie Ferenz; Mgr.: Nick Leyva. Home: Veterans Stadium (64,538). Field distances: 330, l.f. line; 408, c.f.; 330, r.f. line. Spring training: Clearwater, Fla.

SCOUTING REPORT

HITTING: The Phillies' attack improved in 1990, but there's still a long way to go. Although their .255 team batting average ranked near the middle of the NL pack, they were 10th in runs

Catcher Darren Daulton ful-Philled his promise.

(646) and home runs (103), ahead of only the Cardinals and Astros.

Lenny Dykstra (.325, 9, 60, 33 steals) must show that his 1990 season wasn't a fluke. Dale Murphy (.245, 24, 83) seemed rejuvenated after being acquired from the Braves and now the Phillies need him to be a big run producer. Von Hayes (.261, 17, 73) must bounce back from an inconsistent, injury-plagued season.

John Kruk (.291, 7, 67) will get a chance to be the regular first baseman if he keeps producing. Charlie Hayes (.258, 10, 57) should be even better in his second full big-league season. Darren Daulton (.268, 12, 57), coming off a career year, earned a three-year, $6.75-million contract, but now he must prove he deserved it.

PITCHING: This wasn't the NL's worst pitching staff in 1990, but that was only because the Braves, Cubs and Giants all declined. Phillies' pitchers combined for a 4.07 ERA while giving up a league-high 651 walks and 69 wild pitches.

Still, there's reason to believe that better days are ahead. Terry Mulholland (9-10, 3.34) led the team with six complete games, had a no-hitter and posted a 1.99 ERA in his final 10 starts. Pat Combs (10-10, 4.07) could develop into a big winner. Jose DeJesus (7-8, 3.74) was spectacular at times after being called up in June and Jason Grimsley (3-2, 3.30) also showed promise.

Ken Howell (8-7, 4.64), who began 1990 as the Phillies' ace, suffered a strained shoulder and missed the second half. Roger McDowell (6-8, 3.86, 22 Sv) has led the Phillies in saves for two years and Joe Boever (3-6, 3.36) can step in if McDowell stumbles.

FIELDING: The Phillies cut down on their errors and turned the most double plays in the NL in 1990, but there still aren't too many Gold Gloves here. Shortstop Dickie Thon committed 25 errors and his range has diminished. Charlie Hayes made 20 errors at third base. If rookie Mickey Morandini hits enough to be the regular second baseman, he'll improve the infield defense. The outfield is fine as Dykstra can run down balls in center, Murphy is still solid in right and Hayes is more than adequate in left. The catching is in decent shape with Daulton.

OUTLOOK: Nick Leyva's Phillies have come a long way during the past two seasons and they're no longer the division's doormat after last year's 77-85, fourth-place finish. But there still seem to be a few pieces missing from the puzzle, especially on the mound, so the Phils look like longshots in the pennant race.

PHILADELPHIA PHILLIES 1991 ROSTER

MANAGER Nick Leyva
Coaches—Larry Bowa, Hal Lanier, Denis Menke, Johnny Podres, John Vukovich

PITCHERS

No.	Name	1990 Club	W-L	IP	SO	ERA	B-T	Ht.	Wt.	Born
35	Akerfelds, Darrel	Philadelphia	5-2	93	42	3.77	R-R	6-2	210	6/12/62 Denver, CO
—	Ashby, Andy	Reading	10-7	140	94	3.42	R-R	6-5	180	7/11/67 Kansas City, MO
30	Boever, Joe	Atl.-Phil.	3-6	88	33	3.36	R-R	6-1	200	10/4/60 St. Louis, MO
42	*Carman, Don	Philadelphia	6-2	87	58	4.15	L-L	6-3	201	6/14/59 Oklahoma City, OK
—	Carreno, Amalio	Reading	4-13	128	86	3.68	R-R	6-0	170	4/11/64 Venezuela
38	Combs, Pat	Philadelphia	10-10	183	108	4.07	L-L	6-4	200	10/29/66 Newport, RI
54	DeJesus, Jose	Scranton	1-4	56	45	3.38	R-R	6-5	195	1/6/65 Brooklyn, NY
		Philadelphia	7-8	130	87	3.74				
49	Greene, Tommy	Rich.-Scr.	5-8	116	125	3.50	R-R	6-5	225	4/6/67 Lumberton, NC
		Atl.-Phil.	3-3	51	21	5.08				
48	Grimsley, Jason	Scranton	8-5	128	99	3.93	R-R	6-3	180	8/7/67 Cleveland, TX
		Philadelphia	3-2	57	41	3.30				
43	Howell, Ken	Philadelphia	8-7	107	70	4.64	R-R	6-3	230	11/28/60 Detroit, MI
53	Malone, Chuck	Scranton	4-3	76	79	6.39	R-R	6-7	250	7/8/65 Harrisburg, AR
		Philadelphia	1-0	7	7	3.68				
—	Mauser, Tim	Reading	3-4	46	40	3.30	R-R	6-0	185	10/4/66 Fort Worth, TX
		Scranton	5-7	98	54	3.66				
13	McDowell, Roger	Philadelphia	6-8	86	39	3.86	R-R	6-1	182	12/21/60 Cincinnati, OH
51	McElroy, Chuck	Scranton	6-8	76	78	2.72	L-L	6-0	160	10/1/67 Galveston, TX
		Philadelphia	0-1	14	16	7.71				
45	Mulholland, Terry	Scranton	0-1	6	2	3.00	R-L	6-3	207	3/9/63 Uniontown, PA
		Philadelphia	9-10	181	75	3.34				
41	Ontiveros, Steve	Clearwater	0-0	8	2	2.35	R-R	6-0	190	3/5/61 Tularosa, NM
		Reading	0-2	6	8	9.00				
		Philadelphia	0-0	10	6	2.70				
47	Ruffin, Bruce	Philadelphia	6-13	149	79	5.38	S-L	6-2	213	10/4/63 Lubbock, TX
—	Scanlan, Bob	Scranton	8-11	130	74	4.85	R-R	6-7	200	8/6/68 Los Angeles, CA

CATCHERS

No.	Name	1990 Club	H	HR	RBI	Pct.	B-T	Ht.	Wt.	Born
10	Daulton, Darren	Philadelphia	123	12	57	.268	L-R	6-2	190	1/3/62 Arkansas City, KS
24	Fletcher, Darrin	Albuquerque	102	13	65	.291	L-R	6-1	199	10/3/66 Elmhurst, IL
		LA-Phil.	3	0	1	.130				
25	Lake, Steve	Philadelphia	20	0	6	.250	R-R	6-1	199	3/14/57 Inglewood, CA

INFIELDERS

No.	Name	1990 Club	H	HR	RBI	Pct.	B-T	Ht.	Wt.	Born
—	Backman, Wally	Pittsburgh	92	2	28	.292	S-R	5-9	168	9/22/59 Hillsboro, OR
1	Batiste, Kim	Reading	134	6	33	.276	R-R	6-0	175	3/15/68 New Orleans, LA
37	Booker, Rod	Philadelphia	29	0	10	.221	L-R	6-0	175	9/4/58 Los Angeles, CA
8	Hayes, Charlie	Philadelphia	145	10	57	.258	R-R	6-0	205	5/29/65 Hattiesburg, MS
15	Hollins, David	Philadelphia	21	5	15	.184	S-R	6-1	195	5/25/66 Buffalo, NY
17	Jordan, Ricky	Philadelphia	78	5	44	.241	R-R	6-3	208	5/26/65 Richmond, CA
		Scranton	29	2	11	.279				
12	Morandini, Mickey	Scranton	131	1	31	.261	L-R	5-11	170	4/22/66 Kittanning, PA
		Philadelphia	19	1	3	.241				
23	Ready, Randy	Philadelphia	53	1	16	.244	R-R	5-11	184	1/8/60 San Mateo, CA
21	Thon, Dickie	Philadelphia	141	8	48	.255	R-R	5-11	178	6/20/58 South Bend, IN

OUTFIELDERS

No.	Name	1990 Club	H	HR	RBI	Pct.	B-T	Ht.	Wt.	Born
6	Campusano, Sil	Philadelphia	18	2	9	.212	R-R	6-0	190	12/31/66 Dominican Republic
31	Chamberlain, Wes	Buffalo	104	6	52	.250	R-R	6-2	210	4/13/66 Chicago, IL
		Philadelphia	13	2	4	.283				
4	Dykstra, Lenny	Philadelphia	192	9	60	.325	L-L	5-10	193	2/10/63 Santa Ana, CA
9	Hayes, Von	Clearwater	1	0	0	.167	L-R	5-10	186	8/31/58 Stockton, CA
		Philadelphia	122	17	73	.261				
26	Jones, Ron	Scranton	39	3	26	.264	L-R	5-10	214	6/11/64 Sequin, TX
		Philadelphia	16	3	7	.276				
19	Kruk, John	Philadelphia	129	7	67	.291	L-L	5-10	204	2/9/61 Charleston, WV
—	Longmire, Tony	Harrisburg	27	1	13	.297	L-R	5-9	195	8/12/68 Vallejo, CA
3	Murphy, Dale	Atl.-Phil.	138	24	83	.245	R-R	6-4	215	3/12/56 Portland, OR
—	Peguero, Julio	Harr.-Read.	117	1	28	.277	S-R	6-0	160	9/7/68 Dominican Republic

*Free agent at press time

PHILLIE PROFILES

LENNY DYKSTRA 28 5-10 193   Bats L Throws L

In his first full season as an everyday center fielder, "Nails" thrilled Phillies fans with his aggressive style, making a run at NL batting title before finishing fourth at .325 . . . Led league in on-base percentage (.418), tied Brett Butler for most hits (192), was fourth in walks (89) and fifth in runs (106) . . . Stole 33 bases in 38 attempts . . . Batted over .400 with runners in scoring position . . . Hit first inside-the-park homer of his career . . . Batted .523 against Astros . . . Hit .360 for first half . . . Selected to start All-Star Game . . . Had 23-game hitting streak . . . Two months into season, he was hitting .418 . . . Bulked up from 160 to 193 pounds . . . Went 17 straight days in May without striking out . . . Born Feb. 10, 1963, in Santa Ana, Cal. . . . Selected by Mets in 12th round of 1981 draft . . . Traded to Phillies with Roger McDowell for Juan Samuel, June 18, 1989 . . . Earned $725,000 in 1990 . . . Signed new three-year deal in August worth a guaranteed $7.3 million.

Year	Club	Pos.	G	AB	R	H	2B	3B	HR	RBI	SB	Avg.
1985	New York (NL)	OF	83	236	40	60	9	3	1	19	15	.254
1986	New York (NL)	OF	147	431	77	127	27	7	8	45	31	.295
1987	New York (NL)	OF	132	431	86	123	37	3	10	43	27	.285
1988	New York (NL)	OF	126	429	57	116	19	3	8	33	30	.270
1989	N.Y.(NL)-Phil.	OF	146	511	66	121	32	4	7	32	30	.237
1990	Philadelphia . . .	OF	149	590	106	192	35	3	9	60	33	.325
	Totals		783	2628	432	739	159	23	43	232	166	.281

DALE MURPHY 35 6-4 215   Bats R Throws R

One of baseball's classiest players on and off the field . . . Right fielder's career had been on downslide for three years when he agreed to an Aug. 3 trade to Phils . . . After 15 seasons with Braves, he felt a change of scenery would help . . . Seemed rejuvenated by the move, putting together 13-game hitting streak in September while homering in three straight games . . . Filled critical need for Phillies, who were without legitimate cleanup hitter . . . Was batting just .232 with 17 homers and 55 RBI before trade . . . Atlanta's all-time home-run hitter with 371, surpassing Hank Aaron's 335 . . . Won back-to-back MVPs in 1982 and '83 . . . Attended Brigham Young . . . Born March 12, 1956, in Portland, Ore. . . . Fifth player chosen in 1974 draft . . .

Earned $2,000,000 in 1990 . . . Signed new two-year deal with Phillies worth $5 million.

Year	Club	Pos.	G	AB	R	H	2B	3B	HR	RBI	SB	Avg.
1976	Atlanta.......	C	19	65	3	17	6	0	0	9	0	.262
1977	Atlanta.......	C	18	76	5	24	8	1	2	14	0	.316
1978	Atlanta.......	C-1B	151	530	66	120	14	3	23	79	11	.226
1979	Atlanta.......	1B-C	104	384	53	106	7	2	21	57	6	.276
1980	Atlanta.......	OF-1B	156	569	98	160	27	2	33	89	9	.281
1981	Atlanta.......	OF-1B	104	369	43	91	12	1	13	50	14	.247
1982	Atlanta.......	OF	162	598	113	168	23	2	36	109	23	.281
1983	Atlanta.......	OF	162	589	131	178	24	4	36	121	30	.302
1984	Atlanta.......	OF	162	607	94	176	32	8	36	100	19	.290
1985	Atlanta.......	OF	162	616	118	185	32	4	37	111	10	.300
1986	Atlanta.......	OF	160	614	89	163	29	7	29	83	7	.265
1987	Atlanta.......	OF	159	566	115	167	27	1	44	105	16	.295
1988	Atlanta.......	OF	156	592	77	134	35	4	24	77	3	.226
1989	Atlanta.......	OF	154	574	60	131	16	0	20	84	3	.228
1990	Atl.-Phil.	OF	154	563	60	138	23	1	24	83	9	.245
	Totals		1983	7312	1125	1958	315	38	378	1171	160	.268

DARREN DAULTON 29 6-2 190   Bats L Throws R

Showed great timing, putting together his best season just before becoming eligible for free agency and re-signing with Phils at a salary of $6.75 million for three years . . . Led NL catchers in doubles (30) and tied for second in homers (12) . . . Set career highs in hits, runs, homers, doubles, walks, at-bats, RBI and games . . . Batted .327 during three-week period following All-Star break, including four homers, seven doubles, a triple, 17 runs scored, 14 RBI, 10 walks and two stolen bases . . . Credited move from eighth to second in lineup for turning around his season . . . Went 3-for-3, homered and scored four runs against Cardinals Aug. 1 . . . Suffered career-threatening knee injury in 1986 home-plate collision and underwent surgery to repair torn cruciate ligament . . . Made remarkable recovery, returning to action in 10 months . . . Born Jan. 3, 1962, in Arkansas City, Kan. . . . Selected by Phillies in 25th round of 1980 draft . . . Earned $425,000 in 1990.

Year	Club	Pos.	G	AB	R	H	2B	3B	HR	RBI	SB	Avg.
1983	Philadelphia ...	C	2	3	1	1	0	0	0	0	0	.333
1985	Philadelphia ...	C	36	103	14	21	3	1	4	11	3	.204
1986	Philadelphia ...	C	49	138	18	31	4	0	8	21	2	.225
1987	Philadelphia ...	C–1B	53	129	10	25	6	0	3	13	0	.194
1988	Philadelphia ...	C–1B	58	144	13	30	6	0	1	12	2	.208
1989	Philadelphia ...	C	131	368	29	74	12	2	8	44	2	.201
1990	Philadelphia ...	C	143	459	62	123	30	1	12	57	7	.268
	Totals		472	1344	147	305	61	4	36	158	16	.227

VON HAYES 32 6-5 186   **Bats L Throws L**

Ranks among Phillies' all-time leaders in homers, walks, stolen bases and on-base percentage . . . Tied major-league record with five walks in a game June 6 . . . Went nearly two months without a homer until hitting one off John Smiley in Pittsburgh July 28 . . . That homer was also his first extra-base hit in 91 at-bats . . . Addition of Dale Murphy allowed Phillies to remove him from cleanup spot . . . Also switched from right to left field . . . Ended 3-for-35 skid with three hits against Braves July 16 . . . Spent 15 days on disabled list with lacerated finger in June and July . . . Missed 11 games in June with bruised right instep . . . Born Aug. 31, 1958, in Stockton, Cal. . . . Selected by Indians in seventh round of 1979 draft . . . Traded to Phillies before 1983 season for five players, including Julio Franco . . . Was highest-paid Phillie in 1990, earning $2,000,000.

Year	Club	Pos.	G	AB	R	H	2B	3B	HR	RBI	SB	Avg.
1981	Cleveland	OF-3B	43	109	21	28	8	2	1	17	8	.257
1982	Cleveland	OF-3B-1B	150	527	65	132	25	3	14	82	32	.250
1983	Philadelphia . . .	OF	124	351	45	93	9	5	6	32	20	.265
1984	Philadelphia . . .	OF	152	561	85	164	27	6	16	67	48	.292
1985	Philadelphia . . .	OF	152	570	76	150	30	4	13	70	21	.263
1986	Philadelphia . . .	1B-OF	158	610	107	186	46	2	19	98	24	.305
1987	Philadelphia . . .	1B-OF	158	556	84	154	36	5	21	84	16	.277
1988	Philadelphia . . .	1B-OF-3B	104	367	43	100	28	2	6	45	20	.272
1989	Philadelphia . . .	OF-1B-3B	154	540	93	140	27	2	26	78	28	.259
1990	Philadelphia . . .	OF	129	467	70	122	14	3	17	73	16	.261
	Totals		1324	4658	689	1269	250	34	139	646	233	.272

CHARLIE HAYES 25 6-0 205   **Bats R Throws R**

Hit longest 1990 homer by a Phil at Veterans Stadium (426 feet off Mets' Ron Darling) . . . Third baseman also started games at first and second while batting anywhere from third to eighth in lineup . . . Went 6-for-12 with three homers to spark three straight wins at Pittsburgh July 26-28 while swinging a Roger McDowell signature bat after running out of his own model . . . Had first four-hit game of career July 17 at Atlanta . . . Was both goat and hero in Terry Mulholland's no-hitter Aug. 15, committing a throwing error in seventh inning to spoil perfect game but later spearing line drive down third-base line by Gary

Carter to end game... Born May 29, 1965, in Hattiesburg, Miss.... Selected by Giants in fourth round of 1983 draft... Traded to Phillies with Mulholland and Dennis Cook for Steve Bedrosian, June 18, 1989... Earned $120,000 in 1990.

Year	Club	Pos.	G	AB	R	H	2B	3B	HR	RBI	SB	Avg.
1988	San Francisco	OF-3B	7	11	0	1	0	0	0	0	0	.091
1989	S.F.-Phil	3B	87	304	26	78	15	1	8	43	3	.257
1990	Philadelphia ...	3B-1B-2B	152	561	56	145	20	0	10	57	4	.258
	Totals		246	876	82	224	35	1	18	100	7	.256

DICKIE THON 32 5-11 178   Bats R Throws R

Proving again that he has come all the way back from 1984 eye injury which threatened to end his career, he reached 500 at-bats for first time since 1983... After hitting just two homers before All-Star break, he hit three at Astrodome in first series following break when manager Nick Leyva suggested that he go back to pulling the ball... Committed 16th error July 14, equaling his total for 1989... Finished season with 25 errors... Suspended for three games after bumping umpire Terry Tata while arguing called third strike June 26... Led all NL shortstops in homers in 1989 with 15 and was just two shy of Granny Hamner's club record for shortstop... Born June 20, 1958, in South Bend, Ind.... Signed by Angels as amateur free agent in 1975... Traded to Astros in 1981... Signed as free agent with Padres before 1988 season... Contract sold to Phillies before 1989 season ... Earned $1,100,000 in 1990.

Year	Club	Pos.	G	AB	R	H	2B	3B	HR	RBI	SB	Avg.
1979	California	2B-SS-3B	35	56	6	19	33	0	0	8	0	.339
1980	California	SS-2B-3B-1B	80	267	32	68	12	2	0	15	7	.255
1981	Houston......	2B-SS-3B	49	95	13	26	6	0	0	3	6	.274
1982	Houston......	SS-3B-2B	136	496	73	137	31	10	3	36	37	.276
1983	Houston......	SS	154	619	81	177	28	9	20	79	34	.286
1984	Houston......	SS	5	17	3	6	0	1	0	1	0	.353
1985	Houston.......	SS	84	251	26	63	6	1	6	29	8	.251
1986	Houston......	SS	106	278	24	69	13	1	3	21	6	.248
1987	Houston......	SS	32	66	6	14	1	0	1	3	3	.212
1988	San Diego ...	SS-3B-2B	95	258	36	68	12	2	1	18	19	.264
1989	Philadelphia ...	SS	136	435	45	118	18	4	15	60	6	.271
1990	Philadelphia ...	SS	149	552	54	141	20	4	8	48	12	.255
	Totals		1061	3390	399	906	150	34	57	321	138	.267

PAT COMBS 24 6-4 200   Bats L Throws L

Caught everybody's attention in 1989 when, as a September call-up, he went 4-0 . . . Showed flashes of that form in 1990, but often pitched in hard luck . . . In his 10 losses, Phillies scored total of 16 runs . . . Beat Astros, 2-0, June 29 for his second major-league shutout and complete game . . . Pitched well enough in 3-0 loss to Mets June 23 to avoid demotion to minors . . . Made spectacular rise through Phillies' system in 1989, pitching at four levels, compiling 17-8 record and winning every decision after July 24 . . . Member of 1988 USA Olympic team, he was final cut before team left for Seoul . . . Born Oct. 29, 1966, in Newport, R.I. . . . Phillies' first-round pick in 1988 draft . . . Attended Baylor where he was two-time All-Southwest Conference All-Star . . . Also attended Rice . . . Earned $112,000 in 1990.

Year	Club	G	IP	W	L	Pct.	SO	BB	H	ERA
1989	Philadelphia	6	38⅔	4	0	1.000	30	6	36	2.09
1990	Philadelphia	32	183⅓	10	10	.500	108	86	179	4.07
	Totals	38	222	14	10	.583	138	92	215	3.73

JOSE DeJESUS 26 6-5 195   Bats R Throws R

When Phillies sent utility infielder Steve Jeltz to Royals for this guy during spring training 1990, they may have stolen a prize . . . With a fastball clocked at 95 mph, he can be tough when he throws slider for strikes . . . Recalled from Scranton (AAA) on June 12, he moved into rotation and stayed there, making 22 starts . . . Went 3-0 against Mets with two complete games, including a two-hit shutout in which no Met reached second base . . . Was toughest Phillie starter to hit . . . For Scranton, he went 1-4 with 3.38 ERA in 10 games, striking out 45 and walking 39 in 56 innings . . . Selected by American Association managers as top pitching prospect in 1989, when he fanned 158 in 145 innings for Omaha (AAA) . . . Born Jan. 6, 1965, in Brooklyn, N.Y. . . . Signed as amateur free agent with Royals in 1983 . . . Earned major-league minimum of $100,000 in 1990.

Year	Club	G	IP	W	L	Pct.	SO	BB	H	ERA
1988	Kansas City	2	2⅔	0	1	.000	2	5	6	27.00
1989	Kansas City	3	8	0	0	.000	2	8	7	4.50
1990	Philadelphia	22	130	7	8	.467	87	73	97	3.74
	Totals	27	140⅔	7	9	.438	91	86	110	4.22

ROGER McDOWELL 30 6-1 182   Bats R Throws R

A notorious prankster, he has been a major plus on and off the field . . . Led Phillies in saves (22 in 28 chances) for second straight year . . . Pitched 13 consecutive scoreless innings in August . . . Won NL Rolaids Relief Man Award in both April and May . . . Slumped in June, giving up nine runs on 17 hits and five walks in nine-game stretch, and was temporarily relieved of closer's role . . . Went 1-0 with six saves during seven-game stretch in April . . . After giving up six runs in one-third of an inning April 13, he allowed only one earned run over next eight appearances . . . Saved 84 games for Mets from 1985-89 . . . Born Dec. 21, 1960, in Cincinnati . . . Selected by Mets in third round of 1982 draft . . . Traded to Phillies with Lenny Dykstra for Juan Samuel, June 18, 1989 . . . Attended Bowling Green . . . Earned $1,400,000 in 1990, the first season on a three-year contract.

Year	Club	G	IP	W	L	Pct.	SO	BB	H	ERA
1985	New York (NL)	62	127⅓	6	5	.545	70	37	108	2.83
1986	New York (NL)	75	128	14	9	.609	65	42	107	3.02
1987	New York (NL)	56	88⅔	7	5	.583	32	28	95	4.16
1988	New York (NL)	62	89	5	5	.500	46	31	80	2.63
1989	N.Y. (NL)-Phil.	69	92	4	8	.333	47	38	79	1.96
1990	Philadelphia	72	86⅓	6	8	.429	39	35	92	3.86
	Totals	396	611⅓	42	40	.512	299	211	561	3.05

TERRY MULHOLLAND 28 6-3 207   Bats R Throws L

Became first Phillie to pitch no-hitter at home in this century when he hurled 6-0 gem against Giants Aug. 15 . . . Also became first to throw nine-inning no-hitter at Veterans Stadium, which opened in 1971 . . . Had career-high eight strikeouts and faced minimum 27 hitters, but lost bid for perfect game on Charlie Hayes' throwing error in seventh inning . . . In next start, he yielded just one run in 8⅓ innings against Dodgers . . . Pitched first complete game of season July 16 against Braves . . . Placed on 15-day disabled list in June with weakness in pitching arm . . . Gained notoriety as Giant rookie in 1986 for tossing glove, with baseball wedged in it, for out at first base . . . Born March 9, 1963, in Uniontown, Pa. . . . Giants' first-round pick in 1984 draft . . . Traded to Phillies on June 18, 1989, with Charlie Hayes and Dennis Cook, for Steve Bedrosian . . . Posted three-year 30-3 record at Marietta (Ohio) College . . . Earned $150,000 in 1990.

Year	Club	G	IP	W	L	Pct.	SO	BB	H	ERA
1986	San Francisco	15	54⅔	1	7	.125	27	35	51	4.94
1988	San Francisco	9	46	2	1	.667	18	7	50	3.72
1989	S.F.-Phil.	25	115⅓	4	7	.364	66	36	137	4.92
1990	Philadelphia	33	180⅔	9	10	.474	75	42	172	3.34
	Totals.	82	396⅔	16	25	.390	186	120	410	4.06

TOP PROSPECTS

MICKEY MORANDINI 24 5-11 170　　　**Bats L Throws R**
Phillies are hoping he will hit well enough to win job at second base . . . Called up to big leagues Aug. 31, after Tommy Herr was traded to Mets . . . Picked up first hit and scored game-winning run the next day, but batted just .241 in 25 games . . . Batted .261 for Scranton (AAA) with 24 doubles, 10 triples and 16 stolen bases . . . Born April 22, 1966, in Kittanning, Pa. . . . Selected by Phillies in fifth round of 1988 draft . . . Member of 1988 Olympic team . . . Won Paul Owens Award as best player in Phillies organization in 1989, when he hit combined .338 at three levels.

DAVE HOLLINS 24 6-1 195　　　　　**Bats S Throws R**
A four-year pro, he had no major-league experience until 1990, when he made the jump from Double-A after Phillies selected him from Padres in major-league draft . . . Used primarily as pinch-hitter, he may get chance to win job at third base in 1991 . . . Became first Phillie ever to hit pinch homers from each side of plate . . . Born May 25, 1966, in Buffalo, N.Y. . . . Selected by Padres in sixth round of 1987 draft . . . Career .294 hitter in minors . . . Attended University of South Carolina.

WES CHAMBERLAIN 24 6-2 210　　　**Bats R Throws R**
Phillies stole this bright outfield prospect when Pirates mistakenly placed him on irrevocable waivers and were forced to trade him and two other prospects for Carmelo Martinez Aug. 30 . . . Batted .250 with 24 doubles, 52 RBI and 24 steals for Buffalo (AAA) . . . His first major-league homer Sept. 19 at St. Louis and batted .283 in 18 games with Phillies . . . Named Eastern League (AA) MVP in 1989, when he batted .306 with 26 doubles, 21 homers and 87 RBI . . . Born April 13, 1966, in Chicago . . . Selected by Pirates in fourth round of 1987 draft . . . Attended Jackson State.

DARRIN FLETCHER 24 6-2 199   Bats L Throws R
Phillies picked up this highly regarded catching prospect from
Dodgers . . . In 105 games for Albuquerque (AAA), he batted .291
with 13 homers and 65 RBI . . . Born Oct. 3, 1966, in Elmhurst,
Ill. . . . Selected by Dodgers in sixth round of 1987 draft . . . Batted
.273 with 16 doubles in 100 games for Albuquerque in 1989 . . .
Led Texas League catchers in fielding percentage (.992) in 1988
. . . Big 10 Player of the Year at Illinois . . . Traded by Dodgers
for Dennis Cook, Sept. 13, 1990.

MANAGER NICK LEYVA: In his second season as a major-
league manager, he lifted Phillies out of basement, improving their record by 10 games to
77-85 . . . Unlike previous Phillies teams, the
1990 crew got off to a quick start, winning 18
of their first 32 games, and he had them thinking
positively . . . ''Nick has gotten the most out of
the talent,'' said veteran Von Hayes. ''Other
managers tried to do too much and that held us
back. Nick lets us play.'' . . . Club president Bill Giles rewarded
him Aug. 1, extending contract through 1992 . . . Never afraid to
dish out criticism when needed, he occasionally lost patience with
a young pitching staff which led NL in walks with 651 . . . Because
of that inexperienced pitching, his two-year record is 144-180 . . .
A Cardinals coach from 1984-88, he has tried to incorporate some
of Whitey Herzog's methods . . . Managed six years in St. Louis
organization, compiling 350-340 record . . . Named Texas League
Manager of the Year in 1983 . . . Born Aug. 16, 1953, in Ontario,
Cal. . . . Became youngest major-league skipper since 33-year-old
Dave Bristol took over Reds in 1966 . . . Served as minor-league
infielder from 1975-77.

ALL-TIME PHILLIE SEASON RECORDS

BATTING: Frank O'Doul, .398, 1929
HRs: Mike Schmidt, 48, 1980
RBI: Chuck Klein, 170, 1930
STEALS: Juan Samuel, 72, 1984
WINS: Grover Alexander, 33, 1916
STRIKEOUTS: Steve Carlton, 310, 1972

PITTSBURGH PIRATES

TEAM DIRECTORY: Chairman: Douglas Danforth; Pres.: Carl Barger; Sr. VP-GM/Baseball Oper.: Larry Doughty; VP-Pub. Rel.: Rick Cerrone; Trav. Sec.: Greg Johnson; Mgr.: Jim Leyland. Home: Three Rivers Stadium (58,437). Field distances: 335, l.f. line; 375, l.c.; 400, c.f.; 375, r.c.; 335, r.f. line. Spring training: Bradenton, Fla.

SCOUTING REPORT

HITTING: Scoring runs should be no problem for the Pirates—second in the NL with 733 in 1990—if Barry Bonds and Bobby Bonilla come close to duplicating what they did in 1990. NL MVP Bonds (.301, 33, 114) also stole 52 bases while leading the Pirates to a 95-67 finish and a divisional title. Bonilla (.280, 32, 120) has added incentive, because he can become a free agent after this season.

Andy Van Slyke (.284, 17, 77) was almost overlooked last

Bobby Bonds' boy Barry was Killer B as NL MVP.

year, but he's a key contributor and could make the difference in 1991 if the B&B boys tail off. Jeff King (.245, 14, 53) will get a chance to be the regular third baseman after coming on strong during the second half of 1990. Carmelo Martinez (.240, 10, 35), a late-season pickup, and Gary Redus (.247, 6, 23) will play bigger roles this year with Sid Bream having defected to Atlanta as a free agent. Don Slaught (.300, 4, 29) is a weapon vs. left-handed pitching.

PITCHING: Except for Cy Young winner Doug Drabek (22-6, 2.76), no Pirate pitcher won more than 12 games or saved more than 13 in 1990. Eighteen different pitchers won at least one game for the Pirates, but the question is: Can that formula work again?

Drabek figures to have another big year, but he'll need help. The Pirates made a key move by re-signing Zane Smith, who went 6-2 with a 1.30 ERA in 11 games as a Pirate. John Smiley (9-10, 4.64) must shake off a disappointing season in which he was hampered by injury and a lack of offensive support. Neal Heaton (12-9, 3.45) must try to recapture the magic of last year's 10-2 start and forget his slow finish. Bob Walk (7-5, 3.75) pitched well enough down the stretch to get a start in NLCS Game 1. Rookie Randy Tomlin (4-4, 2.55) showed promise in 12 late-season starts.

Bill Landrum (7-3, 2.13, 13 Sv), who had 26 saves in 1989, played a diminished role last year and the Pirates must settle on a closer. Stan Belinda (3-4, 3.55) and September sensation Vicente Palacios are possibilities.

FIELDING: There's still room for improvement, but the Pirates are a better defensive club than they were two years ago, when they led the NL with 160 errors. The left side of the infield is sometimes a problem—shortstop Jay Bell committed 22 errors in 1990 and King had 18 miscues in just 115 games at third.

Jose Lind is an outstanding second baseman, Mike LaValliere is a fine catcher and the outfield is in excellent hands with Van Slyke in center and Bonds in left. Bonilla does far less damage in right than he did at third base. Redus isn't Bream's equal at first.

OUTLOOK: The Pirates' depth was depleted by free-agent defections but Jim Leyland still has enough offensive firepower, with Bonds, Bonilla and Van Slyke, to win a lot of games. It all depends on the pitching. If Drabek comes up big and gets help from Smith, Smiley, Heaton, Walk or Tomlin, the Pirates can win again.

PITTSBURGH PIRATES 1991 ROSTER

MANAGER Jim Leyland
Coaches—Rich Donnelly, Gene Lamont, Milt May, Ray Miller, Tommy Sandt

PITCHERS

No.	Name	1990 Club	W-L	IP	SO	ERA	B-T	Ht.	Wt.	Born
—	Ausanio, Joe	Harrisburg	3-2	54	49	1.83	R-R	6-1	202	12/9/65 Kingston, NY
50	Belinda, Stan	Buffalo	3-1	24	25	1.90	R-R	6-3	200	8/6/66 Huntingdon, PA
		Pittsburgh	3-4	58	55	3.55				
—	Blankenship, Kevin	Iowa	10-9	163	101	3.42	R-R	6-0	185	1/26/63 Anaheim, CA
		Chicago (NL)	0-2	12	5	5.84				
15	Drabek, Doug	Pittsburgh	22-6	231	131	2.76	R-R	6-1	185	7/25/62 Victoria, TX
—	Hancock, Lee	Williamsport	3-2	47	27	2.68	L-L	6-4	225	6/27/67 Van Nuys, CA
		Harrisburg	6-7	118	65	3.44				
		Buffalo	0-0	0	0	—				
26	Heaton, Neal	Pittsburgh	12-9	146	68	3.45	L-L	6-1	195	3/3/60 Jamaica, NY
16	Kipper, Bob	Buffalo	0-0	5	6	7.71	R-L	6-2	180	7/8/64 Aurora, IL
		Pittsburgh	5-2	63	35	3.02				
43	Landrum, Bill	Pittsburgh	7-3	72	39	2.13	R-R	6-2	205	8/17/58 Columbia, SC
—	Minor, Blas	Harrisburg	6-4	94	98	3.06	R-R	6-3	200	3/20/66 Merced, CA
		Buffalo	0-1	3	2	3.38				
—	Neely, Jeff	Salem	0-1	7	11	2.45	R-R	6-4	195	8/9/65 Tacoma, WA
		Harrisburg	4-4	66	62	1.78				
		Buffalo	1-0	9	5	4.15				
58	Palacios, Vicente	Buffalo	13-7	184	137	3.43	R-R	6-3	180	7/19/63 Mexico
		Pittsburgh	0-0	15	8	0.00				
38	Patterson, Bob	Pittsburgh	8-5	95	70	2.95	R-L	6-2	192	5/16/59 Jacksonville, FL
34	Reed, Rick	Buffalo	7-4	91	63	3.46	R-R	6-0	195	8/16/64 Huntington, WV
		Pittsburgh	2-3	54	27	4.36				
—	Rodriguez, Rosario	Chattanooga	2-2	54	39	4.36	R-L	6-0	195	7/6/69 Mexico
		Nashville	0-1	4	1	10.38				
		Cincinnati	0-0	10	6	6.10				
—	Roesler, Mike	Pittsburgh	1-0	6	4	3.00	R-R	6-5	205	9/12/63 Ft. Wayne, IN
		Buffalo	0-3	42	19	4.29				
		Harrisburg	2-1	24	10	4.56				
57	Smiley, John	Pittsburgh	9-10	149	86	4.64	L-L	6-4	200	3/17/65 Phoenixville, PA
41	Smith, Zane	Mont.-Pitt.	12-9	215	130	2.55	L-L	6-2	195	12/28/60 Madison, WI
29	Tomlin, Randy	Harrisburg	9-6	126	92	2.28	L-L	5-11	179	6/14/66 Bainbridge, MA
		Buffalo	0-0	8	3	3.38				
		Pittsburgh	4-4	78	42	2.55				
17	Walk, Bob	Pittsburgh	7-5	130	73	3.75	R-R	6-4	217	11/26/56 Van Nuys, CA
53	York, Mike	Buffalo	8-7	159	130	4.20	R-R	6-1	192	9/6/64 Oak Park, IL
		Pittsburgh	1-1	13	4	2.84				

CATCHERS

No.	Name	1990 Club	H	HR	RBI	Pct.	B-T	Ht.	Wt.	Born
12	LaValliere, Mike	Pittsburgh	72	3	31	.258	L-R	5-10	205	8/18/60 Charlotte, NC
14	Prince, Tom	Pittsburgh	1	0	0	.100	R-R	5-11	185	8/13/64 Kankakee, IL
		Buffalo	64	7	37	.225				
—	Romero, Mandy	Salem	134	17	90	.291	S-R	5-11	196	10/19/67 Miami, FL
11	Slaught, Don	Pittsburgh	69	4	29	.300	R-R	6-1	190	9/11/58 Long Beach, CA

INFIELDERS

No.	Name	1990 Club	H	HR	RBI	Pct.	B-T	Ht.	Wt.	Born
3	Bell, Jay	Pittsburgh	148	7	52	.254	R-R	6-1	180	12/11/65 Pensacola, FL
—	Burdick, Kevin	Buffalo	121	3	41	.282	R-R	5-10	175	12/15/64 Oklahoma City, OK
51	Garcia, Carlos	Harrisburg	67	5	25	.277	R-R	6-1	185	10/15/67 Venezuela
		Buffalo	52	5	18	.264				
		Pittsburgh	2	0	0	.500				
7	King, Jeff	Pittsburgh	91	14	53	.245	R-R	6-1	180	12/26/64 Marion, IN
13	Lind, Jose	Pittsburgh	134	1	48	.261	R-R	5-11	170	5/1/64 Puerto Rico
—	Merced, Orlando	Buffalo	99	9	55	.262	S-R	5-11	170	11/2/66 Puerto Rico
		Pittsburgh	5	0	0	.208				
2	Redus, Gary	Pittsburgh	56	6	23	.247	R-R	6-1	185	11/1/56 Athens, AL
27	Ryal, Mark	Buffalo	124	9	49	.334	L-L	6-1	197	4/28/60 Henrietta, OK
		Pittsburgh	1	0	0	.083				
—	Wehner, John	Harrisburg	147	4	62	.288	R-R	6-3	204	6/29/87 Pittsburgh, PA
—	Wilkerson, Curtis	Chicago (NL)	41	0	16	.220	S-R	5-9	173	4/26/61 Petersburg, VA

OUTFIELDERS

No.	Name	1990 Club	H	HR	RBI	Pct.	B-T	Ht.	Wt.	Born
24	Bonds, Barry	Pittsburgh	156	33	114	.301	L-L	6-1	185	7/24/64 Riverside, CA
25	Bonilla, Bobby	Pittsburgh	175	32	120	.280	S-R	6-3	230	2/23/63 New York, NY
42	Carter, Steve	Buffalo	129	8	45	.303	L-R	6-4	200	12/12/64 Charlottesville, VA
		Pittsburgh	1	0	0	.200				
35	Martinez, Carmelo	Phil.-Pitt.	52	10	35	.240	R-R	6-2	211	7/28/60 Puerto Rico
30	McClendon, Lloyd	Chi. (NL)-Pitt.	18	2	12	.164	R-R	5-11	195	1/11/59 Gary, IN
18	Van Slyke, Andy	Pittsburgh	140	17	77	.284	L-R	6-2	192	12/21/60 Utica, NY

PIRATE PROFILES

BARRY BONDS 26 6-1 185   Bats L Throws L

Demanded to be removed from leadoff spot and then made good on his boasts with an MVP season in No. 5 hole . . . Became first player ever to bat .300, drive in 100 runs, score 100 runs, hit 30 homers and steal 50 bases . . . Played outstanding left field, winning Gold Glove . . . Became first Pirate ever to hit over 20 homers and steal over 40 bases . . . Led team in outfield assists (14) . . . Ranks 10th on Pirates' all-time homer list . . . Had disappointing NLCS, going 3-for-18 with no extra-base hits and one RBI . . . Had at least one homer against every NL opponent . . . Homered in three straight games from Aug. 9-11 . . . Reached previous career high of 62 RBI by All-Star break . . . Born July 24, 1964, in Riverside, Cal . . . Pirates' first pick in 1985 draft . . . Son of former major leaguer Bobby Bonds . . . Attended Arizona State, where he batted .347 with 45 homers, 175 RBI and 57 stolen bases . . . Earned $850,000 in 1990 after losing salary arbitration.

Year	Club	Pos.	G	AB	R	H	2B	3B	HR	RBI	SB	Avg.
1986	Pittsburgh	OF	113	413	72	92	26	3	16	48	36	.223
1987	Pittsburgh	OF	150	551	99	144	34	9	25	59	32	.261
1988	Pittsburgh	OF	144	538	97	152	30	5	24	58	17	.283
1989	Pittsburgh	OF	159	580	96	144	34	6	19	58	32	.248
1990	Pittsburgh	OF	151	519	104	156	32	3	33	114	52	.301
	Totals		717	2601	468	688	156	26	117	337	169	.265

BOBBY BONILLA 28 6-3 230   Bats S Throws R

Formed devastating one-two punch with Barry Bonds . . . Hit safely in 17 straight games in August, longest streak by a Pirate in six years . . . After committing 35 errors at third base in 1989, he made switch to right field . . . Dramatically improved right-handed hitting after All-Star break . . . Second in NL in RBI (120), doubles (39), total bases (324) and runs (112) . . . Finished sixth in homers (32), 10th in hits (175) . . . Home-run production tailed off in final month and he went 4-for-21 in NLCS with one double and one RBI . . . Went 1-for-35 and fanned 16 times in nine games at Montreal . . . Hit first career grand slam May 18 against Braves . . . Born Feb. 23, 1963, in New York . . . Signed by Pirates as non-drafted free agent in 1981

. . . Selected by White Sox in 1985 major-league draft . . . Traded back to Pirates, July 23, 1986 . . . Highest-paid Pirate, earning $1,250,000 in 1990 despite losing arbitration hearing.

Year	Club	Pos.	G	AB	R	H	2B	3B	HR	RBI	SB	Avg.
1986	Chicago (AL)	OF-1B	75	234	27	63	10	2	2	26	4	.269
1986	Pittsburgh	OF-1B-3B	63	192	28	46	6	2	1	17	4	.240
1987	Pittsburgh	3B-OF-1B	141	466	58	140	33	3	15	77	3	.300
1988	Pittsburgh	3B	159	584	87	160	32	7	24	100	3	.274
1989	Pittsburgh	3B-1B-OF	163	616	96	173	37	10	24	86	8	.281
1990	Pittsburgh	OF-3B-1B	160	625	112	175	39	7	32	120	4	.280
	Totals		761	2717	408	757	157	31	98	426	26	.279

JEFF KING 26 6-1 180   Bats R Throws R

Lifted weights during offseason and it paid off as he showed solid power while platooning with Wally Backman at third base during first full year in big leagues . . . After hitting just three homers prior to All-Star break, he had 11 homers and 37 RBI in second half . . . Homered five times in stretch of 25 at-bats in August . . . Hit two homers during 3-1 victory over Mets which completed doubleheader sweep Sept. 5 . . . Committed 18 errors . . . Hampered by bad back in NLCS and had just one single in 10 at-bats . . . Born Dec. 26, 1964, in Marion, Ind. . . . First player chosen in 1986 draft . . . Played three seasons at University of Arkansas, where he batted .372 and set school records for homers (42) and RBI (204) . . . Set single-season school record for RBI (82) and shares home-run record (17) with Kevin McReynolds . . . Earned $112,500 in 1990.

Year	Club	Pos.	G	AB	R	H	2B	3B	HR	RBI	SB	Avg.
1989	Pittsburgh	1B-3B-2B-SS	75	215	31	42	13	1	5	19	4	.195
1990	Pittsburgh	3B-1B	127	371	46	91	17	1	14	53	3	.245
	Totals		202	586	77	133	30	2	19	72	7	.227

ANDY VAN SLYKE 30 6-2 192   Bats L Throws R

One of top defensive center fielders in baseball, he also had solid offensive year, although his statistics were dwarfed by those of Barry Bonds and Bobby Bonilla . . . Batting average reached season-high .337 June 6 . . . Went 5-for-24 in NLCS with double, triple and three RBI . . . His seventh-inning double drove in winning run in Game 1 . . . Didn't hit first homer against a lefty until July 2, when he took Padres' Bruce Hurst deep . . . Hit two homers on Opening Day against Mets, the first two-homer opener by a Pirate since Willie Stargell in 1975 . . . Bounced back from sub-par 1989 when he lost a month to rib-cage muscle strain . . . Won first Gold Glove in 1988 and finished fourth in NL MVP voting . . . Born Dec. 21, 1960, in Utica, N.Y. . . . Selected by Cardinals in first round of 1979 draft . . . Traded to Pirates in Tony Pena deal before 1987 season . . . Second-highest-paid Pirate, earning $1,200,000 and Gold Glove in 1990.

Year	Club	Pos.	G	AB	R	H	2B	3B	HR	RBI	SB	Avg.
1983	St. Louis	OF-1B-3B	101	309	51	81	15	5	8	38	21	.262
1984	St. Louis	OF-1B-3B	137	361	45	88	16	4	7	50	28	.244
1985	St. Louis	OF-1B	146	424	61	110	25	6	13	55	34	.259
1986	St. Louis	OF-1B	137	418	48	113	23	7	13	61	21	.270
1987	Pittsburgh	OF-1B	157	564	93	165	36	11	21	82	34	.293
1988	Pittsburgh	OF	154	587	101	169	23	15	25	100	30	.288
1989	Pittsburgh	OF-1B	130	476	64	113	18	9	9	53	16	.237
1990	Pittsburgh	OF	136	493	67	140	26	6	17	77	14	.284
	Totals		1098	3632	530	979	182	63	113	516	198	.270

JOSE LIND 26 5-11 170   Bats R Throws R

An outstanding athlete with tremendous leaping ability, he regularly turns in spectacular plays at second base and has exceptional range . . . Put together his best offensive season, particularly during first half, batting .297 before All-Star break . . . Was perfect 8-for-8 in stolen bases and is 23-for-24 over past two years . . . Committed just seven errors . . . Hit for cycle in NLCS, going 5-for-21 and driving in two runs . . . Snapped 1-for-21 slump with a double Sept. 3 . . . Had sensational first two months, batting .341 while playing errorless baseball . . . In first full big-league season in 1988, he narrowly missed finishing first in fielding percentage among NL second basemen, was second in putouts, assists and total chances and ended season with 29-game errorless streak . . . Born May 1, 1964, in Toabaja, P.R. . . . Signed by Pirates as non-drafted free agent in 1982 . . . Earned $270,000 in 1990.

Year	Club	Pos.	G	AB	R	H	2B	3B	HR	RBI	SB	Avg.
1987	Pittsburgh	2B	35	143	21	46	8	4	0	11	2	.322
1988	Pittsburgh	2B	154	611	82	160	24	4	2	49	15	.262
1989	Pittsburgh	2B	153	578	52	134	21	3	2	48	15	.232
1990	Pittsburgh	2B	152	514	46	134	28	5	1	48	8	.261
	Totals		494	1846	201	474	81	16	5	156	40	.257

JAY BELL 25 6-1 180   Bats R Throws R

In first full season as Pirates' everyday shortstop, he was solid No. 2 hitter, tying for third on team in doubles (28) . . . Led Pirates with 109 strikeouts . . . Was 5-for-20 in NLCS with a double and a homer . . . Had second most at-bats on team and showed durability, playing all but three of Pirates' games . . . Led majors in sacrifice bunts with 39 . . . Committed 22 errors . . . Was Pirates' Opening Day shortstop in 1989, but was optioned to Buffalo (AAA) after going 1-for-20 . . . Recalled by Pirates in July and batted .309 over final 48 games . . . In just 86 games for Buffalo, he led team in homers (10) and RBI (54) and batted .375 with runners in scoring position . . . Born Dec. 11, 1965, in Pensacola, Fla. . . . Selected by Twins in first round of 1984 draft . . . Traded to Indians in 1985 and to Pirates before 1989 season . . . Earned $180,000 in 1990.

Year	Club	Pos.	G	AB	R	H	2B	3B	HR	RBI	SB	Avg.
1986	Cleveland	2B	5	14	3	5	2	0	1	4	0	.357
1987	Cleveland	SS	38	125	14	27	9	1	2	13	2	.216
1988	Cleveland	SS	73	211	23	46	5	1	2	21	4	.218
1989	Pittsburgh	SS	78	271	33	70	13	3	2	27	5	.258
1990	Pittsburgh	SS	159	583	93	148	28	7	7	52	10	.254
	Totals		353	1204	166	296	57	12	14	117	21	.246

DOUG DRABEK 28 6-1 185   Bats R Throws R

A low-key personality, but a perfectionist on the field, he came within one vote of unanimous selection as Cy Young Award winner while pitching Pirates to NL East title . . . Led league in victories (22), was sixth in ERA (2.76) and tied for second in complete games (9) . . . Pirates scored just nine runs in his six losses . . . Became club's first 20-game winner since John Candelaria in 1977 . . . Had pair of six-game winning streaks . . . Went 10-1 in first 12 starts after All-Star break . . . Was Pirates' most effective starter in NLCS, posting 1.65 ERA while going 1-1, including a 2-1 complete-game loss in Game 2 . . . Had at least one victory against every NL opponent . . . Went 5-0 in July with 2.23 ERA . . . Hit first career homer . . . Born July 25, 1962, in Victoria, Tex. . . . Selected by White Sox in 1983 draft

... Traded to Yankees in 1984 and to Pirates in Rick Rhoden deal before 1987 season... Attended University of Houston... Earned $1,100,000 in 1990.

Year	Club	G	IP	W	L	Pct.	SO	BB	H	ERA
1986	New York (AL)	27	131⅔	7	8	.467	76	50	126	4.10
1987	Pittsburgh	29	176⅓	11	12	.478	120	46	165	3.88
1988	Pittsburgh	33	219⅓	15	7	.682	127	50	194	3.08
1989	Pittsburgh	35	244⅓	14	12	.538	123	69	215	2.80
1990	Pittsburgh	33	231⅓	22	6	.786	131	56	190	2.76
	Totals	157	1003	69	45	.605	577	271	890	3.21

JOHN SMILEY 26 6-4 200   Bats L Throws L

Coming off disappointing season marred by injury and lack of offensive support... Pirates failed to score in four of his 10 losses... Sidelined with broken left hand from May 19 to June 30... In seven starts before injury, he was 3-3 with 3.35 ERA... Did not start in NLCS, but pitched two scoreless innings in Game 3 ... Only Pirate pitcher to reach double figures in losses... Offseason elbow surgery may have contributed to slow start... Pitched three-hitter against Giants April 26 to complete Pirates' first three-game sweep at Candlestick Park in seven years... In 1989, he tied Doug Drabek for club lead in complete games and strikeouts, allowing three earned runs or less in 22 of 28 starts, and had seventh-best ERA in NL... Born March 17, 1965, in Phoenixville, Pa.... Selected by Pirates in 12th round of 1983 draft... Earned $840,000 in 1990.

Year	Club	G	IP	W	L	Pct.	SO	BB	H	ERA
1986	Pittsburgh	12	11⅔	1	0	1.000	9	4	4	3.86
1987	Pittsburgh	63	75	5	5	.500	58	50	69	5.76
1988	Pittsburgh	34	205	13	11	.542	129	46	185	3.25
1989	Pittsburgh	28	205⅓	12	8	.600	123	49	174	2.81
1990	Pittsburgh	26	149⅓	9	10	.474	86	36	161	4.64
	Totals	163	646⅓	40	34	.541	405	185	593	3.73

BILL LANDRUM 32 6-2 205   Bats R Throws R

Led team in saves for second straight season with 13 in 16 chances, but his role diminished as Pirates went to bullpen by committee with eight different pitchers getting saves... Had just one save opportunity in July... Has converted 39 of 45 save opportunities over two seasons... Had team-best 2.13 ERA... Pitched two perfect innings in NLCS, but both came in Pirate losses . . . After yielding just two homers in 81 innings in 1989, he gave up two in his first 21 innings in 1990, but still finished season with only four gopher balls . . . Saved 26 games in 1989, recording at least one save against each NL opponent and registering saves in nine consecutive appearances . . . Born Aug. 17, 1958, in Columbia, S.C. . . . Signed by Cubs as non-drafted free agent in 1980 . . . Signed as free agent with Pirates before 1989 season . . . Was 20-4 in two seasons at University of South Carolina . . . Earned $302,500 in 1990.

Year	Club	G	IP	W	L	Pct.	SO	BB	H	ERA
1986	Cincinnati	10	13⅓	0	0	.000	14	4	23	6.75
1987	Cincinnati	44	65	3	2	.600	42	34	68	4.71
1988	Chicago (NL)	7	12⅓	1	0	1.000	6	3	19	5.84
1989	Pittsburgh	56	81	2	3	.400	51	28	60	1.67
1990	Pittsburgh	54	71⅔	7	3	.700	39	21	69	2.13
	Totals	171	243⅓	13	8	.619	152	90	239	3.11

ZANE SMITH 30 6-2 195   Bats L Throws L

Probably pitched best baseball of career after coming to Pirates from Expos in midseason trade, winning his first four decisions . . . Biggest victory came Sept. 5, when he beat Mets, 1-0, on one-hitter . . . Was 6-7 with 3.23 ERA with Expos . . . Went 6-2 for Pirates, completing only his second full winning season in big leagues . . . "I was in Atlanta so long, I didn't know what it felt like to win," he said . . . Was losing pitcher in NLCS Games 3 and 6, making him only pitcher on either team to lose twice . . . His career-high 15 victories in 1987 were second only to Shane Rawley's 17 among NL left-handers . . . Shoulder and elbow problems ruined his 1988 season and he eventually underwent elbow surgery . . . Born Dec. 28, 1960, in Madison, Wis. . . . Selected by Braves in 1982 draft . . . Traded to Expos in 1989 and to Pirates for three prospects, Aug. 8, 1990 . . . Attended Indiana State . . . Earned $660,000 in 1990 and, as free agent, signed four-year, $10.6-million contract, largest in Pittsburgh history.

Year	Club	G	IP	W	L	Pct.	SO	BB	H	ERA
1984	Atlanta	3	20	1	0	1.000	16	13	16	2.25
1985	Atlanta	42	147	9	10	.474	85	80	135	3.80
1986	Atlanta	38	204⅔	8	16	.333	139	105	209	4.05
1987	Atlanta	36	242	15	10	.600	130	91	245	4.09
1988	Atlanta	23	140⅓	5	10	.333	59	44	159	4.30
1989	Atl.-Mont.	48	147	1	13	.071	93	52	141	3.49
1990	Mont.-Pitt.	33	215⅓	12	9	.571	130	50	196	2.55
	Totals	223	1116⅓	51	68	.429	652	435	1101	3.66

TOP PROSPECTS

RANDY TOMLIN 25 5-11 179   Bats L Throws L
Made major-league debut Aug. 6 with five-hit complete game
against Phillies after making jump from Double-A . . . Started a
dozen games for Pirates down the stretch, going 4-4 with 2.55
ERA . . . Biggest win was three-hitter against Mets Sept. 6 as
Pirates completed three-game sweep . . . Went 9-6 with 2.28
ERA for Harrisburg . . . Born June 14, 1966, in Bainbridge, Md.
. . . Selected by Pirates in 18th round of 1988 draft . . . In 1989,
he struck out 31 batters in 32 innings for Harrisburg, compiling
0.84 ERA, after going 12-6 for Salem (A).

MIKE YORK 26 6-1 192   Bats R Throws R
Made just one start for Pirates, but it was an important one . . . In
major-league debut at Cincinnati Aug. 17, he pitched seven shutout
innings in 7-1 Pirate victory . . . Overall, he pitched in four big-
league games, going 1-1 with 2.84 ERA . . . For Buffalo (AAA),
he went 8-7 with 130 strikeouts in 158⅔ innings . . . Born Sept.
6, 1964, in Oak Park, Ill. . . . Selected by Yankees in 40th round
of 1982 draft . . . Signed as free agent with Pirates before 1987
season . . . Won seven straight decisions for Harrisburg (AA) in
1989, setting club ERA record (2.31).

VICENTE PALACIOS 27 6-3 180   Bats R Throws R
After being called up to majors Sept. 5, he made seven bullpen
appearances, saving three games, finishing four and allowing no
runs while yielding just four hits in 15 innings . . . For Buffalo
(AAA), he won all of his starts in August and September, going
7-0 with 0.94 ERA . . . Made 28 starts and was 13-7 with 137
strikeouts in 183⅔ innings . . . Born July 19, 1963, in Mataloma,
Mexico . . . Obtained by Pirates on waivers from Brewers before
1987 season.

STEVE CARTER 26 6-4 200   Bats L Throws R
A solid outfield prospect, he led American Association with 12
triples and was third in hitting while batting .303 with 19 doubles
and 45 RBI for Buffalo (AAA) . . . Called up to Pirates Sept. 5
and went 1-for-5 . . . Had 16 major-league at-bats in 1989, when
his only two hits were a double and a homer . . . Born Dec. 12,

1964, in Charlottesville, Va. . . . Selected by Pirates in 17th round of 1987 draft . . . Attended University of Georgia . . . Batted .295 with 24 doubles for Buffalo in 1989.

MANAGER JIM LEYLAND: This career minor leaguer's patience and dedication paid off with divisional championship as he and Pirates completed five-year journey from basement to penthouse . . . Club's 95-67 roll earning him NL Manager-of-the-Year honors . . . Set tone during 1989-90 offseason with remarkable display of self-discipline, giving up both coffee and cigarettes, a pledge he maintained despite tension of pennant race . . . Nursed pitching staff with just one consistent starter and a bullpen whose top reliever had just 13 saves and Pirates held off Mets in September . . . His five-year record as Pirates skipper is 398-410 . . . Spent 11 seasons managing in Tigers' farm system and four years as third-base coach with White Sox . . . Close friend of A's manager Tony La Russa, who helped him become big-league manager . . . Inherited Pirates team that lost 104 games in 1985 and immediately began changing attitude in clubhouse . . . Began turnaround in 1987 when Pirates won 27 of last 38 games . . . Made pennant run in 1988, finishing second to Mets . . . Born Dec. 15, 1944, in Toledo, Ohio . . . Was just 26 when he became minor-league manager in 1971.

ALL-TIME PIRATE SEASON RECORDS

BATTING: Arky Vaughan, .385, 1935
HRs: Ralph Kiner, 54, 1949
RBI: Paul Waner, 131, 1927
STEALS: Omar Moreno, 96, 1980
WINS: Jack Chesbro, 28, 1902
STRIKEOUTS: Bob Veale, 276, 1965

ST. LOUIS CARDINALS

TEAM DIRECTORY: Chairman: August A. Busch III; Pres.-CEO: Fred L. Kuhlmann; Exec. VP-Chief Oper. Off.: Mark Sauer; VP/GM: Dal Maxvill; Dir. Player Pers.: Ted Simmons: Dir. Pub. Rel.: Jeff Wehling; Mgr. Pub. Rel.: Brian Barton; Trav. Sec.: C.J. Cherre; Mgr. Joe Torre. Home: Busch Stadium (54,224). Field distances: 330, l.f. line; 414, c.f.; 330, r.f. line. Spring training: St. Petersburg, Fla.

SCOUTING REPORT

HITTING: The offense nearly disappeared last season, when the last-place Cardinals scored just 599 runs (11th in the NL) and hit only 73 home runs (12th). In addition, the Cardinals traded away eventual NL batting champion Willie McGee, an impending free agent, in August and lost free agents Terry Pendleton and Vince Coleman last winter.

Pedro Guerrero (.281, 13, 80), still a force in the middle of the lineup, needs help. Todd Zeile (.244, 15, 57) should be even more productive following a difficult rookie year. Ray Lankford (.286, 3, 12) has played just 39 big-league games, but he and Bernard Gilkey could be good ones. Ozzie Smith (.254, 1, 50) is still a solid contact hitter, though he's past his prime. Jose Oquendo (.252, 1, 37) will get on base, but isn't a run producer.

Switch-hitting Felix Jose (.271, 3, 13 in NL), who played 25 games for the Cardinals after coming from Oakland in the trade for McGee, will be given a chance to be the regular right fielder. Tom Pagnozzi (.277, 2, 23), who takes over as the regular catcher, has just 543 at-bats and 50 RBI after four years in the majors.

PITCHING: Injuries and adversity played havoc with the Cardinals' pitching in 1990 as they slipped toward the bottom of the pack in ERA (3.87). John Tudor (12-4, 2.40) was the only consistent winner and shoulder problems forced him to retire.

Joe Magrane (10-17, 3.59) needs to return to his 1989 form, when he was a Cy Young candidate. Bob Tewksbury (10-9, 3.47) must show that his surprising 1990 performance wasn't a mirage. Jose DeLeon (7-19, 4.43) is 28 games under .500 in his major-league career. Bryn Smith (9-8, 4.27) must bounce back from a disappointing first year as a Card. Ken Hill (5-6, 5.49) must do better, too.

Reliever Lee Smith (3-4, 2.10) saved 27 games and was one

Cards must get lineup protection for Pedro Guerrero.

of the few bright spots in 1990. Todd Worrell is trying to come back after missing an entire season because of elbow surgery. The addition of free agent Juan Agosto (9-8, 4.29 with the Astros) should offset the loss of Ken Dayley, who left for Toronto after six solid years in the St. Louis bullpen.

FIELDING: Defense used to be one of the Cardinals' strong points, but even the fielding declined last season as the Cards made more errors (130) and turned fewer double plays (114).

Smith is still the Wizard at shortstop, although he's lost a step. Oquendo set a record by committing just four errors in 150 games at second base. Lankford has outstanding range in center field and Pagnozzi is an acceptable catcher. But the rest of the defense is average at best and Zeile struggled late last season after switching to third base.

OUTLOOK: During the decade Whitey Herzog managed this team, you always felt the Cardinals would find a way to win. Now, Whitey is gone and so are most of his stars. It's time to rebuild and Joe Torre's Cards will experience growing pains. Anything better than a last-place finish should be regarded as a major achievement after last years' 70-92 facedown.

ST. LOUIS CARDINALS 1991 ROSTER

MANAGER Joe Torre
Coaches—Joe Coleman, Dave Collins, Bucky Dent, Gaylen Pitts, Dave Ricketts, Red Schoendienst

PITCHERS

No.	Name	1990 Club	W-L	IP	SO	ERA	B-T	Ht.	Wt.	Born
49	Agosto, Juan	Houston	9-6	92	50	4.29	L-L	6-2	190	2/23/58 Puerto Rico
44	Carpenter, Cris	St. Louis	0-0	8	6	4.50	R-R	6-1	185	4/5/65 Gainesville, GA
		Louisville	10-8	143	100	3.70				
—	Clark, Mark	St. Petersburg	3-2	62	58	3.05	R-R	6-5	225	5/12/68 Bath, IL
		Arkansas	5-11	115	87	3.82				
48	DeLeon, Jose	St. Louis	7-19	183	164	4.43	R-R	6-3	215	12/20/60 Dominican Republic
35	DiPino, Frank	St. Louis	5-2	81	49	4.56	L-L	6-0	180	10/22/56 Syracuse, NY
68	Ericka, John	St. Petersburg	2-1	23	25	1.57	R-R	6-7	220	9/16/67 Oaklawn, IL
		Arkansas	1-2	15	19	9.39				
43	Hill, Ken	St. Louis	5-6	79	58	5.49	R-R	6-2	175	12/14/65 Lynn, MA
		Louisville	6-1	85	104	1.79				
32	Magrane, Joe	St. Louis	10-17	203	100	3.59	R-L	6-6	230	7/2/64 Des Moines, IA
41	*Niedenfuer, Tom	St. Louis	0-6	65	32	3.46	R-R	6-5	230	8/13/59 St. Louis Park, MN
26	Olivares, Omar	Louisville	10-11	159	88	2.82	R-R	6-1	185	7/6/67 Puerto Rico
		St. Louis	1-1	49	20	2.92				
—	Perez, Mike	Louisville	7-7	67	69	4.28	R-R	6-0	187	10/19/64 Puerto Rico
		St. Louis	1-0	14	5	3.95				
56	Sherrill, Tim	Louisville	4-3	61	57	2.49	L-L	5-11	170	9/10/65 Morrison, AR
		St. Louis	0-0	4	3	6.23				
36	Smith, Bryn	St. Louis	9-8	141	78	4.27	R-R	6-2	205	8/11/55 Marietta, GA
47	Smith, Lee	Boston	2-1	14	17	1.88	R-R	6-6	250	12/4/57 Jamestown, LA
		St. Louis	3-4	69	70	2.10				
37	Terry, Scott	St. Louis	2-6	72	35	4.75	R-R	5-11	195	11/21/59 Hobbs, NM
39	Tewksbury, Bob	Louisville	3-2	41	22	2.43	R-R	6-4	200	11/30/60 Concord, NH
		St. Louis	10-9	145	50	3.47				
38	Worrell, Todd	St. Louis		Injured			R-R	6-5	210	9/28/59 Arcadia, CA

CATCHERS

No.	Name	1990 Club	H	HR	RBI	Pct.	B-T	Ht.	Wt.	Born
19	Pagnozzi, Tom	St. Louis	61	2	23	.277	R-R	6-1	190	7/30/62 Tucson, AZ
54	Stephens, Ray	Louisville	65	3	27	.221	R-R	6-0	190	9/22/62 Houston, TX
27	Zeile, Todd	St. Louis	121	15	57	.244	R-R	6-1	190	9/9/65 Van Nuys, CA

INFIELDERS

No.	Name	1990 Club	H	HR	RBI	Pct.	B-T	Ht.	Wt.	Born
18	Alicea, Luis	St. Petersburg	22	0	12	.232	S-R	5-9	165	7/29/65 Puerto Rico
		Arkansas	14	0	4	.286				
		Louisville	32	0	10	.348				
58	Brewer, Rod	Louisville	129	12	83	.251	L-L	6-3	208	2/24/66 Eustis, FL
		St. Louis	6	0	2	.240				
67	Carmona, Greg	Arkansas	74	0	20	.232	S-R	6-0	150	5/9/68 Dominican Republic
—	Fernandez, Joey	Arkansas	109	14	63	.271	L-R	6-1	190	11/18/65 Tampa, FL
—	Figueroa, Bien	Louisville	95	0	39	.240	R-R	5-10	170	2/7/64 Dominican Republic
28	Guerrero, Pedro	St. Louis	140	13	80	.281	R-R	6-0	197	6/29/56 Dominican Republic
10	Hudler, Rex	Mont.-St. L.	62	7	22	.282	R-R	6-0	180	9/2/60 Tempe, AZ
8	Jones, Tim	St. Louis	28	1	12	.219	L-R	5-10	175	12/1/62 Sumter, SC
59	Martinez, Julian	Louisville	57	2	23	.213	R-R	6-0	175	6/2/67 Dominican Republic
2	Oquendo, Jose	St. Louis	118	1	37	.252	S-R	5-10	160	7/4/63 Puerto Rico
7	Pena, Geronimo	Louisville	97	6	35	.249	S-R	6-1	170	3/29/67 Dominican Republic
		St. Louis	11	0	2	.244				
17	Perry, Gerald	Kansas City	118	8	57	.254	L-R	6-0	190	10/30/60 Savannah, GA
—	Ross, Mike	Arkansas	110	8	56	.252	R-R	6-0	170	10/14/65 Fresno, CA
55	Royer, Stan	Huntsville	136	14	89	.258	R-R	6-3	195	8/31/67 Olney, IL
		Louisville	4	0	4	.267				
1	Smith, Ozzie	St. Louis	130	1	50	.254	S-R	5-10	160	12/26/54 Mobile, AL
21	*Walling, Denny	St. Louis	28	1	19	.220	L-R	6-1	185	4/17/54 Neptune, NJ
12	Wilson, Craig	Louisville	57	2	23	.279	R-R	5-11	175	11/28/64 Anne Arundal, MD
		St. Louis	30	0	7	.248				

OUTFIELDERS

No.	Name	1990 Club	H	HR	RBI	Pct.	B-T	Ht.	Wt.	Born
23	Gilkey, Bernard	Louisville	147	3	46	.295	R-R	6-0	170	9/24/66 St. Louis, MO
		St. Louis	19	1	3	.297				
5	Jose, Felix	Oakland	90	8	39	.264	S-R	6-1	190	5/8/65 Dominican Republic
		St. Louis	23	3	13	.271				
16	Lankford, Ray	Louisville	123	10	72	.260	L-L	5-11	180	6/5/67 Modesto, CA
		St. Louis	36	3	12	.286				
—	Maclin, Lonnie	St. Petersburg	46	2	17	.387	L-L	5-11	160	2/17/67 Clayton, MO
		Arkansas	81	2	25	.308				
		Louisville	18	0	6	.310				
25	Thompson, Milt	St. Louis	91	6	30	.218	L-R	5-11	170	1/5/59 Washington, DC

*Free agent at press time

CARDINAL PROFILES

PEDRO GUERRERO 34 6-0 197   Bats R Throws R

As Cardinals' only big run producer, he had to do it alone last season, without much protection . . . Drove in 20 runs in April, including five during a game against Dodgers . . . Also hit two homers that day, his first against his former teammates . . . Hit 200th career homer June 11 at Pittsburgh . . . Placed on 15-day disabled list in August with lower back strain . . . His grand slam against Phillies April 21 was Cardinals' first since Jack Clark slammed Mike Scott in 1987 . . . First baseman led Cards in batting average and RBI in 1989 . . . Overcame major injury in 1986, rupturing tendon below left knee during spring training . . . Shared 1981 World Series MVP honors with Ron Cey and Steve Yeager . . . Born June 29, 1956, in San Pedro de Macoris, D.R. . . . Signed by Indians in 1973 . . . Contract sold to Dodgers in 1974 . . . Traded to Cardinals for John Tudor, Aug. 16, 1988 . . . Earned $2,083,333 in 1990.

Year	Club	Pos.	G	AB	R	H	2B	3B	HR	RBI	SB	Avg.
1978	Los Angeles . . .	1B	5	8	3	5	0	1	0	1	0	.625
1979	Los Angeles . . .	OF-1B-3B	25	62	7	15	2	0	2	9	2	.242
1980	Los Angeles . . .	OF-INF	75	183	27	59	9	1	7	31	2	.322
1981	Los Angeles . . .	OF-3B-1B	98	347	46	104	17	2	12	48	5	.300
1982	Los Angeles . . .	OF-3B	150	575	87	175	27	5	32	100	22	.304
1983	Los Angeles . . .	3B-1B	160	584	87	174	28	6	32	103	23	.296
1984	Los Angeles . . .	OF-3B-1B	144	535	85	162	29	4	16	72	9	.303
1985	Los Angeles . . .	OF-3B-1B	137	487	99	156	22	2	33	87	12	.320
1986	Los Angeles . . .	OF-1B	31	61	7	15	3	0	5	10	0	.246
1987	Los Angeles . . .	OF-1B	152	545	89	184	25	2	27	89	9	.338
1988	L.A.-St.L	1B-3B-OF	103	364	40	104	14	2	10	65	4	.286
1989	St. Louis	1B	162	570	60	177	42	1	17	117	2	.311
1990	St. Louis	1B	136	498	42	140	31	1	13	80	1	.281
	Totals		1378	4819	679	1470	249	27	206	812	91	.305

JOSE OQUENDO 27 5-10 160   Bats S Throws R

As long as Ryne Sandberg is playing second base in NL, he will always be overshadowed, but he has established himself as one of the very best . . . Led NL second basemen in fielding percentage, making just four errors, a record for 150 or more games . . . Committed only five errors in 1989 . . . After driving in just two runs in May, he picked up 15 RBI in June . . . His average dipped to .212 by the end of May . . . Went

0-for-23 left-handed before singling off Giants' Don Robinson May 24 . . . Saw 65-game errorless streak end in April . . . One of most versatile players in baseball, he played eight different positions in 1987 . . . Spent first full season as second baseman in 1989 . . . Born July 4, 1963, in Rio Piedras, P.R. . . . Signed by Mets as amateur free agent in 1979 . . . Traded to Cardinals before 1985 season . . . Earned $575,000 in 1990.

Year	Club	Pos.	G	AB	R	H	2B	3B	HR	RBI	SB	Avg.
1983	New York (NL)	SS	120	328	29	70	7	0	1	17	8	.213
1984	New York (NL)	SS	81	189	23	42	5	0	0	10	10	.222
1986	St. Louis	SS-2B-3B-OF	76	138	20	41	4	1	0	13	2	.297
1987	St. Louis	INF-OF-P	116	248	43	71	9	0	1	24	4	.286
1988	St. Louis	INF-OF-P-C	148	451	36	125	10	1	7	46	4	.277
1989	St. Louis	2B-SS-1B	163	556	59	162	28	7	1	48	3	.291
1990	St. Louis	2B-SS	156	469	38	118	17	5	1	37	1	.252
	Totals		860	2379	248	629	80	14	11	195	32	.264

TODD ZEILE 25 6-1 190   Bats R Throws R

Entered 1990 as odds-on favorite to win NL Rookie of the Year, but he struggled early . . . His season was further complicated when Cards moved him from catcher to third base late in year as they tried to determine whether he could replace impending free agent Terry Pendleton in 1991 . . . Played 24 games at third, committing three errors in his first seven games . . . Had just 14 hits in first 90 at-bats with runners on base . . . Hit most homers ever by a Cardinal rookie catcher . . . In 1989, he batted .285 with 19 homers and 85 RBI in just 118 games for Louisville (AAA) . . . Led American Association catchers in fielding percentage and threw out 30 percent of would-be base-stealers . . . Born Sept. 9, 1965, in Van Nuys, Cal. . . . Selected by Cardinals in third round of 1986 draft . . . Attended UCLA . . . Named Texas League's best defensive catcher in 1988 . . . Earned major-league-minimum $100,000 in 1990.

Year	Club	Pos.	G	AB	R	H	2B	3B	HR	RBI	SB	Avg.
1989	St. Louis	C	28	82	7	21	3	1	1	8	0	.256
1990	St. Louis	C–3B–1B–OF	144	495	62	121	25	3	15	57	2	.244
	Totals		172	577	69	142	28	4	16	65	2	.246

Even past his prime, Oz is still the Wizard.

OZZIE SMITH 36 5-10 160   Bats S Throws R

Perhaps the greatest athlete ever to play short-stop, the "Wizard" might be slowing down a bit as he reaches his mid-30s . . . Committed 12 errors in 1990 . . . Trails only Marty Marion on Cardinals' all-time games played list at short-stop . . . Very tough to strike out, he whiffed just 33 times . . . Cards' only remaining player from 1982 world champions . . . Stole 20th base Aug. 10, the 13th straight season he has reached that plateau . . . Was caught just six times in 38 steal attempts . . . Batted .333 during 13-game hitting streak that ended in September . . . His goal is to reach 2,000 hits . . . Only NL player to win Gold Glove every year in 1980s and added another in 1990 . . . Selected to play in 10 straight All-Star Games and has been starting shortstop eight consecutive years . . . Born Dec. 26, 1954, in Mobile, Ala. . . . Selected by Padres in fourth round of 1977 draft . . . Traded to Cardinals for Garry Templeton before 1982 season . . . Second-highest-paid Cardinal at $1,975,000 in 1990.

Year	Club	Pos.	G	AB	R	H	2B	3B	HR	RBI	SB	Avg.
1978	San Diego	SS	159	590	69	152	17	6	1	46	40	.258
1979	San Diego	SS	156	587	77	124	18	6	0	27	28	.211
1980	San Diego	SS	158	609	67	140	18	5	0	35	57	.230
1981	San Diego	SS	110	450	53	100	11	2	0	21	22	.222
1982	St. Louis	SS	140	488	58	121	24	1	2	43	25	.248
1983	St. Louis	SS	159	552	69	134	30	6	3	50	34	.243
1984	St. Louis	SS	124	412	53	106	20	5	1	44	35	.257
1985	St. Louis	SS	158	537	70	148	22	3	6	54	31	.276
1986	St. Louis	SS	153	514	67	144	19	4	0	54	31	.280
1987	St. Louis	SS	158	600	104	182	40	4	0	75	43	.303
1988	St. Louis	SS	153	575	80	155	27	1	3	51	57	.270
1989	St. Louis	SS	155	593	82	162	30	8	2	50	29	.273
1990	St. Louis	SS	143	512	61	130	21	1	1	50	32	.254
	Totals ...:..		1926	7019	910	1798	297	52	19	600	464	.256

BOB TEWKSBURY 30 6-4 200   Bats R Throws R

After bouncing around Yankees' and Cubs' organizations for eight years and overcoming shoulder surgery, he finally established himself and earned a spot in Cardinals' rotation for 1991 . . . Recalled from Louisville (AAA) in June, he picked up career-high 10th victory by Sept. 7 . . . Manager Joe Torre called him the team's most consistent pitcher . . . Came within six outs of a perfect game during one-hit, 5-0 victory over Astros . . .

Also blanked Pirates, 6-0 . . . Walked just three batters in last 57 innings . . . Spent most of 1989 with Louisville, where he developed into club's top starter, going 13-5 with 2.43 ERA . . . Born Nov. 30, 1960, in Concord, N.H. . . . Selected by Yankees in 19th round of 1981 draft . . . Signed by Cardinals as six-year minor-league free agent in 1988 . . . Attended Rutgers University and St. Leo (Fla.) College . . . A bargain in 1990, earning major-league-minimum $100,000.

Year	Club	G	IP	W	L	Pct.	SO	BB	H	ERA
1986	New York (AL)	23	130⅓	9	5	.643	49	31	144	3.31
1987	New York (AL)	8	33⅓	1	4	.200	12	7	47	6.75
1987	Chicago (NL)	7	18	0	4	.000	10	13	32	6.50
1988	Chicago (NL)	1	3⅓	0	0	.000	1	2	6	8.10
1989	St. Louis	7	30	1	0	1.000	17	10	25	3.30
1990	St. Louis	28	145⅓	10	9	.526	50	15	151	3.47
	Totals	74	360⅓	21	22	.488	139	78	405	3.90

BRYN SMITH 35 6-2 205   Bats R Throws R

Experienced up-and-down season during first year as a Cardinal . . . Went 3-3 over first six starts as Cards scored total of one run in those losses . . . Retired just one of eight hitters he faced against ex-teammates in 18-2 loss at Montreal . . . Placed on 15-day disabled list July 28 with sore right shoulder . . . Gave up seven runs on eight hits in two innings of 10-1 loss to Mets before going on DL . . . Shaved his beard June 9 and then didn't win another game until July 17 . . . Gave up just two homers in first 56 innings before surrendering four in Atlanta May 21 . . . Picked up first career victory in seven decisions at Dodger Stadium . . . Born Aug. 11, 1955, in Marietta, Ga. . . . Signed by Orioles as non-drafted free agent in 1974 . . . Traded to Expos before 1978 season . . . Signed by Cardinals as free agent, prior to last season . . . Earned $1,633,333 in 1990.

Year	Club	G	IP	W	L	Pct.	SO	BB	H	ERA
1981	Montreal	7	13	1	0	1.000	9	3	14	2.77
1982	Montreal	47	79⅓	2	4	.333	50	23	81	4.20
1983	Montreal	49	155⅓	6	11	.353	101	43	142	2.49
1984	Montreal	28	179	12	13	.480	101	51	178	3.32
1985	Montreal	32	222⅓	18	5	.783	127	41	193	2.91
1986	Montreal	30	187⅓	10	8	.555	105	63	182	3.94
1987	Montreal	26	150⅓	10	9	.526	94	31	164	4.37
1988	Montreal	32	198	12	10	.545	122	32	179	3.00
1989	Montreal	33	215⅔	10	11	.476	129	54	177	2.84
1990	St. Louis	26	141⅓	9	8	.529	78	30	160	4.27
	Totals	310	1541⅔	90	79	.533	916	371	1470	3.37

LEE SMITH 33 6-6 250   Bats R Throws R

Kept Cardinals respectable by saving 27 games in 32 opportunities and finishing 45 of the 53 in which he pitched . . . Obtained from Red Sox for Tom Brunansky in May, he was life saver for Cardinals, who went entire season without injured closer Todd Worrell . . . Pitched 24⅓ innings without allowing an earned run before giving up three Aug. 3 in a 5-4 loss to Mets . . . Saved 17 games in first 19 opportunities . . . Signed three-year contract worth $7.8 million, making him highest-paid Cardinal in history . . . Earned 250th career save July 17 against Dodgers . . . Got off to fast start with Red Sox, striking out 17 in 14 innings while saving four games . . . Saved 30-plus games in four consecutive years with Cubs from 1984-87, including career-high 36 in 1987 . . . Born Dec. 4, 1957, in Jamestown, La. . . . Selected by Cubs in second round of 1975 draft after striking out 124 batters in 53 innings during senior year at Castor (La.) High.

Year	Club	G	IP	W	L	Pct.	SO	BB	H	ERA
1980	Chicago (NL)	18	22	2	0	1.000	17	14	21	2.86
1981	Chicago (NL)	40	67	3	6	.333	50	31	57	3.49
1982	Chicago (NL)	72	117	2	5	.286	99	37	105	2.69
1983	Chicago (NL)	66	103⅓	4	10	.286	91	41	70	1.65
1984	Chicago (NL)	69	101	9	7	.563	86	35	98	3.65
1985	Chicago (NL)	65	97⅔	7	4	.636	112	32	87	3.04
1986	Chicago (NL)	66	90⅓	9	9	.500	93	42	69	3.09
1987	Chicago (NL)	62	83⅔	4	10	.286	96	32	84	3.12
1988	Boston	64	83⅔	4	5	.444	96	37	72	2.80
1989	Boston	64	70⅔	6	1	.857	96	33	53	3.57
1990	Boston	11	14⅓	2	1	.667	17	9	13	1.88
1990	St. Louis.	53	68⅔	3	4	.429	70	20	58	2.10
	Totals.	650	919⅓	55	62	.470	923	363	787	2.88

JOE MAGRANE 26 6-6 230   Bats R Throws L

Entered 1990 as Cardinals' ace but struggled through nightmarish first half . . . In first seven starts, he was 0-6 with 6.45 ERA . . . Allowed 17 earned runs in 13-inning span . . . Picked up first victory with four-hitter against Astros, snapping eight-game losing streak dating back to August 1989 . . . By June 27, he had already suffered career-high 10 losses . . . Pitched 1-0 victory over Mets, beating them for first time since his major-league debut in 1987 . . . Struck out career-high 11 batters in 7-0 win over Cubs, his third career shutout at Wrigley Field . . . Was Cy Young favorite until late slump in 1989 . . . Born July 2, 1964, in Des Moines, Iowa . . . Selected by Cards in first round of 1985 draft . . . Attended University of Arizona, where he pitched no-hitter against NCAA champ Cal State-Fullerton in 1984 . . . Earned $300,000 in 1990.

Year	Club	G	IP	W	L	Pct.	SO	BB	H	ERA
1987	St. Louis.	27	170⅓	9	7	.563	101	60	157	3.54
1988	St. Louis.	24	165⅓	5	9	.357	100	51	133	2.18
1989	St. Louis.	34	234⅔	18	9	.667	127	72	219	2.91
1990	St. Louis.	31	203⅓	10	17	.370	100	59	204	3.59
	Totals.	116	773⅔	42	42	.500	428	242	713	3.07

KEN HILL 25 6-2 175   Bats R Throws R

After starting 33 games as a rookie in 1989, he was demoted to Louisville (AAA) on April 28 of last season . . . Started 12 games for Louisville, going 6-1 with 1.79 ERA and striking out 104 batters in 85 innings while yielding just 47 hits . . . Recalled July 26 and made first start that night against Mets, striking out career-high nine batters in 3-1 victory . . . Pitched 5⅓ innings of no-hit ball at Chicago in another 3-1 win . . . Control was his big problem as a rookie when he led NL with 99 walks . . . Control trouble resurfaced in a 1990 start as he walked four in just one-third of an inning in Philadelphia . . . Fanned 107 hitters in 115 innings for Arkansas (AA) in 1988 . . . Born Dec. 14, 1965, in Lynn, Mass. . . . Signed by Tigers as non-drafted amateur free agent in 1985 . . . Traded to Cardinals, Aug. 10, 1986 . . . Earned major-league-minimum $100,000.

Year	Club	G	IP	W	L	Pct.	SO	BB	H	ERA
1988	St. Louis.	4	14	0	1	.000	6	6	16	5.14
1989	St. Louis.	33	196⅔	7	15	.318	112	99	186	3.80
1990	St. Louis.	17	78⅔	5	6	.455	58	33	79	5.49
	Totals.	54	289⅓	12	22	.353	176	138	281	4.32

TOP PROSPECTS

RAY LANKFORD 23 5-11 180   Bats L Throws L

A good defensive center fielder with outstanding range, he showed what he could do after being promoted Aug. 31 from Louisville

(AAA), where he had batted .260 with 10 homers and 72 RBI
... Reached base by hit or walk in 15 of first 19 big-league games
... Batted .286 with 10 doubles and eight stolen bases in 39 games
for Cards ... Born June 5, 1967, in Modesto, Cal. ... Selected
by Cardinals in third round of 1987 draft ... Named Texas League
MVP in 1989, when he led league in hits (158) and triples (12)
and finished second in RBI (98) and runs (98) for Arkansas (AA).

MIKE PEREZ 26 6-0 187   Bats R Throws R
Set Louisville (AAA) club record for saves with 31 and led American Association ... Struck out 69 in 67 innings ... After being
called up to Cardinals in September, he compiled 3.95 ERA in
13 games with one save ... Born Oct. 19, 1964, in Yauco,
P.R. ... Selected by Cards in 13th round of 1986 draft ... Led
Texas League in saves (33) for Arkansas (AA) in 1989, going 17
consecutive outings without allowing earned run ... Set minor-
league record with 41 saves for Springfield (A) in 1987.

GERONIMO PENA 24 6-1 170   Bats R Throws R
An infielder who can play second or third base, he turned around
his season after an early illness ... Batted .249 with 24 stolen
bases for Louisville (AAA) ... In brief trial with Cardinals, he hit
.244 in 18 games ... Born March 29, 1967, in Distrito Nacional,
D.R. ... Signed by Cards as non-drafted amateur free agent in
1984 ... Hit .296 with nine homers for Arkansas (AA) in 1989,
when he started season by hitting in 19 of 20 games.

BERNARD GILKEY 24 6-0 170   Bats R Throws R
Batted .295 with 26 doubles and 45 stolen bases for Louisville
(AAA), but committed 11 errors in outfield ... In September trial
with Cardinals, he batted .297 with five doubles and six stolen
bases in 18 games ... Born Sept. 24, 1966, in St. Louis ... Signed
by Cardinals as non-drafted free agent in 1984 ... Led Texas
League in stolen bases (53) and runs (104) for Arkansas (AA) in
1989 ... Led league's outfielders with 22 assists ... Led Cardinal
minor leaguers with 54 stolen bases in 1988 and had 17-game
hitting streak for Springfield (A).

MANAGER JOE TORRE: Left Angels' broadcast booth when he accepted Cardinals' managing job Aug. 1, signing contract through 1992 . . . Won eight of first 11 games before Cards went on to their first basement finish since 1918 at 70-92 . . . Hadn't managed since 1984, when he was fired by Braves after one first-place and two second-place finishes . . . Returned to St. Louis where he was star player from 1969-74, winning 1971 MVP . . . Showed an inclination to experiment and shake up a dormant team late in season, moving rookie catcher Todd Zeile to third base, benching Terry Pendleton and switching Vince Coleman to right field . . . Faces massive rebuilding job in 1991 . . . Has added pressure of replacing Whitey Herzog, who won three pennants in 1980s while becoming St. Louis icon . . . Cardinals went 24-34 under him, finishing season with seven straight losses . . . Managed Mets from 1977-81, compiling 286-420 record and never finishing higher than fifth . . . Won NL West title in 1982, his first season managing Braves . . . Overall managerial record is 567-683 . . . Born July 18, 1940, in Brooklyn, N.Y. . . . Batted .297 with 252 homers and 1,185 RBI in 18-year major-league career that he began as a catcher.

ALL-TIME CARDINAL SEASON RECORDS

BATTING: Rogers Hornsby, .424, 1924
HRs: Johnny Mize, 43, 1940
RBI: Joe Medwick, 154, 1937
STEALS: Lou Brock, 118, 1974
WINS: Dizzy Dean, 30, 1934
STRIKEOUTS: Bob Gibson, 274, 1970

INSIDE THE
AMERICAN LEAGUE

By JOHN SHEA and TOM PEDULLA
Marin   *Gannett Newspapers*
Independent Journal

	West	East
PREDICTED ORDER OF FINISH	Oakland Athletics	Toronto Blue Jays
	Kansas City Royals	Detroit Tigers
	Chicago White Sox	Boston Red Sox
	California Angels	Cleveland Indians
	Texas Rangers	Baltimore Orioles
	Seattle Mariners	New York Yankees
	Minnesota Twins	Milwaukee Brewers

Playoff Winner: Toronto

WEST DIVISION

		Owner		Morning Line Manager
1	**ATHLETICS** Make four in a row	Walter A. Haas Jr. Forest green, gold & white	1990 W 103 L 59	2-1 Tony La Russa
2	**ROYALS** Still not enough horses	Ewing Kauffman Royal blue & white	1990 W 75 L 86	3-1 John Wathan
3	**WHITE SOX** Due for letdown	J. Reinsdorf/E. Einhorn Navy, white & scarlet	1990 W 94 L 68	4-1 Jeff Torborg
4	**ANGELS** Time running out	Gene Autry Red, white & navy	1990 W 80 L 82	9-2 Doug Rader
5	**MARINERS** Jr. thoroughbred not enough	Jeff Smulyan Blue, gold & white	1990 W 77 L 85	30-1 Jim Lefebvre
6	**RANGERS** Jockey in trouble	G. Bush./E. Rose Red, white & blue	1990 W 83 L 79	40-1 Bobby Valentine
7	**TWINS** Where has all the power gone?	Carl Pohlad Scarlet, white & blue	1990 W 74 L 88	100-1 Tom Kelly

ATHLETICS make it in photo finish over **ROYALS** as **WHITE SOX** pick up show-oats. **ANGELS** contend until the stretch but **MARINERS** and **RANGERS** are out of the running early in race and **TWINS'** hoofs are caught at the gate.

Canadian Cup

91st Running. American League Race. Distance: 162 games plus playoff. Payoff (based on '90): $112,533 per winning player, World Series: $69,995 per losing player, World Series. A field of 14 entered in two divisions.

Track Record: 111 wins—Cleveland, 1954

EAST DIVISION		Owner		Morning Line Manager
1	**BLUE JAYS** Up close last time	Labatt's, Imp. Trust, CIBC Blue & white	1990 W 86 L 76	2-1 Cito Gaston
2	**TIGERS** Have great jockey	Tom Monaghan Navy, orange & white	1990 W 79 L 83	4-1 Sparky Anderson
3	**RED SOX** Can't repeat	Jean Yawkey Red, white & blue	1990 W 88 L 74	5-1 Joe Morgan
4	**INDIANS** Could surprise	Richard & David Jacobs Black & orange	1990 W 77 L 85	11-2 John Mc- Namara
5	**ORIOLES** Better days ahead	Lawrence Lucchino Black & orange	1990 W 76 L 85	6-1 Frank Robinson
6	**YANKEES** New act doesn't play	George Steinbrenner Navy blue pinstripes	1990 W 67 L 95	40-1 Stump Merrill
7	**BREWERS** Can see them all	Bud Selig Blue, gold & white	1990 W 74 L 88	50-1 Tom Trebel- horn

---

New-look **BLUE JAYS** withstand charge by the **TIGERS** after **RED SOX** falter in the stretch. **INDIANS** show early foot and land in the money ahead of the **ORIOLES**. **YANKEES** are off the pace and **BREWERS** throw jockey midway through race.

CALIFORNIA ANGELS

TEAM DIRECTORY: Chairman: Gene Autry; Pres.: Richard Brown; VP: Jackie Autry; Exec. VP/GM: Mike Port; Dir. Minor League Oper.: Bill Bavasi; Dir. Pub. Rel.: Tim Mead; Trav. Sec.: Frank Sims; Mgr.: Doug Rader. Home: Anaheim Stadium (65,158). Field distances: 333, l.f. line; 386, l.c.; 404, c.f.; 386, r.c.; 333, r.f. line. Spring training: Mesa, Ariz., and Palm Springs, Cal.

SCOUTING REPORT

HITTING: The Angels were in the middle of the pack offensively last year, ranking seventh in the AL in runs (690), sixth in team batting average (.260) and in a tie for fourth in homers (147). That wasn't as bad as you might think given the inadequate showings of the since-traded Devon White (.217, 11, 44), Jack Howell (.228, 8, 33) and Chili Davis (.265, 12, 58), a free agent still unsigned at press time.

Junior Felix (.263, 15, 65 with Blue Jays) was added in the White trade last winter and he'll join ex-Yankees Dave Winfield (.275, 19, 72 as an Angel) and Luis Polonia (.336, 2, 32 as an Angel), Lance Parrish (.268, 24, 70), Wally Joyner (.268, 8, 41) and Dante Bichette (.255, 15, 53). Both Winfield and Polonia responded well to escaping the pressures of New York and playing for George Steinbrenner.

PITCHING: The Angels' starting staff is potentially strong and deep.

There may not be another left-hander in the AL better than Chuck Finley (18-9, 2.40), runnerup in last season's ERA race to Roger Clemens. Finley had seven complete games, logged 236 innings and notched 177 strikeouts.

Despite his 1990 problems, Mark Langston (10-17, 4.40) has an arsenal too lethal not to be overpowering again. Kirk McCaskill (12-11, 3.25) and Jim Abbott (10-14, 4.51) are quality starters, too, and Bert Blyleven (8-7, 5.24) hopes to show he has enough left to be a decent fifth starter.

The bullpen isn't as deep. There's still Bryan Harvey (4-4, 3.22, 25 Sv), but Willie Fraser (5-4, 3.08, 2 Sv) accompanied White to Toronto. Lefty Floyd Bannister (3-2, 4.04 for Yakult Swallows) returns from Japan to contend for a job.

Luis Polonia's .335 average made him a God-ian Angel.

FIELDING: Only the Brewers committed more errors than the Angels (142) last season. The biggest area of improvement figures to be second base, where Luis Sojo—also obtained from Toronto in the White deal—should cover lots more ground than the very limited Johnny Ray. But Felix, who played right for the Blue Jays last year, doesn't figure to be the equal of two-time Gold Glove winner White in center.

OUTLOOK: It will be interesting to see if Doug Rader's Angels improve on last year's 80-82 mark. Winfield—old, but still armed and dangerous—figures to thrive over a full season in a comfort-

CALIFORNIA ANGELS 1991 ROSTER

MANAGER Doug Rader
Coaches—Bruce Hines, Deron Johnson, Bobby Knoop, Marcel Lachemann, Frank Reberger, Jimmie Reese

PITCHERS

No.	Name	1990 Club	W-L	IP	SO	ERA	B-T	Ht.	Wt.	Born
25	Abbott, Jim	California	10-14	212	105	4.51	L-L	6-3	210	9/19/67 Flint, MI
43	Bailes, Scott	California	2-0	35	16	6.37	L-L	6-2	171	12/18/62 Chillicothe, OH
—	Bannister, Floyd	Yakult	3-2	49	31	4.04	L-L	6-1	190	6/10/55 Pierre, SD
28	Blyleven, Bert	California	8-7	134	69	5.24	R-R	6-3	220	4/6/51 Holland
45	Eichhorn, Mark	California	2-5	85	69	3.08	R-R	6-3	210	11/21/60 San Jose, CA
42	Erb, Michael	Midland	1-1	31	25	5.17	R-R	6-4	210	3/19/66 San Diego, CA
		Edmonton	4-4	82	45	4.26				
48	Fetters, Mike	California	1-1	68	35	4.12	R-R	6-4	212	12/19/64 Van Nuys, CA
31	Finley, Chuck	California	18-9	236	177	2.40	L-L	6-6	212	11/26/62 Monroe, LA
44	Grahe, Joe	Midland	7-5	119	58	5.14	R-R	6-0	200	8/14/67 West Palm Beach, FL
		Edmonton	3-0	40	21	1.35				
		California	3-4	43	25	4.98				
34	Harvey, Bryan	California	4-4	64	82	3.22	R-R	6-2	215	6/2/63 Chattanooga, TN
12	Langston, Mark	California	10-17	223	195	4.40	R-L	6-2	190	8/20/60 San Diego, CA
46	Lewis, Scott	California	1-1	16	9	2.20	R-R	6-3	178	12/5/65 Grants Pass, OR
40	Martinez, David	Palm Springs	0-6	55	37	4.72	R-R	6-0	190	9/18/63 Austin, TX
		Midland	6-6	74	53	5.17				
15	McCaskill, Kirk	California	12-11	174	78	3.25	R-R	6-1	196	4/9/61 Canada
33	McClure, Bob	California	2-0	7	6	6.43	R-L	5-11	188	4/29/53 Oakland, CA
38	*Minton, Greg	California	1-1	15	4	2.35	S-R	6-2	207	7/29/51 Lubbock, TX
37	Richardson, Jeff	Edmonton	5-0	48	31	1.86	R-R	6-3	203	8/29/63 Wichita, KS
		California	0-0	1	0	0.00				
35	Young, Cliff	Edmonton	7-4	52	30	2.42	L-L	6-4	210	8/2/64 Willis, TX
		California	1-1	31	19	3.52				

CATCHERS

No.	Name	1990 Club	H	HR	RBI	Pct.	B-T	Ht.	Wt.	Born
14	Orton, John	Edmonton	42	6	26	.241	R-R	6-1	192	12/8/65 Santa Cruz, CA
		California	16	1	6	.190				
13	Parrish, Lance	California	126	24	70	.268	R-R	6-3	220	6/15/56 Clairton, PA

INFIELDERS

No.	Name	1990 Club	H	HR	RBI	Pct.	B-T	Ht.	Wt.	Born
7	Anderson, Kent	California	44	1	5	.308	R-R	6-1	187	8/12/63 Florence, SC
10	Coachman, Pete	Edmonton	122	5	51	.291	R-R	5-9	175	11/11/61 Cottonwood, AL
		California	14	0	5	.311				
51	Cron, Chris	Edmonton	115	17	75	.287	R-R	6-2	200	3/31/64 Albuquerque, NM
		California	5	0	3	.140				
11	DiSarcina, Gary	Edmonton	70	4	37	.212	R-R	6-1	178	11/19/67 Malden, MA
		California	8	0	3	.140				
18	Hill, Donnie	California	93	3	32	.264	S-R	5-10	160	11/12/60 Pomona, CA
16	Howell, Jack	California	72	8	33	.228	L-R	6-0	190	8/18/61 Tucson, AZ
		Edmonton	25	2	15	.333				
21	Joyner, Wally	California	83	8	41	.268	L-L	6-2	198	6/16/62 Atlanta, GA
—	Manrique, Fred	Minnesota	54	5	29	.237	R-R	6-1	175	11/5/61 Venezuela
		California	5	1	2	.385				
6	Rose, Bobby	Edmonton	142	9	68	.283	R-R	5-11	189	3/15/67 Covina, CA
		California	5	1	2	.385				
17	Schofield, Dick	California	79	1	18	.255	R-R	5-10	179	11/21/62 Springfield, IL
20	Schu, Rick	California	42	6	14	.268	R-R	6-0	185	1/26/62 Philadelphia, PA
—	Sojo, Luis	Syracuse	88	6	25	.296	R-R	5-11	165	1/3/66 Venezuela
		Toronto	18	1	9	.225				

OUTFIELDERS

No.	Name	1990 Club	H	HR	RBI	Pct.	B-T	Ht.	Wt.	Born
19	Bichette, Dante	California	89	15	53	.255	R-R	6-3	225	11/18/63 W. Palm Beach, FL
24	**Davis, Chili	California	109	12	58	.265	S-R	6-3	210	1/17/60 Jamaica
52	Davis, Mark	Midland	94	12	41	.266	R-R	6-0	170	11/25/64 Lemon Grove, CA
		Edmonton	49	9	34	.368				
5	*Downing, Brian	California	90	14	51	.273	R-R	5-10	194	10/9/50 Los Angeles, CA
47	Felix, Junior	Toronto	122	15	65	.263	S-R	5-11	180	10/3/67 Dominican Republic
22	Polonia, Luis	NY (AL)-Cal.	135	2	35	.335	L-L	5-8	152	10/12/64 Dominican Republic
9	Stevens, Lee	Edmonton	99	16	66	.293	L-L	6-4	219	7/10/67 Kansas City, MO
		California	53	7	32	.214				
8	Venable, Max	California	49	4	21	.259	L-R	5-10	185	6/6/57 Phoenix, AZ
32	Winfield, Dave	NY (AL)-Cal.	127	21	78	.267	R-R	6-6	239	10/3/51 St. Paul, MN

*Free agent at press time
**New look free agent

able environment. If Joyner can stay healthy and Langston can remember how to win, the Angels could challenge in the AL West. If not, they could fall right in the dumper.

ANGEL PROFILES

DAVE WINFIELD 39 6-6 239   Bats R Throws R

Trade that brought him from Yankees for Mike Witt May 11 was breath of fresh air for the big guy . . . Outfielder ended long and stormy relationship with owner George Steinbrenner . . . Thanks in part to his failure to immediately agree to the trade, he received a new three-year, $9-million contract that begins in '91 . . . Performed better after trade . . . Began season 13-for-61 (.213) with two homers and six RBI . . . In first 32 games, he had just nine RBI . . . Hit .176 with runners in scoring position before All-Star break, .296 after the break . . . Of his 21 homers, 13 were hit in Anaheim Stadium . . . One of 11 major leaguers to collect at least 20 homers, 75 RBI, 70 runs and a .260 average . . . Named Comeback Player of Year by *The Sporting News* . . . Career homer total of 378 ranks 32nd on all-time list . . . His first homer in '91 will tie him with Orlando Cepeda and Tony Perez . . . His 1,516 RBI rank 26th all-time, directly behind Joe DiMaggio (1,537) . . . Born Oct. 3, 1951, in St. Paul, Minn. . . . Made $2,122,890 in '90 after sitting out '89 with bad back.

Year	Club	Pos.	G	AB	R	H	2B	3B	HR	RBI	SB	Avg.
1973	San Diego	OF-1B	56	141	9	39	4	1	3	12	0	.277
1974	San Diego	OF	145	498	57	132	18	4	20	75	9	.265
1975	San Diego	OF	143	509	74	136	20	2	15	76	23	.267
1976	San Diego	OF	137	492	81	139	26	4	13	69	26	.283
1977	San Diego	OF	157	615	104	169	29	7	25	92	16	.275
1978	San Diego	OF-1B	158	587	88	181	30	5	24	97	21	.308
1979	San Diego	OF	159	597	97	184	27	10	34	118	15	.308
1980	San Diego	OF	162	558	89	154	25	6	20	87	23	.276
1981	New York (AL)	OF	105	388	52	114	25	1	13	68	11	.294
1982	New York (AL)	OF	140	539	84	151	24	8	37	106	5	.280
1983	New York (AL)	OF	152	598	99	169	26	8	32	116	15	.283
1984	New York (AL)	OF	141	567	106	193	34	4	19	100	6	.340
1985	New York (AL)	OF	155	633	105	174	34	6	26	114	19	.275
1986	New York (AL)	OF-3B	154	565	90	148	31	5	24	104	6	.262
1987	New York (AL)	OF	156	575	83	158	22	1	27	97	5	.275
1988	New York (AL)	OF	149	559	96	180	37	2	25	107	9	.322
1989	New York (AL)				Did Not Play							
1990	NY (AL)-Cal	OF	132	475	70	127	21	2	21	78	0	.267
	Totals		2401	8896	1384	2548	433	76	378	1516	209	.286

WALLY JOYNER 28 6-2 198   Bats L Throws L

Played in only 83 games, suffering a season-ending injury to his right knee in July... Played every game at first base, pushing career total to 699. Only Rod Carew (720) has played more first base for Angels and only 11 Angels have played as many as 699 games at one position... Four of his eight homers came from May 19-27... Recorded 21 putouts May 28 vs. Cleveland... Committed four errors and posted fielding percentage of .995... Had only 12 RBI in final 135 at-bats... Born June 16, 1962, in Atlanta... Made $1.75 million in 1990.

Year	Club	Pos.	G	AB	R	H	2B	3B	HR	RBI	SB	Avg.
1986	California	1B	154	593	82	172	27	3	22	100	5	.290
1987	California	1B	149	564	100	161	33	1	34	117	8	.285
1988	California	1B	158	597	81	176	31	2	13	85	8	.295
1989	California	1B	159	593	78	167	30	2	16	79	3	.282
1990	California	1B	83	310	35	83	15	0	8	41	2	.268
	Totals		703	2657	376	759	136	8	93	422	26	.286

LUIS POLONIA 26 5-8 152   Bats L Throws L

Seems to have finally found a home in Anaheim... Traded to Angels April 29 for Claudell Washington after rocky stint with Yankees... Began career with Oakland, but was never appreciated as leadoff hitter and outfielder... With Angels, he became more reliable in both roles... Was especially effective against old mates, hitting .419 vs. Oakland and .350 vs. Yanks... Finished at .335, though he was 66 plate appearances shy of qualifying for the batting title... Led league in hitting vs. right-handers at .341... Led Angels in hitting with runners in scoring position at .325... Hit .292 in first 29 games, went over .300 in 30th game and never fell below that mark again... Hit .386 with 21 of 35 RBI in final two months... Both homers were against Yankees, including inside-the-park grand slam... Has 11 career homers, all against AL East teams... Born Oct. 12, 1964, in Santiago City, Dominican Republic... Made $220,000 last season.

Year	Club	Pos.	G	AB	R	H	2B	3B	HR	RBI	SB	Avg.
1987	Oakland	OF	125	435	78	125	16	10	4	49	29	.287
1988	Oakland	OF	84	288	51	84	11	4	2	27	24	.292
1989	Oak.-NY (AL) . .	OF	125	433	70	130	17	6	3	46	22	.300
1990	NY (AL)-Cal	OF	120	403	52	135	7	9	2	35	21	.335
	Totals		454	1559	251	474	51	29	11	157	96	.304

Dave Winfield made it back after missing '89 season.

LANCE PARRISH 34 6-3 220   **Bats R Throws R**

Fine all-around season for veteran catcher . . .
Ranked No. 1 in AL in throwing out runners,
nailing 55 of 117 attempted thieves for 47 percent . . . Had fielding percentage of .993 . . .
His batting average (.268) and homer total (24)
were his best since '85 . . . Hit .304 vs. lefties
. . . Hit .292 with runners on base . . . Was tops
among AL catchers in slugging percentage (.451)
. . . Made $1,916,667 in 1990 . . . Born June 15, 1956, in Clair-

ton, Pa.... Turned down football scholarship to UCLA to sign with Tigers... Once served as a bodyguard for Tina Turner.

Year	Club	Pos.	G	AB	R	H	2B	3B	HR	RBI	SB	Avg.
1977	Detroit	C	12	46	10	9	2	0	3	7	0	.196
1978	Detroit	C	85	288	37	63	11	3	14	41	0	.219
1979	Detroit	C	143	493	65	136	26	3	19	65	6	.276
1980	Detroit	C-1B-OF	144	553	79	158	34	6	24	82	6	.286
1981	Detroit	C	96	348	39	85	18	2	10	46	2	.244
1982	Detroit	C-OF	133	486	75	138	19	2	32	87	3	.284
1983	Detroit	C	155	605	80	163	42	3	27	114	1	.269
1984	Detroit	C	147	578	75	137	16	2	33	98	2	.237
1985	Detroit	C	140	549	64	150	27	1	28	98	2	.273
1986	Detroit	C	91	327	53	84	6	1	22	62	0	.257
1987	Philadelphia	C	130	466	42	114	21	0	17	67	0	.245
1988	Philadelphia	C-1B	123	424	44	91	17	2	15	60	0	.215
1989	California	C	124	433	48	103	12	1	17	50	1	.238
1990	California	C-1B	133	470	54	126	14	0	24	70	2	.268
	Totals		1656	6066	765	1557	265	26	285	947	25	.257

CHILI DAVIS 31 6-3 210   Bats S Throws R

Had much more success at home than on the road... Hit .306 with 10 of his 12 homers at Anaheim Stadium... Overall production slipped... After hitting .322 with runners in scoring position in '89, he hit only .219 during '90... Missed 24 games at end of season with strained lower back... Committed three errors in 52 games in outfield... Spent most of time as designated hitter, batting .284 with six homers and 30 RBI... Born Jan. 17, 1960, in Kingston, Jamaica... Made $1.375 million in 1990, then explored second-look free agency last winter.

Year	Club	Pos.	G	AB	R	H	2B	3B	HR	RBI	SB	Avg.
1981	San Francisco	OF	8	15	1	2	0	0	0	0	2	.133
1982	San Francisco	OF	154	641	86	167	27	6	19	76	24	.261
1983	San Francisco	OF	137	486	54	113	21	2	11	59	10	.233
1984	San Francisco	OF	137	499	87	157	21	6	21	81	12	.315
1985	San Francisco	OF	136	481	53	130	25	2	13	56	15	.270
1986	San Francisco	OF	153	526	71	146	28	3	13	70	16	.278
1987	San Francisco	OF	149	500	80	125	22	1	24	76	16	.250
1988	California	OF	158	600	81	161	29	3	21	93	9	.268
1989	California	OF	154	560	81	152	24	1	22	90	3	.271
1990	California	OF	113	412	58	109	17	1	12	58	1	.265
	Totals		1299	4720	652	1262	214	25	156	659	108	.267

JIM ABBOTT 23 6-3 210   Bats L Throws L

Numbers slipped from fine rookie season, though his 211⅔ innings were 30⅓ more than in 1990 . . . With a little luck, his record would have been better . . . In his 14 losses, the Angels scored only 15 runs while he was on the mound . . . His 9 Ks on Sept. 5 at New York tied career high . . . Allowed more hits (246) than any other AL pitcher . . . Was third in league in most runs allowed (106) and most earned runs allowed (106) . . . Ironically, left-handers hit .318 against him . . . Michigan grad was born Sept. 19, 1957, in Flint, Mich. . . . Eighth overall pick in June 1988 draft, following spectacular career in which he received Sullivan Award in 1988 as nation's top amateur athlete and helped U.S. win gold medal in 1988 Olympics . . . Earned $185,000 in 1990.

Year	Club	G	IP	W	L	Pct.	SO	BB	H	ERA
1989	California	29	181⅓	12	12	.500	115	74	190	3.92
1990	California	33	211⅔	10	14	.417	105	72	246	4.51
	Totals	62	393	22	26	.458	220	146	436	4.24

CHUCK FINLEY 28 6-6 212   Bats L Throws L

Enjoyed second straight strong season . . . Named Angels' MVP by his teammates . . . Posted career-best 18-9 record . . . Should have won 20, but didn't receive support in final weeks . . . Didn't win any of his final three starts, despite allowing a total of three runs . . . First Angel to win as many as 18 since Mike Witt in '86 . . . Angels were 22-10 in his starts . . . For the second straight year, he didn't give up a homer to a lefty . . . Hasn't gone two straight games without a decision since '88 . . . Born Nov. 16, 1962, in Monroe, La. . . . Earned $850,000 in 1990.

Year	Club	G	IP	W	L	Pct.	SO	BB	H	ERA
1986	California	25	46⅓	3	1	.750	37	23	40	3.30
1987	California	35	90⅔	2	7	.222	63	43	102	4.67
1988	California	31	194⅓	9	15	.375	111	82	191	4.17
1989	California	29	199⅔	16	9	.640	156	82	171	2.57
1990	California	32	236	18	9	.667	177	81	210	2.40
	Totals	152	767	48	41	.539	544	311	714	3.22

KIRK McCASKILL 29 6-1 196   Bats R Throws R

For fourth time in six years, he reached double digits in wins . . . Ranked 10th in AL with 3.25 ERA . . . In his 11 losses, he gave up just nine runs before leaving . . . Pitched into the seventh inning 13 times . . . Will always be remembered by the Griffey family as he gave up back-to-back homers to Ken Sr. and Ken Jr. Sept. 14 . . . Underwent postseason surgery to remove spurs from his right elbow . . . Earned $967,500 in 1990 . . . Born April 9, 1961, in Kapuskasing, Ont., Canada . . . Was All-American hockey player for the University of Vermont and the first collegian taken in '81 NHL draft, by Winnipeg Jets.

Year	Club	G	IP	W	L	Pct.	SO	BB	H	ERA
1985	California	30	189⅔	12	12	.500	102	64	189	4.70
1986	California	34	246⅓	17	10	.630	202	92	207	3.36
1987	California	14	74⅔	4	6	.400	56	34	84	5.67
1988	California	23	146⅓	8	6	.571	98	61	155	4.31
1989	California	32	212	15	10	.600	107	59	202	2.93
1990	California	29	174⅓	12	11	.522	78	72	161	3.25
	Totals	162	1043⅓	68	55	.553	643	382	998	3.80

BRYAN HARVEY 27 6-2 215   Bats R Throws R

Became Angels' all-time leader in saves with 67, passing four relievers in '90—Dave LaRoche (65), Donnie Moore (61), Bob Lee (58) and Minnie Rojas (43) . . . Finished season with 25 saves in 31 chances . . . Was successful in seven straight opportunities during one stretch . . . Posted 2.10 ERA in first 48 appearances, but coughed up 10 runs in final six games to finish at 3.22 . . . Averaged 11.5 strikeouts per nine innings . . . Opponents hit just .201 against him—.208 by lefties and .195 by righties . . . Earned $332,500 in 1990 . . . Born June 2, 1963, in Chattanooga, Tenn.

Year	Club	G	IP	W	L	Pct.	SO	BB	H	ERA
1987	California	3	5	0	0	.000	3	2	6	0.00
1988	California	50	76	7	5	.583	67	20	59	2.13
1989	California	51	55	3	3	.500	78	41	36	3.44
1990	California	54	64⅓	4	4	.500	82	35	45	3.22
	Totals	158	200⅓	14	12	.538	230	98	146	2.79

MARK LANGSTON 30 6-2 190   **Bats R Throws L**

What a difference $16 million made . . . Was biggest bust this side of Royals' Mark Davis . . . After signing momentous five-year deal, he lost a career-high 17 games . . . For the first time since 1985, he failed to post 200 strikeouts . . . Gave up at least 100 walks for the fifth straight year . . . Significant stat: Opponents hit .245 with the bases empty against him, but .278 with runners on . . . At least things started well . . . In his debut with Angels April 11 against Seattle, he teamed with Mike Witt to record the first of nine no-hitters thrown in majors last year . . . Threw seven innings and 98 pitches before being relieved in that game . . . Born Aug. 20, 1960, in San Diego.

Year	Club	G	IP	W	L	Pct.	SO	BB	H	ERA
1984	Seattle	35	225	17	10	.630	204	118	188	3.40
1985	Seattle	24	126⅔	7	14	.333	72	91	122	5.47
1986	Seattle	37	239⅓	12	14	.462	245	123	234	4.85
1987	Seattle	35	272	19	13	.594	262	114	242	3.84
1988	Seattle	35	261⅓	15	11	.577	235	110	222	3.34
1989	Seattle	10	73⅓	4	5	.444	60	19	60	3.56
1989	Montreal	24	176⅔	12	9	.571	175	93	138	2.39
1990	California	33	223	10	17	.370	195	104	215	4.40
	Totals	233	1597⅓	96	93	.508	1448	772	1421	3.88

TOP PROSPECTS

DAMION EASLEY 21 5-11 155   **Bats R Throws R**

Quality shortstop played for Quad City (A) last year and is expected to make the jump to Midland (AA) . . . Batted .274 with 10 homers and 56 RBI . . . Selected in 30th round in 1988 draft . . . Born Nov. 11, 1969, in Long Beach, Cal. . . . Attended Long Beach State.

KYLE ABBOTT 23 6-4 200   **Bats L Throws L**

Very close to breaking in with Angels' pitching staff . . . Spent most of season with Midland (AA), where he fashioned a 6-9 record and 4.14 ERA in 24 games . . . For Edmonton (AAA), he was 1-0 in three games . . . Selected in first round of 1989 draft . . . Born Feb. 18, 1968, in Newburyport, Mass.

MARK ZAPPELLI 24 6-0 160   **Bats R Throws R**
Relief pitcher posted 3-4 record and 4.40 ERA in 35 games for
Midland (AA) . . . Also pitched for Palm Springs (A) and went
0-1 with a 2.45 ERA in 21 games . . . In '89, he posted 23 saves
in 48 games for Quad City (A) . . . Was 14th-round draft pick in
1989, out of Cal Poly San Luis Obispo . . . Born July 21, 1966,
in Santa Rosa, Cal.

MANAGER DOUG RADER: His sophomore season with Angels was a far cry from his freshman campaign . . . After guiding his club to 91-71 record in 1989—only the fourth time a manager posted a winning record in his first year with the Angels—he couldn't work the same magic in 1990 . . . Wound up at 80-82 in 1990 as Angels finished 23 games behind the first-place A's . . . His career managerial record is 327-354 . . . Managed Rangers from 1983-85 . . . Won five Gold Gloves as a third baseman . . . Played most of 11 seasons with Astros and finished with Padres and Blue Jays . . . Still among Houston's leaders in hits, doubles, homers, RBI, runs, at-bats, extra-base hits, total bases and slugging percentage . . . Born July 30, 1944, in Chicago.

ALL-TIME ANGEL SEASON RECORDS

BATTING: Rod Carew, .339, 1983
HRs: Reggie Jackson, 39, 1982
RBI: Don Baylor, 139, 1979
STEALS: Mickey Rivers, 70, 1975
WINS: Clyde Wright, 22, 1970
        Nolan Ryan, 22, 1974
STRIKEOUTS: Nolan Ryan, 383, 1973

CHICAGO WHITE SOX

TEAM DIRECTORY: Chairman: Jerry Reinsdorf; Vice Chairman: Eddie Einhorn; Exec. VP: Howard Pizer; VP-Baseball Adm.: Jack Gould; Sr. VP-Major League Oper.: Ron Schueler; VP-Scouting and Minor League Oper.: Larry Monroe; Dir. Baseball Adm.: Dan Evans; Dir. Pub. Rel./Community Affairs: Doug Abel; Mgr. Media Rel.: Dana Noel; Trav. Sec.: Glen Rosenbaum; Mgr.: Jeff Torborg. Home: Comiskey Park (43,000). Field distances: 347, l.f. line; 382, l.c.; 409, c.f.; 382, r.c., 347, r.f. line. Spring training: Sarasota, Fla.

Bobby Thigpen became all-time savior with a record 57.

SCOUTING REPORT

HITTING: No hitting instructor received as much attention last year as Walt Hriniak. A disciple of the late Charley Lau, Hriniak was criticized for changing several players' batting strokes and developing hitters who sacrifice power potential to hit for higher averages. The White Sox were no offensive machine—they ranked ninth in runs (682), 10th in average (.258) and tied for 11th in homers (106)—but they won 94 games.

The White Sox were all but missing from the lists of the AL's departmental leaders. Sammy Sosa (.233, 15, 70) was second in triples with 10 and Ivan Calderon (.273, 14, 74), now gone to Montreal in the Tim Raines trade, was third in doubles with 44. Carlton Fisk (.285, 18, 65) shows no signs of slowing up, young first baseman Frank Thomas (.330, 7, 31) looks like a comer, Dan Pasqua (.274, 13, 58) flashes occasional power and Cory Snyder—obtained from the Indians in a deal last winter—should improve on his 14-homer, 55-RBI totals of 1990.

Raines (.287, 9, 62) will add speed (49 stolen bases in 1990) as leadoff man and should get new life on grass.

PITCHING: Melido Perez (13-14, 4.61) and Jack McDowell (14-9, 3.82) are the top holdovers from an inconsistent starting staff now that Eric King has been dealt to Cleveland. But, last year, the White Sox fashioned the second-lowest ERA in the league (3.61), a dramatic improvement over their 11th-ranked 4.23 mark in 1989.

The big key to the improvement was a deep and talented bullpen, where there are no problems unless overwork becomes a factor. Closer Bobby Thigpen (4-6, 1.83) destroyed the single-season record for saves with 57, but he worked in 77 games.

FIELDING: Nobody played shortstop in 1990 like Ozzie Guillen, who was rewarded with his first Gold Glove. Fisk was just as wonderful handling a young pitching staff and he left strong-armed Ron Karkovice still waiting for his chance behind the plate.

OUTLOOK: Larry Himes, who turned the White Sox into contenders, was a candidate for Executive of the Year, even after his dismissal as GM. New GM Ron Schueler might enjoy more success, because he has been given the go-ahead to spend some money.

But last season, the White Sox proved that lesser-paid guys

CHICAGO WHITE SOX 1991 ROSTER

MANAGER Jeff Torborg
Coaches—Terry Bevington, Sammy Ellis, Walt Hriniak, Dave LaRoche, Joe Nossek

PITCHERS

No.	Name	1990 Club	W-L	IP	SO	ERA	B-T	Ht.	Wt.	Born
—	Alvarez, Wilson	Birmingham	5-1	46	36	4.27	L-L	6-1	175	3/24/70 Venezuela
		Vancouver	7-7	75	35	6.00				
—	Carter, Jeff	Jacksonville	6-3	117	76	1.64	R-R	6-3	195	12/3/64 Tampa, FL
—	Drahman, Brian	Birmingham	6-4	90	72	4.08	R-R	6-3	205	1/7/66 Kenton, KY
45	Edwards, Wayne	Chicago (AL)	5-3	95	63	3.22	L-L	6-5	185	3/7/64 Burbank, CA
32	Fernandez, Alex	Sarasota (GCL)	1-0	10	10	3.60	R-R	6-1	205	2/13/69 Miami, FL
		Sarasota (FSL)	1-1	15	23	1.84				
		Birmingham	4-0	25	27	1.08				
		Chicago (AL)	5-5	88	61	3.80				
—	Garcia, Ramon	Sarasota (FSL)	9-4	157	130	3.95	R-R	6-2	200	12/9/69 Venezuela
		Vancouver	0-0	1	1	0.00				
—	Hall, Grady	Vancouver	13-8	185	108	4.24	L-R	6-4	200	5/29/64 Findlay, OH
—	Harrison, Brian	Riverside	5-2	48	55	1.19	L-L	6-1	180	11/26/66 Bluefield, WV
—	Hernandez, Roberto	Birmingham	8-5	108	64	3.67	R-R	6-4	220	11/11/64 Puerto Rico
		Vancouver	3-5	79	49	2.84				
27	Hibbard, Greg	Chicago (AL)	14-9	211	92	3.16	L-L	6-0	190	9/3/64 New Orleans, LA
	Hough, Charlie	Texas	12-12	219	114	4.07	R-R	6-2	190	1/5/48 Honolulu, HI
52	Kutzler, Jerry	Vancouver	5-7	114	73	4.20	R-L	6-1	175	3/25/65 Waukegan, IL
		Chicago (AL)	2-1	31	21	6.03				
29	McDowell, Jack	Chicago (AL)	14-9	205	165	3.82	R-R	6-5	179	1/16/66 Van Nuys, CA
30	Pall, Donn	Chicago (AL)	3-5	76	39	3.32	R-R	6-1	180	1/11/62 Chicago, IL
34	Patterson, Ken	Chicago (AL)	2-1	66	40	3.39	L-L	6-4	210	7/8/64 Costa Mesa, CA
33	Perez, Melido	Chicago (AL)	13-14	197	161	4.61	R-R	6-4	180	2/15/66 Dominican Republic
43	Peterson, Adam	Vancouver	4-1	43	30	2.09	R-R	6-3	190	12/11/65 Long Beach, CA
		Chicago (AL)	2-5	85	29	4.55				
31	Radinsky, Scott	Chicago (AL)	6-1	52	46	4.82	L-L	6-3	190	3/3/68 Glendale, CA
46	Rosenberg, Steve	Vancouver	6-5	88	74	3.57	L-L	6-0	185	10/31/64 Brooklyn, NY
		Chicago (AL)	1-0	10	4	5.40				
—	Scheid, Rich	Birmingham	2-1	45	37	2.22	L-L	6-3	185	2/3/65 Staten Island, NY
		Vancouver	2-2	39	38	3.20				
37	Thigpen, Bobby	Chicago (AL)	4-6	89	70	1.83	R-R	6-3	195	7/17/63 Tallahassee, FL

CATCHERS

No.	Name	1990 Club	H	HR	RBI	Pct.	B-T	Ht.	Wt.	Born
72	Fisk, Carlton	Chicago (AL)	129	18	65	.285	R-R	6-2	223	12/26/47 Bellows Falls, VT
20	Karkovice, Ron	Chicago (AL)	45	6	20	.246	R-R	6-1	215	8/8/63 Union, NJ
—	Merullo, Matt	Birmingham	110	8	50	.291	L-R	6-2	200	8/4/65 Ridgefield, CT

INFIELDERS

No.	Name	1990 Club	H	HR	RBI	Pct.	B-T	Ht.	Wt.	Born
—	Bernhardt, Cesar	Birmingham	160	6	82	.279	R-R	5-9	148	1/18/69 Dominican Republic
7	Fletcher, Scott	Chicago (AL)	123	4	56	.242	R-R	5-11	173	7/30/58 Ft. Walton Beach, FL
14	Grebeck, Craig	Chicago (AL)	20	1	9	.168	R-R	5-8	160	12/29/64 Johnstown, PA
		Vancouver	8	1	3	.195				
13	Guillen, Ozzie	Chicago (AL)	144	1	58	.279	L-R	5-11	150	1/20/64 Venezuela
12	Lyons, Steve	Chicago (AL)	28	1	11	.192	L-R	6-3	195	6/3/60 Tacoma, WA
24	Martinez, Carlos	Chicago (AL)	61	4	24	.224	R-R	6-5	175	8/11/65 Venezuela
21	Stark, Matt	Birmingham	140	14	109	.309	R-R	6-4	245	1/21/65 Whittier, CA
		Chicago (AL)	4	0	3	.250				
35	Thomas, Frank	Birmingham	114	18	71	.323	R-R	6-4	240	5/27/68 Columbus, GA
		Chicago (AL)	63	7	31	.330				
23	Ventura, Robin	Chicago (AL)	123	5	54	.249	L-R	6-1	192	7/14/67 Santa Maria, CA

OUTFIELDERS

No.	Name	1990 Club	H	HR	RBI	Pct.	B-T	Ht.	Wt.	Born
1	Johnson, Lance	Chicago (AL)	154	1	51	.285	L-L	5-11	155	7/7/63 Cincinnati, OH
—	Lee, Derek	Birmingham	105	7	75	.255	L-R	6-0	195	7/22/66 Tampa, FL
—	Martin, Norberto	Vancouver	35	3	45	.266	S-R	5-10	164	12/10/66 Puerto Rico
44	Pasqua, Dan	Chicago (AL)	89	13	58	.274	L-L	6-0	203	10/17/61 Yonkers, NY
—	Raines, Tim	Montreal	131	9	62	.287	S-R	5-8	185	9/16/59 Sanford, FL
28	Snyder, Cory	Cleveland	102	14	55	.233	R-R	6-3	185	11/11/62 Englewood, CA
25	Sosa, Sammy	Chicago (AL)	124	15	70	.233	R-R	6-0	175	11/10/68 Dominican Republic

can compete with the high rollers like Oakland. The key is for manager Jeff Torborg to maintain that 94-68 chemistry for another season. With such a young team, that can be a tough chore.

WHITE SOX PROFILES

CARLTON FISK 43 6-2 223   Bats R Throws R

Wonderful year for the ageless catcher... "Pudge" became the game's most prolific home-run hitter among catchers, with 333 ... Surpassed Johnny Bench's previous homer record of 327 Aug. 17 at Texas... On the same day, he set all-time White Sox homer record with No. 187, breaking Harold Baines' mark ... His overall homer total is 354, 42nd on the all-time list... Has 50 homers since his 40th birthday; only Darrell Evans (60) had more homers in his 40s... Career hit total is 2,192 ... Although he played 1,078 games for Boston, he has played more for Chicago (1,199)... Stole seven bases, falling four shy of Honus Wagner's all-time record for 42-year-olds... Registered his 1,200th career RBI July 29... Wears No. 72, the reverse of his number in Boston... Salary was $1.75 million in 1990... Born in Bellows Falls, Vt., the day after Christmas in 1947.

Year	Club	Pos.	G	AB	R	H	2B	3B	HR	RBI	SB	Avg.
1969	Boston	C	2	5	0	0	0	0	0	0	0	.000
1971	Boston	C	14	48	7	15	2	1	2	6	0	.313
1972	Boston	C	131	457	74	134	28	9	22	61	5	.293
1973	Boston	C	135	508	65	125	21	0	26	71	7	.246
1974	Boston	C	52	187	36	56	12	1	11	26	5	.299
1975	Boston	C	79	263	47	87	14	4	10	52	4	.331
1976	Boston	C	134	487	76	124	17	5	17	58	12	.255
1977	Boston	C	152	536	106	169	26	3	26	102	7	.315
1978	Boston	C-OF	157	571	94	162	39	5	20	88	7	.284
1979	Boston	C-OF	91	320	49	87	23	2	10	42	3	.272
1980	Boston	C-OF-1B-3B	131	478	73	138	25	3	18	62	11	.289
1981	Chicago (AL) ..	C-1B-3B-OF	96	338	44	89	12	0	7	45	3	.263
1982	Chicago (AL) ..	C-1B	135	476	66	127	17	3	14	65	17	.267
1983	Chicago (AL) ..	C	138	488	85	141	26	4	26	86	9	.289
1984	Chicago (AL) ..	C	102	359	54	83	20	1	21	43	6	.231
1985	Chicago (AL) ..	C	153	543	85	129	23	1	37	107	17	.238
1986	Chicago (AL) ..	OF-C	125	457	42	101	11	0	14	63	2	.221
1987	Chicago (AL) ..	C-1B-OF	135	454	68	116	22	1	23	71	1	.256
1988	Chicago (AL) ..	C	76	253	37	70	8	1	19	50	0	.277
1989	Chicago (AL) ..	C	103	375	47	110	25	2	13	68	1	.293
1990	Chicago (AL) ..	C	137	452	65	129	21	0	18	65	7	.285
	Totals		2278	8055	1220	2192	392	46	354	1231	124	.272

OZZIE GUILLEN 27 5-11 150   Bats L Throws R

Slick-fielding shortstop and team leader won Gold Glove in 1990 . . . Elected co-captain April 2, sharing duties with Carlton Fisk . . . Had only one home run, hitting it off Nolan Ryan, of all people . . . Career homer total is seven . . . Enjoyed a four-hit game May 6 . . . Established career highs in RBI (58), walks (26) and games (160) . . . Had a $1-million contract in 1990 . . . Born Jan. 20, 1964, in Ocumare del Tuy, Venezuela . . . AL Rookie of the Year in '85 . . . A product of the Padres' system, but never played for San Diego . . . Was sent to Chicago in LaMarr Hoyt trade in 1985 . . . It's easy to determine which team made the better deal . . . Began pro career when he was just 17.

Year Club	Pos.	G	AB	R	H	2B	3B	HR	RBI	SB	Avg.
1985 Chicago (AL) ..	SS	150	491	71	134	21	9	1	33	7	.273
1986 Chicago (AL) ..	SS	159	547	58	137	19	4	2	47	8	.250
1987 Chicago (AL) ..	SS	149	560	64	156	22	7	2	51	25	.279
1988 Chicago (AL) ..	SS	156	566	58	148	16	7	0	39	25	.261
1989 Chicago (AL) ..	SS	155	597	63	151	20	8	1	54	36	.253
1990 Chicago (AL) ..	SS	160	516	61	144	21	4	1	58	13	.279
Totals		929	3277	375	870	119	39	7	282	114	.265

RON KARKOVICE 27 6-1 215   Bats R Throws R

A splendid defensive catcher, perhaps the best in baseball, "Karko" would play much more on a club that didn't have Carlton Fisk . . . Played in 68 games and started only 50 . . . Was remarkable in throwing out potential base-stealers . . . In '87, he threw out five straight and 10 of 15 . . . An excellent bunter . . . Has above-average speed for a catcher . . . Most memorable day of 1990 season was Aug. 20, when he sprinted for an inside-the-park grand slam to lift the White Sox past the Twins . . . The only four-hit day in his career was July 14 against New York . . . Six homers were a career high . . . Born Aug. 8, 1963, in Union, N.J. . . . White Sox' No. 1 pick in '82 draft . . . A bargain at $108,000 last year.

Year Club	Pos.	G	AB	R	H	2B	3B	HR	RBI	SB	Avg.
1986 Chicago (AL) ..	C	37	97	13	24	7	0	4	13	1	.247
1987 Chicago (AL) ..	C	39	85	7	6	0	0	2	7	3	.071
1988 Chicago (AL) ..	C	46	115	10	20	4	0	3	9	4	.174
1989 Chicago (AL) ..	C	71	182	21	48	9	2	3	24	0	.264
1990 Chicago (AL) ..	C	68	183	30	45	10	0	6	20	2	.246
Totals		261	662	81	143	30	2	18	73	10	.216

FRANK THOMAS 22 6-5 240   Bats R Throws R

Promoted to the parent club Aug. 1 after a tremendous season in the minors . . . Named Minor League Player of the Year by *Baseball America* . . . First baseman hit .323 with 18 homers and 71 RBI in 353 at-bats for Birmingham (AA) . . . His 112 walks were 16 shy of the Southern League record . . . Although he was 0-for-6 after his promotion, he went on a 15-for-33 tear . . . Had a nine-game hitting streak snapped Sept. 15 . . . Finished the season with a 13-game hitting streak . . . Hit in 45 of 60 games . . . Not surprisingly, his idols are also huge— Dave Parker and Dave Winfield . . . Attended Auburn on a football scholarship, catching three passes as a tight end in his freshman year . . . Also played baseball, drawing comparisons to another Auburn two-sporter, Bo Jackson, but this guy gave up football to concentrate on baseball . . . In three seasons at Auburn, he batted .382 and broke school records for homers (49) and RBI (205) . . . White Sox drafted him No. 1 in the '89 draft, but he thinks the club took too long bringing him to the bigs . . . Born May 27, 1968, in Columbus, Ga.

Year Club	Pos.	G	AB	R	H	2B	3B	HR	RBI	SB	Avg.
1990 Chicago (AL) . .	1B	60	191	39	63	11	3	7	31	0	.330

DAN PASQUA 29 6-0 203   Bats L Throws L

Like so many other White Sox, he had the most productive season of his career . . . Set career highs in RBI (58), doubles (27), multiple-hit games (22) and multiple-RBI games (17) . . . Reached double-digit homers (13) for the fifth straight season . . . Started in right, left and, mostly, as designated hitter . . . Amassed 90 total starts . . . Born Oct. 17, 1961, in Yonkers, N.Y. . . . Salary was $325,000 . . . Won All-American honors at William Paterson College in '81 and '82 . . . Acquired in five-player deal that sent Rich Dotson to Yankees before '88 season . . . Yanks' third-round pick in 1982 draft.

Year Club	Pos.	G	AB	R	H	2B	3B	HR	RBI	SB	Avg.
1985 New York (AL)	OF	60	148	17	31	3	1	9	25	0	.209
1986 New York (AL)	OF-1B	102	280	44	82	17	0	16	45	2	.293
1987 New York (AL)	OF-1B	113	318	42	74	7	1	17	42	0	.233
1988 Chicago (AL) . .	OF-1B	129	422	48	96	16	2	20	50	1	.227
1989 Chicago (AL) . .	OF	73	246	26	61	9	1	11	47	1	.248
1990 Chicago (AL) . .	OF	112	325	43	89	27	3	13	58	1	.274
Totals		589	1739	220	433	79	8	86	267	5	.249

TIM RAINES 31 5-8 185　　　　Bats S Throws R

Twelve-year Expo was traded to White Sox in December with minor leaguer Jeff Carter and minor leaguer to be named for Ivan Calderon and Barry Jones . . . Not quite the game-breaker he was before years on artificial turf caught up to him, "Rock" is still very productive . . . Finished sixth among 1990 NL stolen-base leaders (49) and ranks ninth on all-time list (634), 15 behind Bert Campaneris . . . Left fielder reached numerous milestones last season: 500th RBI, 1,500th hit, 600th steal and 5,000th at-bat . . . Born Sept. 16, 1959, in Sanford, Fla. . . . Selected by Expos in fifth round of 1977 draft . . . Re-signed with Expos as free agent, May 1, 1987 . . . Highest-paid Expo in 1990, earning $2,055,555.

Year	Club	Pos.	G	AB	R	H	2B	3B	HR	RBI	SB	Avg.
1979	Montreal	PR	6	0	3	0	0	0	0	0	2	.000
1980	Montreal	2B-OF	15	20	5	1	0	0	0	0	5	.050
1981	Montreal	OF-2B	88	313	61	95	13	7	5	37	71	.304
1982	Montreal	OF-2B	156	647	90	179	32	8	4	43	78	.277
1983	Montreal	OF-2B	156	615	133	183	32	8	11	71	90	.298
1984	Montreal	OF-2B	160	622	106	192	38	9	8	60	75	.309
1985	Montreal	OF	150	575	115	184	30	13	11	41	70	.320
1986	Montreal	OF	151	580	91	194	35	10	9	62	70	.334
1987	Montreal	OF	139	530	123	175	34	8	18	68	50	.330
1988	Montreal	OF	109	429	66	116	19	7	12	48	33	.270
1989	Montreal	OF	145	517	76	148	29	6	9	60	41	.286
1990	Montreal	OF	130	457	65	131	11	5	9	62	49	.287
	Totals		1405	5305	934	1598	273	81	96	552	634	.301

SAMMY SOSA 22 6-0 175　　　　Bats R Throws R

Posted career highs in homers (15), RBI (70), triples (10), doubles (26), and steals (32) . . . Four of his homers led off games . . . Outfielder displayed strong, accurate arm by collecting 14 assists . . . Earned minimum of $100,000 . . . Obtained in five-player deal that sent Harold Baines to Texas, July 19, 1989 . . . After trade, he hit .367 in 13 games for Vancouver (AAA) and made big-league debut Aug. 22 . . . Born Nov. 10, 1968, in San Pedro de Macoris, Dominican Republic . . . Was only 16 when signed by Rangers.

Year	Club	Pos.	G	AB	R	H	2B	3B	HR	RBI	SB	Avg.
1989	Tex.-Chi. (AL)	OF	58	183	27	47	8	0	4	13	7	.257
1990	Chicago (AL) . .	OF	153	532	72	124	26	10	15	70	32	.233
	Totals		211	715	99	171	34	10	19	83	39	.239

BOBBY THIGPEN 27 6-3 195   Bats R Throws R

Enjoyed the most productive season of any reliever in history . . . His 57 saves set an all-time season record, a record that may be as enduring as Joe DiMaggio's hitting streak and Roger Maris' single-season homer output . . . Eclipsed Dave Righetti's saves record (46 in 1986) Sept. 3 at Kansas City . . . Saved his 40th game quicker than any reliever in history, on Aug. 19 in game No. 118. Bruce Sutter reached 40th save in game No. 141 . . . Shattered White Sox saves record with No. 35 Aug. 4, eclipsing his own mark of 34, reached in both '88 and '89 . . . Had eight blown saves in 1990 . . . Named AL Pitcher of the Month for May . . . Was underpaid at $340,000 . . . Born July 17, 1963, in Tallahassee, Fla. . . . Teamed with Will Clark and Rafael Palmeiro at Mississippi State. . . . Has 148 career saves.

Year	Club	G	IP	W	L	Pct.	SO	BB	H	ERA
1986	Chicago (AL)	20	35⅔	2	0	1.000	20	12	26	1.77
1987	Chicago (AL)	51	89	7	5	.583	52	24	86	2.73
1988	Chicago (AL)	68	90	5	8	.385	62	33	96	3.30
1989	Chicago (AL)	61	79	2	6	.250	47	40	62	3.76
1990	Chicago (AL)	77	88⅔	4	6	.400	70	32	60	1.83
	Totals.	277	382⅓	20	25	.444	251	141	330	2.78

JACK McDOWELL 25 6-5 179   Bats R Throws R

Enjoyed fine '90 season after spending all of '89 working in Triple-A or rehabilitating a hip problem . . . Led staff with 165 strikeouts and four complete games . . . Tossed three-hitter at Oakland Aug. 20 . . . Had a pair of 10-strikeout games . . . Won six straight games between August and September . . . His salary was $130,000 . . . Born Jan. 16, 1966, in Van Nuys, Cal. . . . Led Stanford to College World Series title in 1987 . . . Had three-year college mark of 35-13 with 3.58 ERA . . . After joining White Sox in late '87, he threw 13⅓ scoreless innings out of the gate and was 2-0 with a 1.93 ERA in four starts . . . Struggled throughout '88, posting 5-10 record, and experienced first hip injury in August.

Year	Club	G	IP	W	L	Pct.	SO	BB	H	ERA
1987	Chicago (AL)	4	28	3	0	1.000	15	6	16	1.93
1988	Chicago (AL)	26	158⅔	5	10	.333	84	68	147	3.97
1990	Chicago (AL)	33	205	14	9	.609	165	77	189	3.82
	Totals.	63	391⅔	22	19	.537	264	151	352	3.75

MELIDO PEREZ 25 6-4 180   Bats R Throws R

Highlight of season was no-hitter June 12 vs. Yankees in game that lasted only six innings because of rain . . . It was 38th no-hitter in history that went fewer than nine innings . . . Joined brother Pascual Perez on no-hit list . . . Pascual threw his no-no in 1988 and it was also an abbreviated performance (five innings) . . . Only other brother tandem with no-hitters are Bob and Ken Forsch . . . Last White Sox pitcher with a no-no had been Joe Cowley in 1986 . . . Workhorse of staff, starting 35 games and throwing 197 innings . . . Had a string of 16 scoreless innings . . . First signed by Royals in '83 . . . Traded to White Sox after '87 season . . . Born Feb. 15, 1966, in San Cristobal, Dominican Republic . . . Earned $228,000 in 1990.

Year	Club	G	IP	W	L	Pct.	SO	BB	H	ERA
1987	Kansas City	3	10⅓	1	1	.500	5	5	18	7.84
1988	Chicago (AL)	32	197	12	10	.545	138	72	186	3.79
1989	Chicago (AL)	31	183⅓	11	14	.440	141	90	187	5.01
1990	Chicago (AL)	35	197	13	14	.481	161	86	177	4.61
	Totals	101	587⅔	37	39	.487	445	253	568	4.52

TOP PROSPECTS

WILSON ALVAREZ 21 6-1 175   Bats L Throws L

Starting pitcher began the season with Vancouver (AAA), but was later sent down to Birmingham (AA) . . . Went 7-7 with a 6.00 ERA in 17 games for Vancouver, but his numbers improved to 5-1 and 4.27 in seven games for Birmingham . . . The relative unknown in the Harold Baines deal that also brought Sammy Sosa and Scott Fletcher to White Sox from Texas, July 29, 1989 . . . Born March 24, 1970, in Maracaibo, Venezuela.

CESAR BERNHARDT 22 5-9 150   Bats R Throws R

Named MVP for Birmingham (AA) . . . Second baseman led Southern League in hits . . . Missed only two games all season . . . Hit .279 with six homers and 82 RBI . . . Born Jan. 18, 1969, in San Pedro de Macoris, Dominican Republic.

GREG PERSCHKE 23 6-3 180   Bats R Throws R

Short reliever ranked second among all minor leaguers in ERA, posting combined mark of 1.49 while splitting time between Birmingham (AA) and Sarasota (A) . . . Went 3-1 with 2.60 for Birmingham and 7-3 with 1.21 for Sarasota . . . Posted nine saves for Sarasota . . . Born Aug. 3, 1967, in LaPorte, Ind. . . . Drafted in 24th round of 1989 lottery.

MANAGER JEFF TORBORG: Deserved recipient of AL Manager of the Year honors in 1990 . . . Turned a team that went 69-92 in '89 into one of the best in the majors . . . Club's 1990 record of 94-68 was second-best in the American League and third-best in baseball . . . Proved to be an excellent mentor for a young pitching staff . . . Took over the White Sox after the '88 season, replacing Jim Fregosi . . . Managed three unproductive seasons in Cleveland before being fired in the middle of the '79 season . . . Posted 157-201 mark for Indians . . . During his 10 years between managing stints, he served as a Yankees coach . . . A former Dodger and Angel, he caught three no-hitters—Sandy Koufax ('65), Bill Singer ('70) and Nolan Ryan ('73) . . . A great college player, he hit .537 his senior year at Rutgers, the highest all-time NCAA batting average . . . At Rutgers, he earned a B.S. in education. At Montclair State, he earned a master's in athletic administration . . . Born Nov. 26, 1941, in Westfield, N.J. . . . Overall managerial mark is 320-361.

ALL-TIME WHITE SOX SEASON RECORDS

BATTING: Luke Appling, .388, 1936
HRs: Dick Allen, 37, 1972
         Carlton Fisk, 37, 1985
RBI: Zeke Bonura, 138, 1936
STEALS: Rudy Law, 77, 1983
WINS: Ed Walsh, 40, 1908
STRIKEOUTS: Ed Walsh, 269, 1908

KANSAS CITY ROYALS

TEAM DIRECTORY: Chairman: Ewing Kauffman; Pres.: Joe Burke; Exec. VP-GM: Spencer Robinson; Dir. Scouting: Art Stewart; VP-Dir. Player Pers.: Joe Klein; VP-Pub. Rel.: Dean Vogelaar; VP-Marketing, Broadcasting: Dennis Cryder; Trav. Sec.: Dave Witty; Mgr.: John Watham. Home: Royals Stadium (40,625). Field distances: 330, l.f. line, 385, l.c.; 410, c.f.; 385, r.c.; 330, r.f. line. Spring training: Baseball City Stadium, Orlando, Fla.

SCOUTING REPORT

HITTING: Any lineup that includes George Brett figures to be exciting, even when he's pushing 40. Last season, Brett (.329, 14, 87) was pondering retirement when his average dipped to the low .200s in May, but he exploded in the second half to capture his third AL batting championship. Apparently, he's not finished yet.

George Brett made it three batting titles in three decades.

The Royals ranked sixth in the AL in runs (707), first in doubles (316), second in triples (44), third in slugging percentage (.395) and in a second-place tie in average (.267) last year. However, they were next-to-last in home runs with 100.

Bo Jackson (.272, 28, 78) figures to get some help from free-agent signee Kirk Gibson (.260, 8, 38, 26 steals with the Dodgers) and Danny Tartabull (.268, 15, 60), if the latter isn't traded. Kevin Seitzer (.275, 6, 38) also returns, unlike veterans Willie Wilson, Frank White and Bob Boone.

PITCHING: Something went drastically wrong in 1990 as opponents hit Royals' pitching at a .264 clip, five points above the league average, and the staff posted its highest ERA since 1983 (3.93).

Bret Saberhagen (5-9, 3.27), sore-armed Mark Gubicza (4-7, 4.50) and Storm Davis (7-10, 4.74) all seemed to be AWOL, making the emergence of Kevin Appler (12-8, 2.76) and Tom Gordon (12-11, 3.73) stand out all the more. Now free-agent signee Mike Boddicker (17-8, 3.36 with the Red Sox) offers manager John Wathan an alternative.

The biggest disappointment of all last year was 1989 NL Cy Young winner Mark Davis, who went from a 1.85 ERA and 44 saves for the Padres to a 5.11 ERA and six saves for the Royals. No wonder the entire Royals bullpen posted an AL-low 33 saves last season.

A return to form by Mark Davis, now that he's reunited with his pitching guru Pat Dobson, and continued success by Jeff Montgomery (6-5, 2.39, 24 Sv) are essential with the loss of Steve Farr to the Yankees as a free agent.

FIELDING: The Royals posted a .980 fielding percentage, tying them for sixth in the AL last year. They committed 122 errors, eight more than in 1989, and allowed 88 unearned runs.

Boddicker won a Gold Glove last year. Kurt Stillwell needs to cut down on his error total (24) at short, but Mike Macfarlane is very smooth behind the plate.

OUTLOOK: Having proven that money doesn't always buy pennants in 1990, the Royals continued their wild pending spree when they signed Boddicker, Gibson and lefty reliever Dan Schatzeder as free agents last winter.

Perhaps the most important acquisition was Dobson, who worked in San Diego when Davis was a world-beater for the

KANSAS CITY ROYALS 1991 ROSTER

MANAGER John Wathan
Coaches—Pat Dobson, Glenn Ezell, Adrian Garrett, Lynn Jones, Bob Schaefer

PITCHERS

No.	Name	1990 Club	W-L	IP	SO	ERA	B-T	Ht.	Wt.	Born
55	Appier, Kevin	Omaha	2-0	18	17	1.50	R-R	6-2	190	12/6/67 Lancaster, CA
		Kansas City	12-8	186	127	2.76				
27	Aquino, Luis	Kansas City	4-1	68	28	3.16	R-R	6-1	190	5/19/65 Puerto Rico
52	Boddicker, Mike	Boston	17-8	228	143	3.36	R-R	5-11	188	8/23/57 Cedar Rapids, IA
39	Campbell, Jim	Memphis	5-5	100	79	2.44	L-L	5-11	175	5/19/66 Santa Maria, CA
		Omaha	2-2	27	19	1.32				
		Kansas City	1-0	10	2	8.38				
50	Cole, Victor	Memphis	3-8	108	102	4.35	S-R	5-10	160	1/23/68 Russia
61	Corbin, Archie	St. Lucie	7-8	118	105	2.91	R-R	6-4	190	12/30/67 Beaumont, TX
28	Crawford, Steve	Kansas City	5-4	80	54	4.16	R-R	6-5	225	4/29/58 Pryor, OK
48	Davis, Mark	Kansas City	2-7	69	73	5.11	L-L	6-4	205	10/19/60 Livermore, CA
14	Davis, Storm	Kansas City	7-10	112	62	4.74	R-R	6-4	200	12/26/61 Dallas, TX
36	Gordon, Tom	Kansas City	12-11	195	175	3.73	R-R	5-9	160	11/18/67 Sebring, FL
23	Gubicza, Mark	Kansas City	4-7	94	71	4.50	R-R	6-5	220	8/14/62 Philadelphia, PA
58	Johnston, Joel	Baseball City	2-4	55	60	4.88	R-R	6-4	220	3/8/67 West Chester, PA
		Memphis	0-0	7	6	6.75				
		Omaha	0-0	3	3	0.00				
57	Magnante, Mike	Omaha	2-5	77	56	4.11	L-L	6-1	180	6/17/65 Glendale, CA
59	Maldonado, Carlos	Memphis	4-5	77	77	2.91	R-R	6-1	200	10/18/66 Panama
		Kansas City	0-0	6	9	9.00				
21	Montgomery, Jeff	Kansas City	6-5	94	94	2.39	R-R	5-11	180	1/7/62 Wellston, OH
18	Saberhagen, Bret	Kansas City	5-9	135	87	3.27	R-R	6-1	185	4/11/64 Chicago Heights, IL
—	Schatzeder, Dan	Hou.-NY (NL)	1-3	70	39	2.20	L-L	6-0	175	12/1/54 Elmhurst, IL
30	Stottlemyre, Mel	Omaha	2-1	42	33	1.51	R-R	6-0	190	12/28/63 Prosser, WA
		Kansas City	0-1	31	14	4.88				
34	Wagner, Hector	Memphis	12-4	153	63	2.03	R-R	6-3	185	11/26/68 Dominican Republic
		Kansas City	0-2	23	14	8.10				

CATCHERS

No.	Name	1990 Club	H	HR	RBI	Pct.	B-T	Ht.	Wt.	Born
15	Macfarlane, Mike	Kansas City	102	6	58	.255	R-R	6-1	200	4/12/64 Stockton, CA
49	Mayne, Brent	Memphis	110	2	61	.267	L-R	6-1	195	4/19/68 Loma Linda, CA
		Kansas City	3	0	1	.231				
53	Pedre, Jorge	Memphis	93	9	54	.258	R-R	5-11	210	10/12/66 Culver City, CA
43	Spehr, Tim	Omaha	69	6	34	.225	R-R	6-2	205	7/2/66 Excelsior Springs, MO

INFIELDERS

No.	Name	1990 Club	H	HR	RBI	Pct.	B-T	Ht.	Wt.	Born
47	Berry, Sean	Memphis	142	14	77	.292	R-R	5-11	200	3/22/66 Santa Monica, CA
		Kansas City	5	0	4	.217				
5	Brett, George	Kansas City	179	14	87	.329	L-R	6-0	200	5/15/53 Glendale, WV
19	Conine, Jeff	Memphis	156	15	95	.320	R-R	6-1	205	6/27/66 Tacoma, WA
		Kansas City	5	0	2	.250				
9	de los Santos, Luis	Omaha	146	5	74	.280	R-R	6-5	200	12/29/66 Dominican Republic
46	Hamelin, Bob	Omaha	63	8	30	.232	L-L	6-0	240	11/29/67 Elizabeth, NJ
31	Howard, David	Memphis	96	5	44	.250	S-R	6-0	165	2/26/67 Sarasota, FL
32	Pecota, Bill	Kansas City	58	5	20	.242	R-R	6-2	190	2/16/60 Redwood City, CA
		Omaha	35	4	13	.302				
33	Seitzer, Kevin	Kansas City	171	6	38	.275	R-R	5-11	190	3/26/62 Springfield, IL
3	Shumpert, Terry	Omaha	39	2	12	.255	R-R	5-11	190	8/16/66 Paducah, KY
		Kansas City	25	0	8	.275				
1	Stillwell, Kurt	Kansas City	126	3	51	.249	S-R	5-11	175	6/4/65 Glendale, CA

OUTFIELDERS

No.	Name	1990 Club	H	HR	RBI	Pct.	B-T	Ht.	Wt.	Born
22	Eisenreich, Jim	Kansas City	139	5	51	.280	L-L	5-11	195	4/18/59 St. Cloud, MN
—	Gibson, Kirk	Los Angeles	82	8	38	.260	L-L	6-3	215	5/28/57 Pontiac, MI
16	Jackson, Bo	Kansas City	110	28	78	.272	R-R	6-1	225	11/30/62 Bessemer, AL
56	McRae, Brian	Memphis	126	10	64	.268	S-R	6-0	180	8/27/67 Bradenton, FL
		Kansas City	48	2	23	.286				
45	Morman, Russ	Omaha	130	13	81	.298	R-R	6-4	215	4/28/62 Independence, MO
		Kansas City	10	1	3	.279				
51	Pulliam, Harvey	Omaha	117	16	72	.268	R-R	6-0	210	10/20/67 San Francisco, CA
24	Schulz, Jeff	Omaha	69	4	27	.299	L-R	6-1	190	6/2/61 Evansville, IN
		Kansas City	17	0	6	.258				
4	Tartabull, Danny	Kansas City	84	15	60	.268	R-R	6-1	205	10/30/62 Miami, FL
25	Thurman, Gary	Kansas City	14	0	3	.233	R-R	5-10	175	11/12/64 Indianapolis, IN
		Omaha	126	0	26	.331				

Padres. If the lefty responds to Dobson's touch, the Royals will be in great shape to take major strides in improving on last season's 75-86 finish.

ROYAL PROFILES

GEORGE BRETT 37 6-0 200   Bats L Throws R

Who would have expected anyone hitting .200 on May 7 to win a batting title? . . . But there's only one George Brett . . . First baseman outlasted Rickey Henderson and Rafael Palmeiro in final days of season to claim third batting crown . . . Hit .388 in the second half . . . Became first player to win batting title in three decades . . . Won previous titles in '76 and '80 . . . Became third-oldest player to win title, behind Ted Williams and Honus Wagner . . . Named AL Player of the Month in July, when he hit safely in 16 straight games . . . Hit for the cycle July 25 at Toronto . . . Collected club-record seven hits in doubleheader vs. Milwaukee Aug. 10 . . . Came out swinging in September, going 56 plate appearances without a walk from Sept. 7-24 (he went 24-for-56) . . . Led league with 59 multiple-hit games . . . Tied for first in AL in doubles . . . Collected career hit No. 2,700 . . . Earned $1,838,661 in 1990 . . . Born May 15, 1953, in Glendale, W. Va.

Year	Club	Pos.	G	AB	R	H	2B	3B	HR	RBI	SB	Avg.
1973	Kansas City ...	3B	13	40	2	5	2	0	0	0	0	.125
1974	Kansas City ...	3B-SS	133	457	49	129	21	5	2	47	8	.282
1975	Kansas City ...	3B-SS	159	634	84	195	35	13	11	89	13	.308
1976	Kansas City ...	3B-SS	159	645	94	215	34	14	7	67	21	.333
1977	Kansas City ...	3B-SS	139	564	105	176	32	13	22	88	14	.312
1978	Kansas City ...	3B-SS	128	510	79	150	45	8	9	62	23	.294
1979	Kansas City ...	3B-1B	154	645	119	212	42	20	23	107	17	.329
1980	Kansas City ...	3B-1B	117	449	87	175	33	9	24	118	15	.390
1981	Kansas City ...	3B	89	347	42	109	27	7	6	43	14	.314
1982	Kansas City ...	3B-OF	144	552	101	166	32	9	21	82	6	.301
1983	Kansas City ...	3B-1B-OF	123	464	90	144	38	2	25	93	0	.310
1984	Kansas City ...	3B	104	377	42	107	21	3	13	69	0	.284
1985	Kansas City ...	3B	155	550	108	184	38	5	30	112	9	.335
1986	Kansas City ...	3B-SS	124	441	70	128	28	4	16	73	1	.290
1987	Kansas City ...	1B-3B	115	427	71	124	18	2	22	78	6	.290
1988	Kansas City ...	1B-SS	157	589	90	180	42	3	24	103	14	.306
1989	Kansas City ...	1B-OF	124	457	67	129	26	3	12	80	14	.282
1990	Kansas City ...	1B-OF-3B	142	544	82	179	45	7	14	87	9	.329
	Totals		2279	8692	1382	2707	559	127	281	1398	184	.311

BO JACKSON 28 6-1 225   Bats R Throws R

Finally learning patience at the plate . . . Outfielder struck out a career-low 128 times and drew a career-high 44 walks . . . He also produced his highest batting average to date . . . However, he played the least number of games in his career . . . On disabled list from July 18-Aug. 25 with a bum right shoulder . . . The same night he was injured, he hit three consecutive home runs off Yanks' Andy Hawkins . . . In first at-bat after DL stint, he homered off Randy Johnson, so he became 19th player in history to homer in four straight at-bats . . . Became third Royal to hit 20 homers four straight years, joining Steve Balboni and John Mayberry . . . In one game Aug. 30 at Oakland, he made two diving catches, threw out two runners and belted a game-tying homer off Dennis Eckersley . . . Hit just .239 with runners in scoring position . . . Lost arbitration case and took home $1 million in 1990 . . . Born Nov. 30, 1962, in Bessemer, Ala. . . . After season, he moved to Los Angeles to continue his football career as star running back for Raiders . . . Real first name is Vincent.

Year	Club	Pos.	G	AB	R	H	2B	3B	HR	RBI	SB	Avg.
1986	Kansas City . . .	OF	25	82	9	17	2	1	2	9	3	.207
1987	Kansas City . . .	OF	116	396	46	93	17	2	22	53	10	.235
1988	Kansas City . . .	OF	124	439	63	108	16	4	25	68	27	.246
1989	Kansas City . . .	OF	135	515	86	132	15	6	32	105	26	.256
1990	Kansas City . . .	OF	111	405	74	110	16	1	28	78	15	.272
	Totals		511	1837	278	460	66	14	109	313	81	.250

KIRK GIBSON 33 6-3 215   Bats L Throws L

Dodger free-agent outfielder signed two-year, $3.3-million pact with Royals, who figure to use him primarily as a DH . . . Has never fully recovered from 1988 injuries that set up his dramatic, ninth-inning, game-winning World Series Game 1 home run off Dennis Eckersley . . . Played in just 89 games . . . Started 69 games in center, a position he feels he is no longer physically capable of playing . . . Began the season on the DL, recovering from '89 surgery to repair a tear in left hamstring . . . Didn't make his 1990 debut until June 2 . . . Hit .290 with runners in scoring position and .375 with a man on third . . . Stole 26 bases in 28 attempts . . . Born May 28, 1957, in Pontiac, Mich. . . . Signed three-year, $4.5-million deal with Dodgers' as free agent prior to 1988 season . . . Tigers' first-round pick in 1978 draft . . . Has flair for October dramatics . . . Was named 1984 World Series MVP with Detroit . . . Was All-American at Michigan State in both football and baseball . . . All those years of contact have taken their toll.

Year	Club	Pos.	G	AB	R	H	2B	3B	HR	RBI	SB	Avg.
1979	Detroit	OF	12	38	3	9	3	0	1	4	3	.237
1980	Detroit	OF	51	175	23	46	2	1	9	16	4	.263
1981	Detroit	OF	83	290	41	95	11	3	9	40	17	.328
1982	Detroit	OF	69	266	34	74	16	2	8	35	9	.278
1983	Detroit	OF	128	401	60	91	12	9	15	51	14	.227
1984	Detroit	OF	149	531	92	150	23	10	27	91	29	.282
1985	Detroit	OF	154	581	96	167	37	5	29	97	30	.287
1986	Detroit	OF	119	441	84	118	11	2	28	86	34	.268
1987	Detroit	OF	128	487	95	135	25	3	24	79	26	.277
1988	Los Angeles	OF	150	542	106	157	28	1	25	76	31	.290
1989	Los Angeles	OF	71	253	35	54	8	2	9	28	12	.213
1990	Los Angeles	OF	89	315	59	82	20	0	8	38	26	.260
	Totals		1203	4320	728	1178	196	38	192	641	235	.273

DANNY TARTABULL 28 6-1 205   Bats R Throws R

Endured an injury-plagued season . . . His 88 games were his fewest in five seasons . . . Despite his time on the sideline, this strong outfielder nearly equaled his '89 power numbers, finishing with 15 homers and 60 RBI in only 313 at-bats . . . Homered on Opening Day, then suffered a tear of right plantaris muscle while working out before next game and didn't play again until May 18 . . . Had 12-game hitting streak in June . . . Belted inside-the-park homer at Seattle June 28 . . . Suffered second injury July 13, tearing left groin muscle, and was out until July 31 . . . Sidelined again from Sept. 8-21 with sore right hip flexor . . . Made $1,650,000 in 1990 . . . Born Nov. 30, 1962, in Miami.

Year	Club	Pos.	G	AB	R	H	2B	3B	HR	RBI	SB	Avg.
1984	Seattle	SS-2B	10	20	3	6	1	0	2	7	0	.300
1985	Seattle	SS-3B	19	61	8	20	7	1	1	7	1	.328
1986	Seattle	OF-2B-3B	137	511	76	138	25	6	25	96	4	.270
1987	Kansas City	OF	158	582	95	180	27	3	34	101	9	.309
1988	Kansas City	OF	146	507	80	139	38	3	26	102	8	.274
1989	Kansas City	OF	133	441	54	118	22	0	18	62	4	.268
1990	Kansas City	OF	88	313	41	84	19	0	15	60	1	.268
	Totals		691	2435	357	685	139	13	121	435	27	.281

KEVIN SEITZER 29 5-11 180   Bats R Throws R

Royals' Mr. Durable . . . Led the club in games and at-bats . . . Leadoff man also topped Royals in runs and walks . . . Posted .953 fielding percentage, tops among league third basemen . . . Learning how to play second base . . . Worked at second in Instructional League and debuted there Aug. 10 . . . Posted career-best 17-game hit streak from April 27-May 16 . . . During the streak, he boosted his average from .219 to .271 . . . Sparkled in June, hitting .330 with a four-hit game and a five-hit game . . . Made $1,001,250 in 1990 . . . Born March 26, 1962, in Springfield, Ill.

Year	Club	Pos.	G	AB	R	H	2B	3B	HR	RBI	SB	Avg.
1986	Kansas City . . .	1B-OF-3B	28	96	16	31	4	1	2	11	0	.323
1987	Kansas City . . .	3B-OF-1B	161	641	105	207	33	8	15	83	12	.323
1988	Kansas City . . .	3B-OF	149	559	90	170	32	5	5	60	10	.304
1989	Kansas City . . .	3B-SS-OF-1B	160	597	78	168	17	2	4	48	17	.281
1990	Kansas City . . .	3B-2B	158	622	91	171	31	5	6	38	7	.275
	Totals		656	2515	380	747	117	21	32	240	46	.297

BRET SABERHAGEN 26 6-1 185   Bats R Throws R

A streaky year for "Sabes" . . . Opened season with 1-3 mark before winning four straight starts and then losing four in a row . . . Underwent surgery on right elbow July 23 and spent two months on the disabled list . . . Dropped final six decisions and was winless in final nine starts, the longest drought of his career . . . Struck out 12 batters June 7 against Angels, but lost, 2-1 . . . If his history repeats itself, look out for him in 1991 . . . In odd-numbered years, he has gone 20-6, 18-10 and 23-6. In even-numbered seasons, he has gone 10-11, 7-12, 14-16 and 5-9 . . . Made $1,400,000 last season . . . Born April 11, 1964, in Chicago Heights, Ill.

Year	Club	G	IP	W	L	Pct.	SO	BB	H	ERA
1984	Kansas City	38	157⅔	10	11	.476	73	36	138	3.48
1985	Kansas City	32	235⅓	20	6	.769	158	38	211	2.87
1986	Kansas City	30	156	7	12	.368	112	29	165	4.15
1987	Kansas City	33	257	18	10	.643	163	53	246	3.36
1988	Kansas City	35	260⅔	14	16	.467	171	59	271	3.80
1989	Kansas City	36	262⅓	23	6	.793	193	43	209	2.16
1990	Kansas City	20	135	5	9	.357	87	28	146	3.27
	Totals	224	1464	97	70	.581	957	286	1386	3.23

MIKE BODDICKER 33 5-11 188   Bats R Throws R

A three-year, $9.25-million contract gave Red Sox free agent a Royal flush after a season in which he achieved second-highest victory total of career (17)... Was perfect 6-0 with 2.77 ERA in final nine starts... Fashioned 9-4 record after a Red Sox loss... Red Sox were 22-12 in his 34 starts... Allowed three earned runs or fewer in 26 starts... Pitched well in losing effort in Game 3 of ALCS, limiting Oakland to four runs, two earned, on six hits in eight innings... Born Aug. 23, 1957, in Cedar Rapids, Iowa... Boston acquired him from Baltimore for Brady Anderson and Curt Schilling, July 29, 1988... Began career with Orioles as sixth-round pick in 1978 draft... Earned $675,000 and a Gold Glove in 1990.

Year	Club	G	IP	W	L	Pct.	SO	BB	H	ERA
1980	Baltimore	1	7	0	1	.000	4	5	6	6.43
1981	Baltimore	2	6	0	0	.000	2	2	6	4.50
1982	Baltimore	7	25⅔	1	0	1.000	20	12	25	3.51
1983	Baltimore	27	179	16	8	.667	120	52	141	2.77
1984	Baltimore	34	261⅓	20	11	.645	128	81	218	2.79
1985	Baltimore	32	203⅓	12	17	.414	135	89	227	4.07
1986	Baltimore	33	218⅓	14	12	.538	175	74	214	4.70
1987	Baltimore	33	226	10	12	.455	152	78	212	4.18
1988	Balt.-Bos.	36	236	13	15	.464	156	77	234	3.39
1989	Boston	34	211⅔	15	11	.577	145	71	217	4.00
1990	Boston	34	228	17	8	.680	143	69	225	3.36
	Totals	273	1802⅓	118	95	.554	1180	610	1725	3.66

MARK DAVIS 30 6-4 205   Bats L Throws L

Suffered one of the most amazing reversals in baseball history... Won NL Cy Young Award for Padres in 1989, then signed a four-year, $13-million contract with Royals as free agent and forgot to show up for the season... In a stretch spanning April and May, he failed to convert four of six save chances... Was demoted to long relief and even started three games... On disabled list from Aug. 10-Sept. 4 with elbow tendinitis... Staying in San Diego would have been a wiser choice... Saved 44 games in 48 tries in '89... At the time, it was the third-highest save total in history... Received $2.125 million in

1990 . . . Originally signed by the Phils in 1979 . . . Born Oct. 19, 1960, in Livermore, Cal.

Year	Club	G	IP	W	L	Pct.	SO	BB	H	ERA
1980	Philadelphia	2	7	0	0	.000	5	5	4	2.57
1981	Philadelphia	9	43	1	4	.200	29	24	49	7.74
1983	San Francisco	20	111	6	4	.600	83	50	93	3.49
1984	San Francisco	46	174⅔	5	17	.227	124	54	201	5.36
1985	San Francisco	77	114⅓	5	12	.294	131	41	89	3.54
1986	San Francisco	67	84⅓	5	7	.417	90	34	63	2.99
1987	S.F.-S.D.	63	133	9	8	.529	98	59	123	3.99
1988	San Diego	62	98⅓	5	10	.333	102	42	70	2.01
1989	San Diego	70	92⅔	4	3	.571	92	31	66	1.85
1990	Kansas City	53	68⅔	2	7	.222	73	52	71	5.11
	Totals	469	927	42	72	.368	827	392	829	3.86

KEVIN APPIER 23 6-2 190   Bats R Throws R

Turned in splendid performance as rookie . . . Ranked fourth in league with 2.76 ERA and tied for third with three shutouts . . . Began season in minors, made first start May 11 and moved into rotation permanently June 9 . . . Put together club's longest winning streak, six games from July 3-Aug. 29 . . . Went 4-1 in July and 5-0 in August . . . Tossed one-hitter July 7 at Detroit, with Lou Whittaker's first-inning single the only blemish . . . Also threw a three-hitter and four-hitter . . . Born Dec. 6, 1967, in Lancaster, Cal. . . . Earned $100,000 in 1990.

Year	Club	G	IP	W	L	Pct.	SO	BB	H	ERA
1989	Kansas City	6	21⅔	1	4	.200	10	12	34	9.14
1990	Kansas City	32	185⅔	12	8	.600	127	54	179	2.76
	Totals	38	207⅓	13	12	.520	137	66	213	3.43

TOM GORDON 23 5-9 160   Bats R Throws R

Only Royals starter who didn't miss a start . . . "Flash" was Royals' Pitcher of the Month in April and June . . . Led staff in starts (32), innings (195⅓), complete games (16) and strikeouts (175) . . . Had four straight complete games from Aug. 8-22 . . . Left five games with leads that his bullpen blew . . . Tossed three-hit shutout at Mariners Sept. 2 . . . His ratio of 8.1 strikeouts per nine innings ranked fourth in league . . . Reached season high of nine strikeouts four times . . . Earned $185,000 in

1990 . . . Broke Steve Busby's club rookie record of 16 wins in '89 . . . Born Nov. 18, 1967, in Sebring, Fla.

Year	Club	G	IP	W	L	Pct.	SO	BB	H	ERA
1988	Kansas City	5	15⅔	0	2	.000	18	7	16	5.17
1989	Kansas City	49	163	17	9	.654	153	86	122	3.64
1990	Kansas City	32	195⅓	12	11	.522	175	99	192	3.73
	Totals	86	374	29	22	.569	346	192	330	3.75

MARK GUBICZA 28 6-5 220   Bats R Throws R

His season lasted only three months . . . Left his June 29 start with a partial tear in right rotator cuff . . . Underwent arthroscopic surgery Aug. 2 and spent offseason rehabilitating with former Royals trainer Paul McGannon at a sports rehab center . . . Even before the injury, life wasn't easy for this former 20-game winner . . . Tossed two complete games and lost them both—3-2 to Milwaukee and 4-1 to Boston . . . First time in seven years he hasn't reached double digits in wins . . . Made $2,066,667 in 1990 . . . Born Aug. 14, 1962, in Philadelphia.

Year	Club	G	IP	W	L	Pct.	SO	BB	H	ERA
1984	Kansas City	29	189	10	14	.417	111	75	172	4.05
1985	Kansas City	29	177⅓	14	10	583	99	77	160	4.06
1986	Kansas City	35	180⅔	12	6	.667	118	84	155	3.64
1987	Kansas City	35	241⅔	13	18	.419	166	120	231	3.98
1988	Kansas City	35	269⅔	20	8	.714	183	83	237	2.70
1989	Kansas City	36	255	15	11	.577	173	63	252	3.04
1990	Kansas City	16	94	4	7	.364	71	38	101	4.50
	Totals	215	1407⅓	88	74	.543	921	540	1308	3.57

TOP PROSPECTS

JEFF CONINE 24 6-1 205   Bats R Throws R

First baseman was named Southern League MVP after hitting .320 with 15 homers and 95 RBI for Memphis (AA) . . . Ranked third in league in hitting and second in RBI . . . Promoted to Royals in September and collected five hits in nine games . . . Born June 27, 1966, in Tacoma, Wash.

BRENT MAYNE 22 6-1 195   Bats L Throws R

Good enough to break into the majors in '91, perhaps as the Royals' No. 2 catcher . . . Hit .267 with 61 RBI in 115 games for Memphis (AA) . . . Had three hits in five games with parent club . . . Royals' No. 1 pick in 1989 draft . . . Born April 19, 1968, in Loma Linda, Cal. . . . Has played just two seasons in the minors . . . Attended Orange Coast College and Cal State-Fullerton.

HARVEY PULLIAM 23 6-0 210   Bats R Throws R
Outfielder hit .268 with 16 homers and 72 RBI for Omaha (AAA) . . . Has a decent chance to break camp with the parent club . . . Royals' third-round choice in 1986 draft . . . Born Oct. 20, 1967, in San Francisco.

BRIAN McRAE 23 6-0 180   Bats S Throws R
Son of former Royals star Hal . . . Younger McRae is outfielder who hit .286 in 46 games with Royals . . . Tripled in first at-bat as left-handed batter and singled in first at-bat as right-hander . . . Hit .268 in 116 games for Memphis . . . Born Aug. 27, 1967, in Bradenton, Fla. . . . Royals' first-round pick in 1985 lottery.

MANAGER JOHN WATHAN: Poor man . . . His Royals were supposed to compete for a division title, but barely escaped finishing last at 75-86 . . . Club brass signed expensive free agents, but moves backfired . . . Royals were 21-26 in one-run games and 11-16 in games decided by two runs . . . It was his first losing record over a complete season . . . His three-year mark as Royals manager is 272-248 . . . Ranks as third-winningest skipper in club history, trailing Whitey Herzog and Dick Howser . . . Managed Omaha (AAA) before assuming control of Royals, Aug. 27, 1987 . . . A catcher with Royals from 1976-85 . . . Had 36 steals in '82, setting big-league record for catchers . . . Born Oct. 4, 1949, in Cedar Rapids, Iowa.

ALL-TIME ROYAL SEASON RECORDS

BATTING: George Brett, .390, 1980
HRs: Steve Balboni, 36, 1985
RBI: Hal McRae, 133, 1982
STEALS: Willie Wilson, 83, 1979
WINS: Bret Saberhagen, 23, 1989
STRIKEOUTS: Dennis Leonard, 244, 1977

MINNESOTA TWINS

TEAM DIRECTORY: Owner: Carl Pohlad; Pres.: Jerry Bell; Exec. VP-GM: Andy MacPhail; VP-Player Pers.: Bob Gebhard; VP-Oper.: Dave Moore; Dir. Media Rel.: Tom Mee; Mgr. Tom Kelly. Home: Hubert H. Humphrey Metrodome (55,883). Field distances: 343, l.f. line; 408, c.f.; 327, r.f. line. Spring training: Fort Myers, Fla.

Rick Aguilera split-fingered his way to 32 saves.

SCOUTING REPORT

HITTING: Nearly everyone in the Twins' lineup suffered a down year in 1990. Minnesota hit .276 in 1989, but the figure dropped to .265 last year.

The guilty parties included Kirby Puckett (failed to hit .300 or collect 200 hits for the first time in five years); Greg Gagne (.272 in '89 to .235 in '90); Dan Gladden (.295 in '89 to .275 in '90); Gary Gaetti (.301 in '88 to .251 in '89 to .229 in '90); Brian Harper (.325 in '89 to .294 in '90) and Al Newman (.253 to .242). Gaetti, a second-look free agent, was unsigned at press time.

Kent Hrbek's average improved (.272 to .287), but his power numbers dropped to 22 homers and 79 RBI.

PITCHING: Rick Aguilera (5-3, 2.76) enjoyed a solid year as the closer, registering 32 saves. Aguilera moved to the bullpen after Jeff Reardon departed, but Aguilera may return to the rotation now that the Twins have obtained Steve Bedrosian from the Giants. Bedrosian won the 1987 Cy Young Award with the Phils, but lost his closing role last year with the Giants as he went 9-9 with 17 saves and a 4.20 ERA.

The Twins' rotation could be a good one, with righties Kevin Tapani (12-8, 4.07) and Scott Erickson (8-4, 2.87) and lefties Mark Guthrie (7-9, 3.79) and Allan Anderson (7-18, 4.53) still learning the ropes.

FIELDING: Four-time Gold Glove outfielder Puckett switched from center to right last year, an experimental move that may become permanent to preserve his legs and prolong his career. Shane Mack replaced Puckett in center, but will play left or right if Puckett remains in the middle.

The Twins had an above-average defense last year, committing only 101 errors (fourth-fewest in the league) and fielding at a .983 clip. There were three triple plays in the American League and the Twins turned two of them. Hrbek posted the highest fielding percentage among first basemen (.997).

OUTLOOK: Tom Kelly's young arms need to stay strong throughout the season if the Twins, last at 74-88 in 1990, have any designs on being a .500 team. A veteran such as Bedrosian will help the staff's chemistry.

But the players in the everyday lineup—so many of whom

MINNESOTA TWINS 1991 ROSTER

MANAGER Tom Kelly
Coaches—Terry Crowley, Ron Gardenhire, Tony Oliva, Rick Stelmaszek, Dick Such, Wayne Terwilliger

PITCHERS

No.	Name	1990 Club	W-L	IP	SO	ERA	B-T	Ht.	Wt.	Born
37	Abbott, Paul	Portland	5-14	128	129	4.56	R-R	6-3	185	9/15/67 Van Nuys, CA
		Minnesota	0-5	35	25	5.97				
38	Aguilera, Rick	Minnesota	5-3	65	61	2.76	R-R	6-5	195	12/31/61 San Gabriel, CA
49	Anderson, Allan	Minnesota	7-18	189	82	4.53	L-L	6-0	194	1/7/64 Lancaster, OH
—	Bedrosian, Steve	San Francisco	9-9	79	43	4.20	R-R	6-3	205	12/6/57 Methuen, MA
60	Banks, Willie	Orlando	7-9	163	114	3.93	R-R	6-1	190	2/27/69 Jersey City, NJ
40	**Berenguer, Juan	Minnesota	8-5	100	77	3.41	R-R	5-11	220	11/30/54 Panama
19	Casian, Larry	Portland	9-9	157	89	4.48	R-L	6-0	170	10/28/65 Lynwood, CA
		Minnesota	2-1	22	11	3.22				
54	Drummond, Tim	Minnesota	3-5	91	49	4.35	R-R	6-3	195	12/24/64 LaPlata, MD
39	Dyer, Mike	Portland	0-1	2	0	34.71	R-R	6-3	195	9/8/66 Upland, CA
46	Erickson, Scott	Orlando	8-3	101	69	3.03	R-R	6-4	220	2/2/68 Long Beach, CA
		Minnesota	8-4	113	53	2.87				
41	Garces, Rich	Visalia	2-2	55	75	1.81	R-R	6-0	187	5/18/71 Venezuela
		Orlando	2-1	17	22	2.08				
		Minnesota	0-0	6	1	1.59				
53	Guthrie, Mark	Portland	1-3	42	39	2.98	S-L	6-4	202	9/22/65 Buffalo, NY
		Minnesota	7-9	145	101	3.79				
30	Leach, Terry	Minnesota	2-5	82	46	3.20	R-R	6-0	190	3/13/54 Selma, AL
21	Pittman, Park	Portland	0-1	28	22	6.99	R-R	6-0	175	8/5/65 Richmond, IN
23	Smith, Roy	Minnesota	5-10	153	87	4.81	R-R	6-3	212	9/6/61 Mt. Vernon, NY
36	Tapani, Kevin	Minnesota	12-8	159	101	4.07	R-R	6-0	180	2/18/64 Des Moines, IA
47	Wayne, Gary	Portland	2-4	32	30	3.41	L-L	6-3	192	11/30/62 Dearborn, MI
		Minnesota	1-1	39	28	4.19				
47	Wayne, Gary	Portland	2-4	32	30	3.41	L-L	6-3	192	11/30/62 Dearborn, MI
		Minnesota	1-1	39	28	4.19				
50	West, David	Minnesota	7-9	146	92	5.10	L-L	6-6	220	9/1/64 Memphis, TN

CATCHERS

No.	Name	1990 Club	H	HR	RBI	Pct.	B-T	Ht.	Wt.	Born
12	Harper, Brian	Minnesota	141	6	54	.294	R-R	6-2	208	10/16/59 Los Angeles, CA
0	Ortiz, Junior	Minnesota	57	0	18	.335	R-R	5-11	181	10/24/59 Puerto Rico
16	Parks, Derek	Portland	41	11	27	.177	R-R	6-1	205	9/29/68 Covina, CA
15	Webster, Lenny	Orlando	119	8	71	.262	R-R	5-9	187	2/10/65 New Orleans, LA
		Minnesota	2	0	0	.333				

INFIELDERS

No.	Name	1990 Club	H	HR	RBI	Pct.	B-T	Ht.	Wt.	Born
8	**Gaetti, Gary	Minnesota	132	16	85	.229	R-R	6-0	200	8/19/58 Centralia, IL
7	Gagne, Greg	Minnesota	91	7	38	.235	R-R	5-11	172	11/12/61 Fall River, MA
3	Hale, Chip	Portland	134	3	40	.280	L-R	5-11	180	12/2/64 Santa Clara, CA
		Minnesota	0	0	2	.000				
14	Hrbek, Kent	Minnesota	141	22	79	.287	L-R	6-4	250	5/21/60 Minneapolis, MN
27	Jorgensen, Terry	Portland	114	10	50	.259	R-R	6-4	208	9/2/66 Kewaunee, WI
22	Larkin, Gene	Minnesota	108	5	42	.269	S-R	6-3	205	10/24/62 Astoria, NY
31	Leius, Scott	Portland	81	2	23	.229	R-R	6-3	180	9/24/65 Yonkers, NY
		Minnesota	6	1	4	.240				
2	Liriano, Nelson	Tor.-Minn.	83	1	28	.234	S-R	5-10	172	6/3/64 Dominican Republic
26	Newman, Al	Minnesota	94	0	30	.242	S-R	5-9	188	6/30/60 Kansas City, MO
18	Sorrento, Paul	Portland	107	19	72	.302	L-R	6-2	210	11/17/65 Somerville, MA
		Minnesota	25	5	13	.207				

OUTFIELDERS

No.	Name	1990 Club	H	HR	RBI	Pct.	B-T	Ht.	Wt.	Born
1	Brown, Jarvis	Orlando	137	14	57	.260	R-R	5-7	165	3/26/67 Waukegan, IL
56	Bruett, J. T.	Visalia	134	1	33	.307	L-L	5-11	175	10/8/67 Milwaukee, WI
		Portland	8	0	3	.235				
25	Bush, Randy	Minnesota	44	6	18	.243	L-L	6-1	186	10/5/58 Dover, DE
22	Castillo, Carmen	Minnesota	30	0	12	.219	R-R	6-1	201	6/8/58 Dominican Republic
32	Gladden, Dan	Minnesota	147	5	40	.275	R-R	5-11	181	7/7/57 San Jose, CA
24	Mack, Shane	Minnesota	102	8	44	.326	R-R	6-0	190	12/7/63 Los Angeles, CA
—	*Moses, John	Minnesota	38	1	14	.221	S-L	5-10	174	8/9/57 Los Angeles, CA
5	Munoz, Pedro	Syracuse	101	7	56	.319	R-R	5-11	170	9/19/68 Puerto Rico
		Portland	35	5	21	.318				
		Minnesota	23	0	5	.271				
34	Puckett, Kirby	Minnesota	164	12	80	.298	R-R	5-8	213	3/14/61 Chicago, IL

*Free agent at press time
**New look free agent

were on the 1987 world champions—have to return to their late-80's form. Otherwise, it'll be another dismal year at the Metro-dome.

TWIN PROFILES

KIRBY PUCKETT 30 5-8 213   Bats R Throws R

One of many Twins to suffer sub-par 1990 . . . Slipped significantly after leading the majors in hitting in '89 . . . Hit under .300 for the first time in five years . . . In an effort to protect his legs and prolong his career, this Gold Glove center fielder moved to right field Aug. 17 . . . Last year marked first season on three-year, $9-million contract . . . Was baseball's first $3 million man . . . Played four positions in one game Aug. 16 at Cleveland, rotating from right to short to third to second . . . Was reserve on All-Star team, singling in pinch-hit role . . . Had five-hit games May 14 and June 6 . . . Had six straight hits over two games May 14-15 . . . Posted baseball's third-highest batting average in the '80s. His .3233 followed Wade Boggs' .352 and Tony Gwynn's .332 . . . Born March 14, 1961, in Chicago.

Year	Club	Pos.	G	AB	R	H	2B	3B	HR	RBI	SB	Avg.
1984	Minnesota	OF	128	557	63	165	12	5	0	31	14	.296
1985	Minnesota	OF	161	691	80	199	29	13	4	74	21	.288
1986	Minnesota	OF	161	680	119	223	37	6	31	96	20	.328
1987	Minnesota	OF	157	624	96	207	32	5	28	99	12	.332
1988	Minnesota	OF	158	657	109	234	42	5	24	121	6	.356
1989	Minnesota	OF	159	635	75	215	45	4	9	85	11	.339
1990	Minnesota	OF-2B-SS-3B	146	551	82	164	40	3	12	80	5	.298
	Totals		1070	4395	624	1407	237	41	108	586	89	.320

KENT HRBEK 30 6-4 250   Bats L Throws R

Had better second half than first half . . . Hit just .266 through All-Star break, .309 afterward . . . Club leader in homers . . . Best RBI game came Aug. 28, when he drove home four runs vs. Chicago . . . Posted top fielding percentage among AL first basemen, setting Twins record with .997 mark . . . His weak legs nearly endured the entire season, but he sprained his left ankle Sept. 22 goofing off in the clubhouse . . . Has 223 career homers . . . Made $2.1 million last season on contract that runs through '94 . . . Born May 21, 1960, in Minneapolis.

Year	Club	Pos.	G	AB	R	H	2B	3B	HR	RBI	SB	Avg.
1981	Minnesota	1B	24	67	5	16	5	0	1	7	0	.239
1982	Minnesota	1B	140	532	82	160	21	4	23	92	3	.301
1983	Minnesota	1B	141	515	75	153	41	5	16	84	4	.297
1984	Minnesota	1B	149	559	80	174	31	3	27	107	1	.311
1985	Minnesota	1B	158	593	78	165	31	2	21	93	1	.278
1986	Minnesota	1B	149	550	85	147	27	1	29	91	2	.267
1987	Minnesota	1B	143	477	85	136	20	1	34	90	5	.285
1988	Minnesota	1B	143	510	75	159	31	0	25	76	0	.312
1989	Minnesota	1B	109	375	59	102	17	0	25	84	3	.272
1990	Minnesota	1B-3B	143	492	61	141	26	0	22	79	5	.287
	Totals		1299	4670	685	1353	250	16	223	803	24	.290

DAN GLADDEN 33 5-11 181   Bats R Throws R

Hamstrings didn't set this outfielder back as in previous seasons . . . His .275 average was his second-highest as Twin . . . His 25 steals led club . . . Had six three-hit games . . . Suffered from kidney stone problem in April, spending a night in an Oakland hospital . . . Flew to Anaheim the next day and pinch hit that night . . . Bruised his knee July 6, but didn't miss much action, resting during All-Star break . . . Made $700,000 last year . . . Only player to hit safely in all seven 1987 World Series games . . . Born July 7, 1957, in San Jose, Cal. . . . Originally signed as free agent by Giants in 1979.

Year	Club	Pos.	G	AB	R	H	2B	3B	HR	RBI	SB	Avg.
1983	San Francisco	OF	18	63	6	14	2	0	1	9	4	.222
1984	San Francisco	OF	86	342	71	120	17	2	4	31	31	.351
1985	San Francisco	OF	142	502	64	122	15	8	7	41	32	.243
1986	San Francisco	OF	102	351	55	97	16	1	4	29	27	.276
1987	Minnesota	OF	121	438	69	109	21	2	8	38	25	.249
1988	Minnesota	OF-2B-3B-P	141	576	91	155	32	6	11	62	28	.269
1989	Minnesota	OF-P	121	461	69	136	23	3	8	46	23	.295
1990	Minnesota	OF	136	534	64	147	27	6	5	40	25	.275
	Totals		867	3267	489	900	153	28	48	296	195	.275

BRIAN HARPER 31 6-2 208   Bats R Throws R

Solid season for the well-traveled catcher . . . Nailed 32 of 117 would-be base-stealers (27 percent) . . . Remained in .300 range most of season, before dropping to .294 in final week . . . Had four RBI May 15 and four hits Aug. 25 . . . His 42 doubles led club . . . Earned $450,000 in 1990 . . . Has made the big-league rounds . . . Was drafted by Angels in '77, traded to Pirates in '81, traded to Cards in '84, signed by Tigers as free agent in '86, signed by A's off San Jose Bees' roster in '87 and signed by Twins as free agent in '87 . . . Born Oct. 16, 1959, in Los Angeles.

Year	Club	Pos.	G	AB	R	H	2B	3B	HR	RBI	SB	Avg.
1979	California	DH	1	2	0	0	0	0	0	0	0	.000
1981	California	OF	4	11	1	3	0	0	0	1	1	.273
1982	Pittsburgh	OF	20	29	4	8	1	0	2	4	0	.276
1983	Pittsburgh	OF–1B	61	131	16	29	4	1	7	20	0	.221
1984	Pittsburgh	OF–C	46	112	4	29	4	0	2	11	0	.259
1985	St. Louis	OF–3B-C–1B	43	52	5	13	4	0	0	8	0	.250
1986	Detroit	OF–1B-C	19	36	2	5	1	0	0	3	0	.139
1987	Oakland	OF	11	17	1	4	1	0	0	3	0	.235
1988	Minnesota	C–3B	60	166	15	49	11	1	3	20	0	.295
1989	Minnesota	C-OF–1B–3B	126	385	43	125	24	0	8	57	2	.325
1990	Minnesota	C–3B–1B	134	479	61	141	42	3	6	54	3	.294
	Totals		525	1420	152	406	92	5	28	181	6	.286

AL NEWMAN 30 5-9 188   Bats S Throws R

Club's most versatile player . . . Spent time at second, third, short and left, but his best position is second . . . His best offensive day came July 29 vs. A's, when he had two doubles and a single . . . He's the furthest thing from a power hitter . . . Has gone 1,479 straight at-bats without a home run, the most among active players . . . Only major-league homer came in Atlanta off Zane Smith, July 6, 1986 . . . Was drafted four times— by Angels in January 1979, Rangers in January 1980, Mets in June 1980 and Expos in June 1981 . . . Finally signed with Expos . . . Traded to Padres and then back to Expos before reaching majors . . . Made big-league debut in '85 . . . Was traded to Twins before '87 season . . . Earned $350,000 in 1990 . . . Born June 30, 1960, in Kansas City, Mo.

Year	Club	Pos.	G	AB	R	H	2B	3B	HR	RBI	SB	Avg.
1985	Montreal	2B-SS	25	29	7	5	1	0	0	1	2	.172
1986	Montreal	2B-SS	95	185	23	37	3	0	1	8	11	.200
1987	Minnesota	SS–2B–3B–OF	110	307	44	68	15	5	0	29	15	.221
1988	Minnesota	3B-SS–2B	105	260	35	58	7	0	0	19	12	.223
1989	Minnesota	2B–3B-SS–OF	141	446	62	113	18	2	0	38	25	.253
1990	Minnesota	2B-SS–3B–OF	144	388	43	94	14	0	0	30	13	.242
	Totals		620	1615	214	375	58	7	1	125	78	.232

GREG GAGNE 29 5-11 172   Bats R Throws R

Another Twin whose numbers dipped . . .
Posted lowest average since rookie year of '85
. . . Hit .300 for the first month, but never
reached that level again . . . Was down to .240
by the All-Star break . . . Went through 0-for-18
spell in July . . . Don Baylor helped with his
hitting in '89 and "Gags" posted a career-high
.272 mark. Apparently, he missed Baylor in
'90 . . . Still a very capable shortstop . . . The fastest runner on the
club, he had three steals Aug. 29 vs. Chicago . . . Earned $833,333
last year . . . Was sent to Twins in 1982 trade with Yankees who
had drafted him in fourth round in 1979 . . . Born Nov. 12, 1961,
in Fall River, Mass.

Year	Club	Pos.	G	AB	R	H	2B	3B	HR	RBI	SB	Avg.
1983	Minnesota	SS	10	27	2	3	1	0	0	3	0	.111
1984	Minnesota	PR-PH	2	1	0	0	0	0	0	0	0	.000
1985	Minnesota	SS	114	293	37	66	15	3	2	23	10	.225
1986	Minnesota	SS-2B	156	472	63	118	22	6	12	54	12	.250
1987	Minnesota	SS-OF-2B	137	437	68	116	28	7	10	40	6	.265
1988	Minnesota	SS-OF-2B-3B	149	461	70	109	20	6	14	48	15	.236
1989	Minnesota	SS-OF	149	460	69	125	29	7	9	48	11	.272
1990	Minnesota	SS-OF	138	388	38	91	22	3	7	38	8	.235
	Totals		855	2539	347	628	137	32	54	254	62	.247

SHANE MACK 27 6-0 190   Bats R Throws R

Twins' center fielder of the future . . . Took
over starting job after All-Star break, as Kirby
Puckett moved to right . . . Had been platooned
in right during first half . . . Hit .300 for most
of the season, though he slipped to .284 Aug.
31 . . . Was a fine 13-for-17 in steal attempts
. . . A splendid acquisition . . . Twins drafted
him off Padres' minor-league roster for $50,000
after the 1989 season . . . Never reached potential with Padres . . .
Former Olympian . . . Shows good opposite-field power . . .
Earned $100,000 last year . . . Born Dec. 7, 1963, in Los Angeles
. . . Played at UCLA before Padres made him a first-round pick
in '84 . . . His '89 season was cut short in June because of elbow
surgery.

Year	Club	Pos.	G	AB	R	H	2B	3B	HR	RBI	SB	Avg.
1987	San Diego	OF	105	238	28	57	11	3	4	25	4	.239
1988	San Diego	OF	56	119	13	29	3	0	0	12	5	.244
1990	Minnesota	OF	125	313	50	102	10	4	8	44	13	.326
	Totals		286	670	91	188	24	7	12	81	22	.281

RICK AGUILERA 29 6-5 195   Bats R Throws R

Emerged as most reliable Twins closer in decades . . . Converted 32 of 39 save opportunities last year and had only two blown saves in first 31 opportunities . . . Struck out 61 in 65⅓ innings . . . Issued 19 walks, six of them intentional . . . Acquired from Mets with four other pitchers in Frank Viola trade, July 31, 1989 . . . Relieved in 36 games with Mets, became starter with Twins, then returned to pen in '90 . . . Filled spot vacated by Jeff Reardon, who left for Boston via free agency and now may be headed back into the rotation with the addition of Steve Bedrosian from Giants . . . Born on New Year's Eve, 1961, in San Gabriel, Cal. . . . Earned $648,000 in 1990.

Year	Club	G	IP	W	L	Pct.	SO	BB	H	ERA
1985	New York (NL)	21	122⅓	10	7	.588	74	37	118	3.24
1986	New York (NL)	28	141⅔	10	7	.588	104	36	145	3.88
1987	New York (NL)	18	115	11	3	.786	77	33	124	3.60
1988	New York (NL)	11	24⅔	0	4	.000	16	10	29	6.93
1989	New York (NL)	36	69⅓	6	6	.500	80	21	59	2.34
1989	Minnesota	11	75⅔	3	5	.375	57	17	71	3.21
1990	Minnesota	56	65⅓	5	3	.625	61	19	55	2.76
	Totals	181	614	45	35	.563	469	173	601	3.44

KEVIN TAPANI 26 6-0 180   Bats R Throws R

Twins expect him to develop into dominant starter . . . Had excellent first half and owned 9-5 record at All-Star break . . . Went only 3-3 in the second half as he was hampered by injuries in final months . . . Endured shin, shoulder and rib problems . . . Best game was five-hit shutout May 6 at Milwaukee, when he posted career-high nine strikeouts . . . Earned $100,000 last year . . . Acquired from Mets in Frank Viola deal, July 31, 1989 . . . Originally signed by A's and sent to Mets in three-team deal that sent Bob Welch to the A's and Alfredo Griffin and Jay Howell to the Dodgers . . . Born Feb. 18, 1964, in Des Moines, Iowa . . . Played ball at Central Michigan University, where he earned a degree in finance.

Year	Club	G	IP	W	L	Pct.	SO	BB	H	ERA
1989	New York (NL)	3	7⅓	0	0	.000	2	4	5	3.68
1989	Minnesota	5	32⅔	2	2	.500	21	8	34	3.86
1990	Minnesota	28	159⅓	12	8	.600	101	29	164	4.07
	Totals	36	199⅓	14	10	.583	124	41	203	4.02

STEVE BEDROSIAN 33 6-3 205   Bats R Throws R

Giant relief ace joined Twins following December trade for pitcher Johnny Ard and player to be named . . . Pitched under tremendous strain because his toddler son, Cody, was diagnosed with leukemia on April 13 . . . Two days later, he came to Candlestick for ring ceremony, then stayed and pitched against Padres despite not having thrown for a week and took the loss . . . Successful in his next seven save opportunities . . . Did not record a save in June or July, but still managed to have 17 for the year . . . Saved all three games in a sweep of Padres in September . . . Picked up seven saves and two wins in September to earn Rolaids Relief Man of the Month award . . . Tied with Juan Agosto for NL lead with nine relief wins and tied for sixth in NL with 68 appearances . . . Earned $1.45 million last year . . . Won NL Cy Young Award in 1987, when he saved 40 games for the Phils . . . Born Dec. 6, 1957, in Methuen, Mass. . . . Atlanta's third-round pick in 1978 draft . . . Acquired by Giants from Phils for Dennis Cook, Charlie Hayes and Terry Mulholland, June 18, 1989 . . . Has 178 career saves.

Year	Club	G	IP	W	L	Pct.	SO	BB	H	ERA
1981	Atlanta	15	24	1	2	.333	9	15	15	4.50
1982	Atlanta	64	137⅔	8	6	.571	123	57	102	2.42
1983	Atlanta	70	120	9	10	.474	114	51	100	3.60
1984	Atlanta	40	83⅔	9	6	.600	81	33	65	2.37
1985	Atlanta	37	206⅔	7	15	.318	134	111	198	3.83
1986	Philadelphia	68	90⅓	8	6	.571	82	34	79	3.39
1987	Philadelphia	65	89	5	3	.625	74	28	79	2.83
1988	Philadelphia	57	74⅓	6	6	.500	61	27	75	3.75
1989	Phil.-SF	68	84⅔	3	7	.300	58	39	56	2.87
1990	San Francisco	68	79⅓	9	9	.500	43	44	72	4.20
	Totals	552	989⅔	65	70	.481	779	439	841	3.31

TOP PROSPECTS

RICH GARCES 19 6-0 215   Bats R Throws R

Was most productive reliever in the minors last season, posting 28 saves for Visalia (A) and eight for Orlando (AA) . . . Also had two saves for the Twins late in the season . . . Born May 18, 1971, in Maracay, Venezuela . . . Signed Dec. 29, 1987.

CHUCK KNOBLAUCH 22 5-9 175   Bats R Throws R

Look for this infielder to push for a starting job at second base . . . Hit .290 for Orlando (AA) . . . Twins' scouting director Terry

Ryan said this guy showed during Instructional League that he's ready for majors . . . Was first-round pick in '89 draft . . . All-American at Texas A&M . . . Born July 7, 1968, in Houston.

PEDRO MUNOZ 22 5-11 170   **Bats R Throws R**
Acquired in trade from Toronto, July 27, 1990 . . . Outfielder hit .319 for Blue Jays' farm club in Syracuse (AAA) . . . Moved to Portland (AAA) and hit .318 in 30 games . . . Called up to Twins in September and batted .271 in 22 games . . . Born Sept. 19, 1968, in Ponce, Puerto Rico . . . Signed by Blue Jays as free agent, May 31, 1985.

_____

MANAGER TOM KELLY: Coming off worst season (74-88) in big-league managerial career . . . His club has been steadily falling since '87 World Series . . . Twins finished second in '88, fifth in '89 and last in '90 . . . Was unable to get the most out of his players as several Twins posted career lows . . . It seems like forever since he became the fifth rookie manager to win a World Series . . . Has one year left on contract, but will he last the year? . . . Managed in minor leagues for five seasons, including stops at Tacoma, Visalia and Orlando . . . Left minors in '83 to become Twins' third-base coach . . . Replaced Ray Miller as manager in late '86 . . . Named UPI Manager of the Year in '87 . . . Piloted AL to 2-1 victory in '88 All-Star Game . . . Was minor-league outfielder for 13 seasons . . . Played 49 games for Twins in '75, his only big-league experience . . . Born Aug. 15, 1950, in Graceville, Minn. . . . . Owns 342-319 career mark as big-league manager.

ALL-TIME TWIN SEASON RECORDS

BATTING: Rod Carew, .388, 1977
HRs: Harmon Killebrew, 49, 1964, 1969
RBI: Harmon Killebrew, 140, 1969
STEALS: Rod Carew, 49, 1976
WINS: Jim Kaat, 25, 1966
STRIKEOUTS: Bert Blyleven, 258, 1973

OAKLAND ATHLETICS

TEAM DIRECTORY: Owner/Managing Partner: Walter A. Haas Jr.; Chief Oper. Off.: Wally Haas; VP-Baseball Oper.: Sandy Alderson; Dir. Player Dev.: Karl Kuehl; Dir. Scouting: Dick Bogard; Dir. Media Rel.: Kathy Jacobson; Dir. Baseball Inf.: Jay Alves; Trav. Sec.: Mickey Morabito; Mgr.: Tony La Russa. Home: Oakland Coliseum (48,219). Field distances: 330, l.f. line; 375, l.c.; 400, c.f.; 375, r.c.; 330, r.f. line. Spring training: Phoenix, Ariz.

SCOUTING REPORT

HITTING: What are you going to believe—a 162-game regular season and a four-game ALCS sweep or that shocking four-game World Series facedown? Just because the Reds had their way with the Bash Brothers last fall doesn't mean that AL pitchers will be salivating at the sight of the Athletics' lineup this summer.

The big key for Oakland is the troublesome back of Jose Canseco (.274, 37, 101 in 131 games)—not that he's their only devastating weapon. There's AL MVP Rickey Henderson (.325, 28, 61, 119 runs, 65 steals) to create havoc on the bases and Mark McGwire (.235, 39, 108) to trot around them. Harold Baines (.284, 16, 65) will be on hand for a full season but Carney Lansford (.268, 3, 50), who hit .336 as recently as 1989, injured his left knee in a snowmobile accident and could be lost indefinitly. Ex-Royal Willie Wilson was signed as insurance for free agent Dave Henderson (.271, 20, 63) and then Henderson opted to remain with a three-year contract.

Last year, Oakland ranked third in the AL in runs (733), third in homers (164) and second in stolen bases (141). Tony La Russa's team has more ways to beat you than just about anyone else.

PITCHING: Not only did A's pitchers win the most games in the league (103) and post the lowest staff ERA (3.18), they were also the healthiest group in the majors last season. They used only six starting pitchers in 1990 and only a missed September start by Mike Moore (13-15, 4.65) prevented the A's from becoming the first team since 1965 to use only five starters in a season.

Although Bob Welch (27-6, 2.95) won the Cy Young last year, the ace was Dave Stewart (22-11, 2.56), who won 20 games for the fourth straight season. Stewart, the ultimate workhorse, hasn't missed an assignment since La Russa inserted him into the rotation

Rickey Henderson needs three more swipes to pass Lou Brock.

July 29, 1986—a span of 146 starts.

Eric Show (6-8, 5.67 for the Padres) was signed as a free agent as insurance against the possible loss of Scott Sanderson (17-11, 3.88), a free agent who decided to accept arbitration and then wound up signing with the Yankees. In the bullpen, there's Dennis Eckersley (4-2, 0.61, 48 Sv) to close out every deal in sight. Last year, Athletics' relievers tied a club record with 64 saves and went 14-10 with a 2.35 ERA.

FIELDING: The A's sport one of the finest defensive infields in the majors, with newly crowned Gold Glove winner McGwire at first, Mike Gallego at second, Walt Weiss at shortstop and now doubtful Lansford at third. The A's signed Vance Law, who played in Japan last year, as backup for Lansford. The catching is also solid as Terry Steinbach has developed into an above-average receiver. Canseco can be the weak link in the outfield, as witnessed by his shoddy display in the World Series.

OAKLAND ATHLETICS 1991 ROSTER

MANAGER Tony La Russa
Coaches—Rick Burleson, Dave Duncan, Art Kusnyer, Rene Lachemann, Dave McKay, Tommie Reynolds

PITCHERS

No.	Name	1990 Club	W-L	IP	SO	ERA	B-T	Ht.	Wt.	Born
54	Burns, Todd	Oakland	3-3	79	43	2.97	R-R	6-2	190	7/6/63 Maywood, CA
49	Chitren, Steve	Huntsville	2-4	54	61	1.68	R-R	6-0	180	6/8/67 Japan
		Tacoma	0-0	1	2	0.00				
		Oakland	1-0	18	19	1.02				
43	Eckersley, Dennis	Oakland	4-2	73	73	0.61	R-R	6-2	195	10/3/54 Oakland, CA
57	Harris, Reggie	Hunstville	0-2	30	34	3.03	R-R	6-1	180	8/12/68 Waynesboro, VA
		Oakland	1-0	41	31	3.48				
40	Honeycutt, Rick	Oakland	2-2	63	38	2.70	L-L	6-1	191	6/29/54 Chattanooga,TN
58	Klink, Joe	Oakland	0-0	40	19	2.04	L-L	5-11	175	2/3/62 Johnstown, PA
56	Law, Joe	Tacoma	2-5	61	46	6.16	R-R	6-2	200	2/4/62 Pittsburgh, PA
21	Moore, Mike	Oakland	13-15	199	73	4.65	R-R	6-4	205	11/26/59 Eakly, OK
19	Nelson, Gene	Oakland	3-3	75	38	1.57	R-R	6-0	175	12/3/60 Tampa, FL
—	Show, Eric	San Diego	6-8	106	55	5.76	R-R	6-1	182	5/19/56 Riverside, CA
34	Stewart, Dave	Oakland	22-11	267	166	2.56	R-R	6-2	200	?/19/57 Oakland, CA
—	Van Poppel, Todd	S. Oregon	1-1	24	32	1.13	R-R	6-5	210	12/9/71 Hinsdale, IL
		Madison	2-1	14	17	3.95				
35	Welch, Bob	Oakland	27-6	238	127	2.95	R-R	6-3	195	11/3/56 Detroit, MI
29	Young, Curt	Oakland	9-6	124	56	4.85	R-L	6-1	175	4/16/60 Saginaw, MI

CATCHERS

No.	Name	1990 Club	H	HR	RBI	Pct.	B-T	Ht.	Wt.	Born
52	Afenir, Troy	Tacoma	72	15	47	.249	R-R	6-4	200	9/21/63 Escondido, CA
		Oakland	2	0	2	.143				
27	*Hassey, Ron	Oakland	54	5	22	.213	L-R	6-2	195	2/27/53 Tucson, AZ
6	Quirk, Jamie	Oakland	34	3	26	.281	L-R	6-4	200	10/22/54 Whittier, CA
36	Steinbach, Terry	Oakland	95	9	57	.251	R-R	6-1	195	3/2/62 New Ulm, MN

INFIELDERS

No.	Name	1990 Club	H	HR	RBI	Pct.	B-T	Ht.	Wt.	Born
12	Blankenship, Lance	Tacoma	24	1	9	.258	R-R	6-0	185	12/6/63 Portland, OR
		Oakland	26	0	10	.191				
46	Bordick, Mike	Tacoma	79	2	30	.227	R-R	5-11	170	7/21/65 Marquette, MI
		Oakland	1	0	0	.071				
9	Gallego, Mike	Oakland	80	3	34	.206	R-R	5-8	160	10/31/60 Whittier, CA
31	Hemond, Scott	Tacoma	53	8	35	.243	R-R	6-0	205	11/18/65 Taunton, MA
		Oakland	2	0	1	.154				
23	Howitt, Dann	Tacoma	116	11	69	.265	L-R	6-5	205	2/13/64 Battle Creek, MI
		Oakland	3	0	1	.136				
4	Lansford, Carney	Oakland	136	3	50	.268	R-R	6-2	195	2/7/57 San Jose, CA
—	Law, Vance	Japan					R-R	6-1	190	10/1/56 Boise, ID
25	McGwire, Mark	Oakland	123	39	108	.235	R-R	6-5	225	10/1/63 Pomona, CA
30	*Randolph, Willie	Los Angeles	26	1	9	.271	R-R	5-11	171	7/6/54 Holly Hill, SC
		Oakland	75	1	21	.257				
—	Riles, Ernest	San Francisco	31	8	21	.200	L-R	6-1	175	10/2/60 Bainbridge, GA
7	Weiss, Walt	Oakland	118	2	35	.265	S-R	6-0	175	11/28/63 Tuxedo, NY

OUTFIELDERS

No.	Name	1990 Club	H	HR	RBI	Pct.	B-T	Ht.	Wt.	Born
3	Baines, Harold	Tex.-Oak.	118	16	65	.284	L-L	6-2	195	3/15/59 Easton, MD
33	Canseco, Jose	Oakland	132	37	101	.274	R-R	6-4	240	7/2/64 Cuba
55	Canseco, Ozzie	Huntsville	73	20	67	.225	R-R	6-3	220	7/2/64 Cuba
		Oakland	2	0	1	.105				
42	Henderson, Dave	Oakland	122	20	63	.271	R-R	6-2	210	7/21/58 Dos Palos, CA
24	Henderson, Rickey	Oakland	159	28	61	.325	R-L	5-10	190	12/25/58 Chicago, IL
2	Jennings, Doug	Tacoma	72	6	30	.346	L-R	5-10	170	9/30/64 Atlanta, GA
		Oakland	30	2	14	.192				
—	Wilson, Willie	Kansas City	89	2	42	.290	S-R	6-3	195	7/9/55 Montgomery, AL

*Free agent at press time

OUTLOOK: Unless there are injuries to Stewart and/or Eckersley, the A's don't figure to slide far from last year's 103-59 finish and should win a third straight West flag. But the history books won't be kind if they suffer another postseason letdown.

ATHLETIC PROFILES

RICKEY HENDERSON 32 5-10 190   Bats R Throws L

Left fielder won MVP Award as he continued to make Yankees look bad for trading him to A's in June 1989 for relievers Greg Cadaret and Eric Plunk plus Luis Polonia . . . Enjoyed perhaps his best overall season, finishing among the AL leaders in runs (first with 119), steals (first with 65), on-base percentage (first at .439), hitting (second at .325), slugging percentage (second at .577), walks (fourth with 97) and homers (sixth with 28) . . . Ended the season with 936 career steals . . . Will surpass Lou Brock's all-time record with just three more swipes . . . Broke Ty Cobb's AL steals record May 29, when he stole third vs. Toronto . . . Only five catchers caught him trying to steal in 1990 . . . Scored from second on a grounder to Yankees shortstop Alvaro Espinoza on May 9 and twice scored from third after popups to infielders . . . Battled George Brett for the batting title, losing by four points on the final day . . . Made his ninth All-Star appearance, the most among AL starters . . . Born Christmas Day, 1958, in Chicago . . . Although he signed a four-year, $12-million contract before '90 season, he later declared, "I'm underpaid." . . . One of the few A's to do well in last year's World Series, he hit .333 vs. Reds.

Year	Club	Pos.	G	AB	R	H	2B	3B	HR	RBI	SB	Avg.
1979	Oakland	OF	89	351	49	96	13	3	1	26	33	.274
1980	Oakland	OF	158	591	111	179	22	4	9	53	100	.303
1981	Oakland	OF	108	423	89	135	18	7	6	35	56	.319
1982	Oakland	OF	149	536	119	143	24	4	10	51	130	.267
1983	Oakland	OF	145	513	105	150	25	7	9	48	108	.292
1984	Oakland	OF	142	502	113	147	27	4	16	58	66	.293
1985	New York (AL)	OF	143	547	146	172	28	5	24	72	80	.314
1986	New York (AL)	OF	153	608	130	160	31	5	28	74	87	.263
1987	New York (AL)	OF	95	358	78	104	17	3	17	37	41	.291
1988	New York (AL)	OF	140	554	118	169	30	2	6	50	93	.305
1989	NY (AL)-Oak. . .	OF	150	541	113	148	26	3	12	57	77	.274
1990	Oakland	OF	136	489	119	159	33	3	28	61	65	.325
	Totals		1608	6013	1290	1762	294	50	166	622	936	.293

JOSE CANSECO 26 6-4 240   Bats R Throws R

The $23.5-Million Man was felled by injuries, but still managed to post big numbers... His 37 homers ranked third in AL... Reached 100-RBI level for the fourth time in five seasons ... Enjoyed a wonderful May with 13 homers and 35 RBI... Put on disabled list June 8 and spent time in a hospital with a protruding disc in his back... Right fielder never returned to early-season form... Required two cortisone shots in back... Has 165 career homers... Most awesome homer of season came May 22, when he blasted shot off top of windowed restaurant in center field at the SkyDome... Runnerup came July 8, when he nearly became first player to hit ball into center-field bleachers at Cleveland Stadium... Received more All-Star votes than anyone and made his second career start... Hit only three homers after Aug. 2... Served as DH for 41 games before arrival of Harold Baines... Two years before being eligible for free agency, he signed a five-year contract, worth $23.5 million, the most lucrative package in baseball history... Born July 2, 1964, in Cuba... Twin brother Ozzie spent most of last season with Huntsville (AA), but played nine games for Oakland... Drew tons of criticism for hitting only .182 in ALCS vs. Boston and .083 in World Series vs. Cincinnati... Played so poorly he was benched in Game 4 of World Series.

Year	Club	Pos.	G	AB	R	H	2B	3B	HR	RBI	SB	Avg.
1985	Oakland	OF	29	96	16	29	3	0	5	13	1	.302
1986	Oakland	OF	157	600	85	144	29	1	33	117	15	.240
1987	Oakland	OF	159	630	81	162	35	3	31	113	15	.257
1988	Oakland	OF	158	610	120	187	34	0	42	124	40	.307
1989	Oakland	OF	65	227	40	61	9	1	17	57	6	.269
1990	Oakland	OF	131	481	83	132	14	2	37	101	19	.274
	Totals		699	2644	425	715	124	7	165	525	96	.270

MARK McGWIRE 27 6-5 225   Bats R Throws R

The other "Bash Brother" put up big power numbers, but posted low batting average for second straight season... His .235 was lowest mark among A's starters... Hit 39th homer with 11 games remaining, but couldn't break 40... Became first player in history to hit at least 30 homers in his first four seasons... His homer total was second in AL to Cecil Fielder's

51 . . . Most memorable homer came May 16, when his two-run, two-out, ninth-inning blast off Cleveland relief ace Doug Jones lifted A's to 7-6 victory . . . Led club in RBI (108) and games (156) and led league in walks (110) . . . First baseman says he's most proud of his defensive work . . . Committed only five errors in 1,416 chances, a .996 fielding percentage, making him runnerup to Twins' Kent Hrbek . . . Had errorless streak of 103 straight games before committing one on July 25 . . . Last year was his first million-dollar season as he earned a total of $1.5 million and a Gold Glove . . . Selected as All-Star starter by fans for third straight season . . . Born Oct. 1, 1963, in Pomona, Cal. . . . Hit just .154 in ALCS and .214 in World Series.

Year Club	Pos.	G	AB	R	H	2B	3B	HR	RBI	SB	Avg.
1986 Oakland	3B	18	53	10	10	1	0	3	9	0	.189
1987 Oakland	1B-3B-OF	151	557	97	161	28	4	49	118	1	.289
1988 Oakland	1B-OF	155	550	87	143	22	1	32	99	0	.260
1989 Oakland	1B	143	490	74	113	17	0	33	95	1	.231
1990 Oakland	1B	156	523	87	123	16	0	39	108	2	.235
Totals		623	2173	355	550	84	5	156	429	4	.253

CARNEY LANSFORD 34 6-2 195   Bats R Throws R

Question mark. Snowmobile injury to his left knee could mean long recovery period . . . Captain Carney struggled at the plate, posting his lowest batting average since 1980 and the second-lowest of his career . . . Batted 68 points less than his career high of .336, set in '89 . . . Despite low average, he hit No. 2 in the lineup more than any other Athletic, following Rickey Henderson 80 times . . . Lowered to bottom half of lineup after Willie McGee arrived in August . . . Was 14-for-33 in season's first week, but cooled off in late April . . . Suffered through a .226 June . . . Played one game after the All-Star break before right hamstring tightened and landed him on disabled list for half of July . . . Returned to lineup and improved average to .286 by Aug. 13, but it fell steadily thereafter . . . Soured in season's final weeks, managing just six hits in his last 36 at-bats . . . Once again, his defense was solid . . . Made just nine errors in 126 games and his .970 fielding percentage was tops among AL third basemen for fourth time in five years . . . Since coming to Oakland in '83, he has played in 971 games. Since 1901, only Sal Bando has played in more A's games at third base . . . Earned $1.275 million last year . . . Born Feb. 7, 1957, down the Peninsula from Oakland, in San Jose, Cal. . . . Hit .438 vs. Red Sox in ALCS, but slipped to .267 in the World Series.

Year	Club	Pos.	G	AB	R	H	2B	3B	HR	RBI	SB	Avg.
1978	California	3B	121	453	63	133	23	2	8	52	20	.294
1979	California	3B	157	654	114	188	30	5	19	79	20	.287
1980	California	3B	151	602	87	157	27	3	15	80	14	.261
1981	Boston	3B	102	399	61	134	23	3	4	52	15	.336
1982	Boston	3B	128	482	65	145	28	4	11	63	9	.301
1983	Oakland	3B-SS	80	299	43	92	16	2	10	45	3	.308
1984	Oakland	3B	151	597	70	179	31	5	14	74	9	.300
1985	Oakland	3B	98	401	51	111	18	2	13	46	2	.277
1986	Oakland	3B-1B-2B	151	591	80	168	16	4	19	72	16	.284
1987	Oakland	3B-1B	151	554	89	160	27	4	19	76	27	.289
1988	Oakland	3B-1B-2B	150	556	80	155	20	2	7	57	29	.279
1989	Oakland	3B-1B	148	551	81	185	28	2	2	52	37	.336
1990	Oakland	3B-1B	134	507	58	136	15	1	3	50	16	.268
	Totals		1722	6646	942	1943	302	39	144	798	217	.292

DAVE HENDERSON 32 6-2 220   Bats R Throws R

Was enjoying another strong season as Athletics' center fielder before injuring his right knee Aug. 20 . . . His sliding attempt to catch Carlton Fisk's flyball at Comiskey Park was his last play for a month . . . Required arthrosopic surgery and a stint on the disabled list . . . Injury prompted A's to trade for eventual NL batting champ Willie McGee, who finished the season in center . . . Returned quicker than expected, but bat was slow . . . Ended final week on 5-for-7 tear . . . Healthy for the ALCS, but began Games 1 and 2 on the bench . . . Improved average 21 points over '89 finish last year . . . His three-year averages with the A's: .274, 20 homers and 79 RBI . . . Threw out two Cleveland runners in one inning July 7 . . . Played for a division winner for the fifth straight year ('86 Red Sox, '87 Giants, '88, '89, '90 A's) . . . Does his best work in September and postseason . . . One of 20 players with at least seven postseason homers . . . Most dramatic was his two-out, two-strike, ninth-inning shot in Game 5 of the '86 playoffs that ignited Boston past California . . . Born July 21, 1958, in Dos Palos, Cal. . . . Took a year off from Mr. October exploits in 1990, hitting .167 in ALCS and .231 in World Series . . . Made $850,000 last year in second season of a three-year contract and, as a new-look free agent, signed a three-year, $7-million contract in December.

Year	Club	Pos.	G	AB	R	H	2B	3B	HR	RBI	SB	Avg.
1981	Seattle.......	OF	59	126	17	21	3	0	6	13	2	.167
1982	Seattle.......	OF	104	324	47	82	17	1	14	48	2	.253
1983	Seattle.......	OF	137	484	50	130	24	5	17	55	9	.269
1984	Seattle.......	OF	112	350	42	98	23	0	14	43	5	.280
1985	Seattle.......	OF	139	502	70	121	28	2	14	68	6	.241
1986	Sea.-Bos	OF	139	388	59	103	22	4	15	47	2	.265
1987	Boston	OF	75	184	30	43	10	0	8	25	1	.234
1987	San Francisco	OF	15	21	2	5	2	0	0	1	2	.238
1988	Oakland......	OF	146	507	100	154	38	1	24	94	2	.304
1989	Oakland......	OF	152	579	77	145	24	3	15	80	8	.250
1990	Oakland......	OF	127	450	65	122	28	0	20	63	3	.271
	Totals		1205	3915	559	1024	219	16	147	537	42	.262

HAROLD BAINES 32 6-2 195   Bats L Throws L

Was reunited with favorite manager, Tony La Russa, when A's sent two minor-league pitchers to Texas for him on Aug. 29 . . . La Russa managed Baines in Knoxville (AA) in '78, Iowa (AAA) in '79 and with the White Sox for 4½ years . . . A's were able to acquire him because he cleared the waiver wire, which stunned and embarrassed the second-place White Sox, who failed to make a claim . . . Called "the best clutch hitter in the league" by La Russa . . . Designated hitter hit in cleanup spot, despite all the power around him in A's lineup . . . Enjoyed hottest string from Sept. 5-10, hitting .455 (10-for-22) with four doubles . . . Very effective pinch-hitter, going 4-for-13 for the season and 2-for-2 for Oakland . . . Hit .290 for Texas and .284 overall . . . Locked into contract through '92 that paid him $1.333 million in '90 . . . Born March 15, 1959, in Easton, Md. . . . Homered in Game 3 of World Series.

Year	Club	Pos.	G	AB	R	H	2B	3B	HR	RBI	SB	Avg.
1980	Chicago (AL) ..	OF	141	491	55	125	23	6	13	49	2	.255
1981	Chicago (AL) ..	OF	82	280	42	80	11	7	10	41	6	.286
1982	Chicago (AL) ..	OF	161	608	89	165	29	8	25	105	10	.271
1983	Chicago (AL) ..	OF	156	596	76	167	33	2	20	99	7	.280
1984	Chicago (AL) ..	OF	147	569	72	173	28	10	29	94	1	.304
1985	Chicago (AL) ..	OF	160	640	86	198	29	3	22	113	1	.309
1986	Chicago (AL) ..	OF	145	570	72	169	29	2	21	88	2	.296
1987	Chicago (AL) ..	OF	132	505	59	148	26	4	20	93	0	.293
1988	Chicago (AL) ..	OF	158	599	55	166	39	1	13	81	0	.277
1989	Chi. (AL)-Tex.	OF	146	505	73	156	29	1	16	72	0	.309
1990	Tex.-Oak......	OF	135	415	52	118	15	1	16	65	0	.284
	Totals		1563	5778	731	1665	291	45	205	900	29	.288

DENNIS ECKERSLEY 36 6-2 195   Bats R Throws R

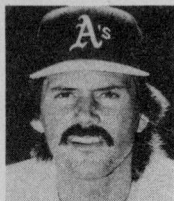

''Eck'' continues to improve with age... Has been game's best reliever over past three seasons, setting new standards in '90... His 48 saves last season were career high and second-highest all-time behind White Sox' Bobby Thigpen, who saved 57 in '90... Saved 19 of Bob Welch's 27 wins, including No. 20... Blew only two save opportunities... Has converted 88 percent of his save opportunities (126-for-143) in last three seasons... Posted microscopic ERA of 0.61... Has uncanny ability to throw strikes, walking only four in 73⅓ innings in 1990... Didn't walk a batter until June 12, snapping a string of 185 innings without issuing a free pass... Has walked only seven batters (one intentional) since passing Dodgers' Mike Davis in fateful ninth inning of 1988 World Series Game 1... Whatever happened to Dave Wilder, Brian Guinn and Mark Leonette, the three guys Oakland sent to the Cubs for him in '87?... Has emerged as club's all-time saves leader, passing Rollie Fingers' mark of 136 on Sept. 15 of last year... One of only six pitchers in 100-100 Club for saves and wins... One of only three pitchers to enjoy two seasons with at least 40 saves... Earned second All-Star save in three years... Made only $787,500 in 1990, but was granted hefty contract extension... Registered two saves in ALCS, but lost World Series Game 2 when he surrendered three straight hits in the 10th inning... Born Oct. 3, 1954, in Oakland.

Year	Club	G	IP	W	L	Pct.	SO	BB	H	ERA
1975	Cleveland	34	187	13	7	.650	152	90	147	2.60
1976	Cleveland	36	199	13	12	.520	200	75	155	3.44
1977	Cleveland	33	247	14	13	.519	191	54	214	3.53
1978	Boston	35	268	20	8	.714	162	71	258	2.99
1979	Boston	33	247	17	10	.630	150	59	234	2.99
1980	Boston	30	198	12	14	.462	121	44	188	4.27
1981	Boston	23	154	9	8	.529	79	35	160	4.27
1982	Boston	33	224⅓	13	13	.500	127	43	228	3.73
1983	Boston	28	176⅓	9	13	.409	77	39	223	5.61
1984	Boston	9	64⅔	4	4	.500	33	13	71	5.01
1984	Chicago (NL)	24	160⅓	10	8	.556	81	36	152	3.03
1985	Chicago (NL)	25	169⅓	11	7	.611	117	19	145	3.08
1986	Chicago (NL)	33	201	6	11	.353	137	43	226	4.57
1987	Oakland	54	115⅔	6	8	.429	113	17	99	3.03
1988	Oakland	60	72⅔	4	2	.667	70	11	52	2.35
1989	Oakland	51	57⅔	4	0	1.000	55	3	32	1.56
1990	Oakland	63	73⅓	4	2	.667	73	4	41	0.61
	Totals	604	2815⅓	169	140	.547	1938	659	2625	3.49

DAVE STEWART 34 6-2 200   Bats R Throws R

Continued to knock on the door to Cooperstown ... Approaching mid-30s, he seems to be getting better and better ... First pitcher to win 20 games for four consecutive seasons since Jim Palmer did it from 1975-78 ... Became 10th pitcher with four straight 20-win seasons since World War II ... His next goal is to become first player since Catfish Hunter to post five straight 20-win campaigns ... Enjoyed best overall season among major leaguers ... Led majors in starts (36) and innings (267), tied for first in shutouts (4) and ranked second in wins (22) ... Was AL co-leader in complete games (11) and ranked third in ERA (2.56) ... Despite Bob Welch's 27 wins, this guy remains A's ace ... Started on Opening Day the last three years ... Started Game 1 in both ALCS and World Series in '88, '89 and '90 ... Especially effective when facing Red Sox' Roger Clemens, whom he has beaten eight straight times ... Was 6-0 in first month of 1990 to extend his April winning streak to 19 straight ... Highly respected off the field, he won Roberto Clemente Award last year ... Especially charitable to people of Oakland, where he was born, Feb. 19, 1957 ... Made $950,000 in 1990, but don't feel sorry for him. He'll make $7 million over the next two years ... After winning ALCS MVP award for beating Boston twice, he lost both of his World Series starts to Reds' Jose Rijo.

Year	Club	G	IP	W	L	Pct.	SO	BB	H	ERA
1978	Los Angeles	1	2	0	0	.000	1	0	1	0.00
1981	Los Angeles	32	43	4	3	.571	29	14	40	2.51
1982	Los Angeles	45	146⅓	9	8	.529	80	49	137	3.81
1983	Los Angeles	46	76	5	2	.714	54	33	67	2.96
1983	Texas	8	59	5	2	.714	24	17	50	2.14
1984	Texas	32	192⅓	7	14	.333	119	87	193	4.73
1985	Texas	42	81⅓	0	6	.000	64	37	86	5.42
1985	Philadelphia	4	4⅓	0	0	.000	2	4	5	6.23
1986	Philadelphia	8	12⅓	0	0	.000	9	4	15	6.57
1986	Oakland	29	149⅓	9	5	.643	102	65	137	3.74
1987	Oakland	37	261⅓	20	13	.606	205	105	224	3.68
1988	Oakland	37	275⅔	21	12	.636	192	110	240	3.23
1989	Oakland	36	257⅔	21	9	.700	155	69	260	3.32
1990	Oakland	36	267	22	11	.667	166	83	226	2.56
	Totals	393	1827⅔	123	85	.591	1202	677	1681	3.52

BOB WELCH 34 6-3 195   Bats R Throws R

AL Cy Young choice was double-figure winner eight times before 1990, but had never won as many as 20 . . . Not only won 20 in '90, but became first AL pitcher to win as many as 27 games since 1968, when Tigers' Denny McClain won 31 . . . Finished at 27-6, the fewest losses he has suffered since '85 . . . As the All-Star Game starter, he tossed two shutout innings . . . Had 13-3 record at the break . . . Won 10 straight games between May 11 and June 30 . . . Combined with Dave Stewart to win 49 games, most by a tandem since Sandy Koufax and Don Drysdale combined for 49 for the '65 Dodgers . . . In 64 of last 66 starts, his battery mate was catcher Ron Hassey. In that time, he has posted a 42-13 record . . . Has lifetime record of 36-8 at the Oakland Coliseum and 24-15 in other AL parks . . . Won his only ALCS start, but was rocked for four runs and nine hits in 7⅓ innings in World Series Game 2 . . . Made $1.133 million last season and became a free agent, re-signing a four-year, $13.8-million contract in December . . . Born Nov. 3, 1956, in Detroit.

Year	Club	G	IP	W	L	Pct.	SO	BB	H	ERA
1978	Los Angeles	23	111	7	4	.636	66	26	92	2.03
1979	Los Angeles	25	81	5	6	.455	64	32	82	4.00
1980	Los Angeles	32	214	14	9	.609	141	79	190	3.28
1981	Los Angeles	23	141	9	5	.643	88	41	141	3.45
1982	Los Angeles	36	235⅔	16	11	.593	176	81	199	3.36
1983	Los Angeles	31	204	15	12	.556	156	72	164	2.65
1984	Los Angeles	31	178⅔	13	13	.500	126	58	191	3.78
1985	Los Angeles	23	167⅓	14	4	.778	96	35	141	2.31
1986	Los Angeles	33	235⅔	7	13	.350	183	55	227	3.28
1987	Los Angeles	35	251⅔	15	9	.625	196	86	204	3.22
1988	Oakland	36	244⅔	17	9	.654	158	81	237	3.64
1989	Oakland	33	209⅔	17	8	.680	137	78	191	3.00
1990	Oakland	35	238	27	6	.818	127	77	214	2.95
	Totals	396	2512⅓	176	109	.618	1714	801	2273	3.16

TOP PROSPECTS

STEVE CHITREN 23 6-0 180   Bats R Throws R

Relief pitcher may one day succeed Dennis Eckersley as Athletics' bullpen closer . . . Saved 27 games for Huntsville (AA), tops in the Southern League . . . Posted 1.68 ERA . . . Pitched 17⅔ innings for Oakland and fashioned 1.02 ERA . . . Born June 8, 1967, in Tokyo, Japan . . . Member of '87 and '88 Stanford teams that won back-to-back College World Series titles . . . Was sixth-round pick in 1989 draft.

MIKE BORDICK 25 6-2 210   **Bats R Throws R**
Highlight of career came in October, when the A's placed him on their World Series roster . . . Replaced injured shortstop Walter Weiss and played in three World Series games . . . Broke camp with the A's, but spent most of the season with Tacoma (AAA) . . . Went 1-for-14 with A's . . . Born July 21, 1965, in Marquette, Mich. . . . Not drafted, but was signed as free agent, July 10, 1986.

TODD VAN POPPEL 19 6-5 196   **Bats R Throws R**
Signed letter of intent to pitch for the University of Texas and requested not to be drafted . . . However, A's made him a first-round pick and offered him an unprecedented $1.2 million over three years, so he changed his mind about college . . . Went 1-1 with 1.13 ERA in five starts for Southern Oregon (A) and 2-1 with 3.95 ERA in three starts for Madison (A) . . . Combined, he posted 49 strikeouts in 37⅔ innings . . . Born Dec. 9, 1971, in Hinsdale, Ill.

MANAGER TONY La RUSSA: Because the A's have been baseball's best team for three years, the job he has done has been somewhat overlooked . . . However, he has done splendid work mixing his superstars and super egos into productive unit . . . Guided the A's to their third straight pennant in 1990 . . . His .594 winning percentages is second in Oakland history behind Dick Williams' .603 and this guy has managed the A's in more games (727) and to more wins (432) . . . Took over

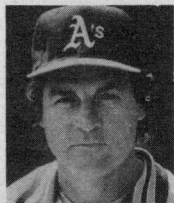

A's in mid-1986, posted 81-81 season in '87 and has won 306 games over past three years . . . Homegrown product . . . Rose to majors with A's in 1963 . . . Managed White Sox from 1979 through part of 1986 . . . One of only five lawyer-managers in history. The other four are in the Hall of Fame—Branch Rickey, Monte Ward, Hughie Jennings and Miller Huggins . . . Born Oct. 4, 1944, in Tampa . . . Played Colt League and American Legion ball with 1990 World Series counterpart Lou Piniella . . . Owns 954-801 overall mark as major-league manager.

ALL-TIME A's SEASON RECORDS

BATTING: Napoleon Lajoie, .422, 1901
HRs: Jimmie Foxx, 58, 1932
RBI: Jimmie Foxx, 169, 1932
STEALS: Rickey Henderson, 130, 1982
WINS: John Coombs, 31, 1910
        Lefty Grove, 31, 1931
STRIKEOUTS: Rube Waddell, 349, 1904

SEATTLE MARINERS

TEAM DIRECTORY: Owner: Jeff Smulyan; Pres.: Gary Kaseff; VP-Baseball Oper.: Woody Woodward; VP-Scouting and Player Dev.: Roger Jongewaard; Dir. Baseball Adm.: Lee Pelekoudas; Farm Dir.: Jim Beattie; Dir. Pub. Rel.: David Aust; Trav. Sec.: Craig Detwiler; Mgr.: Jim Lefebvre. Home: Kingdome (58,150). Field distances: 336, l.f. line; 385, l.c.; 410, c.f.; 375, r.c.; 314, r.f. line. Spring training: Tempe, Ariz.

SCOUTING REPORT

HITTING: The Mariners had problems scoring runs in 1990 as only the Yankees crossed the plate fewer times than Seattle (640). Don't blame Ken Griffey Jr. The kid hit an even .300 and collected 22 homers and 80 RBI. Any year now, he's going to have an MVP season.

There's nothing Junior about Ken Griffey's talents.

Griffey didn't receive a lot of support. Key hitters Alvin Davis (.283, 17, 68) and Pete O'Brien (.224, 5, 27) each slipped from his 1989 production.

One newcomer who picked up part of the slack was Edgar Martinez (.302, 11, 49), who figures to be the Mariners' third baseman for years to come. Harold Reynolds (.252, 5, 55) scored 100 runs as the leadoff hitter.

Jeffrey Leonard has finally worn out his welcome in Seattle, posting a lowly .251 average and 10 homers and receiving his walking papers. But the Mariners wish Jay Buhner would have that big season people have been waiting for.

PITCHING: The Mariners finished at 77-85 and 26 games out of first place in 1990, but their pitching staff was exciting. They had the third-best ERA in the league and lowest in club history (3.69) and led the league in strikeouts (1,064). Three Mariners were among the top eight strikeout pitchers—Erik Hanson (18-9, 3.24, 211 Ks), Randy Johnson (14-11, 3.65, 194 Ks) and free-agent defector Matt Young (176 Ks). In 1991, Hanson and Johnson will be joined by Brian Holman (11-11, 4.03) and shoulder rehab case Scott Bankhead (0-2, 11.08). Mike Schooler (1-4, 2.25), despite missing the final month, was eighth in the AL in saves with 30.

The loss of Young shouldn't hurt, but don't tell the Red Sox, who amazingly forked over $6.3 million to Young for three years, even though Young lost an alarming 18 games last year.

FIELDING: Griffey Jr. proved he's an all-around player by winning his first Gold Glove in center. Only Johnny Bench won a Gold Glove at a younger age than the 21-year-old star. While Griffey Jr. anchors the outfield, Reynolds guides the infield as a crafty second baseman and the Mariners' first three-time Gold Glove winner.

OUTLOOK: Any team built around the younger Griffey has to have a promising future, but Griffey can do only so much. He'll need much more support if Seattle is to post its first winning season. Manager Jim Lefebvre has Mariners fans believing the streak of 14 straight losing years is history after a 77-85 finish in 1990.

Griffey seemed to prosper with his father, Ken Sr., as his teammate. But how long the Griffey-Griffey affair will last is anyone's guess. Griffey Sr., who turns 41 in April, must show that his splurge late last season wasn't a fluke.

SEATTLE MARINERS 1991 ROSTER

MANAGER Jim Lefebvre
Coaches—Ron Clark, Gene Clines, Rusty Kuntz, Mike Paul, Bill Plummer

PITCHERS

No.	Name	1990 Club	W-L	IP	SO	ERA	B-T	Ht.	Wt.	Born
15	Bankhead, Scott	Seattle	0-2	13	10	11.08	R-R	5-10	185	7/31/63 Raleigh, NC
		Calgary	0-1	7	7	6.43				
34	Burba, Dave	Calgary	10-6	114	47	4.67	R-R	6-4	220	7/7/66 Dayton, OH
		Seattle	0-0	8	4	4.50				
32	Comstock, Keith	Seattle	7-4	56	50	2.89	L-L	6-0	175	12/23/55 San Francisco, CA
55	DeLucia, Rich	San Bernardino	4-1	31	35	2.05	R-R	6-0	180	10/7/64 Reading, PA
		Williamsport	6-6	115	76	2.11				
		Calgary	2-2	32	23	3.62				
		Seattle	1-2	36	20	2.00				
23	Gardiner, Mike	Williamsport	12-8	180	149	1.90	S-R	6-0	185	10/19/65 Canada
		Seattle	0-2	13	6	10.66				
31	Givens, Brian	Tidewater	4-6	83	53	4.12	R-L	6-5	220	11/6/65 Lompoc, CA
		Calgary	0-1	6	4	12.71				
39	Hanson, Erik	Seattle	18-9	236	211	3.24	R-R	6-6	210	5/18/65 Kinnelon, NJ
47	Harris, Gene	Calgary	3-0	8	9	2.35	R-R	5-11	190	12/4/64 Sebring, FL
		Seattle	1-2	38	43	4.74				
36	Holman, Brian	Seattle	11-11	190	121	4.03	R-R	6-4	185	1/25/65 Denver, CO
38	Jackson, Mike	Seattle	5-7	77	69	4.54	R-R	6-0	190	12/22/64 Houston, TX
51	Johnson, Randy	Seattle	14-11	220	194	3.65	R-L	6-10	225	9/10/63 Walnut Creek, CA
27	Knackert, Brent	Seattle	1-1	37	28	6.61	R-R	6-3	190	8/1/69 Los Angeles, CA
54	Melendez, Jose	Calgary	11-4	125	95	3.90	R-R	6-2	175	9/2/65 Puerto Rico
		Seattle	0-0	5	7	11.81				
40	Schooler, Mike	Seattle	1-4	56	45	2.25	R-R	6-3	220	8/10/62 Anaheim, CA
37	Swan, Russ	San Francisco	0-1	2	1	3.86	L-L	6-4	215	1/3/64 Fremont, CA
		Phoe.-Calg.	3-6	57	35	4.45				
		Seattle	2-3	47	15	3.64				
18	Swift, Bill	Seattle	6-4	128	42	2.39	R-R	6-0	180	10/27/61 South Portland, ME
33	Walker, Mike	Calgary	5-11	145	64	5.35	R-R	6-3	205	6/23/65 Houston, TX
41	Zavaras, Clint	Seattle	Injured				R-R	6-1	175	1/4/67 Denver, CO

CATCHERS

No.	Name	1990 Club	H	HR	RBI	Pct.	B-T	Ht.	Wt.	Born
9	Bradley, Scott	Seattle	52	1	28	.223	L-R	5-11	185	3/22/60 Montclair, NJ
45	Howard, Chris	Williamsport	95	5	49	.237	R-R	6-2	200	2/27/66 San Diego, CA
35	McGuire, Bill	Calgary	82	7	46	.229	R-R	6-3	215	2/14/64 Omaha, NE
10	Valle, David	Seattle	66	7	33	.214	R-R	6-2	200	10/30/60 Bayside, NY

INFIELDERS

No.	Name	1990 Club	H	HR	RBI	Pct.	B-T	Ht.	Wt.	Born
29	Bolick, Frank	Stockton	51	8	36	.311	S-R	5-10	177	6/28/66 Ashland, PA
		San Bernardino	92	10	66	.332				
43	Cochrane, Dave	Calgary	72	8	36	.275	S-R	6-2	180	1/31/63 Riverside, CA
		Seattle	3	0	0	.150				
21	Davis, Alvin	Seattle	140	17	68	.283	L-R	6-1	190	9/9/60 Riverside, CA
14	Martinez, Edgar	Seattle	147	11	49	.302	R-R	5-11	175	1/2/63 New York, NY
11	Martinez, Tino	Calgary	145	17	93	.320	L-R	6-2	205	12/7/67 Tampa, FL
		Seattle	15	0	5	.221				
12	O'Brien, Pete	Seattle	82	5	27	.224	L-L	6-2	195	2/9/58 Santa Monica, CA
4	Reynolds, Harold	Seattle	162	5	55	.252	S-R	5-11	165	11/26/60 Eugene, OR
2	Schaefer, Jeff	Calgary	41	0	19	.241	R-R	5-10	170	5/31/60 Patchogue, NY
		Seattle	22	0	6	.206				
13	Vizquel, Omar	Calgary	35	0	8	.233	S-R	5-9	165	4/24/67 Venezuela
		Seattle	63	2	18	.247				

OUTFIELDERS

No.	Name	1990 Club	H	HR	RBI	Pct.	B-T	Ht.	Wt.	Born
8	Briley, Greg	Seattle	83	5	29	.246	L-R	5-8	165	5/24/65 Greenville, NC
19	Buhner, Jay	Calgary	7	2	5	.206	R-R	6-3	205	8/13/64 Louisville, KY
		Seattle	45	7	33	.276				
28	Cotto, Henry	Seattle	92	4	33	.259	R-R	6-2	180	1/5/61 Bronx, NY
24	Griffey Jr., Ken	Seattle	179	22	80	.300	L-L	6-3	195	11/21/69 Donora, PA
30	Griffey Sr., Ken	Cincinnati	13	1	8	.206	L-L	6-0	210	4/10/50 Donora, PA
		Seattle	29	3	18	.377				
—	Hood, Dennis	Richmond	96	8	36	.247	R-R	6-2	170	7/3/66 Glendale, CA
25	Jones, Tracy	Det.-Sea.	53	6	24	.260	R-R	6-3	220	3/31/61 Inglewood, CA
26	Lennon, Patrick	San Bernardino	47	8	30	.288	R-R	6-2	200	4/27/68 Whiteville, NC
		Williamsport	49	5	22	.293				

MARINER PROFILES

KEN GRIFFEY Jr. 21 6-3 195   Bats L Throws L

The youngest player in the league last year keeps improving . . . Highlight of season was Aug. 29, when Ken Sr. signed with Mariners and became his son's teammate . . . Two days later, vs. Kansas City, the Griffeys were in the same lineup, the first father-son batting order in major-league history . . . Both Griffeys singled in the first inning . . . On Sept. 14, they hit back-to-back homers off California's Kirk McCaskill . . . With Junior's influence, dad caught fire, too, hitting in 15 of final 19 games . . . Didn't want to be shown up by his old man, so he hit in 21 of 26 games from time dad signed to end of season . . . Slugged four homers in his last 14 games and collected an RBI in seven straight games in late September . . . Center fielder's 179 hits ranked fifth in AL . . . AL Player of the Month in April . . . Became first Mariner ever to be voted onto All-Star team . . . Future millionaire made $180,000 and won a Gold Glove in 1990 . . . Born Nov. 21, 1969, in Donora, Pa. . . . Mariners' first-round pick in 1987 draft.

Year	Club	Pos.	G	AB	R	H	2B	3B	HR	RBI	SB	Avg.
1989	Seattle	OF	127	455	61	120	23	0	16	61	16	.264
1990	Seattle	OF	155	597	91	179	28	7	22	80	16	.300
	Totals		282	1052	152	299	51	7	38	141	32	.284

HAROLD REYNOLDS 30 5-11 165   Bats S Throws R

Improved in almost every offensive category . . . Set club record for most RBI by a second baseman (55) . . . Career highs in homers, RBI, at-bats, runs, doubles and walks . . . Entered the season with six career homers and belted five in '90 . . . All five homers were on the road . . . Began career by going 1,231 at-bats on the road without a home run . . . Hit first career grand slam, Sept. 5 at Baltimore . . . Reached safely in club-record 39 straight games . . . Became only third Mariner in history to score 100 runs. Ruppert Jones ('79) and Phil Bradley ('85, '87) were other century men . . . First Mariner to win Presidential Daily Point of Light Award for outstanding achievement in community . . . Earned $966,667 and a Gold Glove in 1990 . . . Born Nov. 26, 1960, in Eugene, Ore. . . . Brother Don played in Padres' and

Mariners' organizations and brother Larry played with the Rangers
... Mariners made him second player chosen in 1980 draft.

Year Club	Pos.	G	AB	R	H	2B	3B	HR	RBI	SB	Avg.
1983 Seattle.......	2B	20	59	8	12	4	1	0	1	0	.203
1984 Seattle.......	2B	10	10	3	3	0	0	0	0	1	.300
1985 Seattle.......	2B	67	104	15	15	3	1	0	6	3	.144
1986 Seattle.......	2B	126	445	46	99	19	4	1	24	30	.222
1987 Seattle.......	2B	160	530	73	146	31	8	1	35	60	.275
1988 Seattle.......	2B	158	598	61	169	26	11	4	41	35	.283
1989 Seattle.......	2B	153	613	87	184	24	9	0	43	25	.300
1990 Seattle.......	2B	160	642	100	162	36	5	5	55	31	.252
Totals		854	3001	393	790	143	39	11	205	185	.263

ALVIN DAVIS 30 6-1 190   Bats L Throws R

Had another good all-around season... First
Mariner to collect 1,000 hits, getting No. 1,000
July 22 off Milwaukee's Teddy Higuera...
Reached base in 120 of 140 games... Hit
safely in last seven games... Better slugger at
home... Had 12 homers and 40 RBI at Kingdome, but only five homers and 28 RBI on the
road... Hit ninth career grand slam... His
three grand slams set Mariners' single-season record... Excellent
bases-loaded hitter, with .351 career average (27-for-77)
... Highest-paid Mariner at $1.475 million last year... Born
Sept. 9, 1960, in Riverside, Cal.... Received a B.S. degree in
finance at Arizona State.... Sixth-round pick in 1982 draft.

Year Club	Pos.	G	AB	R	H	2B	3B	HR	RBI	SB	Avg.
1984 Seattle.......	1B	152	567	80	161	34	3	27	116	5	.284
1985 Seattle.......	1B	155	578	78	166	33	1	18	78	1	.287
1986 Seattle.......	1B	135	479	66	130	18	1	18	72	0	.271
1987 Seattle.......	1B	157	580	86	171	37	2	29	100	0	.295
1988 Seattle.......	1B	140	478	67	141	24	1	18	69	1	.295
1989 Seattle.......	1B	142	498	84	152	30	1	21	95	0	.305
1990 Seattle.......	1B	140	494	63	140	21	0	17	68	0	.283
Totals		1021	3674	524	1061	197	9	148	598	7	.289

JAY BUHNER 26 6-3 205   Bats R Throws R

Amasses good numbers when healthy, but this
outfielder's season was cut short by injuries...
Missed first two months with a sprained right
ankle... Broke right arm and landed on disabled list from June 17-Aug. 23... Spent 108
total games on DL... Had 33 RBI in 44 starts
... Enjoyed first four-hit game, Sept. 26 at Detroit... Ended season strong, hitting .313 in

final 31 games...Born Aug. 13, 1964, in Louisville, Ky. ...Signed letter of intent to play for University of Texas, but shelved college when drafted by Pirates...Traded to Yankees in 1984, before reaching majors...Joined Mariners in Ken Phelps trade, July 21, 1988...Made $160,000 in 1990.

Year	Club	Pos.	G	AB	R	H	2B	3B	HR	RBI	SB	Avg.
1987	New York (AL)	OF	7	22	0	5	2	0	0	1	0	.227
1988	NY (AL)-Sea. ...	OF	85	261	36	56	13	1	13	38	1	.215
	Totals		92	283	36	61	15	1	13	39	1	.216

PETE O'BRIEN 33 6-2 195   Bats L Throws L

His first year with Mariners was below par... Stats have dropped annually since '87... After signing four-year, $7.6-million deal as free agent, he suffered most disappointing season of his career... His .224 average was career low and his five homers and 27 RBI were also full-season lows... Spent from May 4-June 19 on the disabled list with fractured right thumb ...Played 97 games at first base...Most productive games came when he started in left field as he hit .389 (7-for-18)...Earned $1,187,500 in first year of big contract...Born Feb. 9, 1958, in Santa Monica. Cal....Rangers' 15th-round choice in 1979 draft.

Year	Club	Pos.	G	AB	R	H	2B	3B	HR	RBI	SB	Avg.
1982	Texas	OF-1B	20	67	13	16	4	1	4	13	1	.239
1983	Texas	1B-OF	154	524	53	124	24	5	8	53	5	.237
1984	Texas	1B-OF	142	520	57	149	26	2	18	80	3	.287
1985	Texas	1B	159	573	69	153	34	3	22	92	5	.267
1986	Texas	1B	156	551	86	160	23	3	23	90	4	.290
1987	Texas	1B-OF	159	569	84	163	26	1	23	88	0	.286
1988	Texas	1B	156	547	57	149	24	1	16	71	1	.272
1989	Cleveland	1B	155	555	75	144	24	1	12	55	3	.260
1990	Seattle.	1B-OF	108	366	32	82	18	0	5	27	0	.224
	Totals		1209	4271	526	1140	203	17	131	569	22	.267

EDGAR MARTINEZ 28 5-11 175   Bats R Throws R

A wonderful addition to Mariners' lineup... Third baseman posted highest batting average (.302) among Seattle regulars, topping Ken Griffey Jr. by two points...Ranked sixth in AL in average...Hit .317 in September and led Mariners in hitting after All-Star break at .301...Consistency showed in fact he hit .300 or above for all but 11 days of season...On-

base percentage of .397 ranked third in AL . . . With just one day
in season remaining, he underwent surgery on right knee . . .
Earned $108,000 . . . Born Jan. 2, 1963, in New York City, but
he resides in Dorado, Puerto Rico . . . Cousin Carmelo Martinez
plays for Pirates.

Year Club	Pos.	G	AB	R	H	2B	3B	HR	RBI	SB	Avg.
1987 Seattle.......	3B	13	43	6	16	5	2	0	5	0	.372
1988 Seattle.......	3B	14	32	0	9	4	0	0	5	0	.281
1989 Seattle.......	3B	65	171	20	41	5	0	2	20	2	.240
1990 Seattle.......	3B	144	487	71	147	27	2	11	49	1	.302
Totals.......		236	733	97	213	31	4	13	79	3	.291

ERIK HANSON 25 6-6 210 — Bats R Throws R

Ace of very young staff . . . Produced lowest
ERA (3.24) of any starter in club history,
eclipsing Matt Young's 3.27 mark in '83 . . .
Hurled first career shutout Oct. 2 vs. Twins . . .
Finished season with seven-game winning
streak . . . Became winningest right-hander in
club history with 18 wins . . . Ranked third in
league in strikeouts (211), fourth in wins (18)
and innings (236), sixth in opponents' batting average (.232) and
ninth in ERA . . . Earned $150,000 in 1990 . . . Born May 18,
1965, in Kinnelon, N.J. . . . Second-round selection in 1986 draft.

Year Club	G	IP	W	L	Pct.	SO	BB	H	ERA
1988 Seattle...........	6	41⅔	2	3	.400	36	12	35	3.24
1989 Seattle...........	17	113⅓	9	5	.643	75	32	103	3.18
1990 Seattle...........	33	236	18	9	.667	211	68	205	3.24
Totals............	56	391	29	17	.630	322	112	343	3.22

RANDY JOHNSON 27 6-10 225 — Bats R Throws L

A tough-luck pitcher, but a successful one . . .
Mariners' offense didn't provide him with as
many as four runs until Aug. 31 . . . Over four
straight July starts, he posted 3.41 ERA, but
went 0-4 as Seattle was outscored, 19-2 . . .
Almost had to throw a no-hitter to secure a
victory, so he did . . . Tossed first no-hitter in
Mariners' history when he beat Tigers, 2-0,
June 2 . . . No-hitter was his first career shutout . . . Bettered previous win total by seven . . . Opponents hit only .216 against him,
second-lowest mark in league behind Nolan Ryan . . . His 194
strikeouts ranked sixth in league and were second-most among

lefties . . . On May 1, he became only lefty to strike out Wade Boggs three times in a game . . . Named AL Pitcher of the Month in June after going 5-0, 2.40 . . . Selected to All-Star team, but didn't play . . . Tallest player in big-league history . . . Attended USC on baseball and basketball scholarship, but scratched hoops career in his junior year . . . Made $150,000 in 1990 . . . Born Sept. 10, 1963, in Walnut Creek, Cal. . . . Expos' second-round pick in 1985.

Year	Club	G	IP	W	L	Pct.	SO	BB	H	ERA
1988	Montreal	4	26	3	0	1.000	25	7	23	2.42
1989	Montreal	7	29⅔	0	4	.000	26	26	29	6.67
1989	Seattle	22	131	7	9	.438	104	70	118	4.40
1990	Seattle	33	219⅔	14	11	.560	194	120	174	3.65
	Totals	66	406⅓	24	24	.500	349	223	344	4.03

BRIAN HOLMAN 26 6-4 185   Bats R Throws R

A two-out, ninth-inning hit, a homer by Oakland's Ken Phelps, ruined his chance for a perfect game April 20 . . . Posted career highs in wins (11), innings (189⅔) and strikeouts (121) . . . Lost final four decisions . . . Underwent surgery Sept. 11 to remove bone chips from his right elbow . . . Part of the memorable Mark Langston trade, which sent him, Randy Johnson and Gene Harris from Expos to Mariners, May 26, 1989 . . . Earned $193,000 in 1990 . . . Born Jan. 25, 1965, in Denver. . . . Expos picked him 16th overall in 1983.

Year	Club	G	IP	W	L	Pct.	SO	BB	H	ERA
1988	Montreal	18	100⅓	4	8	.333	58	34	101	3.23
1989	Montreal	10	31⅔	1	2	.333	23	15	34	4.83
1989	Seattle	23	159⅔	8	10	.444	82	62	160	3.44
1990	Seattle	28	189⅔	11	11	.500	121	66	188	4.03
	Totals	79	481⅓	24	31	.436	284	177	483	3.72

MIKE SCHOOLER 28 6-3 220   Bats R Throws R

Bullpen closer finished eighth in AL in saves with 30 and had only four blown saves . . . Set AL record as fastest to reach 50 career saves in terms of appearances, earning No. 50 in his 110th game : . . Missed major-league record by one game as St. Louis' Todd Worrell posted 50th save in 109th game . . . By comparison, Dan Quisenberry needed 133 games to save 50 and Bruce Sutter needed 146 . . . All-time club save leader with

71 . . . Mariners' second-round pick in 1985 draft . . . Earned
$260,000 in 1990 . . . Born Aug. 10, 1962, in Anaheim, Cal.

Year	Club	G	IP	W	L	Pct.	SO	BB	H	ERA
1988	Seattle	40	48⅓	5	8	.385	54	24	45	3.54
1989	Seattle	67	77	1	7	.125	69	19	81	2.81
1990	Seattle	49	56	1	4	.200	45	16	47	2.25
	Totals.	156	181⅓	7	19	.269	168	59	173	2.83

TOP PROSPECTS

TINO MARTINEZ 23 6-2 205   Bats L Throws R
First baseman with power . . . Hit .320 with 17 homers and 93
RBI for Calgary (AAA) . . . Once hit two homers in one inning
. . . Born Dec. 7, 1967, in Tampa . . . First-round pick in 1988
draft.

MIKE GARDINER 25 6-0 185   Bats S Throws R
Enjoyed fine season for Williamsport (AA), prompting call-up to
parent club in September . . . Went 12-8 with 1.90 ERA for Williamsport . . . Has tremendous control . . . In 179⅔ innings, he
walked only 29 batters and struck out 149 . . . Born Oct. 19, 1965,
in Sarnia, Ont., Canada . . . Graduated from Indiana State in 1987
with degree in business . . . Played for Canada in 1984 Olympics.

RICH DeLUCIA 26 6-0 180   Bats R Throws R
Remarkably, he pitched with four different teams in 1990, beginning in Class A and ending in majors . . . Enjoyed success at every
level . . . Was 4-1 with 2.05 ERA for San Bernardino (A) . . . Went
6-6 with 2.11 for Williamsport (AA) . . . Was 2-2, 3.62 for Calgary (AAA) and 1-2, 2.00 with Mariners . . . Was sixth-round pick
in 1986 draft . . . Attended University of Tennessee . . . Born Oct.
7, 1964 in Reading, Pa.

DAVE BURBA 24 6-4 220   Bats R Throws R
On the verge of breaking into majors . . . Went 10-6 with 4.67
ERA for Calgary (AAA) . . . Appeared in 31 games, made 18 starts
and saved two games . . . Earned September promotion to Seattle
. . . Born July 7, 1966, in Dayton, Ohio . . . Second-round pick in
1987 draft . . . Played at Ohio State . . . Uncle Ray Hathaway
pitched for Brooklyn Dodgers in 1945.

MANAGER JIM LEFEBVRE: Accomplished something no other Seattle skipper ever had by improving Mariners' won-lost record for second year in a row . . . His 77-85 record in 1990 bettered Mariners '89 record of 73-89, which topped '88 mark of 68-83 . . . Those 77 wins ranked him second to Dick Williams (78 in 1987) among Seattle managers . . . Ninth manager in club history . . . He'll be expected to improve record once again . . . Becoming player's manager . . . He's highly respected . . . His goodwill move of bringing Ken Griffey Sr. to Seattle turned into a wise decision as Griffey hit .377 in 21 games . . . Co-authored a book, "The Making of a Hitter" . . . Coached with Giants and Dodgers from 1978-82 . . . Later worked as Giants' director of player development and Triple-A manager . . . Joined A's staff in '87 and served as Tony La Russa's third-base coach and hitting instructor . . . Played in majors for eight seasons, all with the Dodgers . . . Named Rookie of Year in '65 . . . Only other pro franchise he played for was Lotte Orions in Japan . . . Born Jan. 7, 1942, in Inglewood, Cal. . . . Has 150-174 career major-league managerial mark.

ALL-TIME MARINER SEASON RECORDS

BATTING: Tom Paciorek, .326, 1981
HRs: Gorman Thomas, 32, 1985
RBI: Alvin Davis, 116, 1984
STEALS: Harold Reynolds, 60, 1987
WINS: Mark Langston, 19, 1987
STRIKEOUTS: Mark Langston, 262, 1987

TEXAS RANGERS

TEAM DIRECTORY: General Partners: George W. Bush, Edward W. (Rusty) Rose; VP-GM: Tom Grieve; VP-Business Oper.: John McMichael; VP-Adm.: Charles Wangner; Asst. GM-Player Pers./Scouting: Sandy Johnson; Dir. Player Dev.: Marty Scott; VP-Pub. Rel.: John Blake; Trav. Sec.: Dan Schimek; Mgr.: Bobby Valentine. Home: Arlington Stadium (43,508). Field distances: 330, l.f. line; 380, l.c.; 400, c.f.; 380, r.c.; 330, r.f. line. Spring training: Port Charlotte, Fla.

SCOUTING REPORT

HITTING: Despite the late-season deal that sent Harold Baines to Oakland, the Rangers still have the foundation for a strong

Nolan Ryan's next no-hitter will be his seventh.

lineup. But more power is needed considering Texas hit its fewest homers (110) since 1983 last year.

Ruben Sierra (.280, 16, 96) needs to relocate his 1989 form, as does Julio Franco (.296, 11, 69), who drove in 23 fewer runs than in 1989 and saw his streak of consecutive .300 seasons end at four. Rafael Palmeiro (.319, 14, 89) improved in his second AL season and maybe youngster Juan Gonzalez (.289, 4, 12 in 90 at-bats) can help Pete Incaviglia (.233, 24, 85) with the power load. A healthy wrist should help Steve Buechele improve on last season's sad .215 showing.

PITCHING: The pitching staff seemed to get better as the season wore on, which might be a good sign for 1991. The Rangers' club ERA was 4.43 in the first half, but a very respectable 3.25 in the second. Texas led the AL with 25 complete games as Bobby Witt (17-10, 3.36) produced seven and Kevin Brown (12-10, 3.60) had six.

The Rangers gave up on knuckleballer Charlie Hough, but Nolan Ryan (13-9, 3.44) doesn't seem to be slowing down, even at age 44.

The bullpen, which was without former stalwart Jeff Russell for most of the season, had just 36 saves in 55 opportunities—15 of them by Kenny Rogers (10-6, 3.13).

FIELDING: Once again, Texas sported one of the league's worst defenses, finishing 12th in the AL with 133 errors. Topping the list were second baseman Franco and shortstop Jeff Huson, both of whom committed 19 miscues. Sierra made 10 errors in the outfield. Texas catchers led the AL in passed balls (35) for the seventh straight year, so Geno Petralli probably isn't heartbroken about the knuckleballer Hough's departure. At least center fielder Gary Pettis didn't make an error after June 7 and ranked fourth among AL outfielders at .993.

OUTLOOK: Bobby Valentine's Rangers have put together back-to-back 83-79 finishes and that's not good enough to compete in the AL West. But the Rangers went 62-47 from June 7 through the end of last season, the third-best mark in baseball over that span, so Ranger fans hope they have reason to believe in 1991.

If all else fails, there's still Hall of Fame shoo-in Ryan around to make more history with, ho hum, another no-hitter or two.

TEXAS RANGERS 1991 ROSTER

MANAGER Bobby Valentine
Coaches—Toby Harrah, Tom House, Davey Lopes, Dave Oliver, Tom Robson

PITCHERS

No.	Name	1990 Club	W-L	IP	SO	ERA	B-T	Ht.	Wt.	Born
49	Alexander, Gerald	Charlotte	6-1	43	39	0.63	R-R	5-11	190	3/26/68 Baton Rouge, LA
		Oklahoma City	13-2	119	94	4.10				
		Texas	0-0	7	8	7.71				
28	Arnsberg, Brad	Oklahoma City	0-4	30	17	5.16	R-R	6-4	210	8/20/63 Seattle, WA
		Texas	6-1	63	44	2.15				
27	Barfield, John	Oklahoma City	1-6	43	25	3.53	L-L	6-1	195	10/15/64 Pine Bluff, AR
		Texas	4-3	44	17	4.67				
45	Bohanon, Brian	Texas	0-3	34	15	6.62	L-L	6-2	215	8/1/68 Denton, TX
		Oklahoma City	1-2	32	22	3.66				
41	Brown, Kevin	Texas	12-10	180	88	3.60	R-R	6-4	188	3/14/65 McIntyre, GA
43	Chiamparino, Scott	Tacoma	13-9	173	100	3.28	L-R	6-2	200	8/22/66 San Mateo, CA
		Texas	1-2	38	19	2.63				
23	Guzman, Jose	Charlotte	0-1	8	7	2.16	R-R	6-3	195	4/9/63 Puerto Rico
		Oklahoma City	0-3	29	26	5.65				
		Tulsa	0-0	3	2	6.00				
30	Jeffcoat, Mike	Texas	5-6	111	58	4.47	L-L	6-2	190	8/3/59 Pine Bluff, AR
—	Manuel, Barry	Charlotte	1-5	56	60	2.88	R-R	5-11	180	8/12/65 Mamou, LA
38	*McMurtry, Craig	Texas	0-3	42	14	4.32	R-R	6-5	195	11/5/59 Temple, TX
—	Nen, Robb	Charlotte	1-4	54	38	3.69	R-R	6-4	190	11/28/69 San Pedro, CA
		Tulsa	0-5	27	21	5.06				
—	Pavlik, Roger	Charlotte	5-3	66	76	2.44	R-R	6-2	185	10/4/67 Houston, TX
		Tulsa	6-5	100	91	2.33				
56	Petkovsek, Mark	Oklahoma City	7-14	151	81	5.25	R-R	6-0	185	11/18/65 Beaumont, TX
37	Rogers, Kenny	Texas	10-6	98	74	3.13	L-L	6-1	205	11/10/64 Savannah, GA
40	Russell, Jeff	Texas	1-5	25	16	4.26	R-R	6-3	210	9/2/61 Cincinnati, OH
		Charlotte	0-1	0	0	—				
34	Ryan, Nolan	Texas	13-9	204	232	3.44	R-R	6-2	210	1/31/47 Refugio, TX
—	Shaw, Cedric	Charlotte	5-3	68	69	1.59	L-L	5-11	160	5/28/67 New Orleans, LA
		Tulsa	4-5	63	41	6.86				
36	Witt, Bobby	Texas	17-10	222	221	3.36	R-R	6-2	205	5/11/64 Arlington, VA

CATCHERS

No.	Name	1990 Club	H	HR	RBI	Pct.	B-T	Ht.	Wt.	Born
33	Haselman, Bill	Tulsa	137	18	80	.319	R-R	6-3	205	5/25/66 Long Branch, NJ
		Texas	2	0	3	.154				
7	Kreuter, Chad	Texas	1	0	2	.045	R-R	6-2	190	8/26/64 Greenbrae, CA
		Oklahoma City	65	7	35	.223				
—	Parent, Mark	San Diego	42	3	16	.222	R-R	6-5	240	9/16/61 Ashland, OR
12	Petralli, Geno	Texas	83	0	21	.255	L-R	6-1	190	9/25/59 Sacramento, CA

INFIELDERS

No.	Name	1990 Club	H	HR	RBI	Pct.	B-T	Ht.	Wt.	Born
22	Buechele, Steve	Texas	54	7	30	.215	R-R	6-2	190	9/26/61 Lancaster, CA
		Oklahoma City	3	1	1	.143				
8	Daugherty, Jack	Texas	93	6	47	.300	S-L	6-0	190	7/3/60 Hialeah, FL
4	Fariss, Monty	Tulsa	73	7	34	.299	R-R	6-4	180	10/13/67 Leedey, OK
		Oklahoma City	68	4	31	.302				
14	Franco, Julio	Texas	172	11	69	.296	R-R	6-1	185	8/23/61 Dominican Republic
57	Green, Gary	Oklahoma City	39	4	25	.234	R-R	6-3	175	1/14/62 Pittsburgh, PA
		Texas	19	0	9	.216				
—	Hernandez, Jose	Charlotte	99	1	44	.255	R-R	6-1	180	7/14/69 Puerto Rico
9	Huson, Jeff	Texas	95	0	28	.240	L-R	6-3	180	8/15/64 Scottsdale, AZ
20	Kunkel, Jeff	Texas	34	3	17	.170	R-R	6-2	180	3/25/62 West Palm Beach, FL
		Oklahoma City	8	0	3	.421				
—	Maurer, Rob	Tulsa	110	21	78	.300	L-L	6-3	200	1/7/67 Evansville, IN
25	Palmiero, Rafael	Texas	191	14	89	.319	L-L	6-0	180	9/24/64 Cuba
16	Palmer, Dean	Tulsa	7	3	9	.292	R-R	6-1	190	12/27/68 Tallahassee, FL
		Oklahoma City	69	12	39	.218				

OUTFIELDERS

No.	Name	1990 Club	H	HR	RBI	Pct.	B-T	Ht.	Wt.	Born
18	Belcher, Kevin	Tulsa	124	11	43	.293	R-R	6-0	175	8/8/67 Waco, TX
		Texas	2	0	0	.133				
19	Gonzalez, Juan	Oklahoma City	128	29	101	.258	R-R	6-3	210	10/16/69 Puerto Rico
		Texas	26	4	12	.289				
29	Incaviglia, Pete	Texas	123	24	85	.233	R-R	6-1	220	4/2/64 Pebble Beach, CA
24	Pettis, Gary	Texas	101	3	31	.239	S-R	6-1	160	4/3/58 Oakland, CA
47	Reimer, Kevin	Oklahoma City	56	4	33	.283	L-R	6-2	220	6/28/64 Macon, GA
		Texas	26	2	15	.260				
—	Scruggs, Tony	Gastonia	84	8	48	.307	R-R	6-1	210	3/19/66 Riverside, CA
		Tulsa	67	4	38	.344				
21	Sierra, Ruben	Texas	170	16	96	.280	S-R	6-1	175	10/6/65 Puerto Rico

*Free agent at press time

RANGER PROFILES

RAFAEL PALMEIRO 26 6-0 180   **Bats L Throws L**

Had best season . . . First Ranger to lead league in hits (191) . . . First baseman was above .300 every day after June 7 . . . Remained in batting race until season's final days, finishing 10 points behind champ George Brett . . . Lost close race for second time in three years as he finished second in NL in '88 . . . Pushed Brett at the end, hitting .325 from Sept. 1 on . . . Career highs in average, hits, homers, RBI . . . Had a pair of five-hit days—June 30 at Boston and Sept. 17 at Seattle . . . Went 47 at-bats without a strikeout . . . Despite hitting left-handed, he batted .339 vs. southpaws . . . Earned $300,000 . . . Born Sept. 24, 1964, in Havana, Cuba . . . Teamed with Will Clark and Bobby Thigpen at Mississippi State . . . Acquired in nine-player deal that sent Mitch Williams to Cubs prior to 1989 season.

Year	Club	Pos.	G	AB	R	H	2B	3B	HR	RBI	SB	Avg.
1986	Chicago (NL) ..	OF	22	73	9	18	4	0	3	12	1	.247
1987	Chicago (NL) ..	OF-1B	84	221	32	61	15	1	14	30	2	.276
1988	Chicago (NL) ..	OF-1B	152	580	75	178	41	5	8	53	12	.307
1989	Texas	1B	156	559	76	154	23	4	8	64	4	.275
1990	Texas	1B	154	598	72	191	35	6	14	89	3	.319
	Totals		568	2031	264	602	118	16	47	248	22	.296

JULIO FRANCO 29 6-1 185   **Bats R Throws R**

First Ranger to win All-Star Game MVP . . . Drove home the winning run with pinch double . . . Following 68-minute rain delay at Wrigley, he came to bat against Rob Dibble and belted two-run double in seventh as AL won, 2-0 . . . Lone Ranger All-Star . . . Four-year streak of .300 averages ended for second baseman . . . Especially effective at Arlington Stadium, hitting .317 at home and .272 on the road . . . Over two seasons, he has hit .335 at Arlington . . . Reached base safely via hit or walk in 31 straight games before an oh-fer in season finale . . . One shy of career high with 96 runs, seventh-most in club history . . . Drew career-high 82 walks . . . Earned $1.25 million . . . Born Aug. 23, 1961, in San Pedro de Macoris, Dominican Republic.

Year	Club	Pos.	G	AB	R	H	2B	3B	HR	RBI	SB	Avg.
1982	Philadelphia . . .	SS-3B	16	29	3	8	1	0	0	3	0	.276
1983	Cleveland	SS	149	560	68	153	24	8	8	80	32	.273
1984	Cleveland	SS	160	658	82	188	22	5	3	79	19	.286
1985	Cleveland	SS-2B	160	636	97	183	33	4	6	90	13	.288
1986	Cleveland	SS-2B	149	599	80	183	30	5	10	74	10	.306
1987	Cleveland	SS-2B	128	495	86	158	24	3	8	52	32	.319
1988	Cleveland	2B	152	613	88	186	23	6	10	54	25	.303
1989	Texas	2B	150	548	80	173	31	5	13	92	21	.316
1990	Texas	2B	157	582	96	172	27	1	11	69	31	.296
	Totals		1221	4720	680	1404	215	37	69	593	183	.297

RUBEN SIERRA 25 6-1 175   Bats S Throws R

Numbers took a dive in '90 . . . Homers (16), RBI (96) and average (.280) all slipped . . . Went from Sept. 12 to Sept. 29 without an extra-base hit, accumulating 20 singles . . . Only one homer after Sept. 6 . . . Most of extra-base hits were early, with at least one in eight straight games from June 27-July 5, a club record . . . Hit in 15 straight games . . . Had fourth career five-RBI game vs. Detroit July 12 . . . Only 14 players hit more home runs before 24th birthday than he did (98) . . . Born Oct. 6, 1965, in Rio Piedras, Puerto Rico . . . Outfielder earned $1,625 million.

Year	Club	Pos.	G	AB	R	H	2B	3B	HR	RBI	SB	Avg.
1986	Texas	OF	113	382	50	101	13	10	16	55	7	.264
1987	Texas	OF	158	643	97	169	35	4	30	109	16	.263
1988	Texas	OF	156	615	77	156	32	2	23	91	18	.254
1989	Texas	OF	162	634	101	194	35	14	29	119	8	.306
1990	Texas	OF	159	608	70	170	37	2	16	96	9	.280
	Totals		748	2882	395	790	152	32	114	470	58	.274

PETE INCAVIGLIA 26 6-1 220   Bats R Throws R

Only Ranger with five seasons of 20-plus homers . . . He's never hit below 20 . . . Outfielder is second to Larry Parrish on Rangers' all-time homer list, with 124 . . . Could catch Parrish (149) in '91 . . . Seventh all-time in RBI (388), but first in strikeouts (788) . . . His rookie mark of 185 Ks still a personal season high and he had 146 in '90 . . . Slumped in final weeks, hitting .176 in final 45 games . . . Has hit more Arlington homers

(68) than anyone but Parrish (73) . . . Earned $800,000 . . . Born April 2, 1964, in Pebble Beach, Cal. . . . At Oklahoma State in '85, he was named NCAA Player of the Year . . . Became only 14th player since inception of amateur draft in 1965 to play first pro game in majors . . . Only other Ranger to do so was David Clyde . . . Father Tom played in Dodgers' system . . . Brother Tony played in Pirates' and Padres' systems.

Year	Club	Pos.	G	AB	R	H	2B	3B	HR	RBI	SB	Avg.
1986	Texas	OF	153	540	82	135	21	2	30	88	3	.250
1987	Texas	OF	139	509	85	138	26	4	27	80	9	.271
1988	Texas	OF	116	418	59	104	19	3	22	54	6	.249
1989	Texas	OF	133	453	48	107	27	4	21	81	5	.236
1990	Texas	OF	153	529	59	123	27	0	24	85	3	.233
	Totals		694	2449	333	607	120	13	124	388	26	.248

JUAN GONZALEZ 21 6-3 210   Bats R Throws R

Power hitter of the future . . . Expected to move into starting outfield spot . . . Started 22 games after promotion from Oklahoma City (AAA) Aug. 31 . . . Hitless in first 11 at-bats, then was 26-for-81 (.321) . . . Led American Association in homers (29) and RBI (101) . . . Named league MVP and Rookie of the Year . . . With Rangers, he played most games in center field . . . Missed final week with back trouble . . . Born Oct. 16, 1969, in Vega Baja, Puerto Rico . . . Signed with the Rangers in 1986 at age 16.

Year	Club	Pos.	G	AB	R	H	2B	3B	HR	RBI	SB	Avg.
1989	Texas	OF	24	60	6	9	3	0	1	7	0	.150
1990	Texas	OF	25	90	11	26	7	1	4	12	0	.289
	Totals		49	150	17	35	10	1	5	19	0	.233

STEVE BUECHELE 29 6-2 190   Bats R Throws R

Broken wrist shelved third baseman for nearly half of season . . . Drilled in wrist by errant pitch from Eric Plunk April 21 . . . Activated May 25, but suffered more wrist problems and returned to disabled list June 1 . . . Activated again July 20 . . . Didn't appear fully recovered until late in season . . . Despite returned health, he finished in slump, hitting .182 over final 36 games . . . Made $550,000 . . . Born Sept. 26, 1961, in Lancaster, Cal. . . . Helped Stanford advance to '82 College World Series, going 10-for-13 in NCAA West Regional . . . Roomed with John Elway in college . . . High school teammate of pitcher Mike Witt.

Year	Club	Pos.	G	AB	R	H	2B	3B	HR	RBI	SB	Avg.
1985	Texas	3B-2B	69	219	22	48	6	3	6	21	3	.219
1986	Texas	3B-2B-0F	153	461	54	112	19	2	18	54	5	.243
1987	Texas	3B-2B-0F	136	363	45	86	20	0	13	50	2	.237
1988	Texas	3B-2B	155	503	68	126	21	4	16	58	2	.250
1989	Texas	3B-2B	155	486	60	114	22	2	16	59	1	.235
1990	Texas	3B-2B	91	251	30	54	10	0	7	30	1	.215
	Totals		759	2283	279	540	98	11	76	272	14	.237

BOBBY WITT 26 6-2 205   Bats R Throws R

Developed into staff ace by season's end . . . Opened 3-8 with 4.97 ERA . . . Closed 14-2 with 2.40 ERA . . . Won 12 straight from June 28-Sept. 6 to set Rangers record . . . Named AL's Co-Pitcher of the Month for July, going 5-0 . . . Struck out 221 batters, teaming with Nolan Ryan to become first Ranger tandem to reach the 200 plateau in same season . . . Earned $415,000 . . . Born May 11, 1964, in Arlington, Va. . . . A member of the 1984 U.S. Olympic team . . . Olympic stats: 3-0, 0.69 ERA, 36 Ks in 26 innings.

Year	Club	G	IP	W	L	Pct.	SO	BB	H	ERA
1986	Texas	31	157⅔	11	9	.550	174	143	130	5.48
1987	Texas	26	143	8	10	.444	160	140	114	4.91
1988	Texas	22	174⅓	8	10	.444	148	101	134	3.92
1989	Texas	31	194⅓	12	13	.480	166	114	182	5.14
1990	Texas	33	222	17	10	.630	221	110	197	3.36
	Totals	143	891⅓	56	52	.519	869	608	757	4.48

NOLAN RYAN 44 6-2 210   Bats R Throws R

Another season, another no-hitter . . . Fired sixth career no-hitter, more than anyone in history . . . In June 11 no-no vs. Oakland, he walked two batters . . . Amazingly, an hour afterward, he was spotted riding a stationary bike in the clubhouse. ''You don't deviate from your routine,'' he said . . . First pitcher to throw no-hitters in three decades and with three teams . . . Oldest pitcher to throw no-no, at 43 years, four months, 12 days . . . One-hitter vs. Chicago April 26 was the 12th of his career, breaking mark he shared with Bob Feller . . . In same game, he set club record with 16 Ks . . . Fanned 10 or more batters eight times, 207 times in career . . . Extended to 14 his big-league record of 200-strikeout seasons . . . Posted 22nd season with at least 100 Ks, another record . . . His 232 Ks led league and were second-most in Rangers' history, behind his 301 in '89 . . . Won 300th game July 31 at Milwaukee . . . Earned $1.4 million . . . Career strikeout total stands at 5,308 . . . Has never allowed Rickey Henderson to steal a base . . . Wonderful season despite being hampered by lower back problems after mid-May . . . Two days after no-hitter, he was diagnosed as having stress fracture in back . . . Disabled from May 18-June 5 . . . Went 2-3 over final nine starts despite 2.19 ERA . . . Born Jan. 31, 1947, in Refugio, Tex.

Year	Club	G	IP	W	L	Pct.	SO	BB	H	ERA
1966	New York (NL)	2	3	0	1	.000	6	3	5	15.00
1968	New York (NL)	21	134	6	9	.400	133	75	93	3.09
1969	New York (NL)	25	89	6	3	.667	92	53	60	3.54
1970	New York (NL)	27	132	7	11	.389	125	97	86	3.41
1971	New York (NL)	30	152	10	14	.417	137	116	125	3.97
1972	California	39	284	19	16	.543	329	157	166	2.28
1973	California	41	326	21	16	.568	383	162	238	2.87
1974	California	42	333	22	16	.578	367	202	221	2.89
1975	California	28	198	14	12	.538	186	132	152	3.45
1976	California	39	284	17	18	.486	327	183	193	3.36
1977	California	37	299	19	16	.543	341	204	198	2.77
1978	California	31	235	10	13	.435	260	148	183	3.71
1979	California	34	223	16	14	.533	223	114	169	3.59
1980	Houston	35	234	11	10	.524	200	98	205	3.35
1981	Houston	21	149	11	5	.688	140	68	99	1.69
1982	Houston	35	250⅓	16	12	.571	245	109	196	3.16
1983	Houston	29	196⅓	14	9	.609	183	101	134	2.98
1984	Houston	30	183⅔	12	11	.522	197	69	143	3.04
1985	Houston	35	232	10	12	.455	209	95	205	3.80
1986	Houston	30	178	12	8	.600	194	82	119	3.34
1987	Houston	34	211⅔	8	16	.333	270	87	154	2.76
1988	Houston	33	220	12	11	.522	228	87	186	3.52
1989	Texas	32	239⅓	16	10	.615	301	98	162	3.20
1990	Texas	30	204	13	9	.591	232	74	137	3.44
	Totals	740	4990⅓	302	272	.526	5308	2614	3629	3.16

KEVIN BROWN 26 6-4 188   Bats R Throws R

Very streaky season . . . Won first five starts of the year, a first in club history . . . Despite the perfect record, ERA was 4.15 in those games . . . Got an assist from Rangers offense, which outscored foes, 45-17 . . . Won five, then lost four, then won four . . . Was 10-6 at All-Star break . . . On disabled list in August with tendinitis in right elbow . . . Didn't pitch after Sept. 4 . . . Earned $218,000 . . . Born March 14, 1965, in Mc-

Intyre, Ga. . . . Majored in chemical engineering at Georgia Tech
. . . In '89, he led all rookies in ERA and complete games.

Year	Club	G	IP	W	L	Pct.	SO	BB	H	ERA
1986	Texas	1	5	1	0	1.000	4	0	6	3.60
1988	Texas	4	23⅓	1	1	.500	12	8	33	4.24
1989	Texas	28	191	12	9	.571	104	70	167	3.35
1990	Texas	26	180	12	10	.545	88	60	175	3.60
	Totals	59	399⅓	26	20	.565	208	138	381	3.52

JEFF RUSSELL 29 6-3 210   Bats R Throws R

Bullpen closer missed most of season after
undergoing elbow surgery in May . . . Sidelined
from May 29-Sept. 10 . . . Replaced by Kenny
Rogers . . . Pitched six times in September, allowing one run and earning two saves . . . Had
10 saves overall . . . Made All-Star team as
starter in '88 and reliever in '89 . . . Only four
other pitchers have been All-Stars in both
roles—Dennis Eckersley, Rich Gossage, Bob Stanley and Hoyt
Wilhelm . . . Born Sept. 2, 1961, in Cincinnati . . . Made $1.25
million.

Year	Club	G	IP	W	L	Pct.	SO	BB	H	ERA
1983	Cincinnati	10	68⅓	4	5	.444	40	22	58	3.03
1984	Cincinnati	33	181⅔	6	18	.250	101	65	186	4.26
1985	Texas	13	62	3	6	.333	44	27	85	7.55
1986	Texas	37	82	5	2	.714	54	31	74	3.40
1987	Texas	52	97⅓	5	5	.556	56	52	109	4.44
1988	Texas	34	188⅔	10	9	.526	88	66	183	3.82
1989	Texas	71	72⅔	6	4	.600	77	24	45	1.98
1990	Texas	27	25⅓	1	5	.167	16	16	23	4.26
	Totals	277	778	40	53	.430	476	303	763	4.03

TOP PROSPECTS

MONTY FARISS 23 6-4 180   Bats R Throws R

Tall, powerful shortstop who made the jump from Tulsa (AA) to
Oklahoma City (AAA) . . . Batted .299 with seven homers for
Tulsa and .302 with four homers for Oklahoma City . . . Born Oct.
13, 1967, in Cordell, Okla. . . . Selected in first round in 1988
draft as the sixth player taken overall . . . Ranks third in Oklahoma
State history in homers (65) and RBI (247), behind Pete Incaviglia
and Robin Ventura.

BILL HASELMAN 24 6-3 200   Bats R Throws R

All-Star catcher in Texas League . . . Hit .319 with 18 homers and
80 RBI for Tulsa (AA) . . . His second strong season at Tulsa

warrants a promotion . . . In 1989, he hit .270 with seven homers and 36 RBI . . . Selected in first round of 1987 draft . . . Born May 25, 1966, in Long Branch, N.J. . . . Played two years at UCLA, including a freshman season in which he won All-American honors as an outfielder . . . Switched to catcher in '87.

GERALD ALEXANDER 23 5-11 190   Bats R Throws R
Promising starting pitcher who posted great stats in '90 . . . For Port Charlotte (A), he amassed a 6-1 record and 0.63 ERA . . . Earned a midseason promotion to Rangers' top farm club in Oklahoma City (AAA) . . . Was just as effective with the 89ers, posting a 13-2 record . . . Attended Tulane . . . Selected in 21st round of 1989 draft . . . Born March 26, 1968, in Baton Rouge, La.

MANAGER BOBBY VALENTINE: Still the pilot, despite another disappointing season . . . An 8-19 May, which pushed the Rangers 13½ games out of first place, virtually ruined club's year . . . Even a 61-46 closing kick left the Rangers at 83-79 and 20 games back . . . Winningest all-time Ranger manager with career mark of 451-487 . . . Has managed more games than any of his 10 Texas predecessors . . . Has second-longest tenure among AL managers, behind Sparky Anderson . . . Named manager May 16, 1985, and was then the youngest in the business at 35 . . . Born May 13, 1950, in Stamford, Conn. . . . Played for five teams, Dodgers, Angels, Padres, Mariners and Mets . . . Wife Mary is daughter of former Dodger Ralph Branca.

ALL-TIME RANGER SEASON RECORDS

BATTING: Mickey Rivers, .333, 1980
HRs: Larry Parrish, 32, 1987
RBI: Ruben Sierra, 119, 1989
STEALS: Bump Wills, 52, 1987
WINS: Ferguson Jenkins, 25, 1974
STRIKEOUTS: Nolan Ryan, 301, 1989

BALTIMORE ORIOLES

TEAM DIRECTORY: Pres.: Lawrence Lucchino; Exec. VP-GM: Roland Hemond; VP-Adm. Pers.: Calvin Hill; VPs: Robert Aylward, Martin Conway; Asst. GM-Player Dev. Dir.: Doug Melvin; Dir. Pub. Rel.: Rick Vaughn; Trav. Sec.: Philip Itzoe; Mgr.: Frank Robinson. Home: Memorial Stadium (53,371). Field distances: 309, l.f. line; 385, l.c.; 405, c.f.; 385, r.c.; 309, r.f. line. Spring training: Sarasota, Fla.

SCOUTING REPORT

HITTING: Cal Ripken Jr. (.250, 21, 84) continues to mean everything to the Orioles. His consistency is remarkable—and that

Gregg Olson's bender makes AL hitters twist and out.

refers to far more than just his consecutive-game streak of 1,411, the second-longest in major-league history to Lou Gehrig's 2,130. Ripken and Dale Murphy are the only major leaguers to belt at least 20 homers each of the last nine seasons.

Beyond Cal and Randy Milligan (.265, 20, 60), the Orioles have plenty of offensive worries, including 1990 disappointment Craig Worthington (.226, 8, 44). But they made a major move when they acquired Astro slugger Glenn Davis (.251, 22, 64). Baltimore must improve on a .245 batting average that ranked next to last in the AL in 1990. The O's stranded 1,230 runners last summer, the third-highest total in the majors, and batted a meager .243 with runners in scoring position. And how much punch can ex-Red Sox DH Dwight Evans provide at 39?

PITCHING: There is no pitcher with more potential than Ben McDonald (8-5, 2.43). If this is the year he blossoms into a dominant ace, it will be enough to propel Baltimore into contention. Former truck driver Dave Johnson (13-9, 4.10) has developed into a quality starter. The Orioles added Jeff Robinson (10-9, 5.96), a four-year starter with Detroit, but gave up two promising pitchers in Pete Harnisch (11-11, 4.34) and Curt Schilling (1-2, 2.54, 3 Sv) in the Davis deal.

The bullpen is a trouble spot. The Orioles hope the winter will revive weary stopper Gregg Olson (6-5, 2.42), who recorded a club-record 37 saves in 42 tries, despite a tired arm that caused him to tail off late in the season. Olson's supporting cast is poor and the Orioles blew 20 saves last year. Only three other major-league teams suffered more blown saves.

FIELDING: Defense is a family affair for the Orioles. Shortstop Cal Ripken Jr. and his brother, second baseman Billy, form a brilliant keystone combination. In fact, Cal is coming off the finest season ever by a player at his position. He committed only three errors en route to a .996 fielding percentage, a record for shortstops. The Ripkens combined for just 11 errors. The Orioles' 93 errors overall represented the third-lowest total in the majors.

OUTLOOK: The Orioles' time has not quite come. Frank Robinson's team began last season averaging 2.8 years of major-league service per player, the lowest experience quotient of any team, and finished 76-85. Memorial Stadium will not house a division winner in its final season as the Birds' nesting place.

BALTIMORE ORIOLES 1991 ROSTER

MANAGER Frank Robinson
Coaches—Elrod Hendricks, Al Jackson, Tom McCraw, Curt Motton, Johnny Oates, Cal Ripken Sr.

PITCHERS

No.	Name	1990 Club	W-L	IP	SO	ERA	B-T	Ht.	Wt.	Born
29	Ballard, Jeff	Baltimore	2-11	133	50	4.93	L-L	6-2	203	8/13/63 Billings, MT
48	Bautista, Jose	Baltimore	1-0	27	15	4.05	R-R	6-2	207	7/25/64 Dominican Republic
		Rochester	7-8	109	50	4.06				
—	De la Rosa, Francisco	Hagerstown	9-5	131	105	2.06	S-R	5-11	185	3/3/66 Dominican Republic
		Rochester	0-0	1	1	0.00				
53	DuBois, Brian	Detroit	3-5	58	34	5.09	L-L	5-10	194	4/18/67 Joliet, IL
		Toledo	5-4	70	41	2.71				
45	Hickey, Kevin	Baltimore	1-3	26	17	5.13	L-L	6-1	201	2/25/66 Chicago, IL
		Rochester	2-1	23	28	5.79				
27	Johnson, Dave	Baltimore	13-9	180	68	4.10	R-R	5-11	183	10/24/59 Baltimore, MD
—	Linskey, Mike	Hagerstown	7-1	55	40	1.47	L-L	6-5	220	6/18/66 Baltimore, MD
		Rochester	7-9	111	54	3.58				
19	McDonald, Ben	Hagerstown	0-1	11	15	6.55	R-R	6-7	212	11/24/67 Baton Rouge, LA
		Rochester	3-3	44	37	2.86				
		Baltimore	8-5	119	65	2.43				
52	Mesa, Jose	Hagerstown	5-5	79	72	3.42	R-R	6-3	219	5/22/66 Dominican Republic
		Rochester	1-2	26	23	2.42				
		Baltimore	3-2	47	24	3.86				
18	Milacki, Bob	Baltimore	5-8	135	60	4.46	R-R	6-4	234	7/28/64 Trenton, NJ
24	Mitchell, John	Rochester	5-0	46	15	1.57	R-R	6-2	189	8/11/65 Dickson, TN
		Baltimore	6-6	114	43	4.64				
—	Myers, Chris	Hagerstown	6-11	110	74	3.52	L-L	6-2	187	4/14/69 Tampa, FL
30	Olson, Gregg	Baltimore	6-5	74	74	2.42	R-R	6-4	211	10/11/66 Omaha, NE
44	Robinson, Jeff	Detroit	10-9	145	73	5.96	R-R	6-6	240	12/14/61 Ventura, CA
50	Telford, Anthony	Frederick	4-2	54	49	1.68	R-R	6-0	184	3/6/66 San Jose, CA
		Hagerstown	10-2	96	73	1.97				
		Baltimore	3-3	36	20	4.95				
32	Williamson, Mark	Baltimore	8-2	85	60	2.21	R-R	6-0	171	7/21/59 Corpus Christi, TX

CATCHERS

No.	Name	1990 Club	H	HR	RBI	Pct.	B-T	Ht.	Wt.	Born
28	Hoiles, Chris	Rochester	86	18	56	.348	R-R	6-0	213	3/20/65 Bowling Green, OH
		Baltimore	12	1	6	.190				
2	Melvin, Bob	Baltimore	73	5	37	.243	R-R	6-4	206	10/28/61 Palo Alto, CA
—	Tackett, Jeff	Rochester	73	4	33	.239	R-R	6-2	210	12/1/65 Fresno, CA

INFIELDERS

No.	Name	1990 Club	H	HR	RBI	Pct.	B-T	Ht.	Wt.	Born
1	Bell, Juan	Rochester	93	6	35	.285	S-R	5-11	170	3/29/68 Dominican Republic
		Baltimore	0	0	0	.000				
7	Davis, Glenn	Houston	82	22	64	.251	R-R	6-3	200	3/28/61 Jacksonville, FL
		Columbus	11	1	8	.297				
11	Gomez, Leo	Rochester	119	26	97	.277	R-R	6-0	202	3/2/67 Puerto Rico
		Baltimore	9	0	1	.231				
88	Gonzales, Rene	Baltimore	22	1	12	.214	R-R	6-3	201	9/3/61 Austin, TX
15	Horn, Sam	Baltimore	61	14	45	.248	L-L	6-5	250	11/2/63 Dallas, TX
		Rochester	24	9	26	.414				
36	Hulett, Tim	Rochester	16	2	4	.372	R-R	6-0	197	1/12/60 Springfield, IL
		Baltimore	39	3	16	.255				
39	Milligan, Randy	Baltimore	96	20	60	.265	R-R	6-1	228	11/27/61 San Diego, CA
3	Ripken, Bill	Baltimore	118	3	38	.291	R-R	6-1	183	12/16/64 Havre de Grace, MD
6	Ripken, Cal	Baltimore	150	21	84	.250	R-R	6-4	225	8/24/60 Havre de Grace, MD
21	Segui, David	Rochester	103	2	51	.336	S-L	6-1	195	7/19/66 Kansas City, KS
		Baltimore	30	2	15	.244				
25	Worthington, Craig	Baltimore	96	8	44	.226	R-R	6-0	200	4/17/65 Los Angeles, CA

OUTFIELDERS

No.	Name	1990 Club	H	HR	RBI	Pct.	B-T	Ht.	Wt.	Born
9	Anderson, Brady	Baltimore	54	3	24	.231	L-L	6-1	185	1/18/64 Silver Spring, MD
12	Devereaux, Mike	Baltimore	88	12	49	.240	R-R	6-0	193	4/10/63 Casper, WY
		Hagerstown	5	0	3	.250				
		Frederick	4	1	3	.500				
—	Evans, Dwight	Boston	111	13	63	.249	R-R	6-3	208	11/3/51 Santa Monica, CA
38	McKnight, Jeff	Rochester	95	7	45	.280	S-R	6-0	188	2/18/63 Conway, AR
		Baltimore	15	1	4	.200				
—	Mercedes, Luis	Hagerstown	139	3	37	.334	R-R	6-0	180	2/20/68 Dominican Republic
6	Orsulak, Joe	Baltimore	111	11	57	.269	L-L	6-1	203	5/31/62 Glen Ridge, NJ

ORIOLE PROFILES

CAL RIPKEN JR. 30 6-4 225   Bats R Throws R

Orioles' franchise player is coming off record-setting season . . . Belted 214th career home run Sept. 15 in Toronto to pass Vern Stephens for most homers by an AL shortstop . . . Ernie Banks holds major-league mark (293) . . . Surpassed Tony Fernandez while setting major-league record for shortstops with .996 fielding percentage . . . Also set standards for consecutive errorless games (95) and consecutive errorless chances (431) . . . Consecutive game streak stands at 1,411, second-longest in major-league history to Lou Gehrig's 2,130 . . . He and Dale Murphy are only major leaguers to belt at least 20 homers each season since 1982 . . . Ran off 8,243 consecutive innings before string ended Sept. 14, 1987 in Toronto . . . Named AL Rookie of the Year in 1982 . . . Born Aug. 24, 1960, in Havre de Grace, Md. . . . Orioles' second-round pick in 1978 draft . . . Orioles' best-paid player in 1990 with $1,366,667 salary.

Year	Club	Pos.	G	AB	R	H	2B	3B	HR	RBI	SB	Avg.
1981	Baltimore	SS-3B	23	39	1	5	0	0	0	0	0	.128
1982	Baltimore	SS-3B	160	598	90	158	32	5	28	93	3	.264
1983	Baltimore	SS	162	663	121	211	47	2	27	102	0	.318
1984	Baltimore	SS	162	641	103	195	37	7	27	86	2	.304
1985	Baltimore	SS	162	642	116	181	32	5	26	110	2	.282
1986	Baltimore	SS	162	627	98	177	35	1	25	81	4	.282
1987	Baltimore	SS	162	624	97	157	28	3	27	98	3	.252
1988	Baltimore	SS	161	575	87	152	25	1	23	81	2	.264
1989	Baltimore	SS	162	646	80	166	30	0	21	93	3	.257
1990	Baltimore	SS	161	600	78	150	28	4	21	84	3	.250
	Totals		1476	5655	871	1552	294	28	225	828	22	.274

BILLY RIPKEN 26 6-1 183   Bats R Throws R

Second baseman will try for encore after best season by far . . . His .291 batting average was 52 points higher than career average before season . . . Matched brother Cal for team lead with 28 doubles . . . Seventeen sacrifices tied him with Oakland's Mike Gallego for AL lead . . . Was batting just .191 May 1, but hit .304 rest of way . . . Enjoyed personal-best 52-game errorless stretch from May 27-Aug. 3 . . . Cracked first Memorial Stadium home run June 8 vs. Yankees . . . Born Dec. 16, 1964,

in Havre de Grace, Md. . . . Orioles' 11th round pick in 1982 draft
. . . Earned $215,000 in 1990.

Year	Club	Pos.	G	AB	R	H	2B	3B	HR	RBI	SB	Avg.
1987	Baltimore	2B	58	234	27	72	9	0	2	20	4	.308
1988	Baltimore	2B-3B	150	512	52	106	18	1	2	34	8	.207
1989	Baltimore	2B	115	318	31	76	11	2	2	26	1	.239
1990	Baltimore	2B	129	406	48	118	28	1	3	38	5	.291
	Totals		452	1470	158	372	66	4	9	118	18	.253

RANDY MILLIGAN 29 6-1 228   Bats R Throws R

First baseman was enjoying outstanding season
before he separated his left shoulder in Aug. 7
collision with Oakland catcher Ron Hassey . . .
Was among AL leaders in walks, on-base percentage, slugging percentage, extra-base hits
and home runs at time of injury . . . Wound up
with .408 on-base percentage and 41 extra-base
hits . . . Seventeen of his 20 homers were solo
shots . . . Received only 83 major-league at-bats in first eight seasons with Mets and Pirates organizations . . . Born Nov. 27, 1961,
in San Diego . . . Acquired from Pittsburgh for Peter Blohm following 1988 season . . . Began career with Mets as first-round
choice in January 1981 draft . . . His 1990 salary was $155,000.

Year	Club	Pos.	G	AB	R	H	2B	3B	HR	RBI	SB	Avg.
1987	New York (NL)	PH-PR	3	1	0	0	0	0	0	0	0	.000
1988	Pittsburgh	1B-OF	40	82	10	18	5	0	3	8	1	.220
1989	Baltimore	1B	124	365	56	98	23	5	12	45	9	.268
1990	Baltimore	1B	109	362	64	96	20	1	20	60	6	.265
	Totals		276	810	130	212	48	6	35	113	16	.262

GLENN DAVIS 30 6-3 200   Bats R Throws R

Slugging first baseman joined Orioles in January trade that sent Pete Harnisch, Curt Schilling and Steve Finley to Astros . . . Was on pace
for his best season in June, when torn muscle
in rib cage sidelined him for two months . . .
Still hit 20-plus homers for the sixth straight
season, but 22 home runs marked his lowest
total since 1985 . . . If stays healthy, he could
put up huge numbers . . . That day could be coming . . . Made
$1,985,000 in 1990 . . . Hit a homer every 14.9 at-bats . . . Born
March 28, 1961, in Jacksonville, Fla. . . . Selected by the Astros
in secondary phase of January 1981 draft . . . Attended University
of Georgia . . . A class act who takes the time to speak out against

child abuse . . . Goes to Korea every year to spend time in orphanages . . . Hit three homers vs. Giants at Candlestick June 1, but Astros still lost that game.

Year	Club	Pos.	G	AB	R	H	2B	3B	HR	RBI	SB	Avg.
1984	Houston.	1B	18	61	6	13	5	0	2	8	0	.213
1985	Houston.	1B-OF	100	350	51	95	11	0	20	64	0	.271
1986	Houston.	1B	158	574	91	152	32	3	31	101	3	.265
1987	Houston.	1B	151	578	70	145	35	2	27	93	4	.251
1988	Houston.	1B	152	561	78	152	26	0	30	99	4	.271
1989	Houston.	1B	158	581	87	156	26	1	34	89	4	.269
1990	Houston.	1B	93	327	44	82	15	4	22	64	8	.251
	Totals		830	3032	427	795	150	10	166	518	23	.262

DWIGHT EVANS 39 6-3 205   Bats R Throws R

For first time in 20-year career, he won't be with Red Sox . . . Free-agent outfielder/designated hitter signed non-guaranteed, one-year, $1.3-million contract . . . Remains clutch hitter despite failing to produce at least 20 homers for first time since 1980 . . . Of 13 homers, 10 tied score or put Sox ahead . . . Batted .306 in last 24 games . . . Delivered 20 of 39 baserunners from third with fewer than two outs . . . Tops all active players with 379 career homers . . . Tied with Tony Perez and Orlando Cepeda for 29th on all-time list . . . Hit disappointing .231 in ALCS . . . Has been hampered by bad back . . . Born Nov. 3, 1951, in Santa Monica, Cal. . . . Boston's fifth selection in June 1969 draft . . . Earned $1.5 million in 1990.

Year	Club	Pos.	G	AB	R	H	2B	3B	HR	RBI	SB	Avg.
1972	Boston	OF	18	57	2	15	3	1	1	6	0	.263
1973	Boston	OF	119	282	46	63	13	1	10	32	5	.223
1974	Boston	OF	133	463	60	130	19	8	10	70	4	.281
1975	Boston	OF	128	412	61	113	24	6	13	56	3	.274
1976	Boston	OF	146	501	61	121	34	5	17	62	6	.242
1977	Boston	OF	73	230	39	66	9	2	14	36	4	.287
1978	Boston	OF	147	497	75	123	24	2	24	63	8	.247
1979	Boston	OF	152	489	69	134	24	1	21	58	6	.274
1980	Boston	OF	148	463	72	123	37	5	18	60	3	.266
1981	Boston	OF	108	412	84	122	19	4	22	71	3	.296
1982	Boston	OF	162	609	122	178	37	7	32	98	3	.292
1983	Boston	OF	126	470	74	112	19	4	22	58	3	.238
1984	Boston	OF	162	630	121	186	37	8	32	104	3	.295
1985	Boston	OF	159	617	110	162	29	1	29	78	7	.263
1986	Boston	OF	152	529	86	137	33	2	26	97	3	.259
1987	Boston	1B-OF	154	541	109	165	37	2	34	123	4	.305
1988	Boston	OF-1B	149	559	96	164	31	7	21	111	5	.293
1989	Boston	OF	146	520	82	148	27	3	20	100	3	.285
1990	Boston	DH	123	445	66	111	18	3	13	63	3	.249
	Totals		2505	8726	1435	2373	474	72	379	1346	76	.272

GREGG OLSON 24 6-4 211   Bats R Throws R

1989 AL Rookie of the Year keeps improving . . . Curveballer's 37 saves in 42 tries last year established a club record . . . Set AL mark for saves by a rookie with 27 in 1989 . . . Already ranks fourth on Orioles' all-time save list with 64 . . . Ran off stretch of 41 scoreless innings spanning 29 appearances from July 31, 1989 through May 7 of last season . . . Will require some scrutiny . . . Experienced tired arm late in season and ERA from Aug. 19 through end of year was worrisome 7.63 . . . Born Oct. 11, 1966, in Omaha, Neb. . . . First-round choice in 1988 draft and the fourth player picked . . . Was an All-American his final two years at Auburn . . . Earned $270,000 in 1990.

Year	Club	G	IP	W	L	Pct.	SO	BB	H	ERA
1988	Baltimore	10	11	1	1	.500	9	10	10	3.27
1989	Baltimore	64	85	5	2	.714	90	46	57	1.69
1990	Baltimore	64	74⅓	6	5	.545	74	31	57	2.42
	Totals.	138	170⅓	12	8	.600	173	87	124	2.11

DAVE JOHNSON 31 5-11 183   Bats R Throws R

Long-time journeyman has established himself as a quality starter . . . Achieved second-highest victory total of nine-year pro career . . . Excelled against AL East, going 8-2 with 2.98 ERA against own division . . . Enjoyed pair of three-game winning streaks, from June 18-July 4 and July 23-Aug. 2 . . . Did permit major-league-high 30 homers, although 20 came with bases empty . . . Made 152 minor-league appearances before major-league debut, May 29, 1987 . . . Employed as truck driver in offseason for first seven years as a pro . . . Born Oct. 24, 1959, in Baltimore . . . Originally signed with Pittsburgh as free agent, June 10, 1982 . . . Made $113,500 in 1990.

Year	Club	G	IP	W	L	Pct.	SO	BB	H	ERA
1987	Pittsburgh	5	6⅓	0	0	.000	4	2	13	9.95
1989	Baltimore	14	89⅓	4	7	.364	26	28	90	4.23
1990	Baltimore	30	180	13	9	.591	68	43	196	4.10
	Totals.	49	275⅔	17	16	.515	98	73	299	4.28

Cal Ripken Jr. has played in 1,411 straight games.

BEN McDONALD 23 6-7 212   **Bats R Throws R**

Has chance to be dominant pitcher... After July 3 recall from Rochester (AAA), he won first five major-league starts... Became first major leaguer to do that since Los Angeles' Fernando Valenzuela in 1981... Fired shutout against Chicago July 21 in major-league debut as starter... Opponents batted .205 against him... First player selected in 1989 draft... Compiled 29-14 record in three years at LSU, including 14-4 as senior... Fanned 373 in 308⅓ collegiate innings... Born Nov. 24, 1967, in Baton Rouge, La.... Despite inexperience, he commanded $241,667 salary in 1990.

Year	Club	G	IP	W	L	Pct.	SO	BB	H	ERA
1989	Baltimore	6	7⅓	1	0	1.000	3	4	8	8.59
1990	Baltimore	21	118⅔	8	5	.615	65	35	88	2.43
	Totals............	27	126	9	5	.643	68	39	96	2.79

TOP PROSPECTS

LEO GOMEZ 24 6-0 180   **Bats R Throws R**
Geared for big-league shot after huge season for Rochester
(AAA)... Topped International League with 97 RBI and tied for
second with 26 home runs... Third baseman was honored as
Orioles' Minor League Player of the Year in 1987, when he led
Carolina League with .326 average for Hagerstown (AA)... Lost
valuable time in 1988 with a stress fracture in his right leg...
Born March 2, 1967, in Canovanas, P.R.... Signed by Orioles
as free agent, Dec. 13, 1985.

DAVID SEGUI 24 6-1 170   **Bats S Throws L**
Son of former major-league pitcher Diego appears set to make
own mark... Hit .336 with two homers and 51 RBI for Rochester
(AAA) and .244 in 123 at-bats with Orioles in 1990... First
baseman was Orioles' Minor League Player of the Year in 1989,
when he batted .317 for Frederick (A) and .324 for Hagerstown
(AA)... Fell just short of qualifying for batting titles in both
leagues... Born July 19, 1966, in Kansas City... Selected by
Baltimore in 19th round of 1987 draft.

MIKE LINSKEY 24 6-5 215   **Bats L Throws L**
Went 7-1 with 1.47 ERA for Hagerstown (AA), but had harder
time for Rochester (AAA), going 7-9 with 3.58 ERA last season
... Could become fast favorite of hometown fans... Born June
18, 1966, in Baltimore... Orioles' Minor League Pitcher of the
Year in 1989, when he compiled 12-8 record in stops at Frederick
(A) and Hagerstown... Selected by Orioles in ninth round of 1987
draft... Attended James Madison.

ANTHONY TELFORD 25 6-0 175   **Bats R Throws R**
Got a good look from Orioles as he went 3-3 with a 4.95 ERA
in 36⅓ innings for parent club after going 10-2, 1.97 for Hag-
erstown (AA)... Orioles' fourth-round choice in 1987 draft...
Made first start of 1988, but lost rest of year to shoulder surgery
... Born March 6, 1966, in San Jose, Cal.

MANAGER FRANK ROBINSON: Will try to get Orioles pointed in right direction again after disappointing 76-85 finish . . . Named AL Manager of the Year in 1989 after overseeing transformation of 54-107 disaster into 87-75 contender . . . Marked third-best, one-season improvement in big-league history . . . Not afraid to go against book . . . Gained distinction as first black manager in history when Cleveland named him player-manager in October 1974 . . . Managed Indians until 1977 before serving stint with San Francisco . . . Composite major-league managerial record stands at 567-727 . . . Enjoyed Hall of Fame career that covered 21 major-league seasons, highlighted by stays with Cincinnati from 1956-65 and Baltimore from 1966-71 . . . Ranks as fourth-leading all-time home run hitter with 586 . . . Only man to be named MVP in each league . . . Won Triple Crown with Baltimore in 1966 . . . Born Aug. 31, 1935, in Beaumont, Tex.

ALL-TIME ORIOLE SEASON RECORDS

BATTING: Ken Singleton, .328, 1977
HRs: Frank Robinson, 49, 1966
RBI: Jim Gentile, 141, 1961
STEALS: Luis Aparicio, 57, 1964
WINS: Steve Stone, 25, 1980
STRIKEOUTS: Dave McNally, 202, 1968

BOSTON RED SOX

TEAM DIRECTORY: Majority Owner and Chairwoman of the Board: Jean R. Yawkey; General Partner: Haywood C. Sullivan; Sr. VP-GM: Lou Gorman; Asst. GM: Elaine C. Weddington; VP-Baseball Dev.: Edward F. Kenney; Dir. Scouting: Eddie Kasko; Dir. Minor League Oper.: Edward P. Kenney; VP-Pub. Rel.: Dick Bresciani; VP-Transportation: Jack Rogers; Mgr.: Joe Morgan. Home: Fenway Park (34,171). Field distances: 315, l.f. line; 379, l.c.; 390, c.f.; 420, deep c.f.; 380, deep r.f.; 302, r.f. line. Spring training: Winter Haven, Fla.

SCOUTING REPORT

HITTING: The Red Sox continue to feature a potent, but hardly overpowering offense. Despite playing in the cozy confines of Fenway, they matched the White Sox for the third-fewest home

Sore-shouldered Roger Clemens' 1.93 ERA led majors.

runs in the AL (106) in 1990 and ranked seventh in runs (699).

While Ellis Burks (.296, 21, 89) and Mike Greenwell (.297, 14, 73) are offensive stars, neither is a real slugger. Wade Boggs' best days appear to be behind him. Last year's .302 average was a career low, his 68 strikeouts were a career high, and his string of 200-hit seasons was snapped at seven. Maybe that's why Boston imported free agent Jack Clark (.266, 25, 62 with the Padres), who should feast on the Green Monster.

Boston did lead the majors with a .272 average and should vie for the honor again. The Red Sox will have to get lots of hits because they lack the speed to make much else happen. They finished last in the AL with 53 steals in 1990.

PITCHING: Boston has won the AL East two of the last three years and Roger Clemens deserves much of the credit. His presence prevents ruinous tailspins as "The Rocket" is 67-18 in his career when he pitches after a Red Sox defeat. He was 21-6 with a major-league-low 1.93 ERA last year and might well have been the AL MVP if not for a late-season shoulder injury.

The departure of Mike Boddicker to the Royals as a free agent was offset by the signing of NL ERA champ Danny Darwin (11-4, 2.21 with the Astros). He'll join 1990 surprise Greg Harris (13-9, 4.00), Dana Kiecker (8-9, 3.97) and Tom Bolton (10-5, 3.38). Also, the addition of Matt Young (8-18, 3.57 with the Mariners) via free agency should help.

The Red Sox must hope 35-year-old closer Jeff Reardon (5-3, 3.16, 21 Sv) is still up to the task, despite chronic back problems. He was injured for part of last season, which helps explain why Boston endured 23 blown saves, tying the Cubs for the most in the majors.

FIELDING: Center fielder Burks will try to repeat a Gold Glove-winning season in which he made only two errors in 333 total chances. Jody Reed looks forward to his first full season at second base. Last year's conversion from shortstop helped him tremendously as he made 10 errors in 177 chances at short and only six in 594 chances at second.

OUTLOOK: Boston is due for a drop after nipping Toronto by two games for the AL East title in 1990 with an 88-74 mark. The Red Sox simply have too many potential trouble spots in their rotation and bullpen to repeat. It doesn't help that players have little respect for hunch-playing manager Joe Morgan, despite his success.

BOSTON RED SOX 1991 ROSTER

MANAGER Joe Morgan
Coaches—Dick Berardino, Al Bumbry, Bill Fischer, Richie Hebner, John McLaren

PITCHERS

No.	Name	1990 Club	W-L	IP	SO	ERA	B-T	Ht.	Wt.	Born
50	Bolton, Tom	Pawtucket	1-0	12	8	3.86	L-L	6-3	175	5/6/62 Nashville, TN
		Boston	10-5	120	65	3.38				
21	Clemens, Roger	Boston	21-6	228	209	1.93	R-R	6-4	220	8/4/62 Dayton, OH
44	Darwin, Danny	Houston	11-4	163	109	2.21	R-R	6-3	190	10/25/55 Bonham, TX
40	Dopson, John	Pawtucket	2-1	22	13	4.91	R-R	6-4	225	7/14/63 Baltimore, MD
		Boston	0-0	18	9	2.04				
—	Fischer, Tom	New Britain	13-10	163	116	4.19	L-L	5-11	195	3/23/67 West Bend, WI
38	Gray, Jeff	Pawtucket	0-0	32	35	3.41	R-R	6-1	190	4/10/63 Richmond, VA
		Boston	2-4	51	50	4.44				
27	Harris, Greg	Boston	13-9	184	117	4.00	R-R	6-0	175	11/2/55 Lynwood, CA
55	Hesketh, Joe	Mont.-Atl.	1-2	34	24	5.29	L-L	6-2	170	2/15/59 Lackawanna, NY
		Boston	0-4	26	26	3.51				
31	Hetzel, Eric	Pawtucket	6-5	109	90	3.64	R-R	6-3	180	9/25/63 Crowley, LA
		Boston	1-4	35	20	5.91				
59	Irvine, Daryl	Pawtucket	2-5	50	35	3.24	R-R	6-3	195	11/15/64 Harrisonburg, VA
		Boston	1-1	17	9	4.67				
19	Kiecker, Dana	Boston	8-9	153	93	3.97	R-R	6-3	180	2/25/61 Sleepy Eye, MN
15	Lamp, Dennis	Boston	3-5	106	49	4.68	R-R	6-3	215	9/23/52 Los Angeles, CA
—	Livernois, Derek	New Britain	9-2	96	67	1.98	R-R	6-2	170	4/17/67 Inglewood, CA
51	Manzanillo, Josias	New Britain	4-4	74	51	3.41	R-R	6-0	190	10/16/67 Dominican Republic
		Pawtucket	4-7	83	77	5.55				
—	Miller, Mike	Jackson	7-7	139	95	2.91	R-R	6-4	200	4/14/67 Kirkwood, MO
—	Murphy, Rob	Boston	0-6	57	54	6.32	L-L	6-2	215	5/26/60 Miami, FL
—	O'Neill, Dan	London	0-0	3	2	3.00	R-L	6-2	175	10/5/64 Holyoke, MA
		New Britain	7-0	60	47	0.60				
—	Owen, Dave	New Britain	7-9	132	88	2.93	L-L	6-2	227	11/7/66 Seattle, WA
		Pawtucket	3-2	42	26	4.71				
—	Plympton, Jeff	New Britain	3-4	64	55	2.67	R-R	6-2	185	11/24/65 Plainville, MA
		Pawtucket	1-0	17	11	0.00				
41	Reardon, Jeff	Boston	5-3	51	33	3.16	R-R	6-0	200	10/1/55 Dalton, MA
—	Taylor, Scott	Lynchburg	5-6	89	120	2.73	L-L	6-1	185	8/2/67 Defiance, OH
		New Britain	0-2	27	27	1.65				
—	Young, Matt	Seattle	8-18	225	176	3.51	L-L	6-3	205	8/9/58 Pasadena, CA

CATCHERS

No.	Name	1990 Club	H	HR	RBI	Pct.	B-T	Ht.	Wt.	Born
20	Marzano, John	Pawtucket	24	2	8	.320	R-R	5-11	197	2/14/63 Philadelphia, PA
		Boston	20	0	6	.241				
42	Matilla, Pedro	Winter Haven	68	3	34	.193	R-R	6-0	205	8/1/68 Cuba
6	Pena, Tony	Boston	129	7	56	.263	R-R	6-0	184	6/4/57 Dominican Republic

INFIELDERS

No.	Name	1990 Club	H	HR	RBI	Pct.	B-T	Ht.	Wt.	Born
26	Boggs, Wade	Boston	187	6	63	.302	L-R	6-2	197	6/15/58 Omaha, NE
—	Clark, Jack	San Diego	89	25	62	.266	R-R	6-3	226	11/10/55 New Brighton, PA
45	Cooper, Scott	Pawtucket	115	12	44	.266	L-R	6-3	200	10/13/67 St. Louis, MO
		Boston	0	0	0	.000				
22	Marshall, Mike	New York (NL)	39	6	27	.239	R-R	6-5	215	1/12/60 Libertyville, IL
		Pawtucket	7	2	4	.304				
		Boston	32	4	12	.286				
11	Naehring, Tim	Pawtucket	78	15	47	.269	R-R	6-2	190	2/1/67 Cincinnati, OH
		Boston	23	2	12	.271				
18	Quintana, Carlos	Boston	147	7	67	.287	R-R	6-2	195	8/26/65 Venezuela
3	Reed, Jody	Boston	173	5	51	.289	R-R	5-9	165	7/26/62 Tampa, FL
2	Rivera, Luis	Boston	78	7	45	.225	R-R	5-9	170	1/3/64 Puerto Rico
12	Robidoux, Billy Jo	Pawtucket	11	3	7	.204	L-R	6-1	200	1/13/64 Ware, MA
		Boston	8	1	4	.182				

OUTFIELDERS

No.	Name	1990 Club	H	HR	RBI	Pct.	B-T	Ht.	Wt.	Born
23	Brunansky, Tom	St. Louis	9	1	2	.158	R-R	6-4	216	8/20/60 Covina, CA
		Boston	123	15	71	.267				
12	Burks, Ellis	Boston	174	21	89	.296	R-R	6-2	202	9/11/64 Vicksburg, MS
39	Greenwell, Mike	Boston	181	14	73	.297	L-R	6-0	200	7/18/63 Louisville, KY
5	Kutcher, Randy	Pawtucket	43	1	14	.316	R-R	5-11	175	4/20/60 Anchorage, AK
		Boston	17	1	5	.230				
—	Pina, Mickey	Pawtucket	94	9	47	.223	R-R	6-0	195	3/8/66 Boston, MA
55	Plantier, Phil	Pawtucket	109	33	79	.253	L-R	6-0	175	1/27/69 Manchester, NH
		Boston	2	0	3	.133				
16	Romine, Kevin	Boston	37	2	14	.272	R-R	5-11	204	5/23/61 Exeter, NH

RED SOX PROFILES

WADE BOGGS 32 6-2 197   Bats L Throws R

Five-time batting champion, including four straight from 1985-88, is in decline . . . String of consecutive 200-hit seasons ended at seven, a modern-day record . . . Third baseman still placed second in AL with career-low 187 hits and was tied for second with 54 multi-hit games . . . Finished with career-low .302 average . . . Also suffered career lows in runs (89) and walks (87) . . . His 68 strikeouts were a career high . . . Injuries hampered him throughout . . . Injured left wrist in May, fractured right toe in August and endured back and hip ailments in September . . . One of few bright spots for Red Sox in ALCS with .438 average, he blasted lone home run of series . . . Born June 15, 1958, in Omaha, Neb. . . . Red Sox' seventh-round pick in 1976 draft . . . Made $1.9 million in 1990.

Year	Club	Pos.	G	AB	R	H	2B	3B	HR	RBI	SB	Avg.
1982	Boston	1B-3B-OF	104	338	51	118	14	1	5	44	1	.349
1983	Boston	3B	153	582	100	210	44	7	5	74	3	.361
1984	Boston	3B	158	625	109	203	31	4	6	55	3	.325
1985	Boston	3B	161	653	107	240	42	3	8	78	2	.368
1986	Boston	3B	149	580	107	207	47	2	8	71	0	.357
1987	Boston	3B-1B	147	551	108	200	40	6	24	89	1	.363
1988	Boston	3B	155	584	128	214	45	6	5	58	2	.366
1989	Boston	3B	156	621	113	205	51	7	3	54	2	.330
1990	Boston	3B	155	619	89	187	44	5	6	63	0	.302
	Totals		1338	5153	912	1784	358	41	70	586	14	.346

JACK CLARK 35 6-3 205   Bats R Throws R

New-look free agent from the Padres signed three-year, $8.7-million contract . . . When healthy, this first baseman is one of the most dangerous hitters in the game . . . Missed 47 games with injuries in 1990 and has missed 348 over last seven years, an average of nearly 50 a year . . . Despite missing so many games, he topped Padres with 25 homers, averaging one per 13 at-bats . . . Led NL in walks with 104 for second straight season . . . "The Ripper" has averaged 26 homers over last 13 years . . . Earned $2 million in 1990 . . . Chastised Tony Gwynn several times during the year . . . Born Nov. 10, 1955, in New

Brighton, Pa. . . . Was 13th-round pick by Giants in 1973 draft . . . Hit .377 against lefties and only .209 vs. righties, but 16 of his 25 homers came against right-handers.

Year	Club	Pos.	G	AB	R	H	2B	3B	HR	RBI	SB	Avg.
1975	San Francisco	OF-3B	8	17	3	4	0	0	0	2	1	.235
1976	San Francisco	OF	26	102	14	23	6	2	2	10	6	.225
1977	San Francisco	OF	136	413	64	104	17	4	13	51	12	.252
1978	San Francisco	OF	156	592	90	181	46	8	25	98	15	.306
1979	San Francisco	OF-3B	143	527	84	144	25	2	26	86	11	.273
1980	San Francisco	OF	127	437	77	124	20	8	22	82	2	.284
1981	San Francisco	OF	99	385	60	103	19	2	17	53	1	.268
1982	San Francisco	OF	157	563	90	154	30	3	27	103	6	.274
1983	San Francisco	OF-1B	135	492	82	132	25	0	20	66	5	.268
1984	San Francisco	OF-1B	57	203	33	65	9	1	11	44	1	.320
1985	St. Louis	1B-OF	126	442	71	124	26	3	22	87	1	.281
1986	St. Louis	1B	65	232	34	55	12	2	9	23	1	.237
1987	St. Louis	1B-OF	131	419	93	120	23	1	35	106	1	.286
1988	New York (AL)	OF-1B	150	496	81	120	14	0	27	93	3	.242
1989	San Diego	1B-OF	142	455	76	110	19	1	26	94	6	.242
1990	San Diego	1B	115	334	59	89	12	1	25	62	4	.266
	Totals		1773	6109	1011	1652	303	38	307	1060	76	.270

MIKE GREENWELL 27 6-0 200   Bats L Throws R

Left fielder came on very strong and was a key figure in drive toward AL East crown . . . Recovered from .221 April and .250 May to pound out 142 hits in final 116 games . . . Finished fourth in AL with 181 hits . . . Excelled at crunch time by batting .438 in last two weeks and was club's top hitter in September with .361 average . . . From Sept. 1 until end of season, he compiled .423 average with 13 RBI with men in scoring position . . . Produced 33 multi-hit efforts in final 69 games . . . Totaled 13 outfield assists, all after June 28 . . . Held hitless in 14 at-bats in ALCS . . . Born July 18, 1963, in Louisville, Ky. . . . Red Sox' sixth pick in 1982 draft . . . Made $1.225 million in 1990.

Year	Club	Pos.	G	AB	R	H	2B	3B	HR	RBI	SB	Avg.
1985	Boston	OF	17	31	7	10	1	0	4	8	1	.323
1986	Boston	OF	31	35	4	11	2	0	0	4	0	.314
1987	Boston	OF-C	125	412	71	135	31	6	19	89	5	.328
1988	Boston	OF	158	590	86	192	39	8	22	119	16	.325
1989	Boston	OF	145	578	87	178	36	0	14	95	13	.308
1990	Boston	OF	159	610	71	181	30	6	14	73	8	.297
	Totals		635	2256	326	707	139	20	73	388	43	.313

ELLIS BURKS 26 6-2 202   Bats R Throws R

Center fielder stayed away from injuries and results were outstanding . . . Ranked among top 10 in AL in seven offensive categories . . . Tied for second with .994 fielding percentage . . . Made only two errors in 333 total chances and won Gold Glove . . . Peak months were June (.337) and July (.338) . . . Led Red Sox with 40 two-out RBI and 36 game-tying and go-ahead RBI . . . Batted .267 in ALCS . . . Born Sept. 11, 1964, in Vicksburg, Miss. . . . Red Sox' first pick in January 1983 draft . . . Due for raise after making only $475,000 in 1990.

Year Club	Pos.	G	AB	R	H	2B	3B	HR	RBI	SB	Avg.
1987 Boston	OF	133	558	94	152	30	2	20	59	27	.272
1988 Boston	OF	144	540	93	159	37	5	18	92	25	.294
1989 Boston	OF	97	399	73	121	19	6	12	61	21	.303
1990 Boston	OF	152	588	89	174	33	8	21	89	9	.296
Totals		526	2085	349	606	119	21	71	301	82	.291

JODY REED 28 5-9 165   Bats R Throws R

Switch from shortstop to second base produced outstanding results . . . After committing 10 errors in 177 total chances at short, he erred just six times in 594 total chances at second base . . . His .990 fielding percentage was third-best among AL second basemen . . . Cracked 45 doubles to tie Kansas City's George Brett for major-league lead . . . Went 5-for-13 with 14 RBI in 16 plate appearances with bases loaded . . . Held to .133 average in ALCS . . . Born July 26, 1962, in Tampa . . . Red Sox' eighth-round pick in 1984 draft . . . Holds criminology degree from Florida State . . . Due for substantial raise after earning $300,000 in 1990.

Year Club	Pos.	G	AB	R	H	2B	3B	HR	RBI	SB	Avg.
1987 Boston	SS-2B-3B	9	30	4	9	1	1	0	8	1	.300
1988 Boston	SS-2B-3B	109	338	60	99	23	1	1	28	1	.293
1989 Boston	SS-2B-3B-OF	146	524	76	151	42	2	3	40	4	.288
1990 Boston	2B-SS	155	598	70	173	45	0	5	51	4	.289
Totals		419	1490	210	432	111	4	9	127	10	.290

ROGER CLEMENS 28 6-4 220   Bats R Throws R

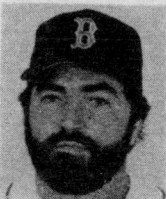

Brilliant season was marred by second-inning ejection in Game 4 of ALCS . . . Heaved without warning after cursing home-plate ump Terry Cooney . . . Was severely criticized for losing cool at critical time, yet detractors should remember Red Sox would never have reached playoffs without the "Rocket" . . . Fashioned major-league-leading 1.93 ERA . . . AL MVP candidate before missing starts with shoulder tendinitis in September . . . Enjoyed winning streaks of seven games (May 9-June 13) and eight games (July 25-Aug. 30) . . . Won 11 of 14 decisions following Red Sox loss and is 67-18 in that situation during his career . . . Red Sox were 22-9 when he started . . . Pitched into seventh inning in 28 of 31 starts . . . Surpassed Cy Young as club's all-time strikeout leader (1,424) . . . Tied for fourth with Smokey Joe Wood on Red Sox' all-time victory list (116) . . . In 1986, he became only pitcher to win league MVP, Cy Young and All-Star Game MVP awards in same season . . . Received Cy Young again in 1987 to join Sandy Koufax (1965-66) and Jim Palmer (1975-76) as only consecutive winners . . . Set club single-season strikeout record with 291 in 1988 . . . Born Aug. 4, 1962, in Dayton, Ohio . . . Red Sox' first pick in 1983 draft, out of University of Texas . . . One of game's best-paid players with $2.6-million salary in 1990 . . . Some of that will pay the $10,000 fine he received along with a five-game suspension for the Cooney confrontation.

Year	Club	G	IP	W	L	Pct.	SO	BB	H	ERA
1984	Boston	21	133⅓	9	4	.692	126	29	146	4.32
1985	Boston	15	98⅓	7	5	.583	74	37	83	3.29
1986	Boston	33	254	24	4	.857	238	67	179	2.48
1987	Boston	36	281⅔	20	9	.690	256	83	248	2.97
1988	Boston	35	264	18	12	.600	291	62	217	2.93
1989	Boston	35	253⅓	17	11	.607	230	93	215	3.13
1990	Boston	31	228⅓	21	6	.778	209	54	193	1.93
	Totals	206	1513	116	51	.695	1424	425	1281	2.89

JEFF REARDON 35 6-0 200   Bats R Throws R

Made remarkable recovery from Aug. 4 back surgery on ruptured disc to play significant role in club's drive to AL East crown . . . Contributed three saves and two wins in final five appearances . . . With team-leading 21 saves, he joined Bruce Sutter as only major-league relievers to notch 20 or more saves for nine consecutive seasons . . . Ranks fourth on all-time list with 287 career saves... Born Oct. 1, 1955, in Dalton, Mass.... Signed by Red Sox as free agent prior to last season ... Began career with Mets as undrafted free agent in June 1977 ... Made $1,633,333 in 1990.

Year	Club	G	IP	W	L	Pct.	SO	BB	H	ERA
1979	New York (NL)......	18	21	1	2	.333	10	9	12	1.71
1980	New York (NL)......	61	110	8	7	.533	101	47	96	2.62
1981	N.Y. (NL)-Mont......	43	70	3	0	1.000	49	21	48	2.19
1982	Montreal..........	75	109	7	4	.636	86	36	87	2.06
1983	Montreal..........	66	92	7	9	.438	78	44	87	3.03
1984	Montreal..........	68	87	7	7	.500	79	37	70	2.90
1985	Montreal..........	63	87⅔	2	8	.200	67	26	68	3.18
1986	Montreal..........	62	89	7	9	.438	67	26	83	3.94
1987	Minnesota.........	63	80⅓	8	8	.500	83	28	70	4.48
1988	Minnesota.........	63	73	2	4	.333	56	15	68	2.47
1989	Minnesota.........	65	73	5	4	.556	46	12	68	4.07
1990	Boston............	47	51⅓	5	3	.625	33	19	39	3.16
	Totals............	694	943⅓	62	65	.488	755	320	796	3.03

MATT YOUNG 6-3 205   Bats L Throws L

Should help compensate for loss of Mike Boddicker... Free agent fled Seattle to sign three-year, $6.4-million contract after a season in which he pitched better than 8-18 record would indicate... Tied for third in AL with seven complete games and was eighth in innings pitched (225⅓)... Rebounded from terrible start during which he went 1-7 with 4.63 ERA in first 13 games... Fashioned 2.82 ERA in final 15 starts but was just 5-7 in that span... Held left-handed hitters to .149 average and has not allowed a home run to a lefty in last 315⅔ innings... Missed all of 1988 and half of '89 due to reconstructive surgery on left elbow... Born Aug. 9, 1958, in Pasadena, Cal. ... Began career as Seattle's second-round choice in June 1980 draft.

Year	Club	G	IP	W	L	Pct.	SO	BB	H	ERA
1983	Seattle...........	33	203⅔	11	15	.423	130	79	178	3.27
1984	Seattle...........	22	113⅓	6	8	.429	73	57	141	5.72
1985	Seattle...........	37	218⅓	12	19	.387	136	76	242	4.91
1986	Seattle...........	65	103⅔	8	6	.571	82	46	108	3.82
1987	Los Angeles.......	47	54⅓	5	8	.385	42	17	62	4.47
1988	Oakland...........					Did Not Play				
1989	Oakland...........	26	37⅓	1	4	.200	27	31	42	6.75
1990	Seattle...........	34	225⅓	8	18	.308	176	107	198	3.51
	Totals...........	264	956	51	78	.395	666	413	971	4.26

DANNY DARWIN 35 6-3 190   Bats R Throws R

Astro new-look free agent signed four-year contract estimated at $12.2 million . . . Led NL in ERA with club-record 2.21 mark, bettering 2.22 showings of Mike Cuellar (1966) and Mike Scott (1986) . . . Pitched 162⅔ innings, the lowest total for ERA champ since Hoyt Wilhelm threw 159 back in 1952 . . . Qualified for ERA title by two-thirds of an inning . . . Opened year in the bullpen . . . Moved to rotation July 1, after 111 straight relief outings . . . First two starts were no-decisions, but went 8-0 with a 1.50 ERA in first 11 starts . . . Became third Houston pitcher in the last five years to win ERA title, joining Scott and Nolan Ryan . . . Secret to success is control . . . Issued fewest walks per nine innings in NL (1.7) . . . Acquired from the Brewers for Don August and Mark Knudson, Aug. 15, 1986 . . . Born Oct. 25, 1955, in Bonham, Tex. . . . Won 11 games in relief in 1989 . . . Signed as a free agent by Texas, May 10, 1976 . . . Made $1,125,000 last season.

Year	Club	G	IP	W	L	Pct.	SO	BB	H	ERA
1978	Texas	3	9	1	0	1.000	8	1	11	4.00
1979	Texas	20	78	4	4	.500	58	30	50	4.04
1980	Texas	53	110	13	4	.765	104	50	98	2.62
1981	Texas	22	146	9	9	.500	98	57	115	3.64
1982	Texas	56	89	10	8	.556	61	37	95	3.44
1983	Texas	28	183	8	13	.381	92	62	175	3.49
1984	Texas	35	223⅔	8	12	.400	123	54	249	3.94
1985	Milwaukee	39	217⅔	8	18	.308	125	65	212	3.80
1986	Milwaukee	27	130⅓	6	8	.429	80	35	120	3.52
1986	Houston	12	54⅓	5	2	.714	40	9	50	2.32
1987	Houston	33	195⅔	9	10	.474	134	69	184	3.59
1988	Houston	44	192	8	13	.381	129	48	189	3.84
1989	Houston	68	122	11	4	.733	104	33	92	2.36
1990	Houston	48	162⅔	11	4	.733	109	31	136	2.21
	Totals	488	1913⅓	111	109	.505	1265	581	1776	3.40

TOM BOLTON 28 6-3 175   Bats L Throws L

Blossomed as a starter after June 13 recall from Pawtucket (AAA), where he was 1-0 with 3.86 ERA . . . Joined rotation on July 17 . . . Won five of first six starts . . . Allowed three earned runs or fewer in 14 of 16 starts . . . Pitched into seventh inning 12 times . . . This lefty excelled at Fenway with 4-1 mark and 2.23 ERA in six starts there . . . Born May 6, 1962, in Nashville, Tenn. . . . Red Sox' 19th choice in 1980 draft . . . Has worked as cabinet maker in family business during offseason . . . Earned approximately $100,000 in 1990.

Year	Club	G	IP	W	L	Pct.	SO	BB	H	ERA
1987	Boston	29	61⅔	1	0	1.000	49	27	83	4.38
1988	Boston	28	30⅓	1	3	.250	21	14	35	4.75
1989	Boston	4	17⅓	0	4	.000	9	10	21	8.31
1990	Boston	21	119⅔	10	5	.667	65	47	111	3.38
	Totals	82	229	12	12	.500	144	98	250	4.21

TOP PROSPECTS

MO VAUGHN 23 6-1 225   **Bats L Throws R**
First baseman should be ready to make impact at big-league level
. . . Ranked fourth in International League in batting average (.295)
and home runs (22) for Pawtucket (AAA) . . . Enjoyed brilliant
three-year collegiate career at Seton Hall, batting .417 with school-
record 57 homers and 218 RBI . . . Honored as Big East Player of
Decade . . . Born Dec. 15, 1967, in Norwalk, Conn. . . . Red Sox'
second pick in 1989 draft.

TIM NAEHRING 24 6-2 190   **Bats R Throws R**
Figures to establish himself as Red Sox shortstop . . . Hit .269 with
15 homers and 47 RBI in 290 at-bats for Pawtucket (AAA) last
year . . . Performed well after his contract was purchased from
Pawtucket July 15, batting .271 with two homers and 12 RBI in
24 games . . . August injury cut short his season . . . Eighth-round
pick in 1988 draft needed only two full years in minors to reach
big leagues . . . Born Feb. 1, 1967, in Cincinnati.

SCOTT COOPER 23 6-3 200   **Bats L Throws R**
Sought-after third baseman is almost ready for prime time . . . Hit
.266 with 12 homers and 44 RBI for Pawtucket (AAA) in
1990 . . . Led New Britain (AA) with 104 hits in 1989 . . . Tied for
Carolina League lead with 148 hits for Lynchburg (A) in '88 and
was named to All-Star team . . . Born Oct. 13, 1967, in St. Louis
. . . Red Sox' third-round pick in 1986 draft.

PHIL PLANTIER 22 6-0 175   **Bats L Throws R**
Outfielder could play prominent role in Red Sox' future . . .

Topped International League with 33 homers, ranked fourth with 79 RBI and hit .253 for Pawtucket (AAA) in 1990 . . . Batted .133 on 2-for-15 in limited time with Red Sox . . . Named Carolina League MVP in 1989, when he hit 27 homers, had 105 RBI and narrowly missed Triple Crown by finishing third with .300 average for Lynchburg (A) . . . Born Jan. 27, 1969, in Manchester, N.H. . . . Red Sox' 11th-round pick in 1987 draft . . . Works as electrician in offseason.

MANAGER JOE MORGAN: Gained second AL East title in three years with 88-74 finish, baffling his many critics . . . Has been severely criticized, even by own players . . . Seems to be little pattern to how he shuffles players, but has knack for pushing proper buttons . . . Relief pitchers justifiably complain that he warms them up too often . . . Was right man at right time when named to replace John McNamara, July 14, 1988 . . . Enjoyed best managerial start in history that year as Red Sox won first 12 games and 19 of first 20 under him en route to AL East title . . . Known for playing hunches . . . Has pinch-hit for five-time AL batting champion Wade Boggs . . . Owns 217-184 career major-league managerial record . . . Spent 15 seasons as minor-league infielder and outfielder . . . Had brief stints in majors with Milwaukee Braves, Kansas City A's, Philadelphia, Cleveland and St. Louis . . . Managed in Pittsburgh system from 1966-73 . . . Joined Red Sox organization in 1974 and managed Pawtucket (AAA) until 1982 . . . Used to plough Massachusetts Turnpike in winter to supplement meager baseball earnings . . . Born Nov. 19, 1930, in Walpole, Mass.

ALL-TIME RED SOX SEASON RECORDS

BATTING: Ted Williams, .406, 1941
HRs: Jimmie Foxx, 50, 1938
RBI: Jimmie Foxx, 175, 1938
STEALS: Tommy Harper, 54, 1973
WINS: Joe Wood, 34, 1912
STRIKEOUTS: Roger Clemens, 291, 1988

CLEVELAND INDIANS

TEAM DIRECTORY: Owners: Richard Jacobs, David Jacobs; Pres.-Chief Oper. Off.: Hank Peters; Dir. Baseball Oper.: John Hart; Dir. Player Dev.: Dan O'Dowd; Dir. Media Rel.: John Maroon; Trav. Sec.: Mike Seghi; Mgr.: John McNamara. Home: Cleveland Stadium (74,483). Field distances: 320, l.f. line; 377, l.c.; 400, c.f.; 395, r.c.; 320, r.f. line. Spring training: Tucson, Ariz.

SCOUTING REPORT

HITTING: The Indians look for continued progress after showing significant offensive improvement last season.

Their 732 runs scored ranked fourth in the AL and represented a 128-run increase from 1989. The Indians stole 33 more bases than the year before to finish with 107 and they rated third in the league with 1,465 hits, 125 more than in 1989. Most impressive was their .267 batting average, the second-highest mark in the majors.

Three additions—Sandy Alomar Jr., Alex Cole and Craig James—made the biggest impact. Alomar batted .290 with nine home runs and 66 RBI and his .376 average against left-handers topped the AL. Cole, who did not make his major-league debut until the end of July, hit .300 and stole 40 bases in 63 games. James (.299, 12, 70) emerged in his first AL season. Brook Jacoby (.293, 14, 75) has proven to be a dependable bat, but with Cory Snyder gone, the Indians might lament their decision to let Candy Maldonado (.273, 22, 95) go elsewhere as a free agent.

PITCHING: The Indians worked during the winter to bolster their rotation, adding Eric King (12-4, 3.28) and Shawn Hillegas from the White Sox in the deal for Snyder and Willie Blair from the Blue Jays.

Right-hander Tom Candiotti (15-11, 3.65), the knuckleballer, has won in double figures four of the last five years. But much of Cleveland's fate will depend on Greg Swindell (12-9, 4.40). He has lots of ability, as he showed by winning 18 games three years ago, but lacks Candiotti's consistency. The Indians need big numbers again from Swindell, who permitted 27 home runs last year, the second-highest total in the AL. It would also help if John Farrell comes back from elbow surgery.

Stopper Doug Jones (5-5, 2.56) anchors the bullpen. An All-

Sandy Alomar Jr. became Tribe chieftain as rookie.

Star each of the last three years, Jones smashed his own club single-season saves record with 43 last year.

FIELDING: Alomar already ranks among the game's finest catchers. He became only the third catcher to gain AL Rookie of the Year honors, joining the great Carlton Fisk and Thurman Munson. Alomar threw out 34 percent of potential base-stealers (33 of 96) and won the Gold Glove in his first year.

Felix Fermin, Brook Jacoby and Jerry Browne are also plusses. Shortstop Fermin slashed his error total from 26 to 16, Jacoby committed only six errors despite playing both first base and third base and Browne is solid at second.

OUTLOOK: Don't be surprised if John McNamara's Indians emerge as a factor after last year's fourth-place, 77-85 finish. They have not finished higher than fourth since 1968, but their 18-13 final-month mark was another encouraging sign better times are on the way.

CLEVELAND INDIANS 1991 ROSTER

MANAGER John McNamara
Coaches—Rich Dauer, Mike Hargrove, Luis Isaac, Jose Morales, Mark Wiley, Billy Williams

PITCHERS

No.	Name	1990 Club	W-L	IP	SO	ERA	B-T	Ht.	Wt.	Born
39	Blair, Willie	Syracuse	0-2	19	6	4.74	R-R	61	185	12/18/65 Paintsville, KY
		Toronto	3-5	69	43	4.06				
49	Candiotti, Tom	Cleveland	15-11	202	128	3.65	R-R	6-2	200	8/31/57 Walnut Creek, CA
56	Cummings, Steve	Syracuse	5-3	81	34	3.11	S-R	6-2	205	7/15/64 Houston, TX
		Toronto	0-0	12	4	5.11				
66	Egloff, Bruce	Canton-Akron	3-2	55	53	1.98	R-R	6-2	215	4/10/65 Denver, CO
52	Farrell, John	Canton-Akron	1-1	10	5	7.20	R-R	6-4	210	8/4/62 Neptune, NJ
		Cleveland	4-5	97	44	4.28				
36	Gozzo, Mauro	Syracuse	3-8	98	62	3.58	R-R	6-3	212	3/7/66 New Britain, CT
		Cleveland	0-0	3	2	0.00				
—	Hillegas, Shawn	Vancouver	5-3	67	52	1.74	R-R	6-2	223	8/21/64 Dos Palos, CA
		Chicago (AL)	0-0	11	5	0.79				
11	Jones, Doug	Cleveland	5-5	84	55	2.56	R-R	6-2	195	6/24/57 Covina, CA
—	King, Eric	Chicago (AL)	12-4	151	70	3.28	R-R	6-2	218	4/10/64 Oxnard, CA
64	Kramer, Tom	Kinston	7-4	98	96	2.85	S-R	6-0	185	1/9/68 Cincinnati, OH
		Canton-Akron	6-3	72	46	3.00				
65	Mutis, Jeff	Canton-Akron	11-10	165	94	3.16	L-L	6-2	185	12/20/66 Allentown, PA
41	Nagy, Charles	Canton-Akron	13-8	175	99	2.52	L-R	6-3	200	5/5/67 Fairfield, CT
		Cleveland	2-4	46	26	5.91				
54	Nichols, Rod	Cleveland	0-3	16	3	7.88	R-R	6-2	190	12/29/64 Burlington, IA
		Colorado Springs	12-9	133	74	5.13				
31	Olin, Steve	Cleveland	4-4	92	64	3.41	R-R	6-2	190	10/10/65 Portland, OR
		Colorado Springs	3-1	27	30	0.66				
47	Orosco, Jesse	Cleveland	5-4	65	55	3.90	R-L	6-2	185	4/21/57 Santa Barbara, CA
32	Seanez, Rudy	Canton-Akron	1-0	17	27	2.16	R-R	5-10	185	10/20/68 Brawley, CA
		Cleveland	2-1	27	24	5.60				
		Colorado Springs	1-4	12	7	6.75				
57	Shaw, Jeff	Colorado Springs	10-3	99	55	4.29	R-R	6-2	185	7/7/66 Washington Court House, OH
		Cleveland	3-4	49	25	6.66				
21	Swindell, Greg	Cleveland	12-9	215	135	4.40	S-L	6-3	225	1/2/65 Fort Worth, TX
33	Valdez, Efrain	Colorado Springs	4-2	76	52	3.81	L-L	5-11	170	6/11/66 Dominican Republic
		Cleveland	1-1	24	13	3.04				
30	Valez, Sergio	Atlanta	0-0	5	3	6.75	R-R	6-1	190	9/7/65 Dominican Republic
		Cleveland	6-6	102	63	4.75				
		Colorado Springs	4-3	43	33	5.19				
48	Walker, Mike	Colorado Springs	2-7	79	50	5.58	R-R	6-1	195	10/4/66 Brooksville, FL
		Canton-Akron	1-0	7	3	0.00				
		Cleveland	2-6	76	34	4.88				
53	Wickander, Kevin	Cleveland	0-1	12	10	3.65	L-L	6-2	202	1/4/65 Fort Dodge, IA

CATCHERS

No.	Name	1990 Club	H	HR	RBI	Pct.	B-T	Ht.	Wt.	Born
15	Alomar, Sandy	Cleveland	129	9	66	.290	R-R	6-5	200	6/18/66 Puerto Rico
4	Skinner, Joel	Cleveland	35	2	16	.252	R-R	6-4	204	2/21/61 LaJolla, CA

INFIELDERS

No.	Name	1990 Club	H	HR	RBI	Pct.	B-T	Ht.	Wt.	Born
9	Baerga, Carlos	Cleveland	81	7	47	.260	S-R	5-11	165	11/4/68 Puerto Rico
		Colorado Springs	19	1	11	.380				
14	Browne, Jerry	Cleveland	137	6	50	.267	S-R	5-10	170	2/13/66 Virgin Islands
16	Fermin, Felix	Cleveland	106	1	40	.256	R-R	5-11	170	10/9/63 Dominican Republic
17	Hernandez, Keith	Cleveland	26	1	8	.200	L-L	6-0	205	10/20/53 San Francisco, CA
		Gulf Coast	5	1	2	.455				
26	Jacoby, Brook	Cleveland	162	14	75	.293	R-R	6-1	195	11/23/59 Philadelphia, PA
61	Magallanes, Ever	Colorado Springs	116	1	63	.308	L-R	5-10	165	11/6/65 Mexico
44	Manto, Jeff	Colorado Springs	94	18	82	.297	R-R	6-3	210	8/23/64 Bristol, PA
		Cleveland	17	2	14	.224				

OUTFIELDERS

No.	Name	1990 Club	H	HR	RBI	Pct.	B-T	Ht.	Wt.	Born
55	Allred, Beau	Colorado Springs	105	13	74	.278	L-L	6-0	193	6/4/65 Mesa, AZ
		Cleveland	3	1	3	.188				
8	Belle, Joey	Cleveland	4	1	3	.174	R-R	6-2	200	8/25/66 Shreveport, LA
		Colorado Springs	33	5	19	.344				
		Canton-Akron	8	0	3	.250				
55	Cockrell, Alan	Port.-Col. Sp.	121	17	71	.323	R-R	6-2	215	12/5/62 Kansas City, KS
2	Cole, Alex	Las Vegas-Col. Sp.	120	0	32	.308	L-L	6-2	170	8/17/65 Fayetteville, NC
		Cleveland	68	0	13	.300				
18	James, Chris	Cleveland	158	12	70	.299	R-R	6-1	190	10/4/62 Rusk, TX
24	Jefferson, Stan	Balt.-Cle.	27	-2	10	.231	S-R	5-11	180	12/4/62 New York, NY
20	Ward, Turner	Colorado Springs	148	6	65	.299	S-R	6-2	200	4/11/65 Orlando, FL
		Cleveland	16	1	10	.348				
23	Webster, Mitch	Cleveland	110	12	55	.252	S-L	6-1	185	5/16/59 Larned, KS

INDIAN PROFILES

SANDY ALOMAR Jr. 24 6-5 200   **Bats R Throws R**

Pointed for stardom after AL Rookie-of-the-Year Campaign . . . Became first rookie catcher to start an All-Star Game and showed he belonged by collecting two hits . . . His 66 RBI were the most by an Indians catcher since 1962 . . . Other than one five-game hitless streak, he did not go more than three games without a hit . . . Threw out 34 percent (33 of 96) of base runners attempting to steal . . . Honored by *Baseball America* as Minor League Player of the Year in both 1988 and '89 . . . Born June 18, 1966, in Salinas, Puerto Rico . . . Acquired from Padres with Chris James and Carlos Baerga for Joe Carter, Dec. 6, 1989 . . . Signed with San Diego as 17-year-old free agent in October 1983 . . . Father Sandy Sr. enjoyed 15-year major-league career . . . Brother Roberto is second baseman for Toronto . . . Earned $115,000 and a Gold Glove last season.

Year	Club	Pos.	G	AB	R	H	2B	3B	HR	RBI	SB	Avg.
1988	San Diego	PH	1	1	0	0	0	0	0	0	0	.000
1989	San Diego	C	7	19	1	4	1	0	1	6	0	.211
1990	Cleveland	C	132	445	60	129	26	2	9	66	4	.290
	Totals		140	465	61	133	27	2	10	72	4	.286

ALEX COLE 25 6-2 170   **Bats L Throws L**

Center fielder proved to be tremendous acquisition . . . Was obtained from St. Louis for Tom Lampkin July 11 . . . Finished fourth in AL with 40 steals, despite playing in only 63 games . . . Succeeded on 81.6 percent of his stolen-base tries while establishing Tribe rookie record for steals . . . Hit safely in 20 of first 22 games . . . Compiled .379 on-base percentage in leadoff situations, fourth-best mark in AL . . . Born Aug. 17, 1965, in Fayetteville, N.C. . . . Cards' second-round pick in 1985 draft . . . Worked on bunting with Rod Carew during offseason . . . Made major-league minimum of $100,000.

Year	Club	Pos.	G	AB	R	H	2B	3B	HR	RBI	SB	Avg.
1990	Cleveland	OF	63	227	43	68	5	4	0	13	40	.300

JERRY BROWNE 25 5-10 170   Bats S Throws R

Second baseman hopes to continue improvement after establishing career highs in RBI (50), runs (92), home runs (6) and walks (72)... Ranked seventh in AL in runs scored... Recovered from .154 April... Enjoyed 44-game errorless string that ended June 25... Voted 1989 Tribe Man of the Year during first full season in Cleveland... Born Feb. 13, 1966, in Christiansted, St. Croix, Virgin Islands... Acquired from Texas with Pete O'Brien and Oddibe McDowell for Julio Franco after 1988 season... Originally signed by Rangers as free agent in March 1983... Earned $310,000 last year.

Year	Club	Pos.	G	AB	R	H	2B	3B	HR	RBI	SB	Avg.
1986	Texas	2B	12	24	6	10	2	0	0	3	0	.417
1987	Texas	2B	132	454	63	123	16	6	1	38	27	.271
1988	Texas	2B	73	214	26	49	9	2	1	17	7	.229
1989	Cleveland	2B	153	598	83	179	31	4	5	45	14	.299
1990	Cleveland	2B	140	513	92	137	26	5	6	50	12	.267
	Totals		510	1803	270	498	84	17	13	153	60	.276

BROOK JACOBY 31 5-11 195   Bats R Throws R

Veteran comes off successful season in which he was named to All-Star team for second time in career... Cited as AL Player of the Month in June, when he hit .394 with six homers and 21 RBI... Led Indians with 18 multi-RBI games... Batted .314 with runners aboard... Made only six errors despite splitting time between first base and third base... Born Nov. 23, 1959, in Philadelphia... Acquired from Braves with Brett Butler and Rick Behenna in Aug. 28, 1983 trade that sent Len Barker to Atlanta... Began career as Atlanta's seventh-round choice in 1979 draft... Earned $987,500 in 1990.

Year	Club	Pos.	G	AB	R	H	2B	3B	HR	RBI	SB	Avg.
1981	Atlanta	3B	11	10	0	2	0	0	0	1	0	.200
1983	Atlanta	3B	4	8	0	0	0	0	0	0	0	.000
1984	Cleveland	3B-SS	126	439	64	116	19	3	7	40	3	.264
1985	Cleveland	3B-2B	161	606	72	166	26	3	20	87	2	.274
1986	Cleveland	3B	158	583	83	168	30	4	17	80	2	.288
1987	Cleveland	3B-1B	155	540	73	162	26	4	32	69	2	.300
1988	Cleveland	3B	152	552	59	133	25	0	9	49	2	.241
1989	Cleveland	3B	147	519	49	141	26	5	13	64	2	.272
1990	Cleveland	3B-1B	155	553	77	162	24	4	14	75	1	.293
	Totals		1069	3810	477	1050	176	23	112	465	14	.276

CHRIS JAMES 28 6-1 190   Bats R Throws R

Made most of first season with Tribe, earning booster club's MVP award . . . Led Indians with .299 batting average, despite woeful .122 start in April . . . Enjoyed big August, posting .357 average, four home runs and 16 RBI . . . Paced Indians with 51 multi-hit games, the ninth-highest total in AL . . . Born Oct. 4, 1962, in Rusk, Tex. . . . Acquired from Padres with Sandy Alomar Jr. and Carlos Baerga for Joe Carter prior to last season . . . Began career by signing with Philadelphia as free agent in October 1981 . . . Brother Craig played as running back with New England Patriots . . . Earned $560,000 last year.

Year	Club	Pos.	G	AB	R	H	2B	3B	HR	RBI	SB	Avg.
1986	Philadelphia . . .	OF	16	46	5	13	3	0	1	5	0	.283
1987	Philadelphia . . .	OF	115	358	48	105	20	6	17	54	3	.293
1988	Philadelphia . . .	OF-3B	150	566	57	137	24	1	19	66	7	.242
1989	Phil.-S.D. . . .	OF-3B	132	482	55	117	17	2	13	65	5	.243
1990	Cleveland	OF	140	528	62	158	32	4	12	70	4	.299
	Totals		553	1980	227	530	96	13	62	260	19	.268

GREG SWINDELL 26 6-3 225   Bats R Throws L

Although he reached double figures in victories for third consecutive year, he has not become the dominant pitcher Indians had hoped he'd be . . . Went winless from April 30 to July 1, a span of 11 starts . . . Surrendered 27 home runs, the second-highest total in AL . . . Showed abilities with 4-1 record and 2.49 ERA in July . . . Led Tribe in starts (34), innings pitched (214⅔) and strikeouts (135) . . . Born Jan. 2, 1965, in Fort Worth, Tex. . . . Chosen by Cleveland in 1986 draft as second player picked overall . . . Three-time All-American at University of Texas, where he compiled 43-8 career record. . . . Earned $840,000 last season.

Year	Club	G	IP	W	L	Pct.	SO	BB	H	ERA
1986	Cleveland	9	61⅔	5	2	.714	46	15	57	4.23
1987	Cleveland	16	102⅓	3	8	.273	97	37	112	5.10
1988	Cleveland	33	242	18	14	.563	180	45	234	3.20
1989	Cleveland	28	184⅓	13	6	.684	129	51	170	3.37
1990	Cleveland	34	214⅔	12	9	.571	135	47	245	4.40
	Totals.	120	805	51	39	.567	587	195	818	3.88

Tom Candiotti is among dying breed of knuckleballers.

TOM CANDIOTTI 33 6-2 200   Bats R Throws R

Knuckleballer has established himself as quality starter . . . Topped Indians with 15 victories, the second-highest total of career, despite missing time in May with inflamed right elbow . . . Has reached double figures in wins four of last five seasons . . . First Indian to throw 200-plus innings for five consecutive seasons since Sam McDowell did it from 1967-71 . . . Spent parts of seven seasons in minors . . . Began developing knuckleball in 1985, with Phil Niekro's help . . . Signed to Triple-A contract by Cleveland after 1985 season . . . Born Aug. 31, 1957, in Walnut Creek, Cal. . . . Earned $1,050,000 last season.

Year	Club	G	IP	W	L	Pct.	SO	BB	H	ERA
1983	Milwaukee	10	55⅔	4	4	.500	21	16	62	3.23
1984	Milwaukee	8	32⅓	2	2	.500	23	10	38	5.29
1986	Cleveland	36	252⅓	16	12	.571	167	106	234	3.57
1987	Cleveland	32	201⅔	7	18	.280	111	93	193	4.78
1988	Cleveland	31	216⅔	14	8	.636	137	53	225	3.28
1989	Cleveland	31	206	13	10	.565	124	55	188	3.10
1990	Cleveland	31	202	15	11	.577	128	55	207	3.65
	Totals	179	1166⅔	71	65	.522	711	388	1147	3.69

DOUG JONES 33 6-2 195   Bats R Throws R

Has established himself as one of AL's finest closers . . . Broke own club single-season record with 43 saves . . . Also set Tribe mark with 64 games finished . . . Ranks as club's all-time saves leader with 121 . . . Converted first 13 save opportunities and did not permit an earned run until May 16 . . . Named to All-Star staff for third consecutive season . . . Not used exclusively as a reliever until 1985 . . . Born June 24, 1957, in Covina, Cal. . . . Began career with Milwaukee as third-round selection in January 1978 draft . . . Signed by Cleveland as free agent, April 3, 1985 . . . Made $950,000 in 1990 . . . Has 121 career saves, a club record.

Year	Club	G	IP	W	L	Pct.	SO	BB	H	ERA
1982	Milwaukee	4	2⅔	0	0	.000	1	1	5	10.13
1986	Cleveland	11	18	1	0	1.000	12	6	18	2.50
1987	Cleveland	49	91⅓	6	5	.545	87	24	101	3.15
1988	Cleveland	51	83⅓	3	4	.429	72	16	69	2.27
1989	Cleveland	59	80⅔	7	10	.412	65	13	76	2.34
1990	Cleveland	66	84⅓	5	5	.500	55	22	66	2.56
	Totals	240	360⅓	22	24	.478	292	82	335	2.65

JOHN FARRELL 28 6-4 210   Bats R Throws R

Hopes to stay healthy after injury-filled 1990 season . . . Removed from game June 24 in Milwaukee with stiff right elbow . . . Sent to Canton (AA) on rehab assignment July 16, but reinjured himself in second start there . . . Was activated Sept. 21 and pitched five shutout innings at Toronto . . . Underwent surgery on right elbow Oct. 4 . . . Born Aug. 4, 1962, in Neptune, N.J. . . . Cleveland's second pick in 1984 draft . . . Earned $320,000 last year.

Year	Club	G	IP	W	L	Pct.	SO	BB	H	ERA
1987	Cleveland	10	69	5	1	.833	28	22	68	3.39
1988	Cleveland	31	210⅓	14	10	.583	92	67	216	4.24
1989	Cleveland	31	208	9	14	.391	132	71	196	3.63
1990	Cleveland	17	96⅔	4	5	.444	44	33	108	4.28
	Totals	89	584	32	30	.516	296	193	588	3.93

TOP PROSPECTS

MARK LEWIS 21 6-1 187   Bats R Throws R
Ready to bid for shortstop job . . . Made stops at Canton (AA) and
Colorado Springs (AAA) last year and did well . . . Batted .272
with 10 homers and 60 RBI for Canton . . . Hit .306 with one
homer and 21 RBI for Colorado Springs . . . Born Nov. 30, 1969,
in Hamilton, Ohio . . . Was second player picked in 1988 draft.

RUDY SEANEZ 22 5-10 185   Bats R Throws R
Hard thrower needs only to develop more consistency to be force
in bullpen . . . Used mid-90-mph fastball to fan 24 in 27⅓ innings
with Indians . . . Hurt himself, however, with 25 walks . . . Was
2-1 with a 5.60 ERA for Cleveland . . . Born Oct. 20, 1968, in
Brawley, Cal. . . . Indians' fourth selection in 1986 draft . . . Went
1-4 with 6.75 ERA for Colorado Springs (AAA) after going 1-0,
2.16 for Canton (AA).

TURNER WARD 25 6-2 200   Bats R Throws R
Outfielder may soon work his way into Indians' plans . . . Batted
.299 with six homers, 65 RBI and 22 stolen bases for Colorado
Springs (AAA) . . . Excelled in short stint with Indians, hitting
.348 with one home run and 10 RBI in 14 games . . . Born April
11, 1965, in Orlando, Fla. . . . Acquired with Joel Skinner from
Yankees for Mel Hall prior to 1989 season.

JOEY BELLE 24 6-2 200   Bats R Throws R
Outfielder has ability to start if he can leave trouble-filled past
behind . . . Missed part of last season to undergo alcohol rehabilitation at Cleveland Clinic . . . Played only 24 games for Colorado
Springs (AAA), compiling .344 average with five homers and 19
RBI . . . Born Aug. 25, 1966, in Shreveport, La. . . . Indians' second selection in 1987 draft.

MANAGER JOHN McNAMARA: Determined to make the most of a limited hand with Indians . . . Tribe responded well to him in his first year on job, despite 77-85 finish . . . Was controversial selection since this is his sixth major-league managerial stop, but he has proven ability . . . Was named AL Manager of the Year in 1986, when he guided Red Sox to pennant . . . Managed Angels in 1983 and 1984 . . . Was minor-league manager for nine years in Kansas City A's organization before being named major-league coach when A's moved to Oakland in 1968 . . . Made major-league managerial debut with Oakland, Sept. 19, 1969 . . . Led A's to second-place finish in 1970 . . . Coaching stints include stops in San Francisco from 1971-73 and California in 1978 . . . Managed young San Diego team from 1974 through May 1977 and Padres' record improved each year . . . Piloted Cincinnati from 1979 through July 1982 and led Reds to NL West titles in 1979 and 1980 . . . Has career major-league managerial mark of 2,025-2,163 . . . Was minor-league catcher and also pitched 14 games . . . Born June 4, 1932, in Sacramento, Cal.

ALL-TIME INDIAN SEASON RECORDS

BATTING: Joe Jackson, .408, 1911
HRs: Al Rosen, 43, 1953
RBI: Hal Trosky, 162, 1936
STEALS: Miguel Dilone, 61, 1980
WINS: Jim Bagby, 31, 1920
STRIKEOUTS: Bob Feller, 348, 1946

DETROIT TIGERS

TEAM DIRECTORY: Chairman Emeritus: John E. Fetzer; Chairman/CEO: Jim Campbell; Owner/Vice Chairman: Tom Monaghan; Pres./Chief Oper. Off.: Bo Schembechler; VP-Operations: William Haase; VP-GM: William Lajoie; VP-Player Procurement Dev.: Joe McDonald; VP-Marketing, Radio-TV, Pub. Rel.: Jeff Odenwald; Dir. Pub. Rel.: Dan Ewald; Trav. Sec.: Bill Brown; Mgr.: Sparky Anderson. Home: Tiger Stadium (52,416). Field distances: 340, l.f. line; 365, l.c.; 440, c.f.; 370, r.c.; 325, r.f. line. Spring training: Lakeland, Fla.

Through thick and thin, Alan Trammell has been a Tiger.

SCOUTING REPORT

HITTING: Much will depend on what kind of encore Cecil Fielder provides. The AL home-run champion will surely suffer a dip from last year's monster 51-homer, 132-RBI season. The question is: How much of a drop?

The Tigers did add another home-run threat by signing Rob Deer as a free agent. Deer collected 27 home runs and 69 RBI for Milwaukee. Detroit's offense figures to continue to be an all-or-nothing affair, however, because both Fielder (182 Ks) and Deer (147 Ks) are frequent strikeout victims.

Alan Trammell (.304, 14, 89) and Lou Whitaker (.237, 18, 60) continue to be key run producers on a club that ranked second in the AL with 750 last year.

PITCHING: Detroit was undermined by its pitching in 1990 and that figures to be the case again. The Tigers were last in the AL with a 4.39 ERA and this staff is loaded with question marks, including free-agent recruit Bill Gullickson (10-14, 3.82 with Astros).

Can 35-year-old Jack Morris (15-18, 4.51), a new-look free agent at press time, still win big without losing big? Is Frank Tanana, 37, capable of improving on a 9-8 record and a 5.31 ERA? What will Walt Terrell, the kid among this trio at 32, provide in a full season? He was 6-4 with a 4.54 ERA after returning to Detroit following his release by Pittsburgh last season. Mike Henneman (8-6, 3.05, 22 Sv) is the key figure in the bullpen.

FIELDING: When it comes to stability, no franchise can match Detroit. The double-play combination of shortstop Trammell and second baseman Whitaker is entering its 14th consecutive season together.

Newcomer Milt Cuyler has the speed necessary to cover Tiger Stadium's vast center field. Defensive standout Travis Fryman, in his first full major-league season, should finally end Detroit's search for a third baseman, leaving Tony Phillips in the role of versatile utility man once again.

OUTLOOK: Detroit made tremendous progress last season, completing a leap from 59-103 in 1989 to 78-83 in 1990. Look for improvement to continue under super manager Sparky Anderson.

DETROIT TIGERS 1991 ROSTER

MANAGER Sparky Anderson
Coaches—Billy Consolo, Alex Grammas, Billy Muffett, Vada Pinson, Dick Tracewski

PITCHERS

No.	Name	1990 Club	W-L	IP	SO	ERA	B-T	Ht.	Wt.	Born
30	Aldred, Scott	Toledo	6-15	158	133	4.90	L-L	6-4	195	6/12/68 Flint, MI
		Detroit	1-2	14	7	3.77				
—	Gakeler, Dan	Indianapolis	5-5	120	89	3.23	R-R	6-6	210	5/1/64 Mt. Holly, NJ
48	Gibson, Paul	Detroit	5-4	97	56	3.05	R-L	6-0	185	1/4/60 Center Moriches, NY
19	Gleaton, Jerry Don	Detroit	1-3	83	56	2.94	L-L	6-3	210	9/14/57 Brownwood, TX
36	Gullickson, Bill	Houston	10-14	193	73	3.82	R-R	6-3	220	2/20/59 Marshall, MN
—	Haas, David	London	13-8	178	116	2.99	R-R	6-1	200	10/19/65 Independence, MO
39	Hennaman, Mike	Detroit	8-6	94	50	3.05	R-R	6-4	205	12/11/61 St. Charles, MO
—	Meacham, Rusty	London	15-9	178	123	3.13	R-R	6-3	155	1/27/68 Stuart, FL
47	**Morris, Jack	Detroit	15-18	250	162	4.51	R-R	6-3	200	5/16/55 St. Paul, MN
—	Munoz, Mike	Albuquerque	4-1	59	40	4.25	L-L	6-3	195	7/12/65 Baldwin Park, CA
		Los Angeles	0-1	6	2	3.18				
37	Nosek, Randy	Toledo	5-8	109	55	5.19	R-R	6-4	216	1/8/67 Omaha, NE
		Detroit	1-1	7	3	7.71				
17	Parker, Clay	Col.-Tol.	2-5	54	34	3.33	R-R	6-2	185	12/19/62 Pistol Thicket, LA
		NY (AL)-Det.	3-3	73	40	3.58				
23	Petry, Dan	Detroit	10-9	150	73	4.45	R-R	6-4	215	11/13/58 Palo Alto, CA
—	Ramos, Jose	London	5-2	52	25	3.12	L-L	6-1	160	1/25/68 Venezuela
		Toledo	0-1	32	16	4.22				
42	Richards, Dave	London	6-6	55	74	4.28	L-L	6-3	195	9/18/67 Rock Island, IL
31	Ritz, Kevin	Toledo	3-6	90	57	5.22	R-R	6-4	195	6/8/65 Eatontown, NJ
		Detroit	0-4	7	3	11.05				
49	Searcy, Steve	Toledo	10-5	105	105	2.92	L-L	6-1	195	6/4/64 Knoxville, TN
		Detroit	2-7	75	66	4.66				
—	Stone, Eric	Toledo	2-4	68	57	3.95	R-R	6-2	190	7/29/67 Parsons, KS
26	Tanana, Frank	Detroit	9-8	176	114	5.31	L-L	6-3	195	7/3/53 Detroit, MI
35	Terrell, Walt	Pittsburgh	2-7	83		5.88	R-R	6-2	205	5/11/58 Jeffersonville, IN
		Detroit	6-4	75	34	4.54				
					30					

CATCHERS

No.	Name	1990 Club	H	HR	RBI	Pct.	B-T	Ht.	Wt.	Born
8	**Heath, Mike	Detroit	100	7	38	.270	R-R	5-11	180	2/5/55 Tampa, FL
12	Rowland, Rich	London	46	8	30	.286	R-R	6-1	210	2/25/67 Cloverdale, CA
		Toledo	50	7	22	.260				
		Detroit	3	0	0	.158				
20	Salas, Mark	Detroit	38	9	24	.232	L-R	6-0	205	3/8/61 Montebello, CA
—	Tettleton, Mickey	Baltimore	99	15	51	.223	S-R	6-2	208	9/16/60 Oklahoma City, OK

INFIELDERS

No.	Name	1990 Club	H	HR	RBI	Pct.	B-T	Ht.	Wt.	Born
—	Bernazard, Tony	Played in Japan					S-R	5-9	160	8/24/56 Puerto Rico
14	Bergman, Dave	Detroit	57	2	26	.278	L-L	6-2	190	6/6/53 Evanston, IL
21	*Coles, Darnell	Sea.-Det.	45	3	20	.209	R-R	6-1	185	6/2/62 San Bernardino, CA
45	Fielder, Cecil	Detroit	159	51	132	.277	R-R	6-3	230	9/21/63 Los Angeles, CA
24	Fryman, Travis	London	84	10	53	.257	R-R	6-1	180	4/25/69 Lexington, KY
		Detroit	69	9	27	.297				
—	Livingstone, Scott	Toledo	94	6	36	.272	L-R	6-0	185	7/15/65 Dallas, TX
4	Phillips, Tony	Detroit	144	8	55	.251	S-R	5-10	175	4/15/59 Atlanta, GA
3	Trammell, Alan	Detroit	170	14	89	.304	R-R	6-0	185	2/21/58 Garden Grove, CA
1	Whitaker, Lou	Detroit	112	18	60	.237	L-R	5-11	180	5/12/57 Brooklyn, NY

OUTFIELDERS

No.	Name	1990 Club	H	HR	RBI	Pct.	B-T	Ht.	Wt.	Born
22	Cuyler, Milt	Toledo	119	2	42	.258	S-R	5-10	175	10/7/68 Macon, GA
		Detroit	13	0	8	.255				
—	Deer, Rob	Milwaukee	92	27	69	.209	R-R	6-3	230	9/29/60 Orange, CA
34	Lemon, Chet	Detroit	83	5	32	.258	R-R	6-0	190	2/12/55 Jackson, MS
7	Lusader, Scott	Toledo	67	4	25	.250	L-L	5-10	165	9/30/64 Chicago, IL
		Detroit	21	2	16	.241				
15	Moseby, Lloyd	Detroit	107	14	51	.248	L-R	6-3	200	11/5/59 Portland, AR
40	Pegues, Steve	London	131	8	63	.271	R-R	6-2	172	5/21/68 Pontotoc, MS
—	Pemberton, Rudy	Fayetteville	126	6	61	.278	R-R	6-1	185	12/17/69 Dominican Republic
9	*Sheets, Larry	Detroit	94	10	52	.261	L-R	6-3	236	12/6/59 Staunton, VA
25	Shelby, John	Los Angeles	6	0	2	.250	S-R	6-1	175	2/23/58 Lexington, KY
		Detroit	55	4	20	.248				
32	*Ward, Gary	Detroit	79	9	46	.256	R-R	6-2	202	12/6/53 Los Angeles, CA

*Free agent at press time
**New-look free agent

TIGER PROFILES

CECIL FIELDER 27 6-3 230   **Bats R Throws R**

Free-agent import returned from Orient to provide baseball's most stunning performance in 1990, becoming 11th player to reach 50-home run mark and first since George Foster slammed 52 for Cincinnati in 1977 . . . Reached plateau in final game, connecting in fourth inning off Yankees' Steve Adkins and adding another homer in eighth inning . . . He and single-season record-holder Roger Maris are the only 50-home-run hitters to finish with batting averages below .300 . . . He and Pittsburgh's Ralph Kiner are the only players to reach the 50-homer milestone for teams with losing records . . . First Tiger to lead AL in RBI (132) since Hank Greenberg in 1946 . . . First baseman took AL by surprise since he had played in Japan in 1989 . . . Slammed 38 home runs for Hanshin Tigers, who had purchased him from Toronto, Dec. 22, 1988 . . . Will be pitched much more carefully this year and faces challenge of making adjustments . . . Born Sept. 21, 1963, in Los Angeles . . . Earned $1.25 million in 1990.

Year	Club	Pos.	G	AB	R	H	2B	3B	HR	RBI	SB	Avg.
1985	Toronto	1B	30	74	6	23	4	0	4	16	0	.311
1986	Toronto	1B–3B–OF	34	83	7	13	2	0	4	13	0	.157
1987	Toronto	1B–3B	82	175	30	47	7	1	14	32	0	.269
1988	Toronto	1B–3B–2B	74	174	24	40	6	1	9	23	0	.230
1990	Detroit	1B	159	573	104	159	25	1	51	132	0	.277
	Totals		379	1079	171	282	44	3	82	216	0	.261

ALAN TRAMMELL 33 6-0 185   **Bats R Throws R**

Rebounded from disappointing 1989 to post sixth .300 season of career . . . Only five other shortstops have enjoyed that many .300 years and all are in Hall of Fame . . . His 89 RBI marked second-best output of career . . . Successfully battled chronic back problems . . . Fashioned huge August, batting .350 with six homers and 21 RBI . . . Earned World Series MVP honors in 1984 by batting .450 with two homers and six RBI . . . Placed second in AL MVP voting in 1987 after batting .416 in September to rally Detroit to AL East crown . . . Born Feb.

21, 1958, in Garden Grove, Cal. . . . Tigers' second-round choice in 1976 draft . . . Made $1.8 million in 1990.

Year	Club	Pos.	G	AB	R	H	2B	3B	HR	RBI	SB	Avg.
1977	Detroit	SS	19	43	6	8	0	0	0	0	0	.186
1978	Detroit	SS	139	448	49	120	14	6	2	34	3	.268
1979	Detroit	SS	142	460	68	127	11	4	6	50	17	.276
1980	Detroit	SS	146	560	107	168	21	5	9	65	12	.300
1981	Detroit	SS	105	392	52	101	15	3	2	31	10	.258
1982	Detroit	SS	157	489	66	126	34	3	9	57	19	.258
1983	Detroit	SS	142	505	83	161	31	2	14	66	30	.319
1984	Detroit	SS	139	555	85	174	34	5	14	69	19	.314
1985	Detroit	SS	149	605	79	156	21	7	13	57	14	.258
1986	Detroit	SS	151	574	107	159	33	7	21	75	25	.277
1987	Detroit	SS	151	597	109	205	34	3	28	105	21	.343
1988	Detroit	SS	128	466	73	145	24	1	15	69	7	.311
1989	Detroit	SS	121	449	54	109	20	3	5	43	10	.243
1990	Detroit	SS	146	559	71	170	37	1	14	89	12	.304
	Totals		1835	6702	1009	1929	329	50	152	810	199	.288

TONY PHILLIPS 31 5-10 175   Bats S Throws R

Free-agent import prior to 1990 season delighted new club with his versatility . . . Began season as regular third baseman, but also started at shortstop and second base as well as in left field and right field . . . Made one appearance in center, too . . . Set career highs in at-bats, RBI, hits, runs, walks and stolen bases . . . Signed with Tigers after nine years with Oakland organization . . . Was a valued member of Oakland's World Series teams in 1988 and 1989 . . . Played every position except pitcher and catcher while with A's . . . Born April 15, 1959, in Atlanta . . . Earned $866,667.

Year	Club	Pos.	G	AB	R	H	2B	3B	HR	RBI	SB	Avg.
1982	Oakland	SS	40	81	11	17	2	2	0	8	2	.210
1983	Oakland	SS-2B-3B	148	412	54	102	12	3	4	35	16	.248
1984	Oakland	SS-2B-OF	154	451	62	120	24	3	4	37	10	.266
1985	Oakland	3B-2B	42	161	23	45	12	2	4	17	3	.280
1986	Oakland	SS-2B-3B	118	441	76	113	14	5	5	52	15	.256
1987	Oakland	2B-3B-SS-OF	111	379	48	91	20	0	10	46	7	.240
1988	Oakland	INF-OF	79	212	32	43	8	4	2	17	0	.203
1989	Oakland	INF-OF	143	451	48	118	15	6	4	47	3	.262
1990	Detroit	3B-2B-SS-OF	152	573	97	144	23	5	8	55	19	.251
	Totals		987	3161	451	793	130	30	41	314	75	.251

LOU WHITAKER 33 5-11 180   Bats L Throws R

Despite posting lowest average since 1980, he continued to be a fine run producer . . . Worked hard to overcome terrible start . . . Was batting .184 through 59 games on June 17 . . . Embarked on a 56-game tear in which he hit .311 . . . Came on strong in August, compiling .329 average with three homers and 11 RBI . . . Second baseman figures to team with Alan Trammell for major-league-record 14th consecutive season in 1991 . . . Named AL Rookie of the Year in 1978 . . . Born May 12, 1957, in Brooklyn, N.Y. . . . Chosen by Tigers in fifth round of 1975 draft . . . Earned $1.8 million in 1990.

Year	Club	Pos.	G	AB	R	H	2B	3B	HR	RBI	SB	Avg.
1977	Detroit.......	2B	11	32	5	8	1	0	0	2	2	.250
1978	Detroit.......	2B	139	484	71	138	12	7	3	58	7	.285
1979	Detroit.......	2B	127	423	75	121	14	8	3	42	20	.286
1980	Detroit.......	2B	145	477	68	111	19	1	1	45	8	.233
1981	Detroit.......	2B	109	335	48	88	14	4	5	36	5	.263
1982	Detroit.......	2B	152	560	76	160	22	8	15	65	11	.286
1983	Detroit.......	2B	161	643	94	206	40	6	12	72	17	.320
1984	Detroit.......	2B	143	558	90	161	25	1	13	56	6	.289
1985	Detroit.......	2B	152	609	102	170	29	8	21	73	6	.279
1986	Detroit.......	2B	144	584	95	157	26	6	20	73	13	.269
1987	Detroit.......	2B	149	604	110	160	38	6	16	59	13	.265
1988	Detroit.......	2B	115	403	54	111	18	2	12	55	2	.275
1989	Detroit.......	2B	148	509	77	128	21	1	28	85	6	.251
1990	Detroit.......	2B	132	472	75	112	22	2	18	60	8	.237
	Totals		1827	6693	1040	1831	301	60	167	781	124	.274

ROB DEER 30 6-3 230   Bats R Throws R

Was the chief power source for the Brewers and a free agent, and the combination brought him into the Tiger lair in November with a three-year, $9.25-million contract . . . Paced Milwaukee in homers for fifth straight year . . . Clouted 20 or more home runs for fifth year in row, tying club mark established by Gorman Thomas (1978-82) . . . Tied for second in majors with 14 outfield assists, trailing only Yankees' Jesse Barfield (16) . . . Made Brewers as non-roster player in 1986 after being

obtained from Giants for Dean Freeland and Eric Pilkington . . .
Selected by San Francisco in fourth round of 1978 draft . . . Earned
$885,000 in 1990 . . . Born Sept. 29, 1960, in Orange, Cal.

Year	Club	Pos.	G	AB	R	H	2B	3B	HR	RBI	SB	Avg.
1984	San Francisco	OF	13	24	5	4	0	0	3	3	1	.167
1985	San Francisco	OF-1B	78	162	22	30	5	1	8	20	0	.185
1986	Milwaukee	OF-1B	134	466	75	108	17	3	33	86	5	.232
1987	Milwaukee	OF-1B	134	474	71	113	15	2	28	80	12	.238
1988	Milwaukee	OF	135	492	71	124	24	0	23	80	9	.252
1989	Milwaukee	OF	130	466	72	98	18	2	26	65	4	.210
1990	Milwaukee	OF-1B	134	440	57	92	15	1	27	69	2	.209
	Totals		758	2524	373	569	94	9	148	408	33	.225

JACK MORRIS 35 6-3 200   Bats R Throws R

Longtime ace begins 1991 season needing only
two more victories for 200 . . . Has paced Tigers
in victories 12 of last 13 years . . . Although
veteran is in decline, he still has plenty of stamina . . . Tied Oakland's Dave Stewart for AL
lead with 11 complete games and placed second
to Stewart with 249⅔ innings pitched . . .
Showed his class by refusing to leave rotation
in order to duck possibility of 20-loss campaign . . . Fired no-hitter
April 7, 1984, blanking White Sox, 4-0, the first no-no by a Tiger
since 1958 . . . Born May 16, 1955, in St. Paul, Minn. . . . Tigers'
fifth selection in 1976 draft . . . Was Tigers' best-paid player in
1990 with $2.1-million salary.

Year	Club	G	IP	W	L	Pct.	SO	BB	H	ERA
1977	Detroit	7	46	1	1	.500	28	23	38	3.72
1978	Detroit	28	106	3	5	.375	48	49	107	4.33
1979	Detroit	27	198	17	7	.708	113	59	179	3.27
1980	Detroit	36	250	16	15	.516	112	87	252	4.18
1981	Detroit	25	198	14	7	.667	97	78	153	3.05
1982	Detroit	37	266⅓	17	16	.515	135	96	247	4.06
1983	Detroit	37	293⅔	20	13	.606	232	83	257	3.34
1984	Detroit	35	240⅓	19	11	.633	148	87	221	3.60
1985	Detroit	35	257	16	11	.593	191	110	212	3.33
1986	Detroit	35	267	21	8	.724	223	82	229	3.27
1987	Detroit	34	266	18	11	.621	208	93	227	3.38
1988	Detroit	34	235	15	13	.536	168	83	225	3.94
1989	Detroit	24	170⅓	6	14	.300	115	59	189	4.86
1990	Detroit	36	249⅔	15	18	.455	162	97	231	4.51
	Totals.	430	3043⅓	198	150	.569	1980	1086	2767	3.73

FRANK TANANA 36 6-3 195   Bats L Throws L

Strong finish helped salvage year in which he failed to win in double figures for first time since 1983 . . . Highlight of season came when he became 88th pitcher in major-league history to win 200 games with 13-5 rout of Milwaukee April 28 . . . Was relegated to bullpen after yielding 46 earned runs in 40⅓ innings from June 8 through July 28, a miserable stretch covering 10 starts . . . Recorded first save of 20-year pro career, vs. Yankees Aug. 2 . . . Celebrated return to rotation Aug. 25 with 14-4 laugher against Oakland . . . Born July 3, 1953, in Detroit . . . Began career with Angels as first-round pick in 1971 draft . . . Ranked second among Tiger pitchers with 1990 salary of $1.1 million.

Year	Club	G	IP	W	L	Pct.	SO	BB	H	ERA
1973	California	4	26	2	2	.500	22	8	20	3.12
1974	California	39	269	14	19	.424	180	77	262	3.11
1975	California	34	257	16	9	.640	269	73	211	2.63
1976	California	34	288	19	10	.655	261	73	212	2.44
1977	California	31	241	15	9	.625	205	61	201	2.54
1978	California	33	239	18	12	.600	137	60	239	3.65
1979	California	18	90	7	5	.583	46	25	93	3.90
1980	California	32	204	11	12	.478	113	45	223	4.15
1981	Boston	24	141	4	10	.286	78	43	142	4.02
1982	Texas	30	194⅓	7	18	.280	87	55	199	4.21
1983	Texas	29	159⅓	7	9	.438	108	49	144	3.16
1984	Texas	35	246⅓	15	15	.500	141	81	234	3.25
1985	Texas-Detroit	33	215	12	14	.462	159	57	220	4.27
1986	Detroit	32	188⅓	12	9	.571	119	65	196	4.16
1987	Detroit	34	218⅔	15	10	.600	146	56	216	3.91
1988	Detroit	32	203	14	11	.560	127	64	213	4.21
1989	Detroit	33	223⅔	10	14	.417	147	74	227	3.58
1990	Detroit	34	176⅓	9	8	.529	114	66	190	5.31
	Totals	541	3580	207	196	.514	2459	1032	3442	3.58

MIKE HENNEMAN 29 6-4 205   Bats R Throws R

Dependable reliever finished with 22 saves . . . Total would undoubtedly have been more impressive with a stronger club . . . Worked 90-plus innings for fourth consecutive year and made 60-plus appearances for third straight season . . . Enjoyed fast start, racking up 15 saves in first 27 appearances . . . Stands fourth on Tigers' all-time save list with 59 . . . Born Dec. 11, 1961, in St. Charles, Mo. . . . Tigers' third-round selection in

1984 draft . . . Attended Oklahoma State and helped Cowboys to College World Series in 1983 and 1984 . . . Salary was $335,000 in 1990.

Year	Club	G	IP	W	L	Pct.	SO	BB	H	ERA
1987	Detroit	55	96⅔	11	3	.786	75	30	86	2.98
1988	Detroit	65	91⅓	9	6	.600	58	24	72	1.87
1989	Detroit	60	90	11	4	.733	69	51	84	3.70
1990	Detroit	69	94⅓	8	6	.571	50	33	90	3.05
	Totals.	249	372⅓	39	19	.672	252	138	332	2.90

WALT TERRELL 32 6-2 205　　　　Bats L Throws R

Released by Pittsburgh July 27, he was signed by Detroit the next day . . . Showed immediate improvement with Tigers, completing six innings in five of first seven starts after finishing six innings in just eight of 16 starts with Pirates . . . Failed to reach 200 innings for first time in a full major-league season . . . Not the dependable pitcher he once was . . . Served as solid starter for Tigers from 1985-88, before splitting the next season between Padres and Yankees . . . Born May 11, 1958, in Jeffersonville, Ind. . . . Made $800,000 on contract he signed with Pirates as free agent prior to last season.

Year	Club	G	IP	W	L	Pct.	SO	BB	H	ERA
1982	New York (NL)	3	21	0	3	.000	8	14	22	3.43
1983	New York (NL)	21	133⅔	8	8	.500	59	55	123	3.57
1984	New York (NL)	33	215	11	12	.478	114	80	232	3.52
1985	Detroit	34	229	15	10	.600	130	95	221	3.85
1986	Detroit	34	217⅓	15	12	.556	93	98	199	4.56
1987	Detroit	35	244⅔	17	10	.630	143	94	254	4.05
1988	Detroit	29	206⅓	7	16	.304	84	78	199	3.97
1989	San Diego	19	123⅓	5	13	.278	63	26	134	4.01
1989	New York (AL)	13	83	6	5	.545	30	24	102	5.20
1990	Pittsburgh	16	82⅔	2	7	.222	34	33	98	5.88
1990	Detroit	13	75⅓	6	4	.600	30	24	86	4.54
	Totals.	250	1631⅓	92	100	.479	788	621	1670	4.13

TOP PROSPECTS

MILT CUYLER 22 5-10 175　　　　Bats S Throws R

Speedster showed he might be Tigers' answer in center field for years . . . Batted .258 with 77 runs scored and 52 steals for Toledo (AAA) in 1990 . . . Already considered a fine stolen-base threat and will improve, but will he hit enough?. . . Born Oct. 7, 1968, in Macon, Ga. . . . Tigers' second-round pick in 1986 draft . . . Hit .296 and stole 50 bases for Lakeland (A) in 1988.

TRAVIS FRYMAN 22 6-2 190   **Bats R Throws R**
Youngster did well after stepping in at third base for Tigers . . . Answered questions about his offense by batting .297 with nine homers and 27 RBI in 232 at-bats . . . Hit .257 with 10 homers and 53 RBI in 327 at-bats for Toledo (AAA) in 1990 . . . Appeared very comfortable at third . . . Was Eastern League All-Star shortstop for London (AA) in 1989 . . . Born April 25, 1969, in Lexington, Ky. . . . Third-round choice in 1987 draft . . . Son of former major-league pitcher Woody.

SCOTT ALDRED 22 6-4 215   **Bats L Throws L**
Went 6-15 with 4.90 ERA and 81 walks in 158 innings for Toledo (AAA) in 1990, but has chance to be dominant pitcher if control improves . . . Has fanned 423 in 521 minor-league innings, including 133 last year . . . Won major-league debut in early September with five scoreless innings vs. Milwaukee . . . Born June 12, 1968, in Flint, Mich. . . . Tigers' 16th selection in 1986 draft.

STEVE SEARCY 26 6-1 190   **Bats L Throws L**
Has lost some luster since being named International League's Most Valuable Pitcher thanks to 13-7 record and 2.59 ERA for Toledo (AAA) in 1988 . . . Slowed at start of 1989, when he required arthroscopic shoulder surgery . . . Went 10-5 with 2.92 ERA for Toledo last year and 2-7, 4.66 for parent club . . . Born June 4, 1964, in Knoxville, Tenn. . . . Tigers' third pick in 1985 draft.

MANAGER SPARKY ANDERSON: Tigers made 20-game improvement last year and he deserves much credit for that . . . Tigers' 79-83 mark represented only his third losing season as a manager, but he has limited club headed in upward direction . . . First manager to win 100 games in a season three times . . . First manager to win World Series in both leagues . . . Led world champion 1984 Tigers to club-record 104 victories . . . Has won 18 League Championship Series games . . . Has

been named Manager of the Year in both leagues . . . First major-league manager to win 700 games with two different teams . . . Boasts 19-year record of 1,837-1,446 . . . Record with Detroit stands at 974-860 . . . Became manager of Tigers, June 12, 1979 . . . Big Red Machine won five NL West titles, four pennants and two World Series under him . . . Born Feb. 22, 1934, in Bridgewater, S.D. . . . Played in minors for six seasons as infielder . . . Played for Philadelphia in 1959, his lone year as major leaguer . . . Only Dodgers' Tommy Lasorda has put in longer continuous service among major-league managers.

ALL-TIME TIGER SEASON RECORDS

BATTING: Ty Cobb, .420, 1911
HRs: Hank Greenberg, 58, 1938
RBI: Hank Greenberg, 183, 1937
STEALS: Ty Cobb, 96, 1915
WINS: Denny McLain, 31, 1968
STRIKEOUTS: Mickey Lolich, 308, 1971

MILWAUKEE BREWERS

TEAM DIRECTORY: Pres.: Allan (Bud) Selig; Exec. VP-GM: Harry Dalton; Sr. Advisor Baseball Oper.: Walter Shannon; Asst. GM-Farm Dir.: Bruce Manno; VP-Int. Baseball Oper.: Ray Poitevint; Assts. to GM: Dee Fondy, Sal Bando; Scouting Dir.: Dick Foster; Coordinator Player Dev. and Pitching: Bob Humphreys; Dir. Publicity: Tom Skibosh; Trav. Sec.: Jimmy Bank; Mgr.: Tom Trebelhorn. Home: Milwaukee County Stadium (53,192). Field distances: 315, l.f. line; 362, l.f.; 392, l.c.; 402, c.f.; 392, r.c.; 362, r.f.; 315, r.f. line. Spring training: Chandler, Ariz.

SCOUTING REPORT

HITTING: The comeback quests of Robin Yount and Paul Molitor will largely determine the extent of the Brewers' success as

DH Dave Parker did his share of bashing for Brewers.

both stalwarts are hoping to rebound from sub-par seasons. Yount posted a career-low .247 batting average and his 17 homers and 77 RBI represented a drop of four homers and 26 RBI from his AL MVP effort of the year before. With Molitor (.285, 12, 45), it's a question of staying healthy. He suffered three different injuries last year.

The addition of free-agent outfielder Franklin Stubbs (.261, 23, 71 with the Astros) will beef up an offense that also features rising star Gary Sheffield (.294, 10, 67) and still-productive veteran Dave Parker (.289, 21, 92). Free-agent defector Rob Deer's home-run bat figures to be missed.

Milwaukee should again vie for the team stolen-base title after topping the AL with 164 steals in 1990. Offense isn't the problem here as evidenced by 732 runs scored last season.

PITCHING: Milwaukee agonized before granting long-time ace Teddy Higuera a four-year contract that kept him from leaving as a free agent last winter. The 32-year-old screwballer remains a key arm, but last year's 11-10 record and 3.76 ERA indicate the lefty is no longer the imposing pitcher he once was.

The Brewers made a great move last season by acquiring Ron Robinson (12-5, 2.91) from Cincinnati for Glenn Braggs. Mark Knudson (10-9, 4.12) is adequate. The condition of Chris Bosio (4-9, 4.00) who twice required surgery on his right knee last year, will be a key for Milwaukee.

Previously reliable closer Dan Plesac (3-7, 4.43) hopes to bounce back from a miserable year during which he blew 11 of 35 save opportunities. The Brewers got him some help by signing free agent Edwin Nunez (3-1, 2.24, 6 Sv with Tigers).

FIELDING: Milwaukee's poor fielding continues to be its downfall. The Brewers ranked last in the AL with a .976 fielding percentage, committing 149 errors last season.

Manager Tom Trebelhorn has addressed this area the last couple of years without any success.

OUTLOOK: Milwaukee, 74-88 in 1990, needs everything to come together just to contend—the rotation must stabilize, Yount and Molitor must have big years and the fielding must improve dramatically. Realistically, the Brewers are looking at a finish near or at the bottom of the AL East.

MILWAUKEE BREWERS 1991 ROSTER

MANAGER Tom Trebelhorn
Coaches—Don Baylor, Ray Burris, Andy Etchebarren, Duffy Dyer, Larry Haney, Fred Stanley

PITCHERS

No.	Name	1990 Club	W-L	IP	SO	ERA	B-T	Ht.	Wt.	Born
60	Austin, Jim	El Paso	11-3	92	77	2.44	R-R	6-2	200	12/7/63 Farmville, VA
29	Bosio, Chris	Beloit	0-0	3	2	3.00	R-R	6-3	235	4/3/63 Carmichael, CA
		Milwaukee	4-9	133	76	4.00				
30	Brown, Kevin	New York (NL)	0-0	0	0	0.00	L-L	6-1	185	3/5/66 Oroville, CA
		Tidewater	10-6	134	109	3.55				
		Milwaukee	1-1	21	12	2.57				
32	Crim, Chuck	Beloit	0-0	2	0	4.50	R-R	6-0	185	7/23/61 Van Nuys, CA
		Milwaukee	3-5	86	39	3.47				
61	Czajkowski, Jim	Harrisburg	0-0	15	6	4.30	S-R	6-4	215	12/18/63 Cleveland, OH
		Salem	1-1	28	26	2.57				
		Beloit	2-0	27	37	1.65				
		Stockton	0-0	3	2	0.00				
35	Elvira, Narciso	Beloit	3-2	38	45	2.35	L-L	5-10	160	10/29/67 Mexico
		El Paso	0-2	18	12	4.50				
		Milwaukee	0-0	5	6	5.40				
59	George, Chris	El Paso	8-3	56	38	1.78	R-R	6-2	200	9/24/66 Pittsburgh, PA
		Denver	1-1	5	4	18.56				
63	Henry, Doug	Stockton	1-0	8	13	1.13	R-R	6-4	185	12/10/63 Sacramento, CA
		El Paso	1-0	31	25	2.93				
		Denver	2-3	51	54	4.44				
49	Higuera, Ted	Milwaukee	11-10	170	129	3.76	S-L	5-10	178	11/9/58 Mexico
—	Holmes, Darren	Albuquerque	12-2	93	99	3.11	R-R	6-0	199	4/25/66 Asheville, NC
		Los Angeles	0-1	17	19	5.19				
66	Johnson, Chris	Stockton	13-6	142	112	2.98	R-R	6-7	200	12/7/68 Chattanooga, TN
41	Knudson, Mark	Milwaukee	10-9	168	56	4.12	R-R	6-5	200	10/28/60 Denver, CO
47	Krueger, Bill	Milwaukee	6-8	129	64	3.98	L-L	6-5	205	4/24/58 Waukegan, IL
34	Lee, Mark	Stockton	1-0	8	7	2.35	L-L	6-3	200	7/20/64 Williston, ND
		Denver	3-1	28	35	2.25				
		Milwaukee	1-0	21	14	2.11				
40	Machado, Julio	New York (NL)	4-1	34	27	3.15	R-R	5-9	165	12/1/65 Venezuela
		Tidewater	0-1	21	24	1.69				
		Milwaukee	0-0	13	12	0.69				
57	Miranda, Angel	Stockton	9-4	108	138	2.66	L-L	6-1	160	11/9/69 Puerto Rico
31	Navarro, Jaime	Denver	2-3	41	28	4.20	R-R	6-4	210	3/27/67 Puerto Rico
		Milwaukee	8-7	149	75	4.46				
—	Nunez, Edwin	Detroit	3-1	80	66	2.24	R-R	6-5	240	5/27/63 Puerto Rico
37	Plesac, Dan	Milwaukee	3-7	69	65	4.43	L-L	6-5	210	2/4/62 Gary, IN
33	Robinson, Ron	Cincinnati	2-2	31	14	4.88	R-R	6-4	235	3/24/62 Woodlake, CA
		Milwaukee	12-5	148	57	2.91				
43	Veres, Randy	Denver	1-6	50	36	5.19	R-R	6-3	189	11/25/65 San Francisco, CA
		Milwaukee	0-3	42	16	3.67				
46	Wegman, Bill	Beloit	0-0	2	2	0.00	R-R	6-5	220	12/19/62 Cincinnati, OH
		Denver	1-0	14	14	3.29				
		Milwaukee	2-2	30	20	4.85				

CATCHERS

No.	Name	1990 Club	H	HR	RBI	Pct.	B-T	Ht.	Wt.	Born
26	McIntosh, Tim	Denver	120	18	74	.288	R-R	5-11	195	3/21/65 Minneapolis, MN
		Milwaukee	1	1	1	.200				
54	Nilsson, Dave	Stockton	104	7	47	.290	S-R	6-3	185	12/14/69 Australia
5	Surhoff, B. J.	Milwaukee	131	6	59	.276	L-R	6-1	200	8/4/64 Bronx, NY

INFIELDERS

No.	Name	1990 Club	H	HR	RBI	Pct.	B-T	Ht.	Wt.	Born
9	Brock, Greg	Milwaukee	91	7	50	.248	L-R	6-3	205	6/14/57 McMinnville, OR
22	Canale, George	Denver	119	12	60	.254	L-R	6-1	190	8/11/65 Memphis,TN
		Milwaukee	1	0	0	.077				
2	Diaz, Edgar	Milwaukee	59	0	14	.271	R-R	6-0	160	2/8/64 Puerto Rico
17	Gantner, Jim	Beloit	11	2	6	.379	L-R	5-11	175	1/5/54 Eden, WI
		Denver	8	0	1	.364				
		Milwaukee	85	0	25	.263				
4	Molitor, Paul	Beloit	2	1	1	.500	R-R	6-0	185	8/22/56 St. Paul, MN
		Milwaukee	119	12	45	.285				
39	Parker, Dave	Milwaukee	176	21	92	.289	L-R	6-5	230	6/9/51 Jackson, MS
11	Sheffield, Gary	Milwaukee	143	10	67	.294	R-R	5-11	190	11/18/68 Tampa, FL
6	Spiers, Bill	Denver	12	1	7	.316	L-R	6-2	190	6/5/66 Orangeburg, SC
		Milwaukee	88	2	36	.242				
7	Sveum, Dale	Denver	63	2	26	.289	S-R	6-3	185	11/23/63 Richmond, CA
		Milwaukee	23	1	12	.197				

OUTFIELDERS

No.	Name	1990 Club	H	HR	RBI	Pct.	B-T	Ht.	Wt.	Born
18	Brantley, Mickey	Calgary	24	1	8	.233	R-R	5-10	187	6/17/61 Catskill, NY
		Denver	19	2	10	.264				
16	Felder, Mike	Milwaukee	65	3	27	.274	S-R	5-8	160	11/18/62 Vallejo, CA
24	Hamilton, Darryl	Milwaukee	46	1	18	.295	L-R	6-1	180	12/3/64 Baton Rouge, LA
—	Stubbs, Franklin	Houston	117	23	71	.261	L-L	6-2	209	10/21/60 Laurinburg, NC
23	Vaughn, Greg	Milwaukee	84	17	61	.220	R-R	6-0	193	7/3/65 Sacramento, CA
19	Yount, Robin	Milwaukee	145	17	77	.247	R-R	6-0	180	9/16/55 Danville, IL

BREWER PROFILES

PAUL MOLITOR 34 6-0 185   Bats R Throws R

Hopes to stay healthy after another injury-filled year... Endured three different injuries last year... Infielder missed most of April with broken right thumb... Fractured knuckle on left index finger in July... Tore a muscle in his left forearm Sept. 26 and underwent surgery for that and an ailing right shoulder two days later... Still very effective when in top form ... Fashioned 19-game hitting streak in August, batting .351... Owns 27 homers leading off games, second to Oakland's Rickey Henderson among active players... His 39-game hitting streak in 1987 was AL's longest since Joe DiMaggio's record 56-game run in 1941... Born Aug. 22, 1956, in St. Paul, Minn.... Selected in first round of 1977 draft... Made $2,433,333 last season.

Year	Club	Pos.	G	AB	R	H	2B	3B	HR	RBI	SB	Avg.
1978	Milwaukee	2B-SS-3B	125	521	73	142	26	4	6	45	30	.273
1979	Milwaukee	2B-SS	140	584	88	188	27	16	9	62	33	.322
1980	Milwaukee	2B-SS-3B	111	450	81	137	29	2	9	37	34	.304
1981	Milwaukee	OF	64	251	45	67	11	0	2	19	10	.267
1982	Milwaukee	3B-SS	160	666	136	201	26	8	19	71	41	.302
1983	Milwaukee	3B	152	608	95	164	28	6	15	47	41	.269
1984	Milwaukee	3B	13	46	3	10	1	0	0	6	1	.217
1985	Milwaukee	3B	140	576	93	171	28	3	10	48	21	.297
1986	Milwaukee	3B-OF	105	437	62	123	24	6	9	55	20	.281
1987	Milwaukee	3B-2B	118	465	114	164	41	5	16	75	45	.353
1988	Milwaukee	3B-2B	154	609	115	190	34	6	13	60	41	.312
1989	Milwaukee	3B-2B	155	615	84	194	35	4	11	56	27	.315
1990	Milwaukee	2B-1B-3B	103	418	64	119	27	6	12	45	18	.285
	Totals		1540	6246	1053	1870	337	66	131	626	362	.299

ROBIN YOUNT 35 6-0 180   Bats R Throws R

Declined sharply after gaining his second AL MVP award in 1989... Had previously earned MVP honors in 1982... Hit career-low .247 ... Dropped four homers and 26 RBI from year before... Rallied in September to bat .327 with four homers and 19 RBI... Played in team-high 158 games... Topped Brewers by driving in team-high 57 percent of runners from third base with fewer than two outs . . . Born Sept. 16, 1955, in Danville, Ill. . . . Selected in first round of 1973 draft . . . Converted from shortstop to center fielder in 1985, after offseason shoulder surgery . . . Brewers' best-paid player in 1990 with $3.2-million salary.

Year	Club	Pos.	G	AB	R	H	2B	3B	HR	RBI	SB	Avg.
1974	Milwaukee	SS	107	344	48	86	14	5	3	26	7	.250
1975	Milwaukee	SS	147	558	67	149	28	2	8	52	12	.267
1976	Milwaukee	SS-OF	161	638	59	161	19	3	2	54	16	.252
1977	Milwaukee	SS	154	605	66	174	34	4	4	49	16	.288
1978	Milwaukee	SS	127	502	66	147	23	9	9	71	16	.293
1979	Milwaukee	SS	149	577	72	154	26	5	8	51	11	.267
1980	Milwaukee	SS	143	611	121	179	49	10	23	87	20	.293
1981	Milwaukee	SS	96	377	50	103	15	5	10	49	4	.273
1982	Milwaukee	SS	156	635	129	210	46	12	29	114	14	.331
1983	Milwaukee	SS	149	578	102	178	42	10	17	80	12	.308
1984	Milwaukee	SS	160	624	105	186	27	7	16	80	14	.298
1985	Milwaukee	OF-1B	122	466	76	129	26	3	15	68	10	.277
1986	Milwaukee	OF-1B	140	522	82	163	31	7	9	46	14	.312
1987	Milwaukee	OF	158	635	99	198	25	9	21	103	19	.312
1988	Milwaukee	OF	162	621	92	190	38	11	13	91	22	.306
1989	Milwaukee	OF	160	614	101	195	38	9	21	103	19	.318
1990	Milwaukee	OF	158	587	98	145	17	5	17	77	15	.247
	Totals		2449	9494	1433	2747	498	116	225	1201	241	.289

GARY SHEFFIELD 22 5-11 190   Bats R Throws R

Immense talent began to realize potential . . . Third baseman placed second on team with 42 multi-hit games . . . Also had 18 multi-RBI games . . . Fashioned 16-game hitting streak from July 13-29 . . . Batted .362 in May, .368 in July . . . Topped club with 25 stolen bases, first time someone other than Paul Molitor has led in that category since 1984 . . . Tied Dave Parker for team lead with 30 doubles . . . Attitude remains a huge question mark . . . Has never been completely at ease in Milwaukee . . . Born Nov. 18, 1968, in Tampa . . . Selected in first round of 1986 draft as the sixth player picked overall . . . Made $115,000 in 1990.

Year	Club	Pos.	G	AB	R	H	2B	3B	HR	RBI	SB	Avg.
1988	Milwaukee	SS	24	80	12	19	1	0	4	12	3	.238
1989	Milwaukee	SS-3B	95	368	34	91	18	0	5	32	10	.247
1990	Milwaukee	3B	125	487	67	143	30	1	10	67	25	.294
	Totals		244	935	113	253	49	1	19	111	38	.271

DAVE PARKER 39 6-5 230   Bats L Throws R

Free-agent signee of a winter ago received $1.2 million in 1990 and more than justified his acquisition . . . Set team record for homers (21) and RBI (89) by a DH . . . Previous standard had been set by Hank Aaron with 12 homers and 60 RBI in 1975 . . . Topped Milwaukee with 51 multi-hit games and with 23 multi-RBI games . . . Recorded 2,500th career hit June 27 at Yankee Stadium . . . Batted .315 before All-Star break, slowed to .263 after it . . . Owns .283 average with one homer and six RBI in 15 World Series games . . . Born June 9, 1951, in Jackson, Miss.

Year	Club	Pos.	G	AB	R	H	2B	3B	HR	RBI	SB	Avg.
1973	Pittsburgh	OF	54	139	17	40	9	1	4	14	1	.288
1974	Pittsburgh	OF-1B	73	220	27	62	10	3	4	29	3	.282
1975	Pittsburgh	OF	148	558	75	172	35	10	25	101	8	.308
1976	Pittsburgh	OF	138	537	82	168	28	10	13	90	19	.313
1977	Pittsburgh	OF-2B	159	637	107	215	44	8	21	88	17	.338
1978	Pittsburgh	OF	148	581	102	194	32	12	30	117	20	.334
1979	Pittsburgh	OF	158	622	109	193	45	7	25	94	20	.310
1980	Pittsburgh	OF	139	518	71	153	31	1	17	79	10	.295
1981	Pittsburgh	OF	67	240	29	62	14	3	9	48	6	.258
1982	Pittsburgh	OF	73	244	41	66	19	3	6	29	7	.270
1983	Pittsburgh	OF	144	552	68	154	29	4	12	69	12	.279
1984	Cincinnati	OF	156	607	73	173	28	0	16	94	11	.285
1985	Cincinnati	OF	160	635	88	198	42	4	34	125	5	.312
1986	Cincinnati	OF	162	637	89	174	31	3	31	116	1	.273
1987	Cincinnati	OF-1B	153	589	77	149	28	0	26	97	7	.253
1988	Oakland	OF-1B	101	377	43	97	18	1	12	55	0	.257
1989	Oakland	OF	144	553	56	146	27	0	22	97	0	.264
1990	Milwaukee	1B	157	610	71	176	30	3	21	92	4	.289
	Totals		2334	8856	1225	2592	500	73	328	1434	151	.293

FRANKLIN STUBBS 30 6-2 209   Bats L Throws L

Astro free agent signed three-year, $6-million pact and will replace departed Rob Deer in right field . . . Had best season in 1990 . . . Average of .261 was highest mark for a full season . . . Outfielder also produced career highs in games (146), at-bats (488), runs (59), hits (117), doubles (23), RBI (71), walks (48) and stolen bases (19) . . . Tied career high with 23 homers, the most by a Houston left-hander since Walt Bond clubbed 20 in 1964 . . . Became the first player other than Glenn Davis to lead the Astros in home runs since 1984 . . . Hit .329 after Aug. 11 . . . Strikes out too much . . . Only four NL players had more whiffs

than his 114 ... Born Oct. 21, 1960, in Laurinburg, N.C. ...
Dodgers' No. 1 selection in 1982 draft ... Earned $450,000 last
year.

Year	Club	Pos.	G	AB	R	H	2B	3B	HR	RBI	SB	Avg.
1984	Los Angeles ...	1B-OF	87	217	22	42	2	3	8	17	2	.194
1985	Los Angeles ...	1B	10	9	0	2	0	0	0	2	0	.222
1986	Los Angeles ...	OF-1B	132	420	55	95	11	1	23	58	7	.226
1987	Los Angeles ...	1B-OF	129	386	48	90	16	3	16	52	8	.233
1988	Los Angeles ...	1B-OF	115	242	30	54	13	0	8	34	11	.223
1989	Los Angeles ...	OF-1B	69	103	11	30	6	0	4	15	3	.291
1990	Houston	1B-OF	146	448	59	117	23	2	23	71	19	.261
	Totals		688	1825	225	430	71	9	82	249	50	.236

RON ROBINSON 29 6-4 235   Bats L Throws R

Obtained from Reds with Bob Sebra for Glenn Braggs and Billy Bates June 9, he excelled with new team ... Went 8-2 after a Brewers loss ... Took 11 of 13 decisions in all ... Earned first AL win June 23 against Cleveland ... Went the distance seven times despite beginning year with only one big-league complete game ... Born March 24, 1962, in Woodlake, Cal. ... Agreed to new three-year contract with Brewers Aug. 22 after making $500,000 in 1990.

Year	Club	G	IP	W	L	Pct.	SO	BB	H	ERA
1984	Cincinnati	12	39⅔	1	2	.333	24	13	35	2.72
1985	Cincinnati	33	108⅓	7	7	.500	76	32	107	3.99
1986	Cincinnati	70	116⅔	10	3	.769	117	43	110	3.24
1987	Cincinnati	48	154	7	5	.583	99	43	148	3.68
1988	Cincinnati	17	78⅔	3	7	.300	38	26	88	4.12
1989	Cincinnati	15	83⅓	5	3	.625	36	28	80	3.35
1990	Cincinnati	6	31⅓	2	2	.500	14	14	36	4.88
1990	Milwaukee.........	22	148⅓	12	5	.706	57	37	158	2.91
	Totals............	223	760⅓	47	34	.580	461	236	762	3.51

TEDDY HIGUERA 32 5-10 178   Bats S Throws L

Not the ace he once was, but the Brewers re-signed him as free agent to a four-year, $13-million contract ... Was 6-2 with 2.26 ERA before All-Star break, but 5-8 with 4.75 ERA after it ... Marked first time he ever had a losing mark in second half ... Became Brewers' all-time strikeout leader Aug. 2, fanning White Sox' Sammy Sosa for No. 930 to overtake Jim Slaton ... Placed second in 1985 AL Rookie of the Year voting ... Contract was purchased from Juarez of Mexican

League, Sept. 13, 1983 . . . Set Milwaukee club record with 240 strikeouts in 1987 . . . Born Nov. 9, 1958, in Los Mochis, Mexico . . . Commanded $2.125 million in 1990.

Year	Club	G	IP	W	L	Pct.	SO	BB	H	ERA
1985	Milwaukee	32	212⅓	15	8	.652	127	63	186	3.90
1986	Milwaukee	34	248⅓	20	11	.645	207	74	226	2.79
1987	Milwaukee	35	261⅔	18	10	.643	240	87	236	3.85
1988	Milwaukee	31	227⅓	16	9	.640	192	59	168	2.45
1989	Milwaukee	22	135⅓	9	6	.600	91	48	125	3.46
1990	Milwaukee	27	170	11	10	.524	129	50	167	3.76
	Totals	181	1255	89	54	.622	986	381	1108	3.34

MARK KNUDSON 30 6-5 200   Bats S Throws R

Was a pleasant surprise, winning career-high 10 games . . . Tossed first major-league shutout July 13, outdueling Oakland's Dave Stewart . . . Game highlighted hot July (3-0, 2.19) . . . Wore down late in year, dropping last three decisions with 12.27 ERA . . . Did not pitch last three weeks after developing shoulder tendinitis . . . Born Oct. 28, 1960, in Denver . . . Acquired from Houston Aug. 21, 1986 to complete trade in which Houston acquired Danny Darwin for Don August . . . Due for raise after earning $150,000 in 1990.

Year	Club	G	IP	W	L	Pct.	SO	BB	H	ERA
1985	Houston	2	11	0	2	.000	4	3	21	9.00
1986	Houston	9	42⅔	1	5	.167	20	15	48	4.22
1986	Milwaukee	4	17⅔	0	1	.000	9	5	22	7.64
1987	Milwaukee	15	62	4	4	.500	26	14	88	5.37
1988	Milwaukee	5	16	0	0	.000	7	2	17	1.13
1989	Milwaukee	40	123⅔	8	5	.615	47	29	110	3.35
1990	Milwaukee	30	168⅓	10	9	.526	56	40	187	4.12
	Totals	105	441⅓	23	26	.469	169	108	493	4.24

DAN PLESAC 29 6-5 210   Bats L Throws L

Will try to rebound from most disappointing season . . . Converted only 24 of 35 save opportunities (69 percent) . . . Allowed 15 of 47 inherited runners (32 percent) to score . . . In May and June, he was 0-2 with 7.71 ERA and 11 saves in 25 games . . . Did not record a save from July 20 through Aug. 12 . . . Born Feb. 14, 1962, in Gary, Ind. . . . Acquired in first round of 1983 draft . . . Has 124 career saves, including club-record 33 in 1989 . . . Earned $1,466,667 in 1990.

Year	Club	G	IP	W	L	Pct.	SO	BB	H	ERA
1986	Milwaukee........	51	91	10	7	.588	75	29	81	2.97
1987	Milwaukee........	57	79⅓	5	6	.455	89	23	63	2.61
1988	Milwaukee........	50	52⅓	1	2	.333	52	12	46	2.41
1989	Milwaukee........	52	61⅓	3	4	.429	52	17	47	2.35
1990	Milwaukee........	66	69	3	7	.300	65	31	67	4.43
	Totals...........	276	353	22	26	.458	333	112	304	2.98

CHRIS BOSIO 27 6-3 235   Bats R Throws R

Will try to recover from dreadful year . . . After going 3-0 with 1.39 ERA in April to run career mark in first month of season to 13-2, he gained only one more victory rest of season . . . Was disabled twice due to injured right knee . . . Underwent surgery to repair knee Aug. 7, then again to remove cyst from knee Oct. 4 . . . Born April 3, 1963, in Carmichael, Cal. . . . Selected in second round of January 1982 draft . . . Tried as reliever before Brewers settled on him as starter . . . Made $710,000 in 1990.

Year	Club	G	IP	W	L	Pct.	SO	BB	H	ERA
1986	Milwaukee........	10	34⅔	0	4	.000	29	13	41	7.01
1987	Milwaukee........	46	170	11	8	.579	150	50	187	5.24
1988	Milwaukee........	38	182	7	15	.318	84	38	190	3.36
1989	Milwaukee........	33	234⅔	15	10	.600	173	48	225	2.95
1990	Milwaukee........	20	132⅔	4	9	.308	76	38	131	4.00
	Totals...........	147	754	37	46	.446	512	187	774	3.94

TOP PROSPECTS

KEVIN BROWN 25 6-1 185   Bats L Throws L

Will get shot at breaking into rotation after impressive effort last September . . . Posted 1-1 record with 2.57 ERA in five games for Brewers . . . Last three appearances were starts . . . Acquired from Mets Sept. 7 with Julio Machado as players to be named later in Aug. 31 deal that sent catcher Charlie O'Brien to Mets . . . Compiled 10-6 record with 3.55 ERA for Tidewater (AAA) . . . Born March 5, 1966, in Oroville, Cal.

NARCISO ELVIRA 23 5-10 160   **Bats L Throws L**
Billed as a young Teddy Higuera . . . Made jump from El Paso
(AA) to Brewers in September . . . Was 0-0 with 5.40 ERA in four
big-league relief efforts . . . Primarily a starter during 37-30 minor-
league career . . . Born Oct. 29, 1967, in Vera Cruz, Mexico . . .
Purchased from Leon of Mexican League in 1987 . . . Pursues kar-
ate as hobby.

TIM McINTOSH 26 5-11 195   **Bats R Throws R**
Catcher is ready for big-league duty . . . Named to American Association postseason All-Star team after batting .288 with 18 home
runs and 74 RBI for Denver (AAA) . . . First big-league hit was
a homer off Yankees' Steve Adkins Sept. 28 . . . Born March 21,
1965, in Minneapolis . . . Selected in third round of 1986 draft.

GEORGE CANALE 25 6-1 190   **Bats L Throws R**
Has done enough to warrant a long look at first base . . . Batted
.254 with 12 home runs and 60 RBI for Denver (AAA) . . . Showed
flashes of brilliance in field after Sept. 4 recall to Brewers . . .
Born Aug. 11, 1965, in Memphis, Tenn. . . . Selected in sixth
round of 1986 draft.

MANAGER TOM TREBELHORN: Job is thought to be in
jeopardy if Brewers don't show almost immediate improvement . . . Club's record dipped to
74-88 after finishing at .500 in 1989 . . . Brewers tend to beat themselves with frequent mistakes, disturbing pattern that reflects poorly on
manager . . . Clubhouse chemistry has been
poor . . . Owns 333-315 record in four full seasons at Brewers' helm, but fortunes have de-
clined steadily . . . Managed Vancouver (AAA) to Pacific Coast
League crown in 1985 . . . Scheduled to direct Brewers' Helena
farm club in Pioneer League in 1986, but became Milwaukee's
third-base coach when Tony Muser was injured in clubhouse ex-
plosion in spring training . . . Officially named manager, succeeding George Bamberger, Oct. 1, 1986 . . . Born Jan. 27, 1948, in
Portland, Ore. . . . Played baseball and basketball at Portland State,

where he was a catcher . . . Played in Northwest League in 1971 and '72 . . . Oakland purchased his contract in 1973 and he played two seasons in Athletics' system . . . Batted .241 in minor-league career . . . Used to be substitute teacher in Portland system in off-season.

ALL-TIME BREWER SEASON RECORDS

BATTING: Paul Molitor, .353, 1987
HRs: Gorman Thomas, 45, 1979
RBI: Cecil Cooper, 126, 1983
STEALS: Paul Molitor, 45, 1987
WINS: Mike Caldwell, 22, 1978
STRIKEOUTS: Ted Higuera, 240, 1987

Ex-Red enigma Ron Robinson made it big in Milwaukee.

NEW YORK YANKEES

TEAM DIRECTORY: Managing General Partner: Robert Neder-
lander; Principal Owner: George Steinbrenner III; VP/GM: Gene
Michael; VP-Baseball Oper.: George Bradley; VP-Player Dev.
and Scouting: Brian Sabean; Dir. Scouting: Bill Livesey; Sr. VP:
Arthur Richman; Dir. Media Rel.: Jeff Idelson; Trav. Sec.: Tony
Bartirome; Mgr.: Stump Merrill. Home: Yankee Stadium
(57,545). Field distances: 312, l.f. line; 379, l.f.; 411, l.c.; 410,
c.f.; 385, r.c.; 310, r.f. line. Spring training: Fort Lauderdale,
Fla.

SCOUTING REPORT

HITTING: If Don Mattingly can return to form, it will make a
vast difference in an offense that ranked last in the AL in batting
average (.241), runs (603), slugging percentage (.366) and on-
base percentage (.300) in 1990. Back problems limited Mattingly
to 102 games, his string of .300 seasons ended at six with a .256
average and he failed to show his usual punch with only five
homers and 42 RBI.

The Yankees have high hopes for 1990 rookie sensation Kevin
Maas (.252, 21, 41) and ever-improving Roberto Kelly (.285, 15,
61). Kelly ranked third in the AL with 183 hits, despite striking
out 148 times.

Jesse Barfield, the team leader in home runs (25) and RBI (78),
returns and the Yankees believe Hensley Meulens, the International League MVP with 26 home runs and 96 RBI, will provide
some sock as the regular left fielder.

PITCHING: The Yankees' pitching took a major turn for the
worse when they lost closer Dave Righetti to San Francisco as a
free agent last winter. Righetti left as the Yankees' all-time saves
leader with 224, including 36 in 39 opportunities last year. Now
Lee Guetterman (11-7, 3.39) must prove he can be more than just
an excellent set-up man.

The Yankees did make several positive moves by signing Scott
Sanderson (17-11, 3.88 with A's) and free agent Steve Farr
(13-7, 1.98 with Royals) and retaining new-look free agent Mike
Witt (5-9, 4.00) and free agent Tim Leary (9-19, 4.11). Farr can
start or finish games and Leary is considerably better than his 1990
record would indicate. He was supported by just 38 runs in his
19 defeats.

Roberto Kelly scored 85 runs and stole 42 bases.

Chuck Cary (6-12, 4.19) was another victim of poor support, but Andy Hawkins (5-12, 5.37) is a rollercoaster ride. Dave Eiland, the International League's biggest winner with 16, may be given a chance to show what he can do as a major-league starter if Pascual Perez' shoulder doesn't prove sound.

FIELDING: The Yankees boast a fine keystone combination in second baseman Steve Sax and shortstop Alvaro Espinoza. They placed second in the AL in double plays (202). Barfield is a defensive weapon in right. He topped the majors with 16 outfield assists and ranked third lifetime among active outfielders (149 assists). When he's healthy, Mattingly is a state-of-the-art first baseman. But third base remains a hole and no one is sure how Meulens will do in left field.

OUTLOOK: The Yankees' 67-95 record last year was their worst since 1912. Outside of pitching, there is little chance for improvement and 1991 would be a success if Stump Merrill can avoid another last-place finish.

NEW YORK YANKEES 1991 ROSTER

MANAGER Stump Merrill
Coaches—Mark Connor, Mike Ferraro, Marc Hill, Frank Howard, Graig Nettles, Buck Showalter

PITCHERS

No.	Name	1990 Club	W-L	IP	SO	ERA	B-T	Ht.	Wt.	Born
43	Adkins, Steve	Columbus	15-7	177	138	2.90	L-L	6-6	205	10/26/64 Chicago, IL
		New York (AL)	1-2	24	14	6.38				
25	Cadaret, Greg	New York (AL)	5-4	121	80	4.15	L-L	6-3	214	2/27/62 Detroit, MI
51	Cary, Chuck	New York (AL)	6-12	157	134	4.19	L-L	6-4	216	3/3/60 Whittier, CA
65	Chapin, Darrin	Albany	3-2	53	61	2.73	R-R	6-0	170	2/1/66 Warren, OH
		Columbus	0-1	9	8	7.27				
26	Eiland, Dave	Columbus	16-5	175	96	2.87	R-R	6-3	205	7/5/66 Dade City, FL
—	Farr, Steve	Kansas City	13-7	127	94	1.98	R-R	5-11	200	12/12/56 Cheverly, MD
35	Guetterman, Lee	New York (AL)	11-7	93	48	3.39	L-L	6-8	227	11/22/58 Chattanooga, TN
57	Habyan, John	Columbus	7-7	112	77	3.21	R-R	6-2	195	1/29/64 Bayshore, NY
		New York (AL)	0-0	9	4	2.08				
40	Hawkins, Andy	New York (AL)	5-12	158	74	5.37	R-R	6-3	219	1/21/60 Waco, TX
64	Johnson, Jeff	Albany	4-3	61	41	1.63	R-L	6-3	200	8/4/66 Durham, NC
		Ft. Lauderdale	6-8	104	84	3.65				
42	**LaPoint, Dave	New York (AL)	7-10	158	67	4.11	L-L	6-3	228	7/29/59 Glens Falls, NY
54	Leary, Tim	New York (AL)	9-19	208	138	4.11	R-R	6-3	190	12/23/58 Santa Monica, CA
56	Leiter, Mark	Columbus	9-4	123	115	3.60	R-R	6-3	210	4/13/63 Joliet, IL
		New York (AL)	1-1	26	21	6.84				
28	Mills, Alan	Columbus	3-3	29	15	3.38	R-R	6-1	190	10/18/66 Lakeland, FL
		New York (AL)	1-5	42	24	4.10				
61	Mmahat, Kevin	Columbus	11-5	115	81	3.76	L-L	6-5	220	11/9/64 Memphis, TN
55	Monteleone, Rich	Edmonton	1-0	14	9	1.93	R-R	6-2	234	3/22/63 Tampa, FL
		Columbus	4-4	64	60	2.24				
34	Perez, Pascual	Columbus	0-1	7	8	6.14	R-R	6-3	183	5/17/57 Dominican Republic
		New York (AL)	1-2	14	12	1.29				
33	Plunk, Eric	New York (AL)	6-3	73	67	2.72	R-R	6-5	217	9/3/63 Wilmington, CA
22	Sanderson, Scott	Oakland	17-11	206	128	3.88	R-R	6-5	200	7/22/66 Dearborn, MI
59	Smith, Willie	Albany	1-1	9	12	0.00	R-R	6-6	240	8/27/67 Savannah, GA
		Columbus	3-1	35	47	6.23				
58	Taylor, Wade	Albany	6-4	84	44	2.88	R-R	6-1	185	10/19/65 Mobile, AL
		Columbus	6-4	99	57	2.19				
36	Witt, Mike	Cal.-NY (AL)	5-9	117	74	4.00	R-R	6-7	210	7/20/60 Fullerton, CA

CATCHERS

No.	Name	1990 Club	H	HR	RBI	Pct.	B-T	Ht.	Wt.	Born
11	Cerone, Rick	New York (AL)	42	2	11	.302	R-R	5-11	195	5/19/54 Newark, NJ
53	Geren, Bob	New York (AL)	59	8	31	.213	R-R	6-3	228	9/22/61 San Diego, CA
38	Nokes, Matt	Det.-NY (AL)	87	11	40	.248	L-L	6-1	191	10/31/63 San Diego, CA
60	Ramos, John	Columbus	0	0	1	.000	R-R	6-0	190	8/6/65 Tampa, FL
		Albany	90	4	45	.314				

INFIELDERS

No.	Name	1990 Club	H	HR	RBI	Pct.	B-T	Ht.	Wt.	Born
45	Balboni, Steve	New York (AL)	51	17	34	.192	R-R	6-3	250	1/5/57 Brockton, MA
21	Blowers, Mike	Columbus	78	6	50	.339	R-R	6-2	210	4/24/65 Germany
		New York (AL)	27	5	21	.188				
20	Espinoza, Alvaro	New York (AL)	98	2	20	.224	R-R	6-0	189	2/19/62 Venezuela
17	Kelly, Pat	Albany	113	8	44	.270	R-R	6-0	180	10/14/67 Philadelphia, PA
12	Leyritz, Jim	Columbus	59	8	32	.269	R-R	6-0	190	12/27/63 Lakewood, OH
		New York (AL)	78	5	25	.257				
14	Maas, Kevin	Columbus	55	13	38	.284	L-L	6-3	203	1/20/65 Castro Valley, CA
		New York (AL)	64	21	41	.252				
23	Mattingly, Don	New York (AL)	101	5	42	.256	L-L	6-0	192	4/20/61 Evansville, IN
6	Sax, Steve	New York (AL)	160	4	42	.260	R-R	5-11	182	1/29/60 W. Sacramento, CA
18	Velarde, Randy	New York (AL)	48	5	19	.210	R-R	6-0	190	11/24/62 Midland, TX

OUTFIELDERS

No.	Name	1990 Club	H	HR	RBI	Pct.	B-T	Ht.	Wt.	Born
29	Barfield, Jesse	New York (AL)	117	25	78	.246	R-R	6-1	200	10/29/59 Joliet, IL
27	Hall, Mel	New York (AL)	93	12	46	.258	L-L	6-1	218	9/16/60 Lyons, NY
39	Kelly, Roberto	New York (AL)	183	15	61	.285	R-R	6-3	182	10/1/64 Panama
31	Meulens, Hensley	Columbus	137	26	96	.285	R-R	6-3	212	6/23/67 Curacao
		New York (AL)	20	3	10	.241				
63	Williams, Bernie	Albany	131	8	54	.281	S-R	6-2	180	9/13/68 Puerto Rico
62	Williams, Gerald	Ft. Lauderdale	59	7	43	.289	R-R	6-2	190	8/10/66 New Orleans, LA
		Albany	81	13	58	.250				

**New-look free agent

YANKEE PROFILES

DON MATTINGLY 29 6-0 192   Bats L Throws L

First baseman must show he can return to being feared hitter he once was . . . Sidelined from July 25-Sept. 14 with flareup of chronic back problems . . . Hit well upon return, but still didn't drive the ball . . . Failed to homer after May 20 . . . Average has dropped for four consecutive years . . . String of .300 seasons ended at six . . . Won batting crown in 1984, his first full major-league season, by outdueling teammate Dave Winfield on final day of season . . . Provided encore in 1985 by taking AL MVP honors and driving in 145 runs, most by a Yankee since Joe DiMaggio's 155 in 1948 . . . Set Yankee records with 238 hits and 53 doubles in 1986 . . . Set long-ball marks in 1987, smashing major-league record with six grand slams and tying major-league mark by homering in eight consecutive games . . . Born April 20, 1961, in Evansville, Ind. . . . Selected in 19th round of 1979 draft . . . Was Yankees' best-paid player with $2.5 million salary in 1990.

Year	Club	Pos.	G	AB	R	H	2B	3B	HR	RBI	SB	Avg.
1982	New York (AL)	OF-1B	7	12	0	2	0	0	0	1	0	.167
1983	New York (AL)	OF-1B-2B	91	279	34	79	15	4	4	32	0	.283
1984	New York (AL)	1B-OF	153	603	91	207	44	2	23	110	1	.343
1985	New York (AL)	1B	159	652	107	211	48	3	35	145	2	.324
1986	New York (AL)	1B-3B	162	677	117	238	53	2	31	113	0	.352
1987	New York (AL)	1B	141	569	93	186	38	2	30	115	1	.327
1988	New York (AL)	1B-OF	144	599	94	186	37	0	18	88	1	.311
1989	New York (AL)	1B-OF	158	631	79	191	37	2	23	113	3	.303
1990	New York (AL)	1B-OF	102	394	40	101	16	0	5	42	1	.256
	Totals		1117	4416	655	1401	288	15	169	759	9	.317

ROBERTO KELLY 26 6-3 182   Bats R Throws R

Center fielder has chance to be star . . . Finished third in AL with 183 hits and led Yankee regulars with .285 average despite 148 strikeouts . . . Ranked third in AL with 42 steals . . . Led club with 85 runs and was second in RBI with 61, despite batting leadoff most of year . . . Played in all 162 games . . . Much better hitter in big leagues than he was in minors, where he compiled .260 lifetime average . . . Born Oct. 1, 1964, in Panama City, Panama . . . Signed as free agent by Yanks in February 1982 . . . Due for raise after earning only $265,000 in 1990.

Year	Club	Pos.	G	AB	R	H	2B	3B	HR	RBI	SB	Avg.
1987	New York (AL)	OF	23	52	12	14	3	0	1	7	9	.269
1988	New York (AL)	OF	38	77	9	19	4	1	1	7	5	.247
1989	New York (AL)	OF	137	441	65	133	18	3	9	48	35	.302
1990	New York (AL)	OF	162	641	85	183	32	4	15	61	42	.285
	Totals		360	1211	171	349	57	8	26	123	91	.288

JESSE BARFIELD 31 6-1 200   Bats R Throws R

Not necessarily an impact player despite some gaudy statistics . . . Right fielder paced Yankees with 25 homers and 78 RBI, but also led club with 150 strikeouts . . . Marked second straight year he fanned 150 times . . . His team-high 82 walks were not a positive as this power hitter seems to prefer taking pass in key situations and leaving it to next man . . . Topped majors in homers with 40 in 1986 and has clouted 20-plus homers six times . . . Topped major-league outfielders with 16 assists . . . Born Oct. 29, 1959, in Joliet, Ill. . . . Acquired from Toronto for Al Leiter, April 30, 1989 . . . His 1990 salary was $1,266,667.

Year	Club	Pos.	G	AB	R	H	2B	3B	HR	RBI	SB	Avg.
1981	Toronto	OF	25	95	7	22	3	2	2	9	4	.232
1982	Toronto	OF	139	394	54	97	13	2	18	58	1	.246
1983	Toronto	OF	128	388	58	98	13	3	27	68	2	.253
1984	Toronto	OF	110	320	51	91	14	1	14	49	8	.284
1985	Toronto	OF	155	539	94	156	34	9	27	84	22	.289
1986	Toronto	OF	158	589	107	170	35	2	40	108	8	.289
1987	Toronto	OF	159	590	89	155	25	3	28	84	3	.263
1988	Toronto	OF	136	468	62	114	21	5	18	56	7	.244
1989	Tor.-NY(AL) . . .	OF	150	521	79	122	23	1	23	67	5	.234
1990	New York (AL)	OF	153	476	69	117	21	2	25	78	4	.246
	Totals		1314	4380	670	1142	202	30	222	661	64	.261

STEVE SAX 31 5-11 182   Bats R Throws R

Team's poor showing appeared to lower level of his play . . . His .260 average was his worst since 1984 and second-lowest of career . . . Still finished second on club with 160 hits and 70 runs . . . Placed second in AL with 43 steals . . . Durable second baseman has played in at least 155 games for five consecutive years . . . NL Rookie of the Year with Los Angeles in 1982

. . . Contributed to Dodgers' world championship in 1988 with .300 average during upset of Oakland . . . Born Jan. 29, 1960, in West Sacramento, Cal. . . . Signed as free agent prior to 1989 season . . . Made $1,066,667 in 1990.

Year	Club	Pos.	G	AB	R	H	2B	3B	HR	RBI	SB	Avg.
1981	Los Angeles . . .	2B	31	119	15	33	2	0	2	9	5	.277
1982	Los Angeles . . .	2B	150	638	88	180	23	7	4	47	49	.282
1983	Los Angeles . . .	2B	155	623	94	175	18	5	5	41	56	.281
1984	Los Angeles . . .	2B	145	569	70	138	24	4	1	35	34	.243
1985	Los Angeles . . .	2B-3B	136	488	62	136	8	4	1	42	27	.279
1986	Los Angeles . . .	2B	157	633	91	210	43	4	6	56	40	.332
1987	Los Angeles . . .	2B-OF-3B	157	610	84	171	22	7	6	46	37	.280
1988	Los Angeles . . .	2B	160	632	70	175	19	4	5	57	42	.277
1989	New York (AL)	2B	158	651	88	205	26	3	5	63	43	.315
1990	New York (AL)	2B	155	615	70	160	24	2	4	42	43	.260
	Totals		1404	5578	732	1583	209	40	39	438	376	.284

KEVIN MAAS 26 6-3 203   Bats L Throws L

Comes off record-setting rookie campaign . . . After June 28 recall from Columbus, he needed fewest at-bats (77) in major-league history to reach 10 home runs . . . Tied Dave Hostetler's major-league mark for most homers in 100 at-bats with 12 . . . Connected for first time as major leaguer July 4, off Kansas City's Bret Saberhagen . . . Of his total of 21 homers, 14 were solo shots . . . Progress was slowed when he needed arthroscopic surgery to repair ligament damage in right knee in August 1989 . . . Yankees' Minor League Player of the Year in 1988, when he collected 28 home runs and 90 RBI in stops at Prince William (A) and Albany (AA) . . . Born Jan. 20, 1965, in Castro Valley, Cal. . . . Selected by Yankees in 22nd round of 1986 draft . . . His 1990 salary was $100,000.

Year	Club	Pos.	G	AB	R	H	2B	3B	HR	RBI	SB	Avg.
1990	New York (AL)	1B	79	254	42	64	9	0	21	41	1	.252

LEE GUETTERMAN 32 6-8 227   Bats L Throws L

Became only pitcher in history to lead team in victories without benefit of a start . . . That says much about his importance . . . Was almost untouchable early in season, permitting one earned run in 22 appearances covering 25⅔ innings from April 27-June 15 . . . Added nine consecutive scoreless outings Aug. 13-Sept. 6 . . . Has led Yankees in appearances last two years . . . Set relief record for scoreless innings at start of a season with 30⅔ innings in 1989 . . . Born Nov. 22, 1958, in Chattanooga, Tenn. . . . Acquired from Seattle with Wade Taylor and Clay Parker for Steve Trout and Henry Cotto after 1987 season . . . Due for raise after collecting $465,000 salary in 1990.

Year	Club	G	IP	W	L	Pct.	SO	BB	H	ERA
1984	Seattle	3	4⅓	0	0	.000	2	2	9	4.15
1986	Seattle	41	76	0	4	.000	38	30	108	7.34
1987	Seattle	25	113⅓	11	4	.733	42	35	117	3.81
1988	New York (AL)	20	40⅔	1	2	.333	15	14	49	4.65
1989	New York (AL)	70	103	5	5	.500	51	26	98	2.45
1990	New York (AL)	64	93	11	7	.611	48	26	80	3.39
	Totals	223	430⅓	28	22	.560	196	133	461	4.10

MIKE WITT 30 6-7 210   Bats R Throws R

Showed he could still be solid starter after May 11 acquisition from Angels for Dave Winfield . . . Worked six-plus innings in 12 of 16 starts . . . Was disabled for first time in nine-plus big-league seasons . . . Suffered strained elbow during June 8 start in Baltimore . . . Returned with victory over Seattle Aug. 7 . . . Displayed impressive ability in final month . . . Pitched 1-0 perfect game against Texas, Sept. 30, 1984 . . . Won 15 or more games for California from 1984-87 . . . Born July 20, 1960, in Fullerton, Cal. . . . California's fourth-round pick in 1978 draft . . . Earned $1.31 million in 1990 and as a new-look free agent, signed a three-year, $8-million contract in January.

Year	Club	G	IP	W	L	Pct.	SO	BB	H	ERA
1981	California	22	129	8	9	.471	75	47	123	3.28
1982	California	33	179⅔	8	6	.571	85	47	177	3.51
1983	California	43	154	7	14	.333	77	75	173	4.91
1984	California	34	246⅔	15	11	.577	196	84	227	3.47
1985	California	35	250	15	9	.625	180	98	228	3.56
1986	California	34	269	18	10	.643	208	73	218	2.84
1987	California	36	247	16	14	.533	192	84	252	4.01
1988	California	34	249⅔	13	16	.448	133	87	263	4.15
1989	California	33	220	9	15	.375	123	48	252	4.54
1990	Cal.-NY (AL)	26	117	5	9	.357	74	47	106	4.00
	Totals	330	2062	114	113	.502	1343	690	2019	3.79

STEVE FARR 34 5-11 200   Bats R Throws R

Enjoyed a career year as a Royal relief pitcher and, as a free agent, turned it into a three-year, $6.3-million contract . . . Posted personal bests in record, ERA, innings and strikeouts . . . His 13 wins topped the club . . . Fifty-one of 57 appearances were in relief . . . Had only one save . . . As a starter, he won five games and posted a 1.51 ERA . . . Threw first career complete game and shutout, Sept. 23 vs. California . . . Royals' Pitcher of the Month in September . . . Pitched 7½ seasons in minors before breaking in with Cleveland in 1984 . . . Signed by Royals as free agent in 1985 . . . Earned $775,000 in 1990 . . . Born Dec. 12, 1956, in Cheverly, Md.

Year	Club	G	IP	W	L	Pct.	SO	BB	H	ERA
1984	Cleveland	31	116	3	11	.214	83	46	106	4.58
1985	Kansas City	16	37⅔	2	1	.667	36	20	34	3.11
1986	Kansas City	56	109⅓	8	4	.667	83	39	90	3.13
1987	Kansas City	47	91	4	3	.571	88	44	97	4.15
1988	Kansas City	62	82⅔	5	4	.556	72	30	74	2.50
1989	Kansas City	51	63⅓	2	5	.286	56	22	75	4.12
1990	Kansas City	57	127	13	7	.650	94	48	99	1.98
	Totals	320	627	37	35	.514	512	249	575	3.33

TIM LEARY 32 6-3 190   Bats R Throws R

Must recover from nightmarish 19-loss season that fell two defeats short of Yankees record . . . Did not pitch after Sept. 19 to keep matters from getting any worse . . . Endured career-high eight-game losing streak from May 28-July 8 . . . Victim of terrible run support . . . Held opposition to one run three times and wound up with two losses and a no-decision . . . Shoddy catching contributed to club-record 23 wild pitches, one shy of Jack Morris' AL mark . . . Played important role in Dodgers' unexpected rise to world championship in 1988 by winning 17 games and pitching six shutouts . . . Born Dec. 23, 1958, in Santa Monica, Cal. . . . Acquired from Reds with Van Snider for Hal Morris and Rodney Imes prior to last season . . . His 1990 salary was $825,000 and he signed five-year, $6-million contract with Yanks as free agent last winter.

Year	Club	G	IP	W	L	Pct.	SO	BB	H	ERA
1981	New York (NL)	1	2	0	0	.000	3	1	0	0.00
1983	New York (NL)	2	10⅔	1	1	.500	9	4	15	3.38
1984	New York (NL)	20	53⅔	3	3	.500	29	18	61	4.02
1985	Milwaukee	5	33⅓	1	4	.200	29	8	40	4.05
1986	Milwaukee	33	188⅓	12	12	.500	110	53	216	4.21
1987	Los Angeles	39	107⅔	3	11	.214	61	36	121	4.76
1988	Los Angeles	35	228⅔	17	11	.607	180	56	201	2.91
1989	LA-Cin.	33	207	8	14	.364	123	68	205	3.52
1990	New York (AL)	31	208	9	19	.321	138	78	202	4.11
	Totals.	199	1039⅓	54	75	.419	682	322	1061	3.79

SCOTT SANDERSON 34 6-5 200   Bats R Throws R

Yankees purchased him from Oakland and signed him to two-year, $4-million contract to be one of the mainstays in their rotation . . . A's dealt him to avoid arbitration hearing that would have resulted in big contract . . . Didn't pitch as well as last year's career-high 17 victories would indicate . . . Benefitted from superior offensive and defensive support of the A's . . . They chose not to give him a postseason start despite regular-season success . . . Dominated Yankees with 3-0 mark and 0.89 ERA . . . Did not make a major-league appearance in 1988 after undergoing back surgery . . . Operation saved his career and he has won in double figures in each of past two seasons . . . Made $750,000 in 1990 . . . Born July 22, 1956, in Dearborn, Mich.

Year	Club	G	IP	W	L	Pct.	SO	BB	H	ERA
1978	Montreal	10	61	4	2	.667	50	21	52	2.51
1979	Montreal	34	168	9	8	.529	138	54	148	3.43
1980	Montreal	33	211	16	11	.593	125	56	206	3.11
1981	Montreal	22	137	9	7	.563	77	31	122	2.96
1982	Montreal	32	224	12	12	.500	158	58	212	3.46
1983	Montreal	18	81⅓	6	7	.462	55	20	98	4.65
1984	Chicago (NL)	24	140⅔	8	5	.615	76	24	140	3.14
1985	Chicago (NL)	19	121	5	6	.455	80	27	100	3.12
1986	Chicago (NL)	37	169⅔	9	11	.450	124	37	165	4.19
1987	Chicago (NL)	32	144⅔	8	9	.471	106	50	156	4.29
1988	Chicago (NL)	11	15⅓	1	2	.133	6	3	13	5.28
1989	Chicago (NL)	37	146⅓	11	9	.550	86	31	155	3.94
1990	Oakland	34	206	17	11	.607	128	66	205	3.88
	Totals.	343	1826⅓	115	100	.534	1209	478	1772	3.57

TOP PROSPECTS

HENSLEY MEULENS 23 6-3 205   **Bats R Throws R**
Figures prominently in Yankees' plans after big year for Columbus
(AAA)... Responded well to move from third base to left field
... Tied for second in International League with 26 home runs
and was one behind RBI leader with 96... Also hit .285... Born
June 23, 1967, in Curacao... Signed as free agent in October
1985.

STEVE ADKINS 26 6-6 200   **Bats R Throws L**
Has a chance to break into Yankees' rotation... Placed second
in International League in victories with 15-7 record and ranked
fourth with 2.90 ERA... Best pitch is elusive knuckle curve, but
often has trouble controlling it... Went 1-2 with 6.38 ERA in
five September starts with Yankees... Born Oct. 26, 1964, in
Chicago... Selected in 15th round of 1986 draft.

DAVE EILAND 24 6-3 205   **Bats R Throws R**
Minor-league ace must show he can do it in big leagues... Topped
International League in victories with 16-5 record and finished
third with 2.87 ERA... Has benefitted from adding sinker to
repertoire... Went 2-1 with 3.56 ERA in five September starts
with Yankees... Born July 5, 1966, in Dade City, Fla.
... Selected in seventh round of 1987 draft.

BERNIE WILLIAMS 22 6-2 180   **Bats S Throws R**
Possesses plenty of ability but needs to develop... Has spent most
of last two years with Albany (AA) and hit .281 with eight homers
and 54 RBI for that club this year... Gifted center fielder also
recorded 39 stolen bases... Improved feel for strike zone resulted
in 98 walks... Born Sept. 13, 1968, in San Juan, Puerto
Rico... Signed as free agent in September 1985.

MANAGER STUMP MERRILL: Received his dream job
when he was named to replace Bucky Dent as
Yankees manager on June 6... Inherited 18-31
disaster and compiled 49-64 record rest of way
... Kept team pushing until end, a credit to
manager... Should be right man to oversee ex-
tensive rebuilding given his experience with
young players and his knowledge of farm system... At time of appointment, he had led

Triple-A Columbus to 35-25 record and first place in Western Division in International League . . . Begins 15th consecutive season in Yankee organization . . . Has proven to be successful minor-league manager in Yankees system as indicated by a 783-544 (.590) career record, seven division titles and three league championships . . . In 1989, he took over at Class-A Prince William in Carolina League on May 21 and led Cannons to 54-43 record and eventual league championship . . . Named minor-league coordinator in 1988, then stepped in as Albany manager (AA) on June 6, leading club to Eastern League title . . . In 1987, he coached first base for Yankees . . . After spending entire six-year playing career as catcher in Philadelphia system, he joined Yankees organization in 1977 as pitching coach at West Haven . . . Prior to beginning professional coaching and managerial career, he spent time at his alma mater, University of Maine, as assistant baseball coach under late Jack Butterfield . . . Joined managerial ranks in 1978 at West Haven and led his clubs to playoffs or outright championships in five of seven years . . . Born Feb. 25, 1944, in Brunswick, Me.

ALL-TIME YANKEE SEASON RECORDS

BATTING: Babe Ruth, .393, 1923
HRs: Roger Maris, 61, 1961
RBI: Lou Gehrig, 184, 1931
STEALS: Rickey Henderson, 93, 1988
WINS: Jack Chesbro, 41, 1904
STRIKEOUTS: Ron Guidry, 248, 1978

TORONTO BLUE JAYS

TEAM DIRECTORY: Chairman: W.R.R. Ferguson; Vice Chairman/CEO: P.N.T. Widdington; Pres./Chief Oper. Off.: Paul Beeston; Exec. VP-Baseball: Pat Gillick; VP-Baseball: Al LaMacchia, Bob Mattick; Dir. Pub. Rel.: Howard Starkman; Trav. Sec.: John Broiux; Mgr.: Cito Gaston. Home: Skydome (50,000). Field distances: 330, l.f. line; 375, l.c.; 400, c.f.; 375, r.c.; 330, r.f. line. Spring training: Dunedin, Fla.

SCOUTING REPORT

HITTING: The stand-pat Blue Jays made stunning changes last winter, dealing their top home-run threat, Fred McGriff, and their

Dave Stieb finally notched that elusive first no-hitter.

greatest source of speed, Tony Fernandez, to San Diego. They also allowed another dangerous offensive player, George Bell, to sign with the Cubs as a free agent.

That's a lot of firepower gone from an attack that led the AL in runs (767), total bases (2,343), triples (50) and slugging percentage (.419) and was second in home runs (167) in 1990.

However, Toronto did receive an excellent run producer from San Diego in Joe Carter (.232, 24, 115) and first baseman McGriff's departure creates a needed spot for John Olerud (.265, 14, 48), who will be something special. Roberto Alomar (.287, 6, 60), the other newcomer from San Diego, is a fine switch-hitter and Kelly Gruber (.274, 31, 118) joins Carter as a top gun in the revamped lineup. Free-agent signee Pat Tabler is versatile and an established big-league hitter.

PITCHING: Ace Dave Stieb (18-6, 2.93) keeps rolling along. He established club records for wins and winning percentage (.750) last year. Jimmy Key (13-7, 4.25) is a winner when he's healthy. Todd Stottlemyre (13-17, 4.34) will undoubtedly improve in his second full major-league season and lefty David Wells (11-6, 3.14) looks forward to his first full season as a starter.

Tom Henke (2-4, 2.17, 32 Sv) heads a formidable bullpen, having registered 20 or more saves for five consecutive years. The Blue Jays ranked third in the AL with a club-record 48 saves in 1990 and the bullpen grew stronger last winter with the addition of free agent left-hander Ken Dayley (4-4, 3.56, 2 Sv with Cards).

FIELDING: Toronto will be hard-pressed to reproduce last year's effort, when it tied pennant-winning Oakland for the AL's best fielding percentage at .986, a club record. The addition of slick center fielder Devon White in a multi-player deal with the Angels will help tremendously. However, neither Manny Lee nor prospect Eddie Zosky is Fernandez' equal at shortstop and Olerud is suspect at first base. At least the Alomar addition finally stabilizes second base.

OUTLOOK: GM Pat Gillick was wise to overhaul the club. Toronto, the only major-league team to post a winning record each of the last eight seasons, has a history of underachievement to show for it. The new-look Jays, coming off an 86-76 finish under Cito Gaston, are in position to win the weak AL East in 1991.

TORONTO BLUE JAYS 1991 ROSTER

MANAGER Cito Gaston
Coaches—Galen Cisco, Rich Hacker, Mike Squires, John Sullivan, Gene Tenace, Hector Torres

PITCHERS

No.	Name	1990 Club	W-L	IP	SO	ERA	B-T	Ht.	Wt.	Born
34	Acker, Jim	Toronto	4-4	92	54	3.83	R-R	6-2	215	9/24/58 Freer, TX
—	Boucher, Denis	Dunedin	7-0	80	82	0.75	R-L	6-1	195	3/7/68 Canada
		Syracuse	8-5	108	80	3.85				
48	*Candelaria, John	Minn.-Tor.	7-6	80	63	3.95	R-L	6-6	225	11/6/53 Brooklyn, NY
38	Cromwell, Nate	Knoxville	5-14	121	79	5.58	L-L	6-1	185	8/23/68 Las Vegas, NV
46	Dayley, Ken	St. Louis	4-4	73	51	3.56	L-L	6-0	180	2/25/59 Jerome, ID
27	Fraser, Willie	California	5-4	76	32	3.08	R-R	6-1	208	5/26/64 New York, NY
50	Henke, Tom	Toronto	2-4	75	75	2.17	R-R	6-5	225	12/21/57 Kansas City, MO
41	Hentgen, Pat	Knoxville	9-5	153	142	3.05	R-R	6-2	200	11/13/68 Detroit, MI
22	Key, Jimmy	Dunedin	2-0	18	14	2.50	R-L	6-1	190	4/22/61 Huntsville, AL
		Toronto	13-7	155	88	4.25				
28	Leiter, Al	Dunedin	0-0	24	14	2.63	L-L	6-3	215	10/23/65 Toms River, NJ
		Syracuse	3-6	78	66	4.62				
		Toronto	0-0	6	5	0.00				
45	MacDonald, Bob	Knoxville	1-2	57	54	1.89	L-L	6-3	206	4/27/65 East Orange, NJ
		Syracuse	0-2	8	6	5.40				
		Toronto	0-0	2	0	0.00				
—	Sanchez, Alex	Syracuse	5-9	112	65	5.71	R-R	6-2	195	4/8/66 Concord, CA
37	Stieb, Dave	Toronto	18-6	209	125	2.93	R-R	6-0	195	7/22/57 Santa Ana, CA
30	Stottlemyre, Todd	Toronto	13-17	203	115	4.34	L-R	6-3	190	5/20/65 Yakima, WA
—	Timlin, Mike	Dunedin	7-2	50	48	1.43	R-R	6-4	205	3/10/66 Midland, TX
		Knoxville	1-2	26	21	1.73				
52	Trucek, Rick	Dunedin	5-8	154	125	3.73	R-R	6-3	200	4/26/69 Houston, TX
31	Ward, Duane	Toronto	2-8	128	112	3.45	R-R	6-4	215	5/28/64 Parkview, NM
36	Wells, David	Toronto	11-6	189	115	3.14	L-L	6-4	215	5/20/63 Torrance, CA
—	Weston, Mickey	Rochester	11-1	109	58	1.98	R-R	6-1	187	3/26/61 Fling, MI
		Baltimore	0-1	21	9	7.71				
44	Wills, Frank	Toronto	6-4	99	72	4.73	R-R	6-2	210	10/26/58 New Orleans, LA

CATCHERS

No.	Name	1990 Club	H	HR	RBI	Pct.	B-T	Ht.	Wt.	Born
10	Borders, Pat	Toronto	99	15	49	.286	R-R	6-2	200	5/14/63 Columbus, OH
—	Diaz, Carlos	Syracuse	51	1	19	.203	R-R	6-3	190	12/24/64 Elizabeth, NJ
		Toronto	1	0	0	.333				
—	Knorr, Randy	Knoxville	108	13	64	.276	R-R	6-2	205	11/12/68 San Gabriel, CA
21	Myers, Greg	Syracuse	2	0	2	.182	L-R	6-2	205	4/14/66 Riverside, CA
		Toronto	59	5	22	.236				

INFIELDERS

No.	Name	1990 Club	H	HR	RBI	Pct.	B-T	Ht.	Wt.	Born
12	Alomar, Roberto	San Diego	168	6	60	.287	S-R	6-0	175	2/5/68 Puerto Rico
17	Gruber, Kelly	Toronto	162	31	118	.274	R-R	6-0	185	2/26/62 Bellaire, TX
4	Lee, Manny	Toronto	95	6	41	.243	S-R	5-9	166	6/17/65 Dominican Republic
5	Mulliniks, Rance	Toronto	28	2	16	.289	L-R	6-0	175	1/15/56 Tulare, CA
—	Olerud, John	Toronto	95	14	48	.265	L-L	6-5	205	8/5/68 Seattle, WA
16	Quinlan, Tom	Knoxville	124	15	51	.258	R-R	6-3	210	3/27/68 St. Paul, MN
		Toronto	1	0	0	.500				
—	Suero, William	Knoxville	127	16	60	.263	R-R	5-9	175	11/7/66 Dominican Republic
—	Tabler, Pat	Kansas City	53	1	19	.272	R-R	6-2	200	2/2/58 Hamilton, OH
		New York (NL)	12	1	10	.279				

OUTFIELDERS

No.	Name	1990 Club	H	HR	RBI	Pct.	B-T	Ht.	Wt.	Born
14	Bell, Derek	Syracuse	105	7	56	.261	R-R	6-2	200	12/11/68 Tampa, FL
—	Carter, Joe	San Diego	147	24	115	.232	R-R	6-3	215	3/7/60 Oklahoma City, OK
20	Ducey, Rob	Syracuse	117	7	47	.267	L-R	6-2	180	5/24/65 Canada
		Toronto	16	0	7	.302				
24	Hill, Glenallen	Toronto	60	12	32	.231	R-R	6-2	210	3/22/65 Santa Cruz, CA
39	White, Devon	California	96	11	44	.217	S-R	6-2	182	12/29/62 Jamaica
		Edmonton	20	0	6	.364				
23	Whiten, Mark	Syracuse	113	14	48	.290	S-R	6-3	215	11/25/66 Pensacola, FL
		Toronto	24	2	7	.273				
12	Williams, Kenny	Det.-Tor.	25	0	13	.161	R-R	6-1	195	4/6/64 Berkeley, CA
3	Wilson, Mookie	Toronto	156	3	51	.265	S-R	5-10	175	2/9/56 Bamberg, SC

*Free agent at press time

BLUE JAY PROFILES

JOE CARTER 31 6-3 215   Bats R Throws R

Blue Jays got veteran outfielder from Padres along with Roberto Alomar for Fred McGriff and Tony Fernandez in December trade . . . Drove in 115 runs in his only year as a Padre, three short of club record established by Dave Winfield in 1979 and third-best mark in the NL . . . Had plenty of chances, because he came to the plate with 413 men on base last year . . . Managed just three RBI in last 14 games . . . His .232 average is one of lowest ever by an NL player with 100 or more RBI . . . Entering second year of three-year, $9.2-million contract . . . Born March 7, 1960, in Oklahoma City, Okla. . . . Came from Indians to San Diego in trade for Sandy Alomar Jr., who became an All-Star catcher; Chris James, who batted .299, and Carlos Baerga, the Indians' starting third baseman . . . Hit 24 homers but only four in last 42 games . . . Played in all 162 games for second straight year and has played in 341 consecutive games, second-highest active streak in majors behind Orioles' Cal Ripken Jr. . . . Hit .320 with runners in scoring position and less than two out and .213 with runners in scoring position and two out . . . Figures to play right field.

Year	Club	Pos.	G	AB	R	H	2B	3B	HR	RBI	SB	Avg.
1983	Chicago (NL) . .	OF	23	51	6	9	1	1	0	1	1	.176
1984	Cleveland	OF-1B	66	244	32	67	6	1	13	41	2	.275
1985	Cleveland	OF-1B-2B-3B	143	489	64	128	27	0	15	59	24	.262
1986	Cleveland	OF-1B	162	663	108	200	36	9	29	121	29	.302
1987	Cleveland	OF-1B	149	588	83	155	27	2	32	106	31	.264
1988	Cleveland	OF	157	621	85	168	36	6	27	98	27	.271
1989	Cleveland	OF-1B	162	651	84	158	32	4	35	105	13	.243
1990	San Diego	OF-1B	162	634	79	147	27	1	24	115	22	.232
	Totals		1024	3941	541	1032	192	24	175	646	149	.262

KELLY GRUBER 29 6-0 185   Bats R Throws R

Earned some consideration in league MVP voting with outstanding season . . . Placed second in AL with team-leading 118 RBI . . . Ranked fifth in AL with 31 home runs, second in total bases (303), second in extra-base hits (73) and sixth in slugging percentage (.512) . . . Finished third among AL third basemen with .955 fielding percentage and was first with 123 putouts

. . . Born Feb. 26, 1962, in Bellaire, Tex. . . . Obtained from Cleveland in major-league draft, Dec. 5, 1983 . . . Had been Indians' first-round pick in 1980 draft . . . Earned $1.15 million in 1990 and was Gold Glove winner.

Year Club	Pos.	G	AB	R	H	2B	3B	HR	RBI	SB	Avg.
1984 Toronto	3B-OF-SS	15	16	1	1	0	0	1	2	0	.063
1985 Toronto	3B-2B	5	13	0	3	0	0	0	1	0	.231
1986 Toronto	3B-2B-OF-SS	87	143	20	28	4	1	5	15	2	.196
1987 Toronto	3B-SS-2B-OF	138	341	50	80	14	3	12	36	12	.235
1988 Toronto	3B-SS-2B-OF	158	569	75	158	33	5	16	81	23	.278
1989 Toronto	3B-OF-SS	135	545	83	158	24	4	18	73	10	.290
1990 Toronto	3B-OF	150	592	92	162	36	6	31	118	14	.274
Totals		688	2219	321	590	111	19	83	326	61	.266

JOHN OLERUD 22 6-5 205   Bats L Throws R

Has tools to be outstanding big-league hitter . . . Toronto's third-round pick in 1989 draft became only 16th player since start of amateur draft in 1965 to make pro debut at major-league level . . . Led all major-league rookies at All-Star break in home runs (10), RBI (33), walks (35), slugging percentage (.465) and on-base average (.375) . . . Takes over at first for departed Fred McGriff . . . Has made dramatic recovery from grave illness . . . Collapsed on Jan. 11, 1989 following workout at Washington State . . . Underwent surgery for removal of aneurism at base of brain . . . Born Aug. 5, 1968, in Seattle . . . Earned $100,000 in 1990.

Year Club	Pos.	G	AB	R	H	2B	3B	HR	RBI	SB	Avg.
1989 Toronto	1B	6	8	2	3	0	0	0	0	0	.375
1990 Toronto	1B	111	358	43	95	15	1	14	48	0	.265
Totals		117	366	45	98	15	1	14	48	0	.268

ROBERTO ALOMAR 23 6-0 175   Bats R Throws R

One of most gifted second basemen in baseball is now a Blue Jay following deal that brought him from San Diego with Joe Carter for Fred McGriff and Tony Fernandez . . . Highlight in 1990 was making All-Star team as one of three Alomars present at game . . . Father Sandy Sr. was third-base coach and brother Sandy Jr. was AL starting catcher . . . Born Feb. 5, 1968, in Salinas, Puerto Rico . . . Signed as a free agent in February 1985

. . . Produced career-high 60 RBI, the most ever by a Padre second baseman . . . Had trouble concentrating early in the year and committed 13 errors by the All-Star break . . . Made just six the rest of the way . . . Finished third on the team in hitting (.287) and second in runs (80) . . . Missed 14 of last 24 games with an elbow injury . . . Earned $390,000 in 1990.

Year	Club	Pos.	G	AB	R	H	2B	3B	HR	RBI	SB	Avg.
1988	San Diego	2B	143	545	84	145	24	6	9	41	24	.266
1989	San Diego	2B	158	623	82	184	27	1	7	56	42	.295
1990	San Diego	2B-SS	147	586	80	168	27	5	6	60	24	.287
	Totals		448	1754	246	497	78	12	22	157	90	.283

TODD STOTTLEMYRE 25 6-3 190   Bats L Throws R

Has famous name and ability to go with it . . . Will only improve . . . Led Jays with four complete games and was second with 203 innings pitched . . . Worked at least six innings in 20 of 33 starts . . . Is much tougher on right-handed hitters than lefties . . . Benefitted from second-best run support in AL per nine innings (5.81) . . . Born May 20, 1965, in Yakima, Wash. . . . Selected in first round (third player picked) of 1985 draft . . . Son of former Yankee pitcher and current Mets pitching coach Mel . . . Brother Mel Jr. pitches for Kansas City . . . Earned $168,500 in 1990.

Year	Club	G	IP	W	L	Pct.	SO	BB	H	ERA
1988	Toronto	28	98	4	8	.333	67	46	109	5.69
1989	Toronto	27	127⅔	7	7	.500	63	44	137	3.88
1990	Toronto	33	203	13	17	.433	115	69	214	4.34
	Totals	88	428⅔	24	32	.429	245	159	460	4.51

TOM HENKE 33 6-5 225   Bats R Throws R

Well-established closer racked up second-highest save total of career . . . Converted 32 of 38 opportunities . . . Averaged better than a strikeout per inning, fifth time in six seasons he's done that . . . Has registered 20 or more saves for five consecutive seasons . . . Opponents batted just .213 against him, .130 with runners in scoring position . . . Born Dec. 21, 1957, in Kansas City, Mo. . . . Selected by Toronto from Texas in compensation pool for loss of free agent Cliff Johnson ... Bricklayer by trade earned $1,166,167 from Jays last year.

Year	Club	G	IP	W	L	Pct.	SO	BB	H	ERA
1982	Texas	8	15⅔	1	0	1.000	9	8	14	1.15
1983	Texas	8	16	1	0	1.000	17	4	16	3.38
1984	Texas	25	28⅓	1	1	.500	25	20	36	6.35
1985	Toronto	28	40	3	3	.500	42	8	29	2.03
1986	Toronto	63	91⅓	9	5	.643	118	32	63	3.35
1987	Toronto	72	94	0	6	.000	128	25	62	2.49
1988	Toronto	52	68	4	4	.500	66	24	60	2.91
1989	Toronto	64	89	8	3	.727	116	25	66	1.92
1990	Toronto	61	74⅔	2	4	.333	75	19	58	2.17
	Totals	381	517	29	26	.527	596	165	404	2.72

DAVID WELLS 27 6-4 225   Bats L Throws L

Shifted to rotation after 126 consecutive relief appearances and responded well ... Compiled second-best ERA among Jays starters at 3.14 ... Worked at least six innings in 20 of 25 starts ... Compiled 10-5 record with 3.11 ERA as starter, 1-1 with 3.38 ERA as reliever ... Before 1990 season, he had not started a game in majors since July 4, 1987 ... Born May 20, 1963, in Torrance, Cal. ... Toronto's second-round choice in 1982 draft ... His 1990 salary: $275,000.

Year	Club	G	IP	W	L	Pct.	SO	BB	H	ERA
1987	Toronto	18	29⅓	4	3	.571	32	12	37	3.99
1988	Toronto	41	64⅓	3	5	.375	56	31	65	4.62
1989	Toronto	54	86⅓	7	4	.636	78	28	66	2.40
1990	Toronto	43	189	11	6	.647	115	45	165	3.14
	Totals	156	369	25	18	.581	281	116	333	3.29

DAVE STIEB 33 6-0 195   Bats R Throws R

Long-time ace established club records for victories and winning percentage with 18-6 record ... Fired first no-hitter in Blue Jays' history, Sept. 2 at Cleveland ... He had come within one out on several previous occasions ... Toronto's all-time leader with 166 victories ... Appeared in All-Star Game for seventh time, tying Early Wynn for most appearances by AL pitcher ... Born July 22, 1957, in Santa Ana, Cal. ... Toronto's fifth-round selection in 1978 draft . . . Toronto's best-paid pitcher in 1990 at $1.6 million.

Year	Club	G	IP	W	L	Pct.	SO	BB	H	ERA
1979	Toronto	18	129	8	8	.500	52	48	139	4.33
1980	Toronto	34	243	12	15	.444	108	83	232	3.70
1981	Toronto	25	184	11	10	.524	89	61	148	3.18
1982	Toronto	38	288⅓	17	14	.548	141	75	271	3.25
1983	Toronto	36	278	17	12	.586	187	93	223	3.04
1984	Toronto	35	267	16	8	.667	198	88	215	2.83
1985	Toronto	36	265	14	13	.519	167	96	206	2.48
1986	Toronto	37	205	7	12	.368	127	87	239	4.74
1987	Toronto	33	185	13	9	.591	115	87	164	4.09
1988	Toronto	32	207⅓	16	8	.667	147	79	157	3.04
1989	Toronto	33	206⅔	17	8	.680	101	76	164	3.35
1990	Toronto	33	208⅔	18	6	.750	125	64	179	2.93
	Totals	390	2667	166	123	.574	1557	937	2337	3.34

KEN DAYLEY 32 6-0 180   Bats L Throws L

After spending entire career in NL, he switched leagues during offseason, signing three-year, $6.3-million contract as free agent . . . Became first free agent signed by Toronto since Dennis Lamp in 1984 . . . Decided to leave Cardinals after being relegated to long relief role in late 1990 despite limiting opposing hitters to .233 batting average . . . Made 58 relief appearances, yet saved just two games as Lee Smith became Cards' closer . . . Finished 17 games, often as mop-up man . . . Saved career-high 12 games in 1989 when injuries sidelined closer Todd Worrell . . . Bounced back from career-threatening elbow surgery in 1987 . . . Born Feb. 25, 1959, in Jerome, Idaho . . . Selected by Braves in first round of 1980 draft . . . Traded to Cardinals along with Mike Jorgensen for Ken Oberkfell, June 15, 1984 . . . Earned $925,000 in 1990.

Year	Club	G	IP	W	L	Pct.	SO	BB	H	ERA
1982	Atlanta	20	71⅓	5	6	.455	34	25	79	4.54
1983	Atlanta	24	104⅔	5	8	.385	70	39	100	4.30
1984	Atl.-St.L.	7	23⅔	0	5	.000	10	11	44	7.99
1985	St. Louis	57	65⅓	4	4	.500	62	18	65	2.76
1986	St. Louis	31	38⅔	0	3	.000	33	11	42	3.26
1987	St. Louis	53	61	9	5	.643	63	33	52	2.66
1988	St. Louis	54	55⅓	2	7	.222	38	19	48	2.77
1989	St. Louis	71	75⅓	4	3	.571	40	30	63	2.87
1990	St. Louis	58	73⅓	4	4	.500	51	30	63	3.56
	Totals	375	568⅔	33	45	.423	401	216	556	3.63

JIMMY KEY 29 6-1 190   **Bats R Throws L**

Continues to be a quality starter, although he is injury-prone ... Pulled right hamstring in late May and was disabled until June 22 ... Rebounded from surgery on Oct. 24, 1989 to repair partial rotator cuff tear ... Jays' all-time leader among left-handers with 83 victories ... Boasted 4-1 strikeout-walk ratio ... Placed second to Boston's Roger Clemens in 1987 Cy Young voting and won league's ERA crown with 2.87 mark ... Born April 22, 1961, in Huntsville, Ala. ... Toronto's third-round choice in 1982 draft ... Wife, Cindy, doubles as his agent ... Earned $1,466,667 in 1990.

Year	Club	G	IP	W	L	Pct.	SO	BB	H	ERA
1984	Toronto	63	62	4	5	.444	44	32	70	4.65
1985	Toronto	35	212⅔	14	6	.700	85	50	188	3.00
1986	Toronto	36	232	14	11	.560	141	74	222	3.57
1987	Toronto	36	261	17	8	.680	161	66	210	2.76
1988	Toronto	21	131⅓	12	5	.706	65	30	127	3.29
1989	Toronto	33	216	13	14	.481	118	27	226	3.88
1990	Toronto	27	154⅔	13	7	.650	88	22	169	4.25
	Totals	251	1269⅔	87	56	.608	702	301	1212	3.47

TOP PROSPECTS

MARK WHITEN 24 6-3 215   **Bats R Throws R**

Right fielder bears close watching after being named top prospect in International League by *Baseball America* ... Batted .290 with 14 homers, 48 RBI and 14 stolen bases for Syracuse (AAA) ... Blessed with rifle arm ... Born Nov. 25, 1966, in Pensacola, Fla. ... Toronto's fifth-round choice in January 1986 draft.

AL LEITER 25 6-3 210   **Bats L Throws L**

Has a chance to work his way into pitching plans ... Performed well for Syracuse (AAA) in final starts there, going 2-2 with 1.15 ERA in last seven starts ... Made four relief appearances for Toronto, supplying 6⅓ scoreless innings ... Born Oct. 23, 1965, in Toms River, N.J. ... Acquired from Yankees, April 30, 1989, for Jesse Barfield.

EDDIE ZOSKY 23 6-0 175　　　　　　**Bats R Throws R**
With Tony Fernandez gone, he has shot at shortstop . . . Batted
.271 with three homers and 45 RBI for Knoxville (AA) . . . Born
Feb. 10, 1968, in Whittier, Cal. . . . Chosen in first round of 1989
draft . . . Donated part of signing bonus to Toronto Hospital for
Sick Children.

TOM QUINLAN 23 6-3 190　　　　　　**Bats R Throws R**
Third baseman has come far since becoming 27th-round pick in
1986 draft . . . Chosen team MVP at Knoxville (AA), batting .258
with 15 home runs, 51 RBI . . . Born March 27, 1968, in St. Paul,
Minn. . . . Also drafted by NHL's Calgary Flames in 1986.

MANAGER CITO GASTON: Narrowly missed guiding
86-76 Jays to second straight AL East crown
. . . Generally acknowledged to have most talented club in division, but Jays are as weak in
fundamentals under him as they were under his
predecessor . . . Soft-spoken manager who
rarely shows emotion . . . Originally signed as
a player by Milwaukee Braves . . . Selected by
San Diego in 1969 NL expansion draft, trig-
gering the start of a 10-year major-league career . . . Represented
San Diego in 1970 All-Star Game . . . Traded by San Diego to
Atlanta following 1974 season . . . Used primarily as utility player
by Atlanta . . . Made coaching debut as Braves' minor-league batting instructor in 1981 . . . Made significant strides working with
Blue Jays' hitters in 1982 . . . Stressed mental aspects of batting
. . . Team average improved 36 points in his first year . . . Born
March 17, 1944, in San Antonio . . . Owns 163-125 major-league
managerial record.

ALL-TIME BLUE JAY SEASON RECORDS

BATTING: Tony Fernandez, .322, 1987
HRs: George Bell, 47, 1987
RBI: George Bell, 134, 1987
STEALS: Damaso Garcia, 54, 1982
WINS: Dave Stieb, 18, 1990
STRIKEOUTS: Dave Stieb, 198, 1984

ALL-TIME MAJOR LEAGUE RECORDS

National	American

Batting (Season)
Average
.438 Hugh Duffy, Boston, 1894 .422 Napoleon Lajoie, Phila., 1901
.424 Rogers Hornsby, St. Louis, 1924

At Bat
701 Juan Samuel, Phila., 1984 705 Willie Wilson, Kansas City, 1980

Runs
196 William Hamilton, Phila., 1894 177 Babe Ruth, New York, 1921
158 Chuck Klein, Phila., 1930

Hits
254 Frank J. O'Doul, Phila., 1929 257 George Sisler, St. Louis, 1920
254 Bill Terry, New York, 1930

Doubles
64 Joseph M. Medwick, St. L., 1936 67 Earl W. Webb, Boston, 1931

Triples
36 J. Owen Wilson, Pitts., 1912 26 Joseph Jackson, Cleve., 1912
26 Samuel Crawford, Detroit, 1914

Home Runs
56 Hack Wilson, Chicago, 1930 61 Roger Maris, New York, 1961

Runs Batted In
190 Hack Wilson, Chicago, 1930 184 Lou Gehrig, New York, 1931

Stolen Bases
118 Lou Brock, St. Louis, 1974 130 Rickey Henderson, Oakland, 1982

Bases on Balls
148 Eddie Stanky, Brooklyn, 1945 170 Babe Ruth, New York, 1923
148 Jim Wynn, Houston, 1969

Strikeouts
189 Bobby Bonds, S.F., 1970 186 Rob Deer, Milwaukee, 1987

Pitching (Season)
Games
106 Mike Marshall, L.A., 1974 88 Wilbur Wood, Chicago, 1968

Innings Pitched
434 Joseph J. McGinnity, N.Y., 1903 464 Edward Walsh, Chicago, 1908

Victories
37 Christy Mathewson, N.Y., 1908 41 Jack Chesbro, New York, 1904

Losses
29 Victor Willis, Boston, 1905 26 John Townsend, Wash., 1904
26 Robert Groom, Wash., 1909

Strikeouts
(Left-hander)
382 Sandy Koufax, Los Angeles, 1965 343 Rube Waddell, Phila., 1904
(Right-hander)
313 J.R. Richard, Houston, 1979 383 Nolan Ryan, Cal., 1973

Bases on Balls
185 Sam Jones, Chicago, 1955 208 Bob Feller, Cleveland, 1938

Earned-Run Average
(Minimum 200 Innings)
1.12 Bob Gibson, St. L., 1968 1.01 Hubert Leonard, Boston, 1914

Shutouts
16 Grover C. Alexander, Phila., 1916 13 John W. Coombs, Phila., 1910

MAJOR LEAGUE YEAR-BY-YEAR LEADERS

NATIONAL LEAGUE MVP

Year	Player, Club
1931	Frank Frisch, St. Louis Cardinals
1932	Chuck Klein, Philadelphia Phillies
1933	Carl Hubbell, New York Giants
1934	Dizzy Dean, St. Louis Cardinals
1935	Gabby Hartnett, Chicago Cubs
1936	Carl Hubbell, New York Giants
1937	Joe Medwick, St. Louis Cardinals
1938	Ernie Lombardi, Cincinnati Reds
1939	Bucky Walters, Cincinnati Reds
1940	Frank McCormick, Cincinnati Reds
1941	Dolph Camilli, Brooklyn Dodgers
1942	Mort Cooper, St. Louis Cardinals
1943	Stan Musial, St. Louis Cardinals
1944	Marty Marion, St. Louis Cardinals
1945	Phil Cavarretta, Chicago Cubs
1946	Stan Musial, St. Louis Cardinals
1947	Bob Elliott, Boston Braves
1948	Stan Musial, St. Louis Cardinals
1949	Jackie Robinson, Brooklyn Dodgers
1950	Jim Konstanty, Philadelphia Phillies
1951	Roy Campanella, Brooklyn Dodgers
1952	Hank Sauer, Chicago Cubs
1953	Roy Campanella, Brooklyn Dodgers
1954	Willie Mays, New York Giants
1955	Roy Campanella, Brooklyn Dodgers
1956	Don Newcombe, Brooklyn Dodgers
1957	Hank Aaron, Milwaukee Braves
1958	Ernie Banks, Chicago Cubs
1959	Ernie Banks, Chicago Cubs
1960	Dick Groat, Pittsburgh Pirates

Year	Player, Club
1961	Frank Robinson, Cincinnati Reds
1962	Maury Wills, Los Angeles Dodgers
1963	Sandy Koufax, Los Angeles Dodgers
1964	Ken Boyer, St. Louis Cardinals
1965	Willie Mays, San Francisco Giants
1966	Roberto Clemente, Pittsburgh Pirates
1967	Orlando Cepeda, St. Louis Cardinals
1968	Bob Gibson, St. Louis Cardinals
1969	Willie McCovey, San Francisco Giants
1970	Johnny Bench, Cincinnati Reds
1971	Joe Torre, St. Louis Cardinals
1972	Johnny Bench, Cincinnati Reds
1973	Pete Rose, Cincinnati Reds
1974	Steve Garvey, Los Angeles Dodgers
1975	Joe Morgan, Cincinnati Reds
1976	Joe Morgan, Cincinnati Reds
1977	George Foster, Cincinnati Reds
1978	Dave Parker, Pittsburgh Pirates
1979	Keith Hernandez, St. Louis Cardinals
	Willie Stargell, Pittsburgh Pirates
1980	Mike Schmidt, Philadelphia Phillies
1981	Mike Schmidt, Philadelphia Phillies
1982	Dale Murphy, Atlanta Braves
1983	Dale Murphy, Atlanta Braves
1984	Ryne Sandberg, Chicago Cubs
1985	Willie McGee, St. Louis Cardinals
1986	Mike Schmidt, Philadelphia Phillies
1987	Andre Dawson, Chicago Cubs
1988	Kirk Gibson, Los Angeles Dodgers
1989	Kevin Mitchell, San Francisco Giants
1990	Barry Bonds, Pittsburgh Pirates

AMERICAN LEAGUE MVP

Year	Player, Club
1931	Lefty Grove, Philadelphia Athletics
1932	Jimmy Foxx, Philadelphia Athletics
1933	Jimmy Foxx, Philadelphia Athletics
1934	Mickey Cochrane, Detroit Tigers
1935	Hank Greenberg, Detroit Tigers
1936	Lou Gehrig, New York Yankees
1937	Charley Gehringer, Detroit Tigers
1938	Jimmy Foxx, Boston Red Sox

Year Player, Club
1939 Joe DiMaggio, New York Yankees
1940 Hank Greenberg, Detroit Tigers
1941 Joe DiMaggio, New York Yankees
1942 Joe Gordon, New York Yankees
1943 Spud Chandler, New York Yankees
1944 Hal Newhouser, Detroit Tigers
1945 Hal Newhouser, Detroit Tigers
1946 Ted Williams, Boston Red Sox
1947 Joe DiMaggio, New York Yankees
1948 Lou Boudreau, Cleveland Indians
1949 Ted Williams, Boston Red Sox
1950 Phil Rizzuto, New York Yankees
1951 Yogi Berra, New York Yankees
1942 Bobby Shantz, Philadelphia Athletics
1953 Al Rosen, Cleveland Indians
1954 Yogi Berra, New York Yankees
1955 Yogi Berra, New York Yankees
1956 Mickey Mantle, New York Yankees
1957 Mickey Mantle, New York Yankees
1958 Jackie Jensen, Boston Red Sox
1959 Nellie Fox, Chicago White Sox
1960 Roger Maris, New York Yankees
1961 Roger Maris, New York Yankees
1962 Mickey Mantle, New York Yankees
1963 Elston Howard, New York Yankees
1964 Brooks Robinson, Baltimore Orioles
1965 Zoilo Versalles, Minnesota Twins
1966 Frank Robinson, Baltimore Orioles
1967 Carl Yastrzemski, Boston Red Sox
1968 Dennis McLain, Detroit Tigers
1969 Harmon Killebrew, Minnesota Twins
1970 Boog Powell, Baltimore Orioles
1971 Vida Blue, Oakland A's
1972 Dick Allen, Chicago White Sox
1973 Reggie Jackson, Oakland A's
1974 Jeff Burroughs, Texas Rangers
1975 Fred Lynn, Boston Red Sox
1976 Thurman Munson, New York Yankees
1977 Rod Carew, Minnesota Twins
1978 Jim Rice, Boston Red Sox
1979 Don Baylor, California Angels
1980 George Brett, Kansas City Royals
1981 Rollie Fingers, Milwaukee Brewers

Year	Player, Club
1982	Robin Yount, Milwaukee Brewers
1983	Cal Ripken Jr., Baltimore Orioles
1984	Willie Hernandez, Detroit Tigers
1985	Don Mattingly, New York Yankees
1986	Roger Clemens, Boston Red Sox
1987	George Bell, Toronto Blue Jays
1988	Jose Canseco, Oakland A's
1989	Robin Yount, Milwaukee Brewers
1990	Rickey Henderson, Oakland A's

AMERICAN LEAGUE
Batting Champions

Year	Player, Club	Avg.
1901	Napoleon Lajoie, Philadelphia Athletics	.422
1902	Ed Delahanty, Washington Senators	.376
1903	Napoleon Lajoie, Cleveland Indians	.355
1904	Napoleon Lajoie, Cleveland Indians	.381
1905	Elmer Flick, Cleveland Indians	.306
1906	George Stone, St. Louis Browns	.358
1907	Ty Cobb, Detroit Tigers	.350
1908	Ty Cobb, Detroit Tigers	.324
1909	Ty Cobb, Detroit Tigers	.377
1910	Ty Cobb, Detroit Tigers	.385
1911	Ty Cobb, Detroit Tigers	.420
1912	Ty Cobb, Detroit Tigers	.410
1913	Ty Cobb, Detroit Tigers	.390
1914	Ty Cobb, Detroit Tigers	.368
1915	Ty Cobb, Detroit Tigers	.370
1916	Tris Speaker, Cleveland Indians	.386
1917	Ty Cobb, Detroit Tigers	.383
1918	Ty Cobb, Detroit Tigers	.382
1919	Ty Cobb, Detroit Tigers	.384
1920	George Sisler, St. Louis Browns	.407
1921	Harry Heilmann, Detroit Tigers	.393
1922	George Sisler, St. Louis Browns	.420
1923	Harry Heilmann, Detroit Tigers	.398
1924	Babe Ruth, New York Yankees	.378
1925	Harry Heilmann, Detroit Tigers	.393
1926	Heinie Manush, Detroit Tigers	.377
1927	Harry Heilmann, Detroit Tigers	.398
1928	Goose Goslin, Washington Senators	.379

Year	Player, Club	Avg.
1929	Lew Fonseca, Cleveland Indians	.369
1930	Al Simmons, Philadelphia Athletics	.381
1931	Al Simmons, Philadelphia Athletics	.390
1932	David Alexander, Detroit Tigers-Boston Red Sox	.367
1933	Jimmy Foxx, Philadelphia Athletics	.356
1934	Lou Gehrig, New York Yankees	.365
1935	Buddy Myer, Washington Senators	.349
1936	Luke Appling, Chicago White Sox	.388
1937	Charlie Gehringer, Detroit Tigers	.371
1938	Jimmy Foxx, Boston Red Sox	.349
1939	Joe DiMaggio, New York Yankees	.381
1940	Joe DiMaggio, New York Yankees	.352
1941	Ted Williams, Boston Red Sox	.406
1942	Ted Williams, Boston Red Sox	.356
1943	Luke Appling, Chicago White Sox	.328
1944	Lou Boudreau, Cleveland Indians	.327
1945	Snuffy Stirnweiss, New York Yankees	.309
1946	Mickey Vernon, Washington Senators	.353
1947	Ted Williams, Boston Red Sox	.343
1948	Ted Williams, Boston Red Sox	.369
1949	George Kell, Detroit Tigers	.343
1950	Billy Goodman, Boston Red Sox	.354
1951	Ferris Fain, Philadelphia Athletics	.344
1952	Ferris Fain, Philadelphia Athletics	.327
1953	Mickey Vernon, Washington Senators	.337
1954	Bobby Avila, Cleveland Indians	.341
1955	Al Kaline, Detroit Tigers	.340
1956	Mickey Mantle, New York Yankees	.353
1957	Ted Williams, Boston Red Sox	.388
1958	Ted Williams, Boston Red Sox	.328
1959	Harvey Kuenn, Detroit Tigers	.353
1960	Pete Runnels, Boston Red Sox	.320
1961	Norm Cash, Detroit Tigers	.361
1962	Pete Runnels, Boston Red Sox	.326
1963	Carl Yastrzemski, Boston Red Sox	.321
1964	Tony Oliva, Minnesota Twins	.323
1965	Tony Oliva, Minnesota Twins	.321
1966	Frank Robinson, Baltimore Orioles	.316
1967	Carl Yastrzemski, Boston Red Sox	.326
1968	Carl Yastrzemski, Boston Red Sox	.301
1969	Rod Carew, Minnesota Twins	.332
1970	Alex Johnson, California Angels	.329
1971	Tony Oliva, Minnesota Twins	.337

Year	Player, Club	Avg.
1972	Rod Carew, Minnesota Twins	.318
1973	Rod Carew, Minnesota Twins	.350
1974	Rod Carew, Minnesota Twins	.364
1975	Rod Carew, Minnesota Twins	.359
1976	George Brett, Kansas City Royals	.333
1977	Rod Carew, Minnesota Twins	.388
1978	Rod Carew, Minnesota Twins	.333
1979	Fred Lynn, Boston Red Sox	.333
1980	George Brett, Kansas City Royals	.390
1981	Carney Lansford, Boston Red Sox	.336
1982	Willie Wilson, Kansas City Royals	.332
1983	Wade Boggs, Boston Red Sox	.361
1984	Don Mattingly, New York Yankees	.343
1985	Wade Boggs, Boston Red Sox	.368
1986	Wade Boggs, Boston Red Sox	.357
1987	Wade Boggs, Boston Red Sox	.363
1988	Wade Boggs, Boston Red Sox	.366
1989	Kirby Puckett, Minnesota Twins	.339
1990	George Brett, Kansas City Royals	.329

NATIONAL LEAGUE
Batting Champions

Year	Player, Club	Avg.
1876	Roscoe Barnes, Chicago	.403
1877	James White, Boston	.385
1878	Abner Dalrymple, Milwaukee	.356
1879	Cap Anson, Chicago	.407
1880	George Gore, Chicago	.365
1881	Cap Anson, Chicago	.399
1882	Dan Brouthers, Buffalo	.367
1883	Dan Brouthers, Buffalo	.371
1884	Jim O'Rourke, Buffalo	.350
1885	Roger Connor, New York	.371
1886	Mike Kelly, Chicago	.388
1887	Cap Anson, Chicago	.421
1888	Cap Anson, Chicago	.343
1889	Dan Brouthers, Boston	.373
1890	Jack Glassock, New York	.336
1891	Billy Hamilton, Philadelphia	.338
1892	Cupid Childs, Cleveland	.335
	Dan Brouthers, Brooklyn	.335

Year	Player, Club	Avg.
1893	Hugh Duffy, Boston	.378
1894	Hugh Duffy, Boston	.438
1895	Jesse Burkett, Cleveland	.423
1896	Jesse Burkett, Cleveland	.410
1897	Willie Keeler, Baltimore	.432
1898	Willie Keeler, Baltimore	.379
1899	Ed Delahanty, Philadelphia	.408
1900	Honus Wagner, Pittsburgh	.380
1901	Jesse Burkett, St. Louis Cardinals	.382
1902	C.H. Beaumont, Pittsburgh Pirates	.357
1903	Honus Wagner, Pittsburgh Pirates	.355
1904	Honus Wagner, Pittsburgh Pirates	.349
1905	J. Bentley Seymour, Cincinnati Reds	.377
1906	Honus Wagner, Pittsburgh Pirates	.339
1907	Honus Wagner, Pittsburgh Pirates	.350
1908	Honus Wagner, Pittsburgh Pirates	.354
1909	Honus Wagner, Pittsburgh Pirates	.339
1910	Sherwood Magee, Philadelphia Phillies	.331
1911	Honus Wagner, Pittsburgh Pirates	.334
1912	Heinie Zimmerman, Chicago Cubs	.372
1913	Jake Daubert, Brooklyn Dodgers	.350
1914	Jake Daubert, Brooklyn Dodgers	.329
1915	Larry Doyle, New York Giants	.320
1916	Hal Chase, Cincinnati Reds	.339
1917	Edd Roush, Cincinnati Reds	.341
1918	Zack Wheat, Brooklyn Dodgers	.335
1919	Edd Roush, Cincinnati Reds	.321
1920	Rogers Hornsby, St. Louis Cardinals	.370
1921	Rogers Hornsby, St. Louis Cardinals	.397
1922	Rogers Hornsby, St. Louis Cardinals	.401
1923	Rogers Hornsby, St. Louis Cardinals	.384
1924	Rogers Hornsby, St. Louis Cardinals	.424
1925	Rogers Hornsby, St. Louis Cardinals	.403
1926	Bubbles Hargrave, Cincinnati Reds	.353
1927	Paul Waner, Pittsburgh Pirates	.380
1928	Rogers Hornsby, Boston Braves	.387
1929	Lefty O'Doul, Philadelphia Phillies	.398
1930	Bill Terry, New York Giants	.401
1931	Chick Hafey, St. Louis Cardinals	.349
1932	Lefty O'Doul, Brooklyn Dodgers	.368
1933	Chuck Klein, Philadelphia Phillies	.368
1934	Paul Waner, Pittsburgh Pirates	.362
1935	Arky Vaughan, Pittsburgh Pirates	.385

Year	Player, Club	Avg.
1936	Paul Waner, Pittsburgh Pirates	.373
1937	Joe Medwick, St. Louis Cardinals	.374
1938	Ernie Lombardi, Cincinnati Reds	.342
1939	Johnny Mize, St. Louis Cardinals	.349
1940	Debs Garms, Pittsburgh Pirates	.355
1941	Pete Reiser, Brooklyn Dodgers	.343
1942	Ernie Lombardi, Boston Braves	.330
1943	Stan Musial, St. Louis Cardinals	.330
1944	Dixie Walker, Brooklyn Dodgers	.357
1945	Phil Cavarretta, Chicago Cubs	.355
1946	Stan Musial, St. Louis Cardinals	.365
1947	Harry Walker, St. L. Cardinals-Phila. Phillies	.363
1948	Stan Musial, St. Louis Cardinals	.376
1949	Jackie Robinson, Brooklyn Dodgers	.342
1950	Stan Musial, St. Louis Cardinals	.346
1951	Stan Musial, St. Louis Cardinals	.355
1952	Stan Musial, St. Louis Cardinals	.336
1953	Carl Furillo, Brooklyn Dodgers	.344
1954	Willie Mays, New York Giants	.345
1955	Richie Ashburn, Philadelphia Phillies	.338
1956	Hank Aaron, Milwaukee Braves	.328
1957	Stan Musial, St. Louis Cardinals	.351
1958	Richie Ashburn, Philadelphia Phillies	.350
1959	Hank Aaron, Milwaukee Braves	.328
1960	Dick Groat, Pittsburgh Pirates	.325
1961	Roberto Clemente, Pittsburgh Pirates	.351
1962	Tommy Davis, Los Angeles Dodgers	.346
1963	Tommy Davis, Los Angeles Dodgers	.326
1964	Roberto Clemente, Pittsburgh Pirates	.339
1965	Roberto Clemente, Pittsburgh Pirates	.329
1966	Matty Alou, Pittsburgh Pirates	.342
1967	Roberto Clemente, Pittsburgh Pirates	.357
1968	Pete Rose, Cincinnati Reds	.335
1969	Pete Rose, Cincinnati Reds	.348
1970	Rico Carty, Atlanta Braves	.366
1971	Joe Torre, St. Louis Cardinals	.363
1972	Billy Williams, Chicago Cubs	.333
1973	Pete Rose, Cincinnati Reds	.338
1974	Ralph Garr, Atlanta Braves	.353
1975	Bill Madlock, Chicago Cubs	.354
1976	Bill Madlock, Chicago Cubs	.339
1977	Dave Parker, Pittsburgh Pirates	.338
1978	Dave Parker, Pittsburgh Pirates	.334

Year	Player, Club	Avg.
1979	Keith Hernandez, St. Louis Cardinals	.344
1980	Bill Buckner, Chicago Cubs	.324
1981	Bill Madlock, Pittsburgh Pirates	.341
1982	Al Oliver, Montreal Expos	.331
1983	Bill Madlock, Pittsburgh Pirates	.323
1984	Tony Gwynn, San Diego Padres	.351
1985	Willie McGee, St. Louis Cardinals	.353
1986	Tim Raines, Montreal Expos	.334
1987	Tony Gwynn, San Diego Padres	.370
1988	Tony Gwynn, San Diego Padres	.313
1989	Tony Gwynn, San Diego Padres	.336
1990	Willie McGee, St. Louis Cardinals	.335

NATIONAL LEAGUE
Home Run Leaders

Year	Player, Club	HRs
1900	Herman Long, Boston Nationals	12
1901	Sam Crawford, Cincinnati Reds	16
1902	Tom Leach, Pittsburgh Pirates	6
1903	Jim Sheckard, Brooklyn Dodgers	9
1904	Harry Lumley, Brooklyn Dodgers	9
1905	Fred Odwell, Cincinnati Reds	9
1906	Tim Jordan, Brooklyn Dodgers	12
1907	Dave Brain, Boston Nationals	10
1908	Tim Jordan, Brooklyn Dodgers	12
1909	Jim Murray, New York Giants	7
1910	Fred Beck, Boston Nationals	10
	Frank Schulte, Chicago Cubs	10
1911	Frank Schulte, Chicago Cubs	21
1912	Heinie Zimmerman, Chicago Cubs	14
1913	Gavvy Cravath, Philadelphia Phillies	19
1914	Gavvy Cravath, Philadelphia Phillies	19
1915	Gavvy Cravath, Philadelphia Phillies	24
1916	Dave Robertson, New York Giants	12
	Cy Williams, Chicago Cubs	12
1917	Gavvy Cravath, Philadelphia Phillies	12
	Dave Robertson, New York Giants	12
1918	Gavvy Cravath, Philadelphia Phillies	8
1919	Gavvy Cravath, Philadelphia Phillies	12
1920	Cy Williams, Philadelphia Phillies	15
1921	George Kelly, New York Giants	23

Year	Player, Club	HRs
1922	Rogers Hornsby, St. Louis Cardinals	42
1923	Cy Williams, Philadelphia Phillies	41
1924	Jack Fournier, Brooklyn Dodgers	27
1925	Rogers Hornsby, St. Louis Cardinals	39
1926	Hack Wilson, Chicago Cubs	21
1927	Cy Williams, Philadelphia Phillies	30
	Hack Wilson, Chicago Cubs	30
1928	Jim Bottomley, St. Louis Cardinals	31
	Hack Wilson, Chicago Cubs	31
1929	Chuck Klein, Philadelphia Phillies	43
1930	Hack Wilson, Chicago Cubs	56
1931	Chuck Klein, Philadelphia Phillies	31
1932	Chuck Klein, Philadelphia Phillies	38
	Mel Ott, New York Giants	38
1933	Chuck Klein, Philadelphia Phillies	28
1934	Rip Collins, St. Louis Cardinals	35
	Mel Ott, New York Giants	35
1935	Wally Berger, Boston Braves	34
1936	Mel Ott, New York Giants	33
1937	Joe Medwick, St. Louis Cardinals	31
	Mel Ott, New York Giants	31
1938	Mel Ott, New York Giants	36
1939	Johnny Mize, St. Louis Cardinals	28
1940	Johnny Mize, St. Louis Cardinals	43
1941	Dolph Camilli, Brooklyn Dodgers	34
1942	Mel Ott, New York Giants	30
1943	Bill Nicholson, Chicago Cubs	29
1944	Bill Nicholson, Chicago Cubs	33
1945	Tommy Holmes, Boston Braves	28
1946	Ralph Kiner, Pittsburgh Pirates	23
1947	Ralph Kiner, Pittsburgh Pirates	51
	Johnny Mize, New York Giants	51
1948	Ralph Kiner, Pittsburgh Pirates	40
	Johnny Mize, New York Giants	40
1949	Ralph Kiner, Pittsburgh Pirates	54
1950	Ralph Kiner, Pittsburgh Pirates	47
1951	Ralph Kiner, Pittsburgh Pirates	42
1952	Ralph Kiner, Pittsburgh Pirates	37
	Hank Sauer, Chicago Cubs	37
1953	Eddie Mathews, Milwaukee Braves	47
1954	Ted Kluszewski, Cincinnati Reds	49
1955	Willie Mays, New York Giants	51
1956	Duke Snider, Brooklyn Dodgers	43

Year	Player, Club	HRs
1957	Hank Aaron, Milwaukee Braves	44
1958	Ernie Banks, Chicago Cubs	47
1959	Eddie Mathews, Milwaukee Braves	46
1960	Ernie Banks, Chicago Cubs	41
1961	Orlando Cepeda, San Francisco Giants	46
1962	Willie Mays, San Francisco Giants	49
1963	Hank Aaron, Milwaukee Braves	44
	Willie McCovey, San Francisco Giants	44
1964	Willie Mays, San Francisco Giants	47
1965	Willie Mays, San Francisco Giants	52
1966	Hank Aaron, Atlanta Braves	44
1967	Hank Aaron, Atlanta Braves	39
1968	Willie McCovey, San Francisco Giants	36
1969	Willie McCovey, San Francisco Giants	45
1970	Johnny Bench, Cincinnati Reds	45
1971	Willie Stargell, Pittsburgh Pirates	48
1972	Johnny Bench, Cincinnati Reds	40
1973	Willie Stargell, Pittsburgh Pirates	44
1974	Mike Schmidt, Philadelphia Phillies	36
1975	Mike Schmidt, Philadelphia Phillies	38
1976	Mike Schmidt, Philadelphia Phillies	38
1977	George Foster, Cincinnati Reds	52
1978	George Foster, Cincinnati Reds	40
1979	Dave Kingman, Chicago Cubs	48
1980	Mike Schmidt, Philadelphia Phillies	48
1981	Mike Schmidt, Philadelphia Phillies	31
1982	Dave Kingman, New York Mets	37
1983	Mike Schmidt, Philadelphia Phillies	40
1984	Mike Schmidt, Philadelphia Phillies	36
1984	Dale Murphy, Atlanta Braves	36
1985	Dale Murphy, Atlanta Braves	37
1986	Mike Schmidt, Philadelphia Phillies	37
1987	Andre Dawson, Chicago Cubs	49
1988	Darryl Strawberry, New York Mets	39
1989	Kevin Mitchell, San Francisco Giants	47
1990	Ryne Sandberg, Chicago Cubs	40

AMERICAN LEAGUE
Home Run Leaders

Year	Player, Club	HRs
1901	Napoleon Lajoie, Philadelphia Athletics	13
1902	Ralph Seybold, Philadelphia Athletics	16
1903	John Freeman, Boston Pilgrims	13
1904	Harry Davis, Philadelphia Athletics	10
1905	Harry Davis, Philadelphia Athletics	8
1906	Harry Davis, Philadelphia Athletics	12
1907	Harry Davis, Philadelphia Athletics	8
1908	Sam Crawford, Detroit Tigers	7
1909	Ty Cobb, Detroit Tigers	9
1910	Garland Stahl, Boston Red Sox	10
1911	Frank (Home Run) Baker, Philadelphia Athletics	9
1912	Frank (Home Run) Baker, Philadelphia Athletics	10
1913	Frank (Home Run) Baker, Philadelphia Athletics	12
1914	Frank (Home Run) Baker, Philadelphia Athletics	8
	Sam Crawford, Detroit Tigers	8
1915	Bob Roth, Cleveland Indians	7
1916	Wally Pipp, New York Yankees	12
1917	Wally Pipp, New York Yankees	9
1918	Babe Ruth, Boston Red Sox	11
	Clarence Walker, Philadelphia Athletics	11
1919	Babe Ruth, Boston Red Sox	29
1920	Babe Ruth, New York Yankees	54
1921	Babe Ruth, New York Yankees	59
1922	Ken Williams, St. Louis Browns	39
1923	Babe Ruth, New York Yankees	41
1924	Babe Ruth, New York Yankees	46
1925	Bob Meusel, New York Yankees	33
1926	Babe Ruth, New York Yankees	47
1927	Babe Ruth, New York Yankees	60
1928	Babe Ruth, New York Yankees	54
1929	Babe Ruth, New York Yankees	46
1930	Babe Ruth, New York Yankees	49
1931	Babe Ruth, New York Yankees	46
	Lou Gehrig, New York Yankees	46
1932	Jimmy Foxx, Philadelphia Athletics	58
1933	Jimmy Foxx, Philadelphia Athletics	48
1934	Lou Gehrig, New York Yankees	49
1935	Hank Greenberg, Detroit Tigers	36
	Jimmy Fox, Philadelphia Athletics	36

Year	Player, Club	HRs
1936	Lou Gehrig, New York Yankees	49
1937	Joe DiMaggio, New York Yankees	46
1938	Hank Greenberg, Detroit Tigers	58
1939	Jimmy Foxx, Boston Red Sox	35
1940	Hank Greenberg, Detroit Tigers	41
1941	Ted Williams, Boston Red Sox	37
1942	Ted Williams, Boston Red Sox	36
1943	Rudy York, Detroit Tigers	34
1944	Nick Etten, New York Yankees	22
1945	Vern Stephens, St. Louis Browns	24
1946	Hank Greenberg, Detroit Tigers	44
1947	Ted Williams, Boston Red Sox	32
1948	Joe DiMaggio, New York Yankees	39
1949	Ted Williams, Boston Red Sox	43
1950	Al Rosen, Cleveland Indians	37
1951	Gus Zernial, Philadelphia Athletics	33
1952	Larry Doby, Cleveland Indians	32
1953	Al Rosen, Cleveland Indians	43
1954	Larry Doby, Cleveland Indians	32
1955	Mickey Mantle, New York Yankees	37
1956	Mickey Mantle, New York Yankees	52
1957	Roy Sievers, Washington Senators	42
1958	Mickey Mantle, New York Yankees	42
1959	Rocky Colavito, Cleveland Indians	42
	Harmon Killebrew, Washington Senators	42
1960	Mickey Mantle, New York Yankees	40
1961	Roger Maris, New York Yankees	61
1962	Harmon Killebrew, Minnesota Twins	48
1963	Harmon Killebrew, Minnesota Twins	45
1964	Harmon Killebrew, Minnesota Twins	49
1965	Tony Conigliaro, Boston Red Sox	32
1966	Frank Robinson, Baltimore Orioles	49
1967	Carl Yastrzemski, Boston Red Sox	44
	Harmon Killebrew, Minnesota Twins	44
1968	Frank Howard, Washington Senators	44
1969	Harmon Killebrew, Minnesota Twins	49
1970	Frank Howard, Washington Senators	44
1971	Bill Melton, Chicago White Sox	33
1972	Dick Allen, Chicago White Sox	37
1973	Reggie Jackson, Oakland A's	32
1974	Dick Allen, Chicago White Sox	32
1975	George Scott, Milwaukee Brewers	36
	Reggie Jackson, Oakland A's	36

Year	Player, Club	HRs
1976	Graig Nettles, New York Yankees	32
1977	Jim Rice, Boston Red Sox	39
1978	Jim Rice, Boston Red Sox	46
1979	Gorman Thomas, Milwaukee Brewers	45
1980	Ben Oglivie, Milwaukee Brewers	41
	Reggie Jackson, New York Yankees	41
1981	Bobby Grich, California Angels	22
	Eddie Murray, Baltimore Orioles	22
	Dwight Evans, Boston Red Sox	22
	Tony Armas, Oakland A's	22
1982	Reggie Jackson, California Angels	39
	Gorman Thomas, Milwaukee Brewers	39
1983	Jim Rice, Boston Red Sox	39
1984	Tony Armas, Boston Red Sox	43
1985	Darrell Evans, Detroit Tigers	40
1986	Jesse Barfield, Toronto Blue Jays	40
1987	Mark McGwire, Oakland A's	49
1988	Jose Canseco, Oakland A's	42
1989	Fred McGriff, Toronto Blue Jays	36
1990	Cecil Fielder, Detroit Tigers	51

CY YOUNG AWARD WINNERS

(Prior to 1967 there was a single overall major league award.)

Year	Player, Club
1956	Don Newcombe, Brooklyn Dodgers
1957	Warren Spahn, Milwaukee Braves
1958	Bob Turley, New York Yankees
1959	Early Wynn, Chicago White Sox
1960	Vernon Law, Pittsburgh Pirates
1961	Whitey Ford, New York Yankees
1962	Don Drysdale, Los Angeles Dodgers
1963	Sandy Koufax, Los Angeles Dodgers
1964	Dean Chance, Los Angeles Angels
1965	Sandy Koufax, Los Angeles Dodgers
1966	Sandy Koufax, Los Angeles Dodgers

AL CY YOUNG

Year	Player, Club
1967	Jim Lonborg, Boston Red Sox
1968	Dennis McLain, Detroit Tigers
1969	Mike Cuellar, Baltimore Orioles
	Dennis McLain, Detroit Tigers
1970	Jim Perry, Minnesota Twins
1971	Vida Blue, Oakland A's
1972	Gaylord Perry, Cleveland Indians
1973	Jim Palmer, Baltimore Orioles
1974	Jim Hunter, Oakland A's
1975	Jim Palmer, Baltimore Orioles
1976	Jim Palmer, Baltimore Orioles
1977	Sparky Lyle, New York Yankees
1978	Ron Guidry, New York Yankees
1979	Mike Flanagan, Baltimore Orioles
1980	Steve Stone, Baltimore Orioles
1981	Rollie Fingers, Milwaukee Brewers
1982	Pete Vuckovich, Milwaukee Brewers
1983	LaMarr Hoyt, Chicago White Sox
1984	Willie Hernandez, Detroit Tigers
1985	Bret Saberhagen, Kansas City Royals
1986	Roger Clemens, Boston Red Sox
1987	Roger Clemens, Boston Red Sox
1988	Frank Viola, Minnesota Twins
1989	Bret Saberhagen, Kansas City Royals
1990	Bob Welch, Oakland A's

NL CY YOUNG

Year	Player, Club
1967	Mike McCormick, San Francisco Giants
1968	Bob Gibson, St. Louis Cardinals
1969	Tom Seaver, New York Mets
1970	Bob Gibson, St. Louis Cardinals
1971	Ferguson Jenkins, Chicago Cubs
1972	Steve Carlton, Philadelphia Phillies
1973	Tom Seaver, New York Mets
1974	Mike Marshall, Los Angeles Dodgers
1975	Tom Seaver, New York Mets
1976	Randy Jones, San Diego Padres
1977	Steve Carlton, Philadelphia Phillies

Year	Player, Club
1978	Gaylord Perry, San Diego Padres
1979	Bruce Sutter, Chicago Cubs
1980	Steve Carlton, Philadelphia Phillies
1981	Fernando Valenzuela, Los Angeles Dodgers
1982	Steve Carlton, Philadelphia Phillies
1983	John Denny, Philadelphia Phillies
1984	Rick Sutcliffe, Chicago Cubs
1985	Dwight Gooden, New York Mets
1986	Mike Scott, Houston Astros
1987	Steve Bedrosian, Philadelphia Phillies
1988	Orel Hershiser, Los Angeles Dodgers
1989	Mark Davis, San Diego Padres
1990	Doug Drabek, Pittsburgh Pirates

NATIONAL LEAGUE
Rookie of Year

Year	Player, Club
1947	Jackie Robinson, Brooklyn Dodgers
1948	Al Dark, Boston Braves
1949	Don Newcombe, Brooklyn Dodgers
1950	Sam Jethroe, Boston Braves
1951	Willie Mays, New York Giants
1952	Joe Black, Brooklyn Dodgers
1953	Junior Gilliam, Brooklyn Dodgers
1954	Wally Moon, St. Louis Cardinals
1955	Bill Virdon, St. Louis Cardinals
1956	Frank Robinson, Cincinnati Reds
1957	Jack Sanford, Philadelphia Phillies
1958	Orlando Cepeda, San Francisco Giants
1959	Willie McCovey, San Francisco Giants
1960	Frank Howard, Los Angeles Dodgers
1961	Billy Williams, Chicago Cubs
1962	Kenny Hubbs, Chicago Cubs
1963	Pete Rose, Cincinnati Reds
1964	Richie Allen, Philadelphia Phillies
1965	Jim Lefebvre, Los Angeles Dodgers
1966	Tommy Helms, Cincinnati Reds
1967	Tom Seaver, New York Mets
1968	Johnny Bench, Cincinnati Reds
1969	Ted Sizemore, Los Angeles Dodgers

Year	Player, Club
1970	Carl Morton, Montreal Expos
1971	Earl Williams, Atlanta Braves
1972	Jon Matlack, New York Mets
1973	Gary Matthews, San Francisco Giants
1974	Bake McBride, St. Louis Cardinals
1975	John Montefusco, San Francisco Giants
1976	Pat Zachry, Cincinnati Reds
	Butch Metzger, San Diego Padres
1977	Andre Dawson, Montreal Expos
1978	Bob Horner, Atlanta Braves
1979	Rick Sutcliffe, Los Angeles Dodgers
1980	Steve Howe, Los Angeles Dodgers
1981	Fernando Valenzuela, Los Angeles Dodgers
1982	Steve Sax, Los Angeles Dodgers
1983	Darryl Strawberry, New York Mets
1984	Dwight Gooden, New York Mets
1985	Vince Coleman, St. Louis Cardinals
1986	Todd Worrell, St. Louis Cardinals
1987	Benito Santiago, San Diego Padres
1988	Chris Sabo, Cincinnati Reds
1989	Jerome Walton, Chicago Cubs
1990	Dave Justice, Atlanta Braves

AMERICAN LEAGUE
Rookie of Year

Year	Player, Club
1949	Roy Sievers, St. Louis Browns
1950	Walt Dropo, Boston Red Sox
1951	Gil McDougald, New York Yankees
1952	Harry Byrd, Philadelphia Athletics
1953	Harvey Kuenn, Detroit Tigers
1954	Bob Grim, New York Yankees
1955	Herb Score, Cleveland Indians
1956	Luis Aparicio, Chicago White Sox
1957	Tony Kubek, New York Yankees
1958	Albie Pearson, Washington Senators
1959	Bob Allison, Washington Senators
1960	Ron Hansen, Baltimore Orioles
1961	Don Schwall, Boston Red Sox
1962	Tom Tresh, New York Yankees

Year	Player, Club
1963	Gary Peters, Chicago White Sox
1964	Tony Oliva, Minnesota Twins
1965	Curt Blefary, Baltimore Orioles
1966	Tommie Agee, Chicago White Sox
1967	Rod Carew, Minnesota Twins
1968	Stan Bahnsen, New York Yankees
1969	Lou Piniella, Kansas City Royals
1970	Thurman Munson, New York Yankees
1971	Chris Chambliss, Cleveland Indians
1972	Carlton Fisk, Boston Red Sox
1973	Al Bumbry, Baltimore Orioles
1974	Mike Hargrove, Texas Rangers
1975	Fred Lynn, Boston Red Sox
1976	Mark Fidrych, Detroit Tigers
1977	Eddie Murray, Baltimore Orioles
1978	Lou Whitaker, Detroit Tigers
1979	John Castino, Minnesota Twins
	Alfredo Griffin, Toronto Blue Jays
1980	Joe Charboneau, Cleveland Indians
1981	Dave Righetti, New York Yankees
1982	Cal Ripken, Jr., Baltimore Orioles
1983	Ron Kittle, Chicago White Sox
1984	Alvin Davis, Seattle Mariners
1985	Ozzie Guillen, Chicago White Sox
1986	Jose Canseco, Oakland A's
1987	Mark McGwire, Oakland A's
1988	Walt Weiss, Oakland A's
1989	Gregg Olson, Baltimore Orioles
1990	Sandy Alomar Jr., Cleveland Indians

WORLD SERIES WINNERS

Year	A. L. Champion	N. L. Champion	World Series Winner
1903	Boston Red Sox	Pittsburgh Pirates	Boston, 5-3
1905	Philadelphia Athletics	New York Giants	New York, 4-1
1906	Chicago White Sox	Chicago Cubs	Chicago (AL), 4-2
1907	Detroit Tigers	Chicago Cubs	Chicago, 4-0-1
1908	Detroit Tigers	Chicago Cubs	Chicago, 4-1
1909	Detroit Tigers	Pittsburgh Pirates	Pittsburgh, 4-3
1910	Philadelphia Athletics	Chicago Cubs	Philadelphia, 4-1
1911	Philadelphia Athletics	New York Giants	Philadelphia, 4-2
1912	Boston Red Sox	New York Giants	Boston, 4-3-1
1913	Philadelphia Athletics	New York Giants	Philadelphia, 4-1
1914	Philadelphia Athletics	Boston Red Sox	Boston, 4-0
1915	Boston Red Sox	Philadelphia Phillies	Boston, 4-1
1916	Boston Red Sox	Brooklyn Dodgers	Boston, 4-1
1917	Chicago White Sox	New York Giants	Chicago, 4-2
1918	Boston Red Sox	Chicago Cubs	Boston, 4-2
1919	Chicago White Sox	Cincinnati Reds	Cincinnati, 5-3
1920	Cleveland Indians	Brooklyn Dodgers	Cleveland, 5-2
1921	New York Yankees	New York Giants	New York (NL), 5-3
1922	New York Yankees	New York Giants	New York (NL), 4-0-1
1923	New York Yankees	New York Giants	New York (AL), 4-2
1924	Washington Senators	New York Giants	Washington, 4-2
1925	Washington Senators	Pittsburgh Pirates	Pittsburgh, 4-3
1926	New York Yankees	St. Louis Cardinals	St. Louis, 4-3
1927	New York Yankees	Pittsburgh Pirates	New York, 4-0
1928	New York Yankees	St. Louis Cardinals	New York, 4-0
1929	Philadelphia Athletics	Chicago Cubs	Philadelphia, 4-2
1930	Philadelphia Athletics	St. Louis Cardinals	Philadelphia, 4-2
1931	Philadelphia Athletics	St. Louis Cardinals	St. Louis, 4-3
1932	New York Yankees	Chicago Cubs	New York, 4-0
1933	Washington Senators	New York Giants	New York, 4-1
1934	Detroit Tigers	St. Louis Cardinals	St. Louis, 4-3
1935	Detroit Tigers	Chicago Cubs	Detroit, 4-2
1936	New York Yankees	New York Giants	New York (AL), 4-2
1937	New York Yankees	New York Giants	New York (AL), 4-1
1938	New York Yankees	Chicago Cubs	New York, 4-0
1939	New York Yankees	Cincinnati Reds	New York, 4-0
1940	Detroit Tigers	Cincinnati Reds	Cincinnati, 4-3
1941	New York Yankees	Brooklyn Dodgers	New York, 4-1
1942	New York Yankees	St. Louis Cardinals	St. Louis, 4-1
1943	New York Yankees	St. Louis Cardinals	New York, 4-1
1944	St. Louis Browns	St. Louis Cardinals	St. Louis (NL), 4-2
1945	Detroit Tigers	Chicago Cubs	Detroit, 4-3
1946	Boston Red Sox	St. Louis Cardinals	St. Louis, 4-3
1947	New York Yankees	Brooklyn Dodgers	New York, 4-3
1948	Cleveland Indians	Boston Braves	Cleveland, 4-2
1949	New York Yankees	Brooklyn Dodgers	New York, 4-1
1950	New York Yankees	Philadelphia Phillies	New York, 4-0
1951	New York Yankees	New York Giants	New York (AL), 4-2
1952	New York Yankees	Brooklyn Dodgers	New York, 4-3
1953	New York Yankees	Brooklyn Dodgers	New York, 4-2
1954	Cleveland Indians	New York Giants	New York, 4-0

Year	A. L. Champion	N. L. Champion	World Series Winner
1955	New York Yankees	Brooklyn Dodgers	Brooklyn, 4-3
1956	New York Yankees	Brooklyn Dodgers	New York, 4-3
1957	New York Yankees	Milwaukee Braves	Milwaukee, 4-3
1958	New York Yankees	Milwaukee Braves	New York, 4-3
1959	Chicago White Sox	Los Angeles Dodgers	Los Angeles, 4-2
1960	New York Yankees	Pittsburgh Pirates	Pittsburgh, 4-3
1961	New York Yankees	Cincinnati Reds	New York, 4-1
1962	New York Yankees	San Francisco Giants	New York, 4-3
1963	New York Yankees	Los Angeles Dodgers	Los Angeles, 4-0
1964	New York Yankees	St. Louis Cardinals	St. Louis, 4-3
1965	Minnesota Twins	Los Angeles Dodgers	Los Angeles, 4-3
1966	Baltimore Orioles	Los Angeles Dodgers	Baltimore, 4-0
1967	Boston Red Sox	St. Louis Cardinals	St. Louis, 4-3
1968	Detroit Tigers	St. Louis Cardinals	Detroit, 4-3
1969	Baltimore Orioles	New York Mets	New York, 4-1
1970	Baltimore Orioles	Cincinnati Reds	Baltimore, 4-1
1971	Baltimore Orioles	Pittsburgh Pirates	Pittsburgh, 4-3
1972	Oakland A's	Cincinnati Reds	Oakland, 4-3
1973	Oakland A's	New York Mets	Oakland, 4-3
1974	Oakland A's	Los Angeles Dodgers	Oakland, 4-1
1975	Boston Red Sox	Cincinnati Reds	Cincinnati, 4-3
1976	New York Yankees	Cincinnati Reds	Cincinnati, 4-0
1977	New York Yankees	Los Angeles Dodgers	New York, 4-2
1978	New York Yankees	Los Angeles Dodgers	New York, 4-2
1979	Baltimore Orioles	Pittsburgh Pirates	Pittsburgh, 4-3
1980	Kansas City Royals	Philadelphia Phillies	Philadelphia, 4-2
1981	New York Yankees	Los Angeles Dodgers	Los Angeles, 4-2
1982	Milwaukee Brewers	St. Louis Cardinals	St. Louis, 4-3
1983	Baltimore Orioles	Philadelphia Phillies	Baltimore, 4-1
1984	Detroit Tigers	San Diego Padres	Detroit, 4-1
1985	Kansas City Royals	St. Louis Cardinals	Kansas City, 4-3
1986	Boston Red Sox	New York Mets	New York, 4-3
1987	Minnesota Twins	St. Louis Cardinals	Minnesota, 4-3
1988	Oakland A's	Los Angeles Dodgers	Los Angeles, 4-1
1989	Oakland A's	San Francisco Giants	Oakland, 4-0
1990	Oakland A's	Cincinnati Reds	Cincinnati, 4-0

1990 WORLD SERIES

Game 1
At CINCINNATI
Tuesday, October 16 (night)

Oakland	000 000 000	0	9 1
Cincinnati	202 030 00x	7	10 0

STEWART, Burns and Nelson (5), Sanderson (7), Eckersley (8)
RIJO, Dibble (8), Myers (9)
HR: Cincinnati (1)-Davis
Time: 2:38
Att: 55,830

Game 2
At CINCINNATI
Wednesday, October 17 (night)

Oakland	103 000 000 0	4	10 2
Cincinnati	200 100 010 1	5	14 2

Welch, Honeycutt (8), ECKERSLEY (10)
Jackson, Scudder, Armstrong (5), Charlton (8), DIBBLE (9)
HR: Oakland (1)-Canseco
Time: 3:31
Att: 55,832

Game 3
At OAKLAND
Friday, October 19 (night)

Cincinnati	017 000 000	8	14 1
Oakland	021 000 000	3	7 1

BROWNING, Dibble (7), Myers (8)
MOORE, Sanderson (3), Klink and Nelson (4), Burns (8), Young (9)
HR: Cincinnati (2)-Sabo 2; Oakland (2)-Baines, R. Henderson
Time: 3:01
Att: 48,269

CINCINNATI REDS

PLAYER	AVG	G	AB	R	H	2B	3B	HR	RBI	SH	SF	HB	BB	SO	SB	CS	E
Bates, B.	1.000	1	1	1	1	0	0	0	0	0	0	0	0	0	0	0	0
Benzinger, T.	.182	4	11	1	2	0	0	0	0	0	0	0	2	0	0	0	0
RIGHT	.500	-	2	-	1												
LEFT	.111	-	9	-	1												
Braggs, G.	.000	2	4	0	0	0	0	0	1	0	0	0	0	2	0	0	0
Davis, E.	.286	2	14	3	4	0	0	1	5	0	0	0	0	2	0	0	0
Duncan, M.	.143	4	14	1	2	0	0	0	0	1	1	0	0	1	0	0	0
Hatcher, B.	.750	4	12	6	9	4	1	0	0	0	0	2	2	0	0	0	0
Larkin, B.	.353	4	17	3	6	1	0	0	1	0	0	0	1	1	0	1	0
Lee, T.	.000	-	1	0	0	0	0	0	0	0	0	0	0	0	0	0	0
Morris, H.	.000	4	14	0	0	0	0	0	0	0	0	0	2	2	0	0	0
Oester, R.	1.000	1	1	0	1	0	0	0	1	0	0	0	0	0	0	0	0
RIGHT	1.000	-	1														
LEFT	.000	-	0														
Oliver, J.	.333	4	18	2	6	1	0	0	2	0	0	0	0	1	0	0	1
O'Neill, P.	.083	4	12	2	1	1	0	0	0	0	0	0	5	2	0	0	0
Quinones, L.	.000	-	1	0	0	0	0	0	0	0	0	0	0	0	0	0	0
RIGHT	.000	-	0														
LEFT	.000	-	1														
Reed, J.	.000	-	1	0	0	0	0	0	0	0	0	0	0	0	0	0	0
Sabo, C.	.563	4	16	4	9	2	0	2	5	0	0	0	0	0	1	0	3
Winningham, H.	.500	2	4	1	2	0	0	0	1	0	0	0	0	1	0	0	0
Jackson, D.	.000	1	1	0	0	0	0	0	0	0	0	0	0	0	0	0	0
Rijo, J.	.333	2	3	0	1	0	0	0	0	2	0	0	0	0	0	0	0
DH	.000	-	7	0	0	0	0	0	0	0	0	0	0	0	0	0	0
REDS	.317	4	142	22	45	9	2	3	22	1	1	15	9	0	2	4	
ATHLETICS	.207	4	135	8	28	4	0	1	8	0	1	12	28	7	0	5	

PITCHER		W	L	ERA	G	GS	CG	SHO	SV	IP	H	R	ER	HR	HB	BB	SO	WP
Armstrong, J.	R	0	0	0.00	1	0	0	0	0	3.0	1	0	0	0	0	2	2	0
Browning, T.	L	0	0	4.50	1	1	0	0	0	6.0	6	3	3	1	0	1	2	0
Charlton, N.	R	0	0	0.00	2	0	0	0	0	1.1	1	0	0	0	0	1	1	0
Dibble, R.	R	1	0	0.00	3	0	0	0	0	4.2	3	0	0	0	0	1	10	0
Jackson, D.	L	0	0	10.13	1	1	0	0	0	2.2	6	4	3	0	1	3	1	0
Mahler, R.	R	-	0	0.00	1	0	0	0	0	0.0	0	0	0	0	0	0	0	0
Myers, R.	L	0	0	0.00	3	0	0	0	0	3.0	2	0	0	0	0	0	2	0
Rijo, J.	R	2	0	0.59	2	2	0	0	0	15.1	9	1	1	0	0	5	14	0
Scudder, S.	R	0	0	0.00	1	0	0	0	0	1.1	1	0	0	0	1	2	2	0
REDS	-	4	0	1.70	4	4	0	1	1	37.0	28	8	7	3	0	12	28	1
ATHLETICS	-	0	4	3.83	4	4	1	0	0	35.1	45	22	15	3	1	15	9	2

Game 4
At Oakland
Saturday, October 20 (night)

											R	H	E
Cincinnati	0	0	0	0	0	0	0	2	0		2	7	1
Oakland	1	0	0	0	0	0	0	0	0		1	2	1

RIJO, Dibble (S) (9)
STEWART
Time: 2:48
Att: 48,613

SCORE BY INNINGS

									R	H	E
Cincinnati	4 1 9	1 3 0	0 3 0	1		22	45	4
Oakland	2 2 4	0 0 0	0 0 0			8	28	5

E-Gallego, Hassey, McGwire 2, Stewart, Jackson, Oliver 3
DP-Cincinnati (2), Oakland (5)
LOB-Cincinnati (32), Oakland (31)
SB-McGee, Lansford, R. Henderson (3), Gallego, Duncan,
O'Neill
S-Lansford, Welch, O'Neill
SF-Hassey, Morris
WP-Sanderson, Burns, Dibble
BK-
PB-
HBP-Hatcher (by Stewart)
ATT-208,544

OAKLAND ATHLETICS

PLAYER	AVG	G	AB	R	H	2B	3B	HR	RBI	SH	SF	HB	BB	SO	SB	CS	E
Baines, H	.143	3	7	1	1	0	0	0	2	0	0	0	0	2	0	0	0
Blankenship, L	.000	1	0	0	0	0	0	0	0	0	0	0	0	0	0	0	0
Bordick, M	.000	3	0	0	0	0	0	0	0	0	0	0	0	0	0	0	0
Canseco, J	.083	4	12	1	1	0	0	1	2	0	0	0	1	3	0	0	0
Gallego, M	.091	4	11	0	1	0	0	0	0	0	0	0	1	1	1	0	2
Hassey, R	.333	3	6	0	2	0	0	0	0	0	1	0	3	0	0	0	1
Henderson, D	.231	4	13	2	3	1	0	0	0	0	0	0	2	3	0	0	0
Henderson, R	.333	4	15	4	5	2	0	0	3	0	0	0	3	1	3	0	0
Jennings, J	1.000	1	1	0	1	0	0	0	0	0	0	0	0	0	0	0	0
Lansford, C	.267	4	15	1	4	0	0	0	1	2	0	0	1	0	1	1	0
McGee, W	.200	4	10	1	2	0	0	0	0	0	0	0	0	1	1	0	0
RIGHT																	
LEFT	.222		9		2									2			
McGwire, M	.214	4	14	0	3	0	0	1	1	0	0	0	4	2	0	0	2
Quirk, J	.000	1	3	0	0	0	0	0	0	0	0	0	0	0	0	0	0
Randolph, W	.267	4	15	1	4	0	0	0	2	0	0	0	0	0	1	0	1
Steinbach, T	.125	3	8	0	1	0	0	0	1	0	0	0	1	2	0	0	0
Weiss, W	.000	4	8	0	0	0	0	0	0	1	0	0	0	1	0	0	0
RIGHT																	
LEFT																	
Stewart, D	.000	2	0	0	0	0	0	0	0	0	0	0	0	1	0	0	0
Welch, B	.000	1	3	0	0	0	0	0	0	1	0	0	0	0	0	0	0
DH	.143	4	7	1	1	0	0	0									
ATHLETICS	.207		135	8	28	4	0	3	8	3	1	0	12	28	7	1	5
REDS	.317		142	22	45	8	2	3	22	1	1	1	15	9	2	4	4

PITCHER		W	L	ERA	G	GS	CG	SHO	SV	IP	H	R	ER	HR	HB	BB	SO	WP
Burns, T	R	0	0	16.20	2	0	0	0	0	1.2	5	3	3	0	1	0	2	1
Eckersley, D	R	0	0	6.75	2	0	0	0	0	1.1	1	1	1	1	0	0	1	0
Honeycutt, R	L	0	0	0.00	3	0	0	0	0	1.2	2	0	0	0	0	1	1	0
Klink, J	L	0	0		2	0	0	0	0	0.0	0	0	0	0	0	1	0	0
Moore, M	R	0	0	6.75	1	1	0	0	0	2.2	3	2	2	0	0	3	2	0
Nelson, G	R	0	0	0.00	2	0	0	0	0	5.0	3	0	0	0	0	1	6	0
Sanderson, S	R	0	0	10.80	2	1	0	0	0	1.2	4	2	2	0	0	2	0	1
Stewart, D	R	0	2	3.46	2	2	1	0	0	13.0	10	6	5	0	1	2	5	0
Welch, B	R	0	0	4.91	1	1	0	0	0	7.1	9	4	4	0	1	2	0	0
Young, C	L	0	0	0.00	1	0	0	0	0	1.0	1	0	0	0	0	2	0	0
ATHLETICS		0	4	3.82	4	4	1	0	0	35.1	45	22	15	3	1	15	9	2
REDS		4	0	1.70	4	4	1	0	1	37.0	28	8	7	3	0	12	28	1

OFFICIAL 1990
NATIONAL LEAGUE RECORDS

COMPILED BY MLB-IBM BASEBALL INFORMATION SYSTEM
Official Statistician: ELIAS SPORTS BUREAU

FINAL STANDINGS

EASTERN DIVISION	W	L	PCT.	GB	WESTERN DIVISION	W	L	PCT.	GB
PITTSBURGH	95	67	.586	-	CINCINNATI	91	71	.562	-
NEW YORK	91	71	.562	4.0	LOS ANGELES	86	76	.531	5.0
MONTREAL	85	77	.525	10.0	SAN FRANCISCO	85	77	.525	6.0
PHILADELPHIA	77	85	.475	18.0	SAN DIEGO	75	87	.463	16.0
CHICAGO	77	85	.475	18.0	HOUSTON	75	87	.463	16.0
ST. LOUIS	70	92	.432	25.0	ATLANTA	65	97	.401	26.0

Championship Series: Cincinnati defeated Pittsburgh, 4 games to 2

Batting

Individual Batting Leaders

Batting Average	.335	McGee	StL
Games	162	J. Carter	SD
At Bats	634	J. Carter	SD
Runs	116	Sandberg	Chi.
Hits	192	Dykstra	Phi.
		Butler	SF
Total Bases	344	Sandberg	Chi.
Singles	160	Butler	SF
Doubles	40	Jefferies	NY
Triples	11	Duncan	Cin.
Home Runs	40	Sandberg	Chi.
Runs Batted In	122	M. Williams	SF
Sacrifice Hits	39	J. Bell	Pit.
Sacrifice Flies	15	Bonilla	Pit.
Hit by Pitch	8	G. Davis	Hou.
Bases on Balls	104	Ja. Clark	SD
Intentional Bases on Balls	21	Dawson	Chi.
		Murray	LA
Strikeouts	169	Galarraga	Mon.
Stolen Bases	77	Coleman	StL.
Caught Stealing	25	Yelding	Hou.
Grounded Into Double Play	22	Murphy	Atl.-Phi.
Slugging Percentage	.565	Bonds	Pit.
On-Base Percentage	.418	Dykstra	Phi.
Longest Batting Streak	23	Dykstra	Phi. (May 15-June 10)

TOP 15 QUALIFIERS FOR BATTING CHAMPIONSHIP

BATTER	TEAM	B	AVG	G	AB	R	H	TB	2B	3B	HR	RBI	SH	SF	HP	BB	IBB	SO	SB	CS	GI DP	SLG	OBP	E
McGee, W.	STL	S	.335	125	501	76	168	219	32	5	3	62	0	4	1	38	6	86	28	8	9	.437	.382	16
Murray, E.	LA	S	.330	155	558	96	184	290	32	3	26	95	0	2	1	82	21	64	8	5	19	.520	.414	10
Magadan, D.	NY	L	.328	144	451	74	148	206	28	6	6	72	4	10	2	74	4	55	2	1	11	.457	.417	3
Dykstra, L.	PHI	L	.325	149	590	106	192	260	35	3	9	60	2	3	7	89	14	48	33	5	5	.441	.418	6
Dawson, A.	CHI	R	.310	147	529	72	164	283	28	5	27	100	0	8	2	42	21	65	16	2	12	.535	.358	5
Roberts, L.	SD	S	.309	149	556	104	172	241	36	3	9	44	4	6	6	55	1	65	46	12	8	.433	.375	13
Grace, M.	CHI	L	.309	157	589	72	182	243	32	1	9	82	1	8	5	59	5	54	15	6	10	.413	.372	12
Gwynn, T.	SD	L	.309	141	573	79	177	238	29	10	4	72	7	7	1	44	20	23	17	8	13	.415	.357	5
Butler, B.	SF	L	.309	160	622	108	192	239	20	9	3	44	7	7	6	90	1	62	51	19	3	.384	.397	6
Sandberg, R.	CHI	R	.306	155	615	116	188	344	30	3	40	100	0	6	1	50	8	84	25	10	8	.559	.354	8
Smith, L.	ATL	R	.305	135	466	72	142	214	27	9	9	42	1	4	6	58	3	69	10	10	2	.459	.384	12
Gant, R.	ATL	R	.303	152	575	107	174	310	34	3	32	84	1	4	1	50	0	86	33	16	8	.539	.357	8
Larkin, B.	CIN	R	.301	158	614	85	185	243	25	6	7	67	4	7	7	49	3	49	30	5	14	.396	.358	17
Bonds, B.	PIT	L	.301	151	519	104	156	293	32	3	33	114	0	6	3	93	15	83	52	13	8	.565	.406	6
Daniels, K.	LA	L	.296	130	450	81	133	239	23	1	27	94	2	3	3	68	1	104	4	3	9	.531	.389	3

INDIVIDUAL BATTING

BATTER	TEAM	B	AVG	G	AB	R	H	TB	2B	3B	HR	RBI	SH	SF	HP	BB	IBB.	SO	SB	CS	GI DP	SLG	OBP	E
Abner, S.	SD	R	.245	91	184	17	45	57	9	0	1	15	2	0	2	9	0	28	2	3	3	.310	.286	1
Agosto, J.	HOU	L	.000	82	0	0	0	0	0	0	0	0	0	0	0	0	0	0	0	0	0	.000	.000	0
Akerfelds, D.	PHI	R	.167	71	6	0	1	1	0	0	0	0	0	0	0	0	0	3	0	0	0	.167	.167	1
Aldrete, M.	MON	L	.242	96	161	22	39	51	7	1	1	18	0	1	2	37	2	31	0	0	2	.317	.385	0
Alomar, R.	SD	S	.287	147	586	80	168	223	27	5	6	60	5	5	0	48	1	72	24	7	16	.381	.340	19
Alou, M.	PIT-MON	R	.200	16	20	4	4	6	0	0	0	0	1	0	0	0	0	3	0	0	0	.300	.200	0
Andersen, L.	HOU	R	.000	50	3	0	0	0	0	0	0	0	1	0	0	0	0	0	0	0	0	.000	.000	1
Anderson, D.	SF	R	.350	60	100	14	35	45	5	1	1	6	1	0	0	3	0	20	1	2	2	.450	.369	1

BATTER	TEAM	B	AVG	G	AB	R	H	TB	2B	3B	HR	RBI	SH	SF	HP	BB	IBB	SO	SB	CS	GI DP	SLG	OBP	E
Anderson, S.	MON	R	.000	4	4	0	0	0	0	0	0	0	1	0	0	0	0	3	0	0	0	.000	.000	0
Anthony, E.	HOU	L	.192	84	239	26	46	84	8	0	10	29	1	6	2	29	3	78	5	0	4	.351	.279	4
Armstrong, J.	CIN	R	.106	29	47	2	5	5	0	0	0	3	13	0	0	2	0	21	0	0	2	.106	.143	0
Assenmacher, P.	CHI	L	.000	74	8	0	0	0	0	0	0	0	2	0	0	0	0	3	0	0	0	.000	.000	0
Avery, S.	ATL	L	.133	21	30	4	4	4	0	0	0	0	2	0	0	1	0	7	0	0	1	.133	.133	2
Backman, W.	PIT	S	.292	104	315	62	92	125	21	3	2	28	2	3	0	42	1	53	6	3	5	.397	.374	12
Baez, K.	NY	R	.167	5	12	2	2	3	1	0	0	0	0	0	0	0	0	2	0	0	0	.250	.167	0
Bailey, M.	SF	R	.143	5	7	1	1	4	0	0	1	3	0	0	0	1	0	1	0	0	0	.571	.143	0
Bair, D.	PIT	R	.000	22	1	0	0	0	0	0	0	0	0	0	0	0	0	0	0	0	0	.000	.000	1
Baldwin, J.	HOU	L	.000	7	8	1	0	0	0	0	0	0	0	0	0	1	0	2	0	0	0	.000	.111	0
Barnes, B.	MON	L	.000	4	9	0	0	0	0	0	0	0	0	0	0	1	0	7	0	0	0	.000	.100	1
Bass, K.	SF	S	.252	61	214	25	54	86	9	1	7	32	2	0	1	14	3	26	2	2	5	.402	.303	3
Bates, B.	CIN	L	.000	8	5	2	0	0	0	0	0	0	0	0	0	0	0	2	2	1	0	.000	.000	0
Bathe, B.	SF	R	.229	52	48	3	11	22	0	0	3	12	0	1	0	7	2	12	0	0	2	.458	.321	0
Bedrosian, S.	SF	R	.500	68	4	0	2	2	0	0	0	1	0	0	0	0	0	1	0	0	0	.500	.500	1
Belcher, T.	LA	R	.163	24	43	5	7	8	1	0	0	0	9	0	0	0	0	15	0	0	1	.186	.200	0
Belinda, S.	PIT	R	.000	55	5	0	0	0	0	0	0	0	0	0	0	0	0	3	0	0	0	.000	.000	0
Bell, J.	PIT	R	.254	159	583	93	148	211	28	7	7	52	39	6	3	65	5	109	10	6	14	.362	.329	22
Bell, M.	ATL	L	.244	36	45	8	11	21	5	1	1	5	1	0	1	6	1	9	0	1	4	.467	.292	2
Belliard, R.	PIT	R	.204	47	54	10	11	14	3	0	0	6	5	0	0	2	1	13	0	2	2	.259	.283	1
Benes, A.	SD	R	.100	32	60	2	6	7	1	0	0	2	5	0	0	0	0	25	0	0	1	.117	.127	1
Benjamin, M.	SF	R	.214	22	56	7	12	23	3	1	2	3	2	0	0	3	0	10	1	0	2	.411	.254	6
Benzinger, T.	CIN	S	.253	118	376	35	95	128	14	2	5	46	2	7	0	19	4	69	3	4	2	.340	.291	0
Berroa, G.	ATL	R	.000	7	4	0	0	0	0	0	0	0	0	0	0	1	0	1	0	0	3	.000	.200	1
Berryhill, D.	CHI	S	.189	17	53	6	10	17	4	0	1	9	1	0	0	5	1	14	0	0	0	.321	.254	0
Bielecki, M.	CHI	R	.163	36	43	3	7	7	0	0	0	2	10	0	0	0	0	20	0	0	3	.163	.200	2
Biggio, C.	HOU	R	.276	150	555	53	153	193	24	2	4	42	9	1	3	53	1	79	25	11	11	.348	.342	13
Bilardello, D.	PIT	R	.054	19	37	2	2	2	0	0	0	0	2	0	0	3	0	10	0	0	0	.054	.146	0
Birtsas, T.	CIN	R	.000	29	4	0	0	0	0	0	0	0	3	0	0	0	0	0	0	0	0	.000	.000	0
Blankenship, K.	CHI	R	.000	3	0	0	0	0	0	0	0	0	0	0	0	0	0	3	0	0	0	.000	.000	1
Blauser, J.	ATL	R	.269	115	386	46	104	158	24	3	8	39	3	0	5	35	1	70	3	5	4	.409	.338	16
Boever, J.	ATL-PHI	R	.000	67	3	0	0	0	0	0	0	0	0	0	0	0	0	0	0	0	0	.000	.000	2
Bonds, B.	PIT	L	.301	151	519	104	156	293	32	3	33	114	0	6	3	93	15	83	52	13	8	.565	.406	6

Player	Team	B	AVG	G	AB	R	H	TB	2B	3B	HR	RBI	SH	IBB	BB	SF	SO	SB	CS	GDP	SLG	OBP	GW
Bonilla, B	PIT	S	.280	160	625	112	175	324	39	7	32	120	0	15	45	9	103	4	3	11	.518	.322	15
Booker, R	PHI	L	.221	73	131	19	29	38	5	2	0	10	2	0	15	7	26	7	1	7	.290	.301	4
Boskie, D	CHI	R	.222	15	36	1	8	11	3	0	0	3	0	0	0	18	8	0	0	0	.306	.222	0
Boston, D	NY	L	.273	115	366	65	100	161	21	1	12	45	2	2	28	3	50	8	5	7	.440	.328	3
Boyd, D	MON	R	.051	31	59	3	3	3	0	0	0	0	0	0	0	0	20	0	0	0	.051	.051	3
Braggs, G	CIN	R	.299	72	201	22	60	89	9	1	6	28	6	2	26	0	43	3	0	1	.443	.385	4
Brantley, J	SF	R	.286	55	7	0	2	2	0	0	0	2	5	0	0	0	1	0	0	0	.286	.286	1
Bream, S	PIT	L	.270	147	389	39	105	177	23	2	15	67	4	7	48	5	65	8	0	13	.455	.349	8
Brewer, R	STL	R	.240	14	25	1	6	7	1	0	0	1	0	0	2	0	4	0	0	0	.280	.240	0
Brooks, H	LA	R	.266	153	568	74	151	241	28	1	20	91	6	6	33	6	108	2	5	10	.424	.307	10
Browning, T	CIN	R	.093	38	75	6	7	9	2	0	0	4	11	0	2	0	29	0	0	0	.120	.117	3
Brunansky, T	STL	R	.158	57	57	5	9	15	0	0	2	10	0	1	12	1	10	0	1	1	.263	.310	2
Bullock, E	MON	L	.500	4	2	0	1	1	0	0	0	0	0	0	0	0	0	0	0	0	.500	.500	0
Burke, T	MON	R	.167	58	6	1	1	1	0	0	0	0	8	0	0	0	3	0	0	0	.167	.286	0
Burkett, J	SF	R	.048	33	63	1	3	3	0	0	0	0	7	0	0	0	35	0	0	0	.048	.118	1
Butler, B	SF	L	.309	160	622	108	192	239	20	9	3	44	7	1	90	1	62	51	19	3	.384	.397	6
Cabrera, F	ATL	R	.277	63	137	30	38	66	5	0	7	25	0	1	5	0	21	9	4	4	.482	.301	3
Caminiti, K	HOU	S	.242	153	541	52	131	167	20	2	4	51	2	1	48	6	97	9	5	15	.309	.302	21
Campusano, S	PHI	R	.212	66	85	10	18	27	1	0	2	9	1	0	6	1	16	7	2	1	.318	.289	3
Candaele, C	HOU	S	.286	130	262	30	75	104	8	2	3	22	3	1	31	1	42	7	2	7	.397	.364	1
Cangelosi, J	PIT	L	.197	58	76	13	15	17	0	1	0	0	0	1	11	0	12	5	2	0	.224	.307	0
Carman, D	PHI	L	.273	59	11	0	3	3	0	0	0	0	0	0	0	0	4	0	0	0	.273	.273	0
Carpenter, C	STL	S	.000	4	0	0	0	0	0	0	0	0	0	0	0	0	0	0	0	0	.000	.000	0
Carr, C	NY	R	.000	2	4	1	0	0	0	0	0	0	0	0	0	0	2	1	0	0	.000	.000	0
Carreon, M	NY	R	.250	82	188	30	47	89	10	0	10	26	2	0	15	2	29	0	0	3	.473	.312	3
Carter, G	SF	R	.254	92	244	24	62	99	10	0	9	27	1	2	25	6	31	1	0	2	.406	.324	11
Carter, J	SD	R	.232	162	634	79	147	248	27	1	24	115	2	7	48	12	93	22	6	6	.391	.290	12
Carter, S	PIT	L	.200	5	5	0	1	1	0	0	0	0	0	0	1	0	1	0	0	0	.200	.200	0
Castillo, T	ATL	R	.143	52	7	1	1	1	0	0	0	0	0	0	0	0	5	0	0	1	.143	.250	1
Cedeno, A	HOU	R	.000	7	8	0	0	0	0	0	0	0	0	0	0	0	5	0	0	0	.000	.000	0
Chamberlain, W	PHI	S	.283	18	46	9	13	22	3	0	2	4	0	0	2	0	9	4	0	1	.478	.298	1
Charlton, N	CIN	R	.135	57	37	4	5	5	0	0	0	2	2	0	3	0	21	0	0	0	.135	.238	0
Clancy, J	HOU	L	.214	33	14	1	3	3	0	0	0	0	5	0	0	0	4	0	0	0	.214	.214	0
Clark, D	CHI	L	.275	84	171	22	47	70	4	0	5	20	0	2	8	2	40	7	4	6	.409	.304	6
Clark, Ja	SD	R	.266	115	334	59	89	178	12	1	25	62	0	5	104	3	91	4	12	0	.533	.441	1
Clark, Je	SD	R	.267	53	101	12	27	48	4	1	4	11	1	0	5	0	24	0	3	6	.475	.299	1

BATTER	TEAM	B	AVG	G	AB	R	H	TB	2B	3B	HR	RBI	SH	SF	HP	BB	IBB	SO	SB	CS	GI DP	SLG	OBP	E
Clark, T	HOU	R	.500	1	2	1	1	1	0	0	0	0	0	0	0	0	0	0	0	0	0	.500	.500	0
Clark, W	SF	L	.295	154	600	91	177	269	25	5	19	95	0	13	3	62	9	97	8	2	7	.448	.357	12
Clary, M	ATL	R	.000	33	28	0	0	0	0	0	0	0	2	0	0	1	0	10	0	0	1	.000	.034	1
Coffman, K	CHI	R	.200	8	5	0	1	1	0	0	0	0	0	0	0	0	0	1	0	0	0	.200	.200	0
Coleman, V	STL	S	.292	124	497	73	145	199	18	9	6	39	4	0	0	35	1	88	77	17	6	.400	.340	5
Collins, D	STL	S	.224	99	58	12	13	14	1	0	0	3	3	0	3	13	2	10	8	0	0	.241	.366	1
Combs, P	PHI	L	.150	32	60	6	9	11	2	0	0	2	4	0	0	3	0	24	0	0	0	.183	.190	0
Cone, D	NY	L	.200	32	70	7	14	15	1	0	0	5	9	0	0	5	0	12	0	0	2	.214	.253	0
Cook, D	PHI-LA	L	.306	48	49	8	15	19	1	0	1	4	4	0	0	0	0	4	0	0	0	.388	.306	3
Cora, J	SD	S	.270	51	100	12	27	30	3	0	0	2	0	0	1	5	1	9	8	3	3	.300	.311	0
Crews, T	LA	R	.000	66	0	0	0	0	0	0	0	0	0	0	0	0	0	0	0	0	0	.000	.000	0
Daniels, K	LA	L	.296	130	450	81	133	239	23	1	27	94	2	3	3	68	1	104	4	3	9	.531	.389	11
Darling, R	NY	R	.129	34	31	2	4	4	0	0	0	2	5	0	0	3	0	12	0	0	0	.129	.206	1
Darwin, D	HOU	R	.132	52	38	5	5	8	0	0	1	0	3	0	0	2	0	18	0	0	3	.211	.175	3
Dascenzo, D	CHI	S	.253	113	241	27	61	83	9	5	1	26	5	3	0	21	2	26	15	6	6	.344	.312	3
Daulton, D	PHI	L	.268	143	459	62	123	191	30	1	12	57	1	3	3	72	9	72	7	1	7	.416	.367	2
Davidson, M	HOU	R	.292	57	130	12	38	48	5	1	1	11	1	0	0	10	0	18	1	0	1	.369	.340	1
Davis, E	CIN	R	.260	127	453	84	118	220	26	2	24	86	0	3	8	60	6	100	21	3	5	.486	.347	0
Davis, G	HOU	R	.251	93	327	44	82	171	15	4	22	64	0	3	0	46	17	54	1	0	11	.523	.357	8
Davis, J	ATL	R	.071	12	28	0	2	2	0	0	0	1	0	0	0	3	0	3	0	0	0	.071	.161	2
Davis, J	SD	R	.000	6	1	0	0	0	0	0	0	0	0	0	0	0	0	0	0	0	0	.000	.000	2
Dawson, A	CHI	R	.310	147	529	72	164	283	28	5	27	100	0	8	4	42	21	65	16	2	12	.535	.358	4
Dayley, K	STL	L	.000	58	6	0	0	0	0	0	0	0	4	0	0	0	0	3	0	0	0	.000	.000	0
DeJesus, J	PHI	R	.079	22	38	1	3	4	1	0	0	2	1	0	0	4	0	21	0	0	0	.105	.167	5
Decker, S	SF	R	.296	15	54	5	16	27	2	0	3	8	0	0	0	1	0	10	0	0	1	.500	.309	1
DeLeon, J	STL	R	.107	32	56	6	6	8	0	1	0	0	5	0	0	0	0	23	0	0	0	.143	.123	2
Dempsey, R	LA	R	.195	62	128	13	25	36	5	0	2	15	0	0	0	23	1	29	1	0	8	.281	.318	1
Deshaies, J	HOU	L	.063	34	63	3	4	4	0	0	0	3	7	1	0	2	0	33	0	0	0	.063	.092	2
Dewey, M	SF	R	.000	14	1	0	0	0	0	0	0	0	0	0	0	1	0	1	0	0	0	.000	.500	2
DeShields, D	MON	L	.289	129	499	69	144	196	28	6	4	45	1	2	4	66	3	96	42	22	10	.393	.375	12
Diaz, M	NY	R	.136	16	22	3	3	4	1	0	0	1	0	1	0	0	0	3	0	0	0	.182	.130	1
Dibble, R	CIN	R	.000	68	7	0	0	0	0	0	0	0	3	0	0	0	0	1	0	0	0	.000	.000	0
Dickson, L	CHI	R	.000	3	3	0	0	0	0	0	0	0	0	0	0	0	0	0	0	0	0	.000	.000	0

Player	Team	B	AVG	G	AB	R	H	TB	2B	3B	HR	RBI	BB	SO	SB	SLG	OBP
DiPino, F.	STL	L	.250	62	4	0	1	2	0	0	0	0	0	2	0	.500	.250
Doran, B.	HOU-CIN	S	.300	126	403	59	121	175	29	2	7	37	79	58	23	.434	.411
Downs, K.	SF	R	.000	13	13	0	0	0	0	0	0	1	1	4	0	.000	.067
Drabek, D.	PIT	R	.214	33	84	18	18	23	2	0	0	6	4	25	0	.274	.258
Duncan, M.	CIN	R	.306	125	435	67	133	207	22	11	10	55	24	67	13	.476	.345
Dunne, M.	SD	L	.000	10	0	0	0	0	0	0	0	0	0	2	0	.000	.000
Dunston, S.	CHI	R	.262	146	545	73	143	232	22	8	17	66	15	87	25	.426	.283
Dykstra, L.	PHI	L	.325	149	590	106	192	260	35	3	9	60	89	48	33	.441	.418
Elster, K.	NY	R	.207	92	314	36	65	114	20	1	9	45	30	54	2	.363	.274
Esasky, N.	ATL	R	.171	9	35	2	6	6	0	0	0	2	4	14	0	.171	.256
Faries, P.	SD	R	.189	14	37	4	7	8	0	0	1	2	0	7	0	.216	.279
Farmer, H.	MON	R	.400	6	5	0	2	2	0	0	0	1	0	1	0	.400	.400
Fernandez, S.	NY	L	.190	30	58	8	11	12	1	0	2	4	0	22	0	.207	.190
Fitzgerald, M.	MON	R	.243	111	313	36	76	123	18	1	9	41	60	60	0	.393	.365
Fletcher, D.	LA-PHI	L	.130	11	23	3	3	4	1	0	1	1	1	6	0	.174	.167
Foley, T.	MON	L	.213	73	164	11	35	39	2	2	0	12	12	22	0	.238	.266
Ford, C.	PHI	L	.111	22	18	0	2	2	0	0	0	1	0	5	0	.111	.158
Franco, J.	NY	L	.000	55	5	0	0	0	0	0	0	0	0	1	0	.000	.000
Freeman, M.	PHI-ATL	R	.000	25	7	0	0	0	0	0	0	0	0	6	0	.000	.000
Frey, S.	MON	R	.000	51	1	0	0	0	0	0	0	0	0	0	0	.000	.000
Galarraga, A.	MON	R	.256	155	579	65	148	237	29	0	20	87	40	169	10	.409	.306
Gant, R.	ATL	R	.303	152	575	107	174	310	34	3	32	84	50	86	33	.539	.357
Garcia, C.	PIT	R	.500	4	4	2	2	2	0	0	0	1	0	2	0	.500	.500
Gardner, M.	MON	R	.114	27	44	5	5	8	1	0	0	1	1	23	0	.182	.114
Garrelts, S.	SF	R	.061	42	66	4	4	5	1	0	0	2	0	28	0	.076	.088
Gedman, R.	HOU	L	.202	40	104	6	21	31	7	0	1	10	15	24	0	.298	.300
Gibson, K.	LA	L	.260	89	315	59	82	126	20	2	8	38	39	65	26	.400	.345
Gilkey, B.	STL	R	.297	18	64	18	19	31	5	2	1	3	3	5	6	.484	.375
Girardi, J.	CHI	R	.270	133	419	36	113	144	24	2	1	38	17	50	8	.344	.300
Glavine, T.	ATL	L	.113	34	62	5	7	9	2	1	0	4	8	24	0	.145	.211
Goff, J.	MON	R	.227	52	119	14	27	37	5	1	1	7	21	36	0	.311	.343
Gonzalez, J.	LA	R	.232	106	99	15	23	40	3	0	2	8	6	27	3	.404	.280
Gonzalez, L.	HOU	R	.190	12	21	1	4	6	2	0	0	4	2	5	0	.286	.261
Gooden, D.	NY	R	.187	35	75	4	14	20	2	0	0	9	2	15	0	.267	.225
Gott, J.	LA	R	.000	50	0	0	0	0	0	0	0	0	0	1	0	.000	.000
Grace, M.	CHI	L	.309	157	589	72	182	243	32	1	9	82	59	54	15	.413	.372

BATTER	TEAM	B	AVG	G	AB	R	H	TB	2B	3B	HR	RBI	SH	SF	HP	BB	IBB	SO	SB	CS	GI DP	SLG	OBP	E
Grant, M.	SD-ATL	R	.333	59	6	2	2	3	1	0	0	1	0	0	1	0	0	2	0	0	0	.333	.500	1
Greene, T.	ATL-PHI	R	.167	15	12	2	2	3	1	0	0	1	3	0	0	1	0	1	0	0	0	.250	.167	1
Gregg, K.	ATL	L	.264	124	239	18	63	93	13	1	5	32	3	2	1	20	4	39	4	3	1	.389	.322	6
Griffey, K.	CIN	L	.206	46	63	6	13	18	2	0	1	8	6	0	2	2	0	5	2	1	0	.286	.235	1
Griffin, A.	LA	S	.210	141	461	38	97	117	11	3	1	35	6	4	0	29	11	65	6	3	5	.254	.258	26
Grimsley, J.	PHI	R	.188	12	16	1	3	3	0	0	0	2	3	0	0	2	0	2	0	0	0	.188	.235	2
Grissom, M.	MON	R	.257	98	288	42	74	101	14	4	2	29	4	1	0	27	0	40	22	2	3	.351	.320	1
Gross, K.	MON	R	.200	32	50	3	10	17	4	0	1	4	7	0	0	2	0	21	0	0	0	.340	.231	2
Guerrero, P.	STL	R	.281	136	498	42	140	212	31	1	13	80	0	11	1	44	14	70	1	1	14	.426	.334	13
Gullickson, B.	HOU	R	.158	32	57	2	9	12	0	0	1	5	7	1	0	4	0	14	0	0	2	.211	.210	0
Gunderson, E.	SF	R	.000	7	6	0	0	0	0	0	0	0	1	0	0	0	0	1	0	0	0	.000	.000	0
Gwynn, C.	LA	L	.284	101	141	19	40	59	2	1	5	22	0	3	0	7	2	28	0	1	2	.418	.311	0
Gwynn, T.	SD	L	.309	141	573	79	177	238	29	10	4	72	7	4	1	44	20	23	17	8	13	.415	.357	5
Hall, D.	MON	R	.000	42	4	0	0	0	0	0	0	0	1	0	0	0	0	4	0	0	0	.000	.000	1
Hamilton, J.	LA	R	.125	7	24	1	3	3	0	0	0	1	1	0	0	0	0	3	0	0	0	.125	.125	0
Hammaker, A.	SF-SD	S	.105	34	19	2	2	2	0	0	0	0	2	0	1	1	0	6	0	0	1	.105	.150	0
Hammond, C.	CIN	L	.000	3	3	0	0	0	0	0	0	0	1	0	0	0	0	1	0	0	0	.000	.000	2
Hansen, D.	LA	L	.143	5	7	0	1	1	0	0	0	1	0	0	0	1	0	3	0	0	0	.143	.143	0
Harkey, M.	CHI	R	.250	27	56	4	14	18	4	0	0	4	8	0	1	1	0	16	0	0	1	.321	.276	1
Harris, G.	SD	R	.083	73	12	1	1	1	0	0	0	0	4	0	0	0	0	8	0	0	0	.083	.083	0
Harris, L.	LA	L	.304	137	431	61	131	161	16	4	2	29	3	1	1	29	2	31	15	10	8	.374	.348	11
Hartley, M.	LA	R	.077	32	13	1	1	1	0	0	0	1	3	0	0	0	0	8	0	0	0	.077	.077	1
Hatcher, B.	CIN	R	.276	139	504	68	139	192	28	5	5	25	3	1	6	33	0	42	30	10	4	.381	.327	1
Hatcher, M.	LA	R	.212	85	132	12	28	33	3	1	0	13	1	2	1	6	1	22	4	1	12	.250	.248	3
Hayes, C.	PHI	R	.258	152	561	56	145	195	20	0	10	57	0	6	2	28	3	91	4	7	10	.348	.293	20
Hayes, V.	PHI	L	.261	129	467	70	122	193	14	3	17	73	0	4	4	87	16	81	16	4	3	.413	.375	6
Heaton, N.	PIT	L	.047	32	43	3	2	2	0	0	0	0	3	0	0	0	0	13	0	0	0	.047	.128	2
Hennis, R.	HOU	R	.000	3	2	0	0	0	0	0	0	0	3	0	0	0	0	1	0	0	0	.000	.000	0
Hernandez, C.	LA	R	.200	10	20	2	4	5	1	0	0	1	0	0	0	2	0	2	0	0	0	.250	.200	0
Hernandez, X.	HOU	R	.333	35	3	0	1	1	0	0	0	0	0	0	0	0	0	1	0	0	0	.333	.333	0
Herr, T.	PHI-NY	S	.261	146	547	48	143	190	26	0	5	60	6	6	2	50	4	58	7	1	11	.347	.324	7
Hershiser, O.	LA	R	.000	4	7	0	0	0	0	0	0	0	1	0	0	0	0	1	0	0	0	.000	.000	0
Hesketh, J.	MON-ATL	L	.000	33	1	0	0	0	0	0	0	0	0	0	0	0	0	1	0	0	0	.000	.000	1

Player	Team	B	AVG	G	AB	R	H	2B	HR	RBI	BB
Hill, K.	STL	R	.211	17	19	0	4	0	0	1	1
Hollins, D.	PHI	S	.184	72	114	14	21	4	5	15	10
Horton, R.	STL	L	.000	32	4	0	0	0	0	0	0
Howard, T.	SD	S	.273	20	44	4	12	2	0	4	4
Howell, J.	LA	R	.000	45	2	0	0	0	0	0	0
Howell, K.	PHI	R	.067	18	30	2	2	0	0	0	2
Hudler, R.	MON-STL	R	.282	93	220	31	62	11	7	22	12
Hughes, K.	NY	L	.000	8	9	0	0	0	0	0	0
Hundley, T.	NY	S	.209	36	67	8	14	6	0	2	6
Hurst, B.	SD	L	.090	33	67	6	6	0	0	1	4
Infante, A.	ATL	S	.036	20	28	3	1	0	0	0	0
Innis, J.	NY	R	.000	18	0	0	0	0	0	0	0
Jackson, D.	CIN	R	.054	23	37	1	2	0	0	0	5
Jackson, D.	SD	R	.257	58	113	10	29	3	3	20	9
Javier, S.	LA	S	.304	104	276	29	84	9	3	24	37
Jefferies, G.	NY	S	.283	153	604	96	171	40	15	68	46
Jelic, C.	NY	R	.091	4	11	1	1	0	0	0	0
Johnson, H.	NY	S	.244	154	590	89	144	37	23	90	69
Johnson, W.	MON	S	.163	47	49	6	8	2	0	7	7
Jones, R.	PHI	L	.276	24	58	5	16	2	0	10	9
Jones, T.	STL	R	.219	67	128	28	28	7	2	14	12
Jordan, R.	PHI	R	.241	92	324	32	78	21	5	44	13
Jose, F.	STL	S	.271	25	85	12	23	4	2	13	8
Justice, D.	ATL	L	.282	127	439	76	124	23	28	78	64
Kennedy, T.	SF	L	.277	107	303	25	84	22	2	26	31
King, J.	PIT	R	.245	127	371	46	91	17	14	53	21
Kingery, M.	SF	L	.295	105	207	24	61	7	0	24	12
Kipper, B.	PIT	L	.143	41	7	0	1	0	0	0	0
Knepper, B.	SF	L	.231	12	13	1	3	1	0	1	0
Komminsk, B.	SF	R	.200	8	5	0	1	0	0	1	0
Kramer, R.	PIT-CHI	R	.000	22	6	0	0	0	0	0	0
Kremers, J.	ATL	L	.110	29	73	7	8	1	0	14	6
Kruk, J.	PHI	L	.291	142	443	52	129	25	7	67	69
LaCoss, M.	SF	R	.043	13	23	2	1	0	0	0	1
Laga, M.	SF	L	.185	23	27	4	5	1	2	5	3
Lake, S.	PHI	R	.250	29	80	9	20	4	0	10	2

BATTER	TEAM	B	AVG	G	AB	R	H	TB	2B	3B	HR	RBI	SH	SF	HP	BB	IBB	SO	SB	CS	GI DP	SLG	OBP	E
Lampkin, T. ......SD	L	.222	26	63	4	14	19	0	1	0	4	0	0	0	4	1	9	0	1	2	.302	.269	3
Lancaster, L. ......CHI	R	.050	55	20	1	1	1	0	0	0	0	4	0	0	3	0	11	0	0	0	.050	.174	0
Landrum, B. ......PIT	R	.111	54	9	2	1	2	1	0	0	0	2	0	0	0	0	5	0	0	1	.222	.111	0
Lankford, R. ......STL	R	.286	39	126	12	36	57	10	1	3	12	4	0	0	13	0	27	8	2	0	.452	.353	1
Larkin, B. ......CIN	R	.301	158	614	85	185	243	25	6	7	67	7	4	7	49	3	49	30	5	14	.396	.358	17
LaValliere, M. ......PIT	L	.258	96	279	27	72	96	15	0	3	31	4	1	2	44	8	20	0	3	6	.344	.362	5
Layana, T. ......CIN	R	.000	55	5	0	0	0	0	0	0	0	0	0	0	0	0	2	0	0	0	.000	.000	0
Leach, R. ......SF	L	.293	78	174	24	51	70	13	0	2	16	0	1	0	21	1	20	2	0	2	.402	.372	1
Lee, T. ......CIN	R	.211	12	19	1	4	5	1	0	0	3	0	0	0	2	0	2	0	0	1	.263	.273	0
Lefferts, C. ......SD	L	.250	56	4	1	1	1	0	0	0	3	5	0	0	0	0	2	0	0	0	.250	.250	1
Leibrandt, C. ......ATL	R	.180	24	50	2	9	9	0	0	0	3	2	0	0	3	0	11	0	1	0	.180	.226	0
Lemke, M. ......ATL	S	.226	102	239	22	54	67	13	0	0	21	4	2	0	21	3	22	0	0	6	.280	.286	4
Leonard, M. ......SF	R	.176	11	17	3	3	7	1	0	0	2	0	2	0	0	0	8	0	0	0	.412	.300	0
Liddell, D. ......NY	R	1.000	1	1	1	1	1	0	0	0	0	0	0	0	0	0	0	0	0	0	1.000	1.000	0
Lilliquist, D. ......ATL-SD	L	.256	29	43	6	11	17	0	0	2	3	2	0	1	0	0	8	0	0	0	.395	.273	0
Lind, J. ......PIT	R	.261	152	514	46	134	175	28	5	1	48	9	7	1	35	19	52	8	2	20	.340	.305	7
Litton, G. ......SF	R	.245	93	204	17	50	64	9	1	1	24	2	1	1	11	0	45	1	0	5	.314	.284	1
Lombardozzi, S. ......HOU	R	.000	2	5	0	0	0	0	0	0	0	0	0	0	0	0	1	0	0	0	.000	.167	0
Long, B. ......CHI	R	.000	42	4	0	0	0	0	0	0	0	0	0	0	0	0	4	0	0	0	.000	.000	1
Lopez, L. ......LA	R	.000	6	6	0	0	0	0	0	0	0	0	0	0	0	0	2	0	0	0	.000	.000	0
Luecken, R. ......ATL	R	.333	36	3	1	1	2	1	0	0	0	1	0	0	0	0	1	0	0	0	.667	.333	0
Lynn, F. ......SD	L	.240	90	196	18	47	70	3	1	6	23	0	3	0	22	2	44	2	0	2	.357	.315	4
Lyons, B. ......NY-LA	R	.235	27	85	9	20	29	3	0	2	9	1	1	2	2	0	10	2	0	2	.341	.261	4
Maddux, G. ......CHI	R	.145	35	83	1	12	12	0	0	0	3	9	0	0	2	0	25	0	1	3	.145	.165	0
Maddux, M. ......LA	R	.000	11	2	0	0	0	0	0	0	0	4	0	0	0	0	0	0	0	0	.000	.000	0
Magadan, D. ......NY	L	.328	144	451	74	148	206	28	0	6	72	4	10	2	74	4	55	0	2	11	.457	.417	3
Magrane, J. ......STL	R	.127	31	55	3	7	9	2	0	0	2	9	0	0	3	0	19	0	1	2	.164	.172	1
Mahler, R. ......CIN	R	.114	35	35	4	4	5	1	0	0	2	5	0	0	0	0	4	0	0	3	.143	.135	1
Mann, K. ......ATL	R	.143	11	28	2	4	8	1	0	1	2	0	0	0	0	0	6	0	0	2	.286	.143	0
Manwaring, K. ......SF	R	.154	8	13	0	2	4	0	0	0	1	1	0	0	0	0	3	0	0	0	.308	.154	0
Marak, P. ......ATL	R	.091	7	11	1	1	1	0	0	0	1	0	0	0	0	0	4	0	0	0	.091	.167	0
Marshall, M. ......NY	R	.239	53	163	24	39	67	8	1	6	27	0	3	1	7	0	40	2	2	2	.411	.278	2
Martinez, C. ......PHI-PIT	R	.240	83	217	26	52	91	9	0	10	35	0	0	0	30	0	42	0	1	3	.419	.332	2

Player	Tm	B	AVG	G	AB	R	H	TB	2B	3B	HR	RBI	SH	SF	HBP	BB	IBB	SO	SB	CS	GDP	SLG	OBP	GW
Martinez, Da	MON	L	.279	118	391	60	109	165	13	5	11	39	3	2	2	24	2	48	13	11	8	.422	.321	3
Martinez, De	MON	R	.103	32	68	7	7	8	1	0	0	6	12	0	1	1	0	25	0	0	3	.118	.129	1
Martinez, R	LA	L	.125	33	80	10	10	10	0	0	0	6	9	0	1	1	1	32	0	0	1	.125	.145	1
Mathews, G	STL	R	.214	12	14	2	3	4	1	0	0	0	1	0	1	0	0	5	0	0	0	.286	.313	1
May, D	CHI	L	.246	17	61	15	15	21	3	0	1	11	0	0	0	8	0	7	5	0	0	.344	.270	0
McCament, R	SF	R	.000	3	1	0	0	0	0	0	0	0	0	0	0	0	0	0	0	0	0	.000	.000	0
McClellan, P	SF	R	.500	4	2	0	1	1	0	0	0	0	0	0	0	0	0	0	0	0	0	.500	.500	1
McClendon, L	CHI-PIT	R	.164	53	110	18	18	27	3	0	2	12	0	1	1	14	1	22	3	2	2	.245	.256	4
McDowell, O	ATL	L	.243	113	305	47	74	109	14	2	7	25	0	1	1	21	0	53	4	0	3	.357	.295	5
McDowell, R	PHI	R	.000	72	2	0	0	0	0	0	0	0	1	0	0	0	0	1	0	0	0	.000	.382	16
McGee, W	STL	S	.335	125	501	76	168	219	32	3	3	62	0	2	0	38	6	86	28	9	9	.437	.353	1
McGriff, T	CIN-HOU	R	.000	6	6	4	0	0	0	0	0	0	0	0	0	0	0	1	0	0	0	.000	.194	3
McReynolds, K	NY	R	.269	147	521	75	140	237	23	1	24	82	0	8	2	71	3	61	9	3	8	.455	.287	0
Meadows, L	HOU-PHI	L	.107	30	28	3	3	3	0	0	0	0	0	0	0	3	0	6	1	0	0	.107	.240	2
Mercado, O	NY-MON	S	.214	25	98	10	21	31	5	1	1	12	0	0	0	6	3	9	0	0	2	.316		0
Merced, O	PIT	L	.208	25	24	3	5	6	1	0	0	2	0	0	0	0	0	9	0	0	2	.250	.240	1
Mercker, K	ATL	L	.000	36	3	0	0	0	0	0	0	0	2	0	0	0	0	2	0	0	0	.000	.000	0
Meyer, B	HOU	R	.000	14	3	0	0	0	0	0	0	0	0	0	0	0	0	1	0	0	0	.000	.000	4
Miller, K	NY	R	.258	88	233	42	60	71	8	1	1	12	0	5	2	23	1	46	16	3	7	.305	.327	9
Mitchell, K	SF	R	.290	140	524	90	152	285	24	2	35	93	0	9	5	58	21	87	4	8	8	.544	.360	0
Mohorcic, D	MON	L	.125	34	8	0	1	1	0	0	0	0	0	0	0	0	0	1	0	0	1	.125	.125	1
Morandini, M	PHI	R	.241	25	79	9	19	26	4	0	1	3	2	0	1	6	0	19	13	3	1	.329	.294	4
Morgan, M	LA	L	.113	33	71	9	8	8	0	0	0	2	5	0	0	6	2	25	0	0	0	.113	.137	0
Morris, H	CIN	R	.340	107	309	50	105	154	22	4	7	36	3	4	0	21	7	32	9	3	12	.498	.381	3
Morris, J	STL	L	.111	18	18	2	2	2	0	0	0	0	0	0	0	3	0	6	0	1	0	.111	.238	0
Mulholland, T	PHI	L	.097	33	62	0	6	7	1	0	0	0	2	0	0	0	0	30	0	0	0	.113	.111	3
Munoz, M	LA	R	.000	8	0	0	0	0	0	0	0	0	0	0	0	0	0	1	0	0	0	.000	.000	0
Murphy, D	ATL-PHI	R	.245	154	563	60	138	235	23	1	24	83	0	4	4	61	14	130	9	9	9	.417	.318	5
Murray, E	LA	S	.330	155	558	96	184	290	22	0	26	95	0	4	4	82	21	64	8	5	8	.520	.414	10
Musselman, J	NY	L	.000	28	1	0	0	0	0	0	0	0	0	0	0	0	0	0	0	0	0	.000	.000	0
Myers, R	CIN	L	.250	66	0	0	0	0	0	0	0	0	2	0	0	0	0	2	0	0	0	.250	.250	1
Nabholz, C	MON	L	.000	11	21	1	3	3	0	0	0	0	0	0	0	0	0	9	0	0	0	.000	.000	0
Neidlinger, J	LA	L	.120	12	25	3	3	3	1	0	0	2	1	0	0	2	0	8	0	0	0	.120	.185	1
Nelson, R	SD	L	.000	5	5	0	0	0	0	0	0	0	0	0	0	0	0	4	0	0	0	.000	.000	0
Nichols, C	HOU	R	.204	32	49	7	13	13	3	0	0	11	1	2	2	8	0	11	3	0	1	.265	.317	3
Niedenfuer, T	STL	R	.000	52	3	0	0	0	0	0	0	0	0	0	0	0	0	2	0	1	0	.000	.000	2

BATTER	TEAM	B	AVG	G	AB	R	H	TB	2B	3B	HR	RBI	SH	SF	HP	BB	IBB	SO	SB	CS	GI DP	SLG	OBP	E
Nieto, T.	PHI	R	.167	17	30	1	5	5	0	0	0	4	3	0	1	3	0	11	0	0	2	.167	.265	1
Nixon, O.	MON	S	.251	119	231	46	58	71	6	2	1	20	3	1	0	28	0	33	50	13	2	.307	.331	1
Noboa, J.	MON	R	.266	81	158	15	42	53	7	2	0	14	3	4	1	7	2	14	4	0	0	.335	.294	2
Noce, P.	CIN	R	1.000	1	1	1	1	1	0	0	0	0	0	0	0	0	0	0	0	0	0	1.000	1.000	0
Novoa, R.	SF	L	.200	7	5	1	1	1	0	0	0	1	0	0	0	1	0	2	0	0	0	.200	.333	0
Nunez, J.	CHI	R	.000	21	11	1	0	0	0	0	0	0	1	0	0	1	0	5	0	0	0	.000	.083	2
Oberkfell, K.	HOU	L	.207	77	150	10	31	42	6	1	0	12	3	1	0	15	1	17	0	1	2	.280	.281	4
O'Brien, C.	NY	R	.162	28	68	6	11	14	0	0	1	9	2	0	0	10	1	8	0	0	0	.206	.272	3
Oester, R.	CIN	S	.299	64	154	10	46	58	10	1	0	13	6	0	0	10	2	29	1	2	1	.377	.339	4
Offerman, J.	LA	S	.155	29	58	7	9	12	1	0	0	7	1	0	0	4	1	14	1	1	0	.207	.210	4
Ojeda, B.	NY	L	.133	38	30	2	4	5	1	0	0	0	1	0	0	0	0	11	0	0	0	.167	.133	2
Olivares, O.	STL	R	.176	9	17	2	3	7	1	0	1	4	0	0	0	0	0	4	0	0	6	.412	.167	0
Oliver, J.	CIN	R	.231	121	364	34	84	131	23	0	8	52	5	1	2	37	15	75	0	0	8	.360	.304	6
Oliveras, F.	SF	R	.000	33	5	0	0	0	0	0	0	0	0	0	0	0	0	4	0	1	0	.000	.000	0
Olson, G.	ATL	R	.262	100	298	36	78	113	12	1	7	36	5	2	1	30	4	51	1	0	8	.379	.332	7
O'Malley, T.	NY	R	.223	82	121	14	27	43	7	0	3	14	0	1	0	11	0	20	0	1	1	.355	.286	2
O'Neal, R.	SF	R	.167	26	6	0	1	1	0	0	0	1	0	0	0	0	0	3	0	0	0	.167	.167	0
O'Neill, P.	CIN	L	.270	145	503	59	136	212	28	0	16	78	1	5	2	53	13	103	13	11	12	.421	.339	2
Oquendo, J.	STL	S	.252	156	469	38	118	148	17	5	1	37	5	5	0	74	8	46	1	1	7	.316	.350	4
Ortiz, J.	HOU	R	.273	30	77	2	21	31	4	0	1	10	5	5	0	12	0	11	0	0	6	.403	.367	4
Owen, S.	MON	S	.234	149	453	55	106	155	24	5	5	35	5	5	3	70	12	60	8	6	12	.342	.333	6
Pagliarulo, M.	SD	L	.254	128	398	29	101	149	23	2	7	38	2	4	3	39	3	66	1	0	3	.374	.322	13
Pagnozzi, T.	STL	R	.277	69	220	20	61	82	15	0	2	23	2	0	1	14	1	37	1	1	6	.373	.321	4
Palacios, V.	PIT	R	.000	3	4	0	0	0	0	0	0	0	0	0	0	0	0	2	0	0	0	.000	.000	0
Paredes, J.	MON	R	.333	6	6	0	2	3	1	0	0	0	0	0	0	0	0	0	0	0	0	.500	.429	1
Parent, M.	SD	R	.222	65	189	13	42	62	11	0	3	16	3	0	1	16	3	29	0	0	2	.328	.283	3
Parker, R.	SF	R	.243	54	107	19	26	37	5	0	2	14	3	1	0	10	0	15	6	1	0	.346	.314	3
Parrett, J.	PHI-ATL	R	.091	67	11	0	1	1	0	0	0	0	2	0	0	0	0	4	0	0	0	.091	.091	4
Patterson, B.	PIT	R	.053	55	19	0	1	1	0	0	0	0	0	0	0	1	0	6	0	0	0	.053	.053	0
Pavlas, D.	CHI	R	.000	13	6	0	0	0	0	0	0	0	0	0	0	0	0	3	0	0	0	.000	.000	0
Pena, A.	NY	R	.167	52	45	2	11	13	0	1	0	2	0	0	0	4	0	14	0	0	0	.167	.286	0
Pena, G.	STL	S	.244	18	45	5	11	13	2	0	0	2	0	1	0	4	0	14	1	1	0	.289	.314	1
Pendleton, T.	STL	S	.230	121	447	46	103	145	20	2	6	58	0	6	1	30	8	58	7	5	12	.324	.277	19

Player	Team	B	AVG	G	AB	R	H	2B	3B	HR	RBI
Perez, M.	STL	R	.000	13	1	0	0	0	0	0	0
Perezchica, T.	SF	R	.333	4	3	1	1	0	0	0	1
Perry, P.	LA	L	.000	7	1	0	0	0	0	0	0
Pico, J.	CHI	R	.273	31	22	2	6	1	0	0	3
Portugal, M.	HOU	R	.136	32	66	6	9	0	1	0	1
Power, T.	PIT	R	.125	40	8	1	1	0	0	0	0
Presley, J.	ATL	R	.242	140	541	59	131	28	1	19	72
Prince, T.	PIT	L	.100	4	10	1	1	0	0	0	1
Puhl, T.	HOU	S	.293	37	41	5	12	1	0	0	5
Quinones, L.	CIN	S	.241	83	145	10	35	7	0	2	17
Quisenberry, D.	SF	R	.000	2	1	0	0	0	0	0	0
Raines, T.	MON	S	.287	130	457	65	131	11	5	9	62
Ramirez, R.	HOU	R	.261	132	445	44	116	19	2	2	37
Ramos, D.	CHI	R	.265	98	226	22	60	5	0	2	17
Randolph, W.	LA	R	.271	26	96	15	26	4	0	1	9
Rasmussen, D.	SD	L	.290	33	62	2	18	3	1	1	8
Ready, R.	PHI	R	.244	101	217	26	53	11	1	1	26
Redus, G.	PIT	R	.247	96	227	32	56	12	5	6	23
Reed, D.	NY	R	.205	26	39	5	8	1	0	1	2
Reed, J.	CIN	L	.251	72	175	44	44	8	1	3	16
Reed, R.	PIT	R	.250	13	16	2	4	0	0	0	3
Reuschel, R.	SF	L	.154	15	26	0	4	0	0	0	0
Reuss, J.	PIT	R	.000	95	0	0	0	0	0	0	0
Reynolds, R.	PIT	L	.288	8	215	25	62	10	1	0	19
Reynolds, R.	SD	R	.067	38	15	0	1	1	0	0	1
Rhodes, K.	HOU	R	.244	29	86	12	21	6	2	0	13
Rijo, J.	CIN	L	.161	92	62	3	10	1	0	0	3
Riles, E.	SF	L	.200	149	155	22	31	1	1	8	21
Roberts, L.	SD	S	.309	149	556	104	172	36	3	9	44
Robinson, D.	SF	R	.143	31	63	4	9	2	0	0	7
Robinson, R.	CIN	R	.091	6	11	1	1	0	0	0	1
Rodriguez, R.	SD	L	.000	32	3	0	0	0	0	0	0
Roesler, M.	PIT	R	.000	5	1	0	0	0	0	0	0
Rohde, D.	HOU	S	.184	59	98	8	18	4	0	0	5
Rojas, M.	MON	R	.000	23	3	0	0	0	0	0	0
Roomes, R.	CIN-MON	R	.227	46	75	6	17	2	0	0	8

BATTER	TEAM	B	AVG	G	AB	R	H	TB	2B	3B	HR	RBI	SH	SF	HP	BB	IBB	SO	SB	CS	GI DP	SLG	OBP	E
Rosario, V	ATL	R	.143	9	7	3	1	1	0	0	0	0	0	0	0	0	0	1	0	0	0	.143	.250	0
Ross, M	PIT	R	.000	9	1	0	0	0	0	0	0	0	0	0	0	1	0	1	0	0	0	.000	.000	0
Ruffin, B	PHI	S	.068	32	44	3	3	3	0	0	0	0	6	0	0	3	0	9	0	0	0	.068	.128	2
Ruskin, S	PIT-MON	R	.250	67	8	3	2	5	1	0	0	1	0	0	0	0	0	5	0	0	0	.625	.250	0
Ryal, M	PIT	L	.083	9	12	0	1	1	0	0	0	0	0	0	0	0	0	3	0	0	0	.083	.083	0
Sabo, C	CIN	R	.270	148	567	95	153	270	38	2	25	71	1	3	4	61	7	58	25	10	8	.476	.343	12
Salazar, L	CHI	R	.254	115	410	44	104	159	13	2	12	47	1	4	4	19	3	59	3	1	4	.388	.293	12
Sampen, B	MON	R	.000	59	8	0	0	0	0	0	0	0	2	0	0	0	0	3	0	0	0	.000	.000	0
Samuel, J	LA	R	.242	143	492	62	119	188	24	3	13	52	0	5	5	51	5	126	38	20	8	.382	.316	16
Sandberg, R	CHI	R	.306	155	615	116	188	344	30	3	40	100	0	8	1	50	8	84	25	7	8	.559	.354	8
Santana, A	SF	S	.000	6	2	0	0	0	0	0	0	1	0	0	0	0	0	0	0	0	0	.000	.000	0
Santiago, B	SD	R	.270	100	344	42	93	144	8	5	11	53	1	7	3	27	2	55	5	5	4	.419	.323	12
Santovenia, N	MON	R	.190	59	163	13	31	54	8	0	6	28	0	5	2	8	2	31	0	3	5	.331	.222	6
Sasser, M	HOU-NY	L	.307	100	270	31	83	115	14	0	6	41	0	1	15	8	9	19	0	1	7	.426	.344	14
Schatzeder, D	HOU-NY	L	.250	51	4	1	1	1	0	0	0	0	0	0	0	0	0	2	0	0	0	.250	.250	1
Schiraldi, C	SD	R	.190	42	21	2	4	9	2	0	1	0	0	0	0	1	0	6	0	0	0	.429	.227	3
Schmidt, D	MON	R	.000	34	3	0	0	0	0	0	0	0	0	0	0	0	0	0	0	0	0	.000	.000	1
Scioscia, M	LA	L	.264	135	435	46	115	176	25	0	12	66	1	4	3	55	14	31	4	0	11	.405	.348	10
Scott, M	HOU	R	.130	32	54	1	7	7	0	0	0	1	6	0	0	4	0	22	1	0	0	.130	.190	1
Scudder, S	CIN	R	.056	21	18	1	1	1	0	0	0	0	1	2	0	2	0	6	0	0	0	.056	.150	1
Searage, R	LA	L	.000	29	2	0	0	0	0	0	0	0	0	0	0	0	0	0	0	0	0	.000	.000	0
Sharperson, M	LA	R	.297	129	357	42	106	133	14	2	3	36	8	3	1	46	6	39	15	6	5	.373	.376	15
Shelby, J	LA	S	.250	25	24	3	6	7	1	0	0	2	0	0	1	7	1	7	1	0	1	.292	.250	0
Show, E	SD	R	.200	39	25	3	5	6	1	0	0	2	2	0	0	0	0	8	0	0	0	.240	.200	0
Simms, M	HOU	R	.308	12	13	4	4	8	1	0	1	3	0	0	0	0	0	4	0	0	1	.615	.308	0
Slaught, D	PIT	R	.300	84	230	27	69	105	18	3	4	29	3	3	4	27	3	27	0	1	2	.457	.375	8
Smiley, J	PIT	L	.122	26	49	1	6	6	0	0	0	3	11	0	0	0	0	15	0	0	2	.122	.173	2
Smith, B	STL	R	.256	26	39	2	10	14	0	0	1	7	3	0	0	1	0	9	0	0	1	.359	.275	1
Smith, D	HOU	R	.000	49	2	0	0	0	0	0	0	0	0	0	0	0	0	0	0	0	0	.000	.333	0
Smith, D	CHI	L	.262	117	290	34	76	109	15	2	6	27	0	2	2	28	1	46	11	6	7	.376	.329	6
Smith, G	CHI	S	.205	18	44	4	9	13	2	1	0	5	0	0	0	2	0	5	1	0	1	.295	.234	3
Smith, L	STL	R	.000	53	2	0	0	0	0	0	0	0	1	0	0	0	0	1	0	0	0	.000	.000	0
Smith, L	ATL	R	.305	135	466	72	142	214	27	9	9	42	1	6	6	58	3	69	10	10	2	.459	.384	12

Player	Team	B	AVG	G	AB	R	H	TB	2B	3B	HR	RBI	GW	SH	SF	BB	IBB	SO	SB	CS	E	SLG	OBP	GDP
Smith, O	STL	S	.254	143	512	61	130	156	21	1	1	50	7	10	2	61	4	33	32	6	8	.305	.330	12
Smith, P	ATL	R	.087	13	23	2	2	2	0	0	0	1	0	4	0	1	0	7	0	0	0	.087	.125	0
Smith, Z	MON-PIT	L	.162	34	68	7	11	16	3	1	0	3	0	8	0	6	0	16	0	0	0	.235	.174	3
Smoltz, J	ATL	R	.162	38	74	2	12	14	1	0	0	1	0	7	0	6	0	32	0	1	1	.189	.225	3
Stephens, R	STL	R	.133	5	15	2	2	6	1	0	0	0	0	0	0	0	0	3	0	0	2	.400	.133	0
Stephenson, P	SD	L	.209	103	182	26	38	61	9	1	4	19	1	2	0	30	2	43	1	1	3	.335	.319	1
Strawberry, D	NY	L	.277	152	542	92	150	281	18	1	37	108	4	0	5	70	15	110	15	3	5	.518	.361	3
Stubbs, F	HOU	L	.261	146	448	59	117	213	23	2	23	71	2	1	2	48	4	114	19	5	4	.475	.334	6
Sutcliffe, R	CHI	R	.000	5	5	0	0	0	0	0	0	0	0	1	0	0	0	2	0	0	0	.000	.286	0
Sutko, G	CIN	L	.000	2	1	0	0	0	0	0	0	0	0	1	0	0	0	1	0	0	0	.000	.000	0
Swan, R	SF	L	.279	17	43	3	12	18	1	0	0	3	0	0	0	8	0	4	0	0	0	.419	.340	0
Tabler, P	NY	R	.248	—	—	—	—	—	—	—	—	—	—	—	—	—	—	—	—	—	—	.362	.280	26
Templeton, G	SD	S	.248	144	505	45	125	183	25	3	9	59	0	1	2	24	3	59	4	2	17	.362	.280	0
Terrell, W	—	L	.107	16	28	3	3	3	0	0	0	0	0	7	0	0	0	13	0	0	1	.107	.138	1
Terry, S	STL	R	.455	50	11	2	5	6	1	0	0	1	1	5	0	0	0	3	0	0	0	.545	.455	4
Teufel, T	NY	R	.246	80	175	28	43	84	11	0	10	24	0	0	1	15	0	33	5	0	5	.480	.304	1
Tewksbury, B	STL	R	.171	28	41	2	7	8	1	0	0	2	0	9	0	4	0	18	0	0	1	.195	.244	10
Thomas, A	ATL	R	.219	84	278	26	61	84	8	0	5	30	1	0	2	11	0	43	2	5	1	.302	.248	7
Thompson, M	STL	L	.218	135	418	42	91	137	14	7	6	30	8	3	0	39	3	60	25	4	10	.328	.292	8
Thompson, R	SF	L	.245	144	498	67	122	195	22	3	15	56	3	6	2	34	6	96	14	9	1	.392	.299	25
Thon, D	PHI	R	.255	149	552	54	141	193	20	4	8	48	1	2	3	37	2	77	12	5	0	.350	.305	1
Thurmond, M	SF	L	.000	43	5	1	1	0	0	0	0	0	0	1	0	0	0	4	0	0	0	.000	.000	0
Tomlin, R	PIT	L	.040	12	25	2	11	1	0	0	0	0	0	2	0	0	0	7	0	1	1	.080	.077	0
Torve, K	NY	L	.289	20	38	1	11	15	2	1	0	4	0	0	0	2	0	9	0	0	1	.395	.386	0
Traxler, B	LA	L	.091	9	—	0	1	2	1	0	0	0	0	0	0	0	0	1	0	0	1	.182	.091	0
Treadway, J	ATL	L	.283	128	474	56	134	191	20	2	11	59	5	1	3	25	4	42	3	2	10	.403	.320	15
Trevino, A	HO-NY-CI	R	.221	58	86	3	19	27	5	1	0	13	1	3	0	7	3	11	1	0	2	.314	.293	4
Tudor, J	STL	L	.152	25	46	7	7	9	2	0	0	2	1	7	0	2	0	19	2	0	0	.196	.188	1
Uribe, J	SF	S	.248	138	415	35	103	126	8	6	1	24	3	4	0	29	0	49	8	9	8	.304	.297	20
Valdez, R	SD	R	.000	3	1	0	0	0	0	0	0	0	0	0	0	0	0	0	0	0	0	.000	.000	0
Valenzuela, F	LA	L	.304	35	69	8	21	29	5	0	1	11	1	7	0	12	0	12	0	0	6	.420	.310	3
Valera, J	NY	R	.200	3	8	0	1	1	0	0	0	0	0	0	0	1	0	1	0	0	1	.200	.200	1
Van Slyke, A	PIT	L	.284	136	493	67	140	229	26	6	17	77	3	0	4	66	2	89	14	6	3	.465	.367	8
Varsho, G	CHI	L	.250	46	48	10	12	16	2	1	0	6	4	3	1	0	0	6	2	1	0	.333	.265	0
Vatcher, J	PHI-ATL	R	.260	57	73	7	19	26	1	0	2	7	0	0	1	5	0	15	0	0	0	.356	.308	0
Villanueva, H	CHI	R	.272	52	114	14	31	58	4	1	7	18	5	0	2	4	2	27	1	3	2	.509	.308	2

BATTER	TEAM	B	AVG	G	AB	R	H	TB	2B	3B	HR	RBI	SH	SF	HP	BB	IBB	SO	SB	CS	GI DP	SLG	OBP	E
Viola, F ....NY	L	.153	35	85	4	13	13	0	0	0	4	7	0	0	4	0	20	0	0	1	.153	.153	1
Vizcaino, J ....LA	S	.275	37	51	3	14	17	1	1	0	2	0	0	0	1	0	8	1	0	1	.333	.327	2
Walk, B ....PIT	R	.162	26	37	3	6	7	1	0	0	4	10	0	1	1	0	13	0	1	1	.189	.205	3
Walker, L .....MON	L	.241	133	419	59	101	182	18	3	19	51	3	2	1	49	5	112	21	7	8	.434	.326	4
Wallach, T ...MON	R	.296	161	626	69	185	295	37	5	21	98	1	3	4	42	11	80	6	9	12	.471	.339	21
Walling, D ....STL	L	.220	78	127	7	28	36	5	0	1	19	0	2	3	8	1	15	0	0	5	.283	.265	0
Walton, J .....CHI	R	.263	101	392	63	103	129	16	2	2	21	1	4	0	50	0	70	14	7	4	.329	.350	6
Wells, T ....LA	L	.000	5	7	0	0	0	0	0	0	0	1	0	0	0	0	4	0	0	0	.000	.000	2
Wetteland, J ...LA	R	.143	22	7	2	1	4	0	0	0	3	1	0	0	0	0	1	0	0	0	.571	.143	1
Whitehurst, W ...NY	R	.250	38	8	0	2	2	0	0	0	0	1	0	0	0	0	0	0	0	0	.250	.250	0
Whitson, E ....SD	R	.149	33	67	6	10	14	1	0	1	4	13	0	0	2	1	16	0	2	1	.209	.174	0
Whitt, E ....ATL	L	.172	67	180	14	31	45	8	0	2	10	3	0	0	23	1	27	2	0	6	.250	.265	3
Wilkerson, C ...CHI	S	.220	77	186	25	41	48	5	1	3	16	3	0	0	7	2	36	2	2	4	.258	.249	14
Williams, E ...SD	R	.286	14	42	5	12	24	3	0	3	4	0	0	0	5	2	6	0	1	0	.571	.362	3
Williams, M ...CHI	L	.000	59	5	1	0	0	0	0	0	0	0	0	0	0	0	0	0	0	0	.000	.000	0
Williams, M ...SF	R	.277	159	617	87	171	301	27	2	33	122	2	5	7	33	9	138	7	4	13	.488	.319	19
Wilson, C ......STL	R	.248	55	121	13	30	32	2	0	0	7	2	2	0	8	0	14	4	2	7	.264	.290	1
Wilson, G ......HOU	R	.245	118	368	42	90	134	14	0	10	55	0	4	1	26	1	64	0	3	16	.364	.293	6
Wilson, S ......CHI	L	.162	45	37	3	6	7	1	0	0	0	5	0	0	3	0	11	0	0	0	.189	.225	2
Wilson, T ......SF	L	.138	27	29	2	4	4	0	0	0	3	5	0	0	2	0	10	0	0	0	.138	.194	2
Winningham, H ...CIN	L	.256	84	160	20	41	68	8	5	3	17	2	1	0	14	1	31	6	4	0	.425	.314	0
Wrona, R ......CHI	R	.172	16	29	3	5	5	0	0	0	0	1	0	0	1	1	11	0	0	0	.172	.226	2
Wynne, M ......CHI	L	.204	92	186	21	38	62	8	2	4	19	1	1	0	14	3	25	3	2	4	.333	.264	1
Yelding, E .....HOU	R	.254	142	511	69	130	152	9	5	1	28	4	5	0	39	1	87	64	25	11	.297	.305	17
York, M ....PIT	R	.333	4	3	1	1	1	0	0	0	0	1	0	0	0	0	1	0	0	0	.333	.333	0
Young, G ......HOU	S	.175	57	154	15	27	36	4	1	1	4	4	1	0	20	0	23	6	3	3	.234	.269	1
Zelle, T ....STL	R	.244	144	495	62	121	197	25	3	15	57	0	6	2	67	3	77	2	4	11	.398	.333	15

CLUB BATTING

CLUB	AVG	G	AB	R	OR	H	TB	2B	3B	HR	GS	RBI	SH	SF	HP	BB	IBB	SO	SB	CS	GI DP	LOB	SHO	SLG	OB
CINCINNATI	.265	162	5525	693	597	1466	2205	284	40	125	1	644	88	42	42	466	73	913	166	66	99	1137	8	.399	.325
CHICAGO	.263	162	5600	690	774	1474	2194	240	36	136	2	649	61	51	30	406	68	869	151	50	100	1124	9	.392	.314
SAN FRANCISCO	.262	162	5573	719	710	1459	2206	221	35	152	3	681	76	45	33	488	61	973	109	56	83	1167	6	.396	.323
LOS ANGELES	.262	162	5491	728	685	1436	2099	288	27	129	4	669	71	48	31	538	78	952	141	65	110	1132	8	.382	.328
PITTSBURGH	.259	162	5388	733	619	1395	2181	288	42	138	5	693	96	66	24	582	64	914	137	59	115	1121	8	.405	.330
SAN DIEGO	.257	162	5554	673	673	1429	2111	243	35	123	4	628	79	48	28	509	75	902	138	53	117	1139	6	.380	.320
NEW YORK	.256	162	5504	775	613	1410	2246	278	21	172	5	734	54	56	32	536	65	851	110	33	89	1114	8	.408	.323
ST. LOUIS	.256	162	5462	599	698	1398	1954	255	41	73	1	554	77	50	21	517	54	844	221	74	101	1164	15	.358	.320
PHILADELPHIA	.255	162	5535	646	729	1410	2010	237	27	103	3	619	59	39	30	582	92	915	108	35	115	1242	11	.363	.327
ATLANTA	.252	162	5504	682	821	1376	2177	263	26	162	3	636	49	31	27	473	36	1010	92	55	101	1074	14	.396	.311
MONTREAL	.250	162	5453	662	598	1363	2018	227	43	114	3	607	87	47	26	576	67	1024	235	99	96	1126	7	.370	.322
HOUSTON	.242	162	5379	573	656	1301	1856	209	32	94	0	536	79	41	28	548	64	997	179	83	107	1132	16	.345	.313
TOTALS	.256	972	65968	8173	8173	16917	25257	2967	405	1521	34	7650	876	564	352	6221	797	11164	1787	727	1233	13672	116	.383	.321

Mets' Greg Jefferies led NL in doubles (40).

Pittsburgh's Doug Drabek (22-6) won Cy Young Award.

Pitching

Individual Pitching Leaders

Games Won	22	Drabek	Pit.
Games Lost	19	DeLeon	StL.
Won-Lost Percentage	.786	Drabek	Pit. (22-6)
Earned Run Average	2.21	Darwin	Hou.
Games	82	Agosto	Hou.
Games Started	35	Maddux	Chi.
		Browning	Cin.
		Viola	NY
Complete Games	12	R. Martinez	LA
Games Finished	60	McDowell	Phi.
Shutouts	4	Morgan	LA
		Hurst	SD
Saves	33	Franco	NY
Innings	249.2	Viola	NY
Hits	242	Maddux	Chi.
Batsmen Faced	1016	Viola	NY
Runs	116	Maddux	Chi.
Earned Runs	104	Valenzuela	LA
Home Runs	28	Rasmussen	SD
Sacrifice Hits	21	Glavine	Atl.
Hit Batsmen	9	Gardner	Mon.
Bases on Balls	90	Smoltz	Atl.
Intentional Bases on Balls	14	Gullickson	Hou.
Strikeouts	233	Cone	NY
Wild Pitches	14	Smoltz	Atl.
Balks	5	Rijo	Cin.
		Armstrong	Cin.
		D. Smith	Hou.
		Kipper	Pit.
		Benes	SD
Games Won, Consecutive	9	Darwin	Hou. (June 10-Aug. 26)
Games Lost, Consecutive	9	Clary	Atl. (May 18-Aug. 11)

TOP 15 QUALIFIERS FOR EARNED RUN AVERAGE LEADERSHIP

PITCHER	TEAM	T	W	L	ERA	G	GS	CG	SHO	GF	SV	IP	H	TBF	R	ER	HR	SH	SF	HB	BB	IBB	SO	WP	BK	OPP AVG
Darwin, D ......HOU	R	11	4	2.21	48	17	3	0	14	2	162.2	136	646	42	40	11	4	2	3	31	4	109	0	2	.225
Smith, Z .....MON-PIT	L	12	9	2.55	33	31	3	2	1	0	215.1	196	860	77	61	15	3	3	1	50	8	130	2	0	.245
Whitson, E ......SD	R	14	9	2.60	32	32	6	3	0	0	228.2	215	918	73	66	13	9	6	1	47	8	127	2	0	.251
Viola, F ......NY	L	20	12	2.67	35	35	7	3	0	0	249.2	227	1016	83	74	15	13	2	2	60	2	182	11	5	.242
Rijo, J ......CIN	R	14	8	2.70	29	29	7	1	0	0	197.0	151	801	65	59	10	8	1	2	78	1	152	0	5	.212
Drabek, D ......PIT	R	22	6	2.76	33	33	9	3	0	0	231.1	190	918	78	71	15	10	3	3	56	6	131	2	3	.225
Martinez, R ......LA	R	20	6	2.92	33	33	12	3	0	0	234.1	191	950	89	76	22	7	5	4	67	5	223	3	3	.221
Boyd, D ......MON	R	10	6	2.93	31	31	3	3	0	0	190.2	164	774	64	62	19	12	4	4	52	10	113	3	3	.234
Martinez, De ......MON	R	10	11	2.95	32	32	7	2	0	0	226.0	191	908	80	74	16	11	3	6	49	5	156	1	1	.228
Hurst, B ......SD	L	11	9	3.14	33	33	9	4	0	0	223.2	188	903	85	78	21	15	1	6	63	9	162	7	1	.228
Leibrandt, C ......ATL	L	9	11	3.16	24	24	5	2	0	0	162.1	164	680	72	57	9	7	6	4	35	3	76	4	3	.261
Cone, D ......NY	R	14	10	3.23	31	30	6	2	1	0	211.2	177	860	84	76	21	4	4	7	65	3	233	10	4	.226
Harkey, M ......CHI	R	12	6	3.27	27	27	6	2	1	0	173.2	153	728	71	63	14	5	4	7	59	8	94	8	1	.234
Mulholland, T ......PHI	L	9	10	3.34	33	26	6	2	2	0	180.2	172	746	78	67	15	5	12	2	42	7	75	7	2	.252
Armstrong, J ......CIN	R	12	9	3.42	29	27	2	1	1	1	166.0	151	704	72	63	9	8	5	6	59	7	110	7	5	.242

INDIVIDUAL PITCHING

PITCHER	TEAM	T	W	L	ERA	G	GS	CG	SHO	GF	SV	IP	H	TBF	R	ER	HR	SH	SF	HB	BB	IBB	SO	WP	BK	OPP AVG
Aase, D ......LA	R	3	1	4.97	32	0	0	0	13	3	38.0	33	163	24	21	5	2	0	0	19	4	24	3	0	.232
Agosto, J ......HOU	L	9	8	4.29	82	0	0	0	29	4	92.1	91	404	46	44	4	7	2	7	39	8	50	1	0	.261
Akerfelds, D ......PHI	R	5	5	3.77	71	0	0	0	18	3	93.0	65	395	45	39	10	9	5	3	54	8	42	7	1	.201
Andersen, L ......HOU	R	5	2	1.95	50	0	0	0	20	6	73.2	61	301	19	16	4	5	1	1	24	5	68	2	0	.229
Andersen, S ......MON	R	0	1	3.00	4	3	0	0	1	1	18.0	12	71	19	6	1	0	1	0	5	0	16	0	0	.188
Armstrong, J ......CIN	R	12	9	3.42	29	27	2	0	1	1	166.0	151	704	72	63	9	8	5	6	59	7	110	7	5	.242
Assenmacher, P ..CHI	L	7	2	2.80	74	1	0	0	21	10	103.0	90	426	33	32	10	10	3	1	36	8	95	2	0	.239

PITCHER	TEAM	T	W	L	ERA	G	GS	CG	SHO	GF	SV	IP	H	TBF	R	ER	HR	SH	SF	HB	BB	IBB	SO	WP	BK	OPP AVG
Avery, S	ATL	L	3	11	5.64	21	20	1	0	1	0	99.0	121	466	79	62	7	14	4	2	45	2	75	5	1	.302
Bair, D	PIT	R	3	1	4.81	22	0	0	0	5	0	24.1	30	112	15	13	3	3	0	0	11	1	19	3	1	.306
Barnes, B	MON	L	1	1	2.89	4	4	1	0	0	0	28.0	25	115	10	9	2	2	0	0	7	0	23	1	0	.236
Bedrosian, S	SF	R	9	9	4.20	68	0	0	0	53	17	79.1	72	349	40	37	6	3	1	2	44	9	43	2	0	.241
Belcher, T	LA	R	9	9	4.00	24	24	5	2	0	0	153.0	136	627	76	68	17	6	6	2	48	0	102	6	1	.240
Belinda, S	PIT	R	3	4	3.55	55	0	0	0	17	8	58.1	48	245	23	23	4	5	6	1	29	3	55	1	0	.227
Benes, A	SD	R	10	11	3.60	32	31	2	0	0	0	192.1	177	811	87	77	18	2	6	1	69	3	140	2	5	.242
Bielecki, M	CHI	R	8	11	4.93	36	29	0	0	1	0	168.0	188	749	101	92	13	16	4	5	70	11	103	11	2	.287
Birtsas, T	CIN	L	1	0	3.86	29	0	0	0	8	0	51.1	69	239	24	22	7	1	1	5	24	6	41	4	0	.325
Blankenship, K	CHI	R	0	2	5.84	3	2	0	0	0	0	12.1	13	57	10	8	1	0	0	0	6	0	5	1	0	.265
Boever, J	ATL-PHI	R	3	6	3.36	67	0	0	0	34	14	88.1	77	388	35	33	6	4	2	0	51	12	75	3	0	.233
Booker, G	SF	R	0	0	13.50	2	0	0	0	1	0	2.0	7	13	3	3	0	0	2	0	1	0	1	1	0	.538
Boskie, S	CHI	R	5	6	3.69	15	15	1	0	0	0	97.2	99	415	42	40	8	8	2	1	31	3	49	3	2	.265
Boyd, D	MON	R	10	6	2.93	31	31	3	3	0	0	190.2	164	774	64	62	19	12	4	3	52	10	113	3	3	.234
Brantley, J	SF	R	5	3	1.56	55	0	0	0	32	19	86.2	77	361	18	15	3	2	2	3	33	6	61	0	3	.240
Brown, K	CIN	R	0	0	4.76	8	0	0	0	2	0	11.1	12	46	6	6	0	1	0	1	3	0	8	0	0	.286
Brown, K	NY	L	0	0	0.00	2	0	0	0	1	0	2.0	2	9	0	0	0	2	0	0	1	0	2	0	0	.250
Browning, T	CIN	L	15	9	3.80	35	35	2	1	0	0	227.2	235	957	98	96	24	13	5	5	52	13	99	5	1	.266
Burke, T	MON	R	3	3	2.52	58	0	0	0	21	20	75.0	71	316	29	21	8	3	5	2	21	6	47	1	3	.247
Burkett, J	SF	R	14	7	3.79	33	32	2	0	0	0	204.0	201	857	90	86	18	6	8	4	61	7	118	3	3	.257
Camacho, E	SF-STL	R	2	0	5.17	14	0	0	0	6	0	15.2	17	72	10	9	3	6	2	1	9	1	15	2	1	.279
Carman, D	PHI	L	6	2	4.15	59	1	0	0	11	0	86.2	69	368	43	40	13	6	4	0	38	7	58	6	0	.218
Carpenter, C	STL	R	0	1	4.50	4	0	0	0	0	0	8.0	5	32	5	4	2	0	0	1	2	1	2	2	0	.167
Castillo, T	ATL	L	5	1	4.23	52	3	0	0	7	1	76.2	93	337	41	36	5	4	4	2	20	3	64	2	2	.302
Charlton, N	CIN	L	12	9	2.74	56	16	1	1	13	2	154.1	131	650	53	47	10	7	2	4	70	4	117	9	1	.231
Clancy, J	HOU	R	2	8	6.51	33	10	0	0	8	0	76.0	100	352	58	55	4	1	4	3	33	9	44	3	0	.322
Clark, T	HOU	R	0	0	13.50	1	1	0	0	0	0	4.0	9	25	7	6	0	0	0	0	3	3	2	0	0	.429
Clark, S	STL	L	0	0	2.70	2	0	0	0	2	0	3.1	2	12	1	1	0	0	0	0	0	0	3	0	0	.167
Clary, M	ATL	R	1	10	5.67	33	14	0	0	5	0	101.2	128	466	72	64	9	5	5	1	39	4	44	5	1	.308
Clements, P	SD	L	0	0	4.15	9	0	0	0	3	0	13.0	20	63	6	6	0	1	0	0	7	1	6	1	0	.357
Coffman, K	CHI	R	0	2	11.29	8	2	0	0	0	0	18.1	26	100	24	23	9	2	1	0	19	1	9	6	4	.338

Player — Team	T	W	L	ERA	G	GS	CG	ShO	Sv	IP	H	R	ER	HR	BB	SO	AVG
Combs, P ....PHI	L	10	10	4.07	32	31	2	1	0	183.1	179	90	83	12	86	108	.257
Cone, D ....NY	R	14	10	3.23	31	31	6	2	0	211.2	177	84	76	21	65	233	.226
Cook, D ....PHI-LA	L	9	4	3.92	47	16	0	0	0	156.0	155	74	68	20	56	64	.262
Costello, J ....STL-MON	R	0	5	5.91	8	0	0	0	0	10.2	12	8	7	3	5	2	.279
Crews, T ....LA	R	4	7	2.77	66	0	0	0	0	107.1	98	40	33	9	24	76	.238
Darling, R ....NY	R	7	9	4.50	33	18	3	1	0	126.0	135	73	63	20	44	99	.273
Darwin, D ....HOU	R	11	4	2.21	48	17	3	3	2	162.2	136	42	40	11	31	109	.225
Dascenzo, D ....CHI	L	0	0	0.00	1	0	0	0	0	1.0	1	0	0	0	0	0	.333
Davis, J ....SD	L	0	0	5.79	6	0	0	0	0	9.1	9	7	6	1	4	7	.257
Dayley, K ....STL	L	4	4	3.56	58	0	0	0	2	73.1	63	32	29	5	30	51	.233
DeJesus, J ....PHI	R	7	8	3.74	22	22	2	0	0	130.0	97	63	54	10	73	87	.211
DeLeon, J ....STL	R	7	19	4.43	32	32	3	0	0	182.2	168	96	90	18	86	164	.246
Deshaies, J ....HOU	L	7	12	3.78	34	34	4	3	0	209.1	186	93	88	21	84	119	.245
Dewey, M ....SF	R	1	0	2.78	14	0	0	0	5	22.2	22	7	7	3	5	11	.259
Dibble, R ....CIN	R	8	3	1.74	68	0	0	0	11	98.0	62	22	19	1	34	136	.183
Dickson, L ....CHI	R	0	3	7.24	3	3	0	0	0	13.2	20	20	11	2	1	4	.370
DiPino, F ....STL	L	5	2	4.56	62	0	0	0	0	81.0	92	45	41	8	31	49	.294
Downs, K ....SF	R	2	6	3.43	13	9	0	0	0	63.0	56	26	24	4	20	31	.233
Drabek, D ....PIT	R	22	6	2.76	33	33	9	3	0	231.1	190	71	71	21	56	131	.225
Dunne, M ....SD	R	0	3	5.65	10	6	0	0	0	28.2	28	21	18	4	17	15	.241
Farmer, H ....MON	R	0	3	7.04	6	6	0	0	0	23.0	26	18	18	1	10	14	.302
Fernandez, S ....NY	L	9	14	3.46	30	30	2	1	0	179.1	130	79	69	18	67	181	.200
Fisher, B ....HOU	R	0	0	7.20	4	0	0	0	0	5.0	9	7	4	1	0	1	.409
Franco, J ....NY	L	5	3	2.53	55	0	0	0	33	67.2	66	22	19	3	21	56	.252
Freeman, M ....PHI-ATL	R	1	8	4.31	25	3	0	0	0	48.0	41	24	23	5	17	38	.224
Frey, S ....MON	L	8	2	2.10	51	0	0	0	9	55.2	44	15	13	3	29	29	.219
Frohwirth, T ....PHI	R	0	1	18.00	5	0	0	0	0	1.0	3	2	2	0	6	1	.500
Gardner, M ....MON	R	7	9	3.42	27	26	1	0	0	152.2	129	62	58	13	61	135	.230
Garrelts, S ....SF	R	12	11	4.15	31	31	4	0	10	182.0	190	91	84	16	70	80	.272
Gideon, B ....MON	R	0	0	9.00	1	0	0	0	0	1.0	2	1	1	0	0	0	.500
Glavine, T ....ATL	L	10	12	4.28	33	33	1	2	0	214.1	232	111	102	18	78	129	.281
Gooden, D ....NY	R	19	7	3.83	34	34	2	3	0	232.2	229	106	99	19	70	223	.258
Gott, J ....LA	R	3	5	2.90	50	0	0	0	3	62.0	70	27	20	5	34	44	.257
Grant, M ....SD-ATL	R	2	3	4.73	59	1	0	0	0	91.1	108	53	48	9	37	69	.298

PITCHER	TEAM	T	W	L	ERA	G	GS	CG	SHO	GF	SV	IP	H	TBF	R	ER	HR	SH	SF	HB	BB	IBB	SO	WP	BK	OPP AVG
Greene, T.	ATL-PHI	R	3	3	5.08	15	9	0	0	1	0	51.1	50	227	31	29	8	5	0	1	26	1	21	1	0	.256
Grimsley, J.	PHI	R	3	2	3.30	11	11	0	0	0	0	57.1	47	255	21	21	2	1	2	1	43	0	41	6	1	.227
Gross, K.	MON	R	9	12	4.57	31	26	2	0	3	0	163.1	171	712	86	83	9	6	9	4	65	7	111	4	1	.272
Gross, K.	CIN	R	0	0	4.26	5	0	0	0	2	0	6.1	6	25	3	3	0	0	0	2	0	0	3	0	0	.273
Gullickson, B.	HOU	R	10	14	3.82	32	32	2	0	1	0	193.1	221	846	100	82	21	6	8	2	61	0	73	3	2	.287
Gunderson, E.	SF	L	1	2	5.49	7	4	0	0	1	0	19.2	24	94	14	12	2	1	8	0	11	0	14	0	0	.293
Hall, D.	MON	L	4	7	5.09	42	0	0	0	13	0	58.1	52	254	35	33	6	6	4	2	29	5	40	3	1	.242
Hammaker, A.	SF-SD	L	4	9	4.36	34	7	0	0	8	0	86.2	85	363	44	42	8	4	0	0	27	5	44	4	1	.259
Hammond, C.	CIN	L	0	2	6.35	3	3	0	0	0	0	11.1	13	56	9	8	2	1	0	0	12	1	9	1	3	.302
Harkey, M.	CHI	R	12	6	3.26	27	27	2	0	0	0	173.2	153	728	71	63	14	9	4	7	59	8	94	8	1	.234
Harris, G.	SD	R	8	8	2.30	73	0	0	0	33	9	117.1	92	488	35	30	8	9	7	4	49	13	97	3	2	.220
Hartley, M.	LA	R	3	2	2.95	32	6	1	0	1	0	79.1	58	325	35	26	7	2	2	2	30	2	76	3	0	.200
Heaton, N.	PIT	L	12	9	3.45	30	24	0	0	2	0	146.0	143	599	66	56	17	10	6	2	38	2	68	4	1	.263
Hennis, R.	HOU	R	0	2	0.00	3	1	0	0	0	0	9.2	1	34	0	0	0	0	0	0	3	0	4	0	0	.033
Henry, D.	ATL	R	2	3	5.63	34	0	0	0	14	0	38.1	41	176	26	24	3	0	4	1	25	0	34	0	1	.273
Hernandez, X.	HOU	R	2	1	4.62	34	4	0	0	10	0	62.1	60	268	32	32	8	2	4	4	24	0	24	6	0	.256
Hershiser, O.	LA	R	1	2	4.26	4	4	0	0	0	0	25.1	26	106	12	12	2	1	0	1	4	0	16	0	0	.260
Hesketh, J.	MON-ATL	L	1	5	5.29	33	6	0	0	15	0	34.0	32	147	23	20	5	5	0	0	14	1	24	5	0	.244
Hill, K.	STL	R	5	6	5.49	17	14	1	0	0	0	78.2	79	343	49	48	7	0	5	3	33	1	58	5	0	.264
Hilton, H.	STL	R	0	0	0.00	2	0	0	0	1	0	3.0	2	14	0	0	0	0	2	0	3	1	2	0	0	.182
Holmes, D.	LA	R	1	1	5.19	14	0	0	0	0	0	17.1	15	77	10	10	3	3	1	1	22	0	19	1	1	.238
Horton, R.	STL	R	1	5	4.93	32	0	0	0	8	0	42.0	52	193	52	23	3	4	2	7	20	7	18	1	0	.315
Howell, J.	LA	L	5	5	2.18	45	0	0	0	35	16	66.0	59	271	17	16	5	6	1	3	20	6	59	4	0	.242
Howell, K.	PHI	R	8	7	4.64	18	18	2	2	0	0	106.2	106	467	60	55	12	6	1	3	49	6	70	8	0	.260
Huismann, M.	PIT	R	0	0	9.00	2	0	0	0	0	0	3.0	6	15	5	3	1	0	1	1	3	0	5	0	1	.462
Hurst, B.	SD	L	11	9	3.14	33	33	9	4	0	0	223.2	188	903	85	78	21	15	2	5	63	5	162	7	1	.228
Innis, J.	NY	R	1	3	2.39	18	0	0	0	12	0	26.1	19	104	9	7	4	6	2	1	10	3	12	1	1	.209
Jackson, D.	CIN	L	6	6	3.61	22	21	0	0	0	0	117.1	119	499	54	47	11	4	5	0	40	4	76	3	0	.266
Jones, J.	STL	R	0	0	6.75	1	0	0	0	1	0	1.1	2	8	2	1	0	0	2	0	2	0	1	0	0	.167
Kerfeld, C.	HOU-ATL	R	3	3	6.62	30	0	0	0	11	2	34.0	40	168	28	25	7	5	2	0	29	4	31	1	0	.303
Kipper, B.	PIT	L	5	2	3.02	41	1	0	0	7	3	62.2	44	260	24	21	7	2	3	0	26	1	35	1	5	.195

Player	T	W	L	ERA	G	GS	CG	ShO	SV	IP	TBF	H	R	ER	HR	BB	SO	BA
Knepper, B. ......SF	L	3	3	5.68	12	7	0	0	0	44.1	202	56	28	28	7	19	24	.311
Kraemer, J. ......CHI	L	0	0	7.20	18	0	0	0	0	25.0	119	31	20	20	2	14	16	.310
Kramer, R. ......PIT-CHI	R	0	3	4.50	22	4	0	0	0	46.0	207	47	25	23	6	21	27	.264
LaCoss, M. ......SF	R	6	4	3.94	13	12	1	0	0	77.2	337	75	37	34	5	39	39	.259
Lancaster, L. ......CHI	R	9	5	4.62	55	0	0	0	6	109.0	479	121	57	56	11	40	65	.283
Landrum, B. ......PIT	R	7	3	2.13	54	0	0	0	13	71.2	292	69	21	17	4	21	39	.262
Layana, T. ......CIN	R	5	3	3.49	55	0	0	0	0	80.0	344	71	34	31	10	44	53	.244
Lefferts, C. ......SD	L	7	5	2.52	56	0	0	0	23	78.2	327	68	24	22	7	22	60	.228
Leibrandt, C. ......ATL	L	9	11	3.16	24	24	5	1	0	162.1	680	164	72	57	9	35	76	.261
Lilliquist, D. ......ATL-SD	L	5	11	5.31	28	18	0	0	0	122.0	537	136	74	72	16	42	63	.285
Long, B. ......CHI	R	6	1	4.37	42	0	0	0	2	55.2	244	66	29	27	8	21	32	.301
Luecken, R. ......ATL	R	1	4	5.77	36	0	0	0	0	53.0	255	73	36	34	5	30	35	.336
Machado, J. ......NY	R	4	1	3.15	27	0	0	0	3	34.1	151	32	13	12	4	17	27	.248
Maddux, G. ......CHI	R	15	15	3.46	35	35	8	2	0	237.0	1011	242	116	91	11	71	144	.265
Maddux, M. ......LA	R	6	2	6.53	11	0	0	0	0	20.2	88	24	15	15	3	11	11	.293
Magrane, J. ......STL	L	10	17	3.59	31	31	3	0	0	203.1	855	204	86	81	10	59	100	.264
Mahler, R. ......CIN	R	7	6	4.28	35	16	0	0	0	134.2	564	134	67	64	16	39	68	.261
Malloy, R. ......MON	R	1	0	0.00	4	0	0	0	0	7.1	34	3	0	0	0	3	1	.143
Malone, C. ......PHI	R	0	1	3.68	8	0	0	0	0	14.0	62	8	6	6	1	11	7	.130
Marak, P. ......ATL	R	1	2	3.69	7	7	0	0	0	39.0	172	44	18	16	2	14	15	.267
Martinez, D. ......MON	L	0	0	54.00	2	0	0	0	0	0.1	5	2	2	2	0	2	0	.667
Martinez, De. ......MON	R	10	11	2.95	32	32	7	2	0	226.0	908	191	80	74	16	49	156	.228
Martinez, R. ......LA	R	20	6	2.92	33	33	12	3	0	234.1	950	191	89	76	22	67	223	.221
Mathews, G. ......STL	L	0	5	5.33	11	7	0	0	0	50.2	229	56	34	30	7	30	18	.277
McCament, R. ......SF	R	0	1	3.00	4	0	0	0	0	6.0	30	8	2	2	2	2	5	.333
McClellan, P. ......SF	R	0	0	11.74	2	0	0	0	0	7.2	44	12	10	10	0	6	2	.389
McDowell, R. ......PHI	R	6	8	3.86	72	0	0	0	22	86.1	373	92	41	37	2	35	39	.286
McElroy, C. ......PHI	L	1	0	7.71	16	0	0	0	0	14.0	76	24	13	12	0	10	16	.369
McGaffigan, A. ......SF	R	0	0	17.36	4	0	0	0	0	4.2	27	9	9	9	2	4	4	.455
Mercker, K. ......ATL	L	4	7	3.17	36	0	0	0	7	48.1	211	44	17	17	1	24	39	.236
Meyer, B. ......HOU	R	0	4	2.21	14	0	0	0	2	20.1	84	16	5	5	3	6	6	.211
Minutelli, G. ......CIN	L	0	0	9.00	2	0	0	0	0	1.0	6	0	1	1	0	2	0	.000
Mohorcic, D. ......MON	R	1	2	3.23	34	0	0	0	0	53.0	226	56	21	19	6	18	29	.286
Moore, B. ......PHI	R	0	0	3.38	3	0	0	0	0	2.2	13	4	1	1	0	2	1	.400

PITCHER	TEAM	T	W	L	ERA	G	GS	CG	SHO	GF	SV	IP	H	TBF	R	ER	HR	SH	SF	HB	BB	IBB	SO	WP	BK	OPP AVG
Morgan, M ....LA		R	11	15	3.75	33	33	6	2	0	0	211.0	216	891	100	88	19	11	4	5	60	5	106	4	1	.266
Mulholland, T ....PHI		L	9	10	3.34	33	26	6	2	1	0	180.2	172	746	78	67	15	7	12	2	42	7	75	7	2	.252
Munoz, M ....LA		L	0	0	3.18	8	0	0	0	3	0	5.2	6	24	2	2	0	1	2	0	0	0	4	0	0	.300
Musselman, J ....NY		L	1	0	5.63	28	0	0	0	5	0	32.0	40	144	22	20	3	1	2	1	11	0	14	3	1	.310
Myers, R ....CIN		L	4	6	2.08	66	0	0	0	59	31	86.2	59	353	24	20	6	4	0	2	38	8	98	2	1	.193
Nabholz, C ....MON		L	6	2	2.83	11	11	1	0	0	0	70.0	43	282	23	22	6	1	3	1	32	1	53	0	1	.176
Neidinger, J ......LA		R	5	3	3.28	12	12	0	0	0	0	74.0	67	301	30	27	4	4	3	1	15	1	46	0	0	.241
Niedenfuer, T ....STL		R	0	6	3.46	52	0	0	0	12	2	65.0	66	276	26	25	3	4	5	0	25	7	32	3	0	.269
Noboa, J ....MON		R	0	0	0.00	1	0	0	0	1	0	0.2	0	2	0	0	0	0	0	0	0	0	0	0	0	.000
Noles, D ....PHI		R	0	0	27.00	1	0	0	0	1	0	0.1	3	3	1	1	0	0	0	0	0	0	0	0	0	.667
Novoa, R ....SF		L	0	1	6.75	7	2	0	0	4	0	18.2	21	88	14	14	0	0	0	0	13	0	14	2	0	.284
Nunez, J ....CHI		R	4	7	6.53	21	10	0	0	2	0	60.2	61	274	47	44	5	11	3	2	34	2	40	2	0	.270
Ojeda, B ....NY		L	7	6	3.66	38	12	0	0	9	0	118.0	123	500	53	48	10	3	3	2	40	2	62	2	3	.272
Olivares, O ......STL		R	1	1	2.92	9	9	0	0	0	0	49.1	45	201	17	16	2	1	3	2	17	2	20	1	1	.249
Oliveras, F ....SF		R	2	2	2.77	33	2	0	0	9	0	55.1	47	231	22	17	5	2	0	2	21	6	41	2	1	.230
O'Neal, R ....SF		R	2	0	3.83	8	8	0	0	0	0	47.0	58	208	23	20	3	3	0	0	18	4	30	4	1	.314
Ontiveros, S .....PHI		R	0	1	2.70	12	0	0	0	1	0	10.0	9	43	3	3	1	0	2	3	3	0	6	3	0	.225
Osuna, A ....HOU		R	2	0	4.76	12	0	0	0	4	3	11.1	10	48	6	6	0	0	5	2	6	0	8	6	0	.270
Palacios, V ....PIT		R	0	0	0.00	7	0	0	0	4	3	15.0	10	50	6	0	0	0	2	0	2	0	8	0	0	.083
Parrett, J ....PHI-ATL		R	5	10	4.64	67	0	0	0	19	0	108.2	119	479	62	56	11	7	3	2	55	10	86	5	1	.290
Patterson, B .....PIT		L	8	5	2.95	55	0	0	0	19	5	94.2	88	386	33	31	9	5	3	1	21	2	70	1	2	.249
Pavlas, D ....CHI		R	2	3	2.11	13	0	0	0	5	0	21.1	23	93	7	5	2	0	2	1	6	1	12	3	0	.271
Pena, A ....NY		R	3	3	3.20	52	0	0	0	32	5	76.0	71	320	31	27	4	1	6	1	22	3	76	0	0	.245
Perez, M ....STL		R	1	0	3.95	13	0	0	0	7	0	13.2	12	55	6	6	0	1	1	1	5	0	5	2	0	.240
Perry, P ....LA		R	0	2	8.10	8	0	0	0	8	2	6.2	9	36	9	6	0	0	1	1	1	1	5	2	0	.310
Pico, J ....CHI		R	4	4	4.79	31	8	0	0	8	2	92.0	120	421	53	49	7	0	7	2	37	10	37	2	1	.321
Poole, J ....LA		L	0	1	4.22	16	0	0	0	4	0	10.2	7	46	5	5	1	0	6	4	8	4	6	2	0	.184
Portugal, M ......HOU		R	11	10	3.62	32	32	1	0	0	0	196.2	187	831	90	79	21	7	2	4	67	4	136	6	1	.250
Power, T ....PIT		R	0	1	3.66	40	0	0	0	25	7	51.2	50	218	23	21	5	3	2	2	17	6	42	2	0	.255
Quisenberry, D ...SD		R	0	1	13.50	5	0	0	0	2	0	6.2	13	37	12	10	1	0	3	0	3	1	4	0	1	.419
Rasmussen, D ....SD		L	11	15	4.51	32	32	3	1	0	0	187.2	217	825	110	94	28	14	4	3	62	4	86	9	1	.292

Name	T	W	L	ERA	G	IP	H	R	ER	BB	SO	BFP	AVG
Reed, R ....PIT	R	2	3	4.36	13	53.2	62	32	26	12	27	238	.279
Reuschel, R ......SF	R	3	6	3.93	15	87.0	102	40	38	31	49	390	.297
Reuss, J ....PIT	L	0	0	3.52	4	7.2	8	3	3	3	1	34	.267
Richards, R ......ATL	R	0	0	27.00	1	1.0	2	3	3	1	0	6	.400
Rijo, J ....CIN	R	14	8	2.70	29	197.0	151	65	59	78	152	801	.212
Robinson, D ......SF	R	10	7	4.57	26	157.2	173	84	80	41	78	667	.280
Robinson, R ......CIN	R	2	2	4.88	6	31.1	36	18	17	14	14	137	.295
Rodriguez, R .....SF	L	0	0	8.10	9	3.1	5	7	3	2	4	16	.357
Rodriguez, R .....CIN	R	0	1	6.10	3	10.1	15	7	7	5	8	47	.357
Rodriguez, R .....SD	L	1	0	2.83	32	47.2	52	17	15	16	22	201	.287
Roesler, M ....PIT	R	1	1	3.00	5	6.0	5	5	2	2	4	25	.217
Rojas, M ....MON	R	3	0	3.60	23	40.0	34	17	16	24	26	173	.234
Ross, M ....PIT	R	0	1	3.55	0	12.2	11	5	5	4	2	50	.244
Ruffin, B ....PHI	L	6	13	5.38	32	149.0	178	99	89	62	79	678	.297
Ruskin, S ....PIT-MON	L	3	2	2.75	67	75.1	75	28	23	38	57	336	.260
Sampen, B ....MON	R	12	7	2.99	59	90.1	94	34	30	33	69	394	.268
Schatzeder, D .HOU-NY	L	1	3	2.20	51	69.2	66	17	23	23	39	283	.261
Schiraldi, C .....SD	R	3	8	4.41	42	104.0	105	59	51	60	74	468	.264
Schmidt, D ....MON	R	9	13	4.31	34	48.0	58	26	23	13	22	213	.299
Scott, M ....HOU	R	9	13	3.81	32	205.2	194	87	87	66	121	871	.246
Scudder, S ....CIN	R	5	5	4.90	21	71.2	74	41	39	30	42	316	.265
Searage, R ....LA	L	1	0	2.78	29	32.1	30	11	10	10	19	136	.250
Sherrill, T ......STL	R	0	8	6.23	0	4.1	10	5	3	4	3	25	.476
Show, E ....SD	R	6	6	5.76	39	106.1	131	74	68	41	55	482	.306
Sisk, D ....ATL	R	0	10	3.86	3	2.1	1	1	1	4	1	13	.143
Smiley, J ....PIT	L	9	8	4.64	26	149.1	161	83	77	36	86	632	.275
Smith, B ....STL	R	9	6	4.27	26	141.1	160	77	67	30	78	605	.286
Smith, D ....HOU	R	6	9	2.39	49	60.1	45	18	16	20	50	239	.210
Smith, L ....STL	R	5	6	2.10	53	68.2	58	20	16	24	70	280	.227
Smith, P ....ATL	R	5	12	4.79	13	77.0	77	45	41	50	56	327	.260
Smith, Z .....MON-PIT	L	12	9	2.55	33	215.1	196	77	61	50	130	860	.245
Smoltz, J ....ATL	R	14	11	3.85	34	231.1	206	109	99	90	170	966	.240
Stanton, M ....ATL	L	0	0	18.00	7	7.0	16	14	14	4	7	42	.444
Sutcliffe, R .....CHI	R	0	2	5.91	5	21.1	25	14	14	11	7	97	.305

PITCHER	TEAM	T	W	L	ERA	G	GS	CG	SHO	GF	SV	IP	H	TBF	R	ER	HR	SH	SF	HB	BB	IBB	SO	WP	BK	OPP BAVG
Swan, R. ...SF		L	0	1	3.86	2	1	0	0	0	0	2.1	6	18	4	1	0	0	0	0	4	0	1	1	0	.429
Terrell, W. ...PIT		R	2	7	5.88	16	16	0	0	0	0	82.2	98	377	59	54	13	6	2	4	33	0	34	7	2	.295
Terry, S. ...STL		R	2	6	4.75	50	2	0	0	26	5	72.0	75	323	45	38	7	3	5	2	27	5	35	2	5	.264
Tewksbury, B. ...STL		R	10	9	3.47	28	20	3	1	1	0	145.1	151	595	67	56	7	5	7	3	15	3	50	2	0	.267
Thompson, R. ...MON		R	0	0	0.00	1	0	0	0	1	0	1.0	1	4	0	0	0	0	0	0	0	0	2	0	0	.250
Thurmond, M. ...SF		L	2	3	3.34	43	0	0	0	16	4	56.2	53	238	26	21	6	8	6	0	18	3	24	0	0	.257
Tibbs, J. ...PIT		R	1	0	2.57	5	0	0	0	3	0	7.0	7	29	2	2	0	0	0	0	2	0	4	1	0	.259
Tomlin, R. ...PIT		L	4	4	2.55	12	12	2	1	0	0	77.2	62	297	24	22	5	2	2	1	12	1	42	0	3	.221
Tudor, J. ...STL		L	12	4	2.40	25	22	1	0	2	0	146.1	120	575	48	39	10	8	1	2	30	4	63	0	0	.225
Valdez, R. ...SD		R	0	1	11.12	3	0	0	0	2	0	5.1	11	30	7	7	4	0	0	0	2	0	3	0	0	.393
Valdez, S. ...ATL		R	0	0	6.75	6	0	0	0	3	0	5.1	6	26	4	4	0	1	0	0	3	0	3	1	0	.273
Valenzuela, F. ...LA		L	13	13	4.59	33	33	5	2	0	0	204.0	223	900	112	104	19	11	4	0	77	4	115	13	1	.276
Valera, J. ...NY		R	1	1	6.92	3	3	0	0	0	0	13.0	20	64	11	10	1	1	0	0	7	0	3	1	0	.351
Viola, F. ...NY		L	20	12	2.67	35	35	7	3	0	0	249.2	227	1016	83	74	15	13	3	2	60	2	182	11	0	.242
Vosberg, E. ...SF		L	1	1	5.55	18	0	0	0	5	0	24.1	21	104	16	15	3	2	3	0	12	2	12	0	3	.233
Walk, B. ...PIT		R	7	5	3.75	26	24	1	1	1	0	129.2	136	549	59	54	17	3	3	2	36	2	73	5	1	.270
Walsh, D. ...LA		L	1	1	3.86	20	0	0	0	7	0	16.1	15	70	7	7	1	1	1	0	6	1	15	1	0	.242
Wells, T. ...LA		L	1	2	7.84	5	0	0	0	0	0	20.2	25	102	23	18	4	1	0	0	14	1	18	1	0	.287
Wetteland, J. ...LA		R	2	4	4.81	22	5	0	0	7	1	43.0	44	190	28	23	6	3	0	0	17	2	36	8	0	.263
Whitehurst, W. ...NY		R	1	0	3.29	38	0	0	0	16	3	65.2	63	263	28	24	5	2	3	1	9	2	46	2	0	.251
Whitson, E. ...SD		R	14	9	2.60	32	32	6	3	0	0	228.2	215	918	73	66	13	9	6	0	47	8	127	2	0	.251
Wilkins, D. ...CHI		R	0	0	9.82	7	0	0	0	3	0	7.1	11	41	8	8	1	0	0	1	3	0	3	3	0	.333
Williams, M. ...CHI		L	0	8	3.93	59	0	0	0	39	16	66.1	60	310	38	29	7	5	3	1	50	6	55	4	2	.239
Wilson, S. ...CHI		L	4	9	4.79	45	15	1	1	5	1	139.0	140	597	74	74	17	9	3	2	43	6	95	2	1	.259
Wilson, T. ...SF		L	8	7	4.00	27	17	3	0	2	0	110.1	87	457	52	49	11	6	2	1	49	3	66	5	1	.218
York, M. ...PIT		R	1	1	2.84	4	1	0	0	0	0	12.2	13	56	5	4	0	2	1	1	5	0	4	0	1	.277

CLUB PITCHING

CLUB	W	L	ERA	G	CG	SHO	REL	SV	IP	H	R	ER	HR	HB	BB	IBB	SO	WP	BK	OPP AVG
MONTREAL	85	77	3.37	162	18	11	341	50	1473.1	1349	598	551	127	38	510	76	991	27	13	.245
CINCINNATI	91	71	3.39	162	14	12	316	50	1456.1	1338	597	549	124	34	543	60	1029	48	26	.246
PITTSBURGH	95	67	3.40	162	18	8	364	43	1447.0	1367	619	546	135	30	413	48	848	42	22	.251
NEW YORK	91	71	3.43	162	18	14	268	41	1440.0	1339	613	548	119	27	444	35	1217	51	14	.246
HOUSTON	75	87	3.61	162	12	6	348	37	1450.0	1396	656	581	130	38	496	74	854	36	15	.255
SAN DIEGO	75	87	3.68	162	21	12	288	35	1461.2	1437	673	597	147	19	507	69	928	39	10	.258
LOS ANGELES	86	76	3.72	162	29	13	339	29	1442.0	1364	685	596	137	28	487	49	1021	63	9	.249
ST. LOUIS	70	92	3.87	162	8	2	364	39	1443.1	1432	698	621	98	34	475	72	833	45	5	.261
PHILADELPHIA	77	85	4.07	162	18	7	374	35	1449.1	1381	729	655	124	29	651	81	840	69	15	.253
SAN FRANCISCO	85	77	4.08	162	14	6	335	45	1446.1	1477	710	655	131	21	553	84	788	37	19	.267
CHICAGO	77	85	4.34	162	13	7	346	42	1442.2	1510	774	695	121	28	572	85	877	62	14	.271
ATLANTA	65	97	4.58	162	17	8	346	30	1429.2	1527	821	727	128	26	579	64	938	61	15	.275
TOTALS	972	972	3.79	972	200	116	4029	476	17381.1	16917	8173	7321	1521	352	6221	797	11164	580	187	.256

OFFICIAL 1990 AMERICAN LEAGUE RECORDS

COMPILED BY MLB-IBM BASEBALL INFORMATION SYSTEM
Official Statistician: ELIAS SPORTS BUREAU

FINAL STANDINGS

AMERICAN LEAGUE EAST					AMERICAN LEAGUE WEST				
CLUB	WON	LOST	PCT.	GB	CLUB	WON	LOST	PCT.	GB
BOSTON	88	74	.543	-	OAKLAND	103	59	.636	-
TORONTO	86	76	.531	2.0	CHICAGO	94	68	.580	9.0
DETROIT	79	83	.488	9.0	TEXAS	83	79	.512	20.0
CLEVELAND	77	85	.475	11.0	CALIFORNIA	80	82	.494	23.0
BALTIMORE	76	85	.472	11.5	SEATTLE	77	85	.475	26.0
MILWAUKEE	74	88	.457	14.0	KANSAS CITY	75	86	.466	27.5
NEW YORK	67	95	.414	21.0	MINNESOTA	74	88	.457	29.0

Championship Series: Oakland defeated Boston, 4 games to 0

Batting

INDIVIDUAL BATTING LEADERS

Batting Average	.329	Brett, K.C.
Games	162	Kelly, N.Y.
At Bats	642	H. Reynolds, Sea.
Runs	119	R. Henderson, Oak.
Hits	191	Palmeiro, Tex.
Total Bases	339	Fielder, Det.
Singles	136	R. Palmeiro, Tex.
Doubles	45	J. Reed, Bos. & Brett, K.C.
Triples	17	T. Fernandez, Tor.
Home Runs	51	Fielder, Det.
Runs Batted In	132	Fielder, Det.
Sacrifice Hits	17	Gallego, Oak. & B. Ripken, Bal.
Sacrifice Flies	14	D. Parker, Mil.
Hit by Pitch	11	P. Bradley, Bal.-Chi.
Bases on Balls	110	McGwire, Oak.
Intentional Bases on Balls	19	Boggs, Bos.
Strikeouts	182	Fielder, Det.
Stolen Bases	65	R. Henderson, Oak.
Caught Stealing	22	L. Johnson, Chi.
Grounded Into Double Plays	26	Calderon, Chi.
Slugging Percentage	.592	Fielder, Det.
On-Base Percentage	.439	R. Henderson, Oak.
Longest Batting Streak	25	Harper, Min. (July 6-Aug. 4)

TOP 15 QUALIFIERS FOR BATTING CHAMPIONSHIP

BATTER	TEAM	B	AVG	G	AB	R	H	TB	2B	3B	HR	RBI	SH	SF	HP	BB	IBB	SO	SB	CS	GI DP	SLG	OBP	E
Brett, G.	KC	L	.329	142	544	82	179	280	45	7	14	87	0	7	0	56	14	63	9	2	18	.515	.387	7
Henderson, R.	OAK	R	.325	136	489	119	159	282	33	3	28	61	2	2	4	97	2	60	65	10	13	.577	.439	5
Palmeiro, R.	TEX	L	.319	154	598	72	191	280	35	6	14	89	3	8	3	40	6	59	3	3	24	.468	.361	7
Trammell, A.	DET	R	.304	146	559	71	170	251	37	1	14	89	2	6	1	68	7	55	12	10	11	.449	.377	14
Boggs, W.	BOS	L	.302	155	619	89	187	259	44	5	6	63	0	6	1	87	19	68	0	1	11	.418	.386	20
Martinez, E.	SEA	R	.302	144	487	71	147	211	27	2	11	49	1	3	5	74	3	62	1	0	14	.433	.397	27
Griffey Jr, K.	SEA	L	.300	155	597	91	179	287	28	7	22	80	1	2	5	63	12	81	16	11	13	.481	.366	7
McGriff, F.	TOR	L	.300	153	557	91	167	295	21	1	35	88	1	4	2	94	12	108	5	3	12	.530	.400	6
James, C.	CLE	R	.299	140	528	71	158	234	32	4	12	70	3	3	4	31	3	71	5	3	7	.443	.341	4
Puckett, K.	MIN	R	.298	146	551	82	164	246	40	3	12	80	3	3	3	57	11	73	5	4	11	.446	.365	7
Greenwell, M	BOS	L	.297	159	610	71	181	265	30	6	14	73	0	3	4	65	12	43	8	7	15	.434	.367	4
Burks, E.	BOS	R	.296	152	588	89	174	286	33	8	21	89	2	2	4	48	3	82	9	11	19	.486	.349	7
Franco, J.	TEX	R	.296	157	582	96	172	234	27	1	11	69	2	2	2	82	4	83	31	11	18	.402	.383	19
Harper, B	MIN	R	.294	134	479	61	141	207	42	3	6	54	0	4	7	19	2	27	3	2	20	.432	.328	11
Sheffield, G	MIL	R	.294	125	487	67	143	205	30	1	10	67	4	9	3	44	1	41	25	10	11	.421	.350	25

INDIVIDUAL BATTING

BATTER	TEAM	B	AVG	G	AB	R	H	TB	2B	3B	HR	RBI	SH	SF	HP	BB	IBB	SO	SB	CS	GI DP	SLG	OBP	E
Afenir, M.	OAK	R	.143	14	14	0	2	2	1	0	0	2	0	0	0	0	0	6	0	0	0	.143	.133	1
Allred, B.	CLE	L	.188	4	16	2	3	7	1	0	1	2	0	0	0	2	0	3	0	0	0	.438	.278	0
Alomar, S.	CLE	R	.290	132	445	60	129	186	26	2	9	66	5	6	2	25	2	46	4	1	10	.418	.326	14
Anderson, B.	BAL	L	.231	89	234	24	54	72	5	2	3	24	4	5	5	31	1	46	15	2	4	.308	.327	2
Anderson, K.	CAL	R	.308	49	143	16	44	55	6	1	1	5	0	1	1	13	0	19	0	2	4	.385	.369	9
Azocar, O.	NY	L	.248	65	214	18	53	76	8	0	5	19	1	1	2	2	0	15	5	0	2	.355	.257	1
Baerga, C.	CLE	S	.260	108	312	46	81	123	17	2	7	47	1	5	4	16	2	57	0	0	4	.394	.300	17
Baines, H.	TEX-OAK	L	.284	135	415	52	118	183	15	1	16	65	0	7	0	67	10	80	0	3	17	.441	.378	1

BATTER	TEAM	B	AVG	G	AB	R	H	TB	2B	3B	HR	RBI	SH	SF	HP	BB	IBB	SO	SB	CS	GI DP	SLG	OBP	E
Baker, D.	MIN	S	.000	3	1	0	0	0	0	0	0	0	0	0	0	0	0	0	0	0	0	.000	.000	0
Balboni, S.	NY	R	.192	116	266	24	51	108	6	0	17	34	1	0	3	35	2	91	0	0	4	.406	.291	3
Barfield, J.	NY	R	.246	153	476	69	117	217	21	2	25	78	2	5	5	82	4	150	4	3	6	.456	.359	9
Barrett, M.	BOS	R	.226	62	159	15	36	40	4	0	0	13	11	2	1	15	1	13	4	0	4	.252	.294	2
Bates, B.	MIL	L	.103	14	29	6	3	4	1	0	0	0	0	1	0	4	0	7	4	0	0	.138	.206	2
Belcher, K.	TEX	R	.133	16	15	4	2	3	1	0	0	0	0	0	0	2	0	6	0	0	0	.200	.235	0
Bell, G.	TOR	R	.265	142	562	67	149	237	25	0	21	86	0	11	1	32	7	80	3	0	14	.422	.303	5
Bell, J.	BAL	S	.000	5	2	1	0	0	0	0	0	0	0	0	0	0	0	1	0	0	0	.000	.000	0
Belle, J.	CLE	R	.174	9	23	1	4	7	0	0	1	3	0	0	0	1	0	6	0	0	1	.304	.208	0
Bergman, D.	DET	L	.278	100	205	21	57	75	10	1	2	26	1	2	0	33	3	17	0	2	7	.366	.375	1
Berry, S.	KC	R	.217	8	23	2	5	8	1	1	0	4	1	0	0	2	0	5	3	0	0	.348	.280	1
Bichette, D.	CAL	R	.255	109	349	40	89	151	15	1	15	53	6	2	3	16	1	79	5	2	9	.433	.292	7
Blankenship, L.	OAK	R	.191	86	136	18	26	29	3	0	0	10	6	1	0	20	0	23	5	1	6	.213	.295	5
Blowers, M.	NY	R	.188	48	144	16	27	46	4	0	5	21	0	1	1	12	0	50	3	0	3	.319	.255	10
Boggs, W.	BOS	L	.302	155	619	89	187	259	44	5	6	63	0	6	1	87	19	68	0	1	14	.418	.386	20
Boone, B.	KC	R	.239	40	117	11	28	31	3	0	0	9	2	0	1	17	2	12	0	1	2	.265	.336	4
Borders, P.	TOR	R	.286	125	346	36	99	172	24	2	15	49	0	3	0	18	2	57	0	1	17	.497	.319	4
Bordick, M.	OAK	R	.071	25	14	0	1	1	0	0	0	0	2	0	0	1	0	4	0	0	0	.071	.133	0
Bosley, T.	TEX	L	.138	30	29	3	4	7	0	0	0	3	0	0	0	4	1	7	1	1	1	.241	.242	0
Boston, D.	CHI	L	.000	5	1	0	0	0	0	0	0	0	0	0	0	0	0	1	0	0	0	.000	.000	0
Bradley, P.	BAL-CHI	R	.256	117	422	59	108	138	14	2	4	31	11	1	11	50	5	61	17	7	11	.327	.349	4
Bradley, S.	SEA	L	.223	101	233	11	52	64	9	0	1	28	3	6	0	15	2	20	1	1	6	.275	.264	2
Braggs, G.	MIL	R	.248	37	113	17	28	42	9	1	1	13	0	3	1	12	2	21	5	3	1	.372	.328	3
Brett, G.	KC	L	.329	142	544	82	179	280	45	5	14	87	1	7	0	56	14	63	9	2	18	.515	.387	7
Briley, G.	SEA	L	.246	125	337	40	83	120	18	2	5	29	4	4	0	37	4	48	16	4	6	.356	.319	2
Brock, G.	MIL	L	.248	123	367	42	91	135	23	2	7	50	2	8	0	43	9	45	4	2	8	.368	.324	5
Brookens, T.	CLE	R	.266	64	154	18	41	55	7	2	1	20	3	0	0	14	1	25	0	0	6	.357	.322	6
Brown, K.	TEX	R	.000	27	1	0	0	0	0	0	0	0	0	0	0	0	0	0	0	0	0	.000	.000	3
Brown, M.	BAL	S	.200	9	15	1	3	3	0	0	0	0	1	0	0	2	0	7	0	0	0	.200	.250	0
Browne, J.	CLE	S	.267	140	513	92	137	191	26	5	6	50	12	2	2	72	1	46	12	7	12	.372	.353	10
Brumley, M.	SEA	S	.224	62	147	19	33	46	5	4	0	7	4	1	0	10	0	22	2	2	5	.313	.272	5
Brunansky, T.	BOS	R	.267	129	461	61	123	202	24	5	15	71	1	8	1	54	7	105	5	10	12	.438	.342	5
Buckner, B.	BOS	L	.186	22	43	4	8	11	0	0	1	3	0	0	0	3	2	2	0	0	1	.256	.234	0

Player	Tm	B	AVG	G	AB	R	H	TB	2B	3B	HR	RBI	BB	SO	SB	SLG	OBP
Buechele, S	TEX	R	.215	91	251	30	54	85	10	0	7	30	27	63	1	.339	.294
Buhner, J	SEA	R	.276	51	163	16	45	78	12	1	7	33	17	50	2	.479	.357
Burks, E	BOS	R	.296	152	588	89	174	286	33	8	21	89	48	82	9	.486	.349
Bush, R	MIN	L	.243	73	181	17	44	70	8	0	6	18	21	27	4	.387	.338
Calderon, I	CHI	R	.273	158	607	85	166	256	44	2	14	74	51	79	32	.422	.327
Canale, G	MIL	L	.077	10	13	1	1	2	0	0	0	0	1	4	0	.154	.200
Canseco, J	OAK	R	.274	131	481	83	132	261	14	2	37	101	72	158	19	.543	.371
Canseco, O	OAK	R	.105	9	19	2	2	3	0	0	0	0	1	10	0	.158	.150
Castillo, C	MIN	R	.219	64	137	11	30	34	4	1	0	12	3	23	1	.248	.239
Cerone, R	NY	R	.302	49	139	12	42	54	6	0	2	11	5	13	0	.388	.324
Coachman, P	CAL	R	.311	16	45	0	14	17	3	0	0	5	1	7	1	.378	.354
Cochrane, D	SEA	S	.150	15	20	3	3	3	0	0	0	0	0	8	0	.150	.150
Cole, A	CLE	L	.300	63	227	43	68	81	5	4	0	13	28	38	40	.357	.379
Coles, D	SEA-DET	R	.209	89	215	22	45	63	7	1	0	20	16	38	1	.293	.265
Conine, J	KC	R	.250	9	20	5	5	7	1	0	0	0	2	5	0	.350	.350
Coolbaugh, S	TEX	R	.200	67	180	21	36	48	6	2	0	13	15	47	1	.267	.264
Cooper, S	BOS	L	.000	2	2	0	0	0	0	0	0	0	0	1	0	.000	.000
Cotto, H	SEA	R	.259	127	355	40	92	124	14	3	4	33	22	52	21	.349	.307
Cuyler, M	DET	S	.258	19	51	8	13	18	3	1	0	8	5	10	1	.353	.316
Daugherty, J	TEX	S	.300	125	310	36	93	135	20	2	6	47	22	49	0	.435	.347
Davis, A	SEA	L	.283	140	494	63	140	212	21	2	17	68	85	68	0	.429	.387
Davis, C	CAL	R	.265	113	412	58	109	164	17	2	12	58	61	89	1	.398	.357
Deer, R	MIL	R	.209	134	440	57	92	190	15	2	27	69	64	147	2	.432	.313
Devereaux, M	BAL	R	.240	108	367	48	88	144	18	1	12	49	28	48	13	.392	.291
Diaz, C	TOR	R	.333	9	3	0	1	1	0	0	0	0	0	2	0	.333	.333
Diaz, E	MIL	R	.271	86	218	27	59	65	12	1	2	14	21	32	4	.298	.338
Disarcina, G	CAL	R	.140	18	57	8	8	11	2	0	0	0	0	10	0	.193	.183
Dorsett, B	NY	R	.143	14	35	5	5	7	2	0	0	0	3	4	0	.200	.189
Downing, B	CAL	R	.273	96	330	47	90	154	18	0	14	51	50	45	0	.467	.374
Ducey, R	TOR	L	.302	19	53	7	16	21	5	2	0	7	7	15	1	.396	.396
Dwyer, J	MIN	L	.190	37	63	7	12	15	0	2	1	5	12	7	0	.238	.320
Eisenreich, J	KC	L	.280	142	496	61	139	197	29	7	5	51	42	51	12	.397	.335
Eppard, J	TOR	L	.200	6	5	0	1	1	0	0	0	0	0	2	0	.200	.333
Espinoza, A	NY	R	.224	150	438	31	98	120	12	2	2	20	16	54	1	.274	.258
Espy, C	TEX	S	.127	52	71	10	9	9	0	2	0	1	10	20	7	.127	.235
Evans, D	BOS	R	.249	123	445	66	111	174	18	3	13	63	67	73	3	.391	.349

BATTER	TEAM	B	AVG	G	AB	R	H	TB	2B	3B	HR	RBI	SH	SF	HP	BB	IBB	SO	SB	CS	GI DP	SLG	OBP	E
Felder, M	MIL	S	.274	121	237	38	65	85	7	2	3	27	8	5	0	22	0	17	20	9	0	.359	.330	5
Felix, J	TOR	S	.263	127	463	73	122	204	23	7	15	65	2	5	2	45	0	99	13	8	4	.441	.328	9
Fermin, F	CLE	R	.256	148	414	47	106	126	13	2	1	40	13	5	0	26	0	22	3	3	13	.304	.297	16
Fernandez, T	TOR	S	.276	161	635	84	175	248	27	17	4	66	2	6	7	71	4	70	26	13	17	.391	.352	8
Fielder, C	DET	R	.277	159	573	104	159	339	25	1	51	132	0	5	5	90	11	182	0	1	15	.592	.377	14
Finley, S	BAL	L	.256	142	464	46	119	152	16	4	3	37	10	5	1	32	8	53	22	9	8	.328	.304	7
Fisk, C	CHI	R	.285	137	452	65	129	204	21	0	18	65	0	1	6	61	3	73	7	2	12	.451	.378	4
Fletcher, S	CHI	R	.242	151	509	54	123	159	18	3	4	56	11	5	3	45	3	63	1	3	10	.312	.304	9
Francona, T	TEX	R	.296	157	582	96	172	234	27	1	11	69	2	5	2	82	3	83	31	10	12	.402	.383	19
Francona, T	MIL	L	.000	3	4	1	0	0	0	0	0	0	2	0	0	0	0	0	0	0	.000	.000	0
Fryman, T	DET	R	.297	66	232	32	69	109	11	1	9	27	1	0	1	17	0	51	3	3	3	.470	.348	14
Gaetti, G	MIN	R	.229	154	577	61	132	217	27	5	16	85	1	8	1	36	1	101	6	8	22	.376	.274	18
Gagne, G	MIN	R	.235	138	388	38	91	140	22	3	7	38	8	2	1	24	0	76	8	5	5	.361	.280	14
Gallagher, D	CHI-BAL	R	.254	68	126	12	32	38	4	1	1	4	7	1	0	7	0	12	1	5	3	.302	.296	2
Gallego, M	OAK	R	.206	140	389	36	80	106	13	0	3	34	17	4	0	35	0	50	5	2	13	.272	.277	13
Gantner, J	MIL	L	.263	88	323	36	85	103	8	2	0	25	4	0	2	29	0	19	18	3	10	.319	.328	9
Gedman, R	BOS	L	.200	17	15	3	3	3	0	0	0	0	0	1	0	5	1	6	0	0	1	.200	.259	1
Geren, R	NY	R	.213	110	277	21	59	90	7	0	8	31	0	2	2	13	0	73	0	1	7	.325	.259	4
Giles, B	SEA	R	.232	45	95	15	22	40	6	0	4	11	6	0	0	15	0	24	2	1	3	.421	.336	3
Gladden, D	MIN	R	.275	136	534	64	147	201	27	6	5	40	1	4	6	26	2	67	25	9	17	.376	.314	6
Gomez, L	MIN	R	.231	12	39	3	9	9	0	0	0	1	1	0	0	8	0	7	0	0	2	.231	.362	4
Gonzales, R	BAL	R	.214	67	103	13	22	30	3	1	1	12	6	1	0	12	0	14	1	0	3	.291	.296	4
Gonzalez, J	TEX	R	.289	25	90	11	26	47	7	1	4	12	0	3	2	2	0	18	0	1	2	.522	.316	2
Grebeck, C	CHI	R	.168	59	119	7	20	28	3	1	1	9	3	3	8	6	0	24	0	0	2	.235	.227	0
Green, G	TEX	R	.216	62	88	10	19	22	3	0	0	8	4	1	0	6	0	18	1	1	2	.250	.263	3
Greenwell, M	BOS	L	.297	159	610	71	181	265	30	6	14	73	0	3	4	65	12	43	8	11	19	.434	.367	5
Griffey Jr, K	SEA	L	.300	155	597	91	179	287	28	7	22	80	0	1	1	63	12	81	16	11	12	.481	.366	7
Griffey Sr, K	SEA	L	.377	21	77	13	29	40	2	0	3	18	0	1	0	10	0	3	0	0	1	.519	.443	1
Gruber, K	TOR	R	.274	150	592	92	162	303	36	6	31	118	1	13	8	48	0	94	14	6	14	.512	.330	19
Guillen, O	CHI	L	.279	160	516	61	144	176	21	4	1	58	15	5	1	26	8	37	13	17	6	.341	.312	17
Hale, C	MIN	L	.000	1	0	0	0	0	0	0	0	2	0	0	0	0	0	1	0	0	0	.000	.000	0
Hall, M	NY	L	.258	113	360	41	93	156	23	0	12	46	0	2	2	6	0	46	0	0	7	.433	.272	2
Hamilton, D	MIL	L	.295	89	156	27	46	54	5	2	1	18	3	0	0	9	2	12	10	3	2	.346	.333	1

Batting statistics (American League). Column headers are not printed on this page; standard abbreviations are used below. Honeycutt, R. is a pitcher with essentially no batting line (games only). Several figures in the sparse/right-hand columns are difficult to read.

Player	Tm	B	AVG	G	AB	R	H	TB	2B	3B	HR	RBI	BB	SO	SB	SLG	OBP
Harper, B.	MIN	R	.294	134	479	61	141	207	42	3	6	54	19	27	3	.432	.328
Haselman, B.	TEX	R	.154	7	13	2	2	2	0	0	0	3	1	5		.154	.214
Hassey, R.	OAK	L	.213	94	254	18	54	76	7	0	5	22	27	29		.299	.288
Heath, M.	DET	R	.270	122	370	46	100	143	18	2	7	38	19	71	7	.386	.311
Heep, D.	BOS	L	.174	41	69	3	12	15	1	1	0	8	7	14		.217	.256
Hemond, S.	OAK	R	.154	7	13	2	2	2	0	0	0	1	0	5		.154	.154
Henderson, D.	OAK	R	.271	127	450	65	122	210	28	0	20	63	40	105	3	.467	.331
Henderson, R.	OAK	R	.325	136	489	119	159	282	33	3	28	61	97	60	65	.577	.439
Hernandez, K.	CLE	L	.200	43	130	7	26	31	2	0	1	8	14	17		.238	.283
Hill, D.	CAL	S	.264	103	352	36	93	124	18	2	3	32	29	27	8	.352	.319
Hill, G.	TOR	R	.231	84	260	47	60	113	11	3	12	32	18	62		.435	.281
Hoiles, C.	BAL	R	.190	23	63	7	12	18	3	0	1	6	5	12		.286	.250
Holman, B.	SEA	R	.000	28	1	0	0	0	0	0	0	0	0	0		.000	.000
Honeycutt, R.	OAK	L		66													
Horn, S.	BAL	L	.248	79	246	30	61	116	13	0	14	45	32	62		.472	.332
Howard, S.	CAL	R	.231	21	52	5	12	16	4	0	0	1	4	17		.308	.286
Howell, J.	OAK	R	.228	105	316	35	72	117	19	1	8	33	46	61		.370	.326
Howell, D.	CAL	L	.136	14	22	3	3	5	1	1	0	3	0	12		.227	.240
Hrbek, K.	MIN	L	.287	143	492	61	141	233	26	0	22	79	69	45	5	.474	.377
Hulett, T.	BAL	R	.255	53	153	8	39	57	7	1	3	16	15	41		.373	.321
Huson, J.	TEX	L	.240	145	396	57	95	111	12	2	0	28	46	54	12	.280	.320
Incaviglia, P.	TEX	R	.233	153	529	59	123	222	27	0	24	85	45	146	3	.420	.342
Jackson, B.	KC	R	.272	111	405	74	110	212	16	1	28	78	44	128	15	.523	.365
Jacoby, B.	CLE	R	.293	155	553	77	162	236	24	4	14	75	63	58	4	.427	.341
James, C.	CLE	R	.299	140	528	62	158	234	32	4	12	70	31	71	4	.443	.347
James, D.	CLE	L	.274	87	248	28	68	90	15	2	1	22	27	23	5	.363	.306
Javier, S.	OAK	S	.242	19	33	4	8	12	2	1	0	3	0	6	3	.364	.295
Jefferson, S.	BAL-CLE	S	.231	59	117	22	27	41	8	0	2	10	3	26		.350	.350
Jeltz, S.	KC	S	.155	74	103	16	16	20	4	0	0	14	20	21		.194	.275
Jennings, J.	OAK	L	.192	64	156	19	30	47	7	2	2	24	6		9	.301	.325
Johnson, L.	CHI	L	.285	151	541	76	154	193	18	9	1	51	33	45	36	.357	.307
Jones, T.	DET-SEA	R	.260	75	204	23	53	81	8			24	9	25	8	.397	.306
Jose, F.	OAK	S	.264	101	341	42	90	126	12	0	8	39	16	65	8	.370	.350
Joyner, W.	CAL	L	.268	83	310	35	83	122	15	0	8	41	41	34	2	.394	.308
Karkovice, R.	CHI	R	.246	68	183	45	45	73	10	0	6	20	16	52		.399	.323
Kelly, R.	NY	R	.285	162	641	85	183	268	32	4	15	61	33	148	42	.418	.323

BATTER	TEAM	B	AVG	G	AB	R	H	TB	2B	3B	IIR	RBI	SH	SF	HP	BB	IBB	SO	SB	CS	GI DP	SLG	OBP	E
Kittle, R. ......CHI-BAL		R	.231	105	338	33	78	148	16	0	18	46	0	2	4	26	2	91	0	1	6	.438	.293	2
Kominsk, B ......BAL		R	.238	46	101	18	24	37	4	0	3	8	2	1	0	14	1	29	1	0	2	.366	.342	0
Kreuter, C ......TEX		R	.045	22	22	1	1	2	1	0	0	2	1	0	2	8	0	9	0	1	2	.091	.280	1
Kunkel, J ......TEX		R	.170	22	200	17	34	56	11	1	3	17	5	1	0	11	0	66	2	1	7	.280	.221	11
Kutcher, R ......BOS		R	.230	63	74	18	17	26	4	1	1	5	3	0	0	13	0	18	3	3	2	.351	.345	0
Lancellotti, R ......BOS		R	.000	8	8	0	0	0	0	0	0	0	0	0	1	0	0	3	0	0	0	.000	.000	0
Lansford, C ......OAK		R	.268	134	507	58	136	162	15	1	3	50	2	4	4	45	4	50	16	14	10	.320	.333	9
Larkin, G ......MIN		S	.269	119	401	46	108	157	26	4	5	42	5	4	2	42	2	55	5	3	6	.392	.343	2
Lawless, T ......TOR		S	.083	15	12	1	1	1	0	0	0	0	1	0	0	0	0	1	1	2	0	.083	.083	1
Lee, M ......TOR		S	.243	117	391	45	95	133	12	4	6	41	5	3	0	26	0	90	3	1	9	.340	.288	4
Lelus, M ......MIN		R	.240	14	25	4	6	10	1	0	0	4	1	0	1	2	0	2	0	0	0	.400	.296	0
Lemon, C ......DET		R	.258	104	322	39	83	122	16	0	5	32	2	3	7	48	3	61	3	2	8	.379	.359	6
Leonard, J ......SEA		R	.251	134	478	39	120	170	20	0	10	75	2	0	3	37	6	97	3	2	20	.356	.305	2
Lewis, D ......OAK		R	.229	25	35	4	8	8	0	0	0	1	3	1	1	7	0	4	4	0	2	.229	.372	0
Leyritz, J ......NY		R	.257	92	303	42	78	108	13	1	5	25	1	0	1	27	1	51	2	0	2	.356	.331	13
Lindeman, J ......DET		R	.219	12	32	5	7	14	1	0	2	8	1	1	0	2	0	13	0	0	1	.438	.265	0
Liriano, N ......TOR-MIN		S	.234	103	355	46	83	116	12	9	1	28	4	2	1	38	0	44	8	7	8	.327	.308	11
Lusader, S ......DET		L	.241	45	87	13	21	29	2	0	2	16	0	3	1	12	0	8	0	0	1	.333	.324	1
Lyons, S ......CHI		L	.192	94	146	22	28	39	6	1	1	11	4	0	1	10	1	41	1	0	1	.267	.245	5
Maas, K ......NY		L	.252	79	254	42	64	136	9	0	21	41	0	2	3	43	10	76	1	2	2	.535	.367	9
Macfarlane, M ......KC		R	.255	124	400	37	102	152	24	4	6	58	1	6	7	25	2	69	1	1	9	.380	.306	6
Mack, S ......MIN		R	.326	125	313	50	102	144	10	4	8	44	6	6	5	29	1	69	13	4	7	.460	.392	3
Maldonado, C ......CLE		R	.273	155	590	76	161	263	32	2	22	95	1	7	5	49	4	134	3	5	13	.446	.330	6
Manrique, F ......MIN		R	.237	69	228	22	54	79	10	2	5	29	1	2	2	4	0	35	2	1	8	.346	.254	2
Manto, J ......CLE		R	.224	30	76	12	17	30	5	1	2	14	0	0	3	21	0	18	1	0	0	.395	.392	7
Marshall, M ......BOS		R	.286	30	112	10	32	52	6	1	4	12	1	1	4	10	2	26	0	0	2	.464	.316	2
Martinez, C ......CHI		R	.224	92	272	18	61	89	6	5	4	24	5	3	1	10	0	40	0	0	4	.327	.252	1
Martinez, E ......SEA		R	.302	144	487	71	147	211	27	2	11	49	2	5	5	74	3	62	1	4	13	.433	.397	8
Martinez, T ......SEA		L	.221	24	68	4	15	19	4	0	0	5	1	1	0	9	0	9	1	0	0	.279	.308	27
Marzano, J ......BOS		R	.241	32	83	8	20	24	4	0	0	6	2	0	3	5	0	10	1	0	3	.289	.281	0
Mattingly, D ......NY		L	.256	102	394	40	101	132	16	0	5	42	0	3	0	28	13	20	1	1	13	.335	.308	3
Mayne, B ......KC		L	.231	5	13	2	3	3	0	0	0	0	2	0	0	3	0	3	0	1	0	.231	.375	1
McCray, R ......CHI		R	.000	32	6	8	0	0	0	0	0	0	1	0	0	1	0	4	6	0	0	.000	.143	0

Player	Club	B	AVG	G	AB	R	H	TB	2B	3B	HR	RBI	BB	SO	SB	CS	GDP	SA	OBA	
McGee, W.	OAK	S	.274	29	113	23	31	38	3	2	0	15	10	18	3	0	4	.336	.333	1
McGriff, F.	TOR	L	.300	153	557	91	167	295	21	1	35	88	94	108	5	3	13	.530	.400	6
McGwire, M.	OAK	R	.235	156	523	87	123	256	16	0	39	108	110	116	2	1	13	.489	.370	5
McIntosh, T.	MIL	R	.200	5	5	1	1	4	0	0	1	1	0	2	1	0	0	.800	.200	1
McKnight, J.	BAL	S	.200	29	75	11	15	20	2	0	1	4	5	17	0	0	1	.267	.259	0
McLemore, M.	CAL-CLE	S	.150	28	60	6	9	12	2	0	0	2	4	15	0	3	5	.183	.203	4
McRae, B.	KC	S	.286	46	168	21	48	68	8	3	2	23	9	29	4	3	8	.405	.318	0
Melvin, B.	BAL	R	.243	93	301	30	73	104	14	0	5	37	11	53	0	0	3	.346	.267	1
Meulens, H.	NY	R	.241	23	83	12	20	36	7	0	3	10	9	25	0	1	0	.434	.337	2
Milligan, R.	BAL	R	.265	109	362	64	96	178	20	1	20	60	88	68	6	3	11	.492	.408	9
Molitor, P.	MIL	R	.285	103	418	64	119	194	27	6	12	45	37	51	18	5	7	.464	.343	10
Morman, R.	KC	R	.270	12	37	1	10	21	4	0	1	3	0	3	0	0	0	.568	.317	0
Moseby, L.	DET	L	.248	122	431	64	107	175	16	2	14	51	48	77	17	9	14	.406	.329	5
Moses, J.	MIN	S	.221	115	172	26	38	46	3	1	1	14	19	19	2	3	4	.267	.303	0
Mulliniks, R.	TOR	L	.289	57	97	11	28	38	4	0	2	16	22	16	2	1	3	.392	.417	2
Munoz, P.	MIN	R	.271	22	85	13	23	29	4	0	0	5	2	16	0	0	2	.341	.281	1
Myers, G.	TOR	L	.236	87	250	33	59	83	7	2	5	22	22	33	0	0	7	.332	.293	3
Naehring, T.	BOS	R	.271	24	85	10	23	35	5	0	2	12	8	15	0	0	12	.412	.333	9
Newman, A.	MIN	S	.242	144	388	43	94	108	14	3	0	30	33	34	13	6	2	.278	.304	13
Nixon, D.	BAL	L	.250	20	20	1	5	7	1	0	0	2	1	7	0	0	7	.350	.286	0
Nokes, M.	DET-NY	L	.248	136	351	33	87	131	9	0	11	40	24	47	2	0	11	.373	.306	2
O'Brien, C.	MIL	R	.186	46	145	11	27	38	7	0	0	11	11	26	0	2	5	.262	.253	2
O'Brien, P.	SEA	L	.224	108	366	32	82	115	18	1	5	27	44	33	0	2	8	.314	.308	5
Olerud, J.	TOR	L	.265	111	358	43	95	154	15	1	14	48	57	75	0	2	3	.430	.364	3
Orsulak, J.	BAL	L	.269	124	413	49	111	164	14	3	11	57	46	48	6	4	3	.397	.343	3
Ortiz, J.	MIN	R	.335	71	170	18	57	66	7	0	0	18	12	16	0	1	2	.388	.384	0
Orton, J.	CAL	R	.190	31	84	8	16	24	5	0	1	6	5	31	0	1	2	.286	.244	2
Palacios, R.	KC	R	.232	41	56	8	13	22	3	2	0	6	5	24	1	0	1	.393	.295	1
Palmeiro, R.	TEX	L	.319	154	598	72	191	280	35	0	14	89	40	59	3	0	7	.468	.361	7
Paredes, J.	DET	R	.125	6	8	1	1	1	0	0	0	0	0	0	0	0	0	.125	.222	1
Parker, D.	MIL	L	.289	157	610	71	176	275	30	0	21	92	41	102	4	5	18	.451	.330	6
Parrish, L.	CAL	R	.268	133	470	54	126	212	14	0	24	70	46	107	2	5	12	.451	.338	3
Pasqua, D.	CHI	L	.274	112	325	43	89	161	27	2	13	58	37	66	1	3	4	.495	.347	5
Pecota, B.	KC	R	.242	87	240	43	58	92	15	2	5	20	33	39	8	6	5	.383	.336	5
Pena, T.	BOS	R	.263	143	491	62	129	171	19	1	7	56	43	71	8	3	23	.348	.322	5
Perry, G.	KC	L	.254	133	465	57	118	168	22	2	8	57	39	56	17	5	14	.361	.313	6

BATTER	TEAM	B	AVG	G	AB	R	H	TB	2B	3B	HR	RBI	SH	SF	HP	BB	IBB	SO	SB	CS	GI DP	SLG	OBP	E
Petralli, G	TEX	L	.255	133	325	28	83	98	13	1	0	21	1	3	3	50	3	49	0	2	12	.302	.357	6
Pettis, G	TEX	S	.239	136	423	66	101	142	16	8	3	31	11	3	4	57	3	118	38	15	6	.336	.333	2
Phelps, K	OAK-CLE	L	.150	56	120	10	18	23	2	0	1	6	0	1	0	22	0	21	0	0	4	.192	.280	1
Phillips, T	DET	S	.251	152	573	97	144	201	23	5	8	55	9	3	2	99	0	85	19	9	10	.351	.364	23
Plantier, P	BOS	L	.133	14	15	1	2	3	1	0	0	3	0	1	1	4	0	6	0	0	1	.200	.333	0
Polidor, G	MIL	R	.067	18	15	1	1	1	0	0	0	1	0	0	0	0	0	6	0	0	0	.067	.067	0
Polonia, L	NY-CAL	L	.335	120	403	52	135	166	7	9	2	35	3	4	1	25	1	43	21	14	9	.412	.372	3
Puckett, K	MIN	R	.298	146	551	82	164	246	40	3	12	80	0	3	3	57	11	73	5	4	15	.446	.365	4
Quinlan, T	TOR	R	.500	1	2	0	1	1	0	0	0	0	0	0	0	0	0	1	0	0	0	.500	.500	0
Quintana, C	BOS	R	.287	149	512	56	147	196	28	0	7	67	4	2	2	52	0	74	1	2	19	.383	.354	17
Quirk, J	OAK	L	.281	56	121	12	34	50	5	1	3	26	5	3	1	14	0	34	0	1	3	.413	.353	5
Randolph, W	OAK	R	.257	93	292	37	75	93	9	3	1	21	7	3	1	32	0	25	6	2	11	.318	.331	7
Ray, J	CAL	S	.277	105	404	47	112	150	23	0	5	43	1	3	2	19	2	44	2	3	10	.371	.308	7
Reed, J	BOS	R	.289	155	598	70	173	233	45	1	5	51	11	3	4	75	0	65	4	1	19	.390	.371	16
Reimer, K	TEX	L	.260	64	100	5	26	43	4	1	5	15	0	1	3	10	3	22	0	1	3	.430	.333	1
Reynolds, H	SEA	S	.252	160	642	100	162	223	36	5	5	55	5	6	3	52	0	52	31	16	9	.347	.336	19
Ripken, B	BAL	R	.291	129	406	48	118	157	28	1	3	38	17	7	4	28	2	43	5	1	7	.387	.342	8
Ripken, C	BAL	R	.250	161	600	78	150	249	28	4	21	84	0	1	5	82	18	66	3	1	12	.415	.341	8
Rivera, L	BOS	R	.225	118	346	38	78	119	20	0	7	45	12	1	1	25	0	58	4	3	10	.344	.279	18
Robidoux, B	BOS	L	.182	27	44	3	8	15	4	0	1	4	0	1	0	6	0	14	0	0	2	.341	.288	1
Romero, E	DET	R	.229	32	70	8	16	19	3	0	0	4	3	1	0	6	0	4	0	0	0	.271	.286	1
Romine, K	BOS	R	.272	70	136	21	37	50	7	0	2	14	0	1	1	12	0	27	4	4	7	.368	.331	2
Rose, B	CAL	R	.385	7	13	5	5	8	1	0	0	2	0	0	0	0	0	1	0	0	0	.615	.467	0
Rowland, R	DET	R	.158	7	19	3	3	4	1	0	0	0	1	0	2	2	0	1	0	0	1	.211	.238	1
Russell, J	TEX	R	.273	68	128	16	35	45	4	0	2	8	6	0	0	11	2	41	0	0	3	.352	.331	3
Salas, M	DET	L	.232	74	164	18	38	68	3	0	9	24	1	1	1	21	1	28	0	1	3	.415	.323	3
Sanders, D	NY	L	.158	57	133	24	21	36	2	2	3	9	0	0	1	13	0	27	8	2	0	.271	.236	2
Santana, R	CLE	R	.231	7	13	3	3	6	0	0	0	3	0	1	0	0	0	0	0	0	0	.462	.231	0
Sax, S	NY	R	.260	155	615	70	160	200	24	2	4	42	6	4	4	49	0	46	43	9	13	.325	.316	10
Schaefer, J	SEA	R	.206	55	107	11	22	25	3	0	0	6	2	1	0	3	0	11	4	1	1	.234	.239	5
Schofield, D	CAL	R	.255	99	310	41	79	92	8	1	1	18	13	2	2	52	3	61	3	4	3	.297	.363	17
Schooler, M	SEA	R	.000	49	1	0	0	0	0	0	0	0	0	0	0	0	0	0	0	0	0	.000	.000	1
Schroeder, B	CAL	R	.224	18	58	7	13	28	3	0	4	9	0	0	0	1	0	10	0	0	3	.483	.237	0

Schu, R	CAL	R	.268	61	157	19	42	68	8	0	6	14	0	1	0	11	0	25	0	0	4	.433	.314	11
Schulz, J	KC	L	.258	30	66	5	17	24	5	1	0	6	1	0	0	6	2	13	0	0	2	.364	.319	2
Segui, D	BAL	S	.244	40	123	14	30	43	7	0	2	15	1	0	1	11	2	15	0	0	12	.350	.311	3
Seitzer, K	KC	R	.275	158	622	91	171	230	31	5	6	38	4	2	2	67	2	66	7	5	11	.370	.346	19
Sheets, L	DET	L	.261	131	360	40	94	145	17	2	10	52	0	4	2	24	2	42	1	3	13	.403	.308	2
Sheffield, G	MIL	R	.294	125	487	67	143	205	30	1	10	67	4	9	3	44	1	41	25	10	11	.421	.350	25
Shelby, J	DET	S	.248	78	222	22	55	82	9	3	4	20	6	0	0	10	0	51	3	5	6	.369	.280	4
Shumpert, T	KC	R	.275	32	91	7	25	33	6	1	0	8	0	2	1	2	0	17	3	3	4	.363	.292	3
Sierra, R	TEX	S	.280	159	608	70	170	259	37	2	16	96	0	8	1	49	13	86	9	0	15	.426	.330	10
Sinatro, M	SEA	R	.300	30	50	2	15	16	1	0	0	4	3	0	0	4	0	10	1	0	3	.320	.352	1
Skinner, J	CLE	R	.252	49	139	16	35	47	4	1	2	16	0	0	0	7	0	44	0	0	2	.338	.288	1
Snyder, C	CLE	R	.233	123	438	46	102	177	27	3	14	55	1	6	2	21	3	118	1	4	11	.404	.268	7
Sojo, L	TOR	R	.225	33	80	14	18	24	3	0	1	9	0	0	0	5	0	5	1	1	1	.300	.271	5
Sorrento, P	MIN	L	.207	41	121	11	25	46	4	1	5	13	0	1	1	12	0	31	1	1	3	.380	.281	1
Sosa, S	CHI	R	.233	153	532	72	124	215	26	10	15	70	2	6	6	33	4	150	32	16	10	.404	.282	13
Spiers, B	MIL	L	.242	112	363	44	88	115	15	3	2	36	6	3	1	16	0	45	11	6	12	.317	.274	12
Springer, S	CLE	R	.167	4	12	1	2	2	0	0	0	1	0	1	0	0	0	6	0	0	0	.167	.154	0
Stanley, M	TEX	R	.249	103	189	21	47	63	8	1	2	19	6	1	0	30	2	25	1	0	4	.333	.350	4
Stark, M	CHI	R	.250	8	16	0	4	5	1	0	0	3	1	0	0	1	0	6	0	0	2	.313	.294	0
Steinbach, T	OAK	R	.251	114	379	32	95	141	15	2	9	57	5	3	4	19	1	66	0	1	11	.372	.291	5
Stevens, L	CAL	L	.214	67	248	28	53	84	10	0	7	32	2	3	0	22	3	75	1	1	8	.339	.275	4
Stillwell, K	KC	S	.249	144	506	60	126	178	35	4	3	51	4	7	4	39	1	60	0	2	11	.352	.304	24
Stone, J	BOS	L	.500	10	2	1	1	1	0	0	0	1	0	0	0	0	0	1	0	1	0	.500	.500	0
Surhoff, B	MIL	L	.276	135	474	55	131	178	21	4	6	59	7	7	1	41	5	37	18	7	8	.376	.331	12
Sveum, D	MIL	S	.197	48	117	15	23	33	7	0	1	12	0	2	2	12	0	30	0	1	2	.282	.278	6
Tabler, P	KC	R	.272	75	195	12	53	70	14	0	1	19	0	3	1	20	2	21	0	2	8	.359	.338	2
Tartabull, D	KC	R	.268	88	313	41	84	148	19	0	15	60	0	3	0	36	0	93	1	1	9	.473	.341	3
Tettleton, M	BAL	S	.223	135	444	68	99	169	21	2	15	51	0	4	5	106	3	160	2	4	7	.381	.376	5
Thomas, F	CHI	R	.330	60	191	39	63	101	11	3	7	31	0	3	2	44	0	54	0	1	5	.529	.454	5
Thurman, G	KC	R	.233	23	60	5	14	17	3	0	0	3	1	0	0	2	0	12	1	1	2	.283	.258	0
Tingley, R	CAL	R	.000	5	3	0	0	0	0	0	0	0	0	0	0	1	0	1	0	0	1	.000	.250	0
Tolleson, W	NY	S	.149	73	74	12	11	14	1	1	0	4	2	1	0	6	0	21	1	0	0	.189	.210	2
Trammell, A	DET	R	.304	146	559	71	170	251	37	1	14	89	3	6	1	68	7	55	12	10	11	.449	.377	14
Valle, D	SEA	R	.214	107	308	37	66	102	15	0	7	33	4	0	7	45	0	48	1	2	11	.331	.328	2
Vaughn, G	MIL	R	.220	120	382	51	84	165	26	2	17	61	7	6	1	33	1	91	7	4	11	.432	.280	7
Velarde, R	NY	R	.210	95	229	21	48	73	6	2	5	19	2	1	1	20	0	53	0	3	6	.319	.275	12

BATTER	TEAM	B	AVG	G	AB	R	H	TB	2B	3B	HR	RBI	SH	SF	HP	BB	IBB	SO	SB	CS	GI DP	SLG	OBP	E
Venable, M	CAL	L	.259	93	189	26	49	76	9	3	4	21	7	2	0	24	2	31	1	5	3	.402	.340	3
Ventura, R	CHI	L	.249	150	493	48	123	157	17	1	5	54	13	3	1	55	2	53	1	4	5	.318	.324	25
Virgil, O	TOR	R	.000	3	5	0	0	0	0	0	0	0	0	0	0	0	0	3	0	1	0	.000	.000	0
Vizquel, O	SEA	S	.247	81	255	19	63	76	3	2	1	18	10	2	0	18	0	22	1	4	7	.298	.295	7
Walewander, J	NY	S	.200	9	5	1	1	2	0	0	0	1	1	0	0	0	0	3	0	1	0	.400	.200	0
Walker, G	CHI-BAL	L	.154	16	39	1	6	6	0	0	0	1	0	0	0	3	0	11	0	1	2	.154	.233	0
Ward, G	DET	R	.256	106	309	32	79	121	11	2	9	46	2	2	1	30	0	50	2	1	12	.392	.322	0
Ward, T	CLE	S	.348	14	46	10	16	23	2	2	1	10	0	0	0	4	0	8	3	0	1	.500	.388	2
Washington, C	CAL-NY	L	.167	45	114	7	19	26	2	1	1	9	0	0	1	1	1	25	0	0	2	.228	.193	1
Webster, L	MIN	R	.333	2	6	1	2	3	1	0	0	0	0	0	0	1	0	1	0	0	0	.500	.429	0
Webster, M	CLE	S	.252	128	437	58	110	178	20	6	12	55	11	6	3	20	1	61	22	6	5	.407	.285	0
Weiss, W	OAK	S	.265	138	445	50	118	143	17	2	1	35	6	4	4	46	5	53	9	3	2	.321	.337	5
Whitaker, L	DET	L	.237	132	472	75	112	192	22	2	18	60	1	5	0	74	5	71	8	2	10	.407	.338	12
White, D	CAL	S	.217	125	443	57	96	152	17	3	11	44	10	3	3	44	5	116	21	6	6	.343	.290	6
White, F	KC	R	.216	82	241	20	52	74	14	1	2	21	0	3	0	10	0	32	1	2	7	.307	.253	9
Whiten, M	TOR	S	.273	33	88	12	24	33	1	0	2	7	0	1	0	7	0	14	2	2	2	.375	.323	8
Williams, J	CHI	L	.000	3	3	0	0	0	0	0	0	0	0	0	0	0	0	2	0	0	1	.000	.000	0
Williams, K	DET-TOR	R	.161	106	155	23	25	35	8	1	0	13	0	2	0	10	0	42	9	4	10	.226	.219	0
Wilson, M	TOR	S	.265	147	588	81	156	209	36	4	3	51	6	4	0	31	1	102	23	6	4	.355	.354	3
Wilson, W	KC	S	.290	115	307	49	89	114	13	2	3	42	3	3	0	30	3	57	24	1	17	.371	.300	0
Winfield, D	NY-CAL	R	.267	132	475	70	127	215	21	3	21	78	1	7	2	52	3	81	0	6	0	.453	.338	0
Witt, B	TEX	R	.000	35	0	1	0	0	0	0	0	0	0	0	0	0	0	0	0	0	0	.000	.000	2
Worthington, C	BAL	R	.226	133	425	46	96	137	17	0	8	44	7	3	3	63	2	96	1	2	13	.322	.328	18
Yount, R	MIL	R	.247	158	587	98	145	223	17	5	17	77	4	8	6	78	6	89	15	8	7	.380	.337	4

TOP 15 DESIGNATED HITTERS
(Minimum: 100 At Bats)

BATTER	TEAM	B	AVG	G	AB	R	H	TB	2B	3B	HR	RBI	SH	SF	HP	BB	IBB	SO	SB	CS	GI DP	SLG	OBP
Larkin, G.......MIN	S	.336	43	140	14	47	62	13	1	0	18	2	3	1	19	2	24	2	2	3	.443	.411
Bergman, D.......DET	L	.322	51	115	15	37	49	7	1	1	15	0	2	0	17	2	13	1	1	3	.426	.403
Calderon, I ....CHI	R	.304	27	112	20	34	59	7	0	6	17	0	1	1	6	1	7	4	2	5	.527	.336
James, C ....CLE	R	.296	124	477	55	141	203	27	4	9	57	2	1	2	30	4	68	4	3	10	.426	.340
Brett, G ....KC	L	.292	32	120	18	35	60	14	1	3	16	0	3	0	9	2	18	2	0	3	.500	.333
Baines, H ....TEX-OAK	L	.287	125	404	52	116	181	15	1	16	61	0	6	0	64	9	77	0	3	17	.448	.380
Davis, C ....CAL	S	.284	60	225	35	64	97	13	1	6	30	0	4	0	34	3	43	4	2	7	.431	.375
Parker, D ....MIL	L	.281	153	597	68	168	266	29	3	21	89	0	14	4	41	11	102	4	7	18	.446	.325
Downing, B ....CAL	R	.280	87	322	47	90	154	18	2	14	51	0	4	6	49	2	44	0	0	11	.478	.381
Davis, A ....SEA	L	.272	87	301	39	82	134	16	0	12	52	0	6	3	57	8	46	0	2	6	.445	.387
Tartabull, D ....KC	R	.271	32	118	13	32	53	9	0	4	19	0	2	0	15	0	30	0	0	4	.449	.348
Horn, S ....BAL	L	.265	63	204	26	54	101	11	0	12	34	0	2	2	26	1	55	0	0	8	.495	.345
Perry, G ....KC	L	.262	68	263	33	69	93	12	0	4	35	0	2	0	22	2	30	10	2	8	.354	.322
Olerud, J ....TOR	L	.258	90	302	34	78	124	14	1	10	38	1	4	1	44	4	66	0	1	5	.411	.350
Evans, D ....BOS	R	.249	122	445	66	111	174	18	3	13	63	0	6	3	67	5	73	3	4	18	.391	.347

CLUB BATTING

CLUB	AVG	G	AB	R	OR	H	TB	2b	3B	HR	GS	RBI	SH	SF	HP	BB	IBB	SO	SB	CS	GI DP	LOB	SHO	SLG	OB
BOSTON	.272	162	5516	699	664	1502	2180	298	31	106	2	660	48	44	28	598	59	795	53	52	174	1233	16	.395	.344
CLEVELAND	.267	162	5485	732	737	1465	2143	266	41	110	2	675	54	61	29	458	33	836	107	52	122	1061	10	.391	.324
KANSAS CITY	.267	161	5488	707	709	1465	2169	316	44	100	3	660	31	54	27	498	32	879	107	62	132	1123	9	.395	.328
MINNESOTA	.265	162	5499	666	729	1458	2117	281	39	100	2	625	40	49	53	445	32	749	96	53	148	1097	14	.385	.324
TORONTO	.265	162	5589	767	661	1479	2343	263	50	167	4	729	18	62	28	526	35	970	111	52	125	1113	10	.419	.328
CALIFORNIA	.260	162	5570	690	706	1448	2180	237	27	147	3	646	58	45	28	566	41	1000	69	43	142	1202	6	.391	.329
SEATTLE	.259	162	5474	640	680	1419	2043	251	26	107	6	610	41	54	40	596	41	749	105	51	140	1227	15	.373	.333
TEXAS	.259	162	5469	676	696	1416	2057	257	27	110	3	641	54	44	34	575	45	1054	115	48	142	1168	11	.376	.331
DETROIT	.259	162	5479	750	754	1418	2239	241	32	172	4	714	36	41	34	634	44	952	82	57	139	1175	7	.409	.337
CHICAGO	.258	162	5402	682	633	1393	2050	251	44	106	1	637	75	47	36	478	50	903	140	90	112	1044	7	.379	.320
MILWAUKEE	.256	162	5503	760	760	1408	2111	247	36	128	1	680	59	71	33	519	46	821	164	72	101	1106	5	.384	.320
OAKLAND	.254	162	5433	733	570	1379	2124	209	22	164	4	693	60	48	46	651	38	992	141	54	122	1195	12	.391	.336
BALTIMORE	.245	161	5410	669	698	1328	2002	234	22	132	3	623	72	41	40	660	50	962	94	52	131	1230	7	.370	.330
NEW YORK	.241	162	5483	603	749	1322	2009	208	19	147	0	561	37	36	53	427	41	1027	119	45	114	1060	15	.366	.300
TOTALS	.259	1133	76800	9746	9746	19900	29767	3559	460	1796	38	9154	683	697	509	7631	587	12689	1503	783	1844	16034	144	.388	.327

Pitching

INDIVIDUAL PITCHING LEADERS

Games Won	27	Welch, Oak.
Games Lost	19	Leary, N.Y.
Won-Lost Percentage	.818	Welch, Oak.
Earned Run Average	1.93	Clemens, Bos.
Games	77	Thigpen, Chi.
Games Started	36	Stewart, Oak. & J. Morris, Det.
Complete Games	11	Stewart, Oak. & J. Morris, Det.
Games Finished	73	Thigpen, Chi.
Shutouts	4	Stewart, Oak. & Clemens, Bos.
Saves	57	Thigpen, Chi.
Innings	267.0	Stewart, Oak.
Hits	246	Abbott, Cal.
Batsmen Faced	1088	Stewart, Oak.
Runs	144	J. Morris, Det.
Earned Runs	125	J. Morris, Det.
Home Runs	30	D. Johnson, Bal.
Sacrifice Hits	12	C. Finley, Cal.
Sacrifice Flies	11	Hough, Tex., LaPoint, N.Y. & R. Smith, Min.
Hit Batsmen	11	Hough, Tex.
Bases on Balls	120	R. Johnson, Sea.
Intentional Bases on Balls	13	J. Morris, Det.
Strikeouts	232	Ryan, Tex.
Wild Pitches	23	Leary, N.Y.
Balks	5	Navarro, Mil.
Games Won, Consecutive	12	B. Witt, Tex. (June 28-Sept. 6)
Games Lost, Consecutive	8	A. Anderson, Min. (May 19-July 11), Leary, N.Y. (May 28-July 8) & Langston, Cal. (June 10-July 27)

TOP 15 QUALIFIERS FOR EARNED RUN AVERAGE CHAMPIONSHIP

PITCHER	TEAM	T	W	L	ERA	G	GS	CG	SHO	GF	SV	IP	H	TBF	R	ER	HR	SH	SF	HB	BB	IBB	SO	WP	BK	OPP AVG
Clemens, R	BOS	R	21	6	1.93	31	31	7	4	0	0	228.1	193	920	59	49	7	7	5	7	54	3	209	8	0	.228
Finley, C	CAL	L	18	9	2.40	32	32	7	2	0	0	236.0	210	962	77	63	17	12	3	2	81	3	177	9	0	.243
Stewart, D	OAK	R	22	11	2.56	36	36	11	4	0	0	267.0	226	1088	84	76	16	10	10	5	83	2	166	8	0	.231
Appier, K	KC	R	12	8	2.76	32	24	3	3	1	0	185.2	179	784	67	57	13	5	9	6	54	2	127	8	0	.252
Stieb, D	TOR	R	18	6	2.93	33	33	2	2	0	0	208.2	179	861	73	68	11	6	3	10	64	6	125	6	0	.230
Welch, B	OAK	R	27	6	2.95	35	35	2	2	0	0	238.0	214	979	90	78	26	6	5	5	77	4	127	5	2	.242
Wells, D	TOR	L	11	6	3.14	43	25	0	0	3	3	189.0	165	759	72	66	14	9	10	5	45	2	115	7	1	.235
Hibbard, G	CHI	L	14	9	3.16	33	33	3	0	0	0	211.0	202	871	80	74	11	8	6	10	55	2	92	7	1	.255
Hanson, E	SEA	R	18	9	3.24	33	33	5	1	0	0	236.0	205	964	88	85	15	5	6	2	68	6	211	10	1	.232
McCaskill, K	CAL	L	12	11	3.25	29	29	2	1	0	0	174.1	161	738	77	63	9	3	1	10	72	6	78	6	1	.244
Boddicker, M	BOS	R	17	8	3.36	34	34	4	0	1	0	228.0	225	956	92	85	16	3	10	6	69	6	143	10	0	.258
Witt, B	TEX	R	17	10	3.37	33	32	7	1	0	0	222.0	197	954	86	83	12	5	4	4	110	3	221	11	2	.238
Ryan, N	TEX	R	13	9	3.44	30	30	5	2	0	0	204.0	137	818	86	78	18	3	6	5	74	2	232	9	1	.188
Young, M	SEA	L	8	18	3.52	34	33	7	1	0	0	225.1	198	963	106	88	15	7	7	6	107	7	176	16	0	.237
Black, B	CLE-TOR	L	13	11	3.57	32	31	5	2	1	0	206.2	181	857	86	82	19	6	7	5	61	1	106	6	1	.233

INDIVIDUAL PITCHING

PITCHER	TEAM	T	W	L	ERA	G	GS	CG	SHO	GF	SV	IP	H	TBF	R	ER	HR	SH	SF	HB	BB	IBB	SO	WP	BK	OPP AVG
Abbott, J	CAL	L	10	14	4.51	33	33	4	0	1	0	211.2	246	925	116	106	16	9	6	5	72	6	105	4	3	.295
Abbott, P	MIN	R	0	5	5.97	7	7	0	0	0	0	34.2	37	162	24	23	0	1	1	1	28	0	25	1	0	.282
Acker, J	TOR	R	4	4	3.83	59	0	0	0	19	0	91.2	103	403	49	39	9	3	1	3	30	5	54	4	1	.281
Adkins, S	NY	L	1	2	6.38	5	5	0	0	0	0	24.0	19	115	18	17	4	0	1	0	29	0	14	2	0	.226
Aguilera, R	MIN	R	5	3	2.76	56	0	0	0	54	32	65.1	55	268	27	20	5	0	4	4	19	6	61	3	0	.224
Aldred, S	DET	L	1	2	3.77	4	3	0	0	0	0	14.1	13	63	6	6	0	0	2	1	10	1	7	0	0	.265
Aldrich, J	BAL	R	1	0	8.25	7	0	0	0	2	1	12.0	17	61	13	11	2	0	2	0	7	3	5	0	0	.327
Alexander, G	TEX	R	0	0	7.71	3	2	0	0	1	0	7.0	14	39	6	6	0	0	1	1	5	0	8	0	0	.438

Name	T	W	L	ERA	G	GS	CG	SHO	SV	IP	H	R	ER	HR	BB	SO	AVG
Andersen, L......BOS	R	0	7	1.23	15	0	0	0	4	22.0	18	3	3	0	3	25	.220
Anderson, A.......MIN	L	7	18	4.53	31	31	5	1	0	188.2	214	106	95	18	39	82	.289
Appier, K.........KC	R	12	8	2.76	32	24	3	1	0	185.2	179	67	57	12	54	127	.252
Aquino, L.........KC	R	4	4	3.16	20	0	0	0	6	68.1	59	25	24	6	27	28	.237
Arnsberg, B.......TEX	R	6	1	2.15	53	0	0	0	5	62.2	56	20	15	7	33	44	.235
August, D.........MIL	R	2	3	6.55	5	1	0	0	0	11.0	13	10	8	1	5	5	.295
Bailes, S.........CAL	L	2	2	6.37	27	0	0	0	1	35.1	46	30	25	5	20	16	.315
Ballard, J........BAL	L	2	11	4.93	44	17	0	0	0	133.1	152	79	73	16	42	50	.290
Baller, J.........KC	R	0	1	15.43	3	0	0	0	0	2.1	4	4	4	1	7	1	.364
Bankhead, S.......SEA	R	0	3	11.08	4	4	0	0	0	13.0	18	16	16	2	13	10	.333
Barfield, J.......TEX	R	4	4	4.67	33	0	0	0	1	44.1	42	25	23	4	15	17	.268
Bautista, J.......BAL	R	1	0	4.05	22	9	0	0	0	26.2	28	15	12	4	2	15	.272
Bearse, K.........CLE	L	0	0	12.91	3	3	0	0	0	7.2	16	11	11	2	5	2	.421
Berenguer, J......MIN	R	8	5	3.41	51	0	0	0	0	100.1	85	43	38	9	58	77	.232
Bitker, J.....OAK-TEX	R	0	0	2.25	5	0	0	0	0	12.0	8	3	3	0	7	8	.190
Black, B......CLE-TOR	L	13	11	3.57	32	31	5	2	0	206.2	181	86	82	20	61	106	.233
Blair, W..........TOR	R	3	5	4.06	27	6	0	0	2	68.2	66	33	31	6	28	43	.250
Blyleven, B.......CAL	R	8	7	5.24	23	23	0	0	0	134.0	163	85	78	16	25	69	.303
Boddicker, M......BOS	R	17	8	3.36	34	34	4	3	0	228.0	225	92	85	16	69	143	.258
Bohanon, B........TEX	L	0	0	6.62	11	0	0	0	0	34.0	40	30	25	6	18	15	.299
Bolton, T.........BOS	L	10	5	3.38	21	16	3	0	0	119.2	111	46	45	6	47	65	.251
Boone, D..........BAL	L	0	0	2.79	16	1	0	0	3	9.2	12	3	3	1	2	2	.308
Bosio, C..........MIL	R	4	9	4.00	20	20	4	0	0	132.2	131	67	59	15	38	76	.258
Brown, K..........TEX	R	12	10	3.60	26	26	6	2	0	180.0	175	84	72	13	60	88	.255
Brown, K..........MIL	R	1	0	2.57	5	3	0	0	0	21.0	14	6	6	1	7	12	.182
Burba, D..........SEA	R	0	0	4.50	2	0	0	0	0	8.0	8	4	4	0	2	4	.267
Burns, T..........OAK	R	3	4	2.97	43	0	0	0	2	78.2	78	28	26	8	32	43	.263
Cadaret, G........NY	L	5	4	4.15	54	6	0	0	3	121.1	120	62	56	9	64	80	.268
Campbell, J.......KC	L	1	0	8.38	6	0	0	0	0	9.2	15	9	9	1	2	2	.349
Candelaria, J.MIN-TOR	L	7	6	3.95	47	2	0	0	5	79.2	87	36	35	11	20	63	.276
Candiotti, T......CLE	R	15	11	3.65	31	29	3	0	0	202.0	207	92	82	23	55	128	.263
Capel, M..........MIL	R	0	0	135.00	2	0	0	0	0	0.1	6	6	5	0	1	0	.857
Cary, M...........NY	L	6	12	4.19	28	27	2	0	0	156.2	155	77	73	21	55	134	.260
Casian, L.........MIN	L	2	1	3.22	5	3	0	0	0	22.1	26	9	8	2	4	11	.306

PITCHER	TEAM	T	W	L	ERA	G	GS	CG	SHO	GF	SV	IP	H	TBF	R	ER	HR	SH	SF	HB	BB	IBB	SO	WP	BK	OPP AVG
Cerutti, J	TOR	L	9	9	4.76	30	23	0	0	1	0	140.0	162	609	77	74	23	5	5	4	49	3	49	4	1	.297
Chiamparino, S	TEX	R	1	2	2.63	6	6	0	0	0	0	37.2	36	160	14	11	2	0	1	2	12	1	19	5	0	.250
Chitren, S	OAK	R	1	0	1.02	8	0	0	0	4	0	17.2	7	64	4	2	1	0	0	1	7	0	19	2	0	.117
Clark, B	SEA	L	2	0	3.27	12	0	0	0	2	0	11.0	9	48	4	4	0	0	2	0	10	0	3	1	0	.237
Clear, M	CAL	R	0	0	5.87	4	0	0	0	1	0	7.2	5	38	7	5	0	0	0	2	8	0	6	2	0	.200
Clemens, R	BOS	R	21	6	1.93	31	31	7	4	0	0	228.1	193	920	59	49	7	5	7	7	54	3	209	8	1	.228
Codiroli, C	KC	R	0	1	9.58	6	2	0	0	0	0	10.1	13	61	11	11	1	1	4	0	17	1	8	2	0	.325
Comstock, K	SEA	L	7	0	2.89	60	0	0	0	19	2	56.0	40	228	22	18	4	5	5	0	26	5	50	2	0	.206
Corbett, S	CAL	L	0	0	9.00	4	0	0	0	2	0	5.0	8	26	5	5	0	3	0	0	5	0	3	1	0	.364
Crawford, S	KC	R	5	4	4.16	46	0	0	0	14	5	80.0	79	341	38	37	7	2	2	3	23	3	54	1	0	.254
Crim, C	MIL	R	3	5	3.47	67	0	0	0	25	11	85.2	88	367	39	33	7	1	4	2	23	4	39	0	1	.261
Cummings, S	CLE	L	2	0	5.11	5	3	0	0	2	0	12.1	22	58	7	7	1	2	2	4	5	3	4	6	0	.431
Davis, M	KC	L	2	7	5.11	53	3	0	0	28	6	68.2	71	334	39	39	9	2	1	0	52	1	73	0	1	.226
Davis, S	KC	R	7	10	4.74	21	20	0	0	0	0	112.0	129	498	66	59	9	2	3	0	35	0	62	4	0	.259
DeLucia, R	SEA	R	0	0	2.00	5	5	0	0	0	0	36.0	30	144	9	8	2	2	1	4	9	0	20	2	0	.281
Dopson, J	BOS	R	0	4	2.04	8	7	0	0	0	0	17.2	13	75	7	4	2	0	0	0	9	1	9	0	0	.200
Dotson, R	KC	R	3	5	8.48	8	0	0	0	1	0	28.2	43	139	29	27	3	4	4	0	14	1	9	0	0	.355
Drummond, T	MIN	R	1	5	4.35	35	4	0	0	14	0	91.0	104	399	46	44	8	2	5	1	36	1	49	2	1	.295
DuBois, B	BAL	L	3	5	5.09	12	11	0	0	0	0	58.1	70	255	37	33	8	2	4	0	22	1	34	5	0	.310
Eave, G	SEA	R	0	3	4.20	8	5	0	0	1	0	30.0	27	134	16	14	5	4	1	0	20	1	16	0	0	.241
Eckersley, D	OAK	R	4	2	0.61	63	0	0	0	61	48	73.1	41	262	9	5	2	1	4	0	4	0	73	1	0	.160
Edens, T	MIL	R	5	3	4.45	35	6	0	0	9	0	89.0	89	387	52	44	6	4	4	3	33	1	40	1	0	.262
Edwards, W	CHI	L	2	5	3.22	42	5	0	0	8	0	95.0	81	396	34	34	8	4	3	3	41	2	63	2	0	.234
Eichhorn, M	CAL	R	2	0	3.08	60	0	0	0	40	13	84.2	98	374	36	29	2	2	4	6	23	9	69	2	0	.289
Eiland, D	NY	R	2	1	3.56	5	5	0	0	0	0	30.1	31	127	14	12	2	0	0	0	5	0	16	0	0	.254
Elvira, N	MIL	L	0	0	5.40	4	0	0	0	2	0	5.0	6	25	5	3	1	0	0	0	4	0	6	0	0	.300
Encarnacion, L	KC	R	0	0	7.84	19	0	0	0	2	0	10.1	14	49	10	9	3	0	0	5	5	0	8	3	1	.311
Erickson, S	MIN	R	8	4	2.87	19	17	1	1	0	0	113.0	108	485	49	36	6	6	2	5	51	4	53	3	0	.256
Farr, S	KC	R	13	7	1.98	57	6	0	0	20	1	127.0	99	515	32	28	9	5	2	1	48	9	94	2	0	.220
Farrell, J	CLE	R	4	5	4.28	17	17	1	0	0	0	96.2	108	418	49	46	10	2	2	1	33	0	44	3	0	.286
Fernandez, A	CHI	R	5	5	3.80	13	13	3	0	0	0	87.2	89	378	40	37	6	0	3	3	34	0	61	1	0	.265

Player	T	W	L	ERA	G	GS	CG	SHO	GF	SV	IP	BFP	H	R	ER	HR			BB	SO	WP	BK	AVG
Fetters, M. ...CAL	R	1	1	4.12	26	2	0	0	10	0	67.2	291	77	33	31	9	0	2	20	35	3	0	.287
Filer, T. ...MIL	R	2	3	6.14	7	4	0	0	0	0	22.0	99	26	17	15	2	0	0	9	8	2	0	.289
Filson, P. ...KC	L	0	4	5.91	8	7	0	0	0	0	35.0	165	42	31	23	6	1	2	13	9	0	1	.282
Finley, C. ...CAL	L	18	9	2.40	32	32	7	2	0	0	236.0	962	210	77	63	17	3	2	81	177	9	0	.243
Flanagan, M. ...TOR	L	2	3	5.31	5	5	0	0	0	0	20.1	94	28	14	12	3	1	2	8	5	0	0	.329
Fossas, T. ...MIL	L	2	2	6.44	32	0	0	0	9	0	29.1	146	44	23	21	5	2	0	10	24	0	0	.331
Fraser, W. ...CAL	R	5	4	3.08	45	0	0	0	20	0	76.0	315	69	29	26	4	3	0	24	32	0	0	.241
Garces, R. ...MIN	R	0	0	1.59	5	0	0	0	3	0	5.2	24	4	2	1	1	0	0	4	1	1	0	.200
Gardiner, M ...SEA	R	0	2	10.66	5	3	0	0	1	0	12.2	66	22	17	15	1	0	2	5	6	0	2	.379
Gardner, W ...BOS	R	3	7	4.89	34	9	0	0	9	0	77.1	340	77	43	42	6	2	2	35	58	1	1	.259
Gibson, P. ...DET	L	5	0	3.05	61	5	0	0	17	0	97.1	422	99	36	33	10	5	1	44	56	2	1	.269
Gilles, T. ...TOR	R	0	3	6.75	2	0	0	0	0	0	1.1	6	6	1	1	0	0	0	0	1	0	0	.333
Gleaton, J. ...DET	L	1	3	2.94	57	0	0	0	34	13	82.2	325	62	27	27	5	4	3	25	56	2	1	.213
Gordon, T. ...KC	R	12	11	3.73	32	32	6	1	0	0	195.1	858	192	99	81	17	8	3	99	175	11	0	.258
Gozzo, G. ...CLE	R	0	0	0.00	2	0	0	0	0	0	3.0	13	10	0	0	0	0	0	2	2	0	1	.182
Grahe, J. ...CAL	R	3	4	4.98	8	8	0	0	0	0	43.1	200	51	30	24	3	0	0	23	25	1	0	.293
Gray, J. ...BOS	R	2	4	4.44	41	0	0	0	28	0	50.2	217	53	27	25	3	2	3	15	50	2	1	.268
Guante, C. ...CLE	R	2	3	5.01	26	0	0	0	6	0	46.2	197	38	26	26	10	4	1	18	30	2	0	.220
Gubicza, M. ...KC	R	4	7	4.50	16	16	1	0	0	0	94.0	409	101	48	47	5	6	1	38	71	2	1	.283
Guetterman, L ...NY	L	11	7	3.39	64	0	0	0	21	2	93.0	376	80	37	35	6	4	4	26	48	2	1	.236
Guthrie, M ...MIN	L	7	9	3.79	24	21	3	0	0	0	144.2	603	154	65	61	8	6	0	39	101	1	0	.276
Habyan, J. ...NY	R	2	2	2.08	6	0	0	0	5	0	14.2	37	10	4	3	0	0	1	2	4	0	0	.294
Hanson, E. ...SEA	R	18	9	3.24	33	33	5	2	0	0	236.0	964	205	88	85	15	6	2	68	211	1	1	.232
Harnisch, P. ...BAL	R	11	11	4.34	31	31	3	0	0	0	188.2	821	189	96	91	17	5	1	86	122	2	2	.261
Harris, G. ...BOS	R	13	9	4.00	34	30	3	0	0	0	184.1	803	186	92	82	13	9	6	77	117	8	1	.265
Harris, G. ...SEA	R	1	2	4.74	25	0	0	0	3	0	38.0	176	31	24	20	5	3	2	21	43	2	0	.217
Harris, R. ...OAK	R	1	1	3.48	16	0	0	0	12	0	41.1	168	25	16	16	5	2	2	21	31	2	0	.176
Harvey, B. ...CAL	R	4	4	3.22	54	0	0	0	47	25	64.1	267	45	24	23	5	4	2	35	82	7	1	.201
Hawkins, A. ...NY	R	5	12	5.37	28	26	2	0	0	0	157.2	692	156	101	94	20	5	5	82	74	6	2	.260
Heep, D. ...BOS	L	0	0	9.00	1	0	0	0	0	0	1.0	6	4	1	1	0	0	0	0	0	0	1	.667
Henke, T. ...TOR	R	2	4	2.17	61	0	0	0	58	32	74.2	297	58	20	18	4	8	2	19	75	6	0	.213
Henneman, M. ...DET	R	8	6	3.05	69	0	0	0	53	22	94.1	399	90	36	32	8	5	3	33	50	3	0	.253
Hesketh, J. ...BOS	L	0	4	3.51	12	0	0	0	0	0	25.2	122	37	12	10	2	2	0	11	26	3	0	.333
Hetzel, E. ...BOS	R	1	4	5.91	9	8	0	0	0	0	35.0	163	39	28	23	3	1	1	21	20	2	0	.281

PITCHER	TEAM	T	W	L	ERA	G	GS	CG	SHO	GF	SV	IP	H	TBF	R	ER	HR	SH	SF	HB	BB	IBB	SO	WP	BK	OPP AVG
Hibbard, G	CHI	L	14	9	3.16	33	33	3	1	0	0	211.0	202	871	80	74	11	8	10	6	55	3	92	2	1	.255
Hickey, K	BAL	L	1	3	5.13	37	0	0	0	9	9	26.1	26	113	16	15	3	1	0	0	13	2	17	1	0	.265
Higuera, T	MIL	L	11	10	3.76	27	27	4	1	0	0	170.0	167	720	80	71	16	10	4	3	50	2	129	2	1	.256
Hill, D	CAL	R	0	0	0.00	1	0	0	0	1	0	1.0	4	4	0	0	0	0	0	0	0	0	1	0	0	.000
Hillegas, S	CHI	R	0	0	0.79	7	0	0	0	3	0	11.1	4	43	1	1	0	1	0	0	5	1	5	0	0	.111
Holman, B	SEA	R	11	11	4.03	28	28	1	0	0	0	189.2	188	804	92	85	17	1	7	0	66	6	121	8	2	.260
Holton, B	BAL	R	2	3	4.50	33	0	0	0	13	0	58.0	68	257	31	29	7	2	1	1	21	2	27	2	2	.292
Honeycutt, R	OAK	L	2	2	2.70	63	0	0	0	13	7	63.1	46	256	23	19	2	2	6	2	22	6	38	1	2	.204
Hoover, J	TEX	R	0	0	11.57	2	0	0	0	1	0	4.2	8	26	6	6	0	1	0	0	3	0	0	1	0	.364
Hough, C	TEX	R	12	12	4.07	32	32	5	0	0	0	218.2	190	950	108	99	24	2	11	11	119	3	114	4	0	.235
Irvine, D	BOS	R	1	1	4.67	11	0	0	0	6	0	17.1	15	75	10	9	2	8	3	1	10	2	9	0	1	.246
Jackson, M	SEA	R	5	7	4.54	63	0	0	0	28	6	77.1	64	338	42	39	8	5	5	2	44	12	69	9	1	.229
Jeffcoat, M	TEX	L	5	6	4.47	44	4	0	0	11	5	110.2	122	466	57	55	12	3	2	2	28	5	58	1	2	.283
Johnson, D	BAL	R	13	9	4.10	30	29	3	0	0	0	180.0	196	758	83	82	30	5	7	2	43	2	68	1	1	.280
Johnson, R	SEA	R	14	11	3.65	33	33	5	2	0	0	219.2	174	944	103	89	26	7	6	2	120	2	194	4	0	.216
Jones, B	CHI	R	11	4	2.31	65	0	0	0	19	2	74.0	62	310	20	19	2	5	1	1	33	7	45	1	0	.235
Jones, D	CLE	R	5	5	2.56	66	0	0	0	64	43	84.1	66	331	26	24	5	2	2	2	22	4	55	0	0	.218
Jones, J	NY	R	1	0	6.30	17	7	0	0	9	0	50.0	72	238	42	35	8	0	4	1	23	3	25	3	0	.344
Kaiser, J	CLE	L	0	2	3.55	5	5	0	0	0	0	12.2	16	60	6	5	1	0	0	1	7	0	9	0	0	.308
Key, J	TOR	L	13	7	4.25	27	27	5	1	0	0	154.2	169	636	79	73	20	5	6	2	22	2	88	1	1	.281
Kiecker, D	BOS	R	8	9	3.97	32	25	3	1	3	0	152.0	145	641	74	67	7	1	5	9	54	2	93	0	0	.253
Kilgus, P	TOR	L	0	2	6.06	11	0	0	0	4	0	16.1	19	74	11	11	2	3	1	6	7	1	7	3	0	.306
King, E	CHI	R	12	4	3.28	25	25	2	2	0	0	151.0	135	623	59	55	10	6	3	6	40	3	70	2	3	.237
Kinzer, M	DET	R	0	0	16.20	1	0	0	0	1	0	1.2	3	11	3	3	0	1	0	0	1	0	1	0	0	.375
Klink, J	OAK	L	0	1	2.04	40	0	0	0	19	1	39.2	34	165	9	9	3	1	2	1	18	2	19	3	1	.233
Knackert, B	SEA	R	1	1	6.51	24	2	0	0	6	0	37.1	50	186	28	27	5	1	2	2	21	0	28	3	0	.313
Knudson, M	MIL	R	10	9	4.12	30	27	4	2	0	0	168.1	187	719	84	77	14	3	9	3	40	6	56	6	0	.282
Krueger, B	MIL	L	6	8	3.98	30	17	0	0	4	0	129.0	137	566	70	57	10	3	10	0	54	1	64	8	0	.276
Kutzler, J	CHI	R	2	1	6.03	7	7	0	0	0	0	31.1	38	141	23	21	2	2	1	0	14	1	21	1	0	.304
LaPoint, J	NY	L	7	10	4.11	28	27	2	0	2	0	157.2	180	694	84	72	11	8	11	1	57	3	67	4	0	.292
Lamp, D	BOS	R	3	5	4.68	47	1	0	0	5	0	105.2	114	453	61	55	10	8	4	3	30	8	49	2	0	.279

Pitcher	T	W	L	ERA	G	GS	CG	ShO	Sv	IP	H	R	ER	HR	SH	SF	HB	BB	IBB	SO	WP	BK	OBA
Langston, M ....CAL	L	10	17	4.40	33	33	5	1	0	223.0	215	120	109	13	6	6	5	104	1	195	8	0	.259
Leach, T ....MIN	R	2	5	3.20	55	0	0	0	2	81.2	84	31	29	2	7	7	1	21	10	46	2	1	.268
Leary, T ....NY	R	9	19	4.11	31	31	6	1	0	208.0	202	105	95	18	4	4	7	78	4	138	23	0	.257
Lee, M ....MIL	L	1	1	2.11	11	0	0	0	1	21.1	20	5	6	1	1	0	0	4	0	14	0	0	.256
Leister, J ....BOS	R	0	0	4.76	2	0	0	0	0	5.2	7	3	3	0	0	0	0	2	0	4	0	1	.304
Leiter, A ....TOR	L	0	0	0.00	4	0	0	0	0	6.1	1	0	0	0	0	0	0	2	0	5	0	0	.050
Leiter, M ....NY	R	1	1	6.84	8	3	0	0	0	26.1	33	20	21	5	2	1	0	9	2	21	2	0	.314
Lewis, S ....CAL	R	1	0	2.20	2	2	0	0	0	16.1	10	4	4	0	0	0	0	2	0	9	0	0	.172
Long, B. ....CHI	R	0	0	6.35	4	0	0	0	0	5.2	6	5	4	1	0	0	0	6	0	2	0	0	.261
Lovelace, V ......SEA	L	0	0	3.86	5	0	0	0	0	2.1	3	1	1	0	0	0	0	1	0	1	2	1	.300
Luecken, R ....TOR	R	0	0	9.00	1	0	0	0	0	1.0	1	1	1	0	0	0	0	3	1	0	0	0	.500
Lugo, R ....DET	R	2	0	7.03	13	0	0	0	0	24.1	30	19	19	9	0	0	0	13	0	12	2	2	.313
Lyons, S ....CHI	R	0	0	4.50	1	0	0	0	0	2.0	2	1	1	0	0	0	0	4	0	1	0	0	.250
MacDonald, B .....TOR	L	0	0	0.00	1	0	0	0	0	2.1	0	0	0	0	0	0	0	8	2	0	1	0	.000
Machado, J ....MIL	R	0	0	0.69	10	0	0	0	0	13.0	9	1	1	0	0	0	0	4	0	12	0	2	.191
Maldonado, C ......KC	R	0	0	9.00	4	0	0	0	0	6.0	9	6	6	0	0	0	0	3	1	9	2	0	.346
Manon, R ....TEX	R	0	1	13.50	1	0	0	0	0	2.0	9	3	3	0	0	0	0	2	0	0	0	0	.333
McCaskill, K ......CAL	R	12	5	3.25	29	29	2	0	0	174.1	161	77	63	6	3	1	0	72	2	78	6	0	.244
McClure, B ....CAL	L	2	0	6.43	11	0	0	0	1	7.0	7	5	5	0	1	0	0	3	0	6	1	0	.269
McCullers, L ...NY-DET	R	2	1	3.02	21	0	0	0	2	44.2	32	19	15	4	3	3	0	19	3	31	0	1	.195
McDonald, B ....BAL	R	8	5	2.43	21	15	2	1	0	118.2	88	36	32	9	5	5	3	35	5	65	3	0	.205
McDonald, J ....CHI	R	1	1	3.82	4	0	0	0	0	7.0	11	5	3	1	0	0	0	3	0	3	0	0	.244
McDowell, J ....CHI	R	14	9	3.09	33	33	4	2	0	205.0	189	93	87	20	7	2	2	77	7	165	5	0	.248
McGaffigan, A ......KC	R	4	3	4.32	24	11	3	0	0	78.2	75	40	40	6	5	2	2	28	2	49	3	1	.281
McMurtry, C ....TEX	R	0	0	9.72	23	3	0	0	6	41.2	43	25	27	4	7	1	2	30	1	14	3	0	.313
McWilliams, L ......KC	L	0	0	6.23	13	0	0	0	2	8.1	10	9	9	2	3	2	0	9	2	7	1	0	.368
Medvin, S ....SEA	R	0	1	11.81	5	0	0	0	3	4.1	7	9	7	2	5	0	0	2	0	7	1	0	.333
Melendez, J ....SEA	R	0	0	3.86	7	0	0	0	0	5.1	8	3	3	0	4	0	1	3	1	7	1	0	.218
Mesa, J ....BAL	R	3	2	3.73	7	7	0	0	0	46.2	37	20	20	2	2	0	1	27	2	24	2	1	.271
Mielke, G ....TEX	R	0	0	4.46	33	0	0	0	8	41.0	42	17	17	4	5	1	2	15	2	13	0	1	.273
Milacki, B ....BAL	R	5	8	4.10	27	33	4	0	0	135.1	143	73	67	18	4	2	0	61	5	60	5	1	.298
Mills, A ....NY	R	1	1	2.35	36	0	0	0	0	41.2	48	21	19	4	1	0	1	33	1	24	1	0	.212
Minton, G ....CAL	R	1	2	3.97	11	0	0	0	3	15.1	61	7	7	1	4	1	1	7	7	4	2	0	.281
Mirabella, P ......MIL	L	4	2	3.97	44	2	0	0	10	59.0	66	32	26	9	2	1	2	27	2	28	9	1	.281
Mitchell, J ....BAL	R	6	6	4.64	24	17	0	0	2	114.1	133	63	59	7	3	6	8	48	3	43	3	3	.300

PITCHER	TEAM	T	W	L	ERA	G	GS	CG	SHO	GF	SV	IP	H	TBF	R	ER	HR	SH	SF	HB	BB	IBB	SO	WP	BK	OPP AVG
Monteleone, R	NY	R	0	1	6.14	5	0	0	0	2	0	7.1	8	31	5	5	1	0	2	0	0	0	8	0	0	.276
Montgomery, J	KC	R	6	5	2.39	73	0	0	0	59	24	94.1	81	400	36	25	6	2	5	5	34	8	94	3	0	.228
Moore, M	OAK	R	13	15	4.65	33	33	3	0	0	0	199.1	204	862	113	103	14	3	3	3	84	2	73	13	0	.267
Morris, J	DET	R	15	18	4.51	36	36	11	0	0	0	249.2	231	1073	144	125	26	4	6	6	97	13	162	16	2	.242
Moses, J	MIN	L	2	0	13.50	2	0	0	0	2	0	2.0	5	13	3	3	0	0	0	0	2	0	0	1	0	.455
Moyer, J	TEX	L	2	6	4.66	33	10	0	0	6	0	102.1	115	447	59	53	9	1	4	4	39	4	58	1	0	.290
Murphy, R	BOS	L	0	6	6.32	68	0	0	0	20	7	57.0	85	285	46	40	6	7	1	3	32	3	54	6	0	.348
Nagy, C	CLE	R	2	4	5.91	9	8	0	0	0	0	45.2	58	208	31	30	10	4	5	2	21	3	26	6	1	.315
Navarro, J	MIL	R	8	7	4.46	32	22	2	0	1	0	149.1	176	654	83	74	11	7	4	5	41	5	75	6	5	.293
Nelson, G	OAK	R	3	3	1.57	51	0	0	0	17	5	74.2	55	291	14	13	5	1	5	3	17	1	38	1	0	.208
Nichols, R	CLE	R	2	3	7.88	4	2	0	0	0	0	16.0	24	79	14	14	5	0	2	2	6	0	3	0	0	.343
Nipper, A	CLE	R	2	3	6.75	9	5	0	0	1	0	24.0	35	125	19	18	2	0	5	2	19	0	12	6	0	.354
Norris, M	OAK	R	1	0	3.00	14	3	0	0	0	0	27.0	24	113	10	9	0	2	1	2	9	0	16	3	2	.242
Nosek, R	DET	R	1	3	7.71	3	0	0	0	0	0	7.0	7	35	7	6	1	0	1	2	3	0	3	1	0	.280
Nunez, E	DET	R	1	1	2.24	42	0	0	0	15	1	80.1	65	343	26	20	4	5	1	2	37	6	66	3	0	.218
Olin, S	CLE	R	4	4	3.41	50	1	0	0	16	1	92.1	96	394	41	35	3	5	2	1	26	7	64	1	0	.270
Olson, G	BAL	R	6	5	2.42	64	0	0	0	58	37	74.1	57	305	20	20	3	0	2	3	31	3	74	0	0	.213
Orosco, J	CLE	L	5	4	3.90	55	0	0	0	28	2	64.2	58	289	35	28	9	0	3	2	38	7	55	5	0	.239
Otto, D	OAK	L	0	0	7.71	2	0	0	0	0	0	2.1	3	13	2	2	0	0	0	0	2	0	2	0	0	.300
Pall, D	CHI	R	3	5	3.32	56	0	0	0	11	2	76.0	63	306	33	28	7	4	3	2	24	8	39	2	0	.232
Parker, C	NY-DET	L	3	1	3.58	29	3	0	0	8	0	73.0	64	308	29	29	11	2	3	1	32	1	40	4	0	.238
Patterson, K	CHI	L	2	1	3.39	43	0	0	0	15	1	66.1	58	283	27	25	6	2	3	2	34	1	40	2	0	.242
Perez, M	CHI	R	13	14	4.61	35	35	3	0	0	0	197.0	177	833	101	101	14	4	6	2	86	1	161	8	4	.241
Perez, P	NY	R	1	2	1.29	3	3	0	0	0	0	14.0	8	52	3	2	0	0	3	0	3	0	12	1	0	.163
Peterson, A	CHI	R	2	5	4.55	20	11	0	0	0	0	85.0	90	357	46	43	12	2	3	0	26	0	29	0	0	.278
Petry, D	DET	R	10	9	4.45	32	23	2	0	2	0	149.2	148	655	78	74	14	8	6	1	77	7	73	10	0	.263
Plesac, D	MIL	L	3	7	4.43	66	0	0	0	52	24	69.0	67	299	36	34	5	2	2	3	31	6	65	2	0	.257
Plunk, E	NY	R	6	3	2.72	47	0	0	0	16	0	72.2	58	310	27	22	6	7	2	2	43	0	67	4	0	.225
Powell, D	SEA-MIL	R	0	4	7.02	11	7	0	0	0	0	42.1	64	214	40	33	8	2	0	2	21	0	23	4	0	.342
Price, J	BAL	L	3	4	3.58	50	0	0	0	12	0	65.1	62	273	29	26	8	2	1	2	24	1	54	1	0	.253
Radinsky, S	CHI	L	6	1	4.82	62	0	0	0	18	4	52.1	47	237	29	28	1	2	2	2	36	1	46	2	1	.241

Pitcher	T	W	L	ERA	G	GS	CG	ShO	GF	SV	IP	H	R	ER	HR	BB	HB	IBB	SO	WP	BK	BA
Reardon, J....BOS	R	5	3	3.16	47	0	0	0	37	21	51.1	39	21	18	5	19	1	4	33	0	0	.206
Reed, J....SEA-BOS	R	2	2	4.82	33	0	0	0	16	2	52.1	63	31	28	2	19	0	2	19	7	1	.300
Richardson, J....CAL	R	0	0	0.00	1	0	0	0	1	0	0.1	2	2	0	0	0	0	2	0	0	0	.500
Righetti, D....NY	L	1	0	3.57	53	0	0	0	47	36	53.0	48	24	21	8	26	0	2	43	3	0	.234
Ritz, K....DET	R	0	4	11.05	4	0	0	0	0	0	7.1	14	9	9	3	14	2	3	3	3	0	.400
Robinson, J....NY	R	3	6	3.45	54	4	0	0	12	0	88.2	82	35	34	8	34	0	9	43	2	1	.248
Robinson, J....DET	R	10	9	5.96	27	27	1	0	0	0	145.0	141	101	96	23	88	1	1	76	16	1	.256
Robinson, R....MIL	R	12	5	2.91	22	22	6	1	0	0	148.1	158	60	48	5	37	6	1	57	2	1	.275
Rochford, M....BOS	L	1	0	18.00	2	0	0	0	0	0	4.0	10	8	8	1	4	0	1	1	0	0	.526
Rogers, K....TEX	L	10	6	3.13	69	0	0	0	46	15	97.2	93	40	34	6	42	1	5	74	5	0	.249
Rosenberg, S....CHI	L	1	0	5.40	6	0	0	0	3	0	10.0	10	6	6	1	5	0	2	4	0	0	.256
Russell, J....TEX	R	1	5	4.26	27	0	0	0	22	0	25.1	23	16	12	3	16	0	2	16	2	1	.253
Ryan, N....TEX	R	13	9	3.44	30	30	5	2	0	0	204.0	137	86	78	18	74	7	2	232	9	1	.188
Saberhagen, B....KC	R	5	9	3.27	20	20	4	0	0	0	135.0	146	52	49	9	28	1	2	87	1	0	.279
Sanchez, I....KC	R	0	0	8.38	11	0	0	0	3	0	9.2	16	9	9	1	3	1	3	5	0	1	.381
Sanderson, S....OAK	R	17	11	3.88	34	34	4	2	0	0	206.1	205	99	89	27	66	4	2	128	7	0	.255
Savage, J....MIN	R	0	2	8.31	17	0	0	0	9	0	26.0	37	26	24	3	11	1	1	12	4	1	.339
Schilling, C....BAL	R	1	2	2.54	35	2	0	0	0	3	46.0	38	13	13	2	19	0	3	32	1	0	.229
Schooler, M....SEA	R	1	0	2.25	49	0	0	0	45	30	56.0	47	18	14	4	16	0	0	45	0	0	.227
Schwabe, M....DET	R	0	0	2.45	1	0	0	0	0	0	3.2	5	4	3	2	0	0	1	1	1	0	.357
Seanez, R....CLE	R	0	1	5.60	24	1	0	0	12	0	27.1	22	17	17	2	25	1	1	24	0	0	.220
Searcy, S....DET	L	2	7	4.66	16	12	0	0	0	0	75.1	76	44	39	9	51	0	3	66	5	0	.270
Sebra, B....MIL	R	1	2	8.18	10	0	0	0	0	0	11.0	20	10	10	1	5	1	2	4	3	1	.408
Shaw, J....CLE	R	3	4	6.66	12	9	0	0	2	0	48.2	73	38	36	11	20	0	0	25	3	0	.356
Smith, D....KC	R	0	1	4.05	2	1	0	0	1	0	6.2	13	3	3	3	4	0	0	6	0	0	.238
Smith, L....BOS	R	2	0	1.88	11	0	0	0	8	0	14.1	4	4	3	3	9	0	2	17	3	0	.236
Smith, M....BAL	R	0	0	12.00	2	0	0	0	1	0	3.0	14	14	4	0	2	0	0	2	1	0	.308
Smith, R....MIN	R	5	10	4.81	32	23	0	1	0	0	153.1	191	91	82	20	47	0	4	87	10	0	.313
Stewart, D....OAK	R	22	11	2.56	36	36	11	1	1	0	267.0	226	84	76	16	83	5	1	166	8	0	.231
Stieb, D....TOR	R	18	6	2.93	33	33	3	4	0	0	208.2	179	73	68	11	64	3	1	125	5	0	.230
Stottlemyre, M....KC	R	6	2	4.88	13	2	0	0	2	0	31.1	35	18	17	6	12	0	4	14	0	0	.280
Stottlemyre, T....TOR	R	13	17	4.34	33	33	5	0	3	0	203.0	214	101	98	18	69	5	4	115	6	1	.274
Swan, R....SEA	L	2	3	3.64	11	0	0	0	0	0	47.0	42	22	19	3	18	0	2	15	0	1	.244
Swift, B....SEA	R	6	4	2.39	55	8	0	0	18	6	128.0	135	46	34	4	21	7	6	42	8	3	.272

PITCHER	TEAM	T	W	L	ERA	G	GS	CG	SHO	GF	SV	IP	H	TBF	R	ER	HR	SH	SF	HB	BB	IBB	SO	WP	BK	OPP BK AVG
Swindell, G ....CLE		L	12	9	4.40	34	34	3	0	0	0	214.2	245	912	110	105	27	8	6	1	47	2	135	3	2	.288
Tanana, F ....DET		L	11	8	5.31	29	29	1	0	4	1	176.1	190	763	104	104	25	3	9	7	66	7	114	5	1	.280
Tapani, K ....MIN		R	12	8	4.07	28	28	0	1	0	0	159.1	164	659	75	72	12	3	2	2	29	2	101	1	0	.264
Taylor, D ....BAL		R	0	3	2.45	8	0	0	0	2	0	3.2	4	18	3	1	0	0	0	0	4	0	4	1	0	.250
Telford, A ....BAL		R	3	3	4.95	8	8	0	0	0	0	36.1	43	168	22	20	4	3	2	1	19	0	20	1	0	.295
Terrell, W ....DET		R	6	4	4.54	13	12	0	0	0	0	75.1	86	333	39	38	7	0	1	8	24	3	30	0	0	.290
Thigpen, B ....CHI		R	4	6	1.83	77	0	0	0	73	57	88.2	60	347	20	18	5	3	3	1	32	3	70	2	0	.195
Tibbs, J ....BAL		L	2	7	5.68	10	10	0	0	0	0	50.2	55	215	34	32	8	2	2	3	14	1	23	1	0	.279
Valdez, E ....CLE		L	1	1	3.04	13	0	0	0	8	0	23.2	20	104	10	8	2	1	0	0	14	3	13	2	0	.233
Valdez, S ....CLE		R	6	6	4.75	24	13	0	0	4	0	102.1	109	440	62	54	17	4	5	1	35	2	63	3	0	.276
Veres, R ....MIL		R	0	0	3.67	26	0	0	0	12	1	41.2	38	175	17	17	5	4	2	1	16	3	16	3	0	.247
Wagner, H ....KC		R	2	0	8.10	5	5	0	0	0	0	23.1	32	112	24	21	5	2	2	0	11	1	14	3	0	.323
Walker, M ....CLE		R	2	6	4.88	18	11	0	0	2	0	75.2	82	350	49	41	6	4	6	2	42	1	34	3	1	.277
Wapnick, S ....DET		R	0	0	6.43	4	0	0	0	1	0	7.0	8	37	5	5	0	0	0	0	6	0	6	1	0	.296
Ward, C ....CLE		R	2	3	4.25	22	0	0	0	7	1	36.0	31	158	17	17	3	0	2	1	10	4	23	0	0	.238
Ward, D ....TOR		R	2	8	3.45	73	0	0	0	39	11	127.2	101	508	51	49	9	9	2	1	42	10	112	6	2	.221
Wayne, G ....MIN		L	1	1	4.19	38	0	0	0	12	0	38.2	38	166	19	18	5	6	2	0	13	2	28	5	1	.255
Wegman, B ....MIL		R	2	2	4.85	8	5	1	0	0	0	29.2	37	132	21	16	8	1	1	0	20	1	20	4	0	.298
Welch, B ....OAK		R	27	6	2.95	35	35	2	2	0	0	238.0	214	979	90	78	26	6	5	5	77	4	127	2	2	.242
Wells, D ....TOR		L	11	6	3.14	43	25	0	0	3	3	189.0	165	759	72	66	14	9	2	7	45	3	115	7	1	.235
West, D ....MIN		L	7	9	5.10	29	27	2	0	0	0	146.1	142	646	88	83	21	6	4	1	78	1	92	4	1	.256
Weston, M ....BAL		R	1	1	7.71	9	2	0	0	4	0	21.0	28	94	20	18	0	6	0	0	6	1	9	1	0	.322
Wickander, K ....CLE		L	0	1	3.65	10	0	0	0	3	0	12.1	14	53	6	5	0	2	1	0	10	0	10	1	0	.304
Williamson, M ....BAL		R	8	4	2.21	49	0	0	0	15	1	85.1	65	343	25	21	8	6	7	1	28	7	60	2	0	.215
Wills, F ....TOR		R	6	4	4.73	44	4	0	0	6	0	99.0	101	422	54	52	13	2	6	1	38	2	72	1	2	.266
Witt, B ....TEX		R	17	10	3.36	33	32	7	1	0	0	222.0	197	954	98	83	9	5	6	4	110	3	221	11	2	.238
Witt, M ....CAL-NY		R	5	9	4.00	26	16	2	0	1	0	117.0	106	498	62	52	9	1	6	5	47	4	74	7	0	.241
Yett, R ....MIN		R	0	0	2.08	4	0	0	0	1	0	4.1	6	19	2	1	1	1	0	1	2	0	2	0	0	.353
Young, C ....OAK		R	9	6	4.85	26	21	0	0	0	0	124.1	124	527	70	67	17	4	2	2	53	1	56	3	0	.266
Young, C ....CAL		L	1	1	3.52	17	0	0	0	5	0	30.2	40	137	14	12	2	7	1	1	7	1	19	1	0	.325
Young, M ....SEA		L	8	18	3.51	34	33	7	1	0	0	225.1	198	963	106	88	15	7	7	6	107	7	176	16	0	.237

CLUB PITCHING

CLUB	W	L	ERA	G	CG	SHO	REL	SV	IP	H	R	ER	HR	HB	BB	IBB	SO	WP	BK	OPP AVG
OAKLAND	103	59	3.18	162	18	16	303	64	1456.0	1287	570	514	123	27	494	19	831	50	7	.238
CHICAGO	94	68	3.61	162	17	10	367	68	1449.1	1313	633	581	106	39	548	27	914	35	11	.244
SEATTLE	77	85	3.69	162	21	7	312	41	1443.1	1319	680	592	120	41	606	55	1064	69	12	.243
BOSTON	88	74	3.72	162	15	13	323	44	1442.0	1439	664	596	92	45	519	47	997	63	6	.261
CALIFORNIA	80	82	3.79	162	21	13	269	42	1454.0	1482	706	613	106	38	544	25	944	50	6	.267
TEXAS	83	79	3.83	162	25	9	302	36	1444.2	1343	696	615	113	44	623	39	997	61	6	.248
TORONTO	86	76	3.84	162	6	9	317	48	1454.0	1434	661	620	143	37	445	44	892	43	5	.260
KANSAS CITY	75	86	3.93	161	18	8	312	33	1420.2	1449	709	621	116	46	560	45	1006	59	5	.264
BALTIMORE	76	85	4.04	161	10	5	357	43	1435.1	1445	698	644	161	16	537	43	776	34	10	.264
MILWAUKEE	74	88	4.08	162	23	13	340	42	1445.0	1558	760	655	121	38	469	39	771	47	7	.275
MINNESOTA	74	88	4.12	162	13	13	310	43	1435.2	1509	729	658	134	27	489	40	872	55	5	.273
NEW YORK	67	95	4.21	162	15	6	342	41	1444.2	1430	749	676	144	26	618	40	909	83	6	.261
CLEVELAND	77	85	4.26	162	12	10	301	47	1427.1	1491	737	676	163	40	518	38	860	50	8	.270
DETROIT	79	83	4.39	162	15	12	300	45	1430.1	1401	754	697	154	45	661	86	856	76	7	.259
TOTALS	1133	1133	3.91	1133	229	144	4455	637	20182.1	19900	9746	8758	1796	509	7631	587	12689	775	101	.259

OFFICIAL 1991 AMERICAN LEAGUE SCHEDULE

BOLD = SUNDAY   ( ) = HOLIDAY   * = NIGHT GAME   TN = TWI-NIGHT DOUBLEHEADER

	AT SEATTLE	AT OAKLAND	AT CALIFORNIA	AT TEXAS	AT KANSAS CITY	AT MINNESOTA	AT CHICAGO
SEATTLE		April 12*,13,14 August 5*,6*,7	April 22*,23*,24 Aug! 2*,3,4	May 30*,31*, June 1,2* Sept. 30*, Oct. 1*,2*	May 20*,21*,22* Sept. 13*,14*,15	April 25*,26*,27,28 August 20*,21,22	June 24*,25*,26*, 27 Sept. 27*,28*,29
OAKLAND	April 19*,20*,21 Aug. 12*,13*,14*,15		April 15*,16*,17*,18* Aug. 9*,10*,11	July 2*,3*,(4*) Oct. 4*,5,6	July 5*,6*,7 Sept. 30* Oct. 1,2*	April 22*,23*,24 Aug. 16*,17*,18*,19*	May 31* June 1*,2*,3* Sept. 17*,18*
CALIFORNIA	April 9*,10*,11 Aug. 16*,17*,18,19*	April 26*,27,28 Aug. 20*,21*,22		July 5*,6*,7 Sept. 17*,18*,19*	June 24*,25*,26* Sept. 26*,27*,28*,29	April 12*,13,14 Aug. 12*,13*,14*,15*	May 28*,29*,30 Sept. 20*,21*,22
TEXAS	May 24*,25*,26 Sept. 23*,24*,25	June 25*,26*,27 Sept. 26*,27*,28,29	June 28*,29*,30 July 1* Sept. 9*,10*,11*		June 4*,5,6 Aug. 22*,23*,24*,25	May 21*,22*,23 Sept. 20*,21*,22	June 20*,21*,22*,23 July 31 Aug. 1*
KANSAS CITY	May 27*, 28*,29 Sept. 19*,20*,21*,22	June 28*,29*,30 July 1* Sept. 23*,24*,25	July 2*,3*(4*) Oct. 4*,5,6	June 17*,18*,19* Aug. 30*,31* Sept. 1		May 24*,25*,26 Sept. 16*,17*,18	June 14*,15*,16 Sept. (2*), 3*,4*,5
MINNESOTA	April 15*,16*,17* Aug. 9*,10*,11	April 9*,10*,11 Aug. 2*,3,4	April 19*,20*,21 Aug. 5*,6*,7	May (27*),28*,29* Sept. 12*,13*,14*,15	May 30*,31* June 1*,2 Sept. 9*,10*,11*		July 5*,6*,7 Sept. 30* Oct. 1*,2*,3
CHICAGO	July 2*,3*(4) Oct. 4*,5*,6	May 23*,24*,25,26 Sept. 9*,10*,11	May 20*,21*,22* Sept. 12*,13*,14,15	June 10*,11*,12*,13* Sept. 6*,7,8	June 7*,8,9 Aug. 26*,27*,28*	June 28*,29*,30 July 1* Sept. 24*,25*	

Team						
MILWAUKEE	June 7;8;9 / Aug. 26*;27*;28*	June 10;11;12 / Sept. 6*;7*;8	April 8;10* / Aug. 9*;10*;11;12*	May 17;18;19 / July 23*;24*;25*	May 14;15;16 / July 26*;27*;28	May 7;8* / July 19*;20*;21;22*
DETROIT	June 13*;14*;15*;16 / Sept. (2),3*	June 10*;11;12 / Aug. 30;31 / Sept. 1	May 13;14*;15* / July 26*;27*;28*	April 29;30* / May 1* / July 19;20;21	May 9*;10*;11;12 / July 29;30	April 18,20,21 / Aug. 19*;20*;21*
CLEVELAND	May 7;8* / July 11*;12*;13*;14	April 30* / May 1* / July 18*;19*;20*;21	April 26*;27*;28 / Aug. 5*;6*;7*	April 8;9*;10 / Aug. 9*;10*;11	June 7;8*;9;10* / Sept. (2),4*	June 18*;19* / Aug. 29*;30*;31* / Sept. 1
TORONTO	July 5*;6*;7 / Sept. 16*;17*;18*	May 20*;21;22 / Sept. 20*;21,22	April 30* / May 1* / July 18*;19*;20*;21*	May 2;3*;4*;5 / July 15*;16*	June 25*;26*;27 / Oct. 4*;5*;6	May 17;18*;19 / July 23*;24*;25
BALTIMORE	May 10;11;12* / July 29*;30*;31*	May 7;8 / July 11*;12*;13,14	April 12;13*;14 / Aug. 19*;20*;21*	June 20;21*;22*;23 / July 17*;18*	June 3*;4*;5;6* / Aug. 30*;31* / Sept. 1	April 22*;23*;24* / Aug. 2*;3*,4
NEW YORK	May 3*;4*;5;6* / July 15;16	April 30* / May 1 / July 18*;19*;20,21	May 7;8* / July 11*;12*;13*;14	June 14;15*;16* / Sept. (2), 3*;4*	April 12*;13;14 / Aug. 19*;20*;21*	April 26*;27*;28 / Aug. 6*;7*;8
BOSTON	June 10*;11*;12 / Aug. 30*;31* / Sept. 1	June 7;8,9 / Aug. 26*;27*;28	June 4*;5*;6 / Aug. 23*;24*;25	May 17;18;19 / July 22*;23*;24*	April 26*;27*;28* / Aug. 5;6*;7*	May 3*;4*;5 / July 15*;16*;17*

1991 ALL-STAR GAME AT THE SKYDOME IN TORONTO, JULY 9

OFFICIAL 1991 AMERICAN LEAGUE SCHEDULE

BOLD = SUNDAY   ' = HOLIDAY   * = NIGHT GAME   TN = TWI-NIGHT DOUBLEHEADER

	AT MILWAUKEE	AT DETROIT	AT CLEVELAND	AT TORONTO	AT BALTIMORE	AT NEW YORK	AT BOSTON
SEATTLE	June 20*,21*,22*,23 July 17*,18	June 4*,5,6 Aug. 23*,24,25	May 14*,15*,16* July 26*,27,28	June 28,29,30 July (1) Sept. 10*,11*	April 29*,30* May 1* July 19*,20*,21	May 17*,18,19 July 23*,24*,25	June 18*,19* Sept. 5*,6*,7,8
OAKLAND	June 14*,15*,16,17* Sept. 3*,4*	June 18*,19* Sept. 5*,6*,7,8	May 17*,18,19 July 23*,24*,25	May 28*,29*,30* Sept. 13*,14,15	May 14*,15*,16* July 26*,27,28	May 10*,11,12,13* July 29*,30*	June 20*,21*,22,23 July 31* Aug. 1*
CALIFORNIA	June 18*,19 Aug. 30*,31* Sept. 1,(2)	June 20*,21*,22*,23* July 31* Aug. 1	May 10*,11,12,13* July 29*,30*	May 31* June 1,2 Sept. 30*, Oct. 1*,2*	May 17*,18,19 July 23*,24*,25*	May 14*,15*,16* July 26*,27,28	June 14*,15,16,17* Sept. 3*,4*
TEXAS	April 23*,24*,25 Aug. 2*,3*,4	May 3*,4,5 July 15*,16*,17	April 16,18* Aug. 16TN,17*,18	May 7*,8* July 11*,12*,13,14*	April 19*,20,21 Aug. 13*,14*,15*	June 7*,8,9 Aug. 26*,27*,28*	May 9*,10*,11,12 July 29*,30
KANSAS CITY	May 10*,11*,12 July 30*,31* Aug. 1	May 7*,8 July 11*,12*,13,14	April 22,23*,24* Aug. 2*,3,4	May 13*,14*,15* July 26*,27,28	June 11*,12*,13* Sept. 6*,7,8	April 19*,20,21 Aug. 13*,14*,15	April 16,17,18 Aug. 16*,17*,18
MINNESOTA	May 2*,3,4,5 July 15*,16*	May 17*,18,19 July 23*,24*,25*	June 14*,15,16 Aug. 26*,27*,28*	July 2*,3*(4) Sept. 27*,28,29	June 17*,18,19 Aug. 23*,24,25	June 21*,22*,23,24* July 31* Aug. 1	May 7*,8* July 18*,19*,20,21
CHICAGO	April 30* May 1 July 11*,12*,13*,14	April 12*,13,14 Aug. 13*,14*,15*	June 4*,5*,6* Aug. 23*,24,25*	May 9*,10*,11,12 July 29*,30*	April 8,10* Aug. 9*,10*,11,12*	April 15*,16*,17 Aug. 16*,17*,18	May 13*,14*,15* July 26*,27,28

	MILWAUKEE	DETROIT	CLEVELAND	TORONTO	BALTIMORE	NEW YORK	BOSTON
MILWAUKEE	—	June 25*,26*,27* / Sept. 20*,21*,22	July (4)5*,6*,7 / Oct. 1*,2*,3*	April 11*,12*,13,14 / Aug. 20*,21*,22*	April 26*,27*,28 / Aug. 5*,6*,7,8*	May 31* / June 1,2 / Sept. 16*,17*,18*	May 20*,21*,22* / Oct. 4*,5,6
DETROIT	May (27),28*,29 / Sept. 12*,13*,14*,15	—	May 31* / June 1,2,3* / Sept. 17*,18*	April 25*,26*,27,28 / Aug. 6*,7*,8*	July 1*,2,3* / Oct. 4*,5,6	April 22*,23*,24* / Aug. 9*,10*,11	July (4)5*,6,7 / Oct. 1*,2*,3*
CLEVELAND	May 23*,24*,25,26* / Sept. 10*,11	June 28*,29,30 / Sept. 23*,24*,25*,26*	—	June 21*,22,23,24 / July 31* / Aug. 1	May (27),28*,29* / Sept. 12*,13*,14*,15	July 1*,2,3* / Oct. 4*,5,6	April 11,13,14,15 / Aug. 19*,20*,21*
TORONTO	April 19*,20,21 / Aug. 13*,14*,15	April 15*,16*,17 / Aug. 16*,17,18	June 11*,12*,13* / Sept. 5*,6*,7,8	—	June 6*,7*,8,9* / Aug. 26*,27*,28*	June 3*,4*,5* / Aug. 29*,30*,31 / Sept. 1	April 22*,23*,24* / Aug. 2*,3,4
BALTIMORE	April 15,17*,18 / Aug. 16*,17*,18	May 20*,21*,22* / Sept. 27*,28,29,30*	June 25*,26*,27* / Sept. 20*,21,22	June 14*,15,16 / Sept. (2),3*,4*	—	July (4)5*,6,7 / Oct. 1*,2*,3*	May 30*,31* / June 1,2 / Sept. 16*,17*,18*
NEW YORK	June 28*,29,30 / Sept. 23*,24*,25*,26*	April 8,10,11 / Aug. 2*,3*,4,5*	May 20*,21*,22* / Sept. 27*,28,29,30*	June 18*,19*,20* / Aug. 23*,24,25	May 24*,25*,26 / Sept. 9*,10*,11	—	June 25*,26*,27* / Sept. 20*,21,22
BOSTON	July 1*,2*,3* / Sept. 27*,28,29,30*	May 23*,24*,25*,26 / Sept. 10*,11	April 8,9*,10* / Aug. 9*,10,11,12*	June 28*,29,30 / Sept. 23*,24*,25*	May 28*,29,30 / Sept. 12*,13*,14*,15*	May (27),28*,29* / Sept. 12*,13*,14,15*	—

1991 ALL-STAR GAME AT THE SKYDOME IN TORONTO, JULY 9

OFFICIAL 1991

EAST

	AT CHICAGO	AT MONTREAL	AT NEW YORK
Chicago		May 31*, June 1*,**2** Aug. 19*,20*,21* Sept. 20*,21*,**22**	May 21*,22*,23* Aug. 2*,3*,4,**5*** Sept. 18*,19*
Montreal	May 24,25*,**26** Aug. 13*,14,15 Sept. 13,14*,**15**		April 11*,12*,13,14 June 25*,26*,27 Sept. 9*,10
New York	May 27,28*,**29** Aug. 9,10,11*,12 Sept. 11,12	April 19*,20,**21*** July 1,2*,3*,**4*** Sept. 16*,17*	
Philadelphia	April 15*,16,17 Aug. 16,17,18 Sept. 23*,24*,25	May 21*,22*,23 Aug. 1*,2*,3*,**4** Sept. 18*,19*	April 8,9,10* June 28*,29*,**30** Sept. 27*,28,29
Pittsburgh	April 12,13,14 July 1*,2,3,**4** Sept. 9,10*	April 23*,24*,**25*** June 28*,29*,**30** Sept. 27*,28*,29	April 26*,27,**28** Aug. 6*,7*,8 Sept. 24*,25*,26*
St. Louis	April 9,10,11 June 28,29,**30** Oct. 4,5,6	April 15,16*,**17*** Aug. 16*,17*,**18** Sept. 30*, Oct. 1*,2*	May 24*,25,**26** Aug. 20*,21*,22* Sept. 20*,21,**22**
Atlanta	May 13*,14*,15 July 26,27,**28**	June 14*,15*,**16** Sept. 2,3*,**4***	June 11*,12*,13* Sept. 6*,7,8
Cincinnati	May 10,11,**12** July 23*,24,25	June 11*,12*,13* Sept. 6*,7*,**8**	June 17*,18*,19* Aug. 23*,24,**25***
Houston	April 30*, May 1 July 11*,12,13,**14**	June 17*,18*,19* Aug. 30*,31*, Sept. 1	June 14*,15*,**16** Sept. 2,3*,**4***
Los Angeles	June 7,8,**9**,10* Aug. 26*,27	April 30*, May 1* July 11*,12*,13*,14	May 7*,8* July 18*,19*,20,**21**
San Diego	June 4*,5,6 Aug. 23,24,**25**	May 3*,4,5 July 15*,16*,17*	April 30*, May 1* July 11*,12*,13*,**14**
San Francisco	June 11,12,13 Sept. 6,7,**8**	May 6*,7*,8* July 19*,20*,21	May 3*,4,5 July 15*,16*,17

* NIGHT GAME
HEAVY BLACK FIGURES DENOTE SUNDAYS
NIGHT GAMES: ANY GAME STARTING AFTER 5:00 P.M.

NATIONAL LEAGUE SCHEDULE

EAST

	AT PHILADELPHIA	AT PITTSBURGH	AT ST. LOUIS
Chicago	May 17*,18*,19* Aug. 6*,7*,8 Sept. 30*, Oct. 1*,2*	April 18*,19*,20,21 June 25*,26*,27* Sept. 16*,17*	April 22*,23*,24* July 5*,6*,7* Sept. 27*,28,29
Montreal	May 27*,28*,29* Aug. 9*,10*,11,12* Sept. 11*,12*	April 8*,9*,10 July 5*,6,*7 Oct. 4*,5*,6	April 26*,27*,28 Aug. 6*,7*,8* Sept. 23*,24*,25*
New York	April 23*,24*,25* July 5*,6*,7 Oct. 4*,5,6	April 15*,16*,17* Aug. 16*,17*,18 Sept. 30*, Oct. 1*,2*	May 31*, June 1*,2 Aug. 13*,14*,15* Sept. 13*,14*,15
Philadelphia		May 24*,25*,26 Aug. 13*,14*,15* Sept. 20*,21*,22	April 18*,19*,20*,21 June 25*,26*,27 Sept. 9*,10*
Pittsburgh	May 31*, June 1*,2 Aug. 20*,21*,22 Sept. 13*,14*,15		May 27,28*,29* Aug. 1*,2*,3,4 Sept. 11*,12*
St. Louis	April 12*,13,14 July 1*,2*,3*,4* Sept. 16*,17*	May 21*,22*,23* Aug. 9*,10*,11,12* Sept. 18*,19*	
Atlanta..........	June 17*,18*,19 Aug. 30*,31*, Sept. 1	May 10*,11*,12 July 22*,23*,24*	April 29*,30*. May 1 July 19*,20*,21
Cincinnati	June 14*,15*,16 Sept. 2*,3*,4*	May 6*,7*,8* July 19*,20*,21*	May 13*,14*,15 July 26*,27*,28
Houston..........	June 20*,21*,22*,23 Aug. 28*,29*	May 3*,4*,5 July 15*,16*,17*	May 17*,18*,19 July 22*,23*,24*
Los Angeles	May 3*,4*,5 July 15*,16*,17	June 11*,12*,13 Sept. 6*,7*,8	June 4*,5*,6* Aug. 23*,24*,25
San Diego	April 26*,27*,28,29* July 30*,31*	June 7*,8*,9,10* Aug. 26*,27	June 21*,22*,23,24* Aug. 28*,29*
San Francisco....	April 30*, May 1* July 11*,12*,13*,14	June 4*,5*,6* Aug. 23*,24*,25	June 7*,8*,9,10 Aug. 26*,27*

JULY 9 — ALL-STAR GAME AT TORONTO

OFFICIAL 1991

WEST

	AT ATLANTA	AT CINCINNATI	AT HOUSTON
Chicago	May 3*,4*,5 July 15*,16*,17*	April 25*,26*,27,28 July 30*,31*	May 6*,7*,8* July 19*,20*,21
Montreal	June 7*,8*,9,10* Aug. 26*,27*	June 20*,21*,22*,23 Aug. 28*,29*	June 4*,5*,6* Aug. 23*,24*,25
New York	June 20*,21*,22*,23 Aug. 28*,29*	June 4*,5*,6* Aug. 30*,31*, Sept. 1	June 7*,8*,9,10* Aug. 26*,27*
Philadelphia	June 4*,5*,6* Aug. 23*,24*,25	June 7*,8*,9,10 Aug. 26*,27*	June 11*,12*,13 Sept. 6*,7*,8
Pittsburgh	May 17*,18*,19 July 29*,30*,31*	April 30*, May 1* July 11*,12*,13*,14	May 14*,15*,16* July 26*,27*,28
St. Louis	May 7*,8* July 11*,12*,13*,14	May 3*,4*,5 July 15*,16*,17*	May 10*,11*,12* July 29*,30*,31*
Atlanta		April 12*,13,14 Aug. 20*,21*,22* Sept. 30*, Oct. 1*,2*	April 26*,27*,28 June 25*,26*,27* Sept. 27*,28*,29
Cincinnati	April 19*,20*,21 July 2*,3*,4* Sept. 24*,25*,26*		April 22*,23*,24* July 5*,6*,7 Sept. 20*,21*,22
Houston	April 15*,16*,17* Aug. 9*,10*,11 Oct. 4*,5*,6	April 8,10*,11* June 28*,29*,30 Sept. 13*,14*,15	
Los Angeles	April 9*,10*,11 June 28*,29*,30* Sept. 13*,14*,15	May 24*,25,26 Aug. 5*,6*,7*,8 Sept. 9*,10*	May 20*,21*,22*,23* Aug. 2*,3*,4 Sept. 11*,12*
San Diego	May 20*,21*,22*,23* Aug. 2*,3*,4 Sept. 11*,12*	May 17*,18*,19 June 25*,26*,27 Sept. 27*,28*,29	May 24*,25*,26 Aug. 5*,6*,7*,8* Sept. 9*,10*
San Francisco	May 24*,25*,26 Aug. 5*,6*,7*,8* Sept. 9*,10*	May 21*,22*,23* Aug. 1*,2*,3*,4* Sept. 11*,12	April 12*,13*,14 Aug. 20*,21*,22 Sept. 23*,24*,25*

* NIGHT GAME
HEAVY BLACK FIGURES DENOTE SUNDAYS
NIGHT GAMES: ANY GAME STARTING AFTER 5:00 P.M.

NATIONAL LEAGUE SCHEDULE

WEST

	AT LOS ANGELES	AT SAN DIEGO	AT SAN FRANCISCO
Chicago	June 17*,18*,19* Aug. 30*,31*, Sept. 1	June 14*,15,16 Sept. 2*,3*,4*	June 20*,21*,22,23 Aug. 28*,29
Montreal	May 13*,14*,15* July 26*,27*,28	May 10*,11*,12 July 23*,24*,25	May 16*,17*,18,19 July 29*,30
New York	May 17*,18,19 July 29*,30*,31*	May 13*,14*,15 July 26*,27*,28	May 10*,11,12 July 23*,24*,25
Philadelphia	May 10*,11*,12 July 23*,24*,25*	May 7*,8*,9 July 19*,20*,21	May 13*,14*,15 July 26*,27,28
Pittsburgh	June 20*,21*,22,23 Aug. 28*,29*	June 17*,18*,19* Aug. 30*,31*, Sept. 1*	June 14*,15,16* Sept. 2,3*,4
St. Louis	June 14*,15*,16 Sept. 2*,3*,4*	June 11*,12*,13 Sept. 5,6*,7*	June 17*,18*,19 Aug. 30*,31, Sept. 1
Atlanta	April 22*,23*,24* July 5*,6*,7 Sept. 20*,21*,22	May 27*,28*,29* Aug. 15,16*,17*,18 Sept. 18*,19*	May 30*,31*, June 1,2 Aug. 12*,13*,14 Sept. 16*,17*
Cincinnati	May 30*,31*, June 1*,2 Aug. 12*,13*,14* Sept. 16*,17*	April 15*,16*,17* Aug. 9*,10*,11 Oct. 4*,5*,6	May 27*,28*,29 Aug. 15*,16*,17,18 Sept. 18*,19
Houston	May 27*,28*,29* Aug. 15*,16*,17*,18 Sept. 18*,19	May 30,31*, June 1*,2 Aug. 12*,13*,14* Sept. 16*,17*	April 19*,20,21 July 2*,3*,4* Sept. 30*, Oct. 1*,2
Los Angeles		April 18,19*,20*,21 July 2*,3*,4* Sept. 24*,25*	April 15*,16*,17 Aug. 9*,10,11 Oct. 4*,5,6
San Diego	April 12,13*,14 Aug. 19*,20*,21 Sept. 30*, Oct. 1*,2*		April 22*,23*,24 July 5*,6,7 Sept. 13*,14,15
San Francisco	April 25*,26*,27*,28 June 25*,26* Sept. 27*,28,29*	April 9*,10*,11 June 28*,29*,30 Sept. 20*,21,22	

JULY 9 — ALL-STAR GAME AT TORONTO

Revised and updated with over 75 all
new sports records and photographs!

THE ILLUSTRATED
SPORTS RECORD BOOK
Zander Hollander and David Schulz

Here, in a single book, are more than 350
all-time sports records with stories and
photos so vivid it's like "being there." All the
sports classics are here: Babe Ruth, Wilt
Chamberlain, Muhammad Ali ... plus the
stories of such active stars as Dwight Gooden
and Wayne Gretzky. This is the authoritative
book on what the great records are, and
who set them——an engrossing, fun-filled
reference guide filled with anecdotes of
hundreds of renowned athletes whose
remarkable records remain as fresh as when
they were set.
